What's Out?

Models, concepts, and topics that don't pass a simple test:
"Does this help students analyze cases and real business situations?"

What's In?

"VRIO" – an integrative framework (see next page for details).

- Broad enough to apply in analyzing a variety of cases and real business settings.
- Simple enough to understand and teach.

The Results?

Provides students with the tools they need to do strategic analysis. Nothing more. Nothing less.

From the Authors

So . . . why write another textbook on Strategic Management? After all, isn't this an already crowded market? Is there really something missing in the current books—something so important that a new book must be written?

We think "yes". But here is the irony—the thing missing in most other textbooks is that *nothing* is missing. Most of these books incorporate virtually every idea, every concept, and every theory that has been mentioned in strategic management literature in the last 20 years. First editions are inclusive. Later editions are more inclusive as authors compare their texts with other texts to make sure that everything "is covered".

Our view in writing this text is different. We believe that because most strategic management texts are missing nothing, they are missing the most important thing—a point of view, a consistent perspective, an integrating framework broad enough to be applied in analyzing a wide variety of cases and business settings, but simple enough to understand and share with others. This text introduces such an integrative framework—The VRIO framework. Many of you already know this framework and its relationship to the resource-based theory of strategy. This is the first undergraduate text that uses such a theory-based, multi-chapter organizing framework to introduce additional structure to the field of strategic management.

Now, don't worry. That much of the text is organized around a single framework doesn't mean that critical ideas and theories are ignored. It's all here—the five forces framework, competitive dynamics, the value chain, generic strategies, corporate strategy, and so forth. In fact, because the VRIO framework provides a simple integrative structure, we are actually able to address issues in this book that are largely ignored elsewhere—including discussions of vertical integration, outsourcing, real options logic, and mergers and acquisitions, to name just a few. In the end, every concept had to pass a simple test to be included in the book: **"Does this concept help students analyze cases and real business situations?"** If "yes," the concept was in. If "no," it was out.

This "less is more" strategy has some obvious implications. First, this book is shorter than the competition (we include fewer, but far more selective cases and tightly integrate them within the parts of the book). Second, instead of buying a huge book and using less than half of it, students using this book will use more of it—both the text and the cases that are closely linked to the text. Third, and most importantly we have included fewer topics albeit more tightly connected through an integrative framework—VRIO. This promotes real understanding versus rote memorization. The result of real understanding is that this book provides students with the tools they need to do strategic analysis. Nothing more. Nothing less.

Other Benefits

Element	Description	Benefit	Example
Chapter Opening Cases	We have chosen firms that are familiar to most students. Opening cases focus on competing strategies in the music download industry; TiVO's challenges in changing the way we watch TV; how Electronic Arts dominates the video game industry; whether or not Wal-Mart can continue its remarkable success; the secret of Victoria's Secret's success; and how HBO is able to produce such successful series as *Sex in the City*, *The Sopranos*, etc. Cases are integrated throughout the chapters.	By having cases tightly linked to the material, students can develop strategic analysis skills by studying firms familiar to them.	3-4
Full Length Cases	This book contains selective, part-ending cases that underscore the concepts in each part. This provides a tight link to the chapter concepts to reinforce understanding of recent research. These are 1) decision oriented, 2) recent, 3) student-recognized companies and 4) cases where the data are only partly analyzed.	Provides a tight link to chapter concepts, facilitating students' ability to apply text ideas to case analysis.	1-56–1-64 *(Concepts and Cases only)*
Strategy in Depth	For professors and students interested in understanding the full intellectual underpinnings of the field (knowledge in strategic management, continuous to evolve rapidly, some beyond what is normally included in an introductory text), we have included an optional *Strategy in Depth* feature in every chapter.	Customize your course as desired to provide enrichment material for advanced students.	282-283
Research Made Relevant	The *Research Made Relevant* feature highlights very current research findings related to some of the strategic topics discussed in that chapter.	Shows students the evolving nature of strategy.	250-251
Challenge Questions	These might be of an ethical or moral nature, forcing students to apply concepts across chapters, apply concepts to themselves, or extend chapter ideas in creative ways.	Requires students to think critically.	110
Problem Set	*Problem Set* asks students to apply theories and tools from the chapter. These often require calculations. They can be thought of as homework assignments. If students struggle with these they might have more trouble with the more complex cases. These problem sets are largely diagnostic in character.	Sharpens quantitative skills, and provides a bridge between chapter material and case analysis.	142-143
Ethics and Strategy	Highlights some of the most important dilemmas faced by firms when creating and implementing strategies.	Helps students make better ethical decisions as managers.	229
Global Perspectives	Most firms, most of the time, need to be concerned about global issues. Thus, we have integrated a global perspective into each chapter in two ways 1) Each chapter has a section that discusses the issues raised in that chapter in a global context; 2) Each chapter includes a *Global Perspectives* feature that provides an extended example of a strategic issue in a global context.	Gets students to think about the global implications of strategic decision making.	193
Strategy in the Emerging Enterprise	Growing number of graduates work for small and medium-sized firms. This feature presents an extended example, in each chapter, of the unique strategic problems facing those employed in small and medium-sized firms.	This feature highlights the unique challenges of doing strategic analysis in emerging enterprises, and small and medium-sized firms.	132-133
Tools for the Professors	We have provided a suite of tools to help support you, the professor. They include: ■ Instructor's Manual ■ Case Teaching Notes ■ Computerized Test Bank ■ Test Bank ■ Companion Web site		

V R I O

"VALUE. RARITY. IMITABILITY. ORGANIZATION."

What Is It?

This book is not just a list of concepts, models and theories. It is the first undergraduate textbook to introduce a **theory-based, multi-chapter organizing framework** to add additional structure to the field of strategic management.

"VRIO" is a mechanism that integrates two existing theoretical frameworks: the positioning perspective and the resource-based view. It is the primary tool for accomplishing internal analysis. It stands for four questions one must ask about a resource or capability to determine its competitive potential:

1. **The Question of Value:** Does a resource enable a firm to exploit an environmental opportunity, and/or neutralize an environmental threat?

2. **The Question of Rarity:** Is a resource currently controlled by only a small number of competing firms?

3. **The Question of Imitability:** Do firms without a resource face a cost disadvantage in obtaining or developing it?

4. **The Question of Organization:** Are a firm's other policies and procedures organized to support the exploitation of its valuable, rare, and costly-to-imitate resources?

What's the Benefit of the VRIO Framework?

The VRIO framework is the organizational foundation of the text. **It creates a decision-making framework for students** to use in analyzing case and business situations.

Students tend to view concepts, models, and theories (in all of their coursework) as fragmented and disconnected. Strategy is no exception. This view encourages rote memorization, not real understanding. VRIO, by serving as a consistent framework, connects ideas together. This encourages real understanding, not memorization.

This understanding enables students to better analyze business cases and situations—the goal of the course.

The VRIO framework makes it possible to discuss the formulation and implementation of a strategy simultaneously, within each chapter.

Because the VRIO framework provides a simple integrative structure, we are actually able to address issues in this book that are largely ignored elsewhere— including discussions of vertical integration, outsourcing, real options logic, and mergers and acquisitions, to name just a few.

Author Biographies

JAY B. BARNEY

Jay B. Barney is a Professor of Management and holder of the Bank One Chair in Strategic Management at the Fisher College of Business, The Ohio State University. He received his undergraduate degree from Brigham Young University, and his master's and Ph.D. from Yale University. After graduation, he served on the faculties at UCLA and at Texas A&M University. Professor Barney moved to Ohio State in 1994 where he teaches business policy and strategy.

He has also taught in a variety of executive programs at Ohio State, Texas A&M, UCLA, Southern Methodist University, Texas Christian University, the University of Michigan, Bocconi University (in Milan, Italy), and for the consulting firm McKinsey and Company. He has received teaching awards at UCLA (1983), Texas A&M (1992), and Ohio State (1995, 1996, 1999, 2000, and 2001).

Professor Barney's research focuses on the relationship between firm resources and capabilities and sustained competitive advantage. He has published over 75 articles in a variety of books and journals. Some of his published work is among the most cited research in the fields of strategic management and entrepreneurship. Professor Barney has also delivered scholarly papers at over 50 universities around the world, won the College of Business Distinguished Research Award at Texas A&M in 1992, received an honorary doctorate degree from Lund University in 1997; and was appointed an Honorary Visiting Professor at Waikato University in Hamilton, New Zealand in 2001. In 2001 he was elected as a Fellow in the Academy of Management and in 2005 was awarded the Irwin Outstanding Educator Award for the Business Policy and Strategy Division of the Academy of Management.

Professor Barney has consulted with a wide variety of public and private organizations, including Hewlett Packard, Texas Instruments, Tenneco, Arco, McKinsey and Company, Nationwide, and the Columbus Public Schools.

WILLIAM S. HESTERLY

William S. Hesterly is the Zeke Dumke Professor of Management in the David Eccles School of Business, the University of Utah. He has twice been selected as the outstanding teacher in the MBA program (1992 and 1997) and also received the Student's Choice Award in 1994. He received the Western Academy of Management Ascendant Scholar Award in 1999. Dr. Hesterly has also received best paper awards from the Western Academy of Management and the Academy of Management.

His research on organizational economics, vertical integration, organizational forms, and entrepreneurial networks has appeared in leading journals including the *Academy of Management Review*, *Organization Science*, *Strategic Management Journal*, the *Journal of Management*, and the *Journal of Economic Behavior and Organization*. Currently, he is studying the sources of value creation in firms and also what determines who capture the value from a firm's competitive advantage. His research on the history of innovation in Major League Baseball recently appeared in the journal *Business History*.

Dr. Hesterly serves on the editorial board of *Strategic Organization* and has previously served on the boards of *Organization Science* and the *Journal of Management*. He has served as Department Chair and also Vice-President and President of the faculty at the David Eccles School of Business at the University of Utah. Professor Hesterly has served as a consultant to *Fortune* 500 firms in the electronic, office equipment, paper, telecommunications, energy, aerospace, and medical equipment industries. He has also consulted with smaller firms in several other industries. After studying at Louisiana State University, he received bachelors and masters degrees from Brigham Young University and a Ph.D. from the University of California, Los Angeles.

Strategic Management and Competitive Advantage

Concepts

Strategic Management and Competitive Advantage
Concepts

Jay B. Barney
The Ohio State University

William S. Hesterly
The University of Utah

PEARSON

Prentice
Hall

Upper Saddle River, New Jersey 07458

Library of Congress Cataloging-in-Publication Data

Barney, Jay B.

Strategic management and competitive advantage: concepts and cases / Jay B. Barney, William S. Hesterly.

   p. cm.

Includes bibliographical references and index.

ISBN 0-13-154274-5

1. Strategic planning.   2. Business planning.   3. Industrial management.

4. Competition.   I. Hesterly, William S.   II. Title.

HD30.28.B36834 2006

658.4′ 012—dc22   2005045936

Senior Acquisitions Editor: Michael Ablassmeir
VP/Editorial Director: Jeff Shelstad
Associate Editor: Melissa Yu
Editorial Assistant: Richard Gomes
Developmental Editor: Erika Rusnak
Media Project Manager: Ashley Santora
VP/Director, Market Development: Annie Todd
Marketing Manager: Anke Braun
Marketing Assistant: Patrick Danzuso
Associate Director Production Editorial: Judy Leale
Production Editor: Mary Ellen Morrell
Permissions Supervisor: Charles Morris
Associate Director, Manufacturing: Vincent Scelta
Production Manager: Arnold Vila
Manufacturing Buyer: Diane Peirano

Design Manager: Maria Lange
Art Director: Janet Slowik
Interior Design: Raven Design
Cover Design: Maria Lange
Cover Illustration: Gary Hovland
Illustrator (Interior): P.J. Loughran, Gary Hovland
Illustrator (Figure Art): ElectraGraphics, Inc.
Director, Image Resource Center: Melinda Reo
Manager, Rights and Permissions: Zina Arabia
Manager, Visual Research: Beth Brenzel
Manager, Cover Visual Research & Permissions: Karen Sanatar
Image Permission Coordinator: Craig A. Jones
Manager, Print Production: Christy Mahon
Composition/Full-Service Project Management: Preparé, Inc.
Printer/Binder: Courier-Kendallville

Credits and acknowledgments borrowed from other sources and reproduced, with permission, in this textbook appear on appropriate page within text.

Pearson Education LTD.
Pearson Education Singapore, Pte. Ltd
Pearson Education, Canada, Ltd
Pearson Education–Japan

Pearson Education Australia PTY, Limited
Pearson Education North Asia Ltd
Pearson Educatión de Mexico, S.A. de C.V.
Pearson Education Malaysia, Pte. Ltd

10 9 8 7 6 5 4 3 2 1
ISBN 0-13-154716-X

This book is dedicated to my expanding family: my wife, Kim; our children, Lindsay, Kristian, and Erin; their spouses, Ryan, Amy, and Dave; and most of all, our four grandchildren, Isaac, Dylanie, Audrey, and Chloe. They all help me remember that no success could compensate for failure in the home.

Jay B. Barney
Columbus, Ohio

This book is for my family who has taught me life's greatest lessons about what matters most. To my wife, Denise; my sons, Drew, Ian, Austin, and Alex; my daughters, Lindsay and Jessica (and their husbands, Matt and John); and grandchildren, Ellie and Owen.

William Hesterly
Salt Lake City, Utah

Brief Contents

Contents

Part 1: THE TOOLS OF STRATEGIC ANALYSIS

Chapter 1: What Is Strategy and the Strategic Management Process? 2

Chapter 2: Evaluating a Firm's External Environment 32

Chapter 3: Evaluating a Firm's Internal Capabilities 74

Part 2: BUSINESS LEVEL STRATEGIES

Chapter 4: Cost Leadership 114

Chapter 5: Product Differentiation   144

Part 3: CORPORATE STRATEGIES

Chapter 6: Vertical Integration   178

Chapter 7: Corporate Diversification 206

Chapter 8: Organizing to Implement Corporate Diversification 244

Chapter 9: Strategic Alliances   276

Chapter 10: Mergers and Acquisitions   308

Acknowledgments

Obviously, a book like this is not written in isolation. We owe a debt of gratitude to all those at Prentice Hall who have supported its development. In particular, we want to thank Jeff Shelstad, VP/Editorial Director; Eric Frank, Director of Marketing; Michael Ablassmeir, Senior Acquisitions Editor; Annie Todd, VP/Director of Market Development; Kathleen McLellan, Market Development Manager; Mary Ellen Morrell, Production Editor; Janet Slowik, Art Director; Judy Leale, Associate Director Production Editorial; Melissa Yu, Associate Editor and Erika Rusnak, Development Editor. We are also grateful to our friend and colleague, Mark Hansen, for his important work on the Instructor's Manual and PowerPoints. Louis Marino helped with the test bank, and Deborah Gilliard has helped with the development of the web site. All these people were instrumental in creating this new approach to teaching strategic management.

Many people were involved in reviewing early drafts of this manuscript. Their efforts undoubtedly improved the manuscript dramatically. Their efforts are largely unsung, but very much appreciated.

Thank you to these professors who participated in early manuscript reviews:

Mainuddin Afza—*Bloomsburg University*

Peter Antoniou—*California State University-San Marcos*

Kendall Artz—*Baylor University*

Susan Barnes—*Washington State University*

Steven Congden—*University of Hartford*

Jim Davis—*University Notre Dame*

David Deeds—*Case Western Reserve University*

Tom Douglas—*Clemson University*

Jon Down—*Oregon State University*

Alan Ellstrand—*University of Arkansas*

James Fiet—*University of Louisville*

Jeff Furman—*Boston University*

Carole Jacobson—*Purdue University*

Joseph Mahoney—*University of Illinois*

Rick Martinez—*Baylor University*

Sharon Matusik—*University of Colorado at Boulder*

Gerry McNamara—*University of California-Riverside*

Elaine Mosakowski—*University of Colorado at Boulder*

Jeffrey Parker—*Jacksonville State University*

Pamela Pommerenke—*Michigan State University*

Peter Ring—*Loyola Marymount University*

Jiten Ruparel—*Otterbein College*

Rhetta Standifer—*University of Missouri*

Edward Ward—*Saint Cloud State University*

Thank you to the following professors who participated in multiple review activities:

Todd Alessandri—*Syracuse University*

Vikas Anand—*University of Arkansas*

Barry Dean Baysinger—*University of Kansas*

James Bloodgood—*Kansas State University*

Brian Boyd—*Arizona State University*

Trevis Certo—*Texas A&M University*

Rebecca Guidice—*University of Nevada-Las Vegas*

Mark Hansen—*Brigham Young University*

Andrew Inkpen—*Thunderbird University*

Constance James—*Pepperdine University*

Janice Joplin—*University of Texas at El Paso*

Franz Kellermanns—*Mississippi State University*

Laura Poppo Lockwood—*Virginia Polytechnic Institute and State University*

Denise Luethge—*University of Michigan-Flint*

Ram Mudambi—*Temple University*

Michael Pitts—*Virginia Commonwealth University*

David Sirmon—*Clemson University*

Jim Thurman—*George Washington University*

Marta White—*Georgia State University*

Thank you to these professors who participated in the Strategic Management Society Focus Groups in 2003 and 2004:

Todd Alessandri—*Syracuse University*

Brian Boyd—*Arizona State University*

Clay Dibrell—*Oregon State University*

Michael Fern—*University of North Carolina*

Marta Geletkanycz—*Boston College*

Amy Hillman—*Arizona State University*

Constance James—*Pepperdine University*

Franz Kellermanns—*Mississippi State*

Ram Mudambi—*Temple University*

Laura Poppo Lockwood—*Virginia Polytechnic Institute and State University*

David Sirmon—*Clemson University*

Jim Thurman—*George Washington University*

1

THE TOOLS
OF STRATEGIC ANALYSIS

What Is Strategy and the Strategic Management Process?

The music business is a mess. U.S. music sales were down 8.2 percent in 2002. Most major record labels have seen their profit margins fall from 15 to 20 percent in the late 1980s to below 5 percent currently. In 2003, many of these labels—including BMG, EMI, and Sony Music—laid off thousands of employees. Even artists like Metallica and Dr. Dre have complained that the structure of the music industry is fundamentally flawed and needs to be redesigned.

Singer-songwriter Sheryl Crow recently observed: "This industry

What Has Napster Wrought?

has been in such a funk. It really needs something . . . to get it going again." In fact, everyone associated with the music business is unhappy—except consumers. Consumers have never been happier.

Of course, it all began with Napster. A Web site where consumers could trade digital music

with each other, Napster opened up the possibility that people could download an entire music library to their hard drive and burn CDs, all for free. Not surprisingly, Napster's founder, Shawn Fanning, got a louder reception than any of the bands when he was introduced at the MTV Music Video Awards.

And while the original Napster was found to violate U.S. copyright laws and was forced out of business, free online downloading continues. Indeed, some researchers suggest that there was a

Learning Objectives

After reading this chapter, you should be able to:

1. Define the concept of strategy.

2. Describe the strategic management process.

3. Define competitive advantage and its relationship to economic value creation.

4. Describe two different measures of competitive advantage.

5. Explain the difference between emergent and intended strategies.

6. Discuss the importance of understanding a firm's strategy even if you are not a senior manager in a firm.

7. Describe how the strategic management process can be extended to include international business activities.

35 percent increase in free downloaded music from 2002 to 2003, despite several well-publicized prosecutions of individual file swappers.

Current free music download Web sites—like KaZaA, eDonkey, and Bit Torrent—operate on the margin of the law. However, since these Web sites do not reside on a single server, their proprietors are difficult to identify and prosecute.

The great irony is that, historically, the creation of new music formats has always enhanced the profitability of record labels. From the 78-rpm single of the 1930s and 1940s, to the 33-rpm long-playing record of the 1950s and 1960s, to the cassette tapes of the 1970s and 1980s, and the compact discs of the 1990s, every time a new recording format has been introduced, record company profits have soared. This has been the case even though some of these formats—including cassette tapes and burnable CDs—were not copy protected. But, so far, no record company has figured out how to make a profit from downloading music off the Internet.

Now, iTunes, Rhapsody, Sony Connect, and Wal-Mart Music Downloads have all recently entered the fee-based Internet music download market. These companies contract with various record companies to make music available to consumers over the Web for a fee. That way, record companies (and artists) are compensated for producing music, these Web sites earn a profit, and consumers have the opportunity to legally download music—albeit for a fee.

These and other fee-based music download firms have adopted two distinct strategies.

Some of them—including Apple iTunes, Sony Connect, and Wal-Mart Music Downloads—have no monthly subscription fee and charge relatively low per-song downloading fees (99 cents per song at Apple iTunes and Sony Connect and 88 cents per song at Wal-Mart Music Downloads), but they require users to purchase a particular brand of hardware to play downloaded songs. Apple iTunes requires users to purchase an Apple iPod; Sony Connect requires users to purchase a Sony player; and Wal-Mart Music Downloads requires users to purchase players that run Microsoft software. Apparently, Apple, Sony, and Wal-Mart are willing to forego some of the revenues associated with monthly subscriptions in the expectation that users will

purchase hardware they either manufacture or sell.

Other firms—including Rhapsody—do not lock users into a particular type of portable player: You can actually burn CDs directly from the Rhapsody Web site. However, they charge a $10-per-month subscription fee, in addition to 79 cents for every song that you burn.

It is too early to tell which, if either, of these strategies may ultimately solve the "free Internet downloading" problem of record companies. Currently, Apple's iTunes Web site has about 70 percent of this fee-based market. However, Sony has a major marketing campaign with McDonald's—every time you buy a Big Mac, you get a free Sony Connect download—so Apple's market share advantage may begin

to shrink. Also, it is difficult to rule out a firm as large and powerful as Wal-Mart. Moreover, the whole strategy of linking music downloads to particular technology standards is inconsistent with the initial vision of music downloading—to make it easy to gain access to music. Thus, Rhapsody's open architecture strategy also has merit. And, despite the efforts of these firms to grow the download-for-a-fee market, consumers currently pay for less than three percent of the music they download from the Web—and record company profits continue to fall.

Sources: D. Bank (2003). "RealNetworks is launching its own online-music network." *Wall Street Journal*, Wednesday, May 28, p. B7; P. Boutin (2004). "It's all groovy, baby." *Wired*, July, p. 91; B. Hindo (2004). "Music pirates: Still on board." *BusinessWeek*, January 26, p. 13; D. Leonard (2003). "Songs in the key of Steve." *Fortune*, May 12, pp. 52 +; W. Mossberg (2004). "The music man." *Wall Street Journal*, Monday, June 14, pp. B1 +.

The problems of the music industry—and the efforts of various firms to profitably solve these problems—exemplify the kinds of strategic management problems that all firms face. "What is happening in our industry?" "What is our competition going to do next?" "How should we respond?" "What can we do to make money in our business?" are among the central questions that all strategic managers—whether they work at Raytheon (one of the largest defense contractors in the United States) or Rhapsody, Sears or Sony Connect, IBM or iTunes Music Store—must address if they are going to survive and prosper. The process by which these questions are answered is the strategic management process. And the answer a firm develops for these questions is a firm's strategy.

Strategy and the Strategic Management Process

While most can agree that a firm's ability to survive and prosper depends critically on choosing and implementing a *good strategy*, there is less agreement about what a *strategy* is, and even less agreement about what constitutes a *good* strategy.

Indeed, there are almost as many different definitions of these concepts as there are books written about them.

Defining Strategy

In this book, a firm's **strategy** is defined as its theory about how to gain competitive advantages.[1] A *good strategy* is a strategy that actually generates such advantages. Apple's, Sony's, and Wal-Mart's *theory* of how to gain a competitive advantage in the music download-for-a-fee business is to use the music download business to help drive sales of their portable digital listening devices. Rhapsody's *theory* is that users will want to download music to a highly flexible format—the burned CD—and will be willing to pay a subscription fee for that opportunity.

Each of these theories of how to gain competitive advantages in the music download-for-a-fee business—like all theories—is based on a set of assumptions and hypotheses about the way competition in this industry is likely to evolve, and how that evolution can be exploited to earn a profit. The greater the extent to which these assumptions and hypotheses accurately reflect how competition in this industry actually evolves, the more likely it is that a firm will gain a competitive advantage from implementing its strategies. If these assumptions and hypotheses turn out not to be accurate, then a firm's strategies are not likely to be a source of competitive advantage.

But here is the challenge. It is usually very difficult to predict precisely how competition in an industry will evolve, and so it is rarely possible to know for sure that a firm is choosing the right strategy. This is why a firm's strategy is almost always a theory—it's a firm's best bet about how competition is going to evolve, and how that evolution can be exploited for competitive advantage.

The Strategic Management Process

While it is usually difficult to know—for sure—that a firm is pursuing the best strategy, it is possible to reduce the likelihood that mistakes are being made. The best way to do this is to choose a firm's strategy carefully and systematically, and to follow the strategic management process. The **strategic management process** is a sequential set of analyses and choices that can increase the likelihood that a firm will choose a *good strategy*, that is, a strategy that generates competitive advantages. An example of the strategic management process is presented in Figure 1.1. Not surprisingly, this book is organized around this strategic management process.

Figure 1.1 The Strategic Management Process

A Firm's Mission

The strategic management process begins when a firm defines its mission. A firm's **mission** is its long- term purpose. Missions define both what a firm aspires to be in the long run and what it wants to avoid in the meantime. Missions are often written down in the form of **mission statements**. Table 1.1 contains examples of several mission statements taken from well-known firms.

Some Missions May Not Affect Firm Performance. As shown in Table 1.1, most mission statements incorporate many common elements. For example, many define the businesses within which a firm will operate—automobiles for Ford; computer hardware, software, and services for IBM. Some define how a firm will compete in those businesses—doing everything direct at Dell, and just winning at the Oakland Raiders. Many even define the core values that a firm espouses—the "soul of Dell" and Anheuser-Busch's values.

Indeed, mission statements often contain so many common elements that some have questioned whether or not having a mission statement actually creates value for a firm.[2] Moreover, even if a mission statement does say something unique about a company, if that mission statement does not influence behavior throughout an organization, it is unlikely to have much impact on a firm's actions. After all, Enron's 1999 annual report includes the following statement of values:

> *Integrity: We work with customers and prospects openly, honestly and sincerely. When we say we will do something, we will do it; when we say we cannot or will not do something, then we won't do it.[3]*

This statement was published at exactly the same time that senior management at Enron was engaging in activities that ultimately defrauded investors, partners, and Enron's own employees—and has landed some Enron executives in jail.[4]

Table 1.1 **Examples of Mission Statements Taken from Several Well-Known Firms**

Anheuser-Busch

Our vision

Through all our products, services, and relationships, we will add to life's enjoyment.

Our mission

Be the world's beer company.
Enrich and entertain a global audience.
Deliver superior returns to our shareholders.

Our values we believe in

Quality in everything we do.
Exceeding customer expectations.
Trust, respect, and integrity in all our relationships.
Continuous improvement, innovation, and embracing change.
Teamwork and open, honest communication.
Each employee's responsibility for contributing to the company's success.
Creating a safe, productive, and rewarding work environment.
Building a high-performing, diverse workforce.
Promoting the responsible consumption of our products.
Preserving and protecting the environment and supporting communities where we do business.

Dell

Dell is building its technology, its business, and its communities through direct relationships with our customers, our employees, and our neighbors. Through this process, we are committed to bringing value to customers and adding value to our company, our neighborhoods, our communities, and our world through diversity, environmental and global citizenship initiatives.

The core elements of the "soul of Dell"

Customers: We believe in creating loyal customers by providing a superior experience at a great value.

The Dell Team: We believe our continued success lies in teamwork and in the opportunity each team member has to learn, develop, and grow.

Direct Relationships: We believe in being direct in all we do.

Global Citizenship: We believe in participating responsibly in the global marketplace.

Winning: We have a passion for winning in everything we do.

Ford Motor Company

Our vision

To become the world's leading consumer company for automotive products and services.

Our mission

We are a global family with a proud heritage passionately committed to providing personal mobility for people around the world.

We anticipate consumer need and deliver outstanding products and services that improve people's lives.

Our values

Our business is driven by our consumer focus, creativity, resourcefulness, and entrepreneurial spirit.

We are an inspired, diverse team. We respect everyone's contribution. The health and safety of our people are paramount.

We are a leader in environmental responsibility. Our integrity is never compromised and we make a positive contribution to society.

We constantly strive to improve in everything we do. Guided by these values, we provide superior returns to our shareholders.

IBM

At IBM, we strive to lead in the invention, development, and manufacture of the industry's most advanced information technologies, including computer systems, software, storage systems, and microelectronics. We translate these advanced technologies into value for our customers through our professional solutions, services, and consulting businesses worldwide.

The Oakland Raiders

Just Win—Baby!

Sources: www.anheuser-busch.com; www.dell.com, used with permission of Dell Computer Corporation; www.ford.com, used with permission of Ford Motor Company; www.ibm.com, used with permission of IBM; www.oaklandraiders.com.

Table 1.2   **A Sample of Visionary Firms**

3M	Marriott
American Express	Merck
Boeing	Motorola
Citicorp	Nordstrom
Ford	Philip Morris
General Electric	Procter & Gamble
Hewlett-Packard	Sony
IBM	Wal-Mart
Johnson & Johnson	Walt Disney

Source: J. C. Collins and J. I. Porras. *Built to last: successful habits of visionary companies.* New York: Harper Collins Publishers Inc. ©1994 James C. Collins and Jerry I. Porras. Reprinted by permission.

Some Missions Can Improve Firm Performance. Despite these caveats, research has identified some firms whose sense of purpose and mission permeates all that they do. Some of these **visionary firms**, or firms whose mission is central to all they do, are presented in Table 1.2.[5] One interesting thing to note about visionary firms is their long-term profitability. From 1926 through 1995, an investment of $1 in one of these firms would have increased in value to $6,536. That same dollar invested in an average firm over this same time period would have been worth $415 in 1995.

These visionary firms earned substantially higher returns than average firms even though many of their mission statements suggest that profit maximizing, while an important corporate objective, is not their primary reason for existence. Consider what Jim Burke, a former CEO at Johnson & Johnson (one of the visionary firms identified in Table 1.2), says about the relationship between profits and his firm's mission and mission statement:

All our management is geared to profit on a day-to-day basis. That's part of the business of being in business. But too often, in this and other businesses, people are inclined to think, "We'd better do this because if we don't, it's going to show up on the figures over the short-term." [Our mission] allows them to say, "Wait a minute. I don't have to do that." The management has told me that they're . . . interested in me operating under this set of principles.[6]

Some Missions Can Hurt Firm Performance. Although some firms have used their missions to develop strategies that create significant competitive advantages, missions can hurt a firm's performance as well. For example, sometimes a firm's mission will be very inwardly focused and defined only with reference to the personal values and priorities of its founders or top managers, independent of whether or not those values and priorities are consistent with the economic realities facing a firm. Strategies derived from such missions or visions are not likely to be a source of competitive advantage.

For example, Ben & Jerry's Ice Cream was founded in 1977 by Ben Cohen and Jerry Greenfield, both as a way to produce super-premium ice cream and as a way to create an organization based on the values of the 1960s counterculture. This strong sense of mission led Ben & Jerry's to adopt some very unusual human resource and other policies. Among these policies, the company adopted a compensation system whereby the highest paid firm employee could earn no more than five times the income of the lowest paid firm employee. Later this ratio was adjusted to seven to one. However, even at this level, such a compensation policy made it very difficult to acquire the senior management talent needed to ensure the growth and profitability of the firm without grossly overpaying the lowest paid employees in the firm. When a new CEO was appointed to the firm in 1995, his $250,000 salary violated this compensation policy.

Indeed, though the frozen dessert market rapidly consolidated through the late 1990s, Ben & Jerry's Ice Cream remained an independent firm, partly because of Cohen's and Greenfield's commitment to maintaining the social values that their firm embodied. Lacking access to the broad distribution network and managerial talent that would have been available if Ben & Jerry's had merged with another firm, the company's growth and profitability lagged. Finally, in April of 2000, Ben & Jerry's Ice Cream was acquired by Unilever. However, the 66 percent premium finally earned by Ben & Jerry's stockholders in April 2000 had been delayed for several years. In this sense, Cohen's and Greenfield's commitment to a set of personal values and priorities was at least partly inconsistent with the economic realities of the frozen dessert market in the United States.[7]

Obviously, since a firm's mission can help, hurt, or have no impact on its performance, missions by themselves do not necessarily lead a firm to choose and implement strategies that generate competitive advantages. Indeed, as suggested in Figure 1.1, while defining a firm's mission is an important step in the strategic management process, it is only the first step in that process.

Objectives

Where a firm's mission is a broad statement of its purpose and values, its **objectives** are specific measurable targets a firm can use to evaluate the extent to which it is realizing its mission. Consider, for example, 3M's mission statement in Table 1.3. This statement emphasizes the importance of finding innovative products and producing high returns for shareholders. However, 3M also lists some objectives associated with its mission: growth in earnings per share averaging 10 percent or better per year, a return on employed capital of 27 percent or better, at least 30 percent of sales from products that are no more than four years old, and so forth.

High-quality objectives are tightly connected to elements of a firm's mission and are relatively easy to measure and track over time. Low-quality objectives either do not exist or are not connected to elements of a firm's mission, are not quantitative, and are difficult to measure or difficult to track over time. Obviously, low-quality objectives cannot be used by management to evaluate how well a mission is being realized. Indeed, one indication that a firm is not that serious about realizing part of its mission statement is when there are no objectives, or only low quality objectives, associated with that part of the mission.

External and Internal Analysis

The next two phases of the strategic management process—external analysis and internal analysis—occur more or less simultaneously. By conducting an **external analysis**, a firm identifies the critical threats and opportunities in its competitive environment. It also examines how competition in this environment is likely to evolve and what implications that evolution has for the threats and opportunities

Table 1.3   **3M's Mission Statement**

We are committed to

Satisfying our **customers** with superior quality and value.

Providing **investors** with an attractive return through sustained, high-quality growth.

Respecting our **social and physical environment**.

Being a company that **employees** are proud to be a part of.

Satisfying our customers with superior quality and value

- Providing the highest quality products and services consistent with our customers' requirements and preferences.
- Making every aspect of every transaction a satisfying experience for our customers.
- Finding innovative ways to make life easier and better for our customers.

Providing investors with an attractive return through sustained, high-quality growth

Our goals are:

- Growth in earnings per share averaging 10 percent a year or better.
- A return on capital employed of 27 percent or better.
- A return on stockholders' equity of between 20 and 25 percent.
- At least 30 percent of our sales each year from products new in the last four years.

Respecting our social and physical environment

- Complying with all laws and meeting or exceeding regulations.
- Keeping customers, employees, investors, and the public informed about our operations.
- Developing products and processes that have a minimal impact on the environment.
- Staying attuned to the changing needs and preferences of our customers, employees, and society.
- Uncompromising honesty and integrity in every aspect of our operations.

Being a company that employees are proud to be a part of

- Respecting the dignity and worth of individuals.
- Encouraging individual initiative and innovation in an atmosphere characterized by flexibility, cooperation, and trust.
- Challenging individual capabilities.
- Valuing human diversity and providing equal opportunity for development.

Source: J. Abrahams (1995). *The mission statement book.* Berkeley, CA: Ten Speed Press, pp. 400–402. Courtesy of 3M Company.

a firm is facing. A considerable literature on techniques for and approaches to conducting external analysis has evolved over the last several years. This literature is the primary subject matter of Chapter 2 of this book.

Where external analysis focuses on the environmental threats and opportunities facing a firm, **internal analysis** helps a firm identify its organizational strengths and weaknesses. It also helps a firm understand which of its resources and capabilities are likely to be sources of competitive advantage and which are less likely to be sources of such advantages. Finally, internal analysis can be used by firms to identify those areas of its organization that require improvement and change. Just as is the case with external analysis, a considerable literature on techniques for and approaches to conducting internal analysis has evolved over the past several years. This literature is the primary subject matter of Chapter 3 of this book.

Strategic Choice

Armed with a mission, objectives, and completed external and internal analyses, a firm is ready to make its strategic choices. That is, a firm is ready to choose its "theory of how to gain competitive advantage."

The strategic choices available to firms fall into two large categories: business-level strategies and corporate-level strategies. **Business-level strategies** are actions firms take to gain competitive advantages in a single market or industry, and are the topic of Part Two of this book. The two most common business-level strategies are cost leadership (Chapter 4) and product differentiation (Chapter 5).

Corporate-level strategies are actions firms take to gain competitive advantages by operating in multiple markets or industries simultaneously and are the topic of Part 3 of this book. Common corporate-level strategies include vertical integration strategies (Chapter 6), diversification strategies (Chapters 7 and 8), strategic alliance strategies (Chapter 9), and merger and acquisition strategies (Chapter 10).

Obviously, the details of choosing specific strategies can be quite complex, and a discussion of these details will be delayed until later in the book. However, the underlying logic of strategic choice is not complex. Based on the strategic management process, the objective when making a strategic choice is to choose a strategy that (1) supports the firm's mission, (2) is consistent with a firm's objectives, (3) exploits opportunities in a firm's environment with a firm's strengths, and (4) neutralizes threats in a firm's environment while avoiding a firm's weaknesses. Assuming this strategy is implemented—the last step of the strategic management process—a strategy that meets these four criteria is very likely to be a source of competitive advantage for a firm.

Strategy Implementation

Of course, simply choosing a strategy means nothing if that strategy is not implemented. **Strategy implementation** occurs when a firm adopts organizational policies and practices that are consistent with its strategy. Three specific organizational policies and practices are particularly important in implementing a strategy: a firm's formal organizational structure, its formal and informal management control systems, and its employee compensation policies. A firm that adopts an organizational structure, management controls, and employee compensation that are consistent with and reinforce its strategies is more likely to be able to implement those strategies than a firm that adopts an organizational structure, management controls, and compensation policies that are inconsistent with its strategies. Specific organizational structures, management controls, and compensation policies used to implement the business-level strategies of cost leadership and product differentiation are discussed in Chapters 4 and 5. How organizational structure, management controls, and compensation can be used to implement corporate-level strategies, including vertical integration, strategic alliance, and merger and acquisition strategies, is discussed in Chapters 6, 9, and 10, respectively. However, there is so much information about implementing diversification strategies that an entire chapter, Chapter 8, is dedicated to the discussion of how this corporate-level strategy is implemented.

What Is Competitive Advantage?

Of course, the ultimate objective of the strategic management process is to enable a firm to choose and implement a strategy that generates a competitive advantage. But what is a competitive advantage? In general, a firm has a **competitive advantage** when it is able to create more economic value than rival firms. **Economic value** is simply the difference between the perceived benefits gained by a customer that purchases a firm's products or services and the full economic cost of these products or services. Thus, the size of a firm's competitive advantage is the difference between the economic value a firm is able to create and the economic value its rivals are able to create.[8]

Consider the two firms presented in Figure 1.2. Both these firms compete in the same market for the same customers. However, Firm I generates $180 of economic value each time it sells a product or service, while Firm II generates $150 of economic value each time it sells a product or service. Since Firm I generates more economic value each time it sells a product or service, it has a com-

Figure 1.2 The Sources of a Firm's Competitive Advantage

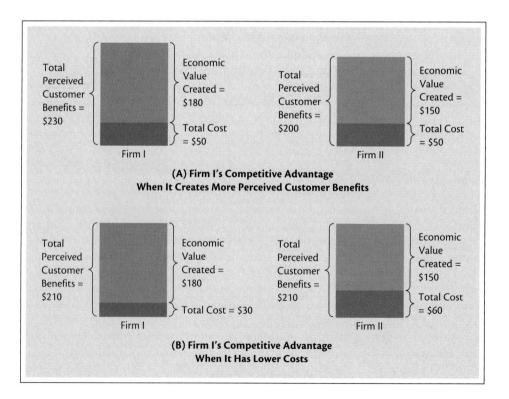

petitive advantage over Firm II. The size of this competitive advantage is equal to the difference in the economic value these two firms create, in this case, $30 ($180 − $150 = $30).

However, as shown in the figure, Firm I's advantage may come from different sources. For example, it might be the case that Firm I creates greater perceived benefits for its customers than Firm II. In panel A of the figure, Firm I creates perceived customer benefits worth $230, while Firm II creates perceived customer benefits worth only $200. Thus, even though both firms' costs are the same (equal to $50 per unit sold), Firm I creates more economic value ($230 − $50 = $180) than Firm II ($200 − $50 = $150). Indeed, it is possible for Firm I, in this situation, to have higher costs than Firm II and still create more economic value than Firm II if these higher costs are offset by Firm I's ability to create greater perceived benefits for its customers.

Alternatively, as shown in panel B of the figure, these two firms may create the same level of perceived customer benefit (equal to $210 in this example), but have different costs. If Firm I's costs per unit are only $30, it will generate $180 worth of economic value ($210 − $30 = $180). If Firm II's costs are $60, it will generate only $150 of economic value ($210 − $60 = $150). Indeed, it might be possible for Firm I to create a lower level of perceived benefits for its customers than Firm II and still create more economic value than Firm II as long as its disadvantage in perceived customer benefits was more than offset by its cost advantage.

A firm's competitive advantage can be temporary or sustained. As summarized in Figure 1.3, a **temporary competitive advantage** is a competitive advantage that lasts for a very short period of time. A **sustained competitive advantage**, on the other hand, can last much longer. How long sustained competitive advantages can last is discussed in the Research Made Relevant feature. Firms that create the same economic value as their rivals experience **competitive parity**. Finally, firms that generate less economic value than their rivals have a **competitive disadvantage**. Not surprisingly, competitive disadvantages can be either temporary or sustained, depending on how long they last.

Figure 1.3   Types of Competitive Advantage

Research Made Relevant

How Sustainable Are Competitive Advantages?

For some time, economists have been interested in how long firms are able to sustain competitive advantages. Traditional economic theory predicts that such advantages should be short-lived in highly competitive markets. This theory suggests that any competitive advantages gained by a particular firm will quickly be identified and imitated by other firms, ensuring competitive parity in the long run. However, in real life, competitive advantages often last longer than what traditional economic theory predicts.

One of the first scholars to examine this issue was Dennis Mueller. In his article, Mueller divided a sample of 472 firms into eight categories, depending on their level of performance in 1949. He then examined the impact of a firm's initial performance on its subsequent performance. The traditional economic hypothesis was that all firms in the sample would converge on an average level of performance. This did not occur. Indeed, firms that were performing well in an earlier time period tended to perform well in later time periods and firms that performed poorly in an earlier time period tended to perform poorly in later time periods as well.

Geoffrey Waring followed up on Mueller's work by explaining why competitive advantages seem to persist longer in some industries than in others. Waring found that, among other factors, firms that operate in industries that (1) are informationally complex; (2) require customers to know a great deal in order to use an industry's products; (3) require a great deal of research and development; and (4) have significant economies of scale are more likely to have sustained competitive advantages compared to firms that operate in industries without these attributes.

Peter Roberts studied the persistence of profitability in one particular industry—the U.S. pharmaceutical industry. Roberts found that not only can firms sustain competitive advantages in this industry, but that the ability to do so is almost entirely attributable to the firms' capacity to innovate by bringing out new and powerful drugs.

In many ways, the difference between traditional economics research and strategic management research is that the former attempts to explain why competitive advantages should not persist while the latter attempts to explain when they can. Thus far, most empirical research suggests that firms, in at least some settings, can sustain competitive advantages.

Sources: D. C. Mueller (1977). "The persistence of profits above the norm." *Economica*, 44, pp. 369–380; P. W. Roberts (1999). "Product innovation, product-market competition, and persistent profitability in the U.S. pharmaceutical industry." *Strategic Management Journal*, 20, pp. 655–670; G. F. Waring (1996). "Industry differences in the persistence of firm-specific returns." *The American Economic Review*, 86, pp. 1253–1265.

The Strategic Management Process, Revisited

With this description of the strategic management process now complete, it is possible to redraw this process, as depicted in Figure 1.1, to incorporate the various options a firm faces as it chooses and implements its strategy. This is done in Figure 1.4. Figure 1.4 is the organizing framework that will be used throughout this book.

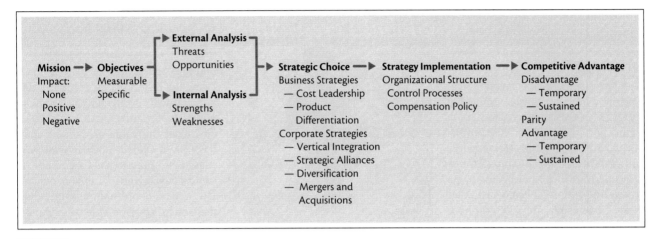

Figure 1.4   Organizing Framework

Measuring Competitive Advantage

A firm has a competitive advantage when it creates more economic value than its rivals, and economic value is the difference between the perceived customer benefits associated with buying a firm's products or services and the cost of producing and selling these products or services. These are deceptively simple definitions. However, these concepts are not always easy to measure directly. For example, the benefits of a firm's products or services are always a matter of customer perception, and perceptions are not easy to measure. Also, the total costs associated with producing a particular product or service may not always be easy to identify or associate with a particular product or service. Despite the very real challenges associated with measuring a firm's competitive advantage, two approaches have emerged. The first estimates a firm's competitive advantage by examining its accounting performance; the second by examining its economic performance. Each of these approaches is discussed below.

Accounting Measures of Competitive Advantage

A firm's **accounting performance** is a measure of its competitive advantage calculated by using information from a firm's published profit and loss and balance sheet statements. A firm's profit and loss and balance sheet statements, in turn, are typically created using widely accepted accounting standards and principles. The application of these standards and principles makes it possible to compare the accounting performance of one firm to the accounting performance of other firms, even if those firms are not in the same industry. However, to the extent that these standards and principles are not applied in generating a firm's accounting statements, or to the extent that different firms use different accounting standards and principles in generating their statements, it can be difficult to compare the accounting performance of firms.

Global Perspectives

Historically, there have been important differences in accounting standards in different countries around the world. These differences can have a significant impact on the profits, losses, and capital stock a firm reports, and thus a significant impact on a firm's performance as measured by its accounting ratios. This suggests that those interested in determining whether, say, Matsushita (a Japanese consumer electronics firm) is outperforming Philips (a Dutch consumer electronics firm) must take into consideration the accounting standards and practices of these two firms.

One of the most important of these accounting differences has to do with how a firm values its current assets. Many countries, including the United States and Japan, require firms to carry assets on their books according to their historical cost, minus depreciation.

**Accounting Around
the World**

However, this approach sometimes understates the true market value of these assets. For example, it may have cost a firm $100 million to construct a

building on a particular piece of land. Using the historical cost approach, this building will be valued at $100 million, minus depreciation, on a firm's books. However, the value of the land may have skyrocketed since it was purchased and used to erect a building. It could now be worth $1 billion, not just $100 million. Some countries—including the United Kingdom, the Netherlands, and Australia—let firms restate the value of their assets on their books to reflect current market values. This can have a significant impact on a firm's balance sheet which, in turn, can affect a firm's accounting ratios.

Another way accounting practices vary around the world is how firms are allowed to value their inventories. Two general approaches to valuing inventories exist: LIFO (last in, first out) and FIFO (first in, first out). When inflation is high, LIFO approaches to valuing inven-

As described in the Global Perspective feature, these issues can be particularly challenging when comparing the performance of firms in different countries around the world.

One way to use a firm's accounting statements to measure its competitive advantage is through the use of accounting ratios. **Accounting ratios** are simply numbers taken from a firm's financial statements that are manipulated in ways that describe various aspects of a firm's performance. Some of the most common accounting ratios that can be used to characterize a firm's performance are presented in Table 1.4. These ratio measures of firm accounting performance can be grouped into four categories: (1) **profitability ratios**, or ratios with some measure of profit in the numerator and some measure of firm size or assets in the denominator; (2) **liquidity ratios**, or ratios that focus on the ability of a firm to meet its short-term financial obligations; (3) **leverage ratios**, or ratios that focus on the level of a firm's financial flexibility, including its ability to obtain more debt; and (4) **activity ratios**, or ratios that focus on the level of activity in a firm's business.

Of course, these ratios, by themselves, say very little about a firm. To tell us how a firm is performing, its accounting ratios must be compared with some standard. In general, that standard is the average of accounting ratios of other firms in the same industry. Using ratio analysis, a firm earns **above average accounting performance** when its performance is greater than the industry tories tend to raise a firm's reported cost of goods sold and reduce its reported profits (and tax liability) compared to FIFO. U.S., Canadian, and Japanese firms can use either LIFO or FIFO methods of accounting for inventory. In the United Kingdom, Brazil, and New Zealand, both methods are legal, but most firms use FIFO; in Australia, LIFO is illegal.

Countries also vary in the extent to which they allow firms to operate multiple sets of books, one for financial reporting and one for tax reporting. For example, in the United States, most firms have two sets of books. The first presents the financial status of the firm to the financial community. The second reports the financial status of the firm to the government for tax purposes. Not surprisingly, it is usually the case that the performance of a firm as reported to the financial community is more positive than the performance of a firm as reported to the government. After all, firms—just like most people—don't like to pay taxes. However, in Germany, firms are not allowed to keep two sets of books. The accounting numbers they report to the financial community are also used to establish their tax liability. In an effort to reduce this liability, it is not uncommon for German firms to engage in accounting practices that have the effect of reducing their reported performance. Thus, when comparing U.S. and German firms in the same industry, it is important to recognize that legal differences between these countries have the effect of biasing the reported performance of the German firms down, when compared to U.S. firms. This means, for example, that just because Daimler-Chrysler's reported accounting performance is, say, lower than Ford's in a given year, the difference between the actual performance of these firms may not be as large as implied by a simple accounting ratio analysis.

All of this greatly complicates the application of accounting measures of competitive advantage for firms that are headquartered in different countries, especially when those countries have important differences in their accounting rules and regulations. However, over time, as markets have become more global, differences in accounting standards have tended to shrink. While we certainly are not in a world where the standard accounting practices of Japan are the same as the standard accounting practices in Germany, these differences have become smaller over time.

Sources: F. Choi (1997). *International accounting and finance handbook,* 2nd ed. New York: Wiley; F. Choi and R. Levich (1990). *The capital market effects of international accounting diversity.* Homewood, IL: Dow-Jones Irwin; R. Griffin and M. Pustay (1999). *International business,* 2nd ed. Reading, MA: Addison-Wesley.

average. Such firms typically have competitive advantages, sustained or otherwise. A firm earns **average accounting performance** when its performance is equal to the industry average. These firms generally enjoy only competitive parity. A firm earns **below average accounting performance** when its performance is less than the industry average. These firms generally experience competitive disadvantages.

Consider, for example, the performance of Apple Computer. Apple's financial statements for 2001 and 2002 are presented in Table 1.5. Losses in this table are presented in parentheses. Several ratio measures of accounting performance are calculated for Apple in these two years in Table 1.6.

Clearly, Apple's accounting performance improved from 2001 to 2002. After all, Apple lost money in 2001 and made a little bit of money in 2002. In fact, while Apple underperformed its industry in 2001, it performed roughly on par with its industry in 2002. The median ROA for firms in the computer and office equipment industry in 2001 and 2002 was zero percent. The median ROE for firms in this industry in 2001 and 2002 was three percent. Apple's current and quick ratio suggests that the firm, despite losing money in 2001, was not threatened with bankruptcy. Indeed, with only 35 percent of its total assets in debt, Apple actually has some debt capacity to grow future business opportunities.

Table 1.4   **Common Ratios to Measure a Firm's Accounting Performance**

Ratio	Calculation	Interpretation
Profitability Ratios		
1. Return on total assets (ROA)	$\dfrac{\text{profits after taxes}}{\text{total assets}}$	A measure of return on total investment in a firm. Larger is usually better.
2. Return on equity (ROE)	$\dfrac{\text{profits after taxes}}{\text{total stockholders' equity}}$	A measure of return on total equity investment in a firm. Larger is usually better.
3. Gross profit margin	$\dfrac{\text{sales} - \text{cost of goods sold}}{\text{sales}}$	A measure of sales available to cover operating expenses and still generate a profit. Larger is usually better.
4. Earnings per share (EPS)	$\dfrac{\text{profits (after taxes)}\ \text{prefered stock dividends}}{\text{number of shares of common stock outstanding}}$	A measure of profit available to owners of common stock. Larger is usually better.
5. Price earnings ratio (p/e)	$\dfrac{\text{current market price/share}}{\text{after-tax earnings/share}}$	A measure of anticipated firm performance— high p/e ratio tends to indicate that the stock market anticipates strong future performance. Larger is usually better.
6. Cash flow per share	$\dfrac{\text{after-tax profits} + \text{depreciation}}{\text{number of common shares outstanding}}$	A measure of funds available to fund activities above current level of costs. Larger is usually better.
Liquidity Ratios		
1. Current ratio	$\dfrac{\text{current assets}}{\text{current liabilities}}$	A measure of the ability of a firm to cover its current liabilities with assets that can be converted into cash in the short term. Recommended in the range of 2 to 3.
2. Quick ratio	$\dfrac{\text{current assets} - \text{inventory}}{\text{current liabilities}}$	A measure of the ability of a firm to meet its short-term obligations without selling off its current inventory. A ratio of 1 is thought to be acceptable in many industries.
Leverage Ratios		
1. Debt to assets	$\dfrac{\text{total debt}}{\text{total assets}}$	A measure of the extent to which debt has been used to finance a firm's business activities. The higher, the greater the risk of bankruptcy.
2. Debt to equity	$\dfrac{\text{total debt}}{\text{total equity}}$	A measure of the use of debt versus equity to finance a firm's business activities. Generally less than 1.
3. Times interest earned	$\dfrac{\text{profits before interest and taxes}}{\text{total interest charges}}$	A measure of how much a firm's profits can decline and still meet its interest obligations. Should be well above 1.
Activity Ratios		
1. Inventory turnover	$\dfrac{\text{sales}}{\text{inventory}}$	A measure of the speed with which a firm's inventory is turning over.
2. Accounts receivable turnover	$\dfrac{\text{annual credit sales}}{\text{accounts receivable}}$	A measure of the average time it takes a firm to collect on credit sales.
3. Average collection period	$\dfrac{\text{accounts receivable}}{\text{average daily sales}}$	A measure of the time it takes a firm to receive payment after a sale has been made.

Table 1.5 **Apple Computer's Financial Statements for 2001 and 2002 (numbers in millions)**

	2002	2001
Net sales	5,742	5,363
Cost of goods sold	4,139	4,128
Gross margin	1,603	1,235
Selling, general and administrative expenses	1,111	1,138
Other operating expenses	475	441
Total operating expenses	1,586	1,579
Operating income (loss)	17	(344)
Other income, net	70	292
Total income (loss), before tax	87	(52)
Provision for (benefit from) income taxes	22	(15)
Net income, after taxes	65	(37)
Inventories	45	11
Total current assets	5,388	5,143
Total assets	6,289	6,021
Total current liabilities	1,658	1,518
Total liabilities	2,203	2,101
Total shareholders' equity	4,095	3,920
Total assets	6,298	6,021

Economic Measures of Competitive Advantage

The great advantage of accounting measures of competitive advantage is that they are relatively easy to compute. All publicly traded firms have to make their accounting statements available to the public. Even privately owned firms will typically release some information about their accounting performance. Once you have access to these statements, it is quite easy to calculate various accounting ratios. Comparing these ratios to industry averages can tell you quite a bit about a firm's competitive position.

However, accounting measures of competitive advantage have at least one significant limitation. Earlier, economic profit was defined as the difference between the perceived benefit associated with purchasing a firm's products or services and the cost of producing and selling that product or service. There is one important component of cost that is typically not included in most accounting measures of competitive advantage: that is the cost of the capital a firm employs to produce and sell its products. The **cost of capital** is the rate of return that a firm promises to pay its suppliers of capital to induce them to invest in the firm. Once

Table 1.6 **Some Accounting Ratios for Apple Computer in 2001 and 2002**

	2002	2001
Return on Assets	0.13	(.006)
Return on Equity	.016	(.009)
Gross Profit Margin	.279	.231
Current Ratio	3.25	3.38
Quick Ratio	3.22	3.38
Debt to Assets	.350	.349
Debt to Equity	.538	.536

these investments are made, a firm can use this capital to produce and sell products and services. However, a firm must provide the promised return to its sources of capital if it expects to obtain more investment capital in the future. **Economic measures of competitive advantage** compare a firm's level of return to its cost of capital instead of to the average level of return in the industry.

Generally, there are two broad categories of sources of capital: **debt** (capital from banks and bondholders) and **equity** (capital from individuals and institutions that purchase a firm's stock). The **cost of debt** is equal to the interest that a firm must pay its debt holders (adjusted for taxes) in order to induce those debt holders to lend money to a firm. The **cost of equity** is equal to the rate of return a firm must promise its equity holders in order to induce these individuals and institutions to invest in a firm. A firm's **weighted average cost of capital** or **WACC** is simply the percentage of a firm's total capital that is debt times the cost of debt plus the percentage of a firm's total capital that is equity times the cost of equity. A simple approach to measuring a firm's WACC is described in the Strategy in Depth feature.

Conceptually, a firm's cost of capital is the level of performance a firm must attain if it is to satisfy the economic objectives of two of its critical stakeholders: debt holders and equity holders. A firm that earns above its cost of capital is likely to be able to attract additional capital, as debt holders and equity holders will scramble to make additional funds available for this firm. Such a firm is said to be earning **above normal economic performance** and will be able to use its access to cheap capital to help grow and expand its business. A firm that earns its cost of capital is said to have **normal economic performance**. This level of performance is said to be "normal" because this is the level of performance that most of a firm's equity and debt holders expect. Firms that have normal economic performance are able to gain access to the capital they need to survive, although they are not prospering. Growth opportunities may be somewhat limited for these firms. In general, firms with competitive parity usually have normal economic performance. A firm that earns less than its cost of capital is in the process of liquidating. Such **below normal economic performance** implies that a firm's debt and equity holders will be looking for alternative ways to invest their money, someplace where they can earn at least what they expect to earn, that is, normal economic performance. Unless a firm having below normal performance changes, its long-term viability will come into question. Obviously, firms that have a competitive disadvantage generally have below normal economic performance.

Measuring a firm's performance relative to its cost of capital has several advantages for strategic analysis. Foremost among these is the notion that a firm that earns at least its cost of capital is satisfying two of its most important stakeholders—debt holders and equity holders. Despite the advantages of comparing a firm's performance to its cost of capital, this approach has some important limitations as well.

For example, it can sometimes be difficult to calculate a firm's cost of capital. This is especially true if a firm is **privately held**—that is, has stock that is not traded on public stock markets, or is a division of a larger company. For example, it would be very difficult to calculate the cost of capital for many of the firms competing in the music download-for-a-fee business. Several of these firms are not publicly traded (e.g., Rhapsody). Some are divisions of publicly traded firms (e.g., iTunes Music Store is a division of Apple Computer). In these situations, it may be necessary to use accounting ratios to measure a firm's performance.

Strategy in Depth

A firm's weighted average cost of capital (WACC) can be an important benchmark against which to compare a firm's performance. However, calculating this number can sometimes be tricky. Fortunately, it is possible to obtain all the information needed to calculate a firm's WACC—at least for publicly traded firms—from information published in outlets such as Moody's, Standard and Poor's, Dun and Bradstreet, and Value Line. These publications are in every major business school library in the world, and are also online.

To calculate a firm's WACC, five pieces of information are required: (1) a firm's debt rating, (2) its marginal tax rate, (3) its Beta, (4) the risk-free and market rates of return in the years you are calculating a firm's WACC, and (5) information about a firm's capital structure.

Typically, a firm's debt rating will be presented in the form of a series of letters, for example, AA or BBB–. Think of these ratings as grades for a firm's riskiness: an "A" is less risky than an "AA" which is less risky than a "BBB+", and so forth. At any given point in time, there is a market-determined interest rate for a firm with a given debt rating. Suppose that the market-determined interest rate for a firm with a BBB debt rating was 7.5 percent. This is a firm's before-tax cost of debt. However, since, in the United States, interest payments are tax deductible, this before-tax cost of debt has to be adjusted for the tax savings a firm has from using debt. If a firm is reasonably large, then it will almost certainly have to pay the

Estimating a Firm's Weighted Average Cost of Capital

largest marginal tax rate, which in the United States has been 39 percent. So, the after-tax cost of debt in this example is (1 − .39) (7.5) or 4.58 percent.

A firm's Beta is a measure of how highly correlated the price of a firm's equity is to the overall stock market. Betas are published for most publicly traded firms. The risk-free rate of return is the rate the U.S. federal government has to pay on its long-term bonds to get investors to buy these bonds, and the market rate of return is the return investors would obtain if they purchased one share of each of the stocks traded on public exchanges. Historically, this risk-free rate of return has been low: around 3 percent. The market rate of return has averaged around 8.5 percent in the United States. Using these numbers, and

assuming that a firm's Beta is equal to 1.2, the cost of a firm's equity capital can be estimated using the Capital Asset Pricing Model, or CAPM, as follows:

Cost of Equity = Risk Free Rate of Return + (Market Rate of Return − Risk Free Rate of Return) Beta

For our example, this equation is:

$$9.6 = 3.0 + (8.5 − 3.0)1.2$$

Since firms obtain no tax advantages from using equity capital, the before- and after-tax cost of equity is the same.

To calculate a firm's WACC, simply multiple the percentage of a firm's total capital that is debt times the after-tax cost of debt and add it to the percentage of a firm's total capital that is equity times the cost of equity. If a firm has total assets of $5 million, and stockholders' equity of $4 million, then it must have debt with a market value of $1 million. The WACC for this hypothetical firm thus becomes:

$$WACC = (Stockholders' Equity/Total$$
Assets) Cost of Equity + (Debt/Total
Assets) After Tax Cost of Debt
$$= 4/5 (9.6) + 1/5 (4.58)$$
$$= 7.68 + .916$$
$$= 8.59$$

Obviously, firms can have a much more complicated capital structure than this hypothetical example. Moreover, the taxes a firm pays can be quite complicated to calculate. There are also some problems using the CAPM to calculate a firm's cost of equity. However, even with these caveats, this approach usually gives a reasonable approximation to a firm's weighted average cost of capital.

Moreover, some have suggested that while accounting measures of competitive advantage understate the importance of a firm's equity and debt holders in evaluating a firm's performance, economic measures of competitive advantage exaggerate the importance of these two particular stakeholders, often to the disadvantage of other stakeholders in a firm. These issues are discussed in more detail in the Ethics and Strategy feature.

The Relationship Between Economic and Accounting Performance Measures

The correlation between economic and accounting measures of competitive advantage is high. That is, firms that perform well using one of these measures usually perform well using the other. Conversely, firms that do poorly using one of these measures normally do poorly using the other. Thus, the relationships between competitive advantage, accounting performance, and economic performance depicted in Figure 1.5 generally hold.

However, it is possible for a firm to have above average accounting performance and simultaneously have below normal economic performance. This could happen, for example, when a firm is not earning its cost of capital but has above industry average accounting performance. Also, it is possible for a firm to have below average accounting performance and above normal economic performance. This could happen when a firm has a very low cost of capital and is earning at a rate in excess of this cost, but still below the industry average

Emergent Versus Intended Strategies

The simplest way of thinking about a firm's strategy is to assume that firms choose and implement their strategies exactly as described by the strategic management process in Figure 1.1. That is, they begin with a well-defined mission and objectives, they engage in external and internal analyses, they make their strategic choices, and then they implement their strategies. And there is no doubt that this describes the process for choosing and implementing a strategy in many firms.

For example, FedEx, the world leader in the overnight delivery business, entered this industry with a very well-developed theory about how to gain competitive advantages in this business. Indeed, Fred Smith, the founder of FedEx (originally known as Federal Express), first articulated this theory as a student in a term paper for an undergraduate business class at Yale University. Legend has it that he only received a "C" on the paper—but the company that was founded on the theory of competitive advantage in the overnight delivery business developed in that paper has done extremely well. Founded in 1971, FedEx had 2004 sales in excess of $24 billion, profits of $838 million, and employed almost 200,000 around the world.[9]

Figure 1.5 Competitive Advantage and Firm Performance

Competitive Advantage	→	Above Average Accounting Performance	→	Above Normal Economic Performance
Competitive Parity	→	Average Accounting Performance	→	Normal Economic Performance
Competitive Disadvantage	→	Below Average Accounting Performance	→	Below Normal Economic Performance

Ethics and Strategy

Considerable debate exists about the role of a firm's equity and debt holders versus its other stakeholders in defining and measuring a firm's performance. These other stakeholders include a firm's suppliers, its customers, its employees, and the communities within which it does business. Like equity and debt holders, these other stakeholders make investments in a firm. They too expect some compensation for making these investments.

On the one hand, some argue that if a firm maximizes the wealth of its equity holders, it will automatically satisfy all of its other stakeholders. This view of the firm depends on what is called the residual claimants view of equity holders. This view is that equity holders only receive payment on their investment in a firm after all the legitimate claims by a firm's other stakeholders are satisfied. Thus, a firm's equity holders, in this view, only receive payment on their investments in a firm after that firm's employees are compensated, after its suppliers are paid, after its customers are satisfied, and after it takes care of its obligations to the communities within which it does business. By maximizing returns to its equity holders, a firm is ensuring that its other stakeholders are fully compensated for investing in a firm.

On the other hand, some argue that the interests of equity holders and

Stockholders Versus Stakeholders

a firm's other stakeholders often collide, and that a firm that maximizes the wealth of its equity holders does not necessarily satisfy its other stakeholders. For example, where a firm's customers may want it to sell higher-quality products at lower prices, a firm's equity holders may want it to sell low-quality products at higher prices—this obviously would increase the amount of money left over to pay off a firm's equity holders. Also, where a firm's employees may want it to adopt policies that lead to steady performance over long periods of time—because this will lead to stable employment—a firm's equity holders may be

more interested in its maximizing its short-term profitability, even if this hurts employment stability. The interests of equity holders and the broader community may also clash, especially when it is very costly for a firm to engage in environment-friendly behavior that could reduce its short-term performance.

This debate manifests itself in a variety of ways. For example, many groups that oppose the globalization of the economy do so on the basis that firms make production, marketing, and other strategic choices in ways that maximize profits for equity holders, often to the detriment of a firm's other stakeholders. These people are concerned about the effects of globalization on employees, on the environment, and on the cultures in the developing economies where global firms sometimes locate their manufacturing and other operations. Managers in global firms respond by saying they have a responsibility to maximize the wealth of their equity holders. Given the passions that surround this debate, it is unlikely that these issues will be resolved soon.

Sources: T. Copeland, T. Koller, and J. Murrin (1995). *Valuation: Measuring and managing the value of companies.* New York Wiley; L. Donaldson (1990). "The ethereal hand: Organizational economics and management theory." *Academy of Review,* 15, pp. 369–381.

Other firms have also begun operations with a well-defined, well-formed strategy, but have found it necessary to modify this strategy so much once it is actually implemented in the marketplace that it bears little resemblance to the theory with which the firm started. **Emergent strategies** are theories of how to gain competitive advantage in an industry that emerge over time or that have been radically reshaped once they are initially implemented.[10] The relationship between a firm's intended and emergent strategies is depicted in Figure 1.6.

Figure 1.6   Mintzberg's Analysis of the Relationship Between Intended and Realized Strategies

Sources: Reprinted from "Strategy formation in an adhocracy," by H. Mintzberg and A. McHugh, published in *Administrative Science Quarterly*, 30, No. 2, June 1985, by permission of *Administrative Science Quarterly*. Copyright © 1985 by *Administrative Science Quarterly*.

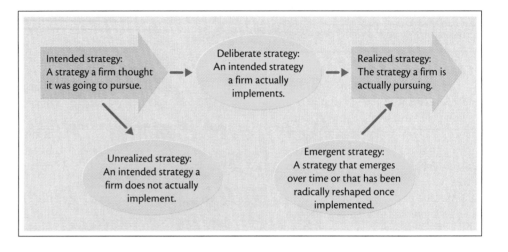

Several well-known firms have strategies that are at least partly emergent. For example, Johnson & Johnson was originally only a supplier of antiseptic gauze and medical plasters. It had no consumer business at all. Then, in response to complaints about irritation caused by some of its medical plasters, J&J began enclosing a small packet of talcum powder with each of the medical plasters it sold. Soon customers were asking to purchase the talcum powder by itself and the company introduced "Johnson's Toilet and Baby Powder." Later an employee invented a ready-to-use bandage for his wife. It seems she often cut herself while using knives in the kitchen. When J&J marketing managers learned of this invention, they decided to introduce it into the marketplace. J&J's Band-Aid products have since become the largest selling brand category at J&J. Overall, J&J's intended strategy was to compete in the medical products market, but its emergent consumer products strategies now generate over 40 percent of total corporate sales.

Another firm with what turns out to be an emergent strategy is the Marriott Corporation. Marriott was originally in the restaurant business. In the late 1930s, Marriott owned and operated eight restaurants. However, one of these restaurants was close to a Washington, D.C., airport. Managers at this restaurant noticed that airline passengers would come into the restaurant to purchase food to eat on their trip. J. Willard Marriott, the founder of the Marriott Corporation, noticed this trend and negotiated a deal with Eastern Airlines whereby Marriott's restaurant would deliver prepackaged lunches directly to Eastern's planes. This arrangement was later extended to include American Airlines. Over time, providing food service to airlines became a major business segment for Marriott. Although Marriott's initial intended strategy was to operate in the restaurant business, it became engaged in the emergent food service business at over 100 airports throughout the world.[11]

Some firms have almost entirely emergent strategies. PEZ Candy, Inc., for example, manufactures and sells small plastic candy dispensers with cartoon and movie character heads, along with candy refills. This privately held firm has made few efforts to speed its growth, yet demand for current and older PEZ products continues to grow. In the 1990s, PEZ doubled the size of its manufacturing operation to keep up with demand. Old PEZ dispensers have become something of a collector's item. Several national conferences on PEZ collecting have been held, and some particularly rare PEZ dispensers were once auctioned at Christie's. This demand has enabled PEZ to raise its prices without increases in advertising, sales personnel, and movie tie-ins so typical in the candy industry.[12]

Of course, one might argue that emergent strategies are only important when a firm fails to implement the strategic management process effectively. After all, if this process is implemented effectively, then would it ever be necessary to fundamentally alter the strategies that a firm has chosen?

In reality, it will often be the case that at the time a firm chooses its strategies, some of the information needed to complete the strategic management process may simply not be available. As suggested earlier, in this setting a firm simply has to make its "best bet" about how competition in an industry is likely to emerge. In such a situation, a firm's ability to change its strategies quickly to respond to emergent trends in an industry may be as important a source of competitive advantage as the ability to complete the strategic management process. For all these reasons, emergent strategies may be particularly important for entrepreneurial firms, as described in the Strategy in the Emerging Enterprise feature.

Why You Need to Know About Strategy

At first glance, it may not be obvious why students would need to know about strategy and the strategic management process. After all, the process of choosing and implementing a strategy is normally the responsibility of senior managers in a firm, and most students are unlikely to be senior managers in large corporations until many years after graduation. Why study strategy and the strategic management process now?

In fact, there are at least three very compelling reasons why it is important to study strategy and the strategic management process now. First, it can give you the tools you need to evaluate the strategies of firms that may employ you. We have already seen how a firm's strategy can have a huge impact on its competitive advantage. Your career opportunities in a firm are largely determined by that firm's competitive advantage. Thus, in choosing a place to begin or continue your career, understanding a firm's theory of how it is going to gain a competitive advantage can be essential in evaluating the career opportunities in a firm. Firms with strategies that are unlikely to be a source of competitive advantage will rarely provide the same career opportunities as firms with strategies that do generate such advantages. Being able to distinguish between these types of strategies can be very important in your career choices.

Second, once you are working for a firm, understanding that firm's strategies, and your role in implementing those strategies, can be very important for your personal success. It will often be the case that expectations of how you perform your function in a firm will change, depending on the strategies a firm is pursuing. For example, as we will see in Part Two of this book, the accounting function plays a very different role in a firm pursuing a cost leadership strategy versus a product differentiation strategy. Marketing and manufacturing also play very different roles in these two types of strategies. Your effectiveness in a firm can

Strategy in the Emerging Enterprise

*E*very entrepreneur—and would-be entrepreneur—is familiar with the drill: If you want to receive financial support for your idea, you need to write a business plan. Business plans are typically 25 to 30 pages long. Most begin with an Executive Summary; then move quickly to describing an entrepreneur's business idea, why customers will be interested in this idea, how much it will cost to realize this idea; and usually end with a series of charts that project a firm's cash flows over the next five years.

Of course, since these business ideas are often new and untried, no one—including the entrepreneur—really knows if customers will like this idea well enough to buy from this firm. No one really knows how much it will cost to build these products or produce these services—they've never been built or produced before. And certainly, no one really knows what a firm's cash flows will look like over the next five years or so. Indeed, it is not unusual for entrepreneurs to constantly revise their business plan to reflect new information they have obtained about their business idea and its viability. It is not even unusual for entrepreneurs to fundamentally revise their central business idea as they begin to pursue it in earnest.

The truth is, most decisions about whether or not to create an entrepreneur-

Emergent Strategies and Entrepreneurship

ial firm take place under conditions of high uncertainty and high unpredictability. In this setting, the ability to adjust on the fly, to be flexible, and to recast your business idea in ways that are more consistent with customer interests may be a central determinant of a firm's ultimate success. This, of course, suggests that emergent strategies are likely to be very important for entrepreneurial firms.

This view of entrepreneurship is different from the popular stereotype. In the popular view, entrepreneurs are assumed to be hit by a "blinding rush of

insight" about a previously unexploited market opportunity. In reality, entrepreneurs are more likely to experience a series of smaller insights about market opportunities. But typically, these periods of insight will be preceded by periods of disappointment, as an entrepreneur discovers that what he or she thought was a new and complete business model is, in fact, either not new or not complete or both. In the popular view, entrepreneurship is all about creativity, about being able to see opportunities others cannot see. In reality, entrepreneurship may be more about tenacity than creativity, as entrepreneurs build their firms step-by-step out of the uncertainty and unpredictability that plague their decision making. In the popular view, entrepreneurs can envision their success well before it occurs. In reality, while entrepreneurs may dream about financial and other forms of success, they usually do not know the exact path they will take, nor what success will actually look like, until after they have arrived.

Sources: S. Alvarez and J. Barney (2004). "Organizing rent generation and appropriation: Toward a theory of the entrepreneurial firm," *Journal of Business Venturing*, 19, pp. 621–636; W. Gartner (1988). "Who is the entrepreneur? is the wrong question." *American Journal of Small Business*, 12, pp. 11–32; S. Sarasvathy (2001). "Causation and effectuation: Toward a theoretical shift from economic inevitability to entrepreneurial contingency." *Academy of Management Review*, 26, pp. 243–264.

be reduced by doing accounting, marketing, and manufacturing as if your firm was pursuing a cost leadership strategy when it is actually pursuing a product differentiation strategy.

Finally, while it is true that strategic choices are generally limited to very experienced senior managers in large organizations, in smaller and entrepreneurial firms many employees end up being involved in the strategic management process. If you choose to work for one of these smaller or entrepreneurial firms—even if it is not right after graduation—you could very easily find yourself to be part of the strategic management team, implementing the strategic management process, and choosing which strategies this firm should implement. In this setting, a familiarity with the essential concepts that underlie the choice and implementation of a strategy may turn out to be very helpful.

The Strategic Management Process in an International Context

Thus far, the description of the strategic management process has ignored the fact that most firms make strategic choices within a global competitive context. Indeed, there are currently relatively few firms that do not have to consider some aspects of global competition when they make their strategic choices. How are these global considerations incorporated into the strategic management process?

There are two ways that this can happen. First, some have suggested that global strategies are a unique category of strategy, separate from the business and corporate strategies listed under the strategic choice section of the strategic management process in Figure 1.4. The logic behind this conclusion is straightforward: Conceiving of and implementing international strategies requires a set of skills that are qualitatively different from the skills required to conceive of and implement either business or corporate strategies. For example, those that pursue international opportunities for competitive advantage must know about legal systems in different countries; must understand differences in consumer tastes and culture; and must be able to operate simultaneously in different time zones, different languages, and different currencies—all while trying to identify and exploit opportunities for competitive advantage around the world.

A second perspective on international strategies acknowledges that these strategies do often place special demands on the managers and firms that pursue them, but that international strategies, in fact, are just one way—albeit a very important way—that firms can pursue their business or corporate strategies. That is, rather than being a separate type of strategy, this perspective suggests that international strategies may be a means by which a firm realizes competitive advantages from implementing its business or corporate strategies.

Take, for example, a cost leadership business strategy. As will be described in detail in Chapter 4, one very common feature of firms that pursue a low-cost strategy is low-cost manufacturing. Now, many low-cost firms develop their own low-cost manufacturing capability. However, more and more, firms are beginning to outsource their manufacturing to firms that have significant manufacturing cost advantages. In many cases, these firms are outsourcing to firms located in China, Malaysia, the Philippines, or other countries in Asia. In this setting, the decision to outsource manufacturing to an Asian company is driven by the desire to have the low-cost manufacturing needed to implement a cost leadership strategy. That is, the decision to "go international" is a means to an end—the implementation of a cost leadership strategy—rather than an end in and of itself.

A similar conclusion can be made about a firm's decision to begin selling in countries outside its home market. If a firm has decided it needs to diversify its operations—a classic corporate strategy that will be discussed in detail in Chapter 7—it may begin to sell into multiple geographic markets. If those geographic markets happen to span country borders, then this firm is pursuing an international strategy. However, as before, the decision to go international in this setting is a means to an end—diversifying a firm's operations—rather than an end in and of itself.

The perspective adopted in this book is that international strategies are typically used by firms to help them realize a particular business or corporate strategy. That said, it is also acknowledged that pursuing a particular business or corporate strategy through international means can create unique challenges, and opportunities, for firms. Thus, each chapter in this book will include a section that examines the challenges and opportunities associated with completing a particular stage of the strategic management process in an international context.

SUMMARY

A firm's strategy is its theory of how to gain competitive advantages. These theories, like all theories, are based on assumptions and hypotheses about how competition in an industry is likely to evolve. When those assumptions and hypotheses are consistent with the actual evolution of competition in an industry, a firm's strategy is more likely to be able to generate a competitive advantage.

One way that a firm can choose its strategies is through the strategic management process. This process is a set of analyses and decisions that increase the likelihood that a firm will be able to choose a "good" strategy, that is, a strategy that will lead to a competitive advantage.

The strategic management process begins when a firm identifies its mission, or its long-term purpose. This mission is often written down in the form of a mission statement. Mission statements, by themselves, can have no impact on performance, can enhance a firm's performance, or can hurt a firm's performance. Objectives are measurable milestones firms use to evaluate whether or not they are accomplishing their mission. External and internal analyses are the processes through which a firm identifies its environmental threats and opportunities and organizational strengths and weaknesses. Armed with these analyses, it is possible for a firm to engage in strategic choice. Strategies can be classified into two categories: business-level strategies (including cost leadership and product differentiation) and corporate-level strategies (including vertical integration, strategic alliances, diversification, and mergers and acquisitions). Strategy implementation follows strategic choice and involves choosing organizational structures, management control policies, and compensation schemes that support a firm's strategies.

The ultimate objective of the strategic management process is the realization of competitive advantage. A firm has a competitive advantage if it is creating more economic value than its rivals. Economic value is defined as the difference between the perceived customer benefits from purchasing a product or service from a firm and the total economic cost of developing and selling that product or service. Competitive advantages can be temporary or sustained. Competitive parity exists when a firm creates the same economic value as its rivals. A competitive disadvantage exists when a firm creates less economic value than its rivals, and it can be either temporary or sustained.

There are two popular measures of a firm's competitive advantage: accounting performance and economic performance. Accounting performance measures competitive advantage using various ratios calculated with a firm's profit and loss and balance sheet statements. A firm's accounting performance is compared with the average level of accounting performance in a firm's industry. Economic performance compares a firm's level of return to its cost of capital. A firm's cost of capital is the rate of return it had to promise to pay to its debt and equity investors to induce them to invest in the firm.

While many firms use the strategic management process to choose and implement strategies, not all strategies are chosen this way. Some strategies emerge over time, as firms respond to unanticipated changes in the structure of competition in an industry.

There are at least three reasons why students need to understand strategy and the strategic management process. First, it can help in deciding where to work. Second, once you have a job, it can help you to be successful in that job. Finally, if you have a job in a small or entrepreneurial firm, you may become involved in strategy and the strategic management process from the very beginning.

While pursuing international opportunities for competitive advantage can create unique challenges and opportunities for firms, in this book such international strategies are analyzed as different ways that firms can realize the competitive advantages associated with the business and corporate strategies identified in the strategic management process. That said, the unique challenges and opportunities associated with using international operations to realize these business and corporate strategies will be examined in each chapter of the book.

CHALLENGE QUESTIONS

1. Some firms widely publicize their corporate mission statements by including them in annual reports, on company letterheads, and in corporate advertising. What, if anything, does this practice say about the ability of these mission statements to be sources of sustained competitive advantage for a firm? Why?

2. There is little empirical evidence that having a formal, written mission statement improves a firm's performance. Yet many firms spend a great deal of time and money developing mission statements. Why?

3. Is it possible to distinguish between an emergent strategy and an ad hoc rationalization of a firm's past decisions?

4. Both external and internal analyses are important in the strategic management process. Is the order in which these analyses are done important? If yes, which should come first—external analysis or internal analysis? If the order is not important, why not?

5. Will a firm that has a sustained competitive disadvantage necessarily go out of business? How about a firm with below average accounting performance over a long period of time? How about a firm with below normal economic performance over a long period of time?

6. Can more than one firm have a competitive advantage in an industry at the same time? Is it possible for a firm to simultaneously have a competitive advantage and a competitive disadvantage?

PROBLEM SET

1. Write objectives for each of the following mission statements.

(a) We will be a leader in pharmaceutical innovation.
(b) Customer satisfaction is our primary goal.
(c) We promise on-time delivery.
(d) Product quality is our first priority.

2. Rewrite each of the following objectives to make them more helpful in guiding a firm's strategic management process.

(a) We will introduce five new drugs.
(b) We will understand our customers' needs.
(c) Almost all of our products will be delivered on time.
(d) The number of defects in our products will fall.

3. Do firms with the following financial results have below normal, normal, or above normal economic performance?

(a) ROA = 14.3%, WACC = 12.8%
(b) ROA = 4.3%, WACC = 6.7%
(c) ROA = 6.5%, WACC = 9.2%
(d) ROA = 8.3%, WACC = 8.3%

4. Do these same firms have below average, average, or above average accounting performance?

(a) ROA = 14.3%, Industry Avg. ROA = 15.2%
(b) ROA = 4.3%, Industry Avg. ROA = 4.1%
(c) ROA = 6.5%, Industry Avg. ROA = 6.1%
(d) ROA = 8.3%, Industry Avg. ROA = 9.4%

5. Is it possible for a firm to simultaneously earn above normal economic returns and below average accounting returns? How about below normal economic returns and above average accounting returns? Why or why not? If this can occur, which measure of performance is more reliable: economic performance or accounting performance? Why?

6. Examine the following corporate Web sites and determine if the strategies pursued by these firms were emergent, deliberate, or both emergent and deliberate. Justify your answer with facts from these Web sites.

(a) www.walmart.com
(b) www.ibm.com
(c) www.homedepot.com
(d) www.cardinal.com

7. Using the information below, calculate this firm's ROA, ROE, Gross Profit Margin, and Quick Ratio. If this firm's WACC is 6.6 percent and the average firm in its industry has an ROA of 8 percent, is this firm earning above or below normal economic performance and above or below average accounting performance?

Net Sales	6,134	Operating Cash	3,226	Net Current Liabilities	1,549
Cost of Goods Sold	(4438)	Accounts Receivable	681	Long-Term Debt	300
Selling, General Admin. Expense	(996)	Inventories	20	Deferred Income Taxes	208
Other Expenses	(341)	Other Current Assets	0	Preferred Stock	0
Interest Income	72	Total Current Assets	3,927	Retained Earnings	0
Interest Expense	(47)	Gross Prop., Plant, Equip.	729	Common Stock	3,104
Provision for Taxes	(75)	Accumulated Depreciation	(411)	Other Liabilities	0
Other Income	245	Book Value of Fixed Assets	318	Total Liabilities and Equity	5,161
Net Income	554	Goodwill	0		
		Net Other Operating Assets	916		
		Total Assets	5,161		

END NOTES

1. This approach to defining strategy was first suggested in Drucker, P. (1994). "The theory of business." *Harvard Business Review*, 75, September/October, pp. 95–105.
2. Bart, C. K., and M. C. Baetz (1998). "The relationship between mission statements and firm performance: An exploratory study." *Journal of Management Studies*, 35(6), pp. 823–854.
3. See www.enron.com.
4. See Emshwiller, J., D. Solomon, and R. Smith (2004). "Lay is indicted for his role in Enron collapse." *Wall Street Journal*, July 8, pp. A1 + and Gilmartin, R. (2005). "The fought the law," *Business Week*, January 10, p. 82–83.
5. These performance results were presented originally in Collins, J. C., and J. I. Porras (1997). *Built to last: Successful habits of visionary companies.* New York: HarperCollins.
6. Quoted in Collins, J. C., and J. I. Porras (1997). *Built to last: successful habits of visionary companies,* New York: HarperCollins.
7. See Theroux, J., and J. Hurstak (1993). "Ben & Jerry's Homemade Ice Cream Inc.: Keeping the mission(s) alive." Harvard Business School, Case no. 9-392-025; and Applebaum, A. (2000). "Smartmoney.com: Unilever feels hungry, buys Ben & Jerry's." *Wall Street Journal*, April 13, pp. B1 +.

8. This definition of competitive advantage has a long history in the field of strategic management. For example, it is closely related to the definitions provided in Barney (1986, 1991) and Porter (1985). It is also consistent with the value-based approach described in Peteraf (2001), Brandenburger and Stuart (1999), and Besanko, Dranove, and Shanley (2000). For more discussion on this definition, see Peteraf and Barney (2004).
9. FedEx's history is described in Trimble, V. (1993). *Overnight success: Federal Express and Frederick Smith, its renegade creator.* New York: Crown.
10. Mintzberg, H. (1978). "Patterns in strategy formulation." *Management Science*, 24(9), pp. 934–948, and Mintzberg, H. (1985). "Of strategies, deliberate and emergent." *Strategic Management Journal*, 6(3), pp. 257–272. Mintzberg has been most influential in expanding the study of strategy to include emergent strategies.
11. The J&J and Marriott emergent strategy stories can be found in Collins, J. C., and J. I. Porras (1997). *Built to last: Successful habits of visionary companies.* New York: HarperCollins.
12. See McCarthy, M. J. (1993). "The PEZ fancy is hard to explain, let alone justify." *Wall Street Journal*, March 10, p. A1, for a discussion of PEZ's surprising emergent strategy.

Evaluating a Firm's External Environment

You want to enter and compete in the consumer electronics industry? Are you out of your mind!? There are few industries as competitive as the worldwide consumer electronics industry. It is populated by huge companies—like Sony, and Mitsubishi, and Philips, and Panasonic, and Sharp, and it goes on and on—all of which have established global brand names and enormous research and development capabilities; they have the world's best and most efficient manufacturing facilities, and enor-

Can TiVo Change the Way You Watch TV?

mous marketing skills. Rivalry in the industry is rabid, with prices constantly dropping and profit margins constantly being squeezed. And yet, this is also an industry characterized by high levels of innovation. Virtually every day, some huge consumer electronics firm somewhere is announcing

a radical new digital technology that will change the way we listen to music, watch TV, take pictures, communicate with others, and so forth.

And TiVo wants to enter this industry. Some may ask, what is TiVo? Founded in 1997, TiVo sells what might be described as a "super VCR." Essentially a box with a large hard drive in it, the TiVo system can be used to record TV shows digitally. Sounds simple enough, but it has some interesting applications—like the ability to "pause" a TV show in order to

Learning Objectives

After reading this chapter, you should be able to:

1. Describe the dimensions of the general environment facing a firm and how this environment can affect a firm's opportunities and threats.

2. Describe how the structure-conduct-performance paradigm suggests that industry structure can influence a firm's competitive choices.

3. Describe the "five forces model of industry attractiveness" and indicators of when each of these forces will improve or reduce the attractiveness of an industry.

4. Describe the difference between rivals and substitutes.

5. Discuss the role of complements in analyzing competition within an industry.

6. Describe four generic industry structures and specific strategic opportunities in those industries.

7. Describe the impact of tariffs, quotas, and other nontariff barriers to entry on the cost of entry into new geographic markets.

8. Describe the differences between multinational, global, and transnational opportunities.

answer the door or the telephone; the ability to record more than one show simultaneously; and most ominously, the ability to enable viewers to skip commercials entirely. To skip commercials, all TiVo users have to do is start recording a show at its normal start time, but start watching the show a few minutes later. Then, when a commercial comes on the recorded show, just touch a button, and the TiVo system automatically skips the commercial. How about that—commercial-free television on commercial channels? The possibility that their expensive commercials are being skipped has forced some firms to rethink their advertising strategies.

The TiVo recorder sounds like a great product, but breaking into the consumer electronics industry is not easy—even if you have a "better mousetrap." Current consumer electronics firms have huge scale advantages in research and development, product differentiation, manufacturing, and distribution. Other firms are beginning to market products that function the same way as TiVo. Substitutes for some of the TiVo's features—including the most widely distributed weekly magazine in the United States, *TV Guide*—are well-entrenched with consumers. And most problematic of all is the TV watcher—the quintessential "couch potato" with a remote in one hand and a beer in the other. Are consumers likely to change the way they watch TV?

So, TiVo faces some tough challenges. But, it is using some clever strategies to try to overcome these problems. For example, instead of just selling its own "box," TiVo is partnering with other large consumer electronics firms—including DirectTV and

Sony—to put TiVo technology in the products of these other firms. Also, to gain access to distribution, TiVo is partnering with firms like Best Buy to make its products more widely available.

By 2002, TiVo had a base of over 422,000 customers and was optimistic that it would have over a million customers in a few years. Most analysts agree that, at one million customers, TiVo will

become a viable consumer electronics firm.

Sources: D. Foust and B. Grow (2004). "Coke: Wooing the TiVo generation." *BusinessWeek*, March 1, 2004, pp. 77 +; S. Kirsner (2002). "Can TiVo go prime time?" *Fast Company*, August 2002, pp. 82 +; www.TiVo.com

T he strategic management process described in Chapter 1 suggested that one of the critical determinants of a firm's strategies is the threats and opportunities in its competitive environment. If a firm understands these threats and opportunities, it is one step closer to being able to choose and implement a "good strategy," that is, a strategy that leads to competitive advantage.

You can see how a knowledge of the threats and opportunities in the global consumer electronics industry helped TiVo choose its strategy—although, it is probably too early to tell if the strategy TiVo has chosen will be a source of competitive advantage. Because TiVo understands the high level of rivalry in this industry, it has partnered with some much larger firms, including Sony and DirecTV, to gain access to some of their competitive strengths. Because TiVo understands the high cost of entry into this market, it has partnered with some important electronics distributors, including Best Buy, to reduce those costs. All these actions have the effect of reducing the competitive threat these firms would have otherwise presented to TiVo as it tried to expand its business.

However, it is not enough to recognize that it is important to understand the threats and opportunities in a firm's competitive environment. What is also required is a set of tools that managers can apply to systematically complete this external analysis part of the strategic management process. Moreover, these tools must be rooted in a strong theoretical base, so that managers know they have not been developed in an arbitrary way. Fortunately, such tools exist and will be described in this chapter.

Understanding a Firm's General Environment

Any analysis of the threats and opportunities facing a firm must begin with an understanding of the general environment within which a firm operates. This **general environment** consists of broad trends in the context within which a firm operates that can have an impact on a firm's strategic choices. As depicted in Figure 2.1, the general environment consists of six interrelated elements: technological change, demographic trends, cultural trends, the economic climate, legal and political conditions, and specific international events. Each of these elements of the general environment is discussed below.

In 1899, Charles H. Duell, Commissioner of the United States patent office, said, "Everything that can be invented has been invented."[1] He was wrong. Technological changes over the last few years have had significant impacts on the ways firms do business and on the products and services they sell. These impacts have been most obvious for technologies that build on digital information—including computers, the Internet, wireless telephones, and so forth. Many of us

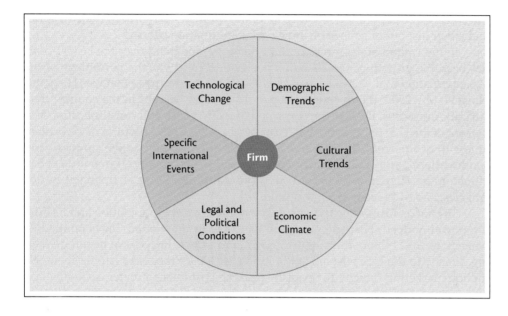

routinely use digital products or services that did not exist just five years ago—including TiVo. However, rapid technological innovation has not been restricted to digital technologies. Biotechnology has also made rapid progress over the last 10 years. New kinds of medicines are now being created. As important, biotechnology holds the promise of developing entirely new ways of both preventing and treating disease.[2]

Technological change creates both opportunity—as firms begin to explore how to use technology to create new products and services—and threats—as technological change forces firms to rethink their technological strategies. Indeed, in Chapter 1 we saw how one technological innovation—downloading digital music from the Internet—has created a threat to the profitability of record companies and an opportunity for firms like Apple's iTunes and Sony Connect to increase the sale of their portable digital listening devices.[3] This is almost always the case with technological change—it creates threats for some firms and opportunities for others.

A second element of the general environment facing firms is demographic trends. **Demographics** is the distribution of individuals in a society in terms of age, sex, marital status, income, ethnicity, and other personal attributes that may determine buying patterns. Understanding this basic information about a population can help a firm determine whether or not its products or services will appeal to customers and how many potential customers for these products or services it might have.

Some demographic trends are very well known. For example, everyone has heard of the "baby boomers"—adults who were born shortly after World War II. This large population has had an impact on the strategies of many firms, especially as they have grown older and have had more disposable income. However, other demographic groups have also had an impact on firm strategies. This is especially true in the automobile industry. For example, minivans were invented to meet the demands of "soccer moms"—women who live in the suburbs and have young children. The 3-series BMW seems to have been designed for "Yuppies"—the young, urban, and upwardly mobile adults of the 1970s and 1980s, while the Jeep Liberty and Nissan Exterra seem to have been designed for the so-called X-generation—young men and women currently in their twenties and either just out of college on anticipating graduation shortly.

In the United States, an important demographic trend over the last 20 years has been the growth of the Hispanic population. In 1990, the percentage of the U.S. population that was black was greater than the percentage that was Hispanic. However, by 2000, there were more people of Latin descent in the country than African Americans. By 2010, it is expected that Hispanics will constitute almost 15 percent of the U.S. population, while the percentage of blacks will remain constant at less than 8 percent. These trends are particularly notable in the southern and southwestern parts of the country. For example, 36 percent of children under 18 in Houston are Hispanic, 39 percent in Miami and San Diego, 53 percent in Los Angeles, and 61 percent in San Antonio.

Of course, firms have become aware of this growing population and its buying power. Indeed, Hispanic disposable income in the United States jumped 29 percent, to $652 billion, from 2001 to 2003. In response, firms have begun marketing directly to the U.S. Hispanic population. In 2003, Procter & Gamble spent $90 million marketing directly to Spanish-speaking customers. Procter & Gamble has also formed a 65-person bilingual team to manage the marketing of products to Hispanics. Indeed, Procter & Gamble expects that the Hispanic population will be the cornerstone of its sales growth in North America.[4]

Firms can try to exploit their understanding of a particular demographic segment of the population to create a competitive advantage—as is the case with Procter & Gamble and the U.S. Hispanic population—but focusing on too narrow a demographic segment can limit the demand for a firm's products. The WB, the alternative television network created by Time Warner in 1995, has faced this dilemma. Initially, the WB found success in producing shows for teens—classics like *Dawson's Creek* and *Buffy the Vampire Slayer*. However, in 2003, the WB saw an 11 percent drop in its viewership and a $25 million drop in its advertising revenues. While not leaving its traditional demographic behind, the WB is currently producing some programs that will appeal to older viewers. Whether or not older viewers will even consider watching a show on the WB is still not known. But, according to Garth Ancier, WB Chair, "To the degree that we have presented ourselves as just a teenage network, that's been a very large mistake on our part."[5]

A third element of a firm's general environment is cultural trends. **Culture** is the values, beliefs, and norms that guide behavior in a society. These values, beliefs, and norms define what is "right and wrong" in a society, what is acceptable and unacceptable, what is fashionable and what is unfashionable. Failure to understand changes in culture, or differences between cultures, can have a very large impact on the ability of a firm to gain a competitive advantage.

This becomes most obvious when firms operate in multiple countries simultaneously. Even seemingly small differences in culture can have an impact. For example, advertisements in the United States that end with a person putting their index finger and thumb together mean that a product is "okay"; in Brazil, the same symbol is vulgar and offensive. Ads in the United States that have a bride dressed in white may be very confusing to the Chinese, because in China white is the traditional color worn at funerals. In Germany, women typically purchase their own engagement rings while in the United States men purchase engagement rings for their fiancées. And what might be appropriate ways to treat women colleagues in Japan or France would land most men in U.S. firms in serious trouble. Understanding the cultural context

Global Perspectives

Pokémon Invades Louis Vuitton

*I*t may have begun with Pokémon, Hello Kitty, and Mighty Morphin Power Rangers, but Japanese style is rapidly becoming an important design feature in many products sold around the world and in the United States. While it is difficult to describe a single simple element of this Japanese style, much of the new Japanese look is derived from a particular form of Japanese cartoon animation called *anime*. Whether in films or in two-inch-thick comic books called *manga*, anime is characterized by highly stylized arts-based movements of characters with white, round, oversized eyes, dark black pupils, and a shock of unruly hair. Colors in anime are bold, the action furious. Characters clash in mythic adventures that pit good against evil in the science fiction of the future.

But this look—stylized, colorful, futuristic—has moved way beyond cartoons, comic books, and action figures. Elements of this Japanese look show up in many products sold around the world. These include the stylized action sequences in a movie like *The Last Samurai*; in

cell phones built by Sony Ericsson that will soon be imported from Japan into the United States; in cars with futuristic designs like Nissan's full-size truck, the Titan; and even in Louis Vuitton's line of Murakami handbags—designed by Japanese artist Takashi Murakami—that now generates $300 million in sales worldwide.

Even cultural icons in the United States are being replaced by Japanese-influenced products. For example, in the 1980s and 1990s, street racers in the United States used to modify their American-made V8 Camaros and Firebirds to race on city streets. But, with the popularity of the movie *Fast and Furious*, American cars are being replaced, more and more often, with modified Japanese cars—Toyotas, Hondas, and Nissans replacing Camaro and Firebirds as the preferred hot rod of today's street racers. A similar transition from Harley-Davidson "Hogs" to Suzuki, Kawasaki, and Honda "pocket rockets" is taking place among those who race motorcycles.

And while it is a long way from Pokémon and Hello Kitty to Murakami handbags and Suzuki motorcycles racing down winding roads, all of these products are connected by a common Japanese look traceable to a uniquely Japanese art form, anime.

Sources: C. Palmeri and N. Byrnes (2004). "Is Japanese style taking over the world?" *BusinessWeek*, July 26, pp. 56 +; G. Parker (2004). "Students used to take Japanese for jobs; now it's for fun." *Wall Street Journal*, August 5, pp. A1 +; C. Matlack, R. Tiplady, D. Brady, R. Berner, and H. Tashiro (2004). "The Vuitton machine." *BusinessWeek*, March 22, pp. 98 +.

within which a firm operates is important in evaluating the ability of a firm to generate competitive advantages.[6]

However, cultural differences can also be a source of opportunity for firms. This is especially the case if a firm in one culture is able to identify and popularize elements taken from a different culture. As described in the Global Perspectives feature, this transfer of cultural elements is beginning to accelerate from the Japanese culture to the U.S. marketplace.

A fourth element of a firm's general environment is the current economic climate. The **economic climate** is the overall health of the economic systems within which a firm operates. The health of the economy varies over time in a distinct pattern: Periods of relative prosperity, when demand for goods and services is high and unemployment is low, are followed by periods of relatively low prosperity, when demand for goods and services is low and unemployment is high. When activity in an economy is relatively low, the economy is said to be in **recession**. A severe recession that lasts for several years is known as a **depression**. This alternating pattern of prosperity followed by recession, followed by prosperity, is called the **business cycle**.

Throughout the 1990s, the world, and especially the United States, enjoyed a period of sustained economic growth. Some observers even speculated that the government had become so skilled at managing demand in the economy through adjusting interest rates that a period of recession did not necessarily have to follow a period of sustained economic growth. Of course, the business cycle reared its ugly head again in 1999 with a sudden downturn in stock markets around the world, beginning with the technology sector in the United States and spreading to the entire world economy by 2000. Over a period of just a few months, much of the economic value that had been created through the 1990s disappeared. CEOs of Internet companies that had once been valued at billions of dollars now found themselves managing Web sites that were treated as virtually worthless in the market.

However, for every downturn in the economic climate, there is an upturn. For example, at one point in 1999, Amazon.com's stock was valued at $100 per share, for a market value of almost $50 billion. At $50 billion, Amazon's market value was greater than the market value of Ford and General Electric. By 2000, Amazon's stock had fallen to $6 per share; but just three years later, in 2003, Amazon's stock had rebounded to $50 per share and its market value to $21 billion. As important, in 2004 it was on track for annual sales of $7 billion and $400 million in earnings.[7] The ability to survive the technology bust of 1999 has positioned Amazon.com—along with other Internet firms including eBay, Google, and Yahoo!—to be a dominant player in the Internet for the foreseeable future.

A fifth element of a firm's general environment is legal and political conditions. The legal and political dimensions of an organization's general environment are the laws and the legal system's impact on business, together with the general nature of the relationship between government and business. These laws and the relationship between business and government can vary significantly around the world. For example, in Japan, business and the government are generally seen has having a consistently close and cooperative relationship. Indeed, some have observed that one of the reasons that the Japanese economy has been growing so slowly over the last decade is the reluctance of the government to impose economic restructuring that would hurt the performance of some Japanese firms—especially the largest Japanese banks. In the United States, on the other hand, the quality of the relationship between business and the government tends to vary over time. In some administrations, rigorous antitrust regulation and tough environmental standards—both seen as inconsistent with the interests of business—dominate. In other administrations, antitrust regulation is less rigorous and the imposition of environmental standards is delayed, suggesting a more "pro-business" perspective.

A final attribute of a firm's general environment is specific international events. These include events such as civil wars, political coups, terrorism, wars between countries, famines, and country or regional economic recessions. All of these specific events can have an enormous impact on the ability of a firm's strategies to generate competitive advantage.

Of course, one of the most important of these specific events to have occurred over the last several decades was the terrorist attacks on New York City and Washington, D.C., on September 11, 2001. Beyond the tragic loss of life, these attacks had important business implications as well. For example, most U.S. airlines have yet to fully recover from the drop in demand that followed 9/11. Insurance companies had to pay out billions of dollars in unanticipated claims as a result of the attacks. Defense contractors saw demand for their products soar as the United States and some of its allies began waging war in Afghanistan and then Iraq.

A firm's general environment defines the broad contextual background within which it operates. Understanding this general environment can help a firm identify some of the threats and opportunities it faces. However, it is usually the case that this general environment has an impact on a firm's threats and opportunities through its impact on a firm's more local environment. Thus, while analyzing a firm's general environment is an important step in any application of the strategic management process, this general analysis must be accompanied by an analysis of a firm's more local environment if the threats and opportunities facing a firm are to be fully understood. Specific tools for analyzing a firm's local environment, together with the theoretical perspectives from which these tools have been derived, are discussed below.

The Structure-Conduct-Performance Model of Firm Performance

In the 1930s, a group of economists began developing an approach for understanding the relationship between a firm's environment, its behavior, and performance. The original objective of this work was to describe conditions under which competition in an industry would *not* develop. Understanding when competition was not developing in an industry assisted government regulators in identifying industries where competition-enhancing regulations should be implemented.[8]

The theoretical framework that developed out of this effort became known as the **structure-conduct-performance model (S-C-P)** and is summarized in Figure 2.2. The term **structure** in this model refers to industry structure, measured by such factors as the number of competitors in an industry, the heterogeneity of products in an industry, the cost of entry and exit in an industry, and so forth. **Conduct** refers to the strategies that firms in an industry implement. **Performance** in the S–C–P model has two meanings: the performance of individual firms and

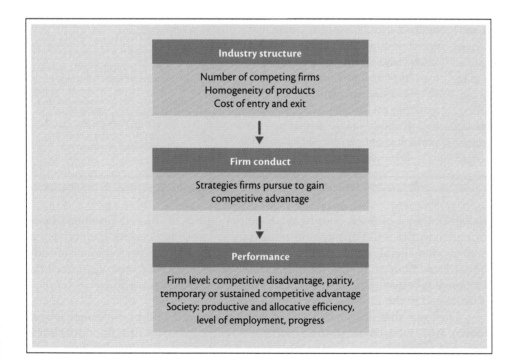

Figure 2.2 The Structure-Conduct-Performance Model

Ethics and Strategy

Is a Firm Gaining a Competitive Advantage Good for Society?

One of the basic tenets of economic theory is that society is better off when industries are very competitive. Industries are very competitive when there are large numbers of firms operating in an industry, when the products and services that these firms sell are similar to each other, and when it is not very costly for firms to enter into or exit these industries. Indeed, as is described in more detail in the Strategy in Depth feature, these industries are said to be perfectly competitive.

The reasons that society is better off when industries are perfectly competitive are well known. In such industries, firms must constantly strive to keep their costs low, their quality high, and, when appropriate, must constantly be innovating if they are to even survive. Low costs, high quality, and appropriate innovation are generally consistent with the interests of a firm's customers and thus consistent with the overall welfare of society.

Indeed, concern for **social welfare**, or the overall good of society, is the primary reason the S-C-P model was developed. This model was to be used to identify industries where perfect competition was not occurring, and thus where social welfare was not being maximized. With these industries identified, the government could

then engage in activities to increase the competitiveness of these industries, thereby increasing social welfare.

Strategic management scholars turned the S-C-P model upside down by using it to describe industries where firms could gain competitive advantages and attain above average performance. However, some have asked, if strategic management is all about creating and exploiting competitive imperfections in industries, is strategic management also all about reducing the overall good of society for advantages to be gained by a few firms? It is not surprising that individuals who are more interested in

improving society than improving the performance of a few firms question the moral legitimacy of the field of strategic management.

However, there is another view about strategic management and social welfare. The S-C-P model assumes that any competitive advantages a firm has in an industry must hurt society. The alternative view is that at least some of the competitive advantages may exist because that firm addresses customer needs more effectively than its competitors. From this perspective, competitive advantages are not bad for social welfare; they are actually good for social welfare.

Of course, both perspectives can be true. For example, a firm like Microsoft has engaged in activities that at least some courts have concluded are inconsistent with social welfare. On the other hand, Microsoft also sells applications software that is routinely ranked among the best in the industry, actions that are consistent with meeting customer needs in ways that maximize social welfare.

Sources: J. B. Barney (1986). "Types of competition and the theory of strategy." *Academy of Management Review*, 11, pp. 791–800; H. Demsetz (1973). "Industry structure, market rivalry, and public policy." *Journal of Law and Economics*, 16, pp. 1–9; M. Porter (1981). "The contribution of industrial organization to strategic management." *Academy of Management Review*, 6, pp. 609–620.

the performance of the economy as a whole. While both these definitions of performance in the S-C-P model are important, as is suggested in Chapter 1, the strategic management process is much more focused on the performance of individual firms than on the performance of the economy as a whole. That said, the relationship between these two types of performance can sometimes be complex, as described in the Ethics and Strategy feature.

The logic that links industry structure to conduct and performance is well known. Attributes of the industry structure within which a firm operates define the range of options and constraints facing a firm. In some industries, firms have very few options and face many constraints. In general, firms in these industries can gain only competitive parity. In this setting, industry structure completely determines both firm conduct and long-run firm performance.

However, in other, less competitive industries firms face fewer constraints and a greater range of conduct options. Some of these options may enable them to obtain competitive advantages. However, even when firms have more conduct options, industry structure still constrains the range of those options. Moreover, as will be shown in more detail later in this chapter, industry structure also has an impact on how long firms can expect to maintain their competitive advantages in the face of increased competition.

The Five Forces Model of Environmental Threats

As a theoretical framework, the S-C-P model has proven to be very useful in informing both research and government policy. However, in this form, this model can sometimes be awkward to use to identify threats in a firm's local environment. Fortunately, several scholars have developed models of environmental threats based on the S-C-P model that are highly applicable in identifying threats facing a particular firm. The most influential of these models was developed by Professor Michael Porter and is known as the "five forces framework."[9] The **five forces framework** identifies the five most common threats faced by firms in their local competitive environments and the conditions under which these threats are more or less likely to be present. The relationship between the S-C-P model and the five forces framework is discussed in the Strategy in Depth feature.

To a firm seeking competitive advantages, an **environmental threat** is any individual, group, or organization outside a firm that seeks to reduce the level of that firm's performance. Threats increase a firm's costs, decrease a firm's revenues, or in other ways reduce a firm's performance. In S-C-P terms, environmental threats are forces that tend to increase the competitiveness of an industry and force firm performance to competitive parity level. The five common environmental threats identified in the "five forces framework" are: (1) the threat of entry, (2) the threat of rivalry, (3) the threat of substitutes, (4) the threat of suppliers, and (5) the threat of buyers. The five forces framework is summarized in Figure 2.3.

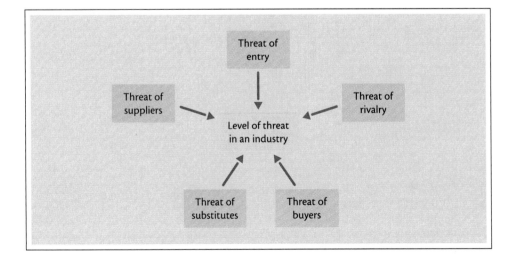

Figure 2.3   Five Forces Model of Environmental Threats

Source: M. E. Porter (1980). Adapted with the permission of The Free Press, a division of Simon & Schuster Adult Publishing Group.

Strategy in Depth

The relationship between the five forces framework and the S-C-P model turns on the relationship between the threats identified in this framework and the nature of competition in an industry. When all five threats are very high, competition in an industry begins to approach what economists call perfect competition. When all five threats are very low, competition in an industry begins to approach what economists call a monopoly. Between perfect competition on the one hand, and monopoly on the other, economists have identified two other types of competition in an industry—monopolistic competition and oligopoly—where the five threats identified in the framework are moderately high. These four types of competition, and the expected performance of firms in these different industries, are summarized in the table below.

Industries are **perfectly competitive** when there are large numbers of competing firms, products being sold are homogeneous with respect to cost and product attributes, and entry and exit are very low cost. Examples of such perfectly competitive industries include the spot market for crude oil.

The S-C-P Model and the Five Forces Framework

Firms in these industries can expect to earn only competitive parity.

In **monopolistically competitive industries**, there are large numbers of competing firms and low-cost entry into and exit from the industry. However, unlike the case of perfect competition, products in these industries are not homogeneous with respect to costs or product attributes. Examples of monopolistically competitive industries include

toothpaste, shampoo, golf balls, and automobiles. Firms in such industries can earn competitive advantages.

Oligopolies are characterized by a small number of competing firms, by homogeneous products, and by costly entry and exit. Examples of oligopolistic industries include the U.S. automobile and steel industries in the 1950s and the U.S. breakfast cereal market today. Currently, the top four producers of breakfast cereal account for about 90 percent of the breakfast cereal sold in the United States. Firms in such industries can earn competitive advantages.

Finally, **monopolistic industries** consist of only a single firm. Entry into this type of industry is very costly. There are few examples of purely monopolistic industries. Historically, for example, the U.S. Post Office had a monopoly on home mail delivery. However, this monopoly has been challenged in small-package delivery by FedEx, larger-package delivery by UPS, and in mail delivery by e-mail. Monopolists can generate competitive advantages—although they are sometimes managed very inefficiently.

Source: J. Barney (2002). *Gaining and sustaining competitive advantage*, 2nd ed. Upper Saddle River, NJ.

Types of Competition and Expected Firm Performance

Type of Competition	Attributes	Examples	Expected Firm Performance
Perfect competition	Large number of firms Homogeneous products Low-cost entry and exit	Stock market Crude oil	Competitive Parity
Monopolistic Competition	Large number of firms Heterogeneous products Low-cost entry and exit	Toothpaste Shampoo Golf balls Automobiles	Competitive Advantage
Oligopoly	Small number of firms Homogenous products Costly entry and exit	U.S. steel and and autos in the 1950s U.S. breakfast cereal	Competitive Advantage
Monopoly	One firm Costly entry	Home mail delivery	Competitive Advantage

The Threat of Entry

The first environmental threat identified in the five forces framework is the threat of new entry. **New entrants** are firms that have either recently begun operations in an industry or that threaten to begin operations in an industry soon. For Amazon.com, in the online book-ordering business, Barnes & Noble.com and Borders.com are new entrants. Amazon largely invented this way of selling books, and both Barnes & Noble and Borders recently entered this market, even though both these firms already operated in the traditional book sales industry. For ESPN in the television sports industry, both the Fox Sports Regional Network and the College Sports Television (CSTV) network are new entrants. The Fox Regional Sports Network consists of several regional sports channels that broadcast both national and regional sporting events, sports news shows, and sports entertainment shows—including *The Best Damn Sports Show, Period.* CSTV is a new (founded in spring of 2003) sports cable and satellite channel that specializes in college sports.

According to the S-C-P model, new entrants are motivated to enter into an industry by the superior profits that some incumbent firms in that industry may be earning. Firms seeking these high profits enter the industry, thereby increasing the level of industry competition and reducing the performance of incumbent firms. With the absence of any barriers, entry will continue as long as any firms in the industry are earning competitive advantages, and entry will cease when all incumbent firms are earning competitive parity.

The extent to which new entry acts as a threat to an incumbent firm's performance depends on the cost of entry. If the cost of entry into an industry is greater than the potential profits a new entrant could obtain by entering, then entry will not be forthcoming, and new entrants are not a threat to incumbent firms. But if the cost of entry is lower than the return from entry, entry will occur until the profits derived from entry are less than the costs of entry.

The threat of entry depends upon the cost of entry, and the cost of entry, in turn, depends upon the existence and "height" of barriers to entry. **Barriers to entry** are attributes of an industry's structure that increase the cost of entry. The greater the cost of entry, the greater the height of these barriers. With significant barriers to entry in place, potential entrants will not enter into an industry even though incumbent firms are earning competitive advantages.

Four important barriers to entry have been identified in the S-C-P and strategy literatures. These four barriers, listed in Table 2.1, are (1) economies of scale, (2) product differentiation, (3) cost advantages independent of scale, and (4) government regulation of entry.[10]

Economies of Scale as a Barrier to Entry

Economies of scale exist in an industry when a firm's costs fall as a function of that firm's volume of production. **Diseconomies of scale** exist when a firm's costs rise as a function of that firm's volume of production. The relationship between

Table 2.1   **Barriers to Entry into an Industry**

1. Economies of scale.
2. Product differentiation.
3. Cost advantages independent of scale.
4. Government regulation of entry.

Figure 2.4   Economies of Scale and the Cost of Production

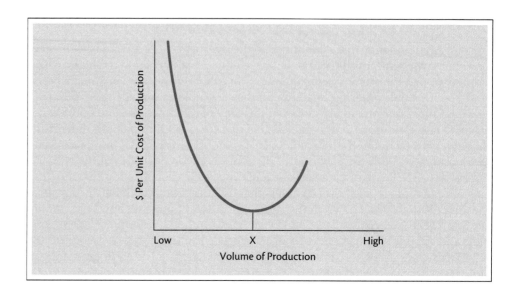

economies of scale, diseconomies of scale, and a firm's volume of production is summarized in Figure 2.4. As a firm's volume of production increases, its costs begin to fall. This is a manifestation of economies of scale. However, at some point, a firm's volume of production becomes too large and its costs begin to rise. This is a manifestation of diseconomies of scale. For economies of scale to act as a barrier to entry, the relationship between the volume of production and firm costs must have the shape of the line in Figure 2.4. This curve suggests that any deviation, positive or negative, from an optimal level of production (point X in Figure 2.4) will lead a firm to experience much higher costs of production.

To see how economies of scale can act as a barrier to entry, consider the following scenario. Imagine an industry with the following attributes. There are five incumbent firms (each firm has only one plant); the optimal level of production in each of these plants is 4,000 units (X = 4,000 units); total demand for the output of this industry is fixed at 22,000 units; the economies-of-scale curve is as depicted in Figure 2.4; and products in this industry are very homogeneous. Total demand in this industry (22,000 units) is greater than total supply (5 × 4,000 units = 20,000). Everyone knows that when demand is greater than supply, prices go up. This means that the five incumbent firms in this industry will have high levels of profit. The S–C–P model suggests that, absent barriers, these superior profits should motivate entry.

However, look at the entry decision from the point of view of potential entrants. Certainly, incumbent firms are earning superior profits, but potential entrants face an unsavory choice. On the one hand, new entrants could enter the industry with an optimally efficient plant and produce 4,000 units. However, this form of entry will lead industry supply to rise to 24,000 units (20,000 + 4,000). Suddenly, supply will be greater than demand (24,000 > 22,000), and all the firms in the industry, including the new entrant, will earn negative profits. On the other hand, the new entrant might enter the industry with a plant of smaller-than-optimal size (for example, 1,000 units). This kind of entry leaves total industry demand larger than industry supply (22,000 > 21,000). However, the new entrant faces a serious cost disadvantage in this case because it does not produce at the low-cost position on the economies-of-scale curve. Faced with these bleak alternatives, the potential entrant simply does not enter even though incumbent firms are earning positive profits.

Of course, there are other options for potential entrants, besides entering at the efficient scale and losing money or entering at an inefficient scale and losing money. For example, potential entrants can attempt to expand the total size of the market (that is, increase total demand from 22,000 to 24,000 units or more) and enter at the optimal size. Potential entrants can also attempt to develop new production technology, shift the economies-of-scale curve to the left (thereby reducing the optimal plant size), and enter. Or, potential entrants may try to make their products seem very special to their customers, enabling them to charge higher prices to offset higher production costs associated with a smaller-than-optimal plant.[11]

Any of these firm actions may enable entry into an industry. However, these actions are costly. If the cost of engaging in these "barrier-busting" activities is greater than the return from entry, entry will not occur, even if incumbent firms are earning positive profits.

Historically, economies of scale acted as a barrier to entry into the worldwide steel market. To fully exploit economies of scale, traditional steel plants had to be very large. If new entrants into the steel market had built these efficient and large steel-manufacturing plants, they would have had the effect of increasing the steel supply over the demand for steel, and the outcome would have been reduced profits for both new entrants and incumbent firms. This discouraged new entry. However, in the 1970s, the development of alternative mini-mill technology shifted the economies-of-scale curve to the left by making smaller plants very efficient in addressing some segments of the steel market. This shift had the effect of decreasing barriers to entry into the steel industry. Recent entrants, including Nucor Steel and Chaparral Steel, now have significant cost advantages over firms still using outdated, less efficient production technology.[12]

Product Differentiation as a Barrier to Entry

Product differentiation means that incumbent firms possess brand identification and customer loyalty that potential entrants do not possess. Brand identification and customer loyalty serve as entry barriers because new entrants not only have to absorb the standard costs associated with starting production in a new industry; they also have to absorb the costs associated with overcoming incumbent firms' differentiation advantages. If the cost of overcoming these advantages is greater than the potential return from entering an industry, entry will not occur, even if incumbent firms are earning positive profits.

There are numerous examples of industries where product differentiation tends to act as a barrier to entry. In the brewing industry, for example, substantial investments by Budweiser, Miller, and Coors (among other incumbent firms) in advertising (will we ever forget the Budweiser frogs?) and brand recognition have made large-scale entry into the U.S. brewing industry very costly.[13] E. & J. Gallo Winery, a U.S. winemaker, faces product differentiation barriers to entry in its efforts to sell Gallo wine in the French market. The market for wine in France is huge—the French consume 16.1 gallons of wine per person per year, for a total consumption of over 400 million cases of wine, while U.S. consumers drink only 1.8 gallons of wine per person per year, for a total consumption of less than 200 million cases. Despite this difference, intense loyalties to local French vineyards have made it very difficult for Gallo to break into this huge French market—a market where American wines are still given as "gag gifts" and only American theme restaurants carry U.S. wines on their menus. Gallo is attempting to overcome this product differentiation advantage of French wineries by emphasizing its California roots—roots that many French consider to be exotic—and downplaying the fact that it is a U.S. company, corporate origins that are less attractive to many French consumers.[14]

Table 2.2   **Sources of Cost Advantage, Independent of Scale, That Can Act as Barriers to Entry**

Proprietary Technology: When incumbent firms have secret or patented technology that reduces their costs below the costs of potential entrants, potential entrants must develop substitute technologies to compete. The cost of developing this technology can act as a barrier to entry.

Managerial Know-how: When incumbent firms have taken-for-granted knowledge, skills, and information that take years to develop, not possessed by potential entrants. The cost of developing this know-how can act as a barrier to entry.

Favorable Access to Raw Materials: When incumbent firms have low-cost access to critical raw materials not enjoyed by potential entrants. The cost of gaining similar access can act as a barrier to entry.

Learning-Curve Cost Advantages: When the cumulative volume of production of incumbent firms gives them cost advantages not enjoyed by potential entrants. These cost disadvantages of potential entrants can act as a barrier to entry.

Cost Advantages Independent of Scale as Barriers to Entry

In addition to the barriers previously cited, incumbent firms may have a whole range of cost advantages, independent of economies of scale, compared to new entrants. These cost advantages can act to deter entry, because new entrants will find themselves at a cost disadvantage vis-à-vis incumbent firms with these cost advantages. New entrants can engage in activities to overcome the cost advantages of incumbent firms, but as the cost of overcoming them increases, the economic profit potential from entry is reduced. In some settings, incumbent firms enjoying cost advantages, independent of scale, can earn superior profits and still not be threatened by new entry because the cost of overcoming those advantages can be prohibitive. Examples of these cost advantages, independent of scale, are presented in Table 2.2 and include: (1) proprietary technology, (2) managerial know-how, (3) favorable access to raw materials, and (4) learning-curve cost advantages.

Proprietary Technology. In some industries, **proprietary** (that is secret or patented) **technology** gives incumbent firms important cost advantages over potential entrants. To enter these industries, potential entrants must develop their own substitute technologies or run the risks of copying another firm's patented technologies. Both of these activities can be costly. Numerous firms in a wide variety of industries have discovered the sometimes substantial economic costs associated with violating another firm's patented proprietary technology. For example, in 1991, Eastman Kodak had to pay Polaroid $873 million for violating patents; in 1997, Intel had to pay Digital $700 million for violating patents; in 2002, Roche Holding had to pay Igen International $505 million for violating patents; and in 2002, Genentech had to pay City of Hope National Medical Center $500 million for violating patents.

Indeed, in the United States, at least 20 firms have had to pay some other firm over $100 million for violating this other firm's patents. And this does not include the numerous patent infringement suits that are settled out of court, suits that involve literally billions of dollars exchanging hands. Obviously, if an industry has several firms with proprietary technologies, these technologies can substantially increase the cost of entry into that industry.[15]

Managerial Know-How. Even more important than technology per se as a barrier to entry is the managerial know-how built up by incumbent firms over their history.[16] **Managerial know-how** is the often-taken-for-granted knowledge and information that are needed to compete in an industry on a day-to-day basis.[17] Know-how includes information about countless details (that has taken years, sometimes decades, to accumulate) in a firm that enables a firm to interact with customers and suppliers, to be innovative and creative, to manufacture quality products, and so forth. Typically, new entrants will not have access to this know-now and it will often be costly for them to build it quickly.

One industry where this kind of know-how is a very important barrier to entry is the pharmaceutical industry. Success in this industry depends critically on having high-quality research and development skills. The development of world-class research and development skills takes decades, as firms accumulate the knowledge, abilities, ideas—the know-how—needed to succeed. New entrants face enormous cost disadvantages for decades as they attempt to develop these abilities, and thus entry into the pharmaceutical industry has been quite limited.[18]

Favorable Access to Raw Materials. Incumbent firms may also have cost advantages, compared to new entrants, based on favorable access to raw materials. If, for example, there are only a few sources of high-quality iron ore in a specific geographic region, steel firms that have access to these sources may have a cost advantage over steel firms that must ship their ore in from distant sources.[19]

Learning-Curve Cost Advantages. It has been shown that in certain industries (such as airplane manufacturing), the cost of production falls with the cumulative volume of production. Over time, as incumbent firms gain experience in manufacturing, their costs fall below those of potential entrants. Potential entrants, in this context, must endure substantially higher costs while they gain experience, and thus they may not enter, despite possible superior profits being earned by incumbent firms. These learning-curve economies are discussed in more detail in Chapter 4.

Government Policy as a Barrier to Entry

Governments, for their own reasons, may decide to increase the cost of entry into an industry. This occurs most frequently when a firm operates as a government-regulated monopoly. In this setting, the government has concluded that it is in a better position to ensure that specific products or services are made available to the population at reasonable prices than competitive market forces. Industries such as electric power generation and elementary and secondary education have been (and to some extent, continue to be) protected from competitive entry by government restrictions on entry.

While the government has acted to restrict competitive entry in many industries in the past, the number of such industries and the level of this entry restriction have both fallen dramatically over the last several years. Indeed, in the United States, deregulation in the electric power generation industry has been occurring at a rapid pace. And while the bankruptcy of Enron may delay the relaxing of government-imposed barriers to entry into this industry, most observers agree that these restrictions will continue to be less important in the future. Entry is even occurring in the primary and secondary school industry with the creation of "charter schools"—often private schools that provide educational alternatives to public school systems.

The Threat of Rivalry

New entrants are an important threat to the ability of firms to maintain or improve their level of performance, but they are not the only threat in a firm's environment. A second environmental threat in the five forces framework is **rivalry**—the intensity of competition among a firm's direct competitors. Both Barnes & Noble .com and Borders.com have become rivals of Amazon.com. CBS, NBC, Fox, USA Networks, and TNN—to name a few—are all ESPN rivals.

Rivalry threatens firms by reducing their economic profits. High levels of rivalry are indicated by such actions as frequent price cutting by firms in an industry (for example, price discounts in the airline industry), frequent introduction of new products by firms in an industry (for example, continuous product introductions in consumer electronics), intense advertising campaigns (for example, Pepsi versus Coke advertising), and rapid competitive actions and reactions in an industry (competing airlines quickly matching the discounts of other airlines).

Some of the attributes of an industry that are likely to generate high levels of rivalry are listed in Table 2.3. First, rivalry tends to be high when there are numerous firms in an industry and these firms tend to be roughly the same size. Such is the case in the laptop personal computer industry. Worldwide, over 120 firms have entered the laptop computer market, and no one firm dominates in market share. Since the early 1990s, prices in the laptop market have been declining 25 to 30 percent a year. Profit margins for laptop personal computer firms that used to be in the 10 to 13 percent range have rapidly fallen to 3 and 4 percent.[20]

Second, rivalry tends to be high when industry growth is slow. When industry growth is slow, firms seeking to increase their sales must acquire market share from established competitors. This tends to increase rivalry. Intense price rivalry emerged in the U.S. fast-food industry—with 99-cent Whoppers at Burger King and "dollar menus" at Wendy's and McDonald's—when the growth in this industry declined.[21]

Third, rivalry tends to be high when firms are unable to differentiate their products in an industry. When product differentiation is not a viable strategic option, firms are often forced to compete only on the basis of price. Intense price competition is typical of high-rivalry industries. In the airline industry, for example, intense competition on longer routes—such as between Los Angeles and New York and Los Angeles and Chicago—has kept prices on these routes down. There are relatively few product differentiation options on these routes. However, by creating hub-and-spoke systems, certain airlines (American, United, Delta) have been able to develop regions of the United States where they are the dominant carrier. These hub-and-spoke systems enable airlines to partially differentiate their products geographically and thus reduce the level of rivalry in segments of this industry.[22]

Finally, rivalry tends to be high when production capacity is added in large increments. If, in order to obtain economies of scale, production capacity must be

Table 2.3   **Attributes of an Industry That Increase the Threat of Rivalry**

1. Large number of competing firms that are roughly the same size
2. Slow industry growth
3. Lack of product differentiation
4. Capacity added in large increments

added in large increments, an industry is likely to experience periods of oversupply after new capacity comes on line. This overcapacity often leads to price cutting. Much of the growing rivalry in the commercial jet industry between Boeing and AirBus can be traced to the large manufacturing capacity additions made by AirBus when it entered the industry.[23]

The Threat of Substitutes

A third environmental threat in the five forces framework is substitutes. The products or services provided by a firm's rivals meet approximately the same customer needs in the same ways as the products or services provided by the firm itself. **Substitutes** meet approximately the same customer needs but do so in different ways. Close substitutes for Amazon.com include Barnes & Noble, Borders, and Waldenbooks book stores. Television is a somewhat more distant substitute for Amazon, because the popularity of television comedies, dramas, and documentaries dampens demand for books. Substitutes for ESPN include sports magazines, sports pages in the newspapers, and actually attending sporting events.

Substitutes place a ceiling on the prices firms in an industry can charge and on the profits firms in an industry can earn. In the extreme, substitutes can ultimately replace an industry's products and services. This happens when a substitute is clearly superior to previous products. Examples include electronic calculators as substitutes for slide rules and mechanical calculators, electronic watch movements as substitutes for pin–lever mechanical watch movements, and compact discs as substitutes for long-playing (LP) records (although some audiophiles continue to argue for the sonic superiority of LPs). An open question remains about the extent to which online downloading of music is a substitute for compact discs.

Substitutes are playing an increasingly important role in reducing the profit potential in a wide variety of industries. For example, in the legal profession, private mediation and arbitration services are becoming viable substitutes for lawyers. Computerized texts are becoming viable substitutes for printed books in the publishing industry. Television news programs, especially services like CNN, are very threatening substitutes for weekly news magazines, including *Time* and *Newsweek*. In Europe, so–called superstores are threatening smaller food shops. Minor league baseball teams are partial substitutes for major league teams. Cable television is a substitute for broadcast television. Groups of "Big Box" retailers are substitutes for traditional shopping centers. Private mail delivery systems (like those in the Netherlands and Australia) are substitutes for government postal services. Home financial planning software is a partial substitute for professional financial planners.[24]

The Threat of Suppliers

A fourth environmental threat in the five forces framework is suppliers. **Suppliers** make a wide variety of raw materials, labor, and other critical assets available to firms. Suppliers can threaten the performance of firms in an industry by increasing the price of their supplies or by reducing the quality of those supplies. Any profits that were being earned in an industry can be transferred to suppliers in this way. For Amazon, book publishers and, more recently, book authors are critical suppliers, along with the employees that provide programming and logistics capabilities to Amazon. Critical suppliers for ESPN include

Table 2.4   **Indicators of the Threat of Suppliers in an Industry**

1. Suppliers' industry dominated by small number of firms.
2. Suppliers sell unique or highly differentiated products.
3. Suppliers are *not* threatened by substitutes.
4. Suppliers threaten forward vertical integration.
5. Firms are *not* important customers for suppliers.

sports leagues—such as the NFL and the NHL—as well as TV personalities that staff ESPN television shows.

Some supplier attributes that can lead to high levels of threat are listed in Table 2.4. First, a firm's suppliers are a greater threat if the *suppliers'* industry is dominated by a small number of firms. In this setting, a firm has little choice but to purchase supplies from these firms. These few firms thus have enormous flexibility to charge high prices, to reduce quality, or in other ways to squeeze the profits of the firms to which they sell. Much of Microsoft's power in the software industry reflects its dominance in the operating system market, where Windows remains the de facto standard for most personal computers. For now, at least, if a company wants to sell personal computers, it is going to need to interact with Microsoft. It will be interesting to see if Linux-based PCs become more powerful, thereby limiting some of Microsoft's power as a supplier.

Conversely, when a firm has the option of purchasing from a large number of suppliers, suppliers have less power to threaten a firm's profits. For example, as the number of lawyers in the United States has increased over the years (up 40 percent since 1981, currently close to one million), lawyers and law firms have been forced to begin competing for work. Some corporate clients have forced law firms to reduce their hourly fees and to handle repetitive simple legal tasks for low flat fees.[25]

Second, suppliers are a greater threat when what they supply is unique or highly differentiated. There was only one Michael Jordan, as a basketball player, as a spokesperson, and as a celebrity (but *not* as a baseball player). Jordan's unique status gave him enormous bargaining power as a supplier and enabled him to extract much of the economic profit that would otherwise have been earned by the Chicago Bulls and Nike. Currently, there is only one Le Bron James. In the same way, Intel's unique ability to develop, manufacture, and sell microprocessors gives it significant bargaining power as a supplier in the personal computer industry.

The uniqueness of suppliers can operate in almost any industry. For example, in the highly competitive world of television talk shows, some guests, as suppliers, can gain surprising fame for their unique characteristics. For example, one woman was a guest on eight talk shows. Her claim to fame: She was the tenth wife of a gay, con-man bigamist. Talk show hosts can also exercise significant power as suppliers. King World, the distributor of the *Oprah* talk show, has depended on *Oprah* for as much as 40 percent of its revenues. This, of course, has given the show's host, Oprah Winfrey, significant leverage in negotiating with King World.[26]

Third, suppliers are a greater threat to firms in an industry when suppliers are *not* threatened by substitutes. When there are no effective substitutes, suppliers can take advantage of their position to extract economic profits from firms they supply. Both Intel (in microprocessors) and Microsoft (in PC operating systems) have been accused of exploiting their unique product positions to extract profits from customers.

When there are substitutes for supplies, supplier power is checked. In the metal can industry, for example, steel cans are threatened by aluminum and plastic containers as substitutes. In order to continue to sell to can manufacturers, steel companies have had to keep their prices lower than what would otherwise have been the case. In this way, the potential power of the steel companies is checked by the existence of substitute products.[27]

Fourth, suppliers are a greater threat to firms when they can credibly threaten to enter into and begin competing in a firm's industry. This is called **forward vertical integration**, where suppliers cease to be suppliers alone and become suppliers *and* rivals. The threat of forward vertical integration is partially a function of barriers to entry into an industry. When an industry has high barriers to entry, suppliers face significant costs of forward vertical integration, and thus forward integration is not as serious a threat to the profits of incumbent firms (vertical integration is discussed in detail in Chapter 6).

Finally, suppliers are a threat to firms when firms are *not* an important part of suppliers' business. Steel companies, for example, are not too concerned with losing the business of a sculptor or of a small construction company. However, they are very concerned about losing the business of the major can manufacturers, major white-goods manufacturers (that is, manufacturers of refrigerators, washing machines, dryers, and so forth), and automobile companies. Steel companies, as suppliers, are likely to be very accommodating and willing to reduce prices and increase quality for can manufacturers, white-goods manufacturers, and auto companies. Smaller, "less important" customers, however, are likely to be subject to greater price increases, lower-quality service, and lower-quality products.

The Threat of Buyers

The final environmental threat in the five forces framework is buyers. **Buyers** purchase a firm's products or services. Where sellers act to increase a firm's costs, buyers act to decrease a firm's revenues. Amazon.com's buyers include all those who purchase books online as well as those who purchase advertising space on Amazon's Web site. ESPN's buyers include all those who watch sports on television as well as those who purchase advertising space on the network. Some of the important indicators of the threat of buyers are listed in Table 2.5.

First, if a firm has only one buyer, or a small number of buyers, these buyers can be very threatening. Firms that sell a significant amount of their output to the U.S. Department of Defense recognize the influence of this buyer on their operations. Reductions in defense spending have forced defense companies to try even harder to reduce costs and increase quality to satisfy government

Table 2.5 **Indicators of the Threat of Buyers in an Industry**

1. Number of buyers is small.
2. Products sold to buyers are undifferentiated and standard.
3. Products sold to buyers are a significant percentage of a buyer's final costs.
4. Buyers are *not* earning significant economic profits.
5. Buyers threaten backward vertical integration.

demands. All these actions reduce the economic profits of these defense-oriented companies.[28] Firms that sell to large retail chains have also found it difficult to maintain high levels of profitability. Powerful retail firms—like Wal-Mart and Home Depot—can make significant and complex logistical and other demands on their suppliers and, if suppliers fail to meet these demands, buyers can "fire" their suppliers. These demands can have the effect of reducing the profits of suppliers.

Second, if the products or services that are being sold to buyers are standard and not differentiated, then the threat of buyers can be greater. For example, farmers sell a very standard product. It is very difficult to differentiate products like wheat, corn, or tomatoes (although this can be done to some extent through the development of new strains of crops, the timing of harvests, no use of pesticides, and so forth). In general, wholesale grocers and food brokers can always find alternative suppliers of basic food products. These numerous alternative suppliers increase the threat of buyers and force farmers to keep their prices and profits low. If any one farmer attempts to raise prices, wholesale grocers and food brokers simply purchase their supplies from some other farmer.

Third, buyers are likely to be more of a threat when the supplies they purchase are a significant portion of the costs of their final products. In this context, buyers are likely to be very concerned about the costs of their supplies and constantly on the lookout for cheaper alternatives. For example, in the canned food industry, the cost of the can itself can constitute up to 40 percent of a product's final price. Not surprisingly, firms like Campbell Soup Company are very concerned about keeping the price of the cans they purchase as low as possible.[29]

Fourth, buyers are likely to be more of a threat when they are *not* earning significant economic profits. In these circumstances, buyers are likely to be very sensitive to costs and insist on the lowest possible cost and the highest possible quality from suppliers. This effect can be exacerbated when the profits suppliers earn are greater than the profits buyers earn. In this setting, a buyer would have a strong incentive to enter into its supplier's business to capture some of the economic profits being earned by the supplier. This strategy of **backward vertical integration** is discussed in more detail in Chapter 6.

Finally, buyers are more of a threat to firms in an industry when they have the ability to vertically integrate backward. In this case, buyers become both buyers and rivals and lock in a certain percentage of an industry's sales. The extent to which buyers represent a threat to vertically integrate, in turn, depends on the barriers to entry that are not in place in an industry. If there are significant barriers to entry, buyers may not be able to engage in backward vertical integration, and their threat to firms is reduced.

The Five Forces Model and Average Industry Performance

The five forces model has three important implications for managers seeking to choose and implement strategies. First, this model describes the most common sources of local environmental threat in industries. These are the threat of entry, the threat of rivalry, the threat of substitutes, the threat of suppliers, and the threat of buyers. Second, this model can be used to characterize the overall level of threat in an industry. Finally, since the overall level of threat in an industry is, according to S-C-P logic, related to the average level of performance of a firm in an industry, the five forces model can also be used to anticipate the average level of performance of firms in an industry.

Of course, it will rarely be the case that all five forces in an industry will be equally threatening at the same time. This can sometimes complicate the anticipation of the

Table 2.6   **Estimating the Level of Average Performance in an Industry**

	Industry I	**Industry II**	**Industry III**	**Industry IV**
Threat of Entry	High	Low	High	Low
Threat of Rivalry	High	Low	Low	High
Threat of Substitutes	High	Low	High	Low
Threat of Suppliers	High	Low	Low	High
Threat of Buyers	High	Low	High	Low
Expected Average Firm Performance	High	Low	?	?

average level of firm performance in an industry. Consider, for example, the four industries in Table 2.6. It is easy to anticipate the average level of performance of firms in the first two industries: In Industry I, this performance will be high; in Industry II, this performance will be low; however, in Industries III and IV it is somewhat more complicated. In these mixed situations, the real question to ask in anticipating the average performance of firms in an industry is: "Are one or more threats in this industry powerful enough to appropriate most of the profits that firms in this industry might generate?" If the answer to this question is yes, then the anticipated average level of performance will be low. If the answer is no, then this anticipated performance will be high.

Even more fundamentally, the five forces framework can be used only to anticipate the average level of firm performance in an industry. This is all right if a firm's industry is the primary determinant of its overall performance. However, as described in the Research Made Relevant feature, research suggests that the industry a firm operates in is far from the only determinant of its performance.

Another Environmental Force: Complementors

Recently, Professors Adam Brandenburger and Barry Nalebuff have suggested that another force needs to be added to Porter's five forces framework.[30] These authors distinguish between competitors and what they call a firm's complementors. If you were the CEO of a firm, this is how you could tell the difference between your competitors and your complementors. Another firm is a **competitor** if your customers value your product less when they have this other firm's product than when they have your product alone. Rivals, new entrants, and substitutes can all be seen as specific examples of competitors. On the other hand, another firm is a **complementor** if your customers value your product more when they have this other firm's product than when they have your product alone.

Consider, for example, the relationship between producers of television programming and cable television companies. The value of these firms' products partially depends on the existence of each other. Television producers need outlets for their programming. The growth in the number of channels on cable television provides more of these outlets and thus increases the value of these production firms. On the other hand, cable television companies can continue to add channels, but those channels need content. So, the value of cable television companies depends partly on the existence of television production firms. Since the value of television producing companies is greater when cable television firms exist, and since the value of cable television companies is greater when television producing companies exist, these types of firms are complements.

Brandenburger and Nalebuff go on to argue that an important difference between complementors and competitors is that a firm's complementors help

Research Made Relevant

For some time now, scholars have been interested in the relative impact of the attributes of the industry within which a firm operates and the attributes of a firm, itself, on its performance. The first work in this area was published by Richard Schmalansee. Using a single year's worth of data, Schmalansee estimated the variance in the performance of firms that was attributable to the industries within which firms operated versus other sources of performance variance. Schmalansee's conclusion was that approximately 20 percent of the variance in firm performance was explained by the industry within which a firm operated—a conclusion consistent with the S-C-P model and its emphasis on industry as a primary determinant of a firm's performance.

Richard Rumelt identified some weaknesses in Schmalansee's research. Most important of these was that Schmalansee had only one year's worth of data with which to examine the effects of industry and firm attributes on firm

The Impact of Industry and Firm Characteristics on Firm Performance

performance. Rumelt was able to use four year's worth of data, which allowed him to distinguish between stable and transient industry and firm effects on firm performance. Rumelt's results were consistent with Schmalansee's in one sense: Rumelt also found that about 16

percent of the variance in firm performance was due to industry effects versus Schmalansee's 20 percent. However, only about half of this industry effect was stable. The rest represented year-to-year fluctuations in the business conditions in an industry. This result is broadly inconsistent with the S-C-P model.

Rumelt also examined the impact of firm attributes on firm performance and found that over 80 percent of the variance in firm performance was due to these firm attributes, but that over half of this 80 percent (46.38%) was due to stable firm effects. The importance of stable firm differences in explaining differences in firm performance is also inconsistent with the S-C-P framework. These results are consistent with another model of firm performance called the Resource-Based View, which will be described in Chapter 3.

Sources: R. P. Rumelt (1991). "How much does industry matter?" *Strategic Management Journal,* 12, pp. 167–185; R. Schmalansee (1985). "Do markets differ much?" *American Economic Review,* 75, pp. 341–351.

increase the size of a firm's market, while a firm's competitors divide this market among a set of firms. Based on this logic, these authors suggest that while it is usually the case that a firm will want to discourage the entry of competitors into its market, it will usually want to encourage the entry of complementors. Returning to the television producers/cable television example, television producers will actually want cable television companies to grow and prosper and constantly add new channels, while cable television firms will want television show producers to grow and constantly create new and innovative programming. If the growth of either of these businesses slows, it hurts the growth of the other.

Of course, the same firm can be a complementor for one firm and a competitor for another. For example, the invention of satellite television and the popularization of DirecTV and the Dish Network represent a competitive challenge to cable television companies. That is, DirecTV and, say, Time Warner Cable, are competitors. However, DirecTV and television production companies are complementors to each other. In deciding whether or not to encourage the entry of new complementors, a firm has to weigh the extra value these new complementors will create against the competitive impact of this entry on a firm's current complementors.

It is also the case that a single firm can be both a competitor and a complementor to the same firm. This is very common in industries where it is important to create technological standards. Without standards about, for example, the size of a CD, how information on a CD will be stored, how this information will be read, and so forth, consumers will often be unwilling to purchase a CD player. With standards in place, however, sales of a particular technology can soar. To develop technology standards, firms must be willing to cooperate. This cooperation means that, with respect to the technology standard, these firms are complementors. And indeed, when these firms act as complementors, their actions have the effect of increasing the total size of the market. However, once these firms cooperate to establish standards, they begin to compete to try to obtain as much of the market they jointly created as possible. In this sense, these firms are also competitors.

Understanding when firms in an industry should behave as complementors and when they should behave as competitors is sometimes very difficult. It is even more difficult for a firm that has interacted with other firms in its industry as a competitor to change its organizational structure, formal and informal control systems, and compensation policy and start interacting with these firms as a complementor, at least for some purposes. Learning to manage what Brandenburger and Nalebuff call the "Jekyll and Hyde" dilemma associated with competitors and complementors can distinguish excellent from only average firms.

Industry Structure and Environmental Opportunities

Identifying environmental threats is only half the task in accomplishing an external analysis. Such an analysis must also identify opportunities. Fortunately, the same S-C-P logic that made it possible to develop tools for the analysis of environmental threats can also be used to develop tools for the analysis of environmental opportunities. However, instead of identifying the threats that are common in most industries, opportunity analysis begins by identifying several generic industry structures and then describing the strategic opportunities that are available in each of these different kinds of industries.[31]

Of course, there are many different generic industry structures. However, four are very common and will be the focus of opportunity analysis in this book. These four are: (1) fragmented industries, (2) emerging industries, (3) mature industries, and (4) declining industries. A fifth industry structure—international industries—will be discussed later in the chapter. The kinds of opportunities typically associated with these industry structures are presented in Table 2.7.

Table 2.7   **Industry Structure and Environmental Opportunities**

Industry structure	Opportunities
Fragmented industry	Consolidation
Emerging industry	First-mover advantages
Mature industry	Product refinement
	Investment in service quality
	Process innovation
Declining industry	Leadership
	Niche
	Harvest
	Divestment

Opportunities in Fragmented Industries: Consolidation

Fragmented industries are industries in which a large number of small or medium-sized firms operate and no small set of firms has dominant market share or creates dominant technologies. Most service industries, including retailing, fabrics, and commercial printing, to name just a few, are fragmented industries.

Industries can be fragmented for a wide variety of reasons. For example, there may be few barriers to entry into a fragmented industry, thereby encouraging numerous small firms to enter. There may be few, if any, economies of scale, and even some important diseconomies of scale, thus encouraging firms to remain small. Also, there may be a need for close local control over enterprises in an industry—for example, local movie houses and local restaurants, to ensure quality and to minimize losses from theft.

The major opportunity facing firms in fragmented industries is the implementation of strategies that begin to consolidate the industry into a smaller number of firms. Firms that are successful in implementing this **consolidation strategy** can become industry leaders and obtain benefits from this kind of effort, if they exist.

Consolidation can occur in several ways. For example, an incumbent firm may discover new economies of scale in an industry. In the highly fragmented funeral home industry, Service Corporation International (SCI) found that the development of a chain of funeral homes gave it advantages in acquiring key supplies (coffins) and in the allocation of scarce resources (morticians and hearses). By acquiring numerous previously independent funeral homes, SCI was able to substantially reduce its costs and gain higher levels of economic performance.[32]

Incumbent firms sometimes adopt new ownership structures to help consolidate an industry. Kampgrounds of America (KOA) uses franchise agreements with local operators to provide camping facilities to travelers in the fragmented private camping grounds industry. KOA provides local operators with professional training, technical skills, and access to brand name reputation. Local operators, in return, provide KOA with local managers who are intensely interested in the financial and operational success of their campgrounds. Similar franchise agreements have been instrumental in the consolidation of other fragmented industries, including fast foods (McDonald's), muffler repair (Midas), and motels (La Quinta, Holiday Inn, Howard Johnson's).[33]

The benefits of implementing a consolidation strategy in a fragmented industry turn on the advantages larger firms in such industries gain from their larger market share. As will be discussed in Chapter 4, firms with large market share can have important cost advantages. Large market share can also help a firm differentiate its products.

Opportunities in Emerging Industries: First-Mover Advantages

Emerging industries are newly created or newly re-created industries formed by technological innovations, changes in demand, the emergence of new customer needs, and so forth. Over the last 30 years, the world economy has been flooded by emerging industries, including the microprocessor industry, the personal computer industry, the medical imaging industry, and the biotechnology industry, to name a few. Firms in emerging industries face a unique set of opportunities, the exploitation of which can be a source of superior performance for some time for some firms.

The opportunities that face firms in emerging industries fall into the general category of first-mover advantages. **First-mover advantages** are advantages that come to firms that make important strategic and technological decisions early in the development of an industry. In emerging industries, many of the rules of the game and standard operating procedures for competing and succeeding have yet to be established. First-moving firms can sometimes help establish the rules of the game and create an industry's structure in ways that are uniquely beneficial to them. In general, first-mover advantages can arise from three primary sources: (1) technological leadership, (2) preemption of strategically valuable assets, and (3) the creation of customer-switching costs.[34]

First-Mover Advantages and Technological Leadership

Firms that make early investments in particular technologies in an industry are implementing a **technological leadership strategy**. Such strategies can generate two advantages in emerging industries. First, firms that have implemented these strategies may obtain a low-cost position based on their greater cumulative volume of production with a particular technology. These cost advantages have had important competitive implications in such diverse industries as the manufacture of titanium dioxide by DuPont and Procter & Gamble's competitive advantage in disposable diapers.[35]

Second, firms that make early investments in a technology may obtain patent protections that enhance their performance.[36] Xerox's patents on the xerography process and General Electric's patent on Edison's original light bulb design were important for these firms' success when these two industries were emerging.[37] However, although there are some exceptions (for example, the pharmaceutical industry and specialty chemicals), patents, per se, seem to provide relatively small profit opportunities for first-moving firms in most emerging industries. One group of researchers found that imitators can duplicate first movers' patent–based advantages for about 65 percent of the first mover's costs.[38] These researchers also found that 60 percent of all patents are imitated within four years of being granted—without legally violating patent rights obtained by first movers. As we will discuss in detail in Chapter 3, patents are rarely a source of sustained competitive advantage for firms, even in emerging industries.

First-Mover Advantages and Preemption of Strategically Valuable Assets

First movers that invest only in technology usually do not obtain sustained competitive advantages. However, first movers that move to tie up strategically valuable resources in an industry before their full value is widely understood can gain sustained competitive advantages. **Strategically valuable assets** are resources required to successfully compete in an industry. Firms that are able to acquire these resources have, in effect, erected formidable barriers to imitation in an industry. Some strategically valuable assets that can be acquired in this way include access to raw materials, particularly favorable geographic locations, and particularly valuable product market positions.

When an oil company like Royal Dutch Shell (because of its superior exploration skills) acquires leases with greater development potential than was expected by its competition, the company is gaining access to raw materials in a way that is likely to generate sustained competitive advantages. When Wal–Mart opens stores in medium-sized cities before the arrival of its competition, Wal–Mart is making it difficult for the competition to enter into this market. And when breakfast cereal companies expand their product lines to include all possible combinations of wheat, oats, bran, corn, and sugar, they are using a first-mover advantage to deter entry.[39]

First-Mover Advantages and Creating Customer-Switching Costs

Firms can also gain first-mover advantages in an emerging industry by creating customer-switching costs. **Customer-switching costs** exist when customers make investments in order to use a firm's particular products or services and when these investments are not useful in accomplishing this. These investments tie customers to a particular firm and make it more difficult for customers to begin purchasing from different firms.[40] Such switching costs are important factors in industries as diverse as applications software for personal computers, prescription pharmaceuticals, and groceries.[41]

In applications software for personal computers, users make very significant investments to learn how to use a particular software package. Once computer users have learned how to operate particular software, they are unlikely to switch to new software, even if that new software system is superior to what they currently use. Such a switch would require learning the new software and how it is similar to and different form the old software. For these reasons, some computer users will continue to use outdated software, even though new software performs much better.

Similar switching costs can exist in some segments of the prescription pharmaceutical industry. Once medical doctors become familiar with a particular drug, its applications, and side effects, they are sometimes reluctant to change to a new drug, even if that new drug promises to be more effective than the older, more familiar drug. Trying the new drug requires learning about its properties and side effects. Even if the new drug has received government approvals, its use requires doctors to be willing to "experiment" with the health of their patients. Given these issues, many physicians are unwilling to rapidly adopt new drug therapies. This is one reason that pharmaceutical firms spend so much time and money using their sales forces to educate their physician customers. This kind of education is necessary if a doctor is going to be willing to switch from an old drug to a new drug.

Customer-switching costs can even play a role in the grocery store industry. Each grocery store has a particular layout of products. Once customers learn where different products in a particular store are located, they are not likely to change stores, because in so doing they would have to relearn the location of products. Many customers want to avoid the time and frustration associated with wandering around a new store looking for some obscure product. Indeed, the cost of switching stores may be large enough to enable some grocery stores to charge higher prices than what would be the case without customer-switching costs.

First-Mover Disadvantages

Of course, the advantages of first moving in emerging industries must be balanced against the risks associated with exploiting this opportunity. Emerging industries are characterized by a great deal of uncertainty. When first-moving firms are making critical strategic decisions, it may not be at all clear what the right decisions are. In such highly uncertain settings, a reasonable strategic alternative to first moving may be retaining flexibility. Where first-moving firms attempt to resolve the uncertainty they face by making decisions early and then trying to influence the evolution of an emerging industry, they use flexibility to resolve this uncertainty by delaying decisions until the economically correct path is clear and then moving quickly to take advantage of that path.

Opportunities in Mature Industries: Product Refinement, Service, and Process Innovation

Emerging industries are often formed by the creation of new products or technologies that radically alter the rules of the game in an industry. However, over time, as these new ways of doing business become widely understood, as technologies diffuse through competitors, and as the rate of innovation in new products and technologies drops, an industry begins to enter the mature phase of its development. As described in the Strategy in the Emerging Enterprise feature, this change in the nature of a firm's industry can be difficult to recognize and can create both strategic and operational problems for a firm.

Common characteristics of **mature industries** include: (1) slowing growth in total industry demand, (2) the development of experienced repeat customers, (3) a slowdown in increases in production capacity, (4) a slowdown in the introduction of new products or services, (5) an increase in the amount of international competition, and (6) an overall reduction in the profitability of firms in the industry.[42]

The fast-food industry in the United States has become mature over the last 10 to 15 years. In the 1960s, there were only three large national fast-food chains in the United States: McDonald's, Burger King, and Dairy Queen. Through the 1980s, all three of these chains grew rapidly, although the rate of growth at McDonald's outstripped the growth rate of the other two firms. During this time period, however, other fast-food chains also entered the market. These included some national chains, such as Kentucky Fried Chicken, Wendy's, and Taco Bell, and some strong regional chains such as Jack in the Box and In and Out Burger. By the early 1990s, growth in this industry had slowed considerably. McDonald's announced that it was having difficulty finding locations for new McDonald's that did not impinge on the sales of already existing McDonald's. Except for non-U.S. operations, where competition in the fast-food industry is not as mature, the profitability of most U.S. fast-food companies did not grow as much in the 1990s as it did in the 1960s through the 1980s. Indeed, by 2002, all the major fast-food chains were either not making very much money, or like McDonald's, actually losing money.[43]

Opportunities for firms in mature industries typically shift from the development of new technologies and products in an emerging industry to a greater emphasis on refining a firm's current products, an emphasis on increasing the quality of service, and a focus on reducing manufacturing costs and increased quality through process innovations.

Refining Current Products

In mature industries such as home detergents, motor oil, and kitchen appliances, there are likely to be few, if any, major technological breakthroughs. However, this does not mean that there is not innovation in these industries. Innovation in these industries focuses on extending and improving current products and technologies. In home detergents, innovation recently has focused on changes in packaging and on selling more highly concentrated detergents. In motor oil, recent packaging changes (from fiber foil cans to plastic containers), additives that keep oil cleaner longer, and oil formulated to operate in four-cylinder engines are recent examples of this kind of innovation. In kitchen appliances, the availability of refrigerators with crushed ice and water through the door, commercial-grade stoves for home use, and dishwashers that automatically adjust the cleaning cycle depending on how dirty the dishes are, are recent improvements.[44]

Strategy in the Emerging Enterprise

*I*t began with a 5,000-word e-mail sent by Steve Balmer, CEO at Microsoft, to all 57,000 employees. Where previous e-mails from Microsoft founder Bill Gates—including one in 1995 calling on the firm to learn how to "ride the wave of the Internet"—inspired the firm to move on to conquer more technological challenges, Balmer's e-mail focused on Microsoft's current state and called on the firm to become more focused and efficient. Balmer also announced that Microsoft would cut its costs by $1 billion during the next fiscal year. One observer described it as the kind of e-mail you would expect to read at Procter & Gamble, not at Microsoft.

And then the other shoe dropped. In a surprise move, Balmer announced that Microsoft would distribute a large portion of its $56 billion cash reserve in the form of a special dividend to stockholders. In what is believed to be the largest such cash dispersion ever, Microsoft will distribute $32 billion to its stockholders, and use an additional $30 billion to buy back stock. Bill Gates, alone, will receive a $3.2 billion cash dividend. These changes would mean that Microsoft's capital structure would be more similar to, say, Procter & Gamble than to an entrepreneurial, high-flying software company.

What is happening at Microsoft? Is it the case that management at Microsoft has concluded that the PC software industry is no longer emerging, but has matured to the point that Microsoft will actually have to alter some of its traditional strategies? Most observers believe

Microsoft Grows Up

that Balmer's e-mail, and the decision to reduce its cash reserves, signal that, in fact, Microsoft has come to this conclusion. In fact, while most of Microsoft's core businesses—its Windows operating systems, its PC applications software, and its server software—are still growing at the rate of about $3 billion a year, if they were growing at historical rates, these businesses would be generating $7 billion in new revenues each year. Moreover, Microsoft's new businesses—video games, Internet services, business software, and software for phones and handheld computers—are adding less than $1 billion in new revenues each year. That is, growth in Microsoft's new businesses is not offsetting slower growth in its traditional businesses.

Other indicators of the growing maturity of the PC software industry, and Microsoft's strategic changes, also

exist. For example, during 2003 and 2004, Microsoft resolved most of the outstanding antitrust litigation it was facing, abandoned its employee stock option plan in favor of a stock-based compensation scheme popular with slower-growth firms, improved its systems for receiving and acting on feedback from customers, and improved the quality of its relationships with some of its major rivals, including Sun Microsystems, Inc. These are all the actions of a firm that recognizes that the rapid growth opportunities that existed in the software industry when Microsoft was a new company do not exist any more.

What Microsoft has to do now is to get its entire organization—all its employees, suppliers, and even its customers—used to the idea that high growth has been abandoned as a goal and replaced by maximizing returns for Microsoft's shareholders. Whether Microsoft will be able to retain all of its high-flying technical and managerial talent in this new world is yet to be seen. Microsoft may also have to get used to not being able to easily attract all the best technical and managerial talent it wants. But, if the PC software industry has really evolved from being an emerging to a mature industry, these are the kinds of strategic changes that a firm like Microsoft will have to make if it wants to retain its place in the industry.

Sources: J. Greene (2004). "Microsoft's midlife crisis." *BusinessWeek*, April 19, 2004, pp. 88 +; R. Guth and S. Thurm (2004). "Microsoft to dole out its cash hoard." *Wall Street Journal*, Wednesday, July 21, 2004, pp. A1 +, S. Hamm (2004). "Microsoft's worst enemy: Success." *BusinessWeek*, July 19, 2004, p. 33.

Emphasis on Service

When firms in an industry have only limited ability to invest in radical new technologies and products, efforts to differentiate products often turn toward the quality of customer service. A firm that is able to develop a reputation for high-quality customer service may be able to obtain superior performance even though the products it sells are not highly differentiated.

This emphasis on service has become very important in a wide variety of industries. For example, in the convenience food industry, one of the major reasons for slower growth in the fast-food segment has been a growth in the so-called "casual dining" segment. This segment includes restaurants such as Chili's and Applebee's. The food sold at fast-food restaurants and casual dining restaurants overlaps—they both sell burgers, soft drinks, salads, chicken, desserts, and so forth—although many consumers believe that the quality of food is superior in the casual dining restaurants. In an addition to any perceived differences in the food, however, the level of service in the two kinds of establishments varies significantly. At fast-food restaurants, food is handed to consumers on a tray; in casual dining restaurants, waiters and waitresses actually bring food to consumers on a plate. This level of service is one reason that casual dining is growing in popularity.[45]

Process Innovation

A firm's **processes** are the activities it engages in to design, produce, and sell its products or services. **Process innovation**, then, is a firms effort to refine and improve its current processes. Several authors have studied the relationship between process innovation, product innovation, and the maturity of an industry.[46] This work, summarized in Figure 2.5, suggests that in the early stages of industry development, product innovation is very important. However, over time, product innovation becomes less important, and process innovations designed to reduce manufacturing costs, increase product quality, and streamline management become more important. In mature industries, firms can often gain an advantage by manufacturing the same product as competitors, but at a lower cost. Alternatively, firms can manufacture a product that is perceived to be of higher quality and do so at a competitive cost. Process innovations facilitate both the reduction of costs and the increase in quality.

The role of process innovation in more mature industries is perhaps best exemplified by the improvement in quality in U.S. automobiles. In the 1980s, Japanese firms like Nissan, Toyota, and Honda sold cars that were of significantly higher quality than U.S. firms General Motors, Ford, and Chrysler. In the face of that competitive disadvantage, these U.S. firms engaged in numerous process reforms to improve the quality of their cars. In the 1980s, U.S. manufacturers were being cited for car body panels that did not fit well, bumpers that were hung crookedly on cars, and for putting the wrong engine in a car. Now, the differences

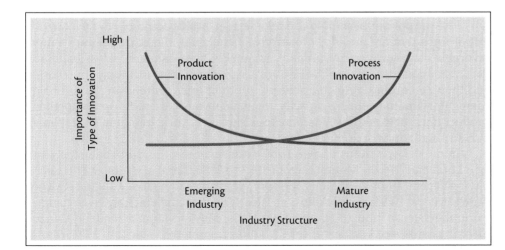

Figure 2.5 Process and Product Innovation and Industry Structure

Source: Taken from Hayes and Wheelwright, "The dynamics of process-product life cycles." *Harvard Business Review*, March-April, pp. 127–136.

in quality between newly manufactured U.S. and Japanese automobiles are very small. Indeed, one well-known judge of initial manufacturing quality—J. D. Powers—now focuses on items like the quality of a car's cup holders and the maximum distance at which a car's keyless entry system still works to establish quality rankings. The really significant quality issues of the 1980s are virtually gone. [47]

Opportunities in Declining Industries: Leadership, Niche, Harvest, and Divestment

A **declining industry** is an industry that has experienced an absolute decline in unit sales over a sustained period of time.[48] One of the most obvious examples of a declining industry is the U.S. defense business. During the Cold War, the U.S. defense industry constituted a significant portion of the country's Gross Domestic Product (GDP). Since the end of the Cold War in 1987, this industry has experienced a significant decline in sales. Between 1987 and 1995, total employment in the U.S. defense business dropped by 800,000, and this does not include 400,000 fewer people serving in the military. While the Gulf War and the Iraq War slowed this rate of decline for a time, the U.S. defense business continues to be a declining industry.

Obviously, firms in a declining industry face more threats than opportunities. Rivalry in a declining industry is likely to be very high, as is the threat of buyers, suppliers, and substitutes. However, even though threats are significant, there are opportunities that firms must recognize and, where appropriate, exploit. The major strategic options that firms in this kind of industry face are leadership, niche, harvest, and divestment.

Market Leadership

An industry in decline is often characterized by overcapacity in manufacturing, distribution, and so forth. Reduced demand often means that firms in this kind of industry will have to endure a significant shakeout period. A **shakeout period** exists when total supply in an industry is reduced by bankruptcies, acquisitions, and business closings. After a shakeout has occurred, a smaller number of lean and focused firms may enjoy a relatively benign environment with few threats and several opportunities. If a firm has decided to wait out the shakeout in hopes of better environmental conditions in the future, it should consider becoming a **market leader** in the pre–shakeout industry, most typically by becoming the firm with the largest market share in that industry.

The purpose of becoming a market leader in this setting is to facilitate the exit of firms that are not likely to survive a shakeout, thereby obtaining a more favorable competitive environment as quickly as possible. Market leaders in declining industries can facilitate exit in a variety of ways, including: purchasing and then de-emphasizing competitors' product lines, purchasing and retiring competitors' manufacturing capacity, manufacturing spare parts for competitors' product lines, and sending unambiguous signals of their intention to stay in an industry and remain a dominant firm.

In the defense industry, two firms seem to exemplify this leadership strategy: Loral and Martin Marietta. From 1987 to 1996, Loral spent over $1.8 billion buying several high-technology military electronics businesses, including Ford Aerospace and LTV's missile division. Clearly, management at Loral was committed to the defense industry. In the early 1990s, Martin Marietta acquired General Electric's aerospace businesses for $1 billion in preferred stock. In 1994, Martin

Marietta consolidated its position even more substantially with its $10 billion merger with Lockheed, and adopted a new name—Lockheed Martin. As is the case at Loral, top management at Lockheed Martin was convinced that the defense business would remain viable—after an industry shakeout—and wanted to be well positioned to exploit any possible opportunities there. Indeed, given the commitment of both Loral and Lockheed Martin to being market leaders in the declining defense industry, it was not too surprising when Lockheed Martin purchased most of Loral's assets for over $10 billion in 1996. This new firm had combined 2004 sales of over $32 billion.[49]

Market Niche

A firm following a leadership strategy in a declining industry attempts to facilitate exit by other firms, but a firm following a **niche strategy** in a declining industry reduces its scope of operations and focuses on narrow segments of the declining industry. If only a few firms choose this niche, then these firms may have a favorable competitive setting, even though the industry as a whole is facing shrinking demand.

In the defense industry, several smaller firms seem to be implementing niche strategies. Applied Signal Technology, a supplier of microwave and radio frequency components to Raytheon and Lockheed Martin, grew from $40 million in sales in 1990 to $117 million in 1997 by acquiring unwanted businesses and divisions from other firms. However, in most of these acquisitions, Applied Signal Technology remained focused on its relatively narrow market segment—microwave and radio frequency components. In 2003, Applied Signal Technology had sales of over $95 million and profits of $8.6 million. It seems likely that Applied Signal Technology will be a major player in this narrow segment of the defense industry.[50]

Harvest

Leadership and niche strategies, though differing along several dimensions, have one attribute in common: Firms that implement these strategies intend to remain in the industry despite its decline. Firms pursuing a **harvest** strategy in a declining industry do not expect to remain in the industry over the long term. Instead, they engage in a long, systematic, phased withdrawal, extracting as much value as possible during the withdrawal period. Firms can implement a harvest strategy by reducing the range of products they sell, reducing their distribution network, eliminating less profitable customers, reducing product quality, reducing service quality, deferring maintenance and equipment repair, and so forth. In the end, after a period of harvesting in a declining industry, firms can either sell their operations in an industry (to a market leader) or simply cease operations.

In the defense industry, GM's Hughes Electronics has been engaging in a harvest strategy. In the late 1990s, Hughes consolidated its four separate missile plants into a single facility. This consolidation enabled Hughes to reduce its R&D expenditures and manufacturing costs, although it also limited the range of missile products the company was manufacturing. GM completed the harvesting of Hughes' defense business by selling it to Raytheon Corporation for $9.5 billion in 1997.[51]

Divestment

The final opportunity facing firms in a declining industry is divestment. Like a harvest strategy, the objective of **divestment** is to extract a firm from a declining industry. However, unlike harvest, divestment occurs quickly, often soon after a pattern of decline is established. Firms without established competitive advantages may find divestment a superior option to harvest, because they have few competitive advantages they can exploit through harvesting.

In the defense business, divestment is the stated strategy of General Dynamics, at least in some of its business segments. General Dynamics' managers recognized early that the shrinking defense industry could not support all the incumbent firms. When General Dynamics concluded that it could not remain a leader in some of its businesses, it decided to divest those, to concentrate on a few remaining businesses. Since 1991, General Dynamics has sold businesses worth over $2.83 billion, including its missile systems business, its Cessna aircraft division, and its tactical aircraft division (maker of the very successful F–16 aircraft and partner in the development of the next generation of fighter aircraft, the F–22). These divestitures have left General Dynamics in just three businesses: armored tanks, nuclear submarines, and space launch vehicles. During this time, General Dynamics has returned almost $4.5 billion to its investors, has seen its stock go as high as $110 per share, and provided a total return to stockholders that at one time totaled 555 percent.[52]

Threat and Opportunity Analysis in an International Context

Obviously, the analysis of threats and opportunities in a firm's environment is not complete until the international dimensions of that environment are considered. Both threat analysis—using the five forces framework and the concept of complementors—and opportunity analysis—focusing on international opportunities—can be applied in this international context. Each of these international extensions will be considered in turn.

Analysis of Environmental Threats in an International Context

All of the threats identified in the five forces framework apply to the analysis of international competitive threats. It is certainly the case that a firm's rivals, new entrants, substitutes, suppliers, and buyers can all be international firms. Indeed, there is nothing in the five forces framework that cannot be applied in understanding international firms as a source of competitive threat.

However, of the five forces identified by Porter, it is usually the case that one of these—the threat of entry—is particularly salient in the analysis of international threats. This is because important barriers to entry still exist in international business. These barriers to entry typically fall into one of three categories: tariffs, quotas, or nontariff trade barriers.

Tariffs as a Barrier to Entry

Tariffs are taxes levied on goods or services imported into a country. Tariffs have the effect of increasing the price of an imported good or service, sometimes well above the price of the same good or service produced by a domestic firm. There are three types of tariffs: **ad valorem tariffs** (where the tariff is calculated as a percentage of the market value of an import, regardless of its weight or volume), **specific tariffs** (where the tariff is calculated as a percentage of the weight or volume of the goods being imported, regardless of its market value), and **compound tariffs** (where both the market value and the weight or volume are used in calculating a tariff).

Calculating the tariffs on specific imported items can be quite complex since different products can have different tariffs, and determining which product category a particular import falls into can be very ambiguous. For example, leather ski gloves imported into the United States are subject to a 5.5 percent ad valorem tariff. But if those ski gloves are designed for cross country skiing, they are subject to only a 3.5 percent ad valorem tariff. In one case, a firm was looking to import "Reindeer Caps" from China. These were hats to be worn primarily at Christmas parties, with fabric reindeer antlers that would play various Christmas carols and shout "Merry Christmas." For tariff purposes, were these caps toys, a hat, or a festive article? These three product categories actually carry different tariffs in the United States.[53]

Quotas as a Barrier to Entry

Quotas are a numerical limit on the number of particular items that are allowed to be imported into a country. Quotas have been used in many countries to protect politically powerful domestic industries, including textiles, automobiles, and agriculture. And while quotas do not raise the price of imported goods directly, they have the effect of reducing the supply of these goods in a particular country. This reduced supply, in turn, typically raises the price of those products or services that are sold within a country.

Nontariff Trade Barriers

Besides quotas, countries can use a variety of other nontariff mechanisms to increase the cost of entry into a geographic market. The other **nontariff trade barriers** include establishing product performance standards that cannot be met by imports, restricting access to domestic distribution channels, imposing local purchasing requirements for government purchases, and a variety of environmental and labor regulations that foreign firms must meet if they are to do business in a country. Often, domestic firms do not have to meet the same standards as firms looking to import into a country. When this is the case, these other nontariffs activities clearly act as a barrier to entry.

For example, entry into Japanese markets has historically been very difficult because of other nontariff trade barriers.[54] In the early 1990s, International Game Technology (IGT), a leading U.S. manufacturer of slot machines, sought entry into the large Japanese gambling market (Japan has over two-thirds of the world's slot machines, approximately 800,000 in total). IGT's entry was deterred, however, because its slot machines did not meet government slot machine standards. Unfortunately, knowledge about what these standards were was available only to members of the Japanese industry's trade association, and to become a member of this trade association, a firm needed to have been manufacturing slot machines in Japan for at least three years. It took several years for IGT to overcome this "Catch-22" barrier to entry.[55]

Similar barriers exist to entry into the Japanese beer industry. Four firms—Kirin, Asahi, Sapporo, and Suntory—dominate this industry with over 78 percent of the Japanese beer market. In order for foreign firms to begin producing beer in Japan, they must obtain a license from the ministry of finance (MOF). However, to obtain such a license, a firm must already be producing 2 million liters of beer in Japan. This barrier to entry has effectively limited non-Japanese beers to the expensive import market in Japan.[56]

Why Do Governments Impose Tariff and Nontariff Barriers to Entry?

Given that the effect of tariff and nontariff barriers to entry is almost always to raise the price of goods or services in a country, an important question becomes: Why would governments choose to erect such barriers? First, like any other tax, tariffs raise revenue for the government. Indeed, tariffs are often more politically palatable than other forms of taxation because they are hidden in the price of the goods or services a person buys. A tariff is not added to the base price of a product or service as is the case with a sales tax. Nor do tax pay-ers receive a bill from the government every six months as is the case with property taxes. Indeed, consumers pay for this tax and they do not even have to file an income tax return to do so.

Second, tariff and nontariff barriers have the effect of strengthening demand for products and services produced by domestic firms. This can give domestic firms time to build their capabilities before engaging in full-fledged global competition. It can also secure higher levels of employment in an indus-try. Both tariff and nontariff barriers to entry can be politically very beneficial to a government.

Analysis of Opportunities in an International Context

Not only can threat analysis be extended to an international context, but opportu-nity analysis can as well. Indeed, it is an assumption of business in the twenty-first century that competitive opportunities are becoming more international in scope. Even industries that appear likely to be national or regional in focus (Broadway plays, for example, are by definition produced only in New York City) have, over the last several years, become more international in character (many major Broadway hits are transfers from the West End in London, and regional traveling companies exhibit these plays throughout the world). International competition has some very obvious effects on the level and kinds of opportunities in an indus-try.[57] Opportunities in international industries generally fall into three large cate-gories: multinational opportunities, global opportunities, and transnational opportunities.

Multinational Opportunities
Firms pursuing **multinational opportunities** in international industries oper-ate simultaneously in several national or regional markets, but these operations are independent of each other and are free to choose how to respond to the spe-cific needs of each national or regional marketplace. Some well-known firms that have pursued multinational international opportunities include Nestlé and General Motors.   Only a small percentage of Nestlé's products are sold throughout the entire world. Rather, managers within each country where Nestlé operates have the responsibility to discern local tastes, design products to be consistent with those tastes, and to market these specially designed prod-ucts locally. In a similar way, GM encourages very little interaction between its U.S. and European operations. Cars designed for the European market and sold under GM's Opal brand name have infrequently been sold in the United States and relatively few Chevrolets and Oldsmobiles designed for the U.S. market are sold in Europe.

Pursuing multinational opportunities in international industries has at least two advantages. First, this strategy enables firms to respond rapidly to changing conditions in a country or region. If threats or opportunities appear in one part of the world but not in others, a multinational firm can quickly move to neutralize threats or exploit opportunities in those geographic regions where it is needed. For example, by operating at least partially as a multinational, McDonald's enables many of its European franchises to sell beer and wine alongside Big Macs and fries. Such sales do not represent an opportunity in McDonald's home market of the United States.

Second, although there are relatively few operational interactions between divisions and headquarters in a multinational company, impressive organizational resources can be quickly marshaled should they be required to exploit an opportunity or neutralize a threat in a particular country or region. McDonald's, for example, has been able to use all of its technological and management skills to open franchises in Moscow and other eastern European cities.[58]

Global Opportunities

Where firms pursuing multinational opportunities operate in countries or regions in an independent manner, those pursuing **global opportunities** seek to optimize production, distribution, and other business functions throughout the world in addressing all the markets in which they operate. If manufacturing costs are very low and quality is very high in plants located in Singapore, global organizations will locate manufacturing facilities there. If particular research and development skills and technology are widely available in Great Britain, global organizations will locate their R&D operations there. If capital is less costly in New York, global organizations will locate their financial functions there. In this manner, the cost and quality of each organizational function can be optimized. Examples of global organizations include IBM and Ford Motor Company. Global strategies have the obvious advantage of locating operations in geographic positions that reduce costs and maximize quality in all business functions.

However, global strategies also have some costs and risks associated with them. First, because the delivery of products or services in a global organization requires inputs from numerous operations all over the world, a global strategy puts a great deal of emphasis on coordination. Coordination can be difficult across divisions within a single country; it can be even more difficult across divisions in different countries or regions. Differences in language, culture, legal systems, and traditional business practices may complicate these coordination efforts.

Second, locating interdependent units in geographically disparate areas can create significant transportation costs. The very low cost of manufacturing automobile transmissions in Mexico may be effectively increased by the need to transport those transmissions to Japan to be installed in automobiles. This is less of a problem for a firm that ships products that are relatively light, small, and have very high profit margins.

Finally, exploiting global strategies may limit a firm's ability to respond to local needs, opportunities, and threats. Firms pursuing global opportunities in international industries are well designed to respond to global markets and less well designed to respond to a series of local markets. If the structure of the markets in which a firm operates does not significantly vary by country or region, a global approach may be a particularly attractive opportunity.

Transnational Opportunities

Recently, another opportunity has been described in international industries: to operate as a transnational firm. Some have argued that the traditional tradeoff between global integration and local responsiveness can be replaced by this transnational approach that exploits the advantages of both global integration and local responsiveness. Firms exploiting a **transnational opportunity** in an international industry treat their global operations as an integrated network of distributed and interdependent resources and capabilities.[59] In this context, a firm's operations in each country are not simply independent activities attempting to respond to local market needs; they are also repositories of ideas, technologies, and management approaches that the firm might be able to use and apply in its other global operations. Put differently, operations in different countries can be thought of as "experiments" in the creation of capabilities. Some of these experiments will work and generate important new capabilities for an entire firm; others will fail to have such benefits for a firm.

When an operation in a particular country develops a capability in manufacturing a particular product, providing a particular service, or engaging in a particular activity that can be used by other countries, the country operating with this capability can achieve global economies of scale by becoming the firm's primarily supplier of this product, service, or activity. In this way, local responsiveness is retained as country managers constantly search for new capabilities that enable them to maximize profits in their particular markets, and global integration and economies of scale are realized as country operations that have developed unique capabilities become suppliers for all other country operations. Firms that pursue transnational strategies include Hewlett-Packard and Honda.

SUMMARY

The strategic management process requires that a firm engage in an analysis of threats and opportunities in its competitive environment before a strategic choice can be made. This analysis begins with understanding the general environment within which a firm operates. This general environment has six components: technological change, demographic trends, cultural trends, economic climate, legal and political conditions, and specific international events. While some of these components of the general environment can affect a firm directly, more frequently they affect a firm through their impact on its local environment.

The theoretical framework that enables the analysis of a firm's local environment and links the structure of the industry within which a firm operates, its strategic alternatives, and firm performance is called the Structure-Conduct-Performance (or S-C-P) model. In this model, structure is defined as industry structure and includes those attributes of a firm's industry that constrain a firm's strategic alternatives and performance. Conduct in this model is defined as a firm's strategies. Performance in this model refers either to the performance of a firm in an industry, or the performance of the entire economy—although the former definition of performance is more important for most strategic management purposes.

The S-C-P model can be used to develop tools for analyzing threats in a firm's competitive environment. The most influential of these tools is called the "five forces framework." These five forces are: the threat of entry, the threat of rivalry, the threat of substitutes, the threat of suppliers, and the threat of buyers. The threat of entry depends on the existence and "height" of barriers to entry. Common barriers to entry include economies of scale, product differentiation, cost advantages independent of scale, and government regulation on entry. The threat of rivalry depends on the number and competitiveness of firms in an industry. The threat of rivalry is high in an industry when there are large numbers of competing firms, competing firms are roughly the same size and have the same influence, growth in an industry is slow, there is no product differentiation, and productive capacity is added in large increments. The threat of substitutes depends on how close substitute products and services are—in performance and cost—to products and services in an industry. Where rivals all meet the same customer needs in approximately the same way, substitutes meet the same customer needs, but do so in very different ways. The threat of suppliers in an industry depends on the number and distinctiveness of the products suppliers provide to an industry. The threat of suppliers increases when a supplier's industry is dominated by a few firms, when suppliers sell unique or highly differentiated products, when suppliers are not threatened by substitutes, when suppliers threaten forward vertical integration, and when firms are not important customers for suppliers. Finally, the threat of buyers depends on the number and size of an industry's customers. The threat of buyers is greater when the number of buyers is small, products sold to buyers are undifferentiated and standard, products sold to buyers are a significant percentage of a buyer's final costs, buyers are not earning significant profits, and when buyers threaten backward vertical integration. Taken together, the level of these threats in an industry can be used to determine the expected average performance of firms in an industry.

One force in a firm's environment not included within the five forces framework is complementors. Where competitors (including rivals, new entrants, and substitutes) compete with a firm to divide profits in a market, complementors increase the total size of the market. If you are a CEO of a firm, you know another firm is a complementor when the value of your products to your customers is higher in combination with this other firm's products than when customers use your products alone. Where firms have strong incentives to reduce the entry of competitors, they can sometimes have strong incentives to increase the entry of complementors.

The S-C-P model can also be used to develop tools for analyzing strategic opportunities in an industry. This is done by identifying generic industry structures and the strategic opportunities available in these different kinds of industries. Four common industry structures are: fragmented industries, emerging industries, mature industries, and declining industries. The primary opportunity in fragmented industries is consolidation. In emerging industries, the most important opportunity is first-mover advantages from technological leadership, preemption of strategically valuable assets, or creation of customer-switching costs. In mature industries, the primary opportunities are product refinement, service, and process innovation; and in declining industries, opportunities include market leadership, niche, harvest, and divestment.

Threat and opportunity analysis can be applied in an international context as well. In this context, all the five forces may be operating. However, barriers to entry are a particularly important consideration for firms contemplating international operations. In this context, barriers to entry can take one of three forms: tariffs, quotas, and other nontariff barriers. All these barriers typically have the effect of increasing the price of goods or services in a country. Finally, in international industries, opportunities include multinational, global, and transnational strategies.

CHALLENGE QUESTIONS

1. Your former college roommate calls you and asks to borrow $10,000 so that he can open a pizza restaurant in his hometown. In justifying this request, he argues that there must be significant demand for pizza and other fast food in his hometown because there are lots of such restaurants already there and three or four new ones are opening each month. He also argues that demand for convenience food will continue to increase and he points to the large number of firms that now sell frozen dinners in grocery stores. Will you lend him the money? Why or why not?

2. According to the five forces model, one potential threat in an industry is buyers. Yet unless buyers are satisfied, they are likely to look for satisfaction elsewhere. Can the fact that buyers can be threats be reconciled with the need to satisfy buyers?

3. Government policies can have a significant impact on the average profitability of firms in an industry. Government, however, is not included as a potential threat in the five forces model. Should the model be expanded to include government (to make a "six forces" model)? If yes, why? If no, why not?

4. How would you add complementors to the five forces model? In particular, if an industry has large numbers of complementors, does that make it a more attractive industry, a less attractive industry, or does it have no impact at all on the attractiveness of an industry? Justify your answer.

5. Opportunities analysis seems to suggest that there are strategic opportunities in almost any industry—even declining industries. If that is true, is it fair to say that there is really no such thing as an unattractive industry? If yes, what implications does this have for the five forces model? If no, describe an industry that has no opportunities.

6. Is the evolution of industry structure from an emerging industry to a mature industry to a declining industry inevitable? Why or why not?

PROBLEM SET

1. Perform a five forces analysis on the following two industries:

The Pharmaceutical Industry

The pharmaceutical industry consists of firms that develop, patent, and distribute drugs. Although there are not significant production economies in this industry, there are important economies in research and development. Product differentiation exists as well, because firms often sell branded products. Firms compete in research and development. However, once a product is developed and patented, competition is significantly reduced. Recently, the increased availability of generic, nonbranded drugs has threatened the profitability of some drug lines. Once an effective drug is developed, there are usually few, if any, alternatives to that drug. Drugs are manufactured from commodity chemicals usually available from numerous suppliers. Major customers include doctors and patients. Recently, increased costs have led the federal government and insurance companies to pressure drug companies to reduce their prices.

The Textile Industry

The textile industry consists of firms that manufacture and distribute fabrics for use in clothing, furniture, carpeting, and so forth. Several firms have invested heavily in sophisticated manufacturing technology, and many lower-cost firms located in Asia have begun fabric production. Textiles are not branded products. Recently, tariffs on some imported textiles have been implemented. There are numerous firms in this industry; the largest have less than 10 percent market share. Traditional fabric materials (such as cotton and wool) have recently been threatened by the development of alternative chemical-based materials (such as nylon and rayon), although many textile companies have begun manufacturing with these new materials as well. Most raw materials are widely available, although some synthetic products may be periodically in short supply. There are numerous textile customers, but textile costs are usually a large percentage of their final product's total costs. Many users shop around the world for the low prices on textiles.

2. Perform an opportunities analysis on the following industries:

Since the tragedies of 9/11, the U.S. airline industry has seen a consistent drop-off in sales. This has forced many U.S. airline companies to cut back their employment, and several—including USAir and United—have had to declare bankruptcy.

The U.S. beer industry is dominated by three companies: Anheuser-Busch, the Miller Brewing Company, and Adolf Coors. In addition, there are several regional brewers and a large number of very small micro-brewers that manufacture and sell beer in small quantities.

There are over 3,000 property and automobile insurance companies in the United States. The largest companies, including GEICO, Progressive, Allstate, and Safeco, control less than 20 percent of the property and automobile market.

Portable memory chips—sometimes worn around the neck like a necklace—may be an important substitute for floppy discs. These memory chips come in various sizes (from 64K to 256K) and range in price from $6 to $150. They plug into a computer's UBS port, self-load, and act like another hard drive in your computer.

In 2003, the German firm DHL acquired the U.S. firm Airborne Express, to become the third largest player in the small-package delivery business—behind UPS and FedEx. Shipments overseas continue to be a growing part of this industry.

3. For each of the following firms, identify at least two competitors (either rivals, new entrants, or substitutes) and two complementors.

(a) Yahoo!
(b) Microsoft
(c) Dell
(d) Boeing
(e) McDonald's

END NOTES

1. See (2003). *The big book of business quotations*. New York: Basic Books, p. 209.
2. See Weintraub, A. (2004). "Repairing the engines of life." *BusinessWeek*, May 24, 2004, pp. 99 + for a discussion of recent developments in biotechnology research and the business challenges they have created.
3. See the opening case in Chapter 1.
4. See Grow, B. (2004). "Hispanic nation." *BusinessWeek*, March 15, 2004, pp. 59 +.
5. Barnes, B. (2004). "The WB grows up." *Wall Street Journal*, July 19, 2004, pp. B1 +.
6. These and other cultural differences are described in Rugman, A., and R. Hodgetts (1995). *International business*. New York: McGraw-Hill. A discussion of the dimensions along which country cultures can vary is presented in a later chapter.
7. See Deutschman, A. (2004). "Inside the mind of Jeff Bezos." *Fast Company*, August 2004, pp. 53 +.
8. Early contributors to the structure-conduct-performance model include Mason, E. S. (1939). "Price and production policies of large scale enterprises." *American Economic Review*, 29, pp. 61—74; and Bain, J. S. (1956). *Barriers to new competition*. Cambridge, MA: Harvard

University Press. The major developments in this framework are summarized in Bain, J. S. (1968). *Industrial organization*. New York: John Wiley & Sons, Inc.; and Scherer, F. M. (1980). *Industrial market structure and economic performance*. Boston: Houghton Mifflin. The links between this framework and work in strategic management are discussed in Porter, M. E. (1981a). "The contribution of industrial organization to strategic management." *Academy of Management Review*, 6, pp. 609–620; and Barney, J. B. (1986c). "Types of competition and the theory of strategy: Toward an integrative framework." *Academy of Management Review*, 1, pp. 791–800.
9. The five forces framework is described in detail in Porter, M. E. (1979). "How competitive forces shape strategy." *Harvard Business Review*, March/April, pp. 137–156; and Porter, M. E. (1980). *Competitive Strategy*. New York: Free Press.
10. These barriers were originally proposed by Bain, J. S. (1968). *Industrial organization*. New York: John Wiley & Sons, Inc.; and Porter, M. E. (1980). *Competitive strategy*. New York: Free Press.. It is actually possible to estimate the "height" of barriers to entry in an industry by comparing the cost of entry into an industry with barriers and the cost of entry into that industry if barriers did not

exist. The difference between these costs is the "height" of the barriers to entry.

11. Another alternative would be for a firm to own and operate more than one plant. If there are economies of scope in this industry, a firm might be able to enter and earn above normal profits. An economy of scope exists when the value of operating in two businesses simultaneously is greater than the value of operating in these two businesses separately. The concept of economy of scope is explored in more detail in Part Three of this book.

12. See Ghemawat, P., and H. J. Stander III (1992). "Nucor at a crossroads." Harvard Business School Case no. 9-793039.

13. See Montgomery, C. A., and B. Wernerfelt (1991). "Sources of superior performance: Market share versus industry effects in the U.S. brewing industry." *Management Science*, 37, pp. 954–959.

14. Stecklow, S. (1999). "Gallo woos French, but don't expect Bordeaux by the jug." *Wall Street Journal*, Friday, March 26, pp. A1 +.

15. See *www.bustpatents.com/awards.html*.

16. See Kogut, B., and U. Zander (1992). "Knowledge of the firm, combinative capabilities, and the replication of technology." *Organization Science*, 3, pp. 383–397; and Dierickx, I., and K. Cool (1989). "Asset stock accumulation and sustainability of competitive advantage." *Management Science*, 35, pp. 1504–1511. Both emphasize the importance of know-how as a barrier to entry into an industry. More generally, intangible resources are seen as particularly important sources of sustained competitive advantage. This will be discussed in more detail in Chapter 5.

17. See Polanyi, M. (1962). *Personal knowledge: Towards a post critical philosophy*. London: Routledge & Kegan Paul; and Itami, H. (1987). *Mobilizing invisible assets*. Cambridge, MA: Harvard University Press.

18. See Henderson, R., and I. Cockburn (1994). "Measuring competence: Exploring firm effects in pharmaceutical research." *Strategic Management Journal*, 15, pp. 361–374.

19. See Scherer, F. M. (1980). *Industrial market structure and economic performance*. Boston: Houghton Mifflin.

20. See Saporito, B. (1992). "Why the price wars never end." *Fortune*, March 23, pp. 68–78; and Allen, M., and M. Siconolfi (1993). "Dell Computer drops planned share offering." *Wall Street Journal*, February 25, p. A3.

21. Chartier, John (2002). "Burger battles." CNN/Money, *http://money.cnn.com*, December 11.

22. See Ghemawat, P., and A. McGahan (1995). "The U.S. airline industry in 1995." Harvard Business School Case No. 9-795-113.

23. Labich, K. (1992). "Airbus takes off." *Fortune*, June 1, pp. 102–108.

24. See Pollock, E. J. (1993). "Mediation firms alter the legal landscape." *Wall Street Journal*, March 22, p. B1; Cox, M. (1993). "Electronic campus: Technology threatens to shatter the world of college textbooks." *Wall Street Journal*, June 1, p. A1; Reilly, P. M. (1993). "At a crossroads: The instant-new age leaves *Time* magazine searching for a mission." *Wall Street Journal*, May 12, p. A1; Rohwedder, C. (1993). "Europe's smaller food shops face finis." *Wall Street Journal*, May 12, p. B1; Fatsis, S. (1995). "Major leagues keep minors at a distance." *Wall Street Journal*, November 8, pp. B1 +; Norton, E., and G. Stern (1995). "Steel and aluminum vie over every ounce in a car's construction." *Wall Street Journal*, May 9, pp. A1 + Paré, T. P. (1995). "Why the banks lined up against Gates.' *Fortune*, May 29, p. 18; "Hitting the mail on the head." *The Economist*, April 30, 1994, pp. 69–70; Pacelle, M. (1996). "'Big Boxes' by discounters are booming." *Wall Street Journal*, January 17, p. A2; and Pope, K., and L. Cauley (1998). "In Battle for TV ads, cable is now the enemy." *Wall Street Journal*, May 6, pp. B1 +.

25. Tully, S. (1992). "How to cut those #$%* legal costs." *Fortune*, September 21, pp. 119–124.

26. Jensen, E. (1993). "Tales are oft told as TV talk shows fill up airtime." *Wall Street Journal*, May 25, p. A1; (1995). Jensen, E. "King World ponders life without Oprah." *Wall Street Journal*, September 26, p. B1.

27. See DeWitt, W. (1997). "Crown Cork & Seal/Carnaud Metalbox." Harvard Business School Case No. 9-296-019.

28. Perry, N. J. (1993). "What's next for the defense industry." *Fortune*, February 22, pp. 94–100.

29. See "Crown Cork and Seal in 1989." Harvard Business School Case No. 5-395-224.

30. See Brandenburger, A., and B. Nalebuff (1996). *Co-opetition*. New York: Doubleday.

31. This approach to studying opportunities was also first suggested in Porter, M. E. (1980). *Competitive strategy*. New York: Free Press.

32. Jacob, R. (1992). "Service Corp. International: Acquisitions done the right way." *Fortune*, November 16, p. 96.

33. Porter, M. E. (1980). *Competitive strategy*. New York: Free Press.

34. For the definitive discussion of first-mover advantages, see Lieberman, M., and C. Montgomery (1988). "First-mover advantages." *Strategic Management Journal*, 9, pp. 41—58.

35. See Ghemawat, P. (1991). *Commitment*. New York: Free Press.

36. See Gilbert, R. J., and D. M. Newbery (1982). "Preemptive patenting and the persistence of monopoly." *American Economic Review*, 72(3), pp. 514–526.

37. See Bresnahan, T. F. (1985). "Post-entry competition in the plain paper copier market." *American Economic Review*, 85, pp. 15–19, for a discussion of Xerox's patents; and Bright, A. A. (1949). *The electric lamp industry*. New York: Macmillan, for a discussion of General Electric's patents.

38. See Mansfield, E., M. Schwartz, and S. Wagner (1981). "Imitation costs and patents: An empirical study." *Economic Journal*, 91, pp. 907–918.

39. See Main, O. W. (1955). *The Canadian nickel industry*. Toronto: University of Toronto Press, for a discussion of asset preemption in the oil and gas industry; Ghemawat, P. (1986). "Wal-Mart store's discount operations." Harvard Business School Case No. 9-387-018, for Wal-Mart's preemption strategy; Schmalansee, R. (1978). "Entry deterrence in the ready-to-eat breakfast cereal industry." *Bell Journal of Economics*, 9(2), pp. 305—327; and Robinson, W. T., and C. Fornell (1985). "Sources of market pioneer advantages in consumer goods industries." *Journal of Marketing Research*, 22(3), pp. 305–307, for a discussion of preemption in the breakfast cereal industry. In this latter case, the preempted valuable asset is shelf space in grocery stores.

40. Klemperer, P. (1986). "Markets with consumer switching costs." Doctoral thesis, Graduate School of Business, Stanford University; and Wernerfelt, B. (1986). "A special case of dynamic pricing policy." *Management Science*, 32, pp. 1562–1566.

41. See Gross, N. (1995). "The technology paradox." *BusinessWeek*, March 6, pp. 691–719; Bond, R. S., and D. F. Lean (1977). *Sales, promotion, and product differentiation in two prescription drug markets*. Washington, D. C.: U.S. Federal Trade Commission; Montgomery, D. B. (1975). "New product distribution: An analysis of supermarket buyer decision." *Journal of Marketing Research*, 12, pp. 255–264; Ries, A., and J. Trout (1986). *Marketing warfare*. New York: McGraw-Hill; and Davidson, J. H. (1976). "Why most new consumer brands fail." *Harvard Business Review*, 54, March/April, pp. 117–122, for a discussion of switching costs in these industries.

42. Porter, M. W. (1980). *Competitive strategy*. New York: Free Press.

43. Gibson, R. (1991). "McDonald's insiders increase their sales of company's stock." *Wall Street Journal*, June 14, p. A1; and Chartier, John (2002). "Burger Battles." CNN/Money, *http://money.cnn.com*, December 11.

44. Descriptions of these product refinements can be found in Demetrakakes, P. (1994). "Household-chemical makers concentrate on downsizing." *Packaging*, 39(1), p. 41; Reda, S. (1995). "Motor oil: Hands-on approach." *Stores*, 77(5), pp. 48–49; and Quinn, J. (1995). "KitchenAid." *Incentive*, 169(5), pp. 46–47.

45. Chartier, John (2002). "Burger Battles." CNN/Money, *http://money.cnn.com*, December 11.

46. See Hayes, R. H., and S. G. Wheelwright (1979). "The Dynamics of process-product life cycles." *Harvard Business Review*, March/April, p. 127.

47. See *www.jdpowers.com*.

48. See Porter, M. E. (1980). *Competitive strategy*. New York: Free Press; and Harrigan, K. R. (1980). *Strategies for declining businesses*. Lexington, MA: Lexington Books.

49. The strategies at Loral and Martin Marietta are described in Perry, N. J. (1993). "What's next for the defense industry." *Fortune*, February 22, pp. 94–100; Pare, T. P. (1994). "The new merger boom." *Fortune*, November 28, pp. 95–106; Brull, S. (1999). "A new

satellite system clambers onto the launchpad." *BusinessWeek*. September 6, p. 35; and Crock, S. (2000). "Can Lockheed Martin pull out of dry dock?" *BusinessWeek*, May 1, p. 148. Lockheed Martin is currently evaluating which of its defense businesses it might want to divest.

50. Perry, N. J. (1993). "What's next for the defense industry." *Fortune*, February 22, pp. 94–100; and *www.appsi.com*.

51. Perry, N. J. (1993). "What's next for the defense industry." *Fortune*, February 22, pp. 94–100; and *www.Raytheon.com*.

52. See Smith, L. (1993). "Can defense pain be turned to gain?" *Fortune*, February 8, pp. 84–96; Perry, N. J. (1993). "What's next for the defense industry." *Fortune*, February 22, pp. 94–100; and Dial, J., and K. J. Murphy (1995). "Incentive, downsizing, and value creation at General Dynamics." *Journal of Financial Economics*, 37, pp. 261–314.

53. U.S. customs decided that this item should be treated as a hat and charge a compound tariff of 37.7 cents per kilogram plus 13.4 percent of the market value of these items. See Griffin, R., and M. Pustay (1999). *International business*. Reading, MA: Addison-Wesley, pp. 215–216.

54. See Tuller, L. W. (1991). *Going global: New opportunities for growing companies to compete in world markets*. Homewood, IL: Irwin. Given Japan's recent economic troubles, some of these difficulties in entering the Japanese markets seem to be going away.

55. Schlesinger, J. M. (1993). "Tough gamble: A slot-machine maker trying to sell in Japan hits countless barriers." *Wall Street Journal*, May 11, p. A1.

56. (1994). "Only here for the Biru." *The Economist*, May 14, pp. 69–70.

57. See Bartlett, C. A., and S. Ghoshal (1989). *Managing across borders: The transnational solution*. Boston: Harvard Business School Press; and Bartlett, C., and S. Ghoshal (1993). "Beyond the M-form: Toward a managerial theory of the firm." *Strategic Management Journal*, 14, pp. 23–46

58. Blackman, A. (1990). "Moscow's Big Mac attack." *Time*, February 5, p. 51; and Bartlett, C. A., and S. Ghoshal (1989). *Managing across borders: The transnational solution*. Boston, MA: Harvard Business School Press.

59. Bartlett, C. A., and S. Ghoshal (1989). *Managing across borders: The transnational solution*. Boston, MA: Harvard Business School Press.

Evaluating a Firm's Internal Capabilities

Electronic Arts– They're in the Game

Video games are serious business, and no one treats them more seriously than Electronic Arts (EA). With 13 production studios around the world, EA is the largest and most successful video game firm in the world. With 27 titles selling more than one million units each, EA had sales of almost $3.0 billion and profits of $577 million in 2004. Some of the best known EA video games include *The Sims* and *Harry Potter* games (each with more than 10 million units sold) and the *FIFA Soccer, James Bond, Madden NFL Football,* and

Medal of Honor games (each with more than five million units sold).

In 2002, domestic video game sales of $10 billion actually outstripped domestic box office receipts—video games are actually a larger industry than the movies! And video games aren't designed just for teenage boys anymore.

One-third of adults over the age of 18 play video games. Twenty-two percent of these people play five or more hours a week. And the development of games like *The Sims*—where players compete by building relationships rather than killing opponents—has helped increase the number of women and girls who play video games. Currently, about 46 percent of those who play video games are female. Moreover, with the introduction of games based on the *Harry Potter* novels, kids younger than 14 are now playing video games.

Learning Objectives

After reading this chapter, you should be able to:

1. Describe the critical assumptions of the resource-based view.

2. Describe four types of resources and capabilities.

3. Apply the VRIO framework to identify the competitive implications of a firm's resources and capabilities.

4. Apply value chain analysis to identify a firm's valuable resources and capabilities.

5. Describe the kinds of resources and capabilities that are likely to be costly to imitate.

6. Describe how a firm uses its structure, formal and informal control processes, and compensation policy to exploit its resources.

7. Discuss how the decision to imitate or not imitate a firm with a competitive advantage affects the competitive dynamics in an industry.

8. Discuss how firms can exploit their current resources or develop new resources through their international operations.

So, how does EA stay at the forefront of this intensely competitive and dynamic industry? Some observers suggest that EA is able to combine the creativity usually associated with Hollywood movies, the technological sophistication usually associated with Silicon Valley firms, and a business discipline usually associated with the best manufacturing firms in the world. Combining these three sometimes very different sets of skills sets EA apart from most of its competitors. Not only does EA routinely produce the most creative games; it is also among the most technically sophisticated, and most surprising of all, they are usually delivered on time and on budget.

The goal at EA is for each major product introduction to have at least one creative innovation (e.g., Snoop Dogg provided original background music for *NBA Live 2003*) and at least one technical innovation (e.g., a new "freestyle joystick" that increases the level of control in *NBA Live 2003*), and to do all of this while bringing a product out on time. After all, 80 percent of EA's revenues are generated during holiday sales. If an EA product misses this sales window, it will have to wait a full year for another opportunity.

The stakes for EA are huge. Each of its best-selling titles takes from 12 to 36 months to develop and costs from $5 to $10 million. But a successful title can generate hundreds of millions in sales. In fact, EA's *FIFA Soccer* has generated more than $1 billion in sales since it was first introduced in 1996. Its *Harry Potter*, *The Sims*, and *James Bond* titles—to name just a few—appear to be on track for this same level of success. But will EA be able to continue to develop its video game blockbusters?

Sources: "Computer games played by one in three adults." *Research Alert*, April 20, p. 10; "EA hits record financials." *Video Business*, May 12, p. 28; C. Salter (2002). "Playing to win." *Fast Company*, December pp. 80 +.

Most firms would like to have the kind of performance that Electronic Arts (EA) enjoys in the video game industry. Such sustained competitive advantages are the objective of the strategic management process described in Chapter 1. But, what is it about EA that enables this firm to gain and sustain its competitive advantage? What are its strengths, and how does it exploit them? What are its weaknesses and how does it avoid them? The purpose of this chapter is to describe a set of tools that can be used to answer these questions.

The Resource-Based View of the Firm

In Chapter 2, we saw that it was possible to take some theoretical models developed in economics—specifically the S-C-P model—and apply them to develop tools for analyzing a firm's external threats and opportunities. The same is true for analyzing a firm's internal strengths and weaknesses. However, where the tools described in Chapter 2 were based on the S-C-P model, the tools described in this chapter are based on the **Resource-Based View** of the Firm, or the **RBV**. The RBV is a model of firm performance that focuses on the resources and capabilities controlled by a firm as sources of competitive advantage.[1]

What Are Resources and Capabilities?

Resources in the RBV are defined as the tangible and intangible assets that a firm controls, which it can use to conceive of and implement its strategies. Examples of resources might include a firm's factories (a tangible asset), its products (a tangible asset), its reputation among customers (an intangible asset), and teamwork among its managers (an intangible asset). EA's tangible assets include its studios and its products. EA's intangible assets include the cooperation among its creative, technical, and business functions.

Capabilities are a subset of a firm's resources and are defined as tangible and intangible assets that enable a firm to take full advantage of other resources it controls. That is, capabilities alone do not enable a firm to conceive of and implement its strategies, but they enable a firm to use other resources to conceive of and implement such strategies. Examples of capabilities might include a firm's marketing skills and teamwork and cooperation among its managers. At EA, the cooperation among the creative, technical, and business functions is an example of a capability.

A firm's resources and capabilities can be classified into four broad categories: financial resources, physical resources, individual resources, and organizational resources. **Financial resources** include all the money, from whatever source, that firms use to conceive of and implement strategies. These financial resources include cash from entrepreneurs, from equity holders, from bondholders, and from banks. **Retained earnings**, or the profit that a firm made earlier in its history and invests in itself, are also an important type of financial resource.

Physical resources include all the physical technology used in a firm. This includes a firm's plant and equipment, its geographic location, and its access to raw materials. Specific examples of plant and equipment that are part of a firm's physical resources are a firm's computer hardware and software technology, robots used in manufacturing, and automated warehouses. Geographic location, as a type of physical resource, is important for firms as diverse as Wal-Mart (with its operations in rural markets generating, on average, higher returns than its operations in more competitive urban markets) and L. L. Bean (a catalogue retail firm that believes that its rural Maine location helps its employees identify with the outdoor lifestyle of many of its customers).[2]

Human resources include the training, experience, judgment, intelligence, relationships, and insight of *individual* managers and workers in a firm.[3] The importance of the human resources of well-known entrepreneurs such as Bill Gates (Microsoft) and Steve Jobs (currently at Apple) is broadly understood. However, valuable human resources are not limited to just entrepreneurs or senior managers. Each employee at a firm like Southwest Airlines is seen as essential for the overall success of the firm. Whether it is the willingness of the gate agent to joke with the harried traveler, or a baggage handler hustling to get a passenger's bag into a plane, or even a pilot's decision to fly in a way that saves fuel—all of these human resources are part of the resource base that has enabled Southwest to gain competitive advantages in the very competitive U.S. airline industry.[4]

Where human resources are an attribute of single individuals, **organizational resources** are an attribute of groups of individuals. Organizational resources include a firm's formal reporting structure; its formal and informal planning, controlling, and coordinating systems; its culture and reputation; as well as informal relations among groups within a firm and between a firm and those in its environment. At Southwest Airlines, relationships among individual resources are an important organizational resource. For example, it is not unusual to see the pilots at Southwest helping to load the bags on an airplane to ensure that the plane leaves on time. This kind of cooperation and dedication shows up in an intense loyalty between Southwest employees and the firm—a loyalty that manifests itself in low employee turnover and high employee productivity, even though over 80 percent of Southwest's employees are unionized.

Critical Assumptions of the Resource-Based View

The RBV rests on two fundamental assumptions about the resources and capabilities that firms may control. First, different firms may possess different bundles of resources and capabilities, even if they are competing in the same industry. This is the assumption of firm **resource heterogeneity**. Resource heterogeneity implies that for a given business activity, some firms may be more skilled in accomplishing this activity than other firms. In manufacturing, for example, Toyota continues to be more skilled than, say, General Motors. In product design, Apple continues to be more skilled than, say, IBM. In video games, EA continues to be more technically innovative and creative than most of its competitors.

Second, some of these resource and capability differences among firms may be long lasting. This is because it may be very costly for firms without certain resources and capabilities to develop or acquire them. This is the assumption of **resource immobility**. For example, Toyota has had its advantage in manufacturing for at least 30 years. Apple has had product design advantages over IBM since Apple was founded in the 1980s. And EA has had its skill advantages for at least 10 years. It is not that GM, IBM, and EA's competitors are unaware of their skill disadvantages. Indeed, some of these firms—notably GM and IBM—have made progress in addressing their disadvantages. However, despite these efforts, Toyota, Apple, and EA continue to enjoy skill advantages over their competition.

Taken together, these two assumptions make it possible to explain why some firms can outperform other firms, even if these firms are all competing in the same

Strategy in Depth

*T*he theoretical roots of the Resource-based View can be traced to research done by David Ricardo in 1817. Interestingly enough, Ricardo was not even studying the profitability of firms way back then; he was interested in the economic consequences of owning more or less fertile farm land.

Unlike many other inputs into the production process, the total supply of land is relatively fixed and cannot be significantly increased in response to higher demand and prices. Such inputs are said to be **inelastic in supply**, because their quantity of supply is fixed and does not respond to price increases. In these settings, it is possible for those that own higher-quality inputs to gain competitive advantages.

Ricardo's argument concerning land as a productive input is summarized in Figure 3.1. Imagine that there are many parcels of land suitable for growing wheat. Also, suppose that the fertility of these different parcels varies from high fertility (low costs of production) to low fertility (high costs of production). It seems obvious that when the market price for wheat is low, it will only pay farmers with the most fertile land to grow wheat. Only these farmers will have costs low enough to make money when the market price for wheat is low. Also,

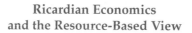

**Ricardian Economics
and the Resource-Based View**

as the market price for wheat goes up, then farmers with progressively less fertile land will be able to use it to grow wheat. These observations lead to market supply curve in panel A of the figure: As prices (*P*) go up, supply (*S*) also goes up. At some point on this supply curve, supply will equal demand (*D*). This point determines the market price for wheat, given supply and demand. This price is called *P** in the figure.

Now consider the situation facing two different kinds of farmers. Ricardo assumed that both these farmers follow

traditional economic logic by producing a quantity (*q*) such that their marginal cost (*MC*) equals their marginal revenue, that is, they produce enough wheat so that the cost of producing the last bushel of wheat equals the revenue they will get from selling that last bushel. However, this decision for the farm with less fertile land (in panel B of the figure) revenues that exactly equal the average total cost (*ATC*) of the only capital this farmer is assumed to employ cost of his land. On the other hand, the farmer with more fertile land (in panel C of the figure) has average total costs (*ATC*) less than the market-determined price and thus is able to earn an above-normal economic profit. This is because at the market determined price, *P**, *MC = ATC* for the farmer with less fertile land, while *MC > ATC* for the farmer with more fetile land.

In traditional economic analysis, the profit earned by the farmer with more fertile land should lead other farmers to enter into this market, to obtain some land and begin producing wheat. However, all the land that can be used to produce wheat in a way that generates at least a normal return given the market price *P** is already in production. In particular, there is no more very fertile land left, and fertile land (by

industry. If a firm possesses valuable resources and capabilities that few other firms possess, and if these other firms find it too costly to imitate these resources and capabilities, the firm that possesses these tangible and intangible assets can gain a sustained competitive advantage. The economic logic that underlies the Resource-Based View is described in more detail in the Strategy in Depth feature.

The VRIO Framework

Armed with the Resource-Based View, it is possible to develop a set of tools for analyzing all the different resources and capabilities a firm might possess and the potential of each of these to generate competitive advantages. In this way, it will

A. Market supply and demand, market quantity (Q^*) and market-determined price (P^*)

B. Performance of firm with less fertile land (higher average total cost – ATC)

C. Performance of firm with more fertile land (lower average total cost – ATC)

MC = marginal costs, ATC = average total costs, Q = aggregate quantity produced in the industry, q = quantity produced by each firm in the industry

Figure 3.1   The Economics of Land with Different Levels of Fertility

assumption) cannot be created. This is what is meant by land being inelastic in supply. Thus, the firm with more fertile land and lower production costs has a sustained competitive advantage over firms with less fertile land and higher production costs and is able to earn an above-normal economic profit.

Of course, at least two events can threaten this sustained competitive advantage. First, market demand may shift down and to the left. This would force farms with less fertile land to cease production and would also reduce the profit of the farms with more fertile land. If demand shifted far enough, this profit might disappear altogether.

Second, farms with less fertile land may discover low-cost ways of increasing their land's fertility, thereby reducing the competitive advantage of the farm with more fertile land. For example, farms with less fertile land may be able to use inexpensive fertilizers to increase their land's fertility. The existence of such low-cost fertilizers suggests that while *land* may be in fixed supply, *fertility* may not be. If enough farms can increase the fertility of their land, then the profits originally earned by the farm with the more fertile land will disappear.

Of course, what the Resource-Based View does is recognize that land is not the only productive input that is inelastic in supply and that farmers are not the only firms that benefit from having such resources at their disposal.

Source: D. Ricardo (1817). *Principles of political economy and taxation.* London: J. Murray.

be possible to identify both a firm's internal strengths and its internal weaknesses. The primary tool for accomplishing this internal analysis is called the VRIO framework.[5] An acronym, the **VRIO framework** stands for four questions you must ask about a resource or capability to determine its competitive potential: the question of **V**alue, the question of **R**arity, the question of **I**mitability, and the question of **O**rganization. These four questions are summarized in Table 3.1.

The Question of Value

The **Question of Value** is: "Do resources and capabilities enable a firm to exploit an external opportunity or neutralize an external threat?" If a firm answers this

Table 3.1   **Questions Needed to Conduct a Resource-Based Analysis of a Firm's Internal Strengths and Weaknesses**

1. *The Question of Value:* Does a resource enable a firm to exploit an environmental opportunity and/or neutralize an environmental threat?
2. *The Question of Rarity:* Is a resource currently controlled by only a small number of competing firms?
3. *The Question of Imitability:* Do firms without a resource face a cost disadvantage in obtaining or developing it?
4. *The Question of Organization:* Are a firm's other policies and procedures organized to support the exploitation of its valuable, rare, and costly-to-imitate resources?

question "yes," then its resources and capabilities are valuable, and can be considered as firm *strengths*. If a firm answers this question "no," its resources and capabilities are *weaknesses*. There is nothing inherently valuable about a firm's resources and capabilities. Rather, they are only valuable to the extent that they enable a firm to enhance its competitive position. Sometimes, the same resources and capabilities can be strengths in one market and weaknesses in another. The Global Perspectives feature discusses this issue in more detail.

Valuable Resources and Firm Performance

Sometimes it is difficult to know for sure whether a firm's resources and capabilities really enable it to exploit its external opportunities or neutralize its external threats. Sometimes this requires detailed operational information that may not be readily available. Other times, the full impact of a firm's resources and capabilities on its external opportunities and threats may not be known for some time. Consider, for example, recent strategic decisions made by Yahoo! and described in the Strategy in the Emerging Enterprise feature on page 82.

One way to track the impact of a firm's resources and capabilities on its opportunities and threats is to examine the impact of using these resources and capabilities on a firm's revenues and costs. In general, firms that use their resources and capabilities to exploit opportunities or neutralize threats will see an increase in their net revenues, or a decrease in their net costs, or both, compared to the situation where they were not using these resources and capabilities to exploit opportunities or neutralize threats. That is, the value of these resources and capabilities will generally manifest itself in either higher revenues or lower costs or both, once a firm starts using them to exploit opportunities or neutralize threats.

Applying the Question of Value

The answer to the question of value, for many firms, has been "yes." That is, many firms have resources and capabilities that are used to exploit opportunities and neutralize threats, and the use of these resources and capabilities enables these firms to increase their net revenues or decrease their net costs. For example, Sony has a great deal of experience in designing, manufacturing, and selling miniaturized electronic technology. Sony has used these resources and capabilities to exploit opportunities, including video games, digital cameras,

Global Perspectives

Despite the best efforts of American college students, the consumption of beer in the United States is no longer growing. In an effort to expand their sales, both Anheuser-Busch and Miller Brewing are trying to enter the European market. Unfortunately, many Europeans don't like American beer. They consider it to be "watered-down" and "tasteless." None of this was helped when these two powerhouse U.S. firms first introduced their "light" beers to Europe. Unfortunately, "light beer" in Europe means "low alcohol content beer," and sales of Bud Light and Miller Light never met expectations. Indeed, Miller changed the name of its light beer in Europe to Miller Pilsner.

In an effort to grow their sales and overcome the perception that American beers are "lightweight," Anheuser-Busch and Miller are adopting very different strategies. Anheuser-Busch is actually playing up its American roots. It uses the same commercials in Europe as it does in the United States. The American eagle remains prominently displayed on the Budweiser can, and the Clydesdales still pull the old-fashioned beer wagon in some Budweiser ads. Anheuser-Busch is signing up European sports stars as spokespersons for Budweiser, and Bud just became the official beer of the 2006 Olympics in

Does It Pay to Be an American Beer in Europe?

Torino, Italy. Anheuser-Busch hopes that the European fascination with U.S. brands—including McDonald's Big Mac—will ultimately transfer to its products and will offset current tensions between the United States and Europe regarding the Iraq War. Currently only imported into Europe, Budweiser is priced as an expensive import beer and saw its market share in the United Kingdom—a critical beer-drinking market in Europe—go from 2.7 percent in 2000 to 2.9 percent in 2002.

Miller, on the other hand, downplays in American roots. Indeed, Miller is trying to be seen as just another European beer company with an upscale product. For example, to serve the Russian market, Miller opened a Russian brewery just 84 miles from Moscow. Also, rather than using U.S.-based ads, Miller has developed a European ad campaign that markets its beer as part of a new, hipper lifestyle that is distinctly European, not made-over American. Miller's sales in Russia increased by 70 percent from 2002 to 2003 while the overall market for upscale beers in that country increased by only 30 percent. Miller is looking to repeat that success in other European countries.

So, is being an American beer a valuable resource or not? As suggested in the text, a resource is not inherently valuable or not valuable. It depends on the specific market demand for that resource. In the United States, being an American beer can be a valuable resource, but it may turn out to be less valuable in Europe.

Sources: J. Barney (2001). "Is the resource-based 'view' a useful perspective for strategic management research? Yes." *Academy of Management Review*, 26, pp. 41–56; D. Bilefsky and C. Lawton (2004). "In Europe, marketing beer as 'American' may not be a plus." *Wall Street Journal*, July 21, pp. B1 +.

computers and peripherals, handheld computers, home video and audio, portable audio, and car audio. 3M has used its resources and capabilities in substrates, coatings, and adhesives, along with an organizational culture that rewards risk-taking and creativity, to exploit opportunities in office products, including invisible tape and Post–it notes. Sony's and 3M's resources and capabilities—including their specific technological skills and their creative organizational cultures—made it possible for these firms to respond to, and even create, new opportunities.[6]

Strategy in the Emerging Enterprise

*E*ntrepreneurial firms, like all other firms, must be able to answer the Question of Value in the affirmative. This can sometimes be very problematic for entrepreneurial firms since the products or services they are providing to consumers may be entirely new. Anticipating whether or not a certain set of resources and capabilities is valuable when you are providing an entirely new product or service to the market can be very difficult. It is not unusual for entrepreneurial firms to adjust their strategies over time as they search for ways in which they can create value with the resources and capabilities they control.

Consider, for example, Yahoo! It began life as an Internet company that repackaged commodity information into formats that were easy for consumers to access. Combining both first-mover advantages and superior technology, Yahoo! became one of the most popular sites on the Web and serviced, over the years, more than 237 million customers. It seems likely that 237 million customers is a potentially valuable resource, and since its inception, Yahoo! has tried to find a way to make money by exploiting this resource.

Yahoo!'s first approach to exploiting this resource was to sell

Who Is Yahoo!?

advertising on its Web site. However, when the tech bubble burst in 1999–2000, it significantly reduced the demand for Web-based advertising, and Yahoo! had to explore alternative ways to use its customer-base resource to create value.

Its second approach was to charge its customers for using its services. Historically, Yahoo!'s services—including its e-mail system, its chat rooms, and its search engines—were free of charge to consumers. Beginning in 2001, Yahoo! began charging for these services. The theory was that if it

could generate $1,000 of revenue per customer a year, it could be a $237 billion company. Unfortunately, Yahoo!'s customers began using low-cost or free alternatives, and it was not able to generate sufficient revenue using its customer resource.

In 2003, Yahoo! decided to begin exploiting information it had about its customer base in a new way by selling its own services and the products and services of its partner firms to those customers. Or, as one observer put it, it became a "direct marketing and solicitation outfit, cold-calling families at dinner time, spamming their e-mail inboxes, and cluttering their mail with targeted appeals." The jury is still out on whether or not this strategy will allow Yahoo! to create value from its resources. On the one hand, it seems very likely that there are numerous firms that will be willing to pay Yahoo! for the information it controls about its 237 million customers. On the other hand, will those customers continue to return to Yahoo! when they know information about them is being sold to the highest bidder?

Sources: J. Ellis, H. Rubin, and K. Hammonds (2002). "FCMC." *Fast Company*, July, p. 113; B. Breen (2003). "She's helping Yahoo act normal." *Fast Company*, May, pp. 92 +; www.Yahoo.com.

Unfortunately, for other firms the answer to the question of value appears to be "no." Touted as a merger (AOL and Time Warner) to create a new kind of entertainment and media company, it is now widely recognized that Time Warner has been unable to marshall the resources necessary to create economic value. Time Warner wrote-off $90 billion in value in 2002; its stock price has been at record low levels, and there have been rumors that it will be broken up. Ironically, many of the segments of this diverse media conglomerate continue to create value. But the company as a whole has not realized the synergies that it was expected to generate when it was created. Put differently, these synergies—as resources and capabilities—are apparently not valuable.[7]

Using Value-Chain Analysis to Identify Potentially Valuable Resources and Capabilities

One way to identify potentially valuable resources and capabilities controlled by a firm is to study that firm's value chain. A firm's **value chain** is the set of business activities in which it engages to develop, produce, and market its products or services. Each step in a firm's value chain requires the application and integration of different resources and capabilities. Because different firms may make different choices about which value-chain activities they will engage in, they can end up developing different sets of resources and capabilities. This can be the case even if these firms are all operating in the same industry. These choices can have implications for the strategies a firm is pursuing, and, as is described in the Ethics and Strategy feature, they can also have implications for society more generally.

Consider, for example, the oil industry. Figure 3.2 provides a simplified list of all the business activities that must be completed if crude oil is to be turned into consumer products, like gasoline. These activities include exploring for crude oil, drilling for crude oil, pumping crude oil, shipping crude oil, buying crude oil, refining crude oil, selling refined products to distributors, shipping refined products, and selling refined products to final customers.

Different firms may make different choices about which of these stages in the oil industry they want to operate. Thus, these firms may have very different resources and capabilities. For example, exploring for crude oil is very expensive and requires substantial financial resources. It also requires access to land (a physical resource), the application of substantial scientific and technical knowledge (individual resources), and an organizational commitment to risk-taking and exploration (organizational resources). Firms that operate in this stage of the oil business are likely to have very different resources and capabilities than firms that, for example, sell refined oil products to final customers. To be successful in the retail stage of this industry, a firm needs retail outlets (such as stores and gas stations), which are costly to build and require both financial and physical resources. These outlets, in turn, need to be staffed by salespeople—individual resources— and marketing these products to customers through advertisements and other means can require a commitment to creativity—an organizational resource.

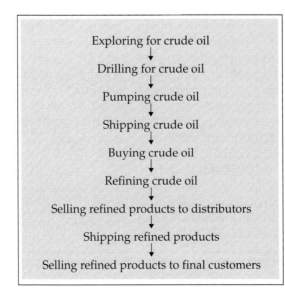

Figure 3.2 A Simplified Value Chain of Activities of Oil-Based Refined Products such as Gasoline and Motor Oil

Ethics and Strategy

Strategic management adopts the perspective of a firm's owners in discussing how to gain and sustain competitive advantages. Even when adopting a stakeholder perspective (see the Ethics and Strategy feature in Chapter 1), how a firm can improve its performance and increase the wealth of its owners still takes center stage.

However, an exclusive focus on the performance of a firm and the wealth of its owners can sometimes have broader effects—on society and on the environment—that are not fully recognized. Economists call these broader effects "externalities" because they are external to the core issue in economics and strategic management about how firms can maximize their performance. They are external to this issue because firms generally do not bear the full costs of the externalities their profit-maximizing behavior creates.

Externalities can take many forms. The most obvious of these has to do with pollution and the environment. If, for example, in the process of maximizing its performance, a firm engages in activities that pollute the environment, the impact of that pollution is an externality. Such pollution reduces our quality of life and hurts the environment, but the firm creating this pollution often does not bear the full costs of doing so.

Other externalities have to do with a firm's impact on the public's health. For example, when tobacco companies maximize their profits by selling tobacco to children, they are also creating a public health externality. Getting children hooked on tobacco early on might be good for the bottom line of a corporation, but it

Externalities and the Broader Consequences of Profit Maximization

increases the chances of these children developing lung cancer, emphysema, heart disease, and the other ailments associated with tobacco. Obviously, these individuals absorb most of the adverse consequences of these diseases, but society suffers as well from the high health care costs that are engendered.

Put differently, while adopting a simple profit-maximizing perspective in choosing and implementing strategies can have positive impacts for a firm, its owners, and its other stakeholders, it can also have negative consequences for society as a whole. Two broad solutions to this problem of externalities have been proposed. First, governments can take on the responsibility of directly monitoring and regulating the behavior of firms in areas where these kinds of externalities are likely to develop. Second, governments can use lawsuits and regulations to

ensure that firms directly bear more of the costs of any externalities their behavior might generate. Once these externalities are "internalized," it is then a matter of self-interest for firms not to engage in activities that generate negative externalities.

Consumers can sometimes also help internalize the externalities generated by a firm's behavior by adjusting their consumption patterns to buy products or services only from companies that do not generate negative externalities. Consumers can even be more proactive and let firms know which firm strategies are particularly troubling. For example, many consumers united to boycott firms with operations in South Africa when South Africa was still implementing a policy of apartheid. Ultimately, this pressure not only changed the strategies of many firms; it also helped change South Africa's domestic policies. More recently, consumer pressures on drug companies have forced these firms to make their AIDs drugs more accessible in less developed countries in Africa, and similar pressures have forced Nike to adjust the wages and working conditions of those individuals that manufacture Nike's shoes. To the extent that sufficient demand for "socially responsible firms" exists in the marketplace, it may make profit-maximizing sense for a firm to engage in socially responsible behavior by reducing the extent to which its actions generate negative externalities.

Sources: "AIDS in Africa." *British Medical Journal,* June 1, p. 456; J. S. Friedman (2003). "Paying for apartheid." *Nation,* June 6, pp. 7 +; L. Lee (2000). "Can Nike still do it?" *BusinessWeek,* February 21, pp. 121 +.

However, even firms that operate in the same set of value-chain activities in an industry may approach these activities very differently and therefore may develop very different resources and capabilities associated with these activities. For example, two firms may sell refined oil products to final customers. However, one of these firms may sell only through retail outlets it owns while the second may sell only through retail outlets it doesn't own. The first firm's financial and physical resources are likely to be very different from the second firm's, although these two firms may have similar individual and organizational resources.

Studying a firm's value chain forces us to think about firm resources and capabilities in a very disaggregated way. Although it is possible to characterize a firm's resources and capabilities more broadly, it is usually more helpful to think about how each of the activities a firm engages in affects its financial, physical, individual, and organizational resources. With this understanding, it is possible to begin to recognize potential sources of competitive advantage for a firm in a much more detailed way.

Because this type of analysis can be so helpful in identifying the financial, physical, individual, and organizational resources and capabilities controlled by a firm, several generic value chains for identifying them have been developed. The first, proposed by the management-consulting firm McKinsey and Company, is presented in Figure 3.3.[8] This relatively simple model suggests that the creation of value almost always involves six distinct activities: technology development, product design, manufacturing, marketing, distribution, and service. Firms can develop distinctive capabilities in any one or any combination of these activities.

Michael E. Porter has developed a second generic value chain.[9] This value chain, presented in Figure 3.4, divides value-creating activities into two large categories: primary activities and support activities. Primary activities include inbound logistics (purchasing, inventory, and so forth), production, outbound logistics (warehousing and distribution), sales and marketing, and service (dealer support and customer service). Support activities include infrastructure (planning, finance, information services, legal), technology development (research and development, product design), and human resource management and development. Primary activities are directly associated with the manufacture and distribution of a product. Support activities assist a firm in accomplishing its primary activities. As is the case with the McKinsey value chain, a firm can develop strengths or weaknesses in any one, or in any combination, of the activities listed in Porter's value chain. These activities, and how they are linked to one another, point to the kinds of resources and capabilities a firm is likely to have developed.

Figure 3.3   The Generic Value Chain Developed by McKinsey and Company

Technology development	Product design	Manufacturing	Marketing	Distribution	Service
Source	Function	Integration	Prices	Channels	Warranty Speed
Sophistication	Physical	Raw materials	Advertising/	Integration	Captive/independent
Patents	characteristics	Capacity	promotion	Inventory	Prices
Product/process	Aesthetics	Location	Sales force	Warehousing	
choices	Quality	Procurement	Package	Transport	
		Parts production	Brand		
		Assembly			

Figure 3.4   The Generic Value Chain Developed by Porter

Sources: Reprinted with permission of The Free Press, a division of Simon and Schuster Adult Publishing Group, from *Competitive Advantage: Creating and Sustaining Superior Performance* by Michael E. Porter. Copyright © 1985 by The Free Press.

Support Activities	Infrastructure activities: Planning, finance, MIS, legal services					
	Technology: Research, development, design					
	Human resource management and development					
Primary Activities	Purchasing Inventory holding Materials handling	Production	Warehousing and distribution	Sales and marketing	Dealer support and customer service	Margin

VRIO   The Question of Rarity

Understanding the value of a firm's resources and capabilities is an important first consideration in understanding a firm's internal strengths and weaknesses. However, if a particular resource or capability is controlled by numerous competing firms, then that resource is unlikely to be a source of competitive advantage for any one of them. Instead, valuable but common (that is, not rare) resources and capabilities are sources of competitive parity. Only when a resource is not controlled by numerous other firms is it likely to be a source of competitive advantage. These observations lead to the **Question of Rarity**: "How many competing firms already possess particular valuable resources and capabilities?"

Consider, for example, competition among television sports channels. All the major networks broadcast sports. In addition, there are several sports-only cable channels, including the best known all-sports channel, ESPN. Several years ago, ESPN began televising what were then called alternative sports—skateboarding, snowboarding, mountain bike riding, and so forth. The surprising popularity of these programs led ESPN to package them into an annual competition called the "X-Games." "X" stands for extreme, and ESPN has definitely gone to the extreme in including sports in the X-Games. The X-Games now include sports such as sky-surfing, competitive high diving, competitive bungee cord jumping, and so forth. ESPN broadcasts both a summer X-Games and a winter X-Games. No other sports outlet has yet made such a commitment to so-called extreme sports, and it has paid handsome dividends for ESPN—extreme sports have very low cost broadcast rights and draw a fairly large audience. This commitment to extreme sports has been a source of at least a temporary competitive advantage for ESPN.

Of course, not all of a firm's resources and capabilities have to be valuable and rare. Indeed, most firms have a resource base that is composed primarily of valuable but common resources and capabilities. These resources cannot be sources of even temporary competitive advantage, but are essential if a firm is to gain competitive parity. Under conditions of competitive parity, although no one firm gains a competitive advantage, firms do increase their probability of survival.

Consider, for example, a telephone system as a resource or capability. Because telephone systems are widely available and because virtually all organizations have access to telephone systems, these systems are not rare and thus not a source of competitive advantage. However, firms that do not possess a telephone system are likely to give their competitors an important advantage and place themselves at a competitive disadvantage.

How rare a valuable firm resource or capability must be in order to have the potential for generating a competitive advantage varies from situation to situation. It is not difficult to see that if a firm's valuable resources and capabilities are absolutely unique among a set of current and potential competitors, they can generate a competitive advantage. However, it may be possible for a small number of firms in an industry to possess a particular valuable resource or capability and still obtain a competitive advantage. In general, as long as the number of firms that possess a particular valuable resource or capability is less than the number of firms needed to generate perfect competition dynamics in an industry, that resource or capability can be considered rare and a potential source of competitive advantage.

The Question of Imitability

V R I O

Firms with valuable and rare resources are often strategic innovators, for they are able to conceive of and engage in strategies that other firms cannot because these other firms lack the relevant resources and capabilities. These firms may gain the first-mover advantages discussed in Chapter 2.

Valuable and rare organizational resources, however, can be sources of sustained competitive advantage only if firms that do not possess them face a cost disadvantage in obtaining or developing them, compared to firms that already possess them. These kinds of resources are **imperfectly imitable**.[10] These observations lead to the **Question of Imitability**: "Do firms without a resource or capability face a cost disadvantage in obtaining or developing it compared to firms that already possess it?"

Imagine an industry with five essentially identical firms. Each of these firms manufactures the same products, uses the same raw materials, and sells the products to the same customers through the same distribution channels. It is not hard to see that firms in this kind of industry will have normal economic performance. Now, suppose that one of these firms, for whatever reason, discovers or develops a heretofore unrecognized valuable resource and uses that resource either to exploit an external opportunity or neutralize an external threat. Obviously, this one firm will gain a competitive advantage over the others.

This firm's competitors can respond to this competitive advantage in at least two ways. First, they can ignore the success of this one firm and continue as before. This action, of course, will put them at a competitive disadvantage. Second, these firms can attempt to understand why this one firm is able to be successful and then duplicate its resources to implement a similar strategy. If competitors have no cost disadvantages in acquiring or developing the needed resources, then this imitative approach will generate competitive parity in the industry.

Sometimes, however, for reasons that are discussed later, competing firms may face an important cost disadvantage in duplicating a successful firm's valuable resources. If this is the case, this one innovative firm may gain a **sustained competitive advantage**—an advantage that is not competed away through strategic imitation. Firms that possess and exploit costly-to-imitate, rare, and valuable resources in choosing and implementing their strategies may enjoy a period of sustained competitive advantage.[11]

For example, other sports networks have observed the success of ESPN's X-Games and are beginning to broadcast these competitions. NBC, for example, has developed its own version of the X-Games, called the "Gravity Games," and even the Olympics have included sports that were previously perceived as being "too extreme" for this mainline sports competition. Several Fox sports channels broadcast programs that feature extreme sports, and at least one new cable channel (Fuel) broadcasts only extreme sports. Whether these efforts will be able to attract the competitors that the X-Games attract, whether winners at these other competitions will gain as much status in their sports as do winners of the X-Games, and whether these other competitions and programs will gain the reputation among viewers enjoyed by ESPN will go a long way to determining whether ESPN's competitive advantage in extreme sports is temporary or sustained.[12]

Forms of Imitation: Direct Duplication and Substitution

In general, imitation occurs in one of two ways: **direct duplication** or **substitution**. Imitating firms can attempt to directly duplicate the resources possessed by the firm with a competitive advantage. Thus, NBC sponsoring an alternative extreme games competition can be thought of as an effort to directly duplicate the resources that enabled ESPN's X-Games to be successful. If the cost of this direct duplication is too high, then a firm with these resources and capabilities may obtain a sustained competitive advantage. If this cost is not too high, then any competitive advantages in this setting will only be temporary.

Imitating firms can also attempt to substitute other resources for a costly-to-imitate resource possessed by a firm with a competitive advantage. Extreme sports shows and an extreme sports cable channel are potential substitutes for ESPN's X-Game strategy. These shows appeal to much the same audience as the X-Games, but do not require the same resources as an X-Game strategy requires (e.g., because they are not competitions, they do not require the network to bring together a large number of athletes all at once). If substitute resources exist, and if imitating firms do not face a cost disadvantage in obtaining them, then the competitive advantage of other firms will only be temporary. However, if these resources have no substitutes, or if the cost of acquiring these substitutes is greater than the cost of obtaining the original resources, then competitive advantages can be sustained.

Why Might It Be Costly to Imitate Another Firm's Resources or Capabilities?

A variety of authors have studied the reasons why it might be costly for one firm to imitate the resources and capabilities of another firm. Four sources of costly imitation have been noted.[13] These are summarized in Table 3.2 and discussed below.

Unique Historical Conditions. It may be the case that a firm was able to acquire or develop its resources and capabilities in a low-cost manner because of its unique historical conditions. The ability of firms to acquire, develop, and use resources often depends upon their place in time and space. Once time and history pass, firms that do not have space-and-time–dependent resources face a significant cost disadvantage in obtaining and developing them, because doing so would require them to re-create history.[14]

ESPN's early commitment to extreme sports is an example of these unique historical conditions. The status and reputation of the X-Games was created because ESPN happened to be the first major sports outlet that took these compe-

Table 3.2 **Sources of Costly Imitation**

Unique Historical Conditions: When a firm gains low-cost access to resources because of its place in time and space, other firms may find these resources to be costly to imitate. Both first-mover advantages and path dependence can create unique historical conditions.

Causal Ambiguity: When competitors cannot tell, for sure, what enables a firm to gain an advantage, that advantage may be costly to imitate. Sources of causal ambiguity include when competitive advantages are based on "taken-for-granted" resources and capabilities, when multiple nontestable hypotheses exist about why a firm has a competitive advantage, and when a firm's advantages are based on complex sets of interrelated capabilities.

Social Complexity: When the resources and capabilities a firm uses to gain a competitive advantage involve interpersonal relationships, trust, culture, and other social resources that are costly to imitate in the short term.

Patents: Only a source of sustained competitive advantage in a few industries, including pharmaceuticals and specialty chemicals.

titions seriously. The X-Games apparently became the most important competition in many of these extreme sports. Indeed, for snow boarders, winning a gold medal in the X-Games is almost as important—if not more important—as winning a gold medal in the Winter Olympics. Other sports outlets that hope to be able to compete with the X-Games will have both the status of ESPN as "the worldwide leader in sports" and its historical advantage in extreme sports to overcome. Overcoming these advantages is likely to be very costly, making competitive threats from direct duplication, at least, less significant.

Of course, firms can also act to increase the costliness of imitating the resources and capabilities they control. ESPN is doing this by expanding its coverage of extreme sports, and by engaging in a "grassroots" marketing campaign that engages young, "extreme athletes" in local competitions. The purpose of these efforts is clear: to keep ESPN's status as the most important source of extreme sports competitions intact.[15]

There are at least two ways that unique historical circumstances can give a firm a sustained competitive advantage. First, it may be that a particular firm is the first in an industry to recognize and exploit an opportunity, and being first gives a firm one or more of the first-mover advantages discussed in Chapter 2. Thus, although in principle other firms in an industry could have exploited an opportunity, that only one firm did so makes it more costly for other firms to imitate this original firm.

A second way that history can have an impact on a firm builds on the concept of **path dependence**.[16] A process is said to be path dependent when events early in the evolution of a process have significant effects on subsequent events. In the evolution of competitive advantage, path dependence suggests that a firm may gain a competitive advantage in the current period based on the acquisition and development of resources in earlier periods. In these earlier periods, it is often not clear what the full future value of particular resources will be. Because of this uncertainty, firms are able to acquire or develop these resources for less than what will turn out to be their full value. However, once the full value of these resources is revealed, other firms seeking to acquire or develop these resources will need to pay their full known value, which (in general) will be greater than the costs incurred by the firm that acquired or developed these resources in some earlier period. The cost of acquiring both duplicate and substitute resources would rise once their full value became known.

Consider, for example, a firm that purchased land for ranching some time ago and discovered a rich supply of oil on this land in the current period. The difference between the value of this land as a supplier of oil (high) and the value of this land for ranching (low) is a source of competitive advantage for this firm. Moreover, other firms attempting to acquire this or adjacent land will now have to pay for the full value of the land in its use as a supply of oil (high) and thus will be at a cost disadvantage compared to the firm that acquired it some time ago for ranching.

Causal Ambiguity. A second reason why a firm's resources and capabilities may be costly to imitate is that imitating firms may not understand the relationship between the resources and capabilities controlled by a firm, and that firm's competitive advantage. In other words, the relationship between firm resources and capabilities and competitive advantage may be **causally ambiguous**.

At first, it seems unlikely that causal ambiguity about the sources of competitive advantage for a firm would ever exist. Managers in a firm seem likely to understand the sources of their own competitive advantage. If managers in one firm understand the relationship between resources and competitive advantage, then it seems likely that managers in other firms would also be able to discover these relationships and thus would have a clear understanding of which resources and capabilities they should duplicate or seek substitutes for. If there are no other sources of cost disadvantage for imitating firms, imitation should lead to competitive parity and normal economic performance.[17]

However, it is not always the case that managers in a particular firm will fully understand the relationship between the resources and capabilities they control and competitive advantage. This lack of understanding could occur for at least three reasons. First, it may be that the resources and capabilities that generate competitive advantage are so taken for granted, so much a part of the day-to-day experience of managers in a firm, that these managers are unaware of them.[18] Organizational resources and capabilities such as teamwork among top managers, organizational culture, relationships among other employees, and relationships with customers and suppliers may be almost "invisible" to managers in a firm.[19] If managers in firms that have such capabilities do not understand their relationship to competitive advantage, managers in other firms face significant challenges in understanding which resources they should imitate.

Second, managers may have multiple hypotheses about which resources and capabilities enable their firm to gain a competitive advantage, but they may be unable to evaluate which of these resources and capabilities, alone or in combination, actually create the competitive advantage. For example, if one asks successful entrepreneurs what enabled them to be successful, they are likely to reply with several hypotheses such as "hard work, willingness to take risks, and a high-quality top management team." However, if one asks what happened to unsuccessful entrepreneurs, they too are likely to suggest that their firms were characterized by "hard work, willingness to take risks, and a high-quality top management team." It may be the case that "hard work, willingness to take risks, and a high-quality top management team" are important resources and capabilities for entrepreneurial firm success, but other factors may also play a role. Without rigorous experiments, it is difficult to establish which of these resources have a causal relationship with competitive advantage and which do not.

Finally, it may be that not just a few resources and capabilities enable a firm to gain a competitive advantage but that literally thousands of these organizational attributes, bundled together, generate these advantages. When the resources and capabilities that generate competitive advantage are complex networks of relationships between individuals, groups, and technology, imitation can be costly.

Consider, again, Electronic Arts—the company with which this chapter began. The broad strategic goals that EA has for each of its major products—to have both creative and technological achievements—are easy to state. But it is the way that EA manages the creative and technological process that makes the achievement of these goals costly for others to imitate. For example, programmers are expected to share computer programs across products when they develop a new feature that might be relevant to other games. A couple of times each year, the senior management team at EA gathers to meet with a diverse group of artists to learn about the creative process. These managers talk about movement with interpretive dancers, they talk about creativity with performance artists, and they talk about structural design with sculptors. Recently, EA hired script writers from Hollywood who introduced a whole new approach to writing the stories associated with their computer games. No single one of these processes by itself would give EA its competitive advantage. But, in combination, these processes and many hundreds of others are very difficult to describe, let alone imitate.[20]

Whenever the sources of competitive advantage are widely diffused across people, locations, and processes in a firm, those sources will be costly to imitate. Perhaps the best example of such a resource is knowledge itself. To the extent that valuable knowledge about a firm's products, processes, customers, and so on, is widely diffused throughout an organization, competitors will have difficulty imitating that knowledge and it can be a source of sustained competitive advantage.[21]

Social Complexity. A third reason that a firm's resources and capabilities may be costly to imitate is that they may be socially complex phenomena, beyond the ability of firms to systematically manage and influence. When competitive advantages are based in such complex social phenomena, the ability of other firms to imitate these resources and capabilities, either through direct duplication or substitution, is significantly constrained. Efforts to influence these kinds of phenomena are likely to be much more costly than they would be if these phenomena developed in a natural way over time in a firm.[22]

A wide variety of firm resources and capabilities may be **socially complex**. Examples include the interpersonal relations among managers in a firm, a firm's culture, and a firm's reputation among suppliers and customers.[23] Notice that in most of these cases it is possible to specify how these socially complex resources add value to a firm. Thus, there is little or no causal ambiguity surrounding the link between these firm resources and capabilities and competitive advantage. However, understanding that an organizational culture with certain attributes or quality relations among managers can improve a firm's efficiency and effectiveness does not necessarily imply that firms lacking these attributes can engage in systematic effort to create them, or that low-cost substitutes for them exist. For the time being, such social engineering may be beyond the abilities of most firms. At the very least, such social engineering is likely to be much more costly than it would be if socially complex resources evolved naturally within a firm.[24]

It is interesting to note that firms seeking to imitate complex physical technology often do not face the cost disadvantages of imitating complex social phenomena. A great deal of physical technology (machine tools, robots, and so forth) can be purchased in supply markets. Even when a firm develops its own unique

Research Made Relevant

Strategic Human Resource Management Research

*M*ost empirical tests of the Resource-Based View have focused on the extent to which history, causal ambiguity, and social complexity have an impact on the ability of firms to gain and sustain competitive advantages. Among the most important of these tests has been research that examines the extent to which human resource practices that are likely to generate socially complex resources and capabilities are related to firm performance. This area of research is known as Strategic Human Resources Management.

The first of these tests was conducted as part of a larger study of efficient low cost manufacturing in the worldwide automobile industry. A group of researchers from the Massachusetts Institute of Technology developed rigorous measures of the cost and quality of over 70 manufacturing plants that assembled mid-size sedans around the world. They discovered that, at the time of their study, only six of these plants had simultaneously low costs and high-quality manufacturing—a position that obviously would give these plants a competitive advantage in their marketplace.

In trying to understand what distinguished these six plants from the others in the sample, these researchers found that, not surprisingly, these six plants had the most modern and up-to-date manufacturing technology. However, so did many of the less effective plants. What distinguished these effective plants was not their manufacturing technology, per se, but their human resource (HR) practices. These six plants all implemented a bundle of such practices that included participative decision making, quality circles, and an emphasis on team production.

One of the results of these efforts—and another distinguishing feature of these six plants—was a high level of employee loyalty and commitment to a plant, together with a belief that plant managers would treat employees fairly. These socially complex resources and capabilities are just the types of resources that the RBV suggests should be sources of sustained competitive advantage.

Later work has followed up on this approach and has examined the impact of HR practices on firm performance outside the manufacturing arena. Using a variety of measures of firm performance and several different measures of HR practices, the results of this research continue to be very consistent with resource-based logic. That is, firms that are able to use HR practices to develop socially complex human and organizational resources are able to gain competitive advantages over firms that do not engage in these practices.

Sources: J. P. Womack, D. I. Jones, and D. Roos (1990). *The machine that changed the world.* New York: Rawson; M. Huselid (1995). "The impact of human resource management practices on turnover, productivity, and corporate financial performance." *Academy of Management Journal,* 38, pp. 635–672; J. B. Barney and P. Wright (1998). "On becoming a strategic partner." *Human Resource Management,* 37, pp. 31–46.

physical technology, reverse engineering tends to diffuse this technology among competing firms in a low-cost manner. Indeed, the costs of imitating a successful physical technology are often lower than the costs of developing a new technology.[25]

Although physical technology is usually not costly to imitate, the application of this technology in a firm is likely to call for a wide variety of socially complex organizational resources and capabilities. These organizational resources may be costly to imitate, and, if they are valuable and rare, the combination of physical and socially complex resources may be a source of sustained competitive advantage. The importance of socially complex resources and capabilities for firm performance has been studied in detail in the field of strategic human resource management, as described in the Research Made Relevant feature.

Patents. At first glance, it might appear that a firm's patents would make it very costly for competitors to imitate its products.[26] Patents do have this effect in some industries. For example, patents in the pharmaceutical and specialty chemical industry effectively foreclose other firms from marketing the same products until a firm's patents expire. As suggested in Chapter 2, patents can raise the cost of imitation in a variety of other industries as well.

However, from another point of view, a firm's patents may decrease, rather than increase, the costs of imitation. When a firm files for patent protection, it is forced to reveal a significant amount of information about its product. Governments require this information to ensure that the technology in question is patentable. By obtaining a patent, a firm may provide important information to competitors about how to imitate its technology.

Moreover, most technological developments in an industry are diffused throughout firms in that industry in a relatively brief period of time, even if the technology in question is patented, because patented technology is not immune from low-cost imitation. Patents may restrict direct duplication for a time, but they may actually increase the chances of substitution by functionally equivalent technologies.[27]

The Question of Organization

`V R I O`

A firm's potential for competitive advantage depends on the value, rarity, and imitability of its resources and capabilities. However, to fully realize this potential, a firm must be organized to exploit its resources and capabilities. These observations lead to the **Question of Organization**: "Is a firm organized to exploit the full competitive potential of its resources and capabilities?"

Numerous components of a firm's organization are relevant to the question of organization, including its formal reporting structure, its formal and informal management control systems, and its compensation policies. A firm's **formal reporting structure** is a description of who in the organization reports to whom; it is often embodied in a firm's **organizational chart**. **Management control systems** include a range of formal and informal mechanisms to ensure that managers are behaving in ways consistent with a firm's strategies. **Formal management controls** include a firm's budgeting and reporting activities that keep people higher up in a firm's organizational chart informed about the actions taken by people lower down in a firm's organizational chart. **Informal management controls** might include a firm's culture and the willingness of employees to monitor each others' behavior. **Compensation policies** are the ways that firms pay employees. Such policies create incentives for employees to behave in certain ways.

These components of a firm's organization are often called **complementary resources and capabilities** because they have limited ability to generate competitive advantage in isolation. However, in combination with other resources and capabilities, they can enable a firm to realize its full potential for competitive advantage.[28]

For example, it has already been suggested that ESPN may have a sustained competitive advantage in the extreme sports segment of the sports broadcasting industry. However, if ESPN's management had not taken advantage of its opportunities in extreme sports by expanding coverage, ensuring that the best competitors come to ESPN competitions, adding additional competitions, and changing up older competitions, then its potential for competitive advantage would not have been fully realized. Of course, the reason that ESPN has done all these things is because it has an appropriate organizational structure, management controls, and employee compensation policies. By themselves, these attributes of ESPN's organization could not be a source of competitive advantage; however, this organization was essential for ESPN to realize its full competitive advantage potential.

Having an appropriate organization in place has enabled ESPN to realize the full competitive advantage potential of its other resources and capabilities. Having an inappropriate organization in place prevented Xerox from taking full advantage of some of its most critical valuable, rare, and costly-to-imitate resources and capabilities.

Through the 1960s and early 1970s, Xerox invested in a series of very innovative technology development research efforts. It managed this research effort by creating a stand-alone research center in Palo Alto, California (Palo Alto Research Center—PARC), and by assembling a large group of highly creative and innovative scientists and engineers to work there. Left to their own devices, these scientists and engineers at Xerox PARC developed an amazing array of technological innovations: the personal computer, the "mouse," Windows-type software, the laser printer, the "paperless office," Ethernet, and so forth. In retrospect, it is clear that the market potential of these technologies was enormous. Moreover, because they were developed at Xerox PARC, they were rare. Xerox might have been able to gain some important first-mover advantages if the organization had been able to translate these technologies into products, thereby increasing the cost to other firms of imitating these technologies.

Xerox possessed the resources and capabilities but did not have an organization in place to take advantage of them. No structure existed whereby Xerox PARC innovations could become known to managers at Xerox. Indeed, most Xerox managers—even many senior managers—were unaware of these technological developments through the mid-1970s. Once they finally became aware of them, very few of the technologies survived Xerox's highly bureaucratic product development process, a process where product development projects were divided into hundreds of minute tasks and progress in each task was reviewed by dozens of large committees. Even innovations that survived the product development process were not exploited by Xerox managers, because management compensation at Xerox depended almost exclusively on maximizing current revenue. Short-term profitability was relatively less important in compensation calculations, and the development of markets for future sales and profitability was essentially irrelevant. Xerox's formal reporting structure, its explicit management control systems, and its compensation policies were all inconsistent with exploiting the valuable, rare, and costly-to-imitate resources it had developed. Not surprisingly, the company failed to exploit any of its potential sources of sustained competitive advantage.[29]

Applying the VRIO Framework

The questions of value, rarity, imitability, and organization can be brought together into a single framework to understand the return potential associated with exploiting any of a firm's resources or capabilities. This is done in Table 3.3. The relationship of the VRIO framework to strengths and weaknesses is presented in Table 3.4.

If a resource or capability controlled by a firm is not valuable, it will not enable a firm to choose or implement strategies that exploit environmental opportunities or neutralize environmental threats. Organizing to exploit this resource will increase a firm's costs or decrease its revenues. These types of resources are

Table 3.3   **The VRIO Framework**

Is a resource or capability:				
Valuable?	**Rare?**	**Costly to imitate?**	**Exploited by organization?**	**Competitive implications**
No	—	—	No	Competitive disadvantage
Yes	No	—	↑	Competitive parity
Yes	Yes	No	↕	Temporary competitive advantage
Yes	Yes	Yes	Yes	Sustained competitive advantage

weaknesses. Firms will either have to fix these weaknesses or avoid using them when choosing and implementing strategies. If firms do exploit these kinds of resources and capabilities, they can expect to put themselves at a competitive disadvantage compared to firms that either do not possess these nonvaluable resources or do not use them in conceiving and implementing strategies.

If a resource or capability is valuable but not rare, exploitation of this resource in conceiving and implementing strategies will generate competitive parity. Exploiting these types of resources will generally not create competitive advantages, but failure to exploit them can put a firm at a competitive disadvantage. In this sense, valuable-but-not-rare resources can be thought of as organizational strengths.

If a resource or capability is valuable and rare but not costly to imitate, exploiting this resource will generate a temporary competitive advantage for a firm. A firm that exploits this kind of resource is, in an important sense, gaining a first-mover advantage, because it is the first firm that is able to exploit a particular resource. However, once competing firms observe this competitive advantage, they will be able to acquire or develop the resources needed to implement this strategy through direct duplication or substitution at no cost disadvantage compared to the first-moving firm. Over time, any competitive advantage that the first mover obtained would be competed away as other firms imitate the resources needed to compete. Consequently, this type of resource or capability can be thought of as an organizational strength and as a **distinctive competence**.

If a resource or capability is valuable, rare, and costly to imitate, exploiting it will generate a sustained competitive advantage. In this case, competing firms face a significant cost disadvantage in imitating a successful firm's resources and

Table 3.4   **The Relationship Between the VRIO Framework and Organizational Strengths and Weaknesses**

Is a resource or capability:				
Valuable?	**Rare?**	**Costly to imitate?**	**Exploited by organization?**	**Strength or weakness**
No	—	—	No	Weakness
Yes	No	—	↑	Strength
Yes	Yes	No	↕	Strength and distinctive competence
Yes	Yes	Yes	Yes	Strength and sustainable distinctive competence

capabilities. As suggested earlier, this competitive advantage may reflect the unique history of the successful firm, causal ambiguity about which resources to imitate, the socially complex nature of these resources and capabilities, or any patent advantages a firm might posses. In any case, attempts to compete away the advantages of firms that exploit these resources will not generate competitive advantage or even competitive parity for imitating firms. Even if these firms are able to acquire or develop the resources or capabilities in question, the very high costs of doing so would put them at a competitive disadvantage. These kinds of resources and capabilities are organizational strengths and **sustainable distinctive competencies**.

The question of organization operates as an adjustment factor in the VRIO framework. For example, if a firm has a valuable, rare, and costly-to-imitate resource and capability but fails to organize itself to take full advantage of this resource, some of its potential competitive advantage could be lost (this is the Xerox example). Extremely poor organization, in this case, could actually lead a firm that has the potential for competitive advantage to gain only competitive parity or competitive disadvantages.

Applying the VRIO Framework to Dell Computer

To examine how the VRIO framework can be applied in analyzing real strategic situations, consider the competition position of Dell Computer. Most observers agree that Dell Computer has been able to gain a sustained competitive advantage in the very competitive personal computer industry. By applying the VRIO framework to Dell's value chain, it is possible to begin to identify the sources of that advantage. Figure 3.5 applies a version of the generic value chain developed by McKinsey and Company (see Figure 3.2) to Dell Computer.[30]

Notice that Dell is not engaged in very many stages of the value chain. Indeed, one of the critical aspects of Dell's ability to generate economic value is

Figure 3.5   An Extended Generic Value Chain for Dell Computers with an Application of the VRIO Framework that it has adopted a strategy that enables it to focus only on those aspects of the value chain where it has either a temporary or sustained competitive advantage. This approach to deciding which stages of the value chain to enter into is discussed in more detail in Chapter 6.

Dell has at least a temporary competitive advantage in purchasing. This advantage stems from several factors, including Dell's volume of sales, which makes it an important customer to its suppliers. Dell can use its volume to obtain price reductions on many of the supplies it purchases. However, although its size is a valuable asset in this function, it is neither rare nor costly to imitate. After all, HP/Compaq and IBM both have large sales and thus enjoy similar volume advantages.

More important than Dell's size is the way that Dell manages its purchasing function. It purchases just the supplies it needs to complete production and expects its suppliers—both large and small—to make numerous deliveries to its production facilities, sometimes several times a day. In this way, Dell has been able to shift the costs of having an inventory of supplies from itself to its suppliers. This approach to purchasing is relatively unusual (that is, rare) in the personal computer industry. However, it is becoming the standard for efficient manufacturing in large numbers of industries, including the automobile industry. For this reason, although purchasing may be a source of temporary competitive advantage, it seems imitable and thus not likely to be a source of sustained competitive advantage.

Dell assembly operations, on the other hand, may be a source of sustained competitive advantage. Attention to detail, increased speed and efficiency, and high quality are all built into Dell assembly operations. This is true even though Dell assembles customized personal computers by offering numerous different option combinations, and often relies on outside companies to do its assembly.

For example, in building one type of computer, Dell engineers were able to reduce the number of times a computer had to be touched during the assembly process from 130 to 60. In another stage of the operation, Dell was able to modify the assembly process so that instead of requiring six screws to secure a subassembly, only a single screw was required—without the loss of quality. This attention to detail has led Dell to receive over 200 patents on assembly operations. And unlike product patents, patents on assembly operations are often costly to imitate because they are usually part of an integrated production system. Using language developed earlier in this chapter, Dell's advantage in assembly is based on numerous little decisions, decisions that are virtually invisible to competitors.

Moreover, Dell's relentless emphasis on process improvement is deeply ingrained in its socially complex culture. These attributes of the assembly process suggest that it is valuable, rare, and costly to imitate, and thus is likely to be a source of sustained competitive advantage for Dell.

Sales and support at Dell are managed through both telephone and Internet operations. Although Dell currently has a head start in these areas of its business, it is unlikely that other personal computer firms will ignore similar opportunities.[31] However, Dell currently does have a reputation for its e-commerce capabilities. This reputation among customers will probably mean that Dell will continue to enjoy these advantages beyond the time that competitors actually catch up to its sales and service strategy.

Dell does not engage in distribution, transportation, inventory holding, and computer applications stages of the value chain. Again, this enables it to concentrate on only those aspects of the value chain that are either a source of temporary or sustained competitive advantage. Given its strategy, it is not surprising that Dell's performance has been outstanding, even though it operates in a very competitive industry.

Imitation and Competitive Dynamics in an Industry

Suppose a firm in an industry has conducted an analysis of its resources and capabilities, concludes that it possesses some valuable, rare, and costly-to-imitate resources and capabilities, and uses these to choose a strategy that it implements with the appropriate organizational structure, formal and informal management controls, and compensation policies. The Resource-Based View suggests that this firm will gain a competitive advantage even if it is operating in what a five forces analysis (see Chapter 2) would suggest is a very unattractive industry. Examples of firms that have competitive advantages in unattractive industries include Southwest Airlines, Nucor Steel, Wal-Mart, and Dell Computers, to name a few.

Given that a particular firm in an industry has a competitive advantage, how should other firms respond? Decisions made by other firms given the strategic choices of a particular firm define the nature of the **competitive dynamics** that exist in an industry. In general, other firms in an industry can respond to the advantages of a competitor in one of three ways. First, they can choose to not respond at all. For example, when Airbus decided to build a super-jumbo airliner designed to dominate international travel for the next 30 years, Boeing did nothing. Second, they can choose to alter some of their business tactics. For example, when Southwest Airlines began operating out of Philadelphia's airport and charged very low airfares, US Airways—the airline that used to dominate the Philadelphia market—lowered its fares as well. Finally, they can choose to alter their strategy—their theory of how to gain competitive advantage (see Chapter 1). For example, when Dell's direct and Internet-based approach to selling personal computers became dominant, Gateway computers decided to abandon its retail stores in favor of a direct and Internet-based approach.[32] The choice of responses a firm makes determines the structure of the competitive dynamics in an industry.

Not Responding to Another Firm's Competitive Advantage

There are at least three reasons why a firm might not respond to another firm's competitive advantage. First, this firm might have its own competitive advantage. By responding to another firm's competitive advantage it might destroy, or at least compromise, its own sources of competitive advantage. For example, digital time keeping has made accurate watches available to most consumers at reasonable prices. Firms like Casio have a competitive advantage in this market because of their miniaturization and electronic capabilities. Indeed, Casio's market share and performance in the watch business continue to climb over the years. How should Rolex—a manufacturer of very expensive, nonelectronic watches—respond to Casio? Rolex's decision has been: Not at all. Rolex appeals to a very different market segment than Casio. Should Rolex change its strategies—even if it replaced its mechanical self-winding design with the technologically superior digital design—it could easily compromise its competitive advantage in its own niche market.[33] In general, when a firm already possesses its own sources of competitive advantage, it will not respond to different sources of competitive advantage controlled by another firm.

Second, a firm may not respond to another firm's competitive advantage because it does not have the resources and capabilities to do so. A firm with insufficient or inappropriate resources and capabilities—be they physical, financial, human, or organizational—will typically not be able to imitate a successful firm's resources either through direct duplication or substitution. This may very well be the case with USAir and Southwest Airlines. Southwest's managerial resources and capabilities may simply be beyond the ability of USAir to imitate. In this setting, USAir is likely to find itself at a sustained competitive disadvantage.[34]

Finally, a firm may not respond to the advantages of a competitor because it is trying to reduce the level of rivalry in an industry. Any actions a firm takes that have the effect of reducing the level of rivalry in an industry and that also do not require firms in an industry to directly communicate or negotiate with each other can be thought of as **tacit cooperation**. Explicit cooperation, where firms do directly communicate and negotiate with each other, is discussed in detail in Chapter 9's analysis of strategic alliances.

Reducing the level of rivalry in an industry can benefit all those firms operating in that industry. This decision can have the effect of reducing the quantity of goods and services provided in an industry to below the competitive level, actions which will have the effect of increasing the prices of these goods or services. When tacit cooperation has the effect of reducing supply and increasing prices, it is known as **tacit collusion**. Tacit collusion can be illegal in some settings. However, firms can also tacitly cooperate along other dimensions besides quantity and price. These actions can also benefit all the firms in an industry and are typically not illegal.[35]

For example, it may be that firms can tacitly agree not to invest in certain kinds of research and development. Some forms of R&D are very expensive, and while these investments might end up generating products or services that could benefit customers, firms might still prefer to avoid the expense and risk. Firms can also tacitly agree not to market their products in certain ways. For example, before regulations compelled them to do so, most tobacco companies had already decided not to put cigarette vending machines in locations usually frequented by children, even though these machines could have generated significant revenues. Also, firms can tacitly cooperate by agreeing not to engage in certain manufacturing practices, such as outsourcing to third world countries and engaging in environmentally unsound practices.

All of these actions can have the effect of reducing the level of rivalry in an industry. And reducing the level of rivalry can have the effect of increasing the average level of performance for a firm in an industry. However, tacit cooperative relationships among firms are sometimes difficult to maintain. Typically, in order for tacit cooperation to work, an industry must have the structural attributes described in Table 3.5. First, there must be relatively few firms in the industry. Informally communicating and coordinating strategies among a few firms is difficult enough; it is even more difficult when there are large numbers of firms in an industry. For this reason, tacit cooperation is a viable strategy only when an industry is an oligopoly (see Chapter 2).

Second, firms in this industry must be homogeneous with respect to the products they sell and their cost structure. Heterogeneous products makes it too

Table 3.5 **Attributes of Industry Structure That Facilitate the Development of Tacit Cooperation**

1. Small Number of Competing Firms
2. Homogeneous Products and Costs
3. Market Share Leader
4. High Barriers to Entry

easy for a firm to "cheat" on its tacitly cooperative agreements by modifying its products, and heterogeneous cost means that the optimal level of output for a particular firm may be very different than the level agreed to through tacit cooperation. In this setting, a firm might have a strong incentive to increase its output and upset cooperative agreements.

Third, there typically has to be a strong market share leader in an industry if firms in that industry are going to tacitly cooperate. This would be a relatively large firm that typically establishes an example of the kind of behavior that will be mutually beneficial in an industry, and other firms in the industry sometimes fall into line with this example. Indeed, it is often this market share leader that will choose not to respond to the competitive actions of another firm in the industry in order to maintain cooperative relations in that industry.

Finally, the maintenance of tacit cooperation in an industry almost always requires the existence of high barriers to entry. If tacit cooperation is successful, the average performance of firms in an industry will improve. However, this higher level of performance can induce other firms to enter into this industry (see Chapter 2). Such entry will increase the number of firms in an industry and make it very difficult to maintain tacitly cooperative relationships. Thus, it must be very costly for new firms to enter into an industry in order for those in that industry to maintain their tacit cooperation. The higher these costs, the higher the barriers to entry.

Changing Tactics in Response to Another Firm's Competitive Advantage

Tactics are the specific actions a firm takes to implement its strategies. Examples of tactics can include decisions firms make about various attributes of their products—including size, shape, color, and price—specific advertising approaches adopted by a firm, and specific sales and marketing efforts. Generally, firms change their tactics much more frequently than they change their strategies.[36]

When competing firms are pursuing approximately the same strategies, the competitive advantages that any one firm might enjoy at a given point in time are most likely due to the tactics that that firm is pursuing. In this setting, it is not unusual for competing firms to change their tactics by imitating the tactics of the firm with an advantage in order to reduce this advantage. While changing one's tactics in this manner will only generate competitive parity, that is usually better than the competitive disadvantage these firms were experiencing previously.

Several industries provide excellent examples of these kinds of tactical interactions. In consumer goods, for example, if one company's sales increase by adding a "lemon scent" to laundry detergent, then lemon scents start showing up in everyone's laundry detergent. When Coke brings out C2—a soft drink with half the sugar and half the carbs of regular Coke—can Pepsi's low sugar/low carb product be far behind? And when Delta Airlines cuts it airfares, can American and United be far behind? Not surprisingly, these kinds of tactical changes, because they initially may be valuable and rare, are seldom costly to imitate and thus are typically only sources of temporary competitive advantage.

Sometimes, rather than simply imitating the tactics of a firm with a competitive advantage, a firm at a disadvantage may "leap frog" its competitors by developing an entirely new set of tactics. Procter & Gamble engaged in this strategy when it introduced its laundry detergent, Tide, in a new, concentrated formula. This new Tide required new manufacturing and packaging equipment—the smaller box could not be filled in the current manufacturing lines in the industry—which meant that Tide's competitors had to take more time in imitating the concentrated laundry detergent tactic than other tactics pursued in this industry. But, nevertheless, in a few short weeks, other firms in this market were introducing their own versions of concentrated laundry detergent.

Indeed, some firms can become so skilled at innovating new products and other tactics that this innovative capability can be a source of sustained competitive advantage. Consider, for example, the performance of Sony. Most observers agree that Sony possesses some special management and coordination skills that enable it to conceive, design, and manufacture high-quality miniaturized consumer electronics. However, virtually every time Sony brings out a new miniaturized product, several of its competitors quickly duplicate that product through reverse engineering, thereby reducing Sony's technological advantage. In what way can Sony's socially complex miniaturization resources and capabilities be a source of sustained competitive advantage when most of Sony's products are quickly imitated through direct duplication?

After Sony introduces each new product, it experiences a rapid increase in profits attributable to the new product's unique features. This increase, however, leads other firms to reverse-engineer the Sony product and introduce their own version. Increased competition results in a reduction in the profits associated with a new product. Thus, at the level of individual products, Sony apparently enjoys only temporary competitive advantages. However, looking at the total returns earned by Sony across all of its new products over time makes clear the source of Sony's sustained competitive advantage: By exploiting its resources and capabilities in miniaturization, Sony is able to constantly introduce new and exciting personal electronics products. No one of these products generates a sustained competitive advantage. But over time, across several such product introductions, Sony's resource and capability advantages lead to sustained competitive advantages.[37]

Changing Strategies in Response to Another Firm's Competitive Advantage

Finally, firms sometimes respond to another firm's competitive advantage by changing their strategies. Obviously, this does not occur very often and it typically only occurs when another firm's strategies usurp a firm's competitive advantage. In this setting a firm will not be able to gain even competitive parity if it maintains its strategy, even if it implements that strategy very effectively.

Changes in consumer tastes, in population demographics, and in the laws that govern a business can all have the effect of rendering what once was a valuable strategy as valueless. However, nothing has this impact more frequently than changes in technology. For example, no matter how well-made a mechanical calculator, is it is simply inferior to an electronic calculator. No matter how efficient the telegraph was in its day, it is an inferior technology to the telephone. And no matter how quickly one's fingers can move the beads on an abacus, an electronic cash register is a better way of keeping track of sales and making change in a store.

When firms change their strategies, they must proceed through the entire strategic management process, as described in Chapter 1. However, these firms will often have difficulty abandoning their traditional strategies. For most firms, their strategy helps define what they do and who they are. Changing its strategy often requires a firm to change its identity and its purposes. These are difficult changes to make and many firms wait to change their strategy until absolutely forced to do so by disastrous financial results. By then these firms not only have to change their strategy—with all that implies—they have to do so in the face of significant financial pressures.

The ability of virtually all strategies to generate competitive advantages typically expires, sooner or later. In general, it is much better for a firm to change its strategy before that strategy is no longer viable. In this way, a firm can make a planned move to a new strategy that maintains whatever resources and capabilities it still possesses while it develops the new resources and capabilities it will need to compete in the future.

Implications of the Resource-Based View

The Resource-Based View and the VRIO framework can be applied to individual firms to understand whether or not these firms will gain competitive advantages, how sustainable these competitive advantages are likely to be, and what the sources of these competitive advantages are. In this way, the Resource-Based View and the VRIO framework can be understood as important complements to the threats and opportunities analyses described in Chapter 2.

However, beyond what these frameworks can say about the competitive performance of a particular firm, the Resource-Based View has some broader implications for managers seeking to gain competitive advantages. Some of these broader implications are listed in Table 3.6 and discussed below.

Where Does the Responsibility for Competitive Advantage in a Firm Reside?

First, the Resource-Based View suggests that competitive advantages can be found in several of the different resources and capabilities a firm controls. These resources and capabilities are not limited to those that are directly controlled by a

Table 3.6 **Broader Implications of the Resource-Based View**

1. The responsibility for competitive advantage in a firm:
   Competitive advantage is every employee's responsibility.
2. Competitive parity and competitive advantage:
   If all a firm does is what its competition does, it can gain only competitive parity. In gaining competitive advantage, it is better for a firm to exploit its own valuable, rare, and costly-to-imitate resources than to imitate the valuable and rare resources of a competitor.
3. Difficult to implement strategies:
   As long as the cost of strategy implementation is less than the value of strategy implementation, the relative cost of implementing a strategy is more important for competitive advantage than the absolute cost of implementing a strategy. Firms can systematically overestimate and underestimate their uniqueness.
4. Socially complex resources:
   Not only can employee empowerment, organizational culture, and teamwork be valuable; they can also be sources of sustained competitive advantage.
5. The role of the organization:
   Organization should support the use of valuable, rare, and costly-to-imitate resources. If conflicts between these attributes of a firm arise, change the organization.

firm's senior managers. Thus, the responsibility for creating, nurturing, and exploiting valuable, rare, and costly-to-imitate resources and capabilities for competitive advantage is not restricted to senior managers, but falls on every employee in a firm. To do this, employees should go beyond defining their jobs in functional terms and instead define their jobs in competitive and economic terms.

Consider a simple example. In a recent visit to a very successful automobile manufacturing plant, the plant manager was asked to describe his job responsibilities. He said, "My job is to manage this plant in order to help the firm make and sell the best cars in the world." In response to a similar question, the person in charge of the manufacturing line also said, "My job is to manage this manufacturing line in order to help the firm make and sell the best cars in the world." A janitor was also asked to describe his job responsibilities. Although he had not been present in the two earlier interviews, the janitor responded, "My job is to keep this facility clean in order to help the firm make and sell the best cars in the world."

Which of these three employees is most likely to be a source of sustained competitive advantage for this firm? Certainly, the plant manager and the manufacturing line manager *should* define their jobs in terms of helping the firm make and sell the best cars in the world. However, it is unlikely that their responses to this question would be any different than the responses of other senior managers at other manufacturing plants around the world. Put differently, while the definition of these two managers' jobs in terms of enabling the firm to make and sell the best cars in the world is valuable, it is unlikely to be rare and thus likely to be a source of competitive parity, not competitive advantage. On the other hand, a janitor that defines his or her job as helping the firm make and sell the best cars in the world instead of simply to clean the facility is, most would agree, quite unusual. Because it is rare, it might be a source of at least a temporary competitive advantage.[38]

Now the value created by one janitor defining his or her job in these competitive terms rather than functional terms is not huge, but suppose that all the employees in this plant defined their jobs in these terms. Suddenly, the value that might be created could be substantial. Moreover, the organizational culture and tradition in a firm that would lead employees to define their jobs in this way is likely to be costly for other firms to imitate. Thus, if this approach to defining job responsibilities is broadly diffused in a particular plant, it seems likely to be valuable, rare, and costly to imitate and thus a source of sustained competitive advantage, assuming the firm is organized to take advantage of this unusual resource.

In the end, it is clear that competitive advantage is too important to remain the sole property of senior management. To the extent that employees throughout an organization are empowered to develop and exploit valuable, rare, and costly-to-imitate resources and capabilities in the accomplishment of their job responsibilities, a firm may actually be able to gain sustained competitive advantages.

Competitive Parity and Competitive Advantage

Second, the Resource-Based View suggests that if all a firm does is create value in the same way as its competitors, the best performance it can ever expect to gain is competitive parity. To do better than competitive parity, firms must engage in valuable and rare activities. They must do things to create economic value that other firms have not even thought of, let alone implemented.

This is especially critical for firms that find themselves at a competitive disadvantage. Such a firm certainly should examine its more successful competition, understand what has made this competition so successful, and, where imitation is very low cost, should imitate the successful actions of its competitors. In this sense, benchmarking a firm's performance against the performance of its competitors can be extremely important.

However, if this is all that a firm does, it can only expect to gain competitive parity. Gaining competitive advantage depends on a firm discovering its own unique resources and capabilities and how they can be used in choosing and implementing strategies. For a firm seeking competitive advantage, it is better to be excellent in how it develops and exploits its own unique resources and capabilities than it is to be excellent in how it imitates the resources and capabilities of other firms.

This does not imply that firms must always be "first movers" to gain competitive advantages. Some firms develop valuable, rare, and costly-to-imitate resources and capabilities in being efficient second movers—that is, in rapidly imitating and improving on the product and technological innovations of other firms. Rather than suggesting that firms must always be first movers, the Resource-Based View suggests that, in order to gain competitive advantages, firms must implement strategies that rely on valuable, rare, and costly-to-imitate resources and capabilities, whatever those strategies or resources might be.

Difficult-to-Implement Strategies

Third, as firms contemplate different strategic options, they often ask how difficult and costly it will be to implement different strategies. As long as the cost of implementing a strategy is less than the value that a strategy creates, the Resource-Based View suggests that the critical question facing firms is not "Is a strategy easy to implement or not?" but rather, "Is this strategy easier for us to implement than it is for our competitors to implement?" Firms that already possess the valuable, rare, and costly-to-imitate resources needed to implement a strategy will, in general, find it easier (that is, less costly) to implement a strategy than firms that first have to develop the required resources and then implement the proposed strategy. For firms that already possess a resource, strategy implementation can be natural and swift.

In understanding the relative costs of implementing a strategy, firms can make two errors. First, they can overestimate the uniqueness of the resources they control. Although every firm's history is unique and no two management teams are exactly the same, this does not always mean that a firm's resources and capabilities will be rare. Firms with similar histories operating in similar industries will often develop similar capabilities. If a firm overestimates the rarity of its resources and capabilities, it can overestimate its ability to generate competitive advantages.

For example, when asked what their most critical sources of competitive advantage are, many firms will cite the quality of their top management team, the quality of their technology, and their commitment to excellence in all that they do. When pushed about their competitors, these same firms will admit that they too have high-quality top management teams, high-quality technology, and a commitment to excellence in all that they do. Although these three attributes can be sources of competitive parity, they cannot be sources of competitive advantage.

Second, firms can sometimes underestimate their uniqueness and thus underestimate the extent to which the strategies they pursue can be sources of sustained competitive advantage. When firms possess valuable, rare, and costly-to-imitate resources, strategy implementation can be relatively easy. In this context, it seems reasonable to expect that other firms will be able to quickly imitate this "easy-to-implement" strategy. Of course, this is not the case if these resources controlled by a firm are, in fact, rare and costly to imitate.

In general, firms must take great care not to overestimate or underestimate their uniqueness. An accurate assessment of the value, rarity, and imitability of a firm's resources is necessary to develop an accurate understanding of the relative costs of implementing a firm's strategies and thus the ability of those strategies to generate competitive advantages. Often, firms must employ outside assistance in helping them describe the rarity and imitability of their resources, even though managers in firms will generally be much more familiar with the resources controlled by a firm than outsiders. However, outsiders can provide a measure of objectivity in evaluating the uniqueness of a firm.

Socially Complex Resources

Over the last several decades much has been written about the importance of employee empowerment, organizational culture, and teamwork for firm performance. Most of this work suggests that firms that empower employees, that have an enabling culture, and that encourage teamwork will, on average, make better strategic choices and implement them more efficiently than firms without these organizational attributes. Using the language of the Resource-Based View, most of this work has suggested that employee empowerment, organizational culture, and teamwork, at least in some settings, are economically valuable.

Resource-based logic acknowledges the importance of the value of these organizational attributes. However, it also suggests that these socially complex resources and capabilities can be rare and costly to imitate—and it is these attributes that make it possible for socially complex resources and capabilities to be sources of sustained competitive advantage. Put differently, the Resource-Based View actually extends and broadens traditional analyses of the socially complex attributes of firms. Not only can these attributes be valuable, but they can also be rare and costly to imitate and thus sources of sustained competitive advantage.

The Role of Organization

Finally, resource-based logic suggests that an organization's structure, control systems, and compensation policies should support and enable a firm's efforts to fully exploit the valuable, rare, and costly-to-imitate resources and capabilities it controls. These attributes of organization, by themselves, are usually not sources of sustained competitive advantage.

These observations suggest that if there is a conflict between the resources a firm controls and that firm's organization, the organization should be changed. However, it is often the case that once a firm's structure, control systems, and compensation policies are put in place they remain, regardless of whether or not they are consistent with a firm's underlying resources and capabilities. In such settings, a firm will not be able to realize the full competitive potential of its underlying resource base. To the extent that a firm's resources and capabilities are continuously evolving, its organizational structure, control systems, and compensation policies must also evolve. For these attributes of organization to evolve, managers must be aware of their link with a firm's resources and capabilities and of organizational alternatives.

Internal Analysis in an International Context

The Resource-Based View and the VRIO framework can also be applied in the analysis of firm decisions to enter into international markets. This logic suggests two broad reasons why firms may begin operating in multiple businesses: (1) to take advantage of current resource and capability advantages in new geographic markets and (2) to develop new resource and capability advantages by beginning to operate in new geographic markets. Organizing to implement these international strategies is also important. However, since exploitation of international markets is almost always a specific example of a corporate diversification strategy, the discussion of how to organize such international ventures will be delayed until Chapter 8's analysis of implementing corporate diversification strategies.

Exploiting Current Resource Advantages in New Markets

Suppose a firm already has a sustained competitive advantage in its domestic market. One logical way for a firm with such an advantage to increase its growth and profitability is to exploit those same capabilities in new geographic markets by beginning international operations. However, that a firm's resources are valuable, rare, and costly to imitate in one country does not necessarily mean they will be in a different country.

Several firms have been successful in using their competitive advantage in one country to gain competitive advantages in another country. Coca-Cola, for example, has used its strong brand name—Coke—as a way of entering markets around the world. Currently, Coca-Cola actually sells more Coke products outside of the United States than it sells domestically. Sony used its technical and innovative capabilities, honed in its hypercompetitive home Japanese market, to become a dominant player in the U.S. consumer electronics market. And BMW used its engineering skills developed by building cars to run at 120 mph on the German autobahn to become an important part of the luxury sports sedan market in the United States. In all these cases, what were valuable, rare, and costly-to-imitate resources or capabilities in a firm's home market also turned out to be valuable, rare, and costly-to-imitate resources in nondomestic markets as well.

However, that a resource or capability is a source of sustained competitive advantage in one country does not guarantee that it will also be valuable, or valuable and rare, or valuable, rare, and costly to imitate in another country. For example, Disney has tried to leverage its brand name and its ability to create and manage theme parks internationally. Its theme park in Asia, Tokyo Disneyland, has been a significant financial success. However, the Disney Company has only a small financial stake in Tokyo Disneyland so this theme park's financial success has not benefited Disney that much. On the other hand, Disney's theme park in Europe, EuroDisney, just outside of Paris, France, has been a financial drag on the Disney Company. After several financial restructuring efforts, EuroDisney is finally beginning to have a positive impact on the financial position of Disney Company. But it has taken many years and many millions of dollars to get EuroDisney on a financially secure footing. Apparently, the "Disney experience" at EuroDisney is simply not as valuable as the "Disney experience" in Florida, California, or Tokyo.[39]

When contemplating the exploitation of a firm's valuable, rare, and costly-to-imitate resources and capabilities in a new geographic market, all four of the VRIO questions are important. Certainly, the value of a firm's resources in a new market may differ from the value of those same resources in its home market.

EuroDisney is an example of this problem. Also, if a firm is contemplating entry into a more competitive market than its home market, it is likely that what were rare and costly-to-imitate resources in the home market will be less rare and less costly to imitate in a new, more competitive, geographic market. As some authors have observed, firms looking to take advantage of their resources in new geographic markets are more likely to be successful if their home markets are highly competitive in the first place.[40] If a firm's valuable resources are a source of sustained competitive advantage in a highly competitive home market they are more likely to be sources of sustained competitive advantage in other, less competitive, geographic markets—assuming, of course, they are still valuable.

Developing New Resources and Capabilities in New Markets

One of the most compelling reasons for firms to begin operations outside their domestic markets is to develop new resources and capabilities. By beginning such operations, firms can gain a greater understanding of their strengths and weakness. By exposing these resources and capabilities to new competitive contexts, traditional resources can be modified and new resources can be developed.

Of course, for international operations to affect a firm's resources and capabilities, firms must learn from their experiences in nondomestic markets. Learning in this context is anything but automatic. Many firms that begin operations in a nondomestic market encounter challenges and difficulties and then immediately withdraw from their international efforts. Other firms continue to try to operate internationally but are unable to learn how to modify and change the core resources. One study identified three critical determinants of the ability of a firm to develop new resources and capabilities through its international operations: the intent to learn, the transparency of learning partners, and the receptivity to learning.[41]

A firm that has a strong intent to learn from its international operations is more likely to learn than a firm without this intent. Moreover, this intent must be communicated to all those who work in a firm's international activities. Compare, for example, a quote from a manager whose firm failed to learn from its international operations with a quote from a manager whose firm was able to learn from these operations.[42]

> *Our engineers were just as good as [our partner's]. In fact, theirs were narrower technically, but they had a much better understanding of what the company was trying to accomplish. They knew they were there to learn, our people didn't.*

> *We wanted to make learning an automatic discipline. We asked the staff every day, "What did you learn from [our partner] today?" Learning was carefully monitored and recorded.*

Obviously, the second firm was in a much better position than the first to learn from its international operations and to develop new resources and capabilities.

The transparency of learning partners is also an important determinant of the ability to develop new resources and capabilities from international operations. Some international business partners are more open and accessible than others. These differences can reflect different organizational philosophies, practices, and procedures, as well as differences in the culture of a firm's home country. For example, knowledge in Japanese and many other Asian cultures tends to be context-specific and deeply embedded in the broader social system. This makes it difficult for many Western managers to understand and appreciate the subtlety of

Japanese business practices and Japanese culture. This, in turn, limits the ability of Western managers to learn from their operations in the Japanese market or from their Japanese partners.[43]

In contrast, knowledge in most Western cultures tends to be less context-specific, less deeply embedded in the broader social system. Such knowledge can be written down, can be taught in classes, and can be transmitted, all at a relatively low cost. Japanese managers working in Western economies are more likely to be able to appreciate and understand Western business practices and thus more able to learn from their operations in the West and from their Western partners.

Finally, firms vary in their receptiveness to learning about new resources and capabilities. A firm's receptiveness to such learning is affected by its culture, its operation procedures, and its history. Research suggests that, before firms can learn from their international operations, they must be prepared to unlearn. Unlearning requires a firm to modify or abandon traditional ways of engaging in business. Unlearning can be difficult, especially if a firm has a long history of success using old patterns of behavior, and if those old patterns of behavior are reflected in its organizational structure, formal and informal management controls, and compensation policies.

SUMMARY

The Resource-Based View (RBV) is an economic theory that suggests that firm performance is a function of the types of resources and capabilities firms control. Resources are the tangible and intangible assets a firm uses to conceive of and implement its strategies. Capabilities are a subset of resources and enable a firm to take advantage of its other resources. Resources and capabilities can be categorized into financial, physical, human, and organizational resource categories.

The RBV makes two assumptions about resources and capabilities: the assumption of resource heterogeneity (that some resources and capabilities may be heterogeneously distributed across competing firms) and the assumption of resource immobility (that this heterogeneity may be long lasting). These two assumptions can be used to describe conditions under which firms will gain competitive advantages by exploiting their resources.

A tool for analyzing a firm's internal strengths and weaknesses can be derived from the RBV. Called the VRIO framework, this tool asks four questions about a firm's resources and capabilities in order to evaluate their competitive potential. These questions are: the Question of Value, the Question of Rarity, the Question of Imitability, and the Question of Organization.

A firm's resources and capabilities are valuable when they enable it to exploit external opportunities or neutralize external threats. Such valuable resources and capabilities are a firm's strengths. Resources and capabilities that are not valuable are a firm's weaknesses. Using valuable resources to exploit external opportunities or neutralize external threats will have the effect of increasing a firm's net revenues or decreasing its net costs.

One way to identify a firm's valuable resources and capabilities is by examining its value chain. A firm's value chain is the list of business activities it engages in to develop, produce, and sell its products or services. Different stages in this value chain require different resources and capabilities, and differences in value-chain choices across firms can lead to important differences among the resources and capabilities controlled by different companies. Two generic value chains have been developed, one by McKinsey and Company and the second by Michael Porter.

Valuable and common (that is, not rare) resources and capabilities can be a source of competitive parity. Failure to invest in such resources can create a competitive disadvantage for a firm. Valuable and rare resources can be a source of at least a temporary competitive advantage. There are fewer firms able to control such a resource and still exploit it as a source of at least temporary competitive advantage than there are firms that will generate perfect competition dynamics in an industry.

Valuable, rare, and costly-to-imitate resources and capabilities can be a source of sustained competitive advantage. Imitation can occur through direct duplication or through substitution. There are at least four reasons a firm's resources and capabilities may be costly to imitate: unique historical circumstances, causal ambiguity, socially complex resources and capabilities, and patents.

To take full advantage of the potential of its resources and capabilities, a firm must be appropriately organized. A firm's organization consists of its formal reporting structure, its formal and informal control processes, and its compensation policy. These are complementary resources in that they are rarely sources of competitive advantage on their own.

The VRIO framework can be used to identify the competitive implications of a firm's resources and capabilities—whether they are a source of competitive disadvantage, competitive parity, temporary competitive advantage, or sustained competitive advantage—and the extent to which these resources and capabilities are strengths or weaknesses.

When a firm faces a competitor that has a sustained competitive advantage, it can not respond, can change its tactics, or change its strategies. There are at least three reasons why a firm may choose not to respond in this setting. First, a response might weaken its own sources of sustained competitive advantage. Second, a firm may not have the resources required to respond. Third, a firm may be trying to create or maintain tacit cooperation within an industry.

The RBV has a series of broader managerial implications as well. For example, this logic suggests that competitive advantage is every employee's responsibility. It also suggests that if all a firm does is what its competition does, it can gain only competitive parity, and that in gaining competitive advantage it is better for a firm to exploit its own valuable, rare, and costly-to-imitate resources than to imitate the valuable and rare resources of a competitor. Also, resource-based logic implies that as long as the cost of strategy implementation is less than the value of strategy implementation, the relative cost of implementing a strategy is more important for competitive advantage than the absolute cost of implementing a strategy. It implies as well that firms can systematically overestimate and underestimate their uniqueness. With regard to a firm's resources and capabilities, resource-based logic suggests that not only can employee empowerment, organizational culture, and teamwork be valuable; they can also be sources of sustained competitive advantage. Also, if conflicts arise between a firm's valuable, rare, and costly-to-imitate resources and a firms organization, the organization should be changed.

Finally, resource-based theory and the VRIO framework can also be applied in an international context. In general, firms pursue international opportunities to either exploit their currently valuable, rare, and costly-to-imitate resources and capabilities in new markets or to develop new resources and capabilities. The ability to develop new resources and capabilities through international operations depends on a firm's intent to learn, the transparency of its international business partners, and its receptiveness to learning.

CHALLENGE QUESTIONS

1. Which approach to strategy formulation is more likely to generate economic profits: (a) evaluating external opportunities and threats and then developing resources and capabilities to exploit these opportunities and neutralize these threats or (b) evaluating internal resources and capabilities and then searching for industries where they can be exploited? Why?

2. Which firm will have a higher level of economic performance: (a) a firm with valuable, rare, and costly-to-imitate resources and capabilities operating in a very attractive industry or (b) a firm with valuable, rare, and costly-to-imitate resources and capabilities operating in a very unattractive industry? Assume both these firms are appropriately organized. Explain your answer.

3. Which is more critical to sustaining human life—water or diamonds? Why do firms that provide water to customers generally earn lower economic performance than firms that provide diamonds?

4. Will a firm currently experiencing competitive parity be able to gain sustained competitive advantages by studying another firm that is currently experiencing sustained competitive advantages? Why or why not?

5. Your former college roommate calls you and asks to borrow $10,000 so that he can open a pizza restaurant in his hometown. He acknowledges that there is a high degree of rivalry in this market, that the cost of entry is low, and that there are numerous substitutes for pizza, but he believes that his pizza restaurant will have some sustained competitive advantages. For example, he is going to have sawdust on his floor, a variety of imported beers, and a late-night delivery service. Will you lend him the money? Why or why not?

6. In the text, it is suggested that Boeing did not respond to Airbus's announcement of the development of a super-jumbo aircraft. Assuming this aircraft will give Airbus a competitive advantage in the segment of the airliner business that supplies airplanes for long international flights, why did Boeing not respond?

a. Does it have its own competitive advantage that it does not want to abandon?

b. Does it not have the resources and capabilities needed to respond?

c. Is it trying to reduce the level of rivalry in this industry?

7. Which firm is more likely to be successful in exploiting its sources of sustained competitive advantage in its home market in a highly competitive, nondomestic market: a firm from a less competitive home country or a firm from a more competitive home country? Why?

8. What are some indicators that a firm is engaging in an international strategy to develop new resources and capabilities?

PROBLEM SET

1. Apply the VRIO framework in the following settings. Will the actions described be a source of competitive disadvantage, parity, temporary advantage, or sustained competitive advantage, and why?

(a) Procter Gamble introduces new, smaller packaging for its laundry detergent Tide.

(b) American Airlines announces a 5 percent across-the-board reduction in airfares.

(c) The Korean automobile firm Hyundai announces a 10-year, 100,000 mile warranty on its cars.

(d) Microsoft makes it easier to transfer data and information from Microsoft Word to Microsoft Excel.

(e) Merck is able to coordinate the work of its chemists and biologists in the development of new drugs.

(f) Ford patents a new kind of brake pad for its cars.

(g) Ashland Chemical, a specialty chemical company, patents a new specialty chemical.

(h) The New York Yankees sign all-star pitcher Randy Johnson to a long-term contract.

(i) Michael Dell uses the money he has made from Dell Computers to purchase the Dallas Cowboys football team.

(j) Ted Turner uses the money he has made from his broadcasting empire to purchase the Atlanta Braves baseball team.

2. Identify three firms you might want to work for. Using the VRIO framework, evaluate the extent to which the resources and capabilities of these firms gives them the potential to realize competitive disadvantages, parity, temporary advantages, or sustained advantages. What implications, if any, does this analysis have for the company you might want to work for?

3. You have been assigned to estimate the present value of a potential construction project for your company. How would you use the VRIO framework to construct the cash flow analysis that is a part of any present-value calculation?

END NOTES

1. The term "the Resource-Based View" was coined by Wernerfelt, B. (1984). "A resource-based view of the firm." *Strategic Management Journal*, 5, pp. 171–180. Some important early contributors to this theory include Rumelt, R. P. (1984). "Toward a strategic theory of the firm." In R. Lamb (ed.), *Competitive strategic Management* (pp. 556–570). Upper Saddle River, NJ: Prentice Hall; and Barney, J. B. (1986). "Strategic factor markets: Expectations, luck and business strategy." *Management Science*, 32, pp. 1512–1514. A second wave of important early resource-based theoretical work includes Barney, J. B. (1991). "Firm resources and sustained competitive advantage." *Journal of Management*, 7, pp. 49–64; Dierickx, I., and K. Cool (1989). "Asset stock accumulation and sustainability of competitive advantage." *Management Science*, 35, pp. 1504–1511; Conner, K. R. (1991). "A historical comparison of resource-based theory and five schools of thought within industrial organization economics: Do we have a new theory of the firm?" *Journal of Management*, 17(1), pp. 121–154; and Peteraf, M. A. (1993). "The cornerstones of competitive advantage: A resource-based view." *Strategic Management Journal*, 14, pp. 179–191. A review of much of this early theoretical literature can be found in Mahoney, J. T., and J. R. Pandian (1992). "The resource-based view within the conversation of strategic management." *Strategic Management Journal*, 13, pp. 363–380. The theoretical perspective has also spawned a growing body of empirical work, including Brush, T. H., and K. W. Artz (1999). "Toward a contingent resource-based theory." *Strategic Management Journal*, 20, pp. 223–250; Marcus, A., and D. Geffen (1998). "The dialectics of competency acquisition." *Strategic Management Journal*, 19, pp. 1145–1168; Brush, T. H., P. Bromiley, and M. Hendrickx (1999). "The relative influence of industry and corporation on business segment performance." *Strategic Management Journal*, 20, pp. 519–547; Yeoh, P.-L., and K. Roth (1999). "An empirical analysis of sustained advantage in the U.S. pharmaceutical industry." *Strategic Management Journal*, 20, pp. 637–653; Roberts, P. (1999). "Product innovation, product-market competition and persistent profitability in the U.S. pharmaceutical industry." *Strategic Management Journal*, 20, pp. 655–670; Gulati, R. (1999). "Network location and learning." *Strategic Management Journal*, 20, pp. 397–420; Lorenzoni, G., and A. Lipparini (1999). "The leveraging of interfirm relationships as a distinctive organizational capability." *Strategic Management Journal*, 20, pp. 317–338; Majumdar, S. (1998). "On the utilization of resources." *Strategic Management Journal*, 19(9) pp. 809–831; Makadok, R. (1997). "Do inter-firm differences in capabilities affect strategic pricing dynamics?" *Academy of Management Proceedings* '97, pp. 30–34; Silverman, B. S., J. A. Nickerson, and J. Freeman (1997). "Profitability, transactional alignment, and organizational mortality in the U.S. trucking industry." *Strategic Management Journal*, 18 (Summer special issue), pp. 31–52; Powell, T. C., and A. Dent-Micallef (1997). "Information technology as competitive advantage." *Strategic Management Journal*, 18(5), pp. 375–405; Miller, D., and J. Shamsie (1996). "The Resource-Based View of the firm in two environments." *Academy of Management Journal*, 39(3), pp. 519–543; and Maijoor, S., and A. Van Witteloostuijn (1996). "An empirical test of the resource-based theory." *Strategic Management Journal*, 17, pp. 549–569; Barnett, W. P., H. R. Greve, and D. Y. Park (1994). "An evolutionary model of organizational performance." *Strategic Management Journal*, 15 (Winter special issue), pp. 11–28; Levinthal, D., and J. Myatt (1994). "Co-evolution of capabilities and industry: The evolution of mutual fund processing." *Strategic Management Journal*, 17, pp. 45–62; Henderson, R., and I. Cockburn (1994). "Measuring competence? Exploring firm effects in pharmaceutical research." *Strategic Management Journal*, 15, pp. 63–84; Pisano, G. P. (1994). "Knowledge, integration, and the locus of learning: An empirical

analysis of process development." *Strategic Management Journal*, 15, pp. 85–100; and Zajac, E. J., and J. D. Westphal (1994). "The costs and benefits of managerial incentives and monitoring in large U.S. corporations: When is more not better?" *Strategic Management Journal*, 15, pp. 121–142.

2. Ghemawat, P. (1986). "Wal-Mart stores' discount operations." Harvard Business School Case No. 9-387-018, on Wal-Mart; Kupfer, A. (1991). "The champion of cheap clones." *Fortune*, September 23, pp. 115–120; and Holder, D. (1989). "L. L. Bean, Inc.—1974." Harvard Business School Case No. 9-676-014, on L. L. Bean. Some of Wal-Mart's more recent moves, especially its international acquisitions, are described in Laing, J. R. (1999). "Blimey! Wal-Mart." *Barron's*, 79, p. 14. L. L. Bean's lethargic performance in the 1990s, together with its turnaround plan, is described in Symonds, W. (1998). "Paddling harder at L.L. Bean." *BusinessWeek*, Dec. 7, p. 72.

3. For an early discussion of the importance of human capital in firms, see Becker, G. S. (1964). *Human capital*. New York: Columbia University Press.

4. Heskett, J. L., and R. H. Hallowell (1993). "Southwest Airlines: 1993 (A)." Harvard Business School Case No. 9-695-023.

5. See Jay Barney (1991). "Firm resources and sustained competitive advantage." *Journal of Management*, 17, pp. 99–120.

6. See Schlender, B. R. (1992). "How Sony keeps the magic going." *Fortune*, February 24, pp. 75–84; and (1999). "The weakling kicks back." *The Economist*, July 3, p. 46, for a discussion at Sony. See Krogh, L., J. Praeger, D. Sorenson, and J. Tomlinson (1988). "How 3M evaluates its R&D programs." *Research Technology Management*, 31, pp. 10–14.

7. George Anders (2002). "AOL's true believers." *Fast Company*, July pp. 96 +.

8. See Grant, R. M. (1991). *Contemporary strategy analysis*. Cambridge, MA: Basil Blackwell.

9. Porter, M. E. (1987). *Competitive advantage*. New York: Free Press.

10. Lipman, S., and R. Rumelt (1982). "Uncertain imitability: An analysis of interfirm differences in efficiency under competition." *Bell Journal of Economics*, 13, pp. 418–438; Barney, J. B. (1986). "Strategic factor markets: Expectations, luck and business strategy." *Management Science*, 32, pp. 1512–1514; and Barney, J. B. (1986). "Organizational culture: Can it be a source of sustained competitive advantage?" *Academy of Management Review*, 11, pp. 656–665.

11. Note that the definition of sustained competitive advantage presented here, though different, is consistent with the definition given in Chapter 1. In particular, a firm that enjoys a competitive advantage for a long period of time (the Chapter 1 definition) does not have its advantage competed away through imitation (the Chapter 3 definition).

12. See Breen, Bill (2003). "What's selling in America." *Fast Company*, January, pp. 80 +.

13. These explanations of costly imitation were first developed by Dierickx, I., and K. Cool (1989). "Asset stock accumulation and sustainability of competitive advantage." *Management Science*, 35, pp. 1504–1511; Barney, J. B. (1991). "Firm resources and sustained competitive advantage." *Journal of Management*, 7, pp. 49–64; Mahoney, J. T., and J. R. Pandian (1992). "The resource-based view within the conversation of strategic management." *Strategic Management Journal*, 13, pp. 363–380; and Peteraf, M. A. (1993). "The cornerstones of competitive advantage: A resource-based view." *Strategic Management Journal*, 14, pp. 179–191.

14. Dierickx, I., and K. Cool (1989). "Asset stock accumulation and sustainability of competitive advantage." *Management Science*, 35,

pp. 1504–1511. In economics, the role of history in determining competitive outcomes was first examined by Arthur, W. B. (1989). "Competing technologies, increasing returns, and lock-in by historical events." *Economic Journal*, 99, pp. 116–131.

15. See Breen, Bill (2003). "What's selling in America." *Fast Company*, January, pp. 80 +.

16. This term was first suggested by Arthur, W. B. (1989). "Competing technologies, increasing returns, and lock-in by historical events." *Economic Journal*, 99, pp. 116–131. A good example of path dependence is the development of Silicon Valley and the important role that Stanford University and a few early firms played in creating the network of organizations that has since become the center of much of the electronics business. See Alley, J. (1997). "The heart of Silicon Valley." *Fortune*, July 7, pp. 86 +.

17. Reed, R., and R. J. DeFillippi (1990). "Causal ambiguity, barriers to imitation, and sustainable competitive advantage." *Academy of Management Review*, 15(1), pp. 88–102, suggest that causal ambiguity about the sources of a firm's competitive advantage need only exist among a firm's competitors for it to be a source of sustained competitive advantage. Managers in a firm, they argue, may fully understand the sources of their advantage. However, in a world where employees freely and frequently move from firm to firm, such special insights into the sources of a firm's competitive advantage would not remain proprietary for very long. For this reason, for causal ambiguity to be a source of sustained competitive advantage, both the firm trying to gain such an advantage and those trying to imitate it must face similar levels of causal ambiguity. Indeed, Wal-Mart recently sued Amazon.com for trying to steal some of its secrets by hiring employees away from Wal-Mart. See Nelson, E. (1998). "Wal-Mart accuses Amazon.com of stealing its secrets in lawsuit." *Wall Street Journal*, October 19, p. B10. For a discussion of how difficult it is to maintain secrets, especially in a world of the World Wide Web, see Farnham, A. (1997). "How safe are your secrets?" *Fortune*, September 8, pp. 114 +. The international dimensions of the challenges associated with maintaining secrets are discussed in Robinson, E. (1998). "China spies target corporate America." *Fortune*, March 30, pp. 118 +.

18. Itami, H. (1987). *Mobilizing invisible assets*, Cambridge, MA: Harvard University Press.

19. See Barney, J. B., and B. Tyler (1990). "The attributes of top management teams and sustained competitive advantage." In M. Lawless and L. Gomez-Mejia (eds.), *Managing the High Technology Firm* (pp. 33–48). Greenwich, CT: JAI Press, on teamwork in top management teams; Barney, J. B. (1986). "Organizational culture: Can it be a source of sustained competitive advantage?" *Academy of Management Review*, 11, pp. 656–665, on organizational culture; Henderson, R. M., and I. Cockburn, (1994). "Measuring competence? Exploring firm effects in pharmaceutical research." *Strategic Management Journal*, 15, pp. 63–84, on relationships among employees; and Dyer, J. H., and H. Singh (1998). "The relational view: Cooperative strategy and sources of interorganizational competitive advantage." *Academy of Management Review*, 23(4), pp. 660–679, on relationships with suppliers and customers.

20. Management at Electronic Arts is described in Salter, Chuck (2002). "Playing to win." *Fast Company*, December, pp. 80 +.

21. For a discussion of knowledge as a source of competitive advantage in the popular business press, see Stewart, T. (1995). "Getting real about brain power." *Fortune*, November 27, pp. 201 +; Stewart, T. (1995). "Mapping corporate knowledge." *Fortune*, October 30, pp. 209 +. For the academic version of this same issue, see Simonin, B. L. (1999). "Ambiguity and the process of knowledge transfer in strategic alliances." *Strategic Management Journal*, 20(7), pp. 595–623; Spender, J. C. (1996). "Making knowledge the basis of a dynamic theory of the firm." *Strategic Management Journal*, 17 (Winter special issue), pp. 109–122; Hatfield, D. D., J. P. Liebeskind, and T. C. Opler (1996). "The effects of corporate restructuring on aggregate industry specialization." *Strategic Management Journal*, 17, pp. 55–72; and Grant, R. M. (1996). "Toward a knowledge-based theory of the firm." *Strategic Management Journal*, 17 (Winter special issue), pp. 109–122.

22. Porras, J., and P. O. Berg (1978). "The impact of organizational development." *Academy of Management Review*, 3, pp. 249–266, have done one of the few empirical studies on whether or not systematic efforts to change socially complex resources are effective. They found that such efforts are usually not effective. Although this study is getting older, it is unlikely that current change methods will be any more effective than the methods examined by these authors.

23. See Hambrick, D. (1987). "Top management teams: Key to strategic success." *California Management Review*, 30, pp. 88–108, on top management teams; Barney, J. B. (1986). "Organizational culture: Can it be a source of sustained competitive advantage?" *Academy of Management Review*, 11, pp. 656–665, on culture; Porter, M. E. (1980). *Competitive strategy*. New York: Free Press; and Klein, B., and K. Leffler (1981). "The role of market forces in assuring contractual performance." *Journal of Political Economy*, 89, pp. 615–641, on relations with customers.

24. See Harris, L. C., and E. Ogbonna (1999). "Developing a market oriented culture: A critical evaluation." *Journal of Management Studies*, 36(2), pp. 177–196.

25. Lieberman, M. B. (1987). "The learning curve, diffusion, and competitive strategy." *Strategic Management Journal*, 8, pp. 441–452, has a very good analysis of the cost of imitation in the chemical industry. See also Lieberman, M. B., and D. B. Montgomery (1988). "First-mover advantages." *Strategic Management Journal*, 9, pp. 41–58.

26. Rumelt, R. P. (1984). "Toward a strategic theory of the firm." In R. Lamb (ed.), *Competitive strategic management* (pp. 556–570). Upper Saddle River, NJ: Prentice Hall, among others, cites patents as a source of costly imitation.

27. There is currently significant debate about the patentability of different kinds of products. For example, while typefaces are not patentable (and cannot be copyrighted), the process for displaying typefaces may be. See Thurm, S. (1998). "Copy this typeface? Court ruling counsels caution." *Wall Street Journal*, July 15, pp. B1 +.

28. For an insightful discussion of these complementary resources, see Amit, R., and P.J.H. Schoemaker (1993). "Strategic assets and organizational rent." *Strategic Management Journal*, 14(1), pp. 33–45.

29. See Kearns, D. T., and D. A. Nadler (1992). *Prophets in the dark*. New York: HarperCollins; and Smith, D. K., and R. C. Alexander (1988). *Fumbling the future*. New York: William Morrow.

30. Information about Dell Computers was taken from Brown, E. (1999). "America's most admired companies." *Fortune*, March 1, pp. 68 +; Kirkpatrick, D. (1998). "The second coming at Apple." *Fortune*, November 9, pp. 96 +; and Hamel, G., and J. Sampler (1998). "The e-corporation." *Fortune*, December 7, pp. 80 +.

31. Indeed, many other firms, including Compaq and Hewlett-Packard, have begun using the net to sell their products. See McWilliams, G. (1998). "Mimicking Dell, Compaq to sell its PC directly." *Wall Street Journal*, November 11, pp. B1 +

32. (2004). "Gateway will close remaining retail stores." *Wall Street Journal*, April 2, p. B2; Michaels, D. (2004). "AA Airbus, picturing huge jet was easy; building it was hard." *Wall Street Journal*, May 27, pp. A1 +; Zeller, W., A. Michael, and L. Woellert (2004). "The airline debate over cheap seats." *Wall Street Journal*, May 24, pp. A1 +.

33. (2004). "Casio." *Marketing*, May 6, p. 95; Weisul, K. (2003). "When time is money—and art." *BusinessWeek*, July 21, p. 86.

34. That said, there have been some "cracks" in Southwest's capabilities armor lately. Its CEO suddenly resigned, and its level of profitability dropped precipitously in 2004. Whether these are indicators that Southwest's core strengths are being dissipated or there are short-term problems is not yet known. However, Southwest's stumbling would give USAir some hope. Trottman, M., S. McCartney, and J. Lublin (2004). "Southwest's CEO abruptly quits 'draining job'." *Wall Street Journal*, July 16, pp. A1 +.

35. One should consult a lawyer before one gets involved in these forms of tacit cooperation.

36. This aspect of the competitive dynamics in an industry is discussed in Smith, K. G., C. M. Grimm, and M. J. Gannon (1992). *Dynamics of competitive strategy*. Newberry Park, CA: Sage.

37. Schlender, B. R. (1992). "How Sony keeps the magic going." *Fortune*, February 24, pp. 75–84.

38. Personal communication.

39. Collis, D. (1988). "The Walt Disney Company (A): Corporate strategy." HBS Case No. 1-388-147; Rukstad, N. M., and D. Collis (2001). "The Walt Disney Company: The entertainment king." HBS Case No. 9-701-035.

40. Porter, M. E. (1990). *The competitive advantage of nations*. New York: Free Press.

41. See Hamel, G. (1991). "Competition for competence and inter-partner learning within international strategic alliances." *Strategic Management Journal*, 12, pp. 83–103.

42. Quoted in Hamel, G. (1991). "Competition for competence and inter-partner learning within international strategic alliances." *Strategic Management Journal*, 12, p. 86.

43. See, for example, Peterson, R. B., and J. Y. Shimada (1978). "Sources of management problems in Japanese-American joint ventures." *Academy of Management Review*, 3, pp. 796–804.

2

BUSINESS LEVEL
STRATEGIES

4

Cost Leadership

It is already the largest firm in the United States, with 2002 revenues of almost $250 billion, profits of over $8 billion, and almost 1.5 million employees. Not bad for a company that began with a single store in 1945, had only 38 stores in 1970, and now has over 4,000 stores!

So, how has Wal-Mart done it, and can it keep it going? At Wal-Mart's current growth rate of 16 percent per year it will be the first company with over $1 trillion in sales within 10 years. At that

Can Wal-Mart Keep It Going?

size, Wal-Mart would have more than 5 million employees—about half the size of the U.S. military during World War II and more people than are employed by the U.S. government. Wal-Mart's sales would approximately equal the Gross Domestic Product (GDP) of the United Kingdom and be sub-

stantially larger than the GDP of Australia, Canada, and Spain; and nearly 10 percent of the GDP of the United States.

The strategy behind this growth is remarkably simple. Wal-Mart exploits its enormous size to get the best prices possible from its suppliers and then passes most of these savings on to customers. This enables people of modest means to purchase items that historically have only been available to wealthier consumers. Only firms with Wal-Mart's huge purchasing power can implement this

114

Learning Objectives

After reading this chapter, you should be able to:

1. Define cost leadership.

2. Identify six reasons firms can differ in their costs.

3. Identify four reasons economies of scale can exist and four reasons diseconomies of scale can exist.

4. Explain the relationship between cost advantages due to learning curve economies and a firm's market share, as well as the limitations of this logic.

5. Identify how cost leadership helps neutralize each of the major threats in an industry.

6. Identify the bases of cost leadership that are more likely to be rare and costly to imitate.

7. Explain how firms use a functional organizational structure to implement business-level strategies like cost leadership.

8. Describe the formal and informal management controls and compensation policies firms use to implement cost leadership strategies.

9. Explain how international operations can affect a firm's cost position.

---

strategy—and there are no other retail firms with Wal-Mart's purchasing power.

Of course, the path to endless growth at Wal-Mart is far from certain. The firm faces both external and internal challenges. Externally, several cities around the United States have successfully fought off Wal-Mart's attempt to build new stores in their communities. These cities argue that Wal-Marts tend to destroy traditional downtown shopping areas, part of a small town lifestyle that citizens in these cities don't want to lose. Also, Wal-Mart has yet to prove that it can export its strategy around the world. While its operations in the United Kingdom are profitable, it has taken years for its operations in Mexico to begin to turn a profit, and there is some uncertainty about Wal-Mart's long term success in Germany.

Internally, Wal-Mart faces the difficult challenge of expanding its size without losing the unique organizational culture that has helped it get to its current level of success. Indeed, many observers have been surprised that Wal-Mart has been able to retain the enthusiastic, down home, "rah-rah" culture originally created by Sam Walton, the founder of Wal-Mart. This culture, which helps create a sense of loyalty between Wal-Mart and its employees, requires continuous investment to remain healthy and vital. And the question remains: "Is it really possible to have a culture that unites 5 million employees?"

Sources: J. Collins (2003). "Bigger, better, faster." *Fast Company*, June, pp. 74 +; B. Breen (2003). "What's selling in America?" *Fast Company*, January, pp. 80 +; P. Ghemewat (1993). "Wal-Mart discount store operations." Harvard Business School Case No. 9-387-018.

Wal-Mart's success has, to this point in time, been almost unimaginable. It is especially striking since one of its major competitors—Kmart—was going through bankruptcy at the same time that Wal-Mart was becoming the largest firm in the United States. And Wal-Mart and Kmart sell just about the same products. Why is it that two firms operating in the same industry, selling the same products to the same customers, can have such different levels of performance? Well, as we have seen, Wal-Mart has been able to use its volume of sales to extract low prices from its suppliers, which it then passes on to customers in the form of lower prices. This is a classic cost leadership strategy, the business strategy that is the topic of this chapter. Kmart has been unable to implement a similar strategy and thus has not enjoyed the same success.

What Is Business-Level Strategy?

Part One of this book introduced you to the basic tools required to conduct a strategic analysis: tools for analyzing external threats and opportunities (in Chapter 2) and tools for analyzing internal strengths and weaknesses (in Chapter 3). Once you have completed these two analyses, it is possible to begin making strategic choices. As was explained in Chapter 1, strategic choices fall into two large categories: business strategies and corporate strategies. **Business-level strategies** are actions firms take to gain competitive advantages in a single market or industry. **Corporate-level strategies** are actions firms take to gain competitive advantages by operating in multiple markets or industries simultaneously.

The two business-level strategies discussed in this book are cost leadership (this chapter) and product differentiation (Chapter 5). The importance of these two business-level strategies is so widely recognized that they are often called **generic business strategies**.

What Is Cost Leadership?

A firm that chooses a **cost leadership business strategy** focuses on gaining advantages by reducing its costs to below those of all its competitors. This does not mean that this firm abandons other business or corporate strategies. Indeed, a single-minded focus on *just* reducing costs can lead a firm to make low-cost products that no one wants to buy. However, a firm pursuing a cost leadership strategy focuses much of its effort on keeping its costs low.

Numerous firms have pursued cost leadership strategies. Wal-Mart clearly follows this strategy, as does Timex and Casio in the watch industry and BIC in the disposable pen and razor market. All these firms advertise their products. However, these advertisements tend to emphasize reliability and low prices—the kinds of product attributes that are usually emphasized by firms pursuing cost leadership strategies.

In automobiles, Hyundai has implemented a cost leadership strategy with its emphasis on low-priced cars for basic transportation. Like Timex, Casio, and BIC, Hyundai spends a significant amount of money advertising its products, but its advertisements tend to emphasize its sporty styling and high gas mileage. Hyundai is positioned as a fun and inexpensive car, not a high-performance sports car or a luxurious status symbol. Hyundai's ability to sell these fun and inexpensive automobiles depends on its design choices (keep it simple) and its low manufacturing costs.[1]

Table 4.1 **Important Sources of Cost Advantages for Firms**

1. Size differences and economies of scale
2. Size differences and diseconomies of scale
3. Experience differences and learning-curve economies
4. Differential low-cost access to productive inputs
5. Technological advantages independent of scale
6. Policy choices

Sources of Cost Advantages

There are many reasons why an individual firm may have a cost advantage over its competitors. Cost advantages are possible even when competing firms produce similar products. Some of the most important of these sources of cost advantage are listed in Table 4.1, and discussed in this section.

Size Differences and Economies of Scale

One of the most widely cited sources of cost advantages for a firm is its size. When there are significant economies of scale in manufacturing, marketing, distribution, service, or other functions of a business, larger firms (up to some point) have a cost advantage over smaller firms. The concept of economies of scale was first defined in Chapter 2. **Economies of scale** are said to exist when the increase in firm size (measured in terms of volume of production) is associated with lower costs (measured in terms of average costs per unit of production), as depicted in Figure 4.1. As the volume of production in a firm increases, the average cost per unit decreases until some optimal volume of production (point X) is reached, after which the average costs per unit of production begin to rise because of **diseconomies of scale** (a concept discussed in more detail later in this chapter).

   If the relationship between volume of production and average costs per unit of production depicted in Figure 4.1 holds, and if a firm in an industry has the largest volume of production (but not greater than the optimal level, X), then that firm will have a cost advantage in that industry. There are several reasons why increasing the volume of production in a firm can reduce a firm's costs.

Figure 4.1 Economies of Scale

Table 4.2   **Why Higher Volumes of Production in a Firm Can Lead to Lower Costs**

With higher production volume . . .
1. firms can use specialized machines . . .
2. firms can build larger plants . . .
3. firms can increase employee specialization . . .
4. firms can spread overhead costs across more units produced . . .
. . . which can lower per unit production costs.

Some of the most important of these reasons are summarized in Table 4.2 and discussed below.

Volume of Production and Specialized Machines. When a firm has high levels of production, it is often able to purchase and use specialized manufacturing tools that cannot be kept in operation in small firms. Manufacturing managers at BIC Corporation, for example, have emphasized this important advantage of high volumes of production. A former director of manufacturing at BIC once observed:

> We are in the automation business. Because of our large volume, one tenth of 1 cent in savings turns out to be enormous. . . . One advantage of the high–volume business is that you can get the best equipment and amortize it entirely over a short period of time (4 to 5 months). I'm always looking for new equipment. If I see a cost–savings machine, I can buy it. I'm not constrained by money.[2]

Only firms with BIC's level of production in the pen industry have the ability to reduce their costs in this manner.

Volume of Production and the Cost of Plant and Equipment. High volumes of production may also allow a firm to build larger manufacturing operations. In some industries, the cost of building these manufacturing operations per unit of production is lower than the cost of building smaller manufacturing operations per unit of production. Thus large-volume firms, other factors being equal, will be able to build lower per unit cost manufacturing operations and will have lower average costs of production.

The link between volume of production and the cost of building manufacturing operations is particularly important in industries characterized by **process manufacturing**—chemical, oil refining, paper and pulp manufacturing, and so forth. Because of the physical geometry of process manufacturing facilities, the costs of constructing a processing plant with increased capacity can be expected to rise as the two–thirds power of a plant's capacity. This is because the area of the surface of some three-dimensional containers (such as spheres and cylinders) increases at a slower rate than the volume of these containers. Thus, larger containers hold greater volumes and require less material per unit volume for the outside skins of these containers. Up to some point, increases in capacity come at a less-than-proportionate rise in the cost of building this capacity.[3]

For example, it might cost a firm $100 to build a plant with a capacity of 1,000 units, for a per-unit average cost of $.01. But, assuming the "two-thirds rule" applies, it might cost a firm $465 to build a plant with a capacity of 10,000 units ($465 = 10,000^{2/3}$), for a per unit average cost of $.0046. The difference between $.01 per unit and $.0046 per unit represents a cost advantage for a large firm.

Volume of Production and Employee Specialization. High volumes of production are also associated with high levels of employee specialization. As workers specialize in accomplishing a narrow task, they can become more and more efficient at this task, thereby reducing their firm's costs. This reasoning applies both in specialized manufacturing tasks (such as the highly specialized manufacturing functions in an assembly line) and in specialized management functions (such as the highly specialized managerial functions of accounting, finance, and sales).

Smaller firms often do not possess the volume of production needed to justify this level of employee specialization. With smaller volumes of production, highly specialized employees may not have enough work to keep them busy an entire workday. This low volume of production is one reason why smaller firms often have employees that perform multiple business functions and often use outside contract employees and part-time workers to accomplish highly specialized functions like accounting, taxes, and human resource management.

Volume of Production and Overhead Costs. A firm with high volumes of production has the luxury of spreading its overhead costs over more units and thereby reducing the overhead costs per unit. Suppose, in a particular industry, that the operation of a variety of accounting, control, and research and development functions, regardless of a firm's size, is $100,000. Clearly, a firm that manufactures 1,000 units is imposing a cost of $100 per unit to cover overhead expenses. However, a firm that manufactures 10,000 units is imposing a cost of $10 per unit to cover overhead. Again, the larger-volume firm's average per unit costs are lower than the small-volume firm's average per unit cost.

Size Differences and Diseconomies of Scale
Just as economies of scale can generate cost advantages for larger firms, important diseconomies of scale can actually increase costs if firms grow too large. As Figure 4.1 shows, if the volume of production rises beyond some optimal point (point X in the figure), this can actually lead to an increase in per-unit costs. If other firms in an industry have grown beyond the optimal firm size, a smaller firm (with a level of production closer to the optimal) may obtain a cost advantage even when all firms in the industry are producing very similar products. Some important sources of diseconomies of scale for a firm are listed in Table 4.3 and discussed in this section.

Physical Limits to Efficient Size. Applying the two–thirds rule to the construction of manufacturing facilities seems to imply, for some industries at least, that larger is always better. However, there are some important physical limitations to the size of some manufacturing processes. Engineers have found, for example, that cement kilns develop unstable internal aerodynamics above 7 million barrels per year capacity. Others have suggested that scaling up nuclear reactors from small installations to huge facilities generates forces and physical processes that, though nondetectable in smaller facilities, can become significant in larger operations. These physical limitations on manufacturing processes reflect the underlying physics and engineering in a manufacturing process and suggest when the cost curve in Figure 4.1 will begin to rise.[4]

Table 4.3 **Major Sources of Diseconomies of Scale**

When the volume of production gets too large . . .
1. physical limits to efficient size . . .
2. managerial diseconomies . . .
3. worker de-motivation. . . .
4. distance to markets and suppliers . . .
. . . can increase per-unit costs.

Managerial Diseconomies. Although the underlying physics and engineering in a manufacturing process have an important impact on a firm's costs, managerial diseconomies are perhaps an even more important cause of these cost increases. As a firm increases in size, it often increases in complexity, and the ability of managers to control and operate it efficiently becomes limited.

One well-known example of a manufacturing plant that grew too large and thus became inefficient is Crown, Cork and Seal's can-manufacturing plant in Philadelphia. Through the early part of this century, this Philadelphia facility handled as many as 75 different can-manufacturing lines. The most efficient plants in the industry, however, were running from 10 to 15 lines simultaneously. The huge Philadelphia facility was simply too large to operate efficiently and was characterized by large numbers of breakdowns, a high percentage of idle lines, and poor-quality products.[5]

Worker De-Motivation. A third source of diseconomies of scale depends on the relationship between firm size, employee specialization, and employee motivation. It has already been suggested that one of the advantages of increased volumes of production is that it allows workers to specialize in smaller and more narrowly defined production tasks. With specialization, workers become more and more efficient at the particular task facing them.

However, a significant stream of research suggests that these types of very specialized jobs can be unmotivating for employees. Based on motivational theories taken from social psychology, this work suggests that as workers are removed further from the complete product that is the end result of a manufacturing process, the role that a worker's job plays in the overall manufacturing process becomes more and more obscure. As workers become mere "cogs in a manufacturing machine," worker motivation wanes, and productivity and quality can both suffer.[6]

Distance to Markets and Suppliers. A final source of diseconomies of scale can be the distance between a large manufacturing facility and the place where the goods in question are to be sold, or the places where essential raw materials are purchased. Any reductions in cost attributable to the exploitation of economies of scale in manufacturing may be more than offset by large transportation costs associated with moving supplies and products to and from the manufacturing facility. Firms that build highly efficient plants without recognizing these significant transportation costs may put themselves at a competitive disadvantage compared to firms with slightly less efficient plants but plants that are located nearer suppliers and key markets.

Experience Differences and Learning-Curve Economies

A third possible source of cost advantages for firms in a particular business depends on their different cumulative levels of production. In some circumstances, firms with the greatest experience in manufacturing a product or service will have the lowest costs in an industry and thus will have a cost-based advantage. The link between cumulative volumes of production and cost has been formalized in the concept of the **learning curve**. The relationship between cumulative volumes of production and per unit costs is graphically represented in Figure 4.2.

The Learning Curve and Economies of Scale. As depicted in Figure 4.2, the learning curve is very similar to the concept of economies of scale. However, there are two important differences. First, where economies of scale focuses on the relationship between the volume of production at a given point in time and average unit costs, the learning curve focuses on the relationship between the *cumulative* volume of production—that is, how much a firm has produced over time—and average unit costs. Second, where diseconomies of scale are presumed to exist if a firm gets too

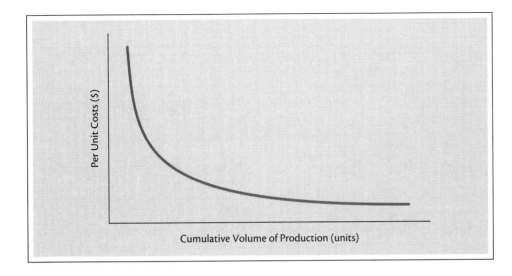

Figure 4.2 The Learning Curve and the Cost of Production

large, there is no corresponding increase in costs in the learning-curve model as the cumulative volume of production grows. Rather, costs continue to fall until they approach the lowest technologically possible cost.

The Learning Curve and Cost Advantages. The learning-curve model is based on the empirical observation that the costs of producing a unit of output fall as the cumulative volume of output increases. This relationship was first observed in the construction of aircraft before World War II. Research then showed that the labor costs per aircraft fell by 20 percent each time the cumulative volume of production doubled.[7] A similar pattern has been observed in numerous industries, although the rate of cost reduction may vary. Some of these industries include the manufacture of ships, computers, spacecraft, and semiconductors. In all these cases, increases in cumulative production have been associated with the improvement of work methods, a fine-tuning of the production operation, and detailed learning about how to make production as efficient as possible.

However, learning-curve cost advantages are not restricted to manufacturing. Learning can be associated with any business function, from purchasing raw materials to distribution and service. Also, there can be important learning effects in service industries as well. The learning curve applies whenever the cost of accomplishing a business activity falls as a function of the cumulative number of times a firm has engaged in that activity.[8]

The Learning Curve and Competitive Advantage. The learning-curve model summarized in Figure 4.2 has been used to develop a model of cost-based competitive advantage that links learning with market share and average production costs. The major proponent of the application of this learning-curve logic to create competitive advantage has been the Boston Consulting Group.[9]

The logic behind this application of the learning-curve model is straightforward: The first firm that successfully moves down the learning curve will obtain a cost advantage over rivals. To move a production process down the learning curve, a firm needs to have higher levels of cumulative volume of production. Of course, firms that are successful at producing high volumes of output need to sell that output to customers. In selling this output, firms are, in effect, increasing their market share. Thus, to drive down the learning-curve and obtain a cost advantage, firms must aggressively acquire market share.

This application of learning-curve logic has been criticized by a wide variety of authors.[10] Two criticisms are particularly salient. First, although the acquisition of market share is likely to allow a firm to reduce its production costs, the acquisition of share itself is expensive. To acquire share, firms must often increase advertising and other marketing expenditures and reduce prices. Indeed, research suggests that the costs that firms will need to absorb in order to acquire market share will often equal the value of that market share in lowering a firm's production costs. Thus, efforts to move down the learning-curve quickly, by acquiring market share, are likely to generate only normal economic performance. This may have occurred in the consolidation of the U. S. beer industry, as described in the Research Made Relevant feature.

The second major criticism of this application of the learning-curve model is that there is, in this logic, no room for any other business or corporate strategies. In other words, this application of the learning-curve implicitly assumes that firms can compete only on the basis of their low costs and that any other strategies are not possible. Most industries, however, are characterized by opportunities for at least some of these other strategies, and thus this strict application of the learning-curve model can be misleading.[11]

These criticisms aside, it is still the case that in many industries, firms with larger cumulative levels of production, other things being equal, will have lower average production costs. Thus, experience in all the facets of production can be a source of cost advantage even if the single–minded pursuit of market share to obtain these cost reductions may not give a firm above-normal economic returns.

Differential Low-Cost Access to Productive Inputs

Besides economies of scale, diseconomies of scale, and learning-curve cost advantages, differential low-cost access to productive inputs may create cost differences among firms producing similar products in an industry. **Productive inputs** are any supplies used by a firm in conducting its business activities; they include, among other things, labor, capital, land, and raw materials. A firm that has differential low-cost access to one or more of these factors is likely to have lower economic costs compared to rivals.

Consider, for example, an oil company with fields in Saudi Arabia compared to an oil company with fields in the North Sea. The cost of obtaining crude oil for the first firm is considerably less than the cost of obtaining crude oil for the second. North Sea drilling involves the construction of giant offshore drilling platforms, housing workers on floating cities, and transporting oil across an often-stormy sea. Drilling in Saudi Arabia requires only the simplest drilling technologies because the oil is found relatively close to the surface.

Of course, in order to create a cost advantage, the cost of acquiring low-cost productive inputs must be less than the cost savings generated by these factors. For example, even though it may be much less costly to drill for oil in Saudi Arabia than in the North Sea, if it is very expensive to purchase the rights to drill in Saudi Arabia compared to the costs of the rights to drill in the North Sea, the potential cost advantages of drilling in Saudi Arabia can be lost. As with all sources of cost advantages, firms must be careful to weigh the cost of acquiring that advantage against the value of that advantage for the firm.

Differential access to raw materials like oil, coal, and copper ore can be important determinants of a cost advantage. However, differential access to other productive inputs can be just as important. For example, it may be easier (that is, less costly) to recruit highly trained electronics engineers for firms located near where these engineers receive their schooling than for firms located some distance

Research Made Relevant

*I*n the 1960s and early 1970s, the U.S. beer market was highly fragmented—with numerous small, regional brewers dominating their local markets. Today, three brewers—Anheuser-Busch, Miller Brewing Company and Coors Brewing Company—dominate the industry, with well over 85 percent of the U.S. beer market. So, how did this industry consolidation occur, and did today's big beer companies create economic value by increasing their market share? This is the subject of an article by Cynthia Montgomery and Birger Wernerfelt.

These authors begin by observing that we know that market share can create value for a firm—among other things, it can reduce costs if learning-curve economies are operating. However, since market share can create value, wouldn't it often be the case that a competitive market for market share might develop? That is, if several firms in an industry were all trying to acquire market share—by increasing their advertising, reducing their prices, and so forth—wouldn't the "price" of acquiring that share go up, to the point perhaps, that the price of acquiring additional share might actually be greater than the value of that share? If this happened, then firms that are successful in acquiring share might actually destroy some of their economic value.

Well, this is exactly what happened in the U.S. beer industry. All but one of the top six brewers in the United States saw at least some increases in their market share—Anheuser-Busch's share increased 10.8 percent and Miller's share increased

The Consolidation of the U.S. Beer Market—Did Bud Pay Too Much?

16.3 percent. Only Schlitz saw a reduction in share, of 2.1 percent. However, using a market-based measure of performance similar to those described in Chapter 1, Montgomery and Wernerfelt showed that increases in market share actually destroyed economic value for firms in the U.S. beer industry. Moreover, the more share a firm acquired, the greater the negative impact on a firm's value: Miller and Anheuser-Busch destroyed more value than Schlitz, a firm that lost 2.1 percentage points in share but saw its economic value actually increase!

None of these results is inconsistent with the notion that high market share can, among other things, reduce a firm's costs. However, these results do suggest that if several equally skilled and resourced firms are all attempting to acquire market share, the price of doing so can sometimes rise to be equal to, or perhaps even greater than, the value that share would create for a firm.

Of course, the performance measure that was used in this research was relatively short term in orientation. It may be the case that Anheuser-Busch and Miller have been able to create value with their market share in ways that could not have been anticipated when they first acquired this share. This suggests that while acquiring market share in a competitive situation may not generate short- to medium-term profits, it may be profitable in the long run—if a firm with large market share is able to leverage that resource in creative ways that were not anticipated when it originally acquired its share advantage.

This research has become very important recently as another wave of consolidations seems to be occurring in the beer industry. Interbrew SA, a European brewer, recently merged with the leading brewer in South America. Anheuser-Busch recently purchased Harbin Brewery Group, Ltd., a regional brewer in China. And Coors and Molson are investigating a possible merger. Whether this current round of consolidations will see firms overpaying for market share, as was the case in the last round of consolidations, is still an open question.

Source: R. Frank, D. Berman, and E. Cherney (2004). "Molson family fight threatens merger with Coors." *Wall Street Journal*, Friday, July 23, pp. A1 +; C. Lawton (2004). "Coors investors may not want to mix drinks." *Wall Street Journal*, Tuesday, July 20, pp. C1 +; C. Montgomery and B. Wernerfelt (1991). "Sources of superior performance: Market share versus industry effects in the U.S. Brewing industry." *Management Science*, 37, pp. 954–959.

away. This lower cost of recruiting is a partial explanation of the development of geographic technology centers like Silicon Valley in California, Route 128 in Massachusetts, and the Research Triangle in North Carolina. In all three cases, firms are located physically close to several universities that train the engineers that are the lifeblood of high-technology companies. The search for low-cost labor can create ethical dilemmas, as described in the Ethics and Strategy feature.

Technological Advantages Independent of Scale

Another possible source of cost advantage in an industry may be the different technologies that firms employ to manage their business. It has already been suggested that larger firms may have technology–based cost advantages reflecting their ability to exploit economies of scale (for example, the two-thirds rule). Here, technology–based cost advantages that do not depend upon economies of scale are discussed.

Traditionally, discussion of technology–based cost advantages has focused on the machines, computers, and other physical tools that firms use to manage their business. Clearly, in some industries, these physical technology differences between firms can create important cost differences—even when the firms in question are approximately the same size in terms of volume of production. In the steel industry, for example, technological advances can substantially reduce the cost of producing steel. Firms with the latest steel-manufacturing technology will typically enjoy some cost advantage compared to similar-sized firms without the latest technology. The same applies in the manufacturing of semiconductors, automobiles, consumer electronics, and a wide variety of other products.[12]

These physical technology cost advantages apply in service firms as well as in manufacturing firms. For example, early in its history, Charles Schwab, a leading discount brokerage, purchased a computer system that enabled Schwab to complete customer transactions more rapidly and at a lower cost than rivals.[13] Kaiser-Permanente, the largest HMO in the United States, has invested in information technology that doctors can use to avoid incorrect diagnoses and procedures that can adversely affect a patient's health. By avoiding these medical mistakes, Kaiser-Permanente can substantially reduce its costs of providing medical service.[14]

However, the concept of technology can be easily broadened to include not just the physical tools that firms use to manage their business, but any processes within a firm used in this way. This concept of firm technology includes not only the **technological hardware** of companies—the machines and robots—but also the **technological software** of firms—things like the quality of relations between labor and management, an organization's culture, and the quality of managerial controls. All these characteristics of a firm can have an impact on a firm's economic costs.[15]

Again, Wal-Mart is an example of a firm that understands the importance of technological software to realize a cost leadership strategy. Wal-Mart's culture of enthusiasm and commitment—complete with Saturday morning employee meetings where the Wal-Mart cheer is shouted and the Wal-Mart song is played—is central to involving all of Wal-Mart's employees in reducing its costs, allowing Wal-Mart to charge lower prices.

Policy Choices

Thus far this discussion has focused on reasons why a firm can gain a cost advantage despite producing products that are similar to competing firms' products. When firms produce essentially the same outputs, differences in economies of scale, learning-curve advantages, differential access to productive inputs, and differences in technology can all create cost advantages (and disadvantages) for

Ethics and Strategy

One of the most important productive inputs in almost all companies is labor. Getting differential low-cost access to labor can give a firm a cost advantage.

This search for low labor costs has led some firms to engage in an international "Race to the Bottom." It is well known that the wage rates of most U.S. and Western European workers are much higher than the wage rates of workers in other, less developed parts of the world. While a firm might have to pay its employees $20 per hour (in wages and benefits) to make sneakers and basketball shoes in the United States, that same firm may only have to pay an employee in the Philippines, or Malaysia, or China $1.00 per day to make the same sneakers and basketball shoes—shoes the firm might be able to sell for $150 a pair in the United States and Europe. Thus, many firms look to overseas manufacturing as a way to keep their labor cost low.

But this search for low labor cost has some important unintended consequences. First, the location of the lowest cost labor rates in the world changes over time. It used to be that Mexico had the lowest labor rates, then Korea and the Philippines, then Malaysia, then China. As the infrastructures of each of these countries evolve to the point that they can support worldwide manufacturing, firms abandon their relation-

The Race to the Bottom

ships with firms in prior countries in search of still lower costs in new countries. The only way former "low-cost centers" can compete is to drive their costs even lower.

This sometimes leads to a second unintended consequence of the "race to the bottom": horrendous working conditions and low wages in these low-cost manufacturing settings. Employees earning $1 for working a 10-hour day, six days a week may look good on the corporate bottom line, but many observers are deeply concerned about the moral and ethical issues associated with this strategy. Indeed, several companies—including Nike and Kmart—have been forced to increase the wages

and improve the working conditions of many of their overseas employees.

An even more horrific result of this "race to the bottom" has been the reemergence of what amounts to slavery in some Western European countries and some parts of the United States. In search of the promise of a better life, illegal immigrants are sometimes brought to Western European countries or the United States and forced to work in illegal, underground factories. These illegal immigrants are sometimes forced to work as many as 20 hours a day, for little or no pay—supposedly to "pay off" the price of bringing them out of their less developed countries. And because of their illegal status and language barriers, they often do not feel empowered to go to the local authorities.

Of course, the people who create and manage these facilities are criminals and deserve contempt. But, what about the companies that purchase the services of these illegal and immoral manufacturing operations? Aren't they also culpable, both legally and morally?

Sources: R. DeGeorge (2000). "Ethics in international business—A contradiction in terms?" *Business Credit*, 102, pp. 50 +; G. Edmondson, K. Carlisle, I. Resch, K. Nickel Anhalt, and H. Dawley (2000). "Workers in bondage." *BusinessWeek*, November 27, pp. 146 +; D. Winter (2000). "Facing globalization." *Ward's Auto World*, 36, pp. 7 +.

them. However, firms can also make choices about the kinds of products and services they will sell—choices that have an impact on their relative cost position. These choices are called **policy choices**.

In general, firms that are attempting to implement a cost leadership strategy will choose to produce relatively simple standardized products that sell for relatively low prices compared to the products and prices firms pursuing other business or corporate strategies choose. These kinds of products often tend to have high volumes of sales, which (if significant economies of scale exist) tend to reduce costs even further.

These kinds of choices in product and pricing tend to have a very broad impact on a cost leader's operations. In these firms, the task of reducing costs is not delegated to a single function or a special task force within the firm but is the responsibility of every manager and employee. Cost reduction sometimes becomes the central objective of the firm. Indeed, in this setting, management must be constantly alert to cost-cutting efforts that reduce the ability of the firm to meet customers' needs. This kind of cost-cutting culture is central to Wal-Mart's ability to implement its cost leadership strategy.

V R I O ## The Value of Cost Leadership

There is little doubt that cost differences can exist among firms, even when those firms are selling very similar products. Policy choices about the kinds of products firms in an industry choose to produce can also create important cost differences. But, under what conditions will these kinds of cost advantages actually create value for a firm?

It was suggested in Chapter 3 that one way to tell if a resource or capability—like the ability of a firm to have a cost advantage—actually creates value for a firm is by whether or not that resource or capability enables a firm to neutralize its external threats or exploit its external opportunities. The ability of a cost leadership position to neutralize external threats will be examined here. The ability of such a position to enable a firm to exploit opportunities will be left as an exercise. The specific economic consequences of cost leadership are discussed in the Strategy in Depth feature.

Cost Leadership and the Threat of Entry

A cost leadership competitive strategy helps reduce the threat of new entrants by creating cost–based barriers to entry. Recall that many of the barriers to entry cited in Chapter 2, including economies of scale and cost advantages independent of scale, assume that incumbent firms have lower costs than potential entrants. If an incumbent firm is a cost leader, for any of the reasons just listed, then new entrants may have to invest heavily to reduce their costs prior to entry. Often, new entrants will enter using another business strategy (for example, product differentiation) rather than attempting to compete on costs.

Cost Leadership and the Threat of Rivalry

Firms with a low-cost position also reduce the threat of rivalry. The threat of rivalry is reduced through pricing strategies that low-cost firms can engage in and through their relative impact on the performance of a low-cost firm and its higher-cost rivals.

Cost leader firms have two choices in pricing their products or services. First, these firms can set their prices equal to the prices of higher-cost competitors. Assuming that there are few opportunities for other firms to implement product differentiation strategies, customers will be indifferent about purchasing goods or services from the low-cost firm or from its high-cost rivals. However, at these competitive prices, high-cost firms are likely to earn normal economic performance, while the cost leader firm is earning above-normal performance.

Second, low-cost firms can price their goods or services slightly below the prices of their high-cost rivals. Again, assuming little product differentiation, customers will no longer be indifferent about which firm they prefer to buy from. Obviously, the lower prices of the low-cost firm will attract numerous customers, rapidly increasing the market share of the low-cost firm.

Strategy in Depth

**The Economics
of Cost Leadership**

*A*nother way to demonstrate that cost leadership can be a source of economic value is to directly examine the economic profits generated by a firm with a cost advantage operating in an otherwise very competitive industry. This is done in Figure 4.3.

The firms depicted in this figure are **price takers**—that is, the price of the products or services they sell is determined by market conditions and not by individual decisions of firms. This implies that there is effectively no product differentiation in this market and that no one firm's sales constitute a large percentage of this market.

The price of goods or services in this type of market (P^*) is determined by aggregate industry supply and demand. This industry price determines the demand facing an individual firm in this market. Because these firms are price takers, the demand facing an individual firm is horizontal—that is, firm decisions about levels of output have a negligible impact on overall industry supply and thus a negligible impact on the market-determined price. As is well known, a firm in this setting maximizes its economic performance by producing a quantity of output (Q) so that marginal revenue equals marginal cost (MC). The ability of firms to earn economic profits in this setting depends upon the relationship between the market-determined price (P^*) and the average total

cost (ATC) of a firm at the quantity it chooses to produce.

Firms in the market depicted in Figure 4.3 fall into two categories. All but one firm have the average-total-cost curve ATC_2 and marginal-cost curve MC_2. However, one firm in this industry has the average-total-cost curve ATC_1 and marginal-cost curve MC_1. Notice that ATC_1 is less than ATC_2 at the performance-maximizing quantities produced by these two kinds of firms (Q_1 and Q_2, respectively). In this particular example, firms with common average-total-cost curves are earning zero economic profits, while the low-cost firm is earning an economic profit (equal to the shaded area in the figure). A variety of other examples could also be constructed: The cost leader firm could be earning zero economic profits while other firms in the market are incurring economic losses; the cost leader firm could be earning substantial economic profits while other firms are earning smaller economic profits; the cost leader firm could be incurring small economic losses while the other firms are incurring substantial economic losses; and so forth. However, in all these examples, the cost leader's economic performance is greater than the economic performance of other firms in the industry. Thus, cost leadership can have an important impact on a firm's economic performance.

Figure 4.3 Cost Leadership and Economic Performance

Each of these alternatives has strengths and weaknesses. Keeping prices equal to the competition's prices enables a low-cost firm to earn large margins on its sales. As important, this pricing approach at least partially conceals the fact that the low-cost firm has a cost advantage. Concealing this information reduces the chances that competitors will imitate the low-cost firm, thereby reducing its cost advantage. However, keeping prices equal to a competitor's prices does sacrifice market share and sales volume.

Setting the low-cost firm's prices below the prices of competing firms has the opposite effects. Such a pricing strategy can significantly increase a firm's market share and total volume of sales, but at the cost of some of the profit margin of the low-cost firm. Also, setting prices to this lower level sends a signal to competitors that lower costs are possible. Such a signal may motivate competitors to try to reduce their costs, either through implementing their own cost leadership competitive strategies or through implementing strategies that reduce costs.

In the end, the choice between these two pricing strategies depends upon the ability of competing firms to respond to the cost advantages of cost leaders. If the potential responses of competing firms are likely to be very detrimental to the cost leader, then this firm should set its prices equal to competitors' prices, sacrificing some market share for increased profit margins and the release of less information. However, if competitive reactions are not likely to threaten the cost leader, then dropping prices below competitors' prices should increase overall economic performance through increased volumes of profitable sales.

More generally, these strategic pricing options, and the potential above-normal economic performance they hold, are available only to cost leaders. These strategies enable a low-cost firm to earn above-normal economic returns even if the industry within which this firm operates is characterized by intense rivalry.

Cost Leadership and the Threat of Substitutes

As suggested in Chapter 2, substitutes become a threat to a firm when their cost and performance, relative to a firm's current products or services, become more attractive to customers. Thus, when the price of crude oil goes up, substitutes for crude oil become more attractive. When the cost and performance of electronic calculators improve, demand for mechanical adding machines disappears.

In this situation, cost leaders have the ability to keep their products and services attractive relative to substitutes. While high-cost firms may have to charge high prices to cover their costs, thus making substitutes more attractive, cost leaders can keep their prices low and still earn normal or above-normal economic profits.

Cost Leadership and the Threat of Suppliers

Suppliers can become a threat to a firm by charging higher prices for the goods or services they supply or by reducing the quality of those goods or services. However, when a supplier sells to a cost leader, that firm has greater flexibility in absorbing higher-cost supplies than does a high-cost firm. Higher supply costs may destroy any above-normal profits for high-cost firms but still allow a cost leader firm to earn an above-normal profit.

Cost leadership based on large volumes of production and economies of scale can also reduce the threat of suppliers. Large volumes of production imply large purchases of raw materials and other supplies. Suppliers are not likely to jeopardize these sales by threatening their customers. Indeed, as was suggested earlier, buyers are often able to use their purchasing volume to extract volume discounts from suppliers.

Cost Leadership and the Threat of Buyers

Cost leadership can also reduce the threat of buyers. Powerful buyers are a threat to firms when they insist on low prices or higher quality and service from their suppliers. Lower prices threaten firm revenues; higher quality can increase a firm's costs. Cost leaders can have their revenues reduced by buyer threats and still have normal or above-normal performance. These firms can also absorb the greater costs of increased quality or service and may still have a cost advantage over their competition.

Buyers can also be a threat through backward vertical integration. Being a cost leader deters buyer backward vertical integration, because a buyer that vertically integrates backward will often not have costs as low as an incumbent cost leader. Rather than vertically integrating backwards and increasing its cost of supplies, powerful buyers usually prefer to continue purchasing from their low-cost suppliers.

Finally, if cost leadership is based on large volumes of production, then the threat of buyers may be reduced, because buyers may depend on just a few firms for the goods or services they purchase. This dependence reduces the willingness of buyers to threaten a selling firm.

Cost Leadership and Sustained Competitive Advantage   V R I O

Given that cost leadership can be valuable, an important question becomes, "Under what conditions will firms implementing this business strategy be able to maintain that leadership to obtain a sustained competitive advantage?" If cost leadership strategies can be implemented by numerous firms in an industry, or if no firms face a cost disadvantage in imitating a cost leadership strategy, then being a cost leader will not generate a sustained competitive advantage for a firm. As was suggested in Chapter 3, the ability of a valuable cost leadership competitive strategy to generate a sustained competitive advantage depends on that strategy being rare and costly to imitate, either through direct duplication or substitution. As suggested in Tables 4.4 and 4.5, the rarity and imitability of a cost leadership strategy depend, at least in part, on the sources of that cost advantage.

The Rarity of Sources of Cost Advantage

Some of the sources of cost advantage listed in Table 4.4 are likely to be rare among a set of competing firms; others are less likely to be rare. Sources of cost advantage that are likely to be rare include learning-curve economies (at least in emerging industries), differential low-cost access to productive inputs, and technological "software." The remaining sources of cost advantage are less likely to be rare.

Table 4.4 **The Rarity of Sources of Cost Advantage**

Likely-to-be-rare sources of cost advantage	Less-likely-to-be-rare sources of cost advantage
Leaving-curve economies of scale (especially in emerging businesses)	Economies of scale (except when efficient plant size approximately equals total industry demand)
Differential low-cost access to productive inputs	Diseconomies of scale
Technological "software"	Technological hardware (unless a firm has proprietary hardware development skills)
	Policy choices

Table 4.5   **Direct Duplication of Cost Leadership**

	Source of cost advantage	Basis for costly duplication		
		History	**Uncertainty**	**Social complexity**
Low-cost duplication possible	1. Economies of scale	—	—	—
	2. Diseconomies of scale	—	—	—
May be costly to duplicate	3. Learning-curve economies	*	—	—
	4. Technological "hardware"	—	*	*
	5. Policy choices	*	—	—
Usually costly to duplicate	6. Differential low-cost access to productive inputs	***	—	**
	7. Technological "software"	***	**	***

— = not a source of costly imitation   * = somewhat likely to be a source of costly imitation   ** = likely to be a source of costly imitation
*** = very likely to be a source of costly imitation

Rare Sources of Cost Advantage

Early in the evolution of an industry, substantial differences in the cumulative volume of production of different firms are not unusual. Indeed, this was one of the major benefits associated with first-mover advantages, discussed in Chapter 2. These differences in cumulative volume of production, in combination with substantial learning-curve economies, suggest that in some settings, learning-curve advantages may be rare and thus a source of at least temporary competitive advantage.

The definition of differential access to productive inputs implies that this access is often rare. Certainly, if large numbers of competing firms have this same access, then it cannot be a source of competitive advantage.

Technological software is also likely to be rare among a set of competing firms. These software attributes represent each firm's path through history. If these histories are unique, then the technological software they create may also be rare. Of course, if several competing firms experience similar paths through history, the technological software in these firms is less likely to be rare.

Less Rare Sources of Cost Advantage

When the efficient size of a firm or plant is significantly smaller than the total size of an industry, there will usually be numerous efficient firms or plants in that industry, and a cost leadership strategy based on economies of scale will not be rare. For example, if the efficient firm or plant size in an industry is 500 units, and the total size of the industry (measured in units produced) is 500,000 units, then there are likely to be numerous efficient firms or plants in this industry, and economies of scale are not likely to give any one firm a cost–based competitive advantage.

Cost advantages based on diseconomies of scale are also not likely to be rare. It is unusual for numerous firms to adopt levels of production in excess of optimal levels. If only a few firms are too large in this sense, then several competing firms in an industry that are *not* too large will have cost advantages over the firms that are too large. However, because several firms will enjoy these cost advantages, they are not rare.

One important exception to this generalization may be when changes in technology significantly reduce the most efficient scale of an operation. Given such changes in technology, several firms may be inefficiently large. If a small number of firms happen to be sized appropriately, then the cost advantages these firms obtain in this way may be rare. Such changes in technology have made large integrated steel producers "too big" relative to smaller mini-mills. Thus, mini-mills have a cost advantage over larger integrated steel firms.

Technological hardware is also not likely to be rare, especially if it is developed by suppliers and sold on the open market. However, if a firm has proprietary technology development skills, it may possess rare technological hardware that creates cost advantages.

Finally, policy choices by themselves are not likely to be a rare source of cost advantage, particularly if the product or service attributes in question are easy to observe and describe.

The Imitability of Sources of Cost Advantage

Even when a particular source of cost advantage is rare, it must be costly to imitate in order to be a source of sustained competitive advantage. Both direct duplication and substitution, as forms of imitation, are important. Again, the imitability of a cost advantage depends, at least in part, on the source of that advantage.

Easy-to-Duplicate Sources of Cost Advantage

In general, economies of scale and diseconomies of scale are relatively easy-to-duplicate bases of cost leadership. As can be seen in Table 4.5, these sources of cost advantage do not build on history, uncertainty, or socially complex resources and capabilities and thus are not protected from duplication for these reasons.

For example, if a small number of firms does obtain a cost advantage based on economies of scale, and if the relationship between production scale and costs is widely understood among competing firms, then firms at a cost disadvantage will rapidly adjust their production to exploit these economies of scale. This can be done by either growing a firm's current operations to the point that the firm exploits economies or by combining previously separate operations to obtain these economies. Both actions enable a firm at a cost disadvantage to begin using specialized machines, reduce the cost of plant and equipment, increase employee specialization, and spread overhead costs more effectively.

Indeed, perhaps the only time economies of scale are not subject to low-cost duplication is when the efficient size of operations is a significant percentage of total demand in an industry. Of course, this is the situation described in Chapter 2's discussion of economies of scale as a barrier to entry. For example, as suggested earlier, BIC Corporation, with its dominant market share in the disposable pen market, has apparently been able to gain and retain an important cost advantage in that market based on economies of scale. BIC's ability to retain this advantage reflects the fact that the optimal plant size in the disposable pen market is a significant percentage of the pen market, and thus economies of scale act as a barrier to entry in that market.

Like economies of scale, in many settings diseconomies of scale will not be a source of sustained competitive advantage for firms that have *not* grown too large. In the short run, firms experiencing significant diseconomies can shrink the size of their operations to become more efficient. In the long run, firms that fail to adjust their size will earn below-normal economic performance and cease operations.

Although in many ways reducing the size of operations to improve efficiency seems like a simple problem for managers in firms or plants, in practice it is often a difficult change to implement. Because of uncertainty, managers in a firm or plant that is too large may not understand that diseconomies of scale have increased their costs. Sometimes, managers conclude that the problem is that employees are not working hard enough, that problems in production can be

Strategy in the Emerging Enterprise

*B*aseball in the United States has a problem. Most observers agree that it is better for fans if there is competitive balance in the league—that is, if, at the beginning of the year, the fans of several teams believe that their team has a chance to go to the World Series and win it all. However, the economic reality of competition in baseball is that only a small number of financially successful teams in large cities—the New York Yankees, the Los Angeles Dodgers—have the resources necessary to compete for a spot in the World Series year after year. So called "small market teams," like the Pittsburgh Pirates or the Milwaukee Brewers—may be able to compete every once in a while, but these exceptions prove the general rule—teams from large markets usually win the World Series.

And then there is Oakland and the Oakland A's. Oakland (with a population of just over 400,000) is the smallest—and least glamorous—of the three cities

The Oakland A's: Inventing a New Way to Play Competitive Baseball

in the San Francisco Bay Area, the other two being San Francisco and San Jose. The A's play in an outdated stadium—Network Associates Coliseum—to an average crowd of 26,787 fans—ranking

eighteenth among the 30 major league baseball teams in the United States. In 2003, the A's player payroll was $49 million, about one-third of the Yankees' player payroll.

Despite these liabilities, from 1998 to 2000, the A's compiled a win–loss record of 456 wins and 353 losses—second in the American league behind the Yankees. And, the team made money!

What is the "secret" to the A's success? Their general manager, William Lamar Beane, says that it has to do with three factors: how players are evaluated, making sure that every personnel decision in the organization is consistent with this approach to evaluation, and ensuring that all personnel decisions are thought of as business decisions.

The criteria used by the A's to evaluate players are easy enough to state. For batters, the A's focus on on-base percentage (i.e., how often a batter reaches base) and total bases (a measure of the ability

fixed, and so forth. These firms or plants may continue their inefficient operations for some time, despite costs that are higher than the industry average.[16]

Other psychological processes can also delay the abandonment of operations that are too large. One of these phenomena is known as **escalation of commitment**: Sometimes, managers committed to an incorrect (cost-increasing or revenue-reducing) course of action *increase* their commitment to this action as its limitations become manifest. For example, a manager who believes that the optimal firm size in an industry is larger than the actual optimal size may remain committed to large operations despite costs that are higher than the industry average.[17]

For all these reasons, firms suffering from diseconomies of scale must often turn to outside managers to assist in reducing costs. Outsiders bring a fresh view to the organization's problems and are not committed to the practices that generated the problems in the first place.[18]

Bases of Cost Leadership That May Be Costly to Duplicate

Although cost advantages based on learning-curve economies are rare (especially in emerging industries), they are usually not costly to duplicate. As suggested in Chapter 2, for learning-curve cost advantages to be a source of sustained competitive advantage, the learning obtained by a firm must be proprietary. Most recent empirical work suggests that in most industries learning is not proprietary and of a batter to hit for power)—that is, they focus on the ability of players to get on base and score. For pitchers, the A's focus on the percentage of first pitches that are strikes and the quality of a pitcher's fast ball. First-pitch strikes and throwing a good fast ball are correlated with keeping runners off base. Thus, not surprisingly, the A's criteria for evaluating pitchers are the reverse of their criteria for evaluating hitters.

While these evaluation criteria are easy to state, getting the entire organization to apply them consistently in scouting, choosing, developing, and managing players is much more difficult. Almost every baseball player and fan has his or her own favorite way to evaluate players. However, if you want to work in the A's organization, you must be willing to let go of your personal favorite and evaluate players the A's way. The result is that players that come through the A's farm system—the minor leagues where younger players are developed until they

are ready to play in the major leagues—learn a single way of playing baseball instead of learning a new approach to the game every time they change managers or coaches. One of the implications of this consistency has been that the A's farm system has been among the most productive in baseball.

This consistent farm system enables the A's to treat personnel decisions—including decisions about whether or not they should re-sign a star player or let him go to another team—as business decisions. The A's simply do not have the resources necessary to play the personnel game the same way as the Los Angeles Dodgers or the New York Yankees. When these teams need a particular kind of player, they go and sign one. Oakland has to rely more on its farm system. But because its farm system performs so well, the A's can let so-called "superstars" go to other teams, knowing that they are likely to have a younger—and cheaper—player in the minor

leagues, just waiting for the chance to play in "the show"—the players' nickname for the major leagues. This allows the A's to keep their payroll costs down and remain profitable, despite relatively small crowds, while still fielding a team that competes virtually every year for the right to play in the World Series.

Of course, an important question becomes: How sustainable is the A's competitive advantage? The evaluation criteria, themselves, are not a source of sustained competitive advantage. However, the socially complex nature of how these criteria are consistently applied throughout the A's organization may be a source of sustained competitive advantage in enabling the A's to gain the differential access to low-cost productive inputs—in this case, baseball players.

Sources: K. Hammonds (2003). "How to play Beane ball." *Fast Company*, May, pp. 84 +; M. Lewis (2003). *Moneyball*. New York; Norton; A. McGahan, J. F. McGuire, and J. Kou (1997). "The baseball strike." Harvard Business Review Case No. 9-796-059.

thus can be rapidly duplicated as competing firms move down the learning-curve by increasing their cumulative volume of production.[19]

However, the fact that learning is not costly to duplicate in *most* industries does not mean it is never costly to duplicate. In some industries the ability of firms to learn from their production experience may vary significantly. For example, some firms treat production errors as failures and systematically punish employees who make those errors. These firms effectively reduce risk-taking among their production employees and thus reduce the chances of learning how to improve their production process. Alternatively, other firms treat production errors as opportunities to learn how to improve their production process. These firms are likely to move rapidly down the learning-curve and retain cost advantages, despite the cumulative volume of production of competing firms. These different responses to production errors reflect the organizational cultures of these different firms. Because organizational cultures are socially complex, they can be very costly to duplicate.[20]

Because technological hardware can usually be purchased across supply markets, it is also not likely to be difficult to duplicate. Sometimes, however, technological hardware can be proprietary, or closely bundled with other unique, costly-to-duplicate resources controlled by a firm. In this case, technological hardware *can* be costly to duplicate.

It is unusual, but not impossible, for policy choices, per se, to be a source of sustained competitive cost advantages for a firm. As suggested earlier, if the policies in question focus on easy-to-observe and easy-to-describe product characteristics, then duplication is likely, and cost advantages based on policy choices will be temporary. However, if policy choices reflect complex decision processes within a firm, teamwork among different parts of the design and manufacturing process, or any of the software commitments discussed previously, then policy choices can be a source of sustained competitive advantage, as long as only a few firms have the ability to make these choices.

Indeed, most of the successful firms that operate in unattractive industries make policy choices that are costly to imitate because they reflect historical, causally ambiguous, and socially complex firm processes. Thus, for example, Dell's low product inventory strategy—a policy with clear low-cost implications—actually reflects the complex linkage between various parts of the value-chain within Dell, an unwavering commitment to manufacturing flexibility and efficiency, and an organizational culture that focuses on Web-based sales. Wal-Mart's supply chain management strategy—again, a policy with clear low-cost implications—actually reflects Wal-Mart's unique history, its socially complex relations with suppliers, and its unique organizational culture. And Southwest Airlines' low-price pricing strategy—a strategy that reflects Southwest's low-cost position—is possible because of the kind of airplane fleet Southwest has built over time, the commitment of its employees to Southwest's success, a charismatic founder (Herb Kelleher), and its unique organizational culture. Because these policies reflect costly-to-imitate attributes of these firms, they can be sources of sustained competitive advantage.

However, for these and other firms, it is not these policy choices, per se, that create sustainable cost leadership advantages. Rather, it is how these policies flow out of the historical, causally ambiguous, and socially complex processes within a firm that makes them costly to duplicate. This has been the case for the Oakland A's baseball team, as described in the Strategy in the Emerging Enterprise Feature.

Costly-to-Duplicate Sources of Cost Advantage

Differential access to low-cost productive inputs and technological software is usually a costly-to-duplicate basis of cost leadership. This is because these inputs often build on historical, uncertain, and socially complex resouces and capabilities. As suggested earlier, differential access to productive inputs often depends on the location of a firm. Moreover, to be a source of economic profits, this valuable location must be obtained before its full value is widely understood. Both these attributes of differential access to productive inputs suggest that if, in fact, it is rare, it will often be costly to duplicate. First, some locations are unique and cannot be duplicated. For example, most private golf clubs would like to own courses with the spectacular beauty of Pebble Beach in Monterey, California, but there is only one Pebble Beach—a course that runs parallel to some of the most beautiful oceanfront scenery in the world. Although "scenery" is an important factor of production in running and managing a golf course, the re-creation of Pebble Beach's scenery at some other location is simply beyond our technology.

Second, even if a location is not unique, once its value is revealed, acquisition of that location is not likely to generate economic profits. Thus, for example, although being located in Silicon Valley provides access to some important low-cost productive inputs for electronics firms, firms that moved to this location after its value was revealed have substantially higher costs than firms that moved there before its full value was revealed. These higher costs effectively reduce the economic profit that otherwise could have been generated. Referring to the discussion in Chapter 3, these arguments suggest that gaining differential access to productive inputs in a way that generates economic profits may reflect a firm's unique path through history.

Technological software is also likely to be difficult to duplicate and often can be a source of sustained competitive advantage. As suggested in Chapter 3, the values, beliefs, culture, and teamwork that constitute this software are socially complex and may be immune from competitive duplication. Firms with cost advantages rooted in these socially complex resources incorporate cost savings in every aspect of their organization; they constantly focus on improving the quality and cost of their operations, and they have employees who are firmly committed to, and understand, what it takes to be a cost leader. Other firms may talk about low costs; these firms live cost leadership. Dell, Wal-Mart, and Southwest are all examples of such firms. If there are few firms in an industry with these kinds of beliefs and commitments, then they can gain a sustained competitive advantage from their cost advantage.

Substitutes for Sources of Cost Advantage

In an important sense, all of the sources of cost advantage listed in this chapter are at least partial substitutes for each other. Thus, for example, one firm may reduce its cost through exploiting economies of scale in large-scale production, and a competing firm may reduce its costs through exploiting learning-curve economies and large cumulative volume of production. If these different activities have similar effects on a firm's cost position, and if they are equally costly to implement, then they are strategic substitutes for each other.

Because of the substitute effects of different sources of cost advantage, it is not unusual for firms pursuing cost leadership to simultaneously pursue *all* the cost-reduction activities discussed in this chapter. Implemention of this *bundle* of cost-reducing activities may have few substitutes. If duplicating this bundle of activities is also rare and difficult, then a firm may be able to gain a sustained competitive advantage from doing so.

Several of the other strategies discussed in later chapters can also have the effect of reducing a firm's costs and thus may be substitutes for the sources of cost reduction discussed in this chapter. For example, one common motivation for firms implementing strategic alliance strategies is to exploit economies of scale in combination with other firms. Thus, a strategic alliance that reduces a firm's costs may be a substitute for a firm exploiting economies of scale on its own to reduce its costs. As is discussed in more detail in Chapter 8, many of the strategic alliances among aluminum mining and smelting companies are motivated by realizing economies of scale and cost reduction. Also, corporate diversification strategies often enable firms to exploit economies of scale across different businesses within which they operate. In this setting, each of these businesses—treated separately—may have scale disadvantages; but collectively, their scale creates the same low-cost position as that of an individual firm that fully exploits economies of scale to reduce costs in a single business (see Chapter 9).

Organizing to Implement Cost Leadership

V R I O

As is the case with all strategies, firms seeking to implement cost leadership strategies must adopt an organizational structure, management controls, and compensation policies that reinforce this strategy. Some key issues associated with using these organizing tools to implement cost leadership are summarized in Table 4.6.

Organizational Structure in Implementing Cost Leadership

As suggested in Table 4.6, firms implementing cost leadership strategies will generally adopt what is known as a **functional organizational structure**.[21] An example of a functional organization structure is presented in Figure 4.4. Indeed, this

Table 4.6   **Organizing to Realize the Full Potential of Cost Leadership Strategies**

Organization structure: Functional structure with
1. Few layers in the reporting structure
2. Simple reporting relationships
3. Small corporate staff
4. Focus on narrow range of business functions

Management control systems
1. Tight cost control systems
2. Quantitative cost goals
3. Close supervision of labor, raw material, inventory, and other costs
4. A cost leadership philosophy

Compensation policies
1. Reward for cost reduction
2. Incentives for all employees to be involved in cost reduction

functional organizational structure is the structure used to implement all business-level strategies a firm might pursue, although this structure is modified when used to implement these different strategies.

In a functional structure, each of the major business functions is managed by a **functional manager**. For example, if manufacturing, marketing, finance, accounting, and sales are all included within a functional organization, then a manufacturing manager leads that function, a marketing manager leads that function, a finance manager leads that function, and so forth. In a functional organizational structure, all these functional managers report to one person. This person has many different titles—including President, CEO, Chair, or Founder. However, for purposes of this discussion, this person will be called the **chief executive officer (CEO)**.

The CEO in a functional organization has a unique status. Everyone else in this company is a functional specialist. The manufacturing people manufacture, the marketing people market, the finance people finance, and so forth. Indeed, there is only one person in the functional organization that has to have a multifunctional perspective—the CEO. This role is so important that sometimes the functional organization is called a **U-form structure**, where the "U" stands for "unitary"—because there is only one person in this organization that has a broad, multifunctional corporate perspective.

When used to implement a cost leadership strategy, this U-form structure is kept as simple as possible. As suggested in Table 4.6, firms implementing cost leadership strategies will have relatively few layers in their reporting structure. Complicated reporting structures, including **matrix structures** where one employee reports to two or more people, are usually avoided.[22] Corporate staff in

Figure 4.4   An Example of the U-form Organizational Structure these organizations is kept small. Such firms do not operate in a wide range of business functions, but instead operate only in those few business functions where they have valuable, rare, and costly-to-imitate resources and capabilities.

One excellent example of a firm pursuing a cost leadership strategy is Nucor Steel. A leader in the mini–mill industry, Nucor has only 5 layers in its reporting structure, compared to 12 to 15 in its major higher-cost competitors. Most operating decisions at Nucor are delegated to plant managers, who have full profit-and-loss responsibility for their operations. Corporate staff at Nucor is small and focuses its efforts on accounting for revenues and costs and on exploring new manufacturing processes to further reduce Nucor's operating expenses and expand its business opportunities. Nucor's former president, Ken Iverson, believed that Nucor does only two things well: build plants efficiently and run them effectively. Thus Nucor focuses its efforts in these areas and subcontracts many of its other business functions, including the purchase of its raw materials, to outside vendors.[23]

Responsibilities of the CEO in a Functional Organization

The CEO in a U-form organization has two basic responsibilities: (1) to formulate the strategy of the firm and (2) to coordinate the activities of the functional specialists in the firm to facilitate the implementation of this strategy. In the special case of a cost leadership strategy, the CEO must decide on which bases such a strategy should be founded—including any of those listed in Table 4.1—and then must coordinate functions within a firm to make sure that the economic potential of this strategy is fully realized.

Strategy Formulation. The CEO in a U-form organization engages in strategy formulation by applying the strategic management process described in Chapter 1. A CEO establishes the firm's mission and associated objectives. He or she evaluates environmental threats and opportunities, understands the firm's strengths and weaknesses, and then chooses one or more of the business and corporate strategies discussed in this book. In the case of a cost leadership strategy, the application of the strategic management process must lead a CEO to conclude that the best chance for achieving a firm's mission is for that firm to adopt a cost leadership business-level strategy.

Although the responsibility for strategy formulation in a U-form organization ultimately rests with the CEO, this individual needs to draw on the insights, analysis, and involvement of functional managers throughout the firm. CEOs who fail to involve functional managers in strategy formulation run several risks. First, strategic choices made in isolation from functional managers may be made without complete information. Second, limiting the involvement of functional managers in strategy formulation can limit their understanding of, and commitment to, the chosen strategy. This can severely limit their ability, and willingness, to implement any strategy—including cost leadership—that is chosen.[24]

Coordinating Functions for Strategy Implementation. Even the best formulated strategy is competitively irrelevant if it is not implemented. And the only way that strategies can be effectively implemented is if all the functions within a firm are aligned in a way consistent with this strategy.

For example, compare two firms pursuing a cost leadership strategy. All but one of the first firm's functions—marketing—are aligned with this cost leadership strategy. All of the second firm's functions—including marketing—are aligned with this cost leadership strategy. Because marketing is not aligned with the first firm's cost leadership strategy, this firm is likely to advertise products that it does not sell. That is, this firm might advertise its products on the basis of their style and performance, but sell products that are reliable (but

Table 4.7   **Common Misalignments Between Business Functions and a Cost Leadership Strategy**

	When Function is *Aligned* with Cost Leadership Strategies	When Function is *Misaligned* with Cost Leadership Strategies
Manufacturing	Lean, low cost, good quality	Inefficient, high cost, poor quality
Marketing	Emphasize value, reliability, and price	Emphasize style and performance
R&D	Focus on product extensions and process improvements	Focus on radical new technologies and products
Finance	Focus on low cost and stable financial structure	Focus on non-traditional financial instruments
Accounting	Collect cost data and adopt conservative accounting principles	Collect no-cost data and adopt very aggressive accounting principles
Sales	Focus on value, reliability, and low price	Focus on style and performance and high price

not stylish) and inexpensive (but not high performers). A firm that markets products it does not actually sell is likely to disappoint its customers. On the other hand, the second firm that has all of its functions—including marketing—aligned with its chosen strategy is more likely to advertise products it actually sells and thus is less likely to disappoint its customers. In the long run, it seems reasonable to expect this second firm to outperform the first firm, at least with respect to implementing a cost leadership strategy.

Of course, alignment is required of all of a firm's functional areas, not just marketing. Also, misalignment can emerge in any of a firm's functional areas. Some common misalignments between a firm's cost leadership strategy and its functional activities are listed in Table 4.7.

Management Controls in Implementing Cost Leadership

As suggested in Table 4.6, cost leadership firms are typically characterized by very tight cost-control systems; frequent and detailed cost-control reports; an emphasis on quantitative cost goals and targets; and close supervision of labor, raw materials, inventory, and other costs. Again, Nucor is an example of a cost leadership firm that has implemented these kinds of control systems. At Nucor, groups of employees are given weekly cost and productivity improvement goals. Groups that meet or exceed these goals receive extra compensation. Plant managers are held responsible for cost and profit performance. A plant manager who does not meet corporate performance expectations cannot expect a long career at Nucor. Similar group-oriented cost-reduction systems are in place at some of Nucor's major competitors, including Chaparral Steel.[25]

Less formal management control systems also drive a cost-reduction philosophy at cost leadership firms. For example, although Wal-Mart is one of the most successful retail operations in the world, its Arkansas headquarters is plain and simple. Indeed, some have suggested that Wal-Mart's headquarters looks like a warehouse. Its style of interior decoration was once described as "early bus station." Regional vice presidents at Wal-Mart travel every week, from Monday to Thursday, meet all day Friday, attend a company-wide meeting on Saturday morning, and then have late Saturday and Sunday off, just in time to start traveling again on Monday. This schedule enables Wal-Mart to reduce its costs by 2 percent of sales by *not* opening independent regional offices. Wal-Mart even involves its customers in reducing costs by asking them to "help keep your costs low" by returning shopping carts to the designated areas in Wal-Mart's parking lots.[26]

Compensation Policies and Implementing Cost Leadership Strategies

As suggested in Table 4.6, compensation in cost leadership firms is usually tied directly to cost-reducing efforts. Such firms often provide incentives for employees to work together to reduce costs and increase or maintain quality, and they expect *every* employee to take responsibility for both costs and quality. For example, an important expense for retail stores like Wal-Mart is "shrinkage"—a nice way of saying people steal stuff. About half the shrinkage in most stores comes from employees stealing their own companies' products.

Wal-Mart used to have a serious problem with shrinkage. Among other solutions (including hiring "greeters" whose real job is to discourage shoplifters), Wal-Mart developed a compensation scheme that took half the cost savings created by reduced shrinkage and shared it with employees in the form of a bonus. With this incentive in place, Wal-Mart's shrinkage problems dropped significantly.

Even apparently small cost savings can be important for firms implementing a cost leadership strategy. Ford Motor used compensation policies to help discover cost reductions in manufacturing the Ford Taurus. Cost reductions included redesigning door hinge pins (to save $2 per car), the use of splash shields under wheel wells made out of recycled plastic (to save 45 cents per car), and the use of a part from the Lincoln Continental to reinforce sheet metal under seats (to save $1.50 per car). Collectively, these small improvements have trimmed $180 from the cost of producing each Taurus. This could lead to additional profits of almost $73 million for the Taurus line of products.[27]

Cost Leadership in an International Context

As has already been suggested in this chapter, one of the most common reasons that a firm begins international operations is to reduce its cost position. International operations can reduce a firm's costs in at least three ways: (1) by increasing sales to realize economies of scale, (2) by gaining access to low-cost labor, and (3) by gaining access to low-cost raw materials.

Gaining access to new customers for a firm's current products or services can increase a firm's volume of sales. If a firm's production process is sensitive to economies of scale, this increased volume of sales can reduce its costs and enable it to gain cost advantages in both its domestic and nondomestic operations. Many scholars, over many years, have pointed out the potential of international operations to generate economies of scale.[28] Most recognize that the realization of economies of scale from international operations requires a high degree of integration across firm borders. Integration must focus on those aspects of a firm's operations where economies of scale can be realized. For example, McDonald's attempts to generate training-based economies of scale through the operation of a single management training center for all of its international operations. Firms in the float glass, color television, and chemical industries have all attempted to exploit manufacturing economies of scale through their international operations.[29]

Many firms in the worldwide automobile industry have attempted to realize manufacturing economies of scale through their international operations. According to one estimate, the minimum efficient scale of a single compact-car manufacturing plant is 400,000 units per year.[30] Such a plant would produce approximately 20 percent of all the automobiles sold in Britain, Italy, or France. Obviously, to exploit this 400,000-cars-per-year manufacturing efficiency, European automobile firms have had to sell cars in more than just a single-country market. Thus, the implementation of an international strategy has been essential if these firms were to recognize manufacturing economies of scale.

Global Perspectives

The Rise of the Maquiladora

One interesting example of firms gaining access to low labor costs through their international strategies is maquiladoras. Maquiladoras are manufacturing plants owned by non-Mexican companies operated in Mexico near the U.S. border. The primary driver behind maquiladora investment is lower labor costs than similar plants located in the United States. In addition, firms exporting from maquiladoras to the United States have to pay duties only on the value added that was created in Mexico; maquiladoras do not have to pay Mexican taxes on the goods processed in Mexico. Also, the cost of the land on which plants are built in Mexico is substantially lower than the cost would be in the United States. However, despite these other advantages, a study by the Banco de Mexico suggests that without the 20 percent cost-of-labor advantage, most maquiladoras would not be profitable.

Given the cost advantages in operating maquiladoras, it is not surprising that investment in this particular international strategy has increased substantially over time. In 1965, there were only 12 maquiladora plants. By 1990, approximately 1,700 were in operation. By 1999, over 3,100 maquiladoras, employing over 1 million people, were in operation. Most of these were U.S. firms operating plants in Mexico. Currently, only oil generates more foreign currency for Mexico than maquiladoras.

Sources: A. DePalma (1994). "Trade pact is spurring Mexican deals in the U.S." *New York Times*, March 17, pp. C1, 3; M. Celestino (1999). "Manufacturing in Mexico." *World Trade*, 12, July, pp. 36–42.

Similar economies of scale through international operations can be found through research and development and marketing.

It has already been suggested that firms can engage in international operations to gain access to low-cost labor. As the lowest cost labor in the world shifted from Japan (right after World War II) to South Korea, then to Taiwan, Singapore, and Malaysia, and still later to China, Mexico, and Vietnam, some firms have changed their manufacturing operations accordingly. For example, Mineba, a Japanese ball bearing company, began manufacturing in Japan, shifted its operations to Singapore in the 1970s, and has been operating in Thailand since the 1980s. Hewlett-Packard operates manufacturing and assembly operations in Malaysia and Mexico, Mitsubishi Motors recently opened a manufacturing operation in Vietnam, General Motors operates assembly plants in Mexico, and Motorola has operations in China. All these investments were motivated, at least partly, by the availability of low-cost labor in these countries.[31] One interesting approach to gaining access to the low-cost labor market while still remaining close to the boundaries of the United States is described in the Global Perspectives feature.

Finally, firms can engage in international operations to gain access to low-cost raw materials. Indeed, historically, this was the most traditional reason that firms began international operations. For example, in 1600, the British East India Company was formed with an initial investment of 70,000 £ to manage trade between England and the Far East, including India. In 1601, the third British East India Company fleet sailed for the Indies to buy cloves, pepper, silk, coffee, saltpeter, and other products. This fleet generated a return on investment of 234 percent. These profits led to the formation of the Dutch East India Company in 1602 and the French East India Company in 1664. Similar firms were organized to manage trade in the New World. The Hudson Bay Company was chartered in 1670 to manage the fur trade, and the rival North West Company was organized in 1784 for the same purpose. All these organizations were created to gain access to low-cost raw materials and products that were available only in nondomestic markets.[32]

Gaining access to low-cost raw materials is still an important reason why some firms engage in international enterprise. In some industries, including the oil and gas industry, virtually the only reason why firms have begun international operations is to gain access to low-cost raw materials.

SUMMARY

There are several reasons that firms producing essentially the same products can have different costs. Some of the most important of these are: (1) size differences and economies of scale, (2) size differences and diseconomies of scale, (3) experience differences and learning-curve economies, (4) differential access to productive inputs, and (5) technological advantages independent of scale. In addition, firms competing in the same industry can make policy choices about the kinds of products and services to sell that can have an important impact on their relative cost position. Cost leadership in an industry can be valuable by assisting a firm in reducing the threat of each of the five forces in an industry outlined in Chapter 2.

Each of the sources of cost advantage discussed in this chapter can be a source of sustained competitive advantage if it is rare and costly to imitate. Overall, leaning-curve economies, differential access to productive inputs, and technological "software" are more likely to be rare than other sources of cost advantage. Differential access to productive inputs and technological "software" is more likely to be costly to imitate—either through direct duplication or through substitution—than the other sources of cost advantage. Thus, differential access to productive inputs and technological "software" will often be more likely to be a source of sustained competitive advantage than cost advantages based on other sources.

Of course, to realize the full potential of these competitive advantages, a firm must be organized appropriately. Organizing to implement a strategy always involves a firm's organizational structure, its management control systems, and its compensation policies. The organizational structure used to implement cost leadership—and other business strategies—is called a functional or U-form structure. The CEO is the only person in this structure who has a corporate perspective. The CEO has two responsibilities: to formulate a firm's strategy and to implement it by coordinating functions within a firm. Ensuring that a firm's functions are aligned with its strategy is essential to successful strategy implementation.

When used to implement a cost leadership strategy, the U-form structure generally has few layers, simple reporting relationships, a small corporate staff; and it focuses on a narrow range of business functions. The management control systems used to implement these strategies generally include tight cost controls; quantitative cost goals; close supervision of labor, raw materials, inventory and other costs; and a cost leadership culture and mentality. Finally, compensation policies in these firms typically reward cost reduction and provide incentives for everyone in the organization to be part of the cost-reduction effort.

Firms often pursue a cost leadership strategy by engaging in international operations, and such operations can affect their cost structure in at least three ways: (1) firms can use international sales to exploit economies of scale, (2) firms can operate facilities around the world to gain access to low-cost labor, and (3) firms can operate internationally to gain access to low-cost raw materials.

CHALLENGE QUESTIONS

1. Wal-Mart, Timex, Casio, and Hyundai are all cited as examples of firms pursuing cost leadership strategies, but these firms make substantial investments in advertising, which seems more likely to be associated with a product differentiation strategy. Are these firms really pursuing a cost leadership strategy or are they pursuing a product differentiation strategy by emphasizing their lower costs?

2. When economies of scale exist, firms with large volumes of production will have lower costs than firms with smaller volumes of production. The realization of these economies of scale, however, is far from automatic. What actions can firms take to ensure that they realize whatever economies of sale are created by their volume of production?

3. Firms engage in an activity called "forward pricing" when they estab-lish, during the early stages of the learning-curve, a price for their prod-ucts that is lower than their actual costs, in anticipation of lower costs later on, after significant learning has occurred. Under what conditions, if any, does forward pricing make sense? What risks, if any, do firms engaging in forward pricing face?

4. One way of thinking about orga-nizing to implement cost leadership strategies is that firms that pursue this strategy should be highly centralized, have high levels of direct supervision, and keep employee wages to an absolute minimum. Another approach is to decentralize decision-making authority—to ensure that individuals who know the most about reducing costs make decisions about how to reduce costs. This, in turn, would imply less direct supervision and somewhat higher levels of employee wages (why?). Which of these two approaches seems more reasonable? Under what conditions would these different approaches make more or less sense?

5. International operations can reduce a firm's costs by generating economies of scale that it would not otherwise enjoy or by giving a firm access to low-cost labor and/or raw materials. The first of these strategies involves mostly exporting products made in a firm's home country to a nondomestic mar-ket while the second involves mostly importing products made outside a firm's home market to its home market. Describe the differences between these two strategies in terms of the types of investments that firms following these two strategies must make in their non-domestic markets and the different man-agement control problems these firms are likely to face.

PROBLEM SET

1. The economies of scale curve in Figure 4.1 can be represented algebraically in the fol-lowing equation:

$$\text{Average costs} = a + bQ + cQ^2$$

where Q is the quantity produced by a firm.; and a, b, and c are coefficients that are esti-mated from industry data. For example, it has been shown that that economies of scale curve for savings and loan companies in the U.S. is:

$$\text{Average costs} = 2.38 - .615A + .54A^2$$

where A is a savings and loan's total assets. Using this equation, what is the optimal size of a savings and loan? (Hint: Plug in different values of A and calculate Average costs. The lowest possible Average costs is the optimal size for a savings and loan.)

2. The learning-curve depicted in Figure 4.2 can be represented algebraically in the fol-lowing equation:

$$\text{Average time to produce x units} = ax^{-\beta}$$

where x is the total number of units produced by a firm in its history, a is the amount of time it took a firm to produce its first unit, and β is a coefficient that describes the rate of learning in a firm.

Suppose it takes a team of workers 45 hours to assemble their first product (a = 45) and 40.5 hours to assemble their second product. When a firm doubles its production (in this case, from one to two units) and cuts its production time (in this case, from 45 hours to 40.5

hours), learning is said to have occurred (in this case a 40.5/45 or 90% learning-curve). The β for a 90% learning-curve is .3219. Thus, this firm's learning-curve is:

$$\text{Average time to produce x units} = 45x^{-.3219}$$

What is the average amount of time it will take this firm to produce 6 products? (Hint: Simply plug "6" in for "X" in the equation and solve.) What is the total time it took this firm to produce these 6 products? (Hint: Simply multiply the number of units produced "6" by the average time it will take to produce these 6 products.) What is the average time it will take this firm to produce 5 products? What is the total time it will take this firm to produce 5 products? So, what is the total time it will take this firm to produce its sixth product? (Hint: Subtract the total time needed to produce five products from the total time needed to produce six products.)

Suppose a new firm is going to start producing these same products. Assuming this new firm doesn't learn anything from established firms, what will its cost disadvantage be when it assembles its first product? (Hint: Compare the costs of the experienced firm's sixth product with the cost of the new firm's first product.)

END NOTES

1. Weiner, S. (1987). "The road most traveled." *Forbes*, October 19, pp. 60–64.
2. Christensen, C. R., N. A. Berg, and M. S. Salter (1980). *Policy formulation and administration: A casebook of senior management problems in business*, 8th ed. Homewood, IL: Irwin, p. 163.
3. Scherer, F. M. (1980). *Industrial market structure and economic Performance*. Boston: Houghton Mifflin; Moore, F. T. (1959). "Economies of scale: Some statistical evidence." *Quarterly Journal of Economics*, 73, pp. 232–245; and Lau, L. J., and S. Tamura (1972). "Economies of scale, technical progress, and the nonhomothetic leontief production function." *Journal of Political Economy*, 80, pp. 1167–87.
4. Scherer, F. M. (1980). *Industrial market structure and economic performance*. Boston: Houghton Mifflin; and Perrow, C. (1984). *Normal accidents: Living with high-risk technologies*. New York: Basic Books.
5. Hamermesh, R. G., and R. S. Rosenbloom (1989). "Crown Cork and Seal Co., Inc." Harvard Business School Case No. 9-388-096.
6. See Hackman, J. R., and G. R. Oldham (1980). *Work redesign*. Reading, MA: Addison-Wesley.
7. This relationship was first noticed in 1925 by the commander of Wright-Patterson Air Force Base in Dayton, Ohio.
8. Learning-curves have been estimated for numerous industries. Boston Consulting Group (1970). "Perspectives on experience." Boston: BCG, presents learning curves for over 20 industries while Lieberman, M. (1984). "The learning curve and pricing in the chemical processing industries". *Rand Journal of Economics*, 15, pp. 213–228, estimates learning curves for 37 chemical products.
9. Henderson, B. (1974). *The experience curve reviewed III—How does it work?* Boston: Boston Consulting Group; and Boston Consulting Group (1970). "Perspectives on experience". Boston: BCG.
10. Hall, G., and S. Howell (1985). "The experience curve from the economist's perspective." *Strategic Management Journal*, 6, pp. 197–212.
11. Hill, C. W. L. (1988). "Differentiation versus low-cost or differentiation and low-cost: A contingency framework". *Academy of Management Review*, 13(3), pp. 401–412.
12. See Ghemawat, P., and H. J. Stander III (1992). "Nucor at a crossroads." Harvard Business School Case No. 9-793-039 on technology in steel manufacturing and cost advantages; Shaffer, R. A. (1995). "Intel as conquistador." *Forbes*, February 27, p. 130 on technology in semiconductor manufacturing and cost advantages; Monteverde, K., and D. Teece (1982). "Supplier switching costs and vertical integration in the automobile industry." *Rand Journal of Economics*, 13(1), pp. 206–213; and McCormick, J., and N. Stone (1990). "From national champion to global competitor: An interview with Thomson's Alain Gomez." *Harvard Business Review*, May/June, pp. 126–135 on technology in consumer electronic manufacturing and cost advantages.
13. Schultz, E. (1989). "Climbing high with discount brokers." *Fortune*, Fall (special issue), pp. 219–223.
14. Schonfeld, Erick (1998). "Can computers cure health care?" *Fortune*, March 30, pp. 111 +.
15. Ibid.
16. See Meyer, M. W., and L. B. Zucker (1989). *Permanently failing organizations*. Newbury Park, CA: Sage.
17. Staw, B. M. (1981). "The escalation of commitment to a course of action." *Academy of Management Review*, 6, pp. 577–587.
18. Hesterly, W. S. (1989). *Top management succession as a determinant of firm performance and de-escalation: An agency problem*, Unpublished doctoral dissertation, University of California, Los Angeles.
19. Barney, J. B. (1986). "Organizational culture: Can it be a source of sustained competitive advantage?" *Academy of Management Review*, 11, pp. 656–665.
20. See Spence, A. M. (1981). "The learning-curve and competition." *Bell Journal of Economics*, 12, pp. 49–70, on why learning needs to be proprietary; Mansfield, E. (1985). "How rapidly does new industrial technology leak out?" *Journal of Industrial Economics*, 34(2), pp. 217–223; Lieberman, M. B. (1982). *The learning-curve, pricing and market structure in the chemical processing industries*. Unpublished doctoral dissertation, Harvard University; Lieberman, M. B. (1987). "The learning curve, diffusion, and competitive strategy." *Strategic Management Journal*, 8, pp. 441–452 on why it usually is not proprietary.
21. Williamson, O. (1975). *Markets and hierarchies*. New York: Free Press.
22. Davis, S. M., and P. R. Lawrence (1977). *Matrix*. Reading, MA: Addison-Wesley.
23. See Ghemawat, P., and H. J. Stander III (1992). "Nucor at a crossroads." Harvard Business School Case No. 9-793-039.
24. See Floyd, S. W. and B. Woldridge (1992). "Middle management involvement in strategy and its association with strategic type: A research note." *Strategic Management Journal*, 13, pp. 153–167.
25. Ibid.
26. Walton, S. (1992). *Sam Walton, made in America: My story*. New York: Doubleday.
27. See Suris, O. (1996). "How Ford cut costs on its 1997 Taurus, little by little." *Wall Street Journal*, July 18, pp. B1 +.
28. See Fayerweather, J. (1969). *International business management*. New York: McGraw-Hill, and Porter, M. E. (1982). "How global companies win out." *Harvard Business Review*, September/October, pp. 98–108.
29. See Serwer, A. (1994). "McDonald's conquers the world." *Fortune*, October 17, pp. 103–116; Prahalad, C. K., and Y. Doz (1987). *The multinational mission*. New York: Free Press; and Bartlett, C. A., and S. Shoshal (1989). *Managing across borders: The transnational solution*. Boston: Harvard Business School Press.
30. See Porter, M. E. (1986). "Competition in international industries: A conceptual framework." In M. E. Porter (ed.), *Competition in international industries*. Boston: Harvard Business School Press.
31. See Collis, D. J. (1991). "A resource-based analysis of international competition: The case of the bearing industry." *Strategic Management Journal*, 12 (Summer Special Issue), pp. 49–68; and Engardio, P. (1993). "Motorola in China: A great leap forward." *BusinessWeek*, May 17, pp. 58–59.
32. See Trager, J. (1992). *The people's chronology*. New York: Henry Holt.

5

Product Differentiation

S exy. Glamorous. Mysterious. Victoria's Secret is the world's leading specialty retailer of lingerie and beauty products. With 2002 sales of almost $3.6 billion, and operating profits of $614 million, Victoria's Secret sells its mix of sexy lingerie, prestige fragrances, and fashion-inspired collections through over 1,000 retail stores and through the almost 400 million catalogues it distributes each year.

But all this glamour and success leaves the two central questions about this firm unanswered: "Who is Victoria?" and "What is her secret?"

Who Is Victoria, and What Is Her Secret?

It turns out that Victoria is a retired fashion model who lives in an up-and-coming fashionable district in London. She has a committed relationship and is thinking about starting a family. However, these maternal instincts are balanced by Victoria's adventurous and sexy side. She loves good food, classical music, and great wine. She travels frequently and is as much at home in New York, Paris, and Los Angeles as she is in London. Her fashion tastes are edgy enough to never be boring, but practical enough to never be extreme. Her lingerie is an essential part of her wardrobe. Sexy and alluring while never cheap, trashy, or vulgar, Victoria's lingerie is the perfect complement to her overall lifestyle. Most importantly, while Victoria knows she is beautiful and sexy, she also knows that it is

Learning Objectives

After reading this chapter, you should be able to:

1. Define product differentiation.

2. Describe eleven bases of product differentiation and how they can be grouped into three categories.

3. Describe how product differentiation is ultimately limited only by managerial creativity.

4. Describe how product differentiation can be used to neutralize environmental threats and exploit environmental opportunities.

5. Describe those bases of product differentiation that are not likely to be costly to duplicate, those that may be costly to duplicate, and those that will often be costly to duplicate.

6. Describe the main substitutes for product differentiation strategies.

7. Describe how organizational structure, control processes, and compensation policies can be used to implement product differentiation strategies.

8. Discuss whether or not it is possible for a firm to implement cost leadership and product differentiation strategies simultaneously, and why or why not.

9. Discuss the trade-off between local responsiveness and international integration as firms pursue product differentiation strategies around the world.

---

her brains, not her looks, that have enabled her to succeed in life.

This is who Victoria is. This is the woman that Victoria's Secret's designers design for, the woman Victoria's Secret's marketers create advertising for, and the woman to whom all Victoria's Secret's sales associates are trained to sell.

And this is her secret— Victoria doesn't really exist. Or, more precisely, the number of real women in the entire world who are like Victoria is very small—no more than a handful. So why would a company like Victoria's Secret organize all of its design, marketing, and sales efforts

around meeting the lingerie needs of a woman who, for all practical purposes, doesn't really exist?

Victoria's Secret knows how few of its actual customers are like Victoria. However, it is convinced that many of its customers would like to be treated as if they were Victoria, if only for a few hours, when they come into a Victoria's Secret store. Victoria's Secret is not just selling lingerie; it is selling an opportunity, almost a fantasy, to be like Victoria—to live in an exciting and sexy city, to travel the world, to

have refined yet edgy tastes. To buy and wear Victoria's Secret lingerie is—if only for a moment or two— an opportunity to experience life as Victoria experiences life.

Practically speaking, building an entire company around meeting the needs of a customer who does not actually exist creates some interesting problems. You can't just call Victoria on the phone and ask her about trends in her lifestyle; you can't form a focus group of people like Victoria and ask them to evaluate new lines of lingerie. In a sense, not only has Victoria's Secret invented Victoria; it also had to invent Victoria's lifestyle—and the lingerie, fragrances, and accessories that go along with that lifestyle. And as long as the lifestyle that the Company invents for Victoria is desirable to, but just beyond the reach of, its actual customers, Victoria's Secret will continue to be able to sell a romantic fantasy—along with its bras and panties.

Source: www.limitedbrands.com; www.victoriassecret.com.

V ictoria's Secret uses the fictional character "Victoria" to help implement its product differentiation strategy.

What Is Product Differentiation?

Where Wal-Mart exemplifies a firm pursuing a cost leadership strategy, Victoria's Secret exemplifies a firm pursuing a product differentiation strategy. **Product differentiation** is a business strategy whereby firms attempt to gain a competitive advantage by increasing the perceived value of their products or services relative to the perceived value of other firms' products or services. These other firms can be either that firm's rivals or firms that provide substitute products or services. By increasing the perceived value of its products or services, a firm will be able to charge a higher price than it would otherwise. This higher price can increase a firm's revenues and can generate competitive advantages.

A firm's attempts to create differences in the relative perceived value of its products or services often are made by altering the objective properties of those products or services. Rolex attempts to differentiate its watches from Timex and Casio watches by manufacturing them with solid gold cases. Mercedes attempts to differentiate its cars from Hyundai's cars through sophisticated engineering and high performance. Victoria's Secret attempts to differentiate its shopping experience from Wal-Mart, and other retailers, through the merchandise it sells and the way it sells it.

While firms often alter the objective properties of their products or services in order to implement a product differentiation strategy, the existence of product differentiation, in the end, is *always* a matter of customer perception. Products sold by two different firms may be very similar, but if customers believe the first is more valuable than the second, then the first product has a differentiation advantage.

In the world of "craft" or "microbrewery" beers for example, image among consumers about where a beer is brewed may be very different from how a beer for example is actually brewed. Boston Beer Company, for example, sells Samuel Adams Beer. Customers can tour the Boston Beer Company, where they will see a small row of fermenting tanks and two 10-barrel kettles being tended by a brewmaster wearing rubber boots. However, Samuel Adams Beer is not actually brewed in this small factory. Instead, it is brewed—in 200-barrel steel tanks—in Cincinnati, Ohio, by the Hudepohl-Schoenling Brewing Company, a contract brewing firm that also manufactures Hudy Bold Beer and Little Kings Cream Ale. Maui Beer Company's Aloha Lager brand is brewed in Portland, Oregon, and Pete's Wicked Ale (a craft beer that claims it is brewed "one batch at a time. Carefully.") is brewed in batches of 400 barrels each by Stroh Brewery Company, makers of Old Milwaukee Beer. However, the more consumers believe there are important differences between these "craft" beers and more traditional brews—despite many of their common manufacturing methods—the more willing they will be to pay more for a craft beer. This willingness to pay more suggests that an important "perceptual" basis of product differentiation exists for these craft beers.[1] If products or services are *perceived* as being different in a way that is valued by consumers, then product differentiation exits.

Just as perceptions can create product differentiation between products that are essentially identical, the lack of perceived differences between products with very different characteristics can prevent product differentiation. For example, consumers with an untrained palate may not be able to distinguish between two different wines, even though expert wine tasters would be very much aware of their differences. Those who are not aware of these differences, even if they exist, will not be willing to pay more for one wine over the other. In this sense, for these consumers at least, these two wines, though different, are not differentiated.

Product differentiation is always a matter of customer perceptions, but firms can take a variety of actions to influence these perceptions. These actions can be thought of as different bases of product differentiation.

Bases of Product Differentiation

A wide variety of authors, drawing on both theory and empirical research, have developed lists of ways firms can differentiate their products or services.[2] Some of these are listed in Table 5.1. While the purpose of all these bases of product differentiation is to create the perception that a firm's products or services are unusually valuable, different bases of product differentiation attempt to accomplish this objective in different ways. For example, the first four bases of product differentiation listed in Table 5.1 attempt to create this perception by focusing directly on the attributes of the products or services a firm sells. The second three attempt to create this perception by developing a relationship between a firm and its customers. The last five attempt to create this perception through linkages within and between firms. Of course, these bases of product differentiation are not mutually exclusive. Indeed, firms will often attempt to differentiate their products or services along multiple dimensions simultaneously. An empirical method for identifying ways that firms have differentiated their products is discussed in the Research Made Relevant feature.

Table 5.1   **Ways Firms Can Differentiate Their Products**

To differentiate their products, firms can focus directly on the attributes of it products or services, or

1. Product features
2. Product complexity
3. Timing of product introduction
4. Location

on relationships between itself and its customers, or

5. Product customization
6. Consumer marketing
7. Product reputation

on linkages within or between firms

8. Linkages among functions within a firm
9. Linkages with other firms
10. Product mix
11. Distribution channels
12. Service and support

Source: M.C. Porter, (1980). *Competitive Strategy*-New York: Free Press. And R.E. Caves, and P. Williamson (1985). "What is product differentiation, really?" *Journal of Industrial Economics*, 34, pp. 113–132.

Research Made Relevant

Of all the possible bases of product differentiation that might exist in a particular market, how does one pinpoint those bases of product differentiation that have actually been used to differentiate products in that market? Research in strategic management and marketing has shown that the bases of product differentiation can be identified using multiple regression analysis to estimate what are called **hedonic prices**. A hedonic price is that part of the price of a product or service that is attributable to a particular characteristic of that product or service.

The logic behind hedonic prices is straightforward. If customers are willing to spend more for a product with a particular attribute than they are willing to spend for that same product without that attribute, then that attribute differentiates the first product from the second. That is, this attribute is a basis of product differentiation in this market.

Consider, for example, the price of used cars. The market price of a used car can be determined through the use of a variety of used car buying guides. These guides typically establish the base price of a used car. This base price typically includes product features that are common to almost all cars—a radio, a standard engine, a

**Discovering the Bases
of Product Differentiation**

heater/defroster. Because these product attributes are common to virtually all cars, they are not a basis for product differentiation.

However, in addition to these common features, the base price of an automobile is adjusted depending on some less common features—a high-end stereo system, a larger engine, air conditioning. How much the base price of the car is adjusted when these features are added—$300 for a high-end stereo, $500 for a larger engine, $200 for air conditioning—are the hedonic prices of these product attributes. These product attributes differen-

tiate well-equipped cars from less-well-equipped cars and, since consumers are willing to pay more for well-equipped cars, can be thought of as bases of product differentiation in this market.

Multiple regression techniques are used to estimate these hedonic prices in the following way. For the simple car example above, the following regression equation is estimated:

$$Price = a_1 + b_1(Stereo) + b_2(Engine) + b_3(AC)$$

where Price is the retail price of cars, Stereo is a variable describing whether or not a car has a high-end stereo, Engine is a variable describing whether or not a car has a large engine, and AC is a variable describing whether or not a car has air conditioning. If the hedonic prices for these features are those suggested earlier, the results of running this regression analysis would be:

$$Price = \$7,800 + \$300(Stereo) + \$500(Engine) + \$200(AC)$$

where $7,800 is the base price of this type of used car.

Source: D. Hay and D. Morris (1979). *Industrial economics: Theory and evidence.* Oxford: Oxford University Press; K. Cowling and J. Cubbin (1971). "Price, quality, and advertising competition." *Economica*, 38, pp. 378–394.

Focusing on the Attributes of a Firm's Products or Services

Product Features. The most obvious way that firms can try to differentiate their products is by altering the features of the products they sell. One industry where firms are constantly modifying product features to attempt to differentiate their products is the automobile industry. Chrysler, for example, introduced the "cab forward" design to try to give its cars a distinctive look, while Audi went with a more radical flowing and curved design to differentiate its cars. For emergency situations, General Motors introduced the "On Star" system which instantly connects drivers to GM operators 24 hours a day, while Mercedes-Benz continued to develop its "crumple zone" system to ensure passenger safety in a crash. In body construction, General Motors continues to develop its "uni-body" construction system, where different parts of a car are welded to each other rather than built on a single frame, while Jaguar introduced a 100 percent aluminum body to help differentiate its top-of-the-line model from other luxury cars. Mazda continues to tinker with the motor and suspension of its sporty Miata, while Nissan introduced the 350 Z—a continuation of the famous 240 Z line—and Porsche changed from air-cooled to water-cooled engines in its 911 series of sports cars. All these—and many more—changes in the attributes of automobiles are examples of firms trying to differentiate their products by altering product features.

Product Complexity. Product complexity can be thought of as a special case of altering a product's features to create product differentiation. In a given industry, products can vary significantly in their complexity. The BIC "crystal pen" for example, has only a handful of parts, while a Cross pen or a Mount Blanc pen has many more parts. To the extent that these differences in product complexity convince consumers that the products of some firms are more valuable than the products of other firms, product complexity can be a basis of product differentiation.

Timing of Product Introduction. Introducing a product at the right time can also help create product differentiation. As suggested in Chapter 2, in some industry settings (that is, in emerging industries) *the* critical issue is to be a first mover—to introduce a new product before all other firms. Being first in emerging industries can enable a firm to set important technological standards, preempt strategically valuable assets, and develop customer-switching costs. These first-mover advantages can create a perception among customers that the products or services of the first-moving firm are somehow more valuable than the products or services of other firms.[3]

First moving has been an important determinant of perceived differences in the quality of education at universities in the United States and worldwide. In the United States, the first few universities founded (for example, Harvard and Yale) are seen as more prestigious than more recently founded state schools. In the United Kingdom, the oldest universities (including Oxford and Cambridge) are also widely perceived to be superior to more recently founded universities. Regardless of whether the date of founding of a university has an impact on the quality of education one receives, if there is a *perceived* link between founding date and quality, founding date acts as a timing-based source of product differentiation.[4]

Timing-based product differentiation, however, does not depend only on being a first mover. Sometimes, a firm can be a later mover in an industry but introduce products or services at just the right time and thereby gain a competitive advantage. This can happen when the ultimate success of a product or service depends on the availability of complementary products or technologies. For example, the domination of Microsoft's MS-DOS operating system, and thus ultimately, the domination of Windows, was only possible because IBM introduced its version of the personal computer. Without the IBM PC, it would have been difficult for any operating system—including MS-DOS—to have such a large market presence.[5]

Location. The physical location of a firm can also be a source of product differentiation.[6] Consider, for example, Disney's operations in Orlando, Florida. Beginning with The Magic Kingdom and Epcot Center, Disney built a world-class destination resort in Orlando. Over the years, Disney has added numerous attractions to its core entertainment activities, including MGM Studios, over 11,000 Disney-owned hotel rooms, a $100 million sports center, an automobile racing track, an after-hours entertainment district, and most recently, a $1 billion theme park called "The Animal Kingdom"—all in and around Orlando. Now, families can travel from around the world to Orlando, knowing that in a single location they can enjoy a full range of Disney adventures.[7]

Focusing on the Relationship Between a Firm and Its Customers

Product Customization. Products can also be differentiated by the extent to which they are customized for particular customer applications. Product customization is an important basis for product differentiation in a wide variety of industries, from enterprise software to bicycles.

Enterprise software is software that is designed to support all of a firm's critical business functions, including human resources, payroll, customer service, sales, quality control, and so forth. Major competitors in this industry include PeopleSoft and Oracle. However, although these firms sell basic software packages, most firms find it necessary to customize these basic packages to meet their specific business needs. The ability to build complex software packages that can also be customized to meet the specific needs of a particular customer is an important basis of product differentiation in this marketplace.

In the bicycle industry, consumers can spend as little as $50 on a bicycle, and as much as—well, almost as much as you want on a bicycle, easily in excess of $10,000. High-end bicycles use, of course, the very best components—like brakes and gears. But what really distinguishes these bicycles is their customized fit. Firms that sell these customized bicycles build a strong and lightweight frame that is custom fit to you and to your individual riding style. Much of the competition in this high end of the industry focuses on different ways of customizing this fit and different space-age materials that can be used to build the frames. Once a serious rider becomes accustomed to a particular customization approach, it is very difficult for that rider to switch to suppliers that might have an alternative approach to customization.

Consumer Marketing. Differential emphasis on consumer marketing has been a basis for product differentiation in a wide variety of industries. Through advertising and other consumer marketing efforts, firms attempt to alter the perceptions of current and potential customers, whether or not specific attributes of a firm's products or services are altered.

For example, in the soft drink industry, Mountain Dew—a product of PepsiCo—was originally marketed as a fruity, lightly carbonated drink, that tasted as light as a "morning dew in the mountains." However, beginning in the late 1990s, Mountain Dew's marketing efforts changed dramatically. "As light as a morning dew in the mountains" became "Do the Dew," and Mountain Dew focused its marketing efforts on young, mostly male, extreme sports-oriented consumers. Young men riding snowboards, roller blades, mountain bikes, and skateboards—mostly upside down—became central to most Mountain Dew commercials. Mountain Dew became a sponsor of a wide variety of extreme sports contests and an important sponsor of the X-games on ESPN. And will we ever forget the confrontation between the young Dew enthusiast and a mountain ram over a can of Mountain Dew in a meadow? Note that this radical repositioning of Mountain Dew depended entirely on changes in consumer marketing. The features of the underlying product were not changed at all.

Reputation. Perhaps the most important relationship between a firm and its customers depends on a firm's reputation in its marketplace. Indeed, a firm's **reputation** is really no more than a socially complex relationship between a firm and its customers. Once developed, a firm's reputation can last a long time, even if the basis for that reputation no longer exists.[8]

A firm that has tried to exploit its reputation for cutting-edge entertainment is MTV, a division of Viacom, Inc. While several well-known video artists—including Madonna—have had their videos banned from MTV, it has still been able to develop a reputation for risk-taking on television. MTV believes that its viewers have come to expect the unexpected in MTV programming. One of the first efforts to exploit, and reinforce, this reputation for risk-taking was *Beavis and Butthead*, an animated series on MTV starring two teenage boys with serious social and emotional development problems. More recently, MTV exploited its reputation by inventing an entirely new genre of television—"reality TV"—through its *Real World* and *House Rules* programs. Not only are these shows cheap to produce, they build on the reputation that MTV has for providing entertainment that is a little risky, a little sexy, and a little controversial. Indeed, MTV has been so successful in providing this kind of entertainment that it had to form an entirely new cable station—MTV 2—to actually show music videos.[9]

Focusing on Links Within and Between Firms

Linkages Between Functions. A less obvious but still important way in which a firm can attempt to differentiate its products is through linking different functions within the firm. For example, research in the pharmaceutical industry suggests that firms vary in the extent to which they are able to integrate different scientific specialties—such as genetics, biology, chemistry, and pharmacology—to develop new drugs. Firms that are able to form effective multidisciplinary teams to explore new drug categories have what some have called an **architectural competence**, that is, the ability to use organizational structure to facilitate coordination among scientific disciplines to conduct research. Firms that have this competence are able to more effectively pursue product differentiation strategies—by introducing new and powerful drugs—compared to firms that do not have this competence. And in the pharmaceutical industry, where firms that introduce such drugs can experience very large positive returns, the ability to coordinate across functions is an important source of competitive advantage.[10]

Links with Other Firms. Another basis of product differentiation is linkages with other firms. Here, instead of differentiating products or services on the basis of linkages between functions within a single firm or linkages between different products, differentiation is based on explicit linkages between one firm's products and the products or services of other firms.

This form of product differentiation has increased in popularity over the last several years. For example, with the growth in popularity of stock car racing in the United States, more and more corporations are looking to link their products or services with famous names and cars in NASCAR. Firms such as Kodak, Circuit City, Gatorade, McDonald's, Home Depot, The Cartoon Network, True Value, and Pfizer (manufacturers of Viagra) have all been major sponsors of NASCAR teams. In one year, the Coca-Cola Corporation filled orders for over 200,000 NASCAR-themed vending machines. Visa struggled to keep up with demand for its NASCAR affinity cards, and over 1 million NASCAR Barbies were once sold by Mattel—generating revenues of about $50 million. Notice that none of these firms sells products for automobiles. Rather, these firms seek to associate themselves with NASCAR because of the popularity of this sport.[11]

Another product with which firms often seek to link their own products and services is movies, especially summer "blockbuster" movies. This can be done in at least two ways. First, firms may **co-brand** their product with a movie.[12] That is, they may tie the brand of their product to the brand of another firm's product. For example, McDonald's often uses characters from movies as toys in its Happy Meals. This first occurred in 1979, when a McDonald's Happy Meal featured action figures from *Star Trek: The Motion Picture*. Second, firms can attempt to place their products in a movie. Such product placements can be as simple as having an actor drink from a can of Coca-Cola after defeating the bad guys or as complicated as introducing a new product to the market by having an actor use this product in a movie. Both BMW and Aston-Martin used this kind of product placement in James Bond movies to introduce new cars to the automobile market—although the cars that were actually sold did not include machine guns and rockets.

In general, linkages between firms that differentiate their products are examples of cooperative strategic alliance strategies. The conditions under which cooperative strategic alliances create value and are sources of sustained competitive advantage are discussed in detail in Chapter 9.

Product Mix. One of the outcomes of links among functions within a firm and links between firms can be changes in the mix of products a firm brings to the market. This mix of products or services can be a source of product differention, especially when (1) those products or services are technologically linked or (2) when a single set of customers purchases several of a firm's products or services.

For example, technological interconnectivity is an extremely important selling point in the information technology business and thus an important basis of potential product differentiation. However, seamless interconnectivity—where Company A's computers talk to Company B's computers across Company C's data line merging a database created by Company D's software with a database created by Company E's software to be used in a calling center that operates with Company F's technology—has been extremely difficult to realize. For this reason, some information technology firms try to realize the goal of interconnectivity by adjusting their product mix, that is, by selling a bundle of products whose interconnectivity they can control and guarantee to customers. This goal of selling a bundle of interconnected technologies can influence a firm's research and development, strategic alliance, and merger and acquisition strategies, since all these activities can influence the set of products a firm brings to market.

Shopping malls are an example of the second kind of linkage among a mix of products—where products have a common set of customers. Many customers prefer to go to one location, to shop at several stores at once, rather than travel to a series of locations to shop. This one-stop shopping reduces travel time and helps turn shopping into a social experience. Mall development companies have recognized that the value of several stores brought together in a particular location is greater than the value of those stores if they were isolated, and they have invested to help create this mix of retail shopping opportunities.[13]

Distribution Channels. Linkages within and between firms can also have an impact on how a firm chooses to distribute its products, and distribution channels can be a basis of product differentiation. For example, in the soft drink industry, Coca-Cola, PepsiCo, and Seven-Up all distribute their drinks through a network of independent and company-owned bottlers. These firms manufacture key ingredients for their soft drinks and ship these ingredients to local bottlers, who add carbonated water, package the drinks in bottles or cans, and distribute the final product to soft drink outlets in a given geographic area. Each local bottler has exclusive rights to distribute a particular brand in a geographic location.

Canada Dry has adopted a completely different distribution network. Instead of relying on local bottlers, Canada Dry packages its final product in several locations and then ships its soft drinks directly to wholesale grocers, who distribute them to local grocery stores, convenience stores, and other retail outlets.

One of the consequences of these alternative distribution strategies is that Canada Dry has a relatively strong presence in grocery stores but a relatively small presence in soft drink vending machines. The vending machine market is dominated by Coca-Cola and PepsiCo. These two firms have local distributors that maintain and stock vending machines. Canada Dry has no local distributors and is able to get its products into vending machines only when they are purchased by local Coca-Cola or Pepsi distributors. These local distributors are likely to purchase and stock Canada Dry products such as Canada Dry ginger ale, but they are contractually prohibited from purchasing Canada Dry's various cola products.[14]

Service and Support. Finally, products have been differentiated by the level of service and support associated with them. Some firms in the home appliance market, including General Electric, have not developed their own service and support network and instead rely on a network of independent service and support operations throughout the United States. Other firms in the same industry, including Sears, have developed their own service and support network.[15]

Differences in service and support have recently become a major point of differentiation in the automobile industry. Such firms as Lexus (a division of Toyota) and Saturn (a division of General Motors) compete not only on the basis of product quality but also on the basis of the level of service and support they provide. To emphasize its willingness to provide service and support, Saturn once advertised that one of its customers needed to replace a defective seat in a Saturn car. The customer lived in the Alaskan wilderness, and Saturn sent a customer service representative there for just a single day to replace the defective seat.

Product Differentiation and Creativity

The bases of product differentiation listed earlier in Table 5.1 indicate a broad range of ways in which firms can differentiate their products and services. In the end, however, any effort to list all possible ways to differentiate products and services is doomed to failure. Product differentiation is ultimately an expression of the creativity of individuals and groups within firms. It is limited only by the opportunities that exist, or that can be created, in a particular industry and by the willingness and ability of firms to creatively explore ways to take advantage of those opportunities. It is not unreasonable to expect that the day some academic researcher claims to have developed the definitive list of bases of product differentiation, some creative engineer, marketing specialist, or manager will think of yet another way to differentiate his or her product.

The Value of Product Differentiation

VRIO

In order to have the potential for generating competitive advantages, the bases of product differentiation upon which a firm competes must be valuable. The market conditions under which product differentiation can be valuable are discussed in the Strategy in Depth feature. More generally, in order to be valuable, bases of product differentiation must enable a firm to neutralize its threats and/or exploit its opportunities.

Product Differentiation and Environmental Threats

Successful product differentiation helps a firm respond to each of the environmental threats identified in the five forces framework. For example, product differentiation helps reduce the threat of new entry by forcing potential entrants to an industry to absorb not only the standard costs of beginning business but also

Strategy in Depth

The two classic treatments of the relationship between product differentiation and firm value, developed independently and published at approximately the same time, are by Edward Chamberlin and Joan Robinson.[16]

Both Chamberlin and Robinson examine product differentiation and firm performance relative to perfect competition. As explained in Chapter 2, under perfect competition, there are assumed to be numerous firms in an industry, each controlling a small proportion of the market, and the products or services sold by these firms are assumed to be identical. Under these conditions, firms face a horizontal demand curve (because they have no control over the price of the products they sell), and they maximize their economic performance by producing and selling output such that marginal revenue equals marginal costs. The maximum economic performance a firm in a perfectly competitive market can obtain, assuming no cost differences across firms, is normal economic performance.

When firms sell differentiated products, they gain some ability to adjust their prices. A firm can sell its output at very high prices and produce relatively smaller amounts of output, or it can sell its output at very low prices and produce relatively greater amounts of output. These trade-offs

**The Economics
of Product Differentiation**

between price and quantity produced suggest that firms selling differentiated products face a downward-sloping demand curve, rather than the horizontal demand curve for firms in a perfectly competitive market. Firms selling differentiated products and facing a downward-sloping demand curve are in an industry structure described by Chamberlin as **monopolistic competition**. It is as if, within the market niche defined by a firm's differentiated product, a firm possesses a monopoly.

Firms in monopolistically competitive markets still maximize their economic profit by producing and selling a quantity of products such that

marginal revenue equals marginal cost. The price that firms can charge at this optimal point depends on the demand they face for their differentiated product. If demand is large, then the price that can be charged is greater; if demand is low, then the price that can be charged is lower. However, if a firm's average total cost is below the price it can charge (that is, if average total cost is less than the demand-determined price), then a firm selling a differentiated product can earn an above-normal economic profit.

Consider the example presented in Figure 5.1. Several curves are relevant in this figure. First, notice that the demand (*D*) facing a firm in this industry is downward sloping. This means that the industry is not perfectly competitive and that a firm has some control over the prices it will charge for its products. Also, the marginal-revenue curve (*MR*) is downward sloping and everywhere lower than the demand curve. Marginal revenue is downward sloping because in order to sell additional levels of output of a single product, a firm must be willing to lower its price. The marginal-revenue curve is lower than the demand curve because this lower price applies to all the products sold by a firm, not just to any additional products the firm sells. The marginal-cost curve (*MC*) is upward sloping, indicating that in order to produce

the additional costs associated with overcoming incumbent firms' product differentiation advantages. The relationship between product differentiation and new entry has already been discussed in Chapter 2.

Product differentiation reduces the threat of rivalry, because each firm in an industry attempts to carve out its own unique product niche. Rivalry is not reduced to zero, for these products still compete with one another for a common set of customers, but it is somewhat attenuated because the customers each firm seeks are different. For example, both a Rolls Royce and a Hyundai satisfy the same basic additional outputs, a firm must accept additional costs. The average-total-cost curve (ATC) can have a variety of shapes, depending on the economies of scale, the cost of productive inputs, and other cost phenomena described in Chapter 4.

These four curves (demand, marginal revenue, marginal cost, and average total cost) can be used to determine the level of economic profit for a firm under monopolistic competition. In order to maximize profit, the firm produces an amount (Q_e) such that marginal costs equal marginal revenues. To determine the price of a firm's output at this level of production, a vertical line is drawn from the point where marginal costs equal marginal revenues. This line will intersect with the demand curve. Where this vertical line intersects demand, a horizontal line is drawn to the vertical (price) axis to determine the price a firm can charge. In the figure, this price is P_e. At the point P_e, average total cost is less than the price. The total revenue obtained by the firm in this situation (price x quantity) is indicated by the shaded area in the figure. The economic profit portion of this total revenue is indicated by the cross-hatched section of the shaded portion of the figure. Because this cross-hatched section is above average total costs in the figure, it represents a competitive advantage. If this section was below average total costs, it would represent a competitive disadvantage.

Chamberlin and Robinson go on to discuss the impact of entry into the market niche defined by a firm's differentiated product. As discussed in Chapter 2, a basic assumption of S-C-P models is that the existence of above-normal economic performance motivates entry into an industry or into a market niche within an industry. In monopolistically competitive industries, such entry means that the demand curve facing incumbent firms shifts downward and to the left. This implies that an incumbent firm's customers will buy less of its output if it maintains its prices or (equivalently) that a firm will have to lower its prices to maintain its current volume of sales. In the long run, entry into this market niche can lead to a situation where the price of goods or services sold when a firm produces output such that marginal cost equals marginal revenue is exactly equal to that firm's average total cost. At this point, a firm earns zero economic profits even if it still sells a differentiated product.

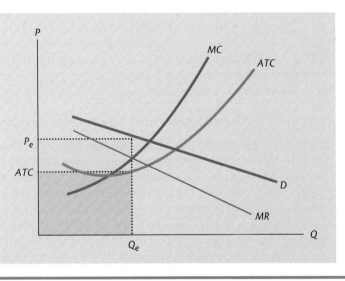

Sources: E. H. Chamberlin (1933). *The economics of monopolistic competition.* Cambridge, MA: MIT Press; J. Robinson (1934). "What is perfect competition?" *Quarterly Journal of Economics,* 49, pp. 104–120.

Figure 5.1 Product Differentiation and Firm Performance: The Analysis of Monopolistic Competition

consumer need—transportation—but it is unlikely that potential customers of Rolls Royce will also be interested in purchasing a Hyundai or vice versa.

Product differentiation also helps firms reduce the threat of substitutes by making a firm's current products appear more attractive than substitute products. For example, fresh food can be thought of as a substitute for frozen processed foods. In order to make its frozen processed foods more attractive than fresh foods, products like Stouffer's and Swanson are marketed heavily through television advertisements, newspaper ads, point-of-purchase displays, and coupons.

Product differentiation can also reduce the threat of suppliers. Powerful suppliers can raise the prices of the products or services they provide. Often, these increased supply costs must be passed on to a firm's customers in the form of higher prices if a firm's profit margin is not to deteriorate. A firm without a highly differentiated product may find it difficult to pass its increased costs on to customers, because these customers will have numerous other ways to purchase similar products or services from a firm's competitors. However, a firm with a highly differentiated product may have loyal customers or customers who are unable to purchase similar products or services from other firms. These types of customers are more likely to accept increased prices. Thus, a powerful supplier may be able to raise its prices, but, up to some point, these increases will not reduce the profitability of a firm selling a highly differentiated product.

The relationship between sugar suppliers and soft drink manufacturers over the last 30 years has had many of these characteristics. In the 1970s, sugar was a major ingredient in soft drinks. However, in the early 1980s, sugar prices rose suddenly. At first, soft drink companies were able to pass these increased costs on to customers in the form of increased prices. Customer loyalty to soft drink brands, and dislike for soft drink substitutes, kept customers purchasing soft drinks despite increased prices. However, as sugar prices continued to rise, several alternatives to sugar were developed. First, expensive sugar from sugar cane was supplemented by less expensive high-fructose corn syrup. Second, aspartame, a low-calorie sugar substitute (marketed under the brand name NutraSweet) was developed. Thus, although soft drink firms could raise their prices in response to increased sugar costs, at some point these higher prices led to the development of sugar substitutes that reduced the power of sugar suppliers over the soft drink industry.[17]

Finally, product differentiation can reduce the threat of buyers. When a firm sells a highly differentiated product, it enjoys a "quasi-monopoly" in that segment of the market. Buyers interested in purchasing this particular product must buy it from a particular firm. Any potential buyer power is reduced by the ability of a firm to withhold highly valued products or services from a buyer.

Product Differentiation and Environmental Opportunities

Product differentiation can also help a firm take advantage of environmental opportunities. For example, in fragmented industries firms can use product differentiation strategies to help consolidate a market. In the office-paper industry, Xerox has used its brand name to become the leading seller of paper for office copy machines and printers. Arguing that its paper is specially manufactured to avoid jamming in its own copy machines, Xerox was able to brand what had been a commodity product and facilitate the consolidation of what had been a very fragmented industry.[18]

The role of product differentiation in emerging industries has been discussed in Chapter 2. By being a first mover in these industries, firms can gain product differentiation advantages based on perceived technological leadership, preemption of strategically valuable assets, and buyer loyalty due to high switching costs.

In mature industries, product differentiation efforts often switch from attempts to introduce radically new technologies to product refinement as a basis of product differentiation. For example, in the mature retail gasoline market, firms attempt to differentiate their products by selling slightly modified gasoline (cleaner-burning gasoline, gasoline that cleans fuel injectors, and so forth) and by altering the product mix (linking gasoline sales with convenience stores). In mature markets, it is sometimes difficult to find ways to actually refine a product or service. In such settings, firms can sometimes be tempted to exaggerate the extent to which they have

Ethics and Strategy

*O*ne of the most common ways to try to differentiate a product is to make claims about that product's performance. In general, high-performance products command a price premium over low-performance products. However, the potential price advantages enjoyed by high-performance products can sometimes lead firms to make claims about their products that, at the least, strain credibility, and at the most, simply lie about what their products can do.

Some of these claims are easily dismissed as harmless exaggerations. Few people actually believe that using a particular type of whitening toothpaste is going to make your in-laws like you, or that not wearing a particular type of deodorant is going cause patrons in a bar to collapse when you lift your arms in victory after a foosball game. These exaggerations are harmless and present few ethical challenges.

However, in the field of health care, exaggerated product performance claims can have serious consequences. This can happen when a patient takes a medication with exaggerated performance claims in lieu of a medication with more modest, although accurate, performance claims. A history of false medical performance claims in the United States led to the formation of the Federal Drug Administration (FDA), a federal regulatory agency charged with evaluating the efficacy of drugs before they are marketed. Historically, the FDA has adopted the "gold standard" of drug approval—not only must a drug demon-

Product Claims and the Ethical Dilemmas in Health Care

strate that it does what it claims, it must also demonstrate that it does not do any significant harm to the patient. Patients can be confident that drugs that pass the FDA approval process meet the highest standards in the world.

However, this "gold standard" of approval creates important ethical dilemmas—mostly stemming from the time it takes a drug to pass FDA inspections. This process can take between five and seven years. During FDA trials, patients that might otherwise benefit from a drug are not allowed to use it because it hasn't yet received FDA approval. Thus, while the FDA approval process may work very well for people who may need a drug sometime in the future, it works less well for those who need a drug right now.

A growing suspicion among some consumers that the FDA process may prevent effective drugs from being marketed has helped feed the growth of alternative treatments—usually based on some herbal or more natural formula. Such treatments are careful to note that their claims—everything from re-growing hair to losing weight to enhancing athletic performance to quitting smoking—have not been tested by the FDA. And yet, these claims are still made.

Some of these performance claims seem at least reasonable. For example, it is now widely accepted that ephedra does behave as an amphetamine, and thus is likely to enhance strength and athletic performance. Others—including those that claim that a mixture of herbs can actually increase the size of male genitals—seem far-fetched, at best. Indeed, a recent analysis of herbal treatments making this claim found no ingredients that could have this effect, and found an unacceptably high concentration of bacteria from animal feces that can cause serious stomach disorders. Firms that sell products on the basis of exaggerated and unsubstantiated claims face their own ethical dilemmas. And without the FDA to ensure product safety and efficacy, the adage "caveat emptor"—or, let the buyer beware—seems like good advice.

Sources: J. Angwin (2003). "Some 'enlargement pills' pack impurities." *Wall Street Journal*, April 8, p. B1; G. Pisano (1991). "Nucleon, Inc." Harvard Business School Case No. 9-692-041.

refined and improved their products or services. The implications of these exaggerations are discussed in the Ethics and Strategy feature.

Product differentiation can also be an important strategic option in a declining industry. Product-differentiating firms may be able to become leaders in this kind of industry (based on their reputation, on unique product attributes, or on some other product differentiation basis). Alternatively, highly differentiated firms may be able to discover a viable market niche that will enable them to survive despite the overall decline in the market.

Finally, the decision to implement a product differentiation strategy can have a significant impact on how a firm acts in a global industry. For example, several firms in the retail clothing industry with important product differentiation advantages in their home markets are beginning to enter into the U.S. retail clothing market. These firms include Sweden's H & M Hennes & Mauritz AB with its emphasis on "cheap chic," the Dutch firm Mexx (a division of Liz Claiborne), the Spanish company Zara (a division of Inditex SA), and the French sportswear company Lacoste (a division of Devanlay SA).[19]

V R I O   Product Differentiation and Sustained Competitive Advantage

Product differentiation strategies add value by enabling firms to charge for their products or services prices that are greater than its average total cost. Firms that implement this strategy successfully can reduce a variety of environmental threats and exploit a variety of environmental opportunities. However, as discussed in Chapter 3, the ability of a strategy to add value to a firm must be linked with rare and costly-to-imitate organizational strengths in order to generate a sustained competitive advantage. Each of the bases of product differentiation listed earlier in this chapter varies with respect to how likely it is to be rare and costly to imitate.

Rare Bases for Product Differentiation

The concept of product differentiation generally assumes that the number of firms that have been able to differentiate their products in a particular way is, at some point in time, smaller than the number of firms needed to generate perfect competition dynamics. Indeed, the reason that highly differentiated firms can charge a price for their product that is greater than average total cost is because these firms are using a basis for product differentiation that few competing firms are also using.

Ultimately, the rarity of a product differentiation strategy depends on the ability of individual firms to be creative in finding new ways to differentiate their products. As suggested earlier, highly creative firms will be able to discover or create new ways to do this. These kinds of firms will always be one step ahead of the competition, for rival firms will often be trying to imitate these firms' last product differentiation move while creative firms are working on their next one.

The Imitability of Product Differentiation

Valuable and rare bases of product differentiation must be costly to imitate if they are to be sources of sustained competitive advantage. Both direct duplication and substitution, as approaches to imitation, are important in understanding the ability of product differentiation to generate competitive advantages.

Direct Duplication of Product Differentiation

As discussed in Chapter 4, firms that successfully implement a cost leadership strategy can choose whether or not they want to reveal this strategic choice to their competition by adjusting their prices. If they keep their prices high—despite their cost advantages—the existence of those cost advantages may not be revealed to competitors. Of course, other firms—like Wal-Mart—who are confident that their cost advantages cannot be duplicated at low cost are willing to reveal their cost advantage through charging lower prices for their products or services.

Firms pursuing product differentiation strategies usually do not have this option. More often than not, the act of selling a highly differentiated product or service reveals the basis upon which a firm is trying to differentiate its products. In fact, most firms go to great lengths to let their customers know how they are differentiating their products; and in the process of informing potential customers they also inform their competitors. Indeed, if competitors are not sure how a firm is differentiating its product, all they need to do is purchase that product themselves. Their own experience with the product—its features and other attributes—will tell them all they need to know about this firm's product differentiation strategy.

Knowing how a firm is differentiating its products, however, does not necessarily mean that competitors will be able to duplicate the strategy at low cost. The ability to duplicate a valuable and rare product differentiation strategy depends on the basis upon which a firm is differentiating its products. As suggested in Table 5.2, some bases of product differentiation—including the use of product features—are almost always easy to duplicate. Others—including product mix, links with other firms, product customization, product complexity, and consumer marketing—can sometimes be costly to duplicate. Finally, still other bases of product differentiation— including links between functions, timing, location, reputation, distribution channels, and service and support—are usually costly to duplicate.

How costly it is to duplicate a particular basis of product differentiation depends on the kinds of resources and capabilities that basis uses. When those resources and capabilities are acquired in unique historical settings, when there is some uncertainty about how to build these resources and capabilities, or when these resources and capabilities are socially complex in nature, then product differentiation strategies that exploit these kinds of resources and capabilities will be costly to imitate. These strategies can be a source of sustained competitive advantage for a firm. However, when a product differentiation strategy exploits resources and capabilities that do not possess these attributes, then those strategies are likely to be less costly to duplicate, and even if they are valuable and rare, will only be sources of temporary competitive advantage.

Bases of Product Differentiation That Are Easy to Duplicate. The one basis of product differentiation in Table 5.2 that is identified as almost always being easy to duplicate is product features. This is ironic since product features are by far the most popular way for firms to try to differentiate their products. Rarely do product features, by themselves, enable a firm to gain sustained competitive advantages from a product differentiation strategy.

For example, virtually every one of the product features used in the automobile industry to differentiate the products of different automobile companies has been duplicated. Chrysler's "cab forward" design has been incorporated in the design of many manufacturers. The curved, sporty styling of the Audi has surfaced in cars manufactured by Lexus and General Motors. GM's "On Star" system has been duplicated by Mercedes. Mercedes' crumple zone technology has become the industry standard as has GM's uni-body construction method. Indeed, only the Mazda Miata, Nissan 350 Z, and the Porsche 911 have remained unduplicated—and this has little to do with the product features of these cars and much more to do with their reputation.

The only time product features, per se, can be a source of sustained competitive advantage for a firm is when those features are protected by patents. However, as was discussed in Chapters 2 and 3, even patents provide only limited protection from direct duplication, except in very unusual settings.

Table 5.2　**Bases of Product Differentiation and the Cost of Duplication**

	History	Uncertainty	Social complexity
Low-cost duplication usually possible			
1. Product features	—	—	—
May be costly to duplicate			
2. Product mix	*	*	*
3. Links with other firms	*	—	**
4. Product customization	*	—	**
5. Product complexity	*	—	*
6. Consumer marketing	—	**	—
Usually costly to duplicate			
7. Links between functions	*	*	**
8. Timing	***	*	—
9. Location	***	—	—
10. Reputation	***	**	***
11. Distribution channels	**	*	**
12. Service and support	*	*	**

— = Not likely to be a source of costly duplication   * = Somewhat likely to be a source of costly duplication
** = Likely to be a source of costly duplication   *** = Very likely to be a source of costly duplication

While product features, by themselves, are usually not a source of sustained competitive advantage, they can be a source of a temporary competitive advantage. During the period of time when a firm has a temporary competitive advantage from implementing a product differentiation strategy based on product features, it may be able to attract new customers. Once these customers try this product, they may discover other features of a firm's products that make them attractive. If these other features are costly to duplicate, then they can be a source of sustained competitive advantage, even though the features that originally attracted a customer to a firm's products will often be rapidly duplicated by competitors.

Bases of Product Differentiation That May Be Costly to Duplicate. On the other hand, some bases of product differentiation may sometimes be costly to duplicate, at least in some circumstances. The first of these, listed in Table 5.2, is product mix.

Duplicating the features of another firm's products is usually not difficult. However, if that firm brings a series of products to market, if each of these products has unique features, and most importantly, if the products are highly integrated with each other, then this mix of products may be costly to duplicate. Certainly, the technological integration of the mix of information technology products sold by IBM and other firms has been relatively difficult to duplicate for firms that do not manufacture all these products themselves.

On the other hand, when this basis of a product mix advantage is a common customer, then duplication is often less difficult. Thus, while having a mall that brings several stores together in a single place is a source of competitive advantage over stand-alone stores, it is not a competitive advantage over other malls that provide the same service. Since there continue to be opportunities to build such malls, the fact that malls make it easier for a common set of customers to shop does not give any one mall a sustained competitive advantage.

Links with other firms may also be costly to duplicate, especially when those links depend on socially complex relationships. Setting up a racing team to compete in NASCAR requires a great deal of time and effort. However, most of the skills needed to set up a team are widely available and thus not likely to be a source of competitive advantage for any one firm. The same is probably true for fast-food companies—like McDonald's marketing its Happy Meals using characters from a single summer movie. However, to develop a marketing relationship between a firm and a movie studio such that a firm can plan its marketing efforts years in advance requires a great deal of coordination and cooperation. Thus, to the extent that McDonald's has that kind of relationship with a movie studio, or to the extent that BMW and Aston Martin coordinate their product development cycle with the release of a particular movie, these links with other firms may be costly to duplicate and a source of sustained competitive advantage.

The extent to which interfirm links can provide sources of sustained competitive advantage is discussed in more detail in Chapter 9.

In the same way, product customization and product complexity are often easy-to-duplicate bases of product differentiation. However, sometimes the ability of a firm to customize its products for one of its customers depends on the close relationships it has developed with those customers. Product customization of this sort depends on the willingness of a firm to share often-proprietary details about its operations, products, research and development, or other characteristics with a supplying firm. Willingness to share this kind of information, in turn, depends on the ability of each firm to trust and rely on the other. The firm opening its operations to a supplier must trust that that supplier will not make this information broadly available to competing firms. The firm supplying customized products must trust that its customer will not take unfair advantage of it. If two firms have developed these kinds of socially complex relationships, and few other firms have them, then links with other firms will be costly to duplicate and a source of sustained competitive advantage.

The product customization seen in both enterprise software and in high-end customized bicycles has these socially complex features. In a real sense, when these products are purchased, a relationship with a supplier is being established—a relationship that is likely to last a long period of time. Once this relationship is established, partners are likely to be unwilling to abandon it, unless, of course, a party to the exchange tries to take unfair advantage of another party to that exchange. This possibility is discussed in detail in Chapter 9.

Finally, consumer marketing, though a very common form of product differentiation, is often easy to duplicate. Thus, while Mountain Dew has established itself as the "Extreme Games" drink, other drinks, including Gatorade, have also begun to tap into this market segment. Of course, every once in a while an advertising campaign or slogan, a point-of-purchase display, or some other attribute of a consumer marketing campaign will unexpectedly catch on and create greater-than-expected product awareness. In beer, marketing campaigns such as "Tastes great, less filling," "Why ask why," the "Budweiser Frogs," and "What's Up?" have had these unusual effects. If a firm, in relation with its various consumer marketing agencies, is systematically able to develop these superior consumer marketing campaigns, then it may be able to obtain a sustained competitive advantage. However, if such campaigns are unpredictable and largely a matter of a firm's good luck, they cannot be expected to be a source of sustained competitive advantage.

Bases of Product Differentiation That Are Usually Costly to Duplicate. The remaining bases of product differentiation listed in Table 5.2 are usually costly to duplicate. Firms that differentiate their products on these bases may be able to obtain sustained competitive advantages.

Linkages across functions within a single firm are usually a costly-to-duplicate basis of product differentiation. Where linkages with other firms can be either easy or costly to duplicate, depending on the nature of the relationship that exists between firms, linkages across functions within a single firm usually require socially complex, trusting relations. There are numerous built-in conflicts between functions and divisions within a single firm. Organizations that have a history and culture that support cooperative relations among conflicting divisions may be able to set aside functional and divisional conflicts to cooperate in delivering a differentiated product to the market. However, firms with a history of conflict across functional and divisional boundaries face a significant, and costly, challenge in altering these socially complex, historical patterns.

Indeed, the research on architectural competence in pharmaceutical firms suggests that not only do some firms possess this competence, but that other firms do not. Moreover, despite the significant advantages that accrue to firms with this competence, firms without this competence have, on average, been unable to develop it. All this suggests that such a competence, if it is also rare, is likely to be costly to duplicate and thus a source of sustained competitive advantage.

Timing is also a difficult-to-duplicate basis of product differentiation. As suggested in Chapter 3, it is difficult (if not impossible) to recreate a firm's unique history. If that history endows a firm with special resources and capabilities it can use to differentiate its products, this product differentiation strategy can be a source of sustained competitive advantage. Rivals of a firm with such a timing-based product differentiation advantage may need to seek alternative ways to differentiate their products. Thus, it is not surprising that universities that compete with the oldest universities in the country find alternative ways to differentiate themselves—through their size, the quality of the extramural sports, through their diversity—rather than relying on their age.

Location is often a difficult-to-duplicate basis of product differentiation. This is especially the case when a firm's location is unique. For example, research on the hotel preferences of business travelers suggests that location is a major determinant of the decision to stay in a hotel. Hotels that are convenient to both major transportation and commercial centers in a city are preferred, other things being equal, to hotels in other types of locations. Indeed, location has been shown to be a more important decision criterion for business travelers than price. If only a few hotels in a city have these prime locations, and if no further hotel development is possible, then hotels with these locations can gain sustained competitive advantages.

Of all the bases of product differentiation listed in this chapter, perhaps none is more difficult to duplicate than a firm's reputation. As suggested earlier, a firm's reputation is actually a socially complex relationship between a firm and its customers, based on years of experience, commitment, and trust. Reputations are not built quickly, nor can they be bought and sold. Rather, they can only be developed over time by consistent investment in the relationship between a firm and its customers. A firm with a positive reputation can enjoy a significant competitive advantage, whereas a firm with a negative reputation, or no reputation, may have to invest significant amounts over long periods of time to match the differentiated firm.

Distribution channels can also be a costly-to-duplicate basis of product differentiation, for at least two reasons. First, relations between a firm and its distribution channels are often socially complex and thus costly to duplicate. Second, the supply of distribution channels may be limited. Firms that already have access to these channels may be able to use them, but firms that do not have such access may be forced to create their own or develop new channels. Creating new channels, or developing entirely new means of distribution, can be difficult and costly undertakings.[20] These costs are one of the primary motivations underlying many international joint ventures (see Chapter 9).

Finally, level of service and support can be a costly-to-duplicate basis of product differentiation. In most industries, it is usually not too costly to provide a minimum level of service and support. In home electronics, this minimum level of service can be provided by a network of independent electronic repair shops. In automobiles, this level of service can be provided by service facilities associated with dealerships. In fast foods, this level of service can be provided by a minimum level of employee training.

However, moving beyond this minimum level of service and support can be difficult for at least two reasons. First, increasing the quality of service and support may involve substantial amounts of costly training. McDonald's has created a sophisticated training facility (Hamburger University) to maintain its unusually high level of service in fast foods. General Electric has invested heavily in training for service and support over the last several years. Many Japanese automakers spent millions on training employees to help support auto dealerships, before they opened U.S. manufacturing facilities.[21]

More important than the direct costs of the training needed to provide high-quality service and support, these bases of product differentiation often reflect the attitude of a firm and its employees toward customers. In many firms throughout the world, the customer has become "the bad guy." This is, in many ways, understandable. Employees tend to interact with their customers less frequently than they interact with other employees. When they do interact with customers, they are often the recipients of complaints directed at the firm. In these settings, hostility toward the customer can develop. Such hostility is, of course, inconsistent with a product differentiation strategy based on customer service and support.

In the end, high levels of customer service and support are based on socially complex relations between firms and customers. Firms that have conflicts with their customers may face some difficulty duplicating the high levels of service and support provided by competing firms.

Substitutes for Product Differentiation

The bases of product differentiation outlined in this chapter vary in how rare they are likely to be and in how difficult they are to duplicate. However, the ability of the bases of product differentiation to generate a sustained competitive advantage also depends on whether low-cost substitutes exist.

Substitutes for bases of product differentiation can take two forms. First, many of the bases of product differentiation listed in Table 5.1 can be partial substitutes for each other. For example, product features, product customization, and product complexity are all very similar bases of product differentiation and thus can act as substitutes for each other. A particular firm may try to develop a competitive advantage by differentiating its products on the basis of product customization only to find that its customization advantages are reduced as another firm alters the features of its products. In a similar way, linkages between functions, linkages between firms, and product mix, as bases of product differentiation, can also be substitutes for each other. IBM links its sales, service, and consulting functions to differentiate itself in the computer market. Other computer firms, however, may develop close relationships with computer service companies and consulting firms to close this product differentiation advantage. Given that different bases of product differentiation are often partial substitutes for each other, it is not surprising that firms pursue these multiple bases of product differentiation simultaneously.

Second, other of the strategies discussed throughout this book can be substitutes for many of the bases of product differentiation listed in Table 5.1. One firm may try to gain a competitive advantage through adjusting its product mix, and another firm may substitute strategic alliances to create the same type of product differentiation. For example, Southwest Airline's continued emphasis on friendly, on-time, low cost service and United Airlines' emphasis on its links to Lufthansa and other worldwide airlines through the Star Alliance can both be seen as product differentiation efforts that are at least partial substitutes.[22]

In contrast, some of the other bases of product differentiation discussed in this chapter have few obvious close substitutes. These include timing, location, distribution channels, and service and support. To the extent that these bases of product differentiation are also valuable, rare, and difficult to duplicate, they may be sources of sustained competitive advantage.

VRIO

Organizing to Implement Product Differentiation

As was suggested in Chapter 3, the ability to implement a strategy depends on the adjustment of a firm's structure, its management controls, and its compensation policies to be consistent with that strategy. Where strategy implementation for firms adopting a cost leadership strategy focuses on reducing a firm's costs and increasing its efficiency, strategy implementation for a firm adopting a product differentiation strategy must focus on innovation, creativity, and product performance. Where cost-leading firms are all about customer value, product-differentiating firms are all about style. How the need for style is reflected in a firm's structure, controls, and compensation policies is summarized in Table 5.3.

Organizational Structure and Implementing Product Differentiation

Both cost leadership and product differentiation strategies are implemented through the use of a functional or U-form organizational structure. However, where the U-form structure used to implement a cost leadership strategy has few layers, simple reporting relationships, a small corporate staff, and focuses on only a few business functions, the U-form structure for a firm implementing a product differentiation strategy can be somewhat more complex. For example, these firms often use temporary cross-divisional *and* cross-functional teams to manage the development and implementation of new, innovative, and highly differentiated products. These teams bring individuals from different businesses and different functional areas together to cooperate on a particular new product or service.

One firm that has used these cross-divisional and cross-functional teams effectively is the British advertising agency WPP. WPP owns several very large advertising agencies, several public relations firms, several marketing research companies, and so forth. Each of these businesses operates relatively independently in most areas. However, the corporation has identified a few markets where cross-divisional and cross-functional collaboration is important. One of these is the health care market. To

Table 5.3 **Organizing to Implement Product Differentiation Strategies**

Organizational Structure:
1. Cross-divisional/cross-functional product development teams
2. Complex matrix structures
3. Isolated pockets of intense creative efforts: Skunk works

Management Control Systems:
1. Broad decision-making guidelines
2. Managerial freedom within guidelines
3. A policy of experimentation

Compensation Policies:
1. Rewards for risk-taking, not punishment for failures
2. Rewards for creative flair
3. Multidimensional performance measurement

exploit opportunities in this health care market, WPP, the corporation, forms teams of advertising specialists, market research specialists, public relations specialists, and so on, drawn from each of the businesses it owns. The resulting cross-divisional teams are given the responsibility of developing new and highly differentiated approaches to developing marketing strategies for their clients in the health care industry.[23]

The creation of cross-divisional, or cross-functional teams often implies that a firm has implemented some form of matrix structure. As suggested in Chapter 4, a **matrix structure** exists when individuals in a firm have two or more "bosses" simultaneously. Thus, for example, if a person from one of WPP's advertising agencies is assigned temporarily to a or cross-divisional team, that person has two bosses: the head of the temporary team he/she has been assigned to and his/her boss back in the advertising agency. Managing two bosses simultaneously can be very challenging, especially when they have conflicting interests, and, as we will see in Chapter 8, the interests of these multiple bosses *will* often conflict.

A particularly important form of the cross-divisional or cross-functional team exists when this team is relieved of all other responsibilities in the firm and focuses all its attention on developing a new innovative product or service. The best known example of this approach to developing a differentiated product occurred at the Lockheed Corporation during the 1950s and 1960s when small groups of engineers were put on very focused teams to develop sophisticated and top secret military aircraft. These teams would have a section of the Lockheed facility dedicated to their efforts and designated as off-limits to almost all other employees. The joke was that these intensive creative efforts were so engaging that members of these teams actually would forget to shower—hence their name "**Skunk Works**." Such skunk works have been used by numerous firms to focus the creative energy required to develop and introduce highly differentiated products.[24]

Management Controls and Implementing Product Differentiation

The first two management controls helpful for implementing product differentiation listed in Table 5.3—broad decision-making guidelines and managerial freedom within those guidelines—often go together, even though they sound somewhat contradictory. These potential contradictions are discussed in the Strategy in the Emerging Enterprise feature. Managing these contradictions is one of the central challenges of firms looking to implement product differentiation strategies.

Broad decision-making guidelines help bring order to what otherwise might be a chaotic decision-making process. When managers have no constraints in their decision making, they can make decisions that are disconnected from each other and inconsistent with a firm's overall mission and objectives. This results in decisions that are either not implemented or not implemented well.

On the other hand, if these decision-making guidelines become too narrow, they can stifle creativity within a firm. As was suggested earlier, a firm's ability to differentiate its products is limited only by its creativity. Thus, decision guidelines must be narrow enough to ensure that the decisions made are consistent with a firm's mission and objectives. However, these guidelines must be broad enough so that managerial creativity is not destroyed. In well-managed firms implementing product differentiation strategies, as long as managerial decisions fall within the broad decision-making guidelines in a firm, managers have the right—in fact, are expected—to make creative decisions.

A firm that has worked hard to reach this balance between chaos and control is 3M. In an effort to provide guiding principles that define the range of acceptable decisions at 3M, its senior managers have developed a set of innovating principles. These are presented in Table 5.4 and define the boundaries of innovative chaos at

Strategy in the Emerging Enterprise

*I*n the 1950s, a well-known economist named Joseph Schumpeter suggested that only very large and profitable companies have the resources necessary to invest in creating new and highly innovative products and services. His conclusion suggested that the social evils caused by economic power being concentrated in the hands of a relatively few large and powerful organizations was simply the price society had to pay for innovations that could benefit consumers.

The economic history of the last 30 years or so suggests that one of Schumpeter's key assumptions—that only large firms can afford to be innovative—is wrong. Indeed, over this time period, it is clear that a great deal of innovation has occurred through the creation of entrepreneurial firms. Firms such as Dell, Microsoft, Intel, Apple, Home Depot, Cisco, Gateway, Sun, Office Depot, Nike, Oracle, PeopleSoft, Foot Locker, Amazon.com, and Starbucks have all been sources of major innovations in their industries, and all were begun as entrepreneurial ventures in the last 30 years. Indeed, given the impact of these and other entrepreneurial ventures on the worldwide economy during this time period, it is possible to call the last 30 years the "era of the entrepreneur."

What is it about entrepreneurial firms that enables them to develop innovations that sometimes come to dominate a market? Some scholars have sug-

Can Only Small Firms Be Innovative?

gested that the small size and lack of resources that characterize entrepreneurial start-ups, far from limiting their innovativeness, actually facilitate innovation.

For example, entrepreneurial firms have relatively little to lose when engaging in innovation. If the market accepts their innovation, great; if it doesn't, move on to the next innovation. Established firms, on the other hand, may have a significant stake in an older technology, an older distribution system, or an older type of customer. Established firms may be unwilling to cannibalize the sales of their current products for new and innovative products.

Moreover, small entrepreneurial firms have relatively few bureaucratic controls. Information and ideas flow freely in these organizations. Such information flow tends to facilitate innovation. Larger firms, on the other hand, have usually installed numerous bureaucratic controls that impede cross-functional communication, and thus slow innovation.

Indeed, some have even argued that the types of people that are attracted to small entrepreneurial firms tend to be more innovative than people that are attracted to larger, more stable companies. People who are comfortable with risk-seeking and creativity may be attracted to an entrepreneurial firm, while people who are less comfortable with risk-seeking and creativity may be attracted to larger, more stable firms.

Whatever the reasons, many large firms have come to realize that they cannot afford to be "out-innovated" and "out-maneuvered" by entrepreneurial start-ups. In response, larger firms have begun to adopt policies and procedures that try to create the kind of innovativeness and creativity one often sees in entrepreneurial firms. Some firms—like 3M (see Table 5.4)—have been quite successful in this effort. Others have been less successful.

Sources: C. Christensen (1997). *The innovator's dilemma*. Boston: Harvard Business School Press; J. Schumpeter (1942). *Capitalism, socialism and democracy*. New York: Harper and Rowe; T. Zenger and E. Rasmusen (1990). "Diseconomies of scale in employment contracts." *Journal of Law, Economics, and Organization*, 6, pp. 65–98.

3M. Within these boundaries, managers and engineers are expected to be creative and innovative in developing highly differentiated products and services.[25]

Another firm that has managed this tension well is British Airways (BA). BA has extensive training programs to teach its flight attendants how to provide world-class service, especially for its business-class customers. This training constitutes standard operating procedures that give purpose and structure to BA's efforts to provide a differentiated service in the highly competitive airline industry. Interestingly, however, BA also trains its flight attendants in when to violate these standard policies and procedures. By recognizing that no set of management controls can ever anticipate all the special situations that can occur when provid-

Table 5.4   **Guiding Innovative Principles at 3M***

1. **Vision.** Declare the importance of innovation; make it part of the company's self-image. "Our efforts to encourage and support innovation are proof that we really do intend to achieve our vision of ourselves . . . that we intend to become what we want to be . . . as a business and as creative individuals."

2. **Foresight.** Find out where technologies and markets are going. Identify articulated and unarticulated needs of customers. "If you are working on a next-generation medical imaging device, you'll probably talk to radiologists, but you might also sit down with people who enhance images from interplanetary space probes."

3. **Stretch goals.** Set goals that will make you and the organization stretch to make quantum improvements. Although many projects are pursued, place your biggest bets on those that change the basis of competition and redefine the industry. "We have a number of stretch goals at 3M. The first states that we will drive 30 percent of all sales from products introduced in the past 4 years. . . . To establish a sense of urgency, we've recently added another goal, which is that we want 10 percent of our sales to come from products that have been in the market for just 1 year . . . Innovation is time sensitive . . . you need to move quickly."

4. **Empowerment.** Hire good people and trust them, delegate responsibilities, provide slack resources, and get out of the way. Be tolerant of initiative and the mistakes that occur because of that initiative. "William McKnight [a former chairman of 3M] came up with one way to institutionalize a tolerance of individual effort. He said that all technical employees could devote 15 percent of their time to a project of their own invention. In other words, they could manage themselves for 15 percent of the time. . . . The number is not so important as the message, which is this: The system has some slack in it. If you have a good idea, and the commitment to squirrel away time to work on it and the raw nerve to skirt your lab manager's expressed desires, then go for it.
   Put another way, we want to institutionalize a bit of rebellion in our labs. We can't have all our people off totally on their own . . . we do believe in

discipline . . . but at the same time 3M management encourages a healthy disrespect for 3M management. This is not the sort of thing we publicize in our annual report, but the stories we tell—with relish—are frequently about 3Mers who have circumvented their supervisors and succeeded.
   We also recognize that when you let people follow their own lead . . . everyone doesn't wind up at the same place. You can't ask people to have unique visions and march in lockstep. Some people are very precise, detail-oriented people . . . and others are fuzzy thinkers and visionaries . . . and this is exactly what we want."

5. **Communications.** Open, extensive exchanges according to ground rules in forums that are present for sharing ideas and where networking is each individual's responsibility. Multiple methods for sharing information are necessary. "When innovators communicate with each other, you can leverage their discoveries. This is critically important because it allows companies to get the maximum return on their substantial investments in new technologies. It also acts as a stimulus to further innovation. Indeed, we believe that the ability to combine and transfer technologies is as important as the original discovery of a technology."

6. **Rewards and recognition.** Emphasize individual recognition more than monetary rewards through peer recognition and by choice of managerial or technical promotion routes. "Innovation is an intensely human activity."
   "I've laid out six elements of 3M's corporate culture that contribute to a tradition of innovation: vision, foresight, stretch goals, empowerment, communication, and recognition. . . . The list is . . . too orderly. Innovation at 3M is anything but orderly. It is sensible, in that our efforts are directed at reaching our goals, but the organization . . . and the process . . . and sometimes the people can be chaotic. We are managing in chaos, and this is the right way to manage if you want innovation. It's been said that the competition never knows what we are going to come up with next. The fact is, neither do we."

*As expressed by W. Coyne (1996) *Building a tradition of innovation*. The Fifth U.K. Innovation Lecture, Department of Trade and Industry, London. Cited in Van de Ven et al. (1999), pp. 198–200.

ing service to customers, BA empowers its employees to meet specific customer needs. This enables BA to have both a clearly defined product differentiation strategy and the flexibility to adjust this strategy as the situation dictates.[26]

Firms can also facilitate the implementation of a product differentiation strategy by adopting a **policy of experimentation**. Such a policy exists when firms are committed to engage in several related product differentiation efforts simultaneously. That these product differentiation efforts are related suggests that a firm has some vision about how a particular market is likely to unfold over time. However, that there are several of these product differentiation efforts occurring simultaneously suggests that a firm is not overly committed to a particular narrow vision about how a market is going to evolve. Rather, several different experiments facilitate the exploration of different futures in a marketplace. Indeed, successful experiments can actually help define the future evolution of a marketplace.

Consider, for example, Charles Schwab, the innovative discount broker. In the face of increased competition from full-service and Internet-based brokerage firms, Schwab engaged in a series of experiments to discover the next generation of products it could offer to its customers and the different ways it could differentiate those products. Schwab investigated a software for simplifying online mutual fund selection, online futures trading, and online company research. It also formed an exploratory alliance with Goldman Sachs to evaluate the possibility of enabling Schwab customers to trade in initial public offerings. Not all of Schwab's experiments led to the introduction of highly differentiated products. For example, based on some experimental investments, Schwab decided not to get into the credit card market. However, by experimenting with a range of possible product differentiation moves, it was able to develop a range of new products for the fast-changing financial services industry.[27]

Compensation Policies and Implementing Product Differentiation Strategies

The compensation policies used to implement product differentiation listed in Table 5.3 very much complement the organizational structure and managerial controls listed in that table. For example, a policy of experimentation has little impact on the ability of a firm to implement product differentiation strategies if every time an innovative experiment fails, individuals are punished for taking risks. Thus, compensation policies that reward risk-taking and celebrate a creative flair help to enable a firm to implement its product differentiation strategy.

Consider, for example, Nordstrom's. Nordstrom's is a department store that celebrates the risk-taking and creative flair of its associates as they try to satisfy their customers' needs. The story is often told of a Nordstrom's sales associate who allowed a customer to return a set of tires to the store because she wasn't satisfied with them. What makes this story interesting—whether or not it is true—is that Nordstrom's doesn't sell tires. But this sales associate felt empowered to make what is obviously a risky decision, and this decision is celebrated within Nordstrom's as an example of the kind of service that Nordstrom's customers should expect.

The last compensation policy listed in Table 5.4 is multidimensional performance measurement. In implementing a cost leadership strategy, compensation should focus on providing appropriate incentives for managers and employees to reduce costs. Various forms of cash payments, stock, and stock options can all be tied to the attainment of specific cost goals and thus can be used to create incentives for realizing cost advantages. Similar techniques can be used to create incentives for helping a firm implement its product differentiation advantage. However, since the implementation of a product differentiation strategy generally involves the integration of multiple business functions, often through the use of product development teams, compensation schemes designed to help implement this strategy must generally recognize its multifunctional character.

Thus, rather than focusing only on a single dimension of performance, these firms often examine employee performance along multiple dimensions simultaneously. Examples of such dimensions include not only a product's sales and profitability, but customer satisfaction, an employee's willingness to cooperate with other businesses and functions within a firm, an employee's ability to effectively facilitate cross-divisional and cross-functional teams, and an employee's ability to engage in creative decision making.

Can Firms Implement Product Differentiation and Cost Leadership Simultaneously?

The arguments developed in Chapter 4 and in this chapter suggest that cost leadership and product differentiation business strategies, under certain conditions, can both create sustained competitive advantages. Given the beneficial impact of both strategies on a firm's competitive position, an important question becomes: "Can a single firm simultaneously implement both strategies?" After all, if each separately can improve a firm's performance, wouldn't it be better for a firm to implement both?

No: These Strategies Cannot Be Implemented Simultaneously

A quick comparison of the organizational requirements for the successful implementation of cost leadership strategies and product differentiation strategies presented in Table 5.5 summarizes one perspective on the question of whether or not these strategies can be implemented simultaneously. In this view the organizational requirements of these strategies are essentially contradictory. Cost leadership requires simple reporting relationships, but product differentiation requires cross-divisional/cross-functional linkages. Cost leadership requires intense labor supervision, but product differentiation requires less intense supervision of creative employees. Cost leadership requires rewards for cost reduction, but product

Table 5.5 **The Organizational Requirements for Implementing Cost Leadership and Product Differentiation Strategies**

Cost leadership	Product differentiation
Organizational structure	**Organizational structure**
1. Few layers in the reporting structure	1. Cross-divisional/cross-functional product development teams
2. Simple reporting relationships	2. Willingness to explore new structures to exploit new opportunities
3. Small corporate staff	3. Isolated pockets of intense creative efforts
4. Focus on narrow range of business functions	
Management control systems	**Management control systems**
1. Tight cost-control systems	1. Broad decision-making guidelines
2. Quantitative cost goals	2. Managerial freedom within guidelines
3. Close supervision of labor, raw material, inventory, and other costs	3. Policy of experimentation
4. A cost leadership philosophy	
Compensation policies	**Compensation policies**
1. Reward for cost reduction	1. Rewards for risk-taking, not punishment for failures
2. Incentives for all employees to be involved in cost reduction	2. Rewards for creative flair
	3. Multidimensional performance measurement

Figure 5.2 Simultaneous Implementation of Cost Leadership and Product Differentiation Competitive Strategies: Being "Stuck in the Middle"

Source: M. E. Porter (1980). *Competitive strategy: techniques for analyzing industries and competitors.* New York: Free Press, a Division of Simon & Schuster Adult Publishing Group.

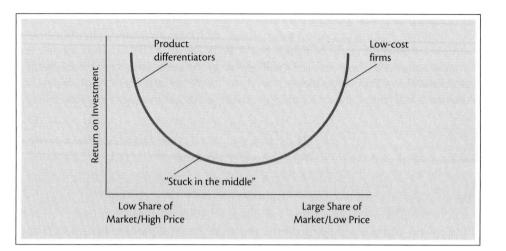

differentiation requires rewards for creative flair. It is reasonable to ask, "Can a single firm combine these multiple contradictory skills and abilities?"

Some have argued that firms that attempt to implement both strategies will end up doing neither well. This logic leads to the curve pictured in Figure 5.2. This figure suggests that there are often only two ways to earn superior economic performance within a single industry: (1) by selling high-priced products and gaining small market share (product differentiation) or (2) by selling low-priced products and gaining large market share (cost leadership). Firms that do not make this choice of strategies (medium price, medium market share) or that attempt to implement both strategies will fail. These firms are said to be "stuck in the middle."[28]

Yes: These Strategies Can Be Implemented Simultaneously

More recent work contradicts assertions about being "stuck in the middle." This work suggests that firms that are successful in both cost leadership and product differentiation can often expect to gain a sustained competitive advantage. This advantage reflects at least two processes.

Differentiation, Market Share, and Low-Cost Leadership
First, firms that are able to successfully differentiate their products and services are likely to see an increase in their volume of sales. This is especially the case if the basis of product differentiation is attractive to a large number of potential customers. Thus, product differentiation can lead to increased volumes of sales. It has already been established (in Chapter 4) that an increased volume of sales can lead to economies of scale, learning, and other forms of cost reduction. So, successful product differentiation can, in turn, lead to cost reductions and a cost leadership position.[29]

This is the situation that best describes McDonald's. McDonald's has traditionally followed a product differentiation strategy, emphasizing cleanliness, consistency, and fun in its fast-food outlets. Over time, McDonald's has used its differentiated product to become the market share leader in the fast-food industry. This market position has enabled it to reduce its costs, so that it is now the cost leader in fast foods as well. Thus, McDonald's level of profitability depends both on its product differentiation strategy and its low-cost strategy. Either one of these two strategies by itself would be difficult to overcome; together they give McDonald's a very costly-to-imitate competitive advantage.[30]

Managing Organizational Contractions

Product differentiation can lead to high market share and low costs. It may also be the case that some firms develop special skills in managing the contradictions that are part of simultaneously implementing low-cost and product differentiation strategies. Some recent research on automobile manufacturing helps describe these special skills.[31] Traditional thinking in automotive manufacturing was that plants could either reduce manufacturing costs by speeding up the assembly line or increase the quality of the cars they made by slowing the line, emphasizing team-based production, and so forth. In general, it was thought that plants could not simultaneously build low-cost/high-quality (that is low cost *and* highly differentiated) automobiles.

Several researchers at the Massachusetts Institute of Technology examined this traditional wisdom. They began by developing rigorous measures of the cost and quality performance of automobile plants and then applied these measures to over 70 auto plants throughout the world that assembled mid-size sedans. What they discovered was six plants in the entire world that had, at the time this research was done, very low costs *and* very high quality.[32]

In examining what made these six plants different from other auto plants, the researchers focused on a broad range of manufacturing policies, management practices, and cultural variables. Three important findings emerged. First, these six plants had the best manufacturing technology hardware available—robots, laser-guided paint machines, and so forth. However, since many of the plants in the study had these same technologies, manufacturing technology by itself was not enough to make these six plants special. In addition, policies and procedures at these plants implemented a range of highly participative, group-oriented management techniques, including participative management, team production, and total quality management. As important, employees in these plants had a sense of loyalty and commitment toward the plant they worked for—a belief that they would be treated fairly by their plant managers.

What this research shows is that firms *can* simultaneously implement cost leadership and product differentiation strategies if they learn how to manage the contradictions inherent in these two strategies. The management of these contradictions, in turn, depends on socially complex relations among employees, between employees and the technology they use, and between employees and the firm for which they work. These relations are not only valuable (because they enable a firm to implement cost leadership and differentiation strategies) but also socially complex and thus likely to be costly to imitate and a source of sustained competitive advantage.

Recently, many scholars have backed away from the original "stuck in the middle" arguments and now suggest that low-cost firms must have competitive levels of product differentiation to survive, and that product differentiation firms must have competitive levels of cost to survive.[33] So, for example, a firm like the fashion design company Versace—the ultimate product differentiating firm—has recently had to hire a new CEO and controller to help control its costs.[34]

Product Differentiation in an International Context

The tension that sometimes exists between cost leadership and product differentiation strategies domestically can also exist internationally. Here, this tension is manifest by the need for firms to simultaneously be responsive to local market needs while still integrating operations across multiple countries. On the one hand, local responsiveness enables a firm to implement a product differentiation strategy internationally, and failure to do so can lead to marketing blunders, some of which are described in the Global Perspectives feature. On the other hand, global integration can enable a firm to gain the cost advantages associated with international operations, as described in Chapter 4.

Global Perspectives

International Marketing Blunders

Lack of local responsiveness has led to some well-known—and sometimes quite funny—international product differentiation blunders. For example, General Motors once introduced the Chevrolet Nova to South America, even though "No va" in Spanish means "it won't go." When Coca-Cola was first introduced in China, it was translated into Ke-kou-ke-la, which turns out to mean either "bite the wax tadpole" or "female horse stuffed with wax," depending on which dialect was being spoken. Coca-Cola reintroduced its product with the name Ke-kou-ko-le, which roughly translates into "happiness in the mouth."

Coca-Cola is not the only beverage firm to run into problems internationally. Pepsi's slogan "Come alive with the Pepsi generation" was translated into "Pepsi will bring your ancestors back from the dead" in Taiwan. In Italy, a marketing campaign for Schweppes tonic water was translated into Schweppes toilet water—not a terribly appealing drink. Bicardi developed a fruity drink called "Pavian." Unfortunately, "Pavian" means baboon in German. Coors used its "Turn it loose" slogan when selling beer in Spain and Latin America.

Unfortunately, "Turn it loose" was translated into "Suffer from diarrhea."

Food companies have had similar problems. Kentucky Fried Chicken's slogan "Finger-lickin' good" translates into "eat your fingers off" in Chinese. In Arabic, the "Jolly Green Giant" translates into "Intimidating Green Ogre." Frank Perdue's famous catch phrase—"It takes a tough man to make a tender chicken"—takes on a slightly different meaning when translated into Spanish—

"It takes a sexually stimulated man to make a chicken affectionate." And Gerber found that it was unable to sell its baby food—with pictures of cute babies on the jar—in Africa because the tradition in Africa is to put pictures of what is inside the jar on the label. Think about it.

Other product differentiation blunders include Colgate's decision to introduce Cue toothpaste in France, even though Cue is the name of a French pornographic magazine; an American T-shirt manufacturer who wanted to print up T-shirts in Spanish that said "I saw the Pope" (el Papa) but instead printed up T-shirts that said "I saw the potato" (la papa); and Salem cigarettes, whose slogan "Salem—feeling free" translated into Japanese as "When smoking Salem, you feel so refreshed that your mind seems to be free and empty." What were they smoking?

However, of all these marketing blunders, perhaps none tops Electrolux—a Scandinavian vacuum cleaner manufacturer. While its marketing slogan for the U.S. market does rhyme—"Nothing sucks like an Electrolux"—it doesn't really communicate what the firm had in mind.

Source: www.relojournal.com.

Traditionally, it has been thought that firms had to choose between local responsiveness and international integration. For example, firms like CIBA-Geigy (a Swiss chemical company), Nestlé (a Swiss food company), and Philips (a Dutch consumer electronics firm) have chosen to emphasize local responsiveness. Nestlé, for example, owns nearly 8,000 brand names worldwide. However, of those 8,000 brands, only 750 are registered in more than 1 country, and only 80 are registered in more than 10 countries. Nestlé adjusts its product attributes to the needs of local consumers, adopts brand names that resonate with those consumers, and builds its brands for long-run profitability by country. For example, in the United States, Nestlé's condensed milk carries the brand name "Carnation" (obtained through the acquisition of the Carnation Company); in Asia, this same product carries the brand name "Bear Brand." Nestlé delegates brand management authority to country managers, who can (and do) adjust traditional marketing and manufacturing strategies in accordance with local tastes and preferences. For example, Nestlé's Thailand management group dropped traditional coffee-marketing efforts that focused on taste, aroma, and stimulation and instead began selling coffee as a drink that promotes relaxation and romance. This marketing strategy resonated with Thais experiencing urban stress, and it prompted Nestlé coffee sales in Thailand to jump dramatically.[35]

Of course, all this local responsiveness comes at a cost. Firms that emphasize local responsiveness are often unable to realize the full economic value possible by integrating their operations across country borders. Numerous firms have focused on appropriating this economic value and have pursued a more integrated international strategy. Examples of such firms include IBM, General Electric, Toyota Motor Corporation, and most major pharmaceutical firms, to name just a few.

Internationally integrated firms locate business functions and activities in countries that have a comparative advantage in these functions or activities. For example, the production of components for most consumer electronics is research intensive, capital intensive, and subject to significant economies of scale. To manage component manufacturing successfully, most internationally integrated consumer electronics firms have located their component operations in technologically advanced countries like the United States and Japan. However, because the assembly of these components into consumer products is labor intensive, most internationally integrated consumer electronics firms have located their assembly operations in countries with relatively low labor costs, including Mexico and China.

Of course, one of the costs of locating different business functions and activities in different geographic locations is that these different functions and activities must be coordinated and integrated. Operations in one country might very efficiently manufacture certain components. However, if the wrong components are shipped to the assembly location, or if the right components are shipped at the wrong time, any advantages that could have been obtained from exploiting the comparative advantages of different countries can be lost. Shipping costs can also reduce the returns on international integration.

To ensure that different operations in internationally integrated firms are appropriately coordinated, these firms typically manufacture more standardized products, using more standardized components, than do locally responsive firms. Standardization enables these firms to realize substantial economies of scale and other advantages, but it can limit their ability to respond to the specific needs of individual markets. When international product standards exist, as in the personal computer industry and the semiconductor chip industry, such standardization is not problematic. Also, when local responsiveness requires only a few modifications of a standardized product (for example, changing the shape of the electric plug or changing the color of a product), international integration can be very effective. However, when local responsiveness requires a great deal of local knowledge and product modifications, international integration can create problems for a firm pursuing an international product differentiation strategy.

Recently, it has been suggested that the traditional trade-off between international integration and local responsiveness can be replaced by a **transnational strategy** that exploits all the advantages of both international integration and local responsiveness.[36] Firms implementing a transnational strategy treat their international operations as an integrated network of distributed and interdependent resources and capabilities. In this context, a firm's operations in each country are not simply independent activities attempting to respond to local market needs; they are also repositories of ideas, technologies, and management approaches that the firm might be able to use and apply in its other international operations. Put differently, operations in different countries can be thought of as "experiments" in the creation of new resources and capabilities. Some of these experiments will work and generate important new resources and capabilities; others will fail to have such benefits for a firm.

When a particular country operation develops a competence in manufacturing a particular product, providing a particular service, or engaging in a particular activity that can be used by other country operations, the country operation with this competence can achieve international economies of scale by becoming the firm's primary supplier of this product, service, or activity. In this way, local responsiveness is retained as country managers constantly search for new competencies that enable them to maximize profits in their particular markets, and international integration and economies are realized as country operations that have developed unique competencies become suppliers for all other country operations.

SUMMARY

Product differentiation exists when customers perceive a particular firm's products to be more valuable than other firms' products. Although differentiation can have several bases, it is, in the end, always a matter of customer perception. Bases of product differentiation include: (1) attributes of the products or services a firm sells (including product features, product complexity, the timing of product introduction, and location); (2) relations between a firm and its customers (including product customization, consumer marketing, and reputation); and (3) links within and between firms (including links between functions, links with other firms, a firm's product mix, its distribution system, and its level of service and support). However, in the end, product differentiation is limited only by the creativity of a firm's managers.

Product differentiation is valuable to the extent that it enables a firm to set its prices higher than what it would otherwise be able to. Each of the bases of product differentiation identified can be used to neutralize environmental threats and exploit environmental opportunities. The rarity and imitability of bases of product differentiation vary. Highly imitable bases of product differentiation include product features. Somewhat imitable bases include product mix, links with other firms, product customization, and consumer marketing. Costly-to-imitate bases of product differentiation include linking business functions, timing, location, reputation, and service and support.

The implementation of a product differentiation strategy involves management of organizational structure, management controls, and compensation policies. Structurally, it is not unusual for firms implementing product differentiation strategies to use cross-divisional and cross-functional teams, together with teams that are focused exclusively on a particular product differentiation effort, so-called "skunk works." Managerial controls that provide free managerial decision-making within broad decision-making guidelines can be helpful in implementing product differentiation strategies, as is a policy of experimentation. Finally, compensation policies that tolerate risk-taking and a creative flair and that measure employee performance along multiple dimensions simultaneously can also be helpful in implementing product differentiation strategies.

A variety of organizational attributes is required to successfully implement a product differentiation strategy. Some have argued that contradictions between these organizational characteristics and those required to implement a cost leadership strategy mean that firms that attempt to do both will perform poorly. More recent research notes the relationship between product differentiation, market share, and low costs and observes that some firms have learned to manage the contradictions between cost leadership and product differentiation.

These same tensions can manifest themselves for firms pursuing international strategies. Product differentiation, internationally, requires responsiveness to local markets; cost leadership, internationally, requires a firm to integrate its global operations. Some authors have suggested that a transnational strategy can enable a firm to be both locally responsive and globally integrated.

CHALLENGE QUESTIONS

1. Although cost leadership is, perhaps, less relevant for firms pursuing product differentiation, costs are not totally irrelevant. What advice about costs would you give a firm pursuing a product differentiation strategy?

2. Product features are often the focus of product differentiation efforts. Yet product features are among the easiest-to-imitate bases of product differentiation and thus among the least likely bases of product differentiation to be a source of sustained competitive advantage. Does this seem paradoxical to you? If no, why not? If yes, how can you resolve this paradox?

3. What are the strengths and weaknesses of using regression analysis and hedonic prices to describe the bases of product differentiation?

4. "Monopolistic competition" is the term that Chamberlin developed to describe firms pursuing a product differentiation strategy in a competitive industry. However, it is usually the case that firms that operate in monopolies are less efficient and less competitive than firms that operate in more competitive settings (see Chapter 3). Does this same problem exist for firms operating in a "monopolistic competition" context? Why or why not?

5. Implementing a product differentiation strategy seems to require just the right mix of control and creativity. How do you know if a firm has the right mix? Is it possible to evaluate this mix before problems associated with being out of balance manifest themselves? If yes, how? If no, why not?

6. A firm with a highly differentiated product can increase the volume of its sales. Increased sales volumes can enable a firm to reduce its costs. High volumes with low costs can lead a firm to have very high profits, some of which the firm can use to invest in further differentiating its products. What advice would you give a firm whose competition is enjoying this product differentiation and cost leadership advantage?

7. What kinds of organizational and management problems is a firm trying to implement a transnational strategy (as a way to resolve conflicts between product differentiation and cost leadership strategies internationally) likely to face? (Hint: See Table 5.5.)

8. Is a firm implementing a transnational strategy just "stuck in the middle" internationally? If yes, why? If no, why not?

PROBLEM SET

1. For each of the listed products, describe at least two ways they are differentiated.

(a) Ben & Jerry's ice cream
(b) The Hummer H2
(c) The X-Games
(d) The Back Street Boys
(e) The movies *Animal House* and *Caddyshack*
(f) Fredrick's of Hollywood
(g) Taco Bell

2. Which, if any of these bases of product differentiation (in question #1) are likely to be sources of sustained competitive advantage, and why?

3. Suppose you obtained the following regression results, where the starred (*) coefficients are statistically significant. What could you say about the bases of product differentiation in this market? (Hint: A regression coefficient is statistically significant when it is so large that its effect is very unlikely to have emerged by chance.)

House Price = $125,000* + $15,000*(More than 3 bedrooms)
+ $18,000*(More than 3,500 square feet)
+ $150(Has plumbing) + $180(Has lawn)
+ $17,000*(Lot larger than 1/2 acre)

How much would you expect to pay for a 4-bedroom, 3,800-square-foot house on a one-acre lot? How much for a 4-bedroom, 2,700-square-foot house on a 1/4-acre lot? Do these results say anything about the sustainability of competitive advantages in this market?

4. Which of the following management controls and compensation policies is consistent with implementing cost leadership? With product differentiation? With both cost leadership and product differentiation? With neither cost leadership nor product differentiation?

(a) Firm-wide stock options

(b) Compensation that rewards each function separately for meeting its own objectives

(c) A detailed financial budget plan

(d) A document that describes, in detail, how the innovation process will unfold in a firm

(e) A policy that reduces the compensation of a manager who introduces a product that fails in the market

(f) A policy that reduces the compensation of a manager who introduces several products that fail in the market

(g) The creation of a purchasing council to discuss how different business units can reduce their costs

5. Identify three industries or markets that have the volume–profit relationship described in Figure 5.2. Which firms in this industry are implementing cost leadership strategies? Which are implementing product differentiation strategies? Are there any firms "stuck in the middle?" If yes, who are they? If no, why not? Are there any firms implementing both cost leadership and product differentiation strategies? If yes, who? If no, why not?

END NOTES

1. See Ono, Y. (1996). "Who really makes that cute little beer? You'd be surprised." *Wall Street Journal*, April 15, pp. A1 +. Since this 1996 article, some of these craft beer companies have changed the way they manufacture the beers to be more consistent with the image they are trying to project.
2. See Porter, M. E. (1980). *Competitive strategy*. New York: Free Press, and Caves R. E., and P. Williamson (1985). "What is product differentiation, really?" *Journal of Industrial Organization Economics*, 34, pp. 113–132.
3. Lieberman, M. B., and D. B. Montgomery (1988). "First-mover advantages." *Strategic Management Journal*, 9, pp. 41–58.
4. London, H. (1995). "Bait and switch in academe." *Forbes*, May 22, p. 120.
5. Carroll, P. (1993). *Big blues: The unmaking of IBM*. New York: Crown Publishers.
6. These ideas were first developed in Hotelling, H. (1929). "Stability in competition." *Economic Journal*, 39, pp. 41–57; Ricardo, D. (1817). *Principles of political economy and taxation*. London: J. Murray.
7. See Gunther, M. (1998). "Disney's Call of the Wild." *Fortune*, April 13, pp. 120–124.
8. The idea of reputation is explained in Klein, B., and K. Leffler (1981). "The role of market forces in assuring contractual performance." *Journal of Political Economy*, 89, pp. 615–641.
9. See Robichaux M., (1995). "It's a book! A T-shirt! A toy! No, just MTV trying to be Disney." *Wall Street Journal*, February 8, pp. A1 +.
10. See Henderson, R., and I. Cockburn (1994). "Measuring competence? Exploring firm effects in pharmaceutical research." *Strategic Management Journal*, 15, pp. 63–84.
11. See Johnson, R. (1999). "Speed sells." *Fortune*, April 12, pp. 56–70. In fact, NASCAR fans either love or hate Jeff Gordon.
12. See Carvell, T. (1998). "How Sony created a monster." *Fortune*, June 8, pp. 162 +; and Gibson, R. (1999). "Star Wars' tie-in is more a menace than a hit at Tricon." *Wall Street Journal*, July 21, p. A5.
13. Kotler, P. (1986). *Principles of marketing*. Upper Saddle River, NJ: Prentice Hall.
14. Porter, M. E., and R. Wayland (1991). "Coca-Cola vs. Pepsi-Cola and the soft drink industry." Harvard Business School Case No. 9-391-179.
15. Ghemawat, P. (1993). "Sears, Roebuck and Company: The merchandise group." Harvard Business School Case No. 9-794-039.
16. Chamberlin, E. H. (1933). *The theory of monopolistic competition*. Cambridge, MA: Harvard University Press; Robinson, J. (1934). "What is perfect competition?" *Quarterly Journal of Economics*, 49, pp. 104–120.
17. Casey, J. (1976). "High fructose corn syrup." *Research Management*, 19, pp. 27–32.
18. Welsh, J. (1998). "Office-paper firms pursue elusive goal: Brand loyalty." *Wall Street Journal*, September 21, p. B6.
19. See White, E., and K. Palmer (2003). "U.S. retailing 101." *Wall Street Journal*, August 12, pp. B1 +.
20. See Hennart, J. F. (1988). "A transaction cost theory of equity joint ventures." *Strategic Management Journal*, 9, pp. 361–374.
21. Deutsch, C. H. (1991). "How is it done? For a small fee…." *New York Times*, October 27, p. 25; Armstrong, L. (1991). "Services: The customer as 'Honored Guest'." *BusinessWeek*, October 25, p. 104.
22. See Rankin, A. (1998). "Dave Mathews band succeeds by marching to its own drummer." *Columbus Dispatch*, August 2, pp. F1 +; and Yoffie, D. (1994). "Swissair's alliances (A)." Harvard Business School Case No. 9-794-152.
23. "WPP—Integrating icons." Harvard Business School Case No. 9-396-249.
24. Orosz, J. J. (2002). "Big funds need a 'Skunk Works' to stir ideas." *Chronicle of Philanthropy*, June 27, p. 47.
25. Van de Ven, A., D. Polley, R. Garud, and S. Venkatraman (1999). *The innovation journey*. New York: Oxford, pp. 198-200.
26. Prokesch, S. (1995). "Competing on customer service: An interview with British Airways' Sir Colin Marshall." *Harvard Business Review*, November/December, p. 101.
27. Position, L. L. (1999). "David S. Pottruck." *BusinessWeek*, September 27, EB 51.
28. Porter, M. E. (1980). *Competitive strategy*. New York: Free Press.
29. Hill, C. W. L. (1988). "Differentiation versus low cost or differentiation and low cost: A contingency framework." *Academy of Management Review*, 13(3), pp. 401–412.
30. Gibson, R. (1995). "Food: At McDonald's, new recipes for buns, eggs." *Wall Street Journal*, June 13, p. B1.
31. Originally discussed in the Strategy in Depth feature in Chapter 3.
32. Womack, J. P., D. I. Jones, and D. Roos (1990). *The machine that changed the world*. New York: Rawson.
33. Porter, M. E. (1985). *Competitive advantage*. New York: Free Press.
34. Agins, Teri, and Alessandra Galloni (2003). "Facing a squeeze, Versace struggles to trim the fat." *Wall Street Journal*, September 30, pp. A1 +.
35. Rapoport, C. (1994). "Nestlé's brand building machine." *Fortune*, September 19, pp. 147–156.
36. See Bartlett, C. A., and S. Ghoshal (1989). *Managing across borders: The transnational solution*. Boston: Harvard Business School Press.

3
CORPORATE STRATEGIES

6

Vertical Integration

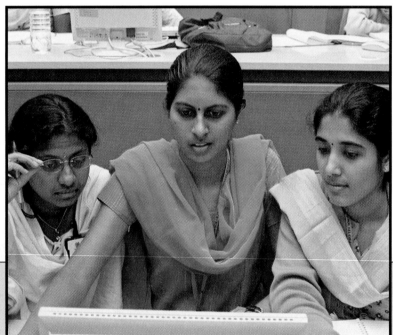

The box promised that it would be easy to install. It promised that your new software would be "plug-and-play compatible" with your system. But, here you are; three hours into installation and all you get is helpful error messages like "System Error No. 1257-3"—whatever that means. So, you decide to call the help line. But who are you calling?

The package from your tax service arrived on time. All it requires is your signature, and you can safely file your taxes. And then—the tax refund. Those tickets to Cancun are

Who Am I Calling?

just dying to be purchased. However, as you look over your return, you are not sure about how a certain deduction is calculated. A mistake on your tax return can be very costly, so you decide to call the help line. But who are you calling?

Last month was a great month—concerts, new music, new clothes, a road trip. But it was very

expensive—maybe too expensive. The day of reckoning—when the credit card bill comes in the mail—finally arrives. $1,600! How can the bill be that much? You quickly look over the list of charges and see that you were double billed for that great hotel in Florida. Well, this will be easy to fix—just call the customer service line. But who are you calling?

Until recently, it was easy to know who you were calling to receive these kinds of services. If, for example, your software was an IBM product and you called the

Learning Objectives

After reading this chapter, you should be able to:

1. Define vertical integration, forward vertical integration, and backward vertical integration.

2. Discuss how vertical integration can create value by reducing the threat of opportunism.

3. Discuss how vertical integration can create value by enabling a firm to exploit its valuable, rare, and costly-to-imitate resources and capabilities.

4. Discuss how vertical integration can create value by enabling a firm to retain its flexibility.

5. Describe conditions under which vertical integration may be rare and costly to imitate.

6. Describe how the functional organization structure, management controls, and compensation policies are used to implement vertical integration.

7. Describe different degrees of vertical integration in an international context.

IBM help line, you would talk to an IBM employee located somewhere in the United States. If you had a problem with you tax return, you would call your tax preparer—a firm like H&R Block—and talk to an employee located somewhere in the United States. And if you had a problem with your credit card bill, you would call the credit card company and talk to one of its employees in the United States.

But in the last ten years, all of this has changed. First, large corporations started to hire smaller companies to staff and manage their call centers. Firms like Convergys locate call centers near universities and colleges and hire engineering and computer science students to answer questions about software; they hire accounting students to answer questions about tax returns and other students to answer questions about credit card bills. All this is cheaper than these large corporations hiring full-time employees to answer these questions—and the quality of these services can be very good.

However, the search for high-quality, low-cost services has led some corporations to look beyond the borders of the United States for companies to manage their call centers and help lines. Many of these services are now provided by companies operating out of India. That's right—you may call the same 800 help line number you always have, but the person you get on the other end may actually live in India.

Research shows that shifting operations to firms in India can reduce a corporation's costs by 40 to 60 percent. And with India's schools turning out

260,000 well-trained engineers each year, the quality of the service you receive on the other end of the line that connects you to a call center in India may be just as good as the service you received in the past.

And it isn't just call centers that are moving to India. Some of the Web sites you visit, the electronics you use, the financial analyses you read—even your credit worthiness—are designed, written, and evaluated by firms in India. One study estimates that by 2008, the information technology and back-office work done in India will

employ over 4 million people, be worth over $57 billion, and account for 7 percent of India's Gross Domestic Product (GDP). Currently, GE Capital employs 16,000 people in India to help manage paper work; GE's John Welch Technology Center employs 1,800 people in India to develop and design new products; IBM employs 10,000 people in India to provide information technology services and software; Oracle employs 6,000 people in India to develop new software and provide software services; and Intel employs 1,700 people in India to help design chips

and software. These trends are likely to continue for some time.

So, the next time you call a help line to install your software, update your tax return, or check your credit card bill, ask the people on the other end of the line who they are and where they live. More and more, they are not likely to be employees of the firm you thought you were calling. And more and more, they don't even live in the United States.

Sources: M. Kripalani and P. Engardio (2003). "The rise of India." *BusinessWeek*, December 8, pp. 66 +; C. Hawn (2004). "The global razor's edge." *Fast Times*, February, pp. 27 +; K. J. Delaney (2003). "Outsourcing jobs—and workers—to India." *Wall Street Journal*, October 13, pp. B1 +.

The decision to hire another company to provide services for a firm's customers is an example of a decision that determines the level of a firm's vertical integration. This is the case, whether the company that is hired to perform these services is located in the United States or India.

What Is Corporate Strategy?

Vertical integration is the first corporate strategy examined in detail in this book. As suggested in Chapter 1, **business strategy** is a firm's theory of how to gain competitive advantage in a single business or industry. The two business strategies discussed in this book are cost leadership and product differentiation. **Corporate strategy** is a firm's theory of how to gain competitive advantage by operating in several businesses simultaneously. Decisions about whether or not to vertically integrate often determine whether or not a firm is operating in a single business or industry or multiple businesses or industries. Other corporate strategies discussed in this book include strategic alliances, diversification, and mergers and acquisitions.

What Is Vertical Integration?

The concept of a firm's value chain was first introduced in Chapter 3. As a reminder, a **value chain** is that set of activities that must be accomplished to bring a product or service from raw materials to the point that it can be sold to a final customer. A simplified value chain of the oil and gas industry, originally presented in Figure 3.1, is reproduced in Figure 6.1.

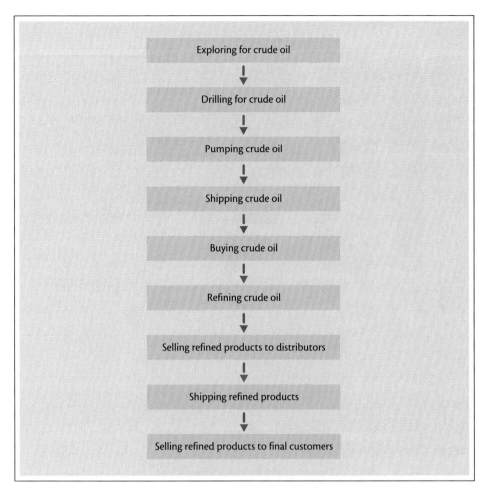

A firm's level of **vertical integration** is simply the number of steps in this value chain that a firm accomplishes within its boundaries. More vertically integrated firms accomplish more stages of the value chain within their boundaries than less vertically integrated firms. A more sophisticated approach to measuring the degree of a firm's vertical integration is presented in the Strategy in Depth feature.

A firm engages in **backward vertical integration** when it incorporates more stages of the value chain within its boundaries and those stages bring it closer to the beginning of the value chain, that is, closer to gaining access to raw materials. When computer companies developed all their own software, they were engaging in backward vertical integration, because these actions are close to the beginning of the value chain. When they began using independent companies operating in India to develop this software, they were less vertically integrated backward.

A firm engages in **forward vertical integration** when it incorporates more stages of the value chain within its boundaries and those stages bring it closer to the end of the value chain, that is, closer to interacting directly with final customers. When companies staffed and operated their own call centers in the United States, they were engaging in forward vertical integration, because these activities brought them closer to the ultimate customer. When they started using independent companies in India to staff and operate these centers, they were less vertically integrated forward.

Strategy in Depth

*I*t is sometimes possible to directly observe which stages of the value chain a firm is engaging in and thus the level of that firm's vertical integration. Sometimes, however, it is more difficult to directly observe a firm's level of vertical integration. This is especially the case when a firm believes that its level of vertical integration is a potential source of competitive advantage and thus is not likely to reveal this information freely to competitors.

In this situation, it is possible to get a sense of the degree of a firm's vertical integration—though not a complete list of the steps in the value chain integrated by the firm—from a close examination of the firm's **value added as a percentage of sales**. Valued added as a percentage of sales measures that percentage of a firm's sales that is generated by activities done within the boundaries of a firm. A firm with a high ratio between value added and sales has brought many of the value-creating activities associated with its business inside its boundaries, consistent with a high level of vertical integration. A firm with a low ratio between value added and sales does not have, on average, as high a level of vertical integration.

Value added as a percentage of sales is computed using the following equation in Exhibit 1.

The sum of net income and income taxes is subtracted in both the

Measuring Vertical Integration

numerator and the denominator in this equation to control for inflation and changes in the tax code over time. Net income, income taxes, and sales can all be taken directly from a firm's profit-and-loss statement. Value added can be calculated using the equation in Exhibit 2.

Again, most of the numbers needed to calculate value added can be found either in a firm's profit-and-loss statement or in its balance sheet.

Sources: A. Laffer (1969). "Vertical integration by corporations: 1929–1965." *Review of Economics and Statistics*, 51, pp. 91– 93; I. Tucker and R. P. Wilder (1977). "Trends in vertical integration in the U.S. manufacturing sector." *Journal of Industrial Economics*, 26, pp. 81–94; K. Harrigan (1986). "Matching vertical integration strategies to competitive conditions." *Strategic Management Journal*, 7, pp. 535–555.

Exhibit 1

$$\text{vertical integration}_i = \frac{\text{value added}_i - \left(\text{net income}_i + \text{income taxes}_i\right)}{\text{sales}_i - \left(\text{net income}_i + \text{income taxes}_i\right)}$$

where,

$\text{vertical integration}_i$ = the level of vertical integration for firm_i

value added_i = the level of value added for firm_i

net income_i = the level of net income for firm_i

income taxes_i = firm_i's income taxes

sales_i = firm_i's sales

Exhibit 2

value added = depreciation + amortization + fixed charges + interest expense + labor and related expenses + pension and retirement expenses + income taxes + net income (after taxes) + rental expense

Of course, in choosing how to organize its value chain, a firm has more choices than just to vertically integrate or not vertically integrate. Indeed, between these two extremes, a wide range of somewhat vertically integrated options exist. These alternatives include various types of strategic alliances and joint ventures, the primary topic of Chapter 9.

The Value of Vertical Integration

The question of vertical integration—which stages of the value chain should be included within a firm's boundaries and why—has been studied by many scholars for almost 100 years. The reason this question has been of such interest was first articulated by Nobel Prize–winning economist Ronal Coase. In a famous article originally published in 1937, Coase asked a simple question: Given how efficiently markets can be used to organize economic exchanges among thousands, even hundreds of thousands, of separate individuals, why would markets, as a method for managing economic exchanges, ever be replaced by firms? In markets, almost as if by magic, Adam Smith's "invisible hand" coordinates the quantity and quality of goods and services produced with the quantity and quality of goods and services demanded through the adjustment of prices—all without a centralized controlling authority. In firms, on the other hand, centralized bureaucrats monitor and control subordinates who, in turn battle each other for "turf" and control of inefficient internal "fiefdoms." Why would the "beauty" of the invisible hand ever be replaced by the clumsy "visible hand" of the modern corporation?[1]

Coase began to answer his own question when he observed that sometimes the cost of using a market to manage an economic exchange must be higher than the cost of using vertical integration and bringing an exchange within the boundary of a firm. Over the years, efforts have focused on identifying the conditions under which this would be the case. The resulting work has described several different situations where vertical integration can either increase a firm's revenues or decrease its costs compared to not vertically integrating, that is, several situations where vertical integration can be valuable. Three of the most influential of these explanations of when vertical integration can create value for a firm are discussed here.

Vertical Integration and the Threat of Opportunism

One of the best known explanations of when vertical integration can be valuable focuses on using vertical integration to reduce the threat of opportunism.[2] **Opportunism** exists when a firm is unfairly exploited in an exchange. Examples of opportunism include when a party to an exchange expects a high level of quality in a product it is purchasing, only to discover it has received a lower level of quality than it expected; when a party to an exchange expects to receive a service by a particular point in time and that service is delivered late (or early); and when a party to an exchange expects to pay a price to complete this exchange and its exchange partner demands a higher price than what was previously agreed to.

Obviously, when one of its exchange partners behaves opportunistically, this reduces the economic value of a firm. One way to reduce the threat of opportunism is to bring an exchange within the boundary of a firm, that is, to vertically integrate into this exchange. This way, managers in a firm can directly monitor and control this exchange instead of relying on the market to manage it. If the exchange that is brought within the boundary of a firm brings a firm closer to its ultimate suppliers, it is an example of backward vertical integration. If the exchange that is brought within the boundary of a firm brings a firm closer to its ultimate customer, it is an example of forward vertical integration.

Of course, firms should only bring market exchanges within their boundaries when the cost of vertical integration is less than the cost of opportunism. If the cost of vertical integration is greater than the cost of opportunism, then firms should not vertically integrate into an exchange. This is the case for both backward and forward vertical integration decisions.

So, when will the threat of opportunism be large enough to warrant vertical integration? Research has shown that the threat of opportunism is greatest when a party to an exchange has made what are called transaction-specific investments. A **transaction-specific investment** is any investment in an exchange that has significantly more value in the current exchange than it does in alternative exchanges. Perhaps the easiest way to understand the concept of a transaction-specific investment is through an example.

Consider the economic exchange between an oil refining company and an oil pipeline building company, depicted in Figure 6.2. As can be seen in the figure, this oil refinery is built on the edge of a deep-water bay. Because of this, the refinery has been receiving supplies of crude oil from large tanker ships. However, an oil field exists several miles distant from the refinery, but the only way to transport crude oil from the oil field to the refinery is with trucks—a very expensive way to move crude oil, especially compared to large tankers. But, if the oil refining company could find a way to get crude oil from this field cheaply, it would probably make this refinery even more valuable.

Enter the pipeline company. Suppose this pipeline company approaches the refinery and offers to build a pipeline from the oil field to the refinery. In return, all the pipeline company expects is for the refinery to promise to buy a certain number of barrels of crude at an agreed-to price for some period of time, say, five years, through the pipeline. If reasonable prices can be negotiated, the oil refinery is likely to find this offer attractive, for the cost of crude oil carried by the pipeline is likely to be lower than the cost of crude oil delivered by ship or by truck. Based on this analysis, so far, the refinery and the oil pipeline company are likely to cooperate and the pipeline is likely to be built.

Now, five years go by, and it's time to renegotiate the contract. Which of these two firms has made the largest transaction-specific investments? Remember

Figure 6.2 The Exchange Between an Oil Refinery and an Oil Pipeline Company

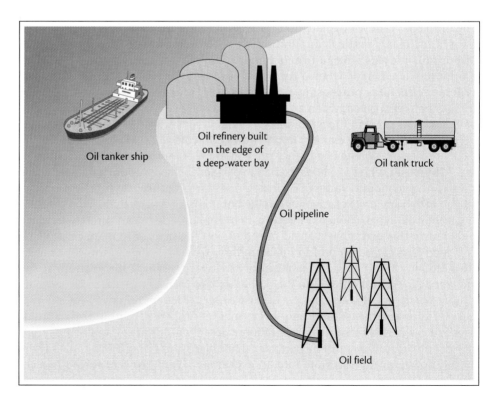

that a transaction-specific investment is any investment in an exchange that is more valuable in that particular exchange than in alternative exchanges.

What specific investments has the refinery made? Well, how much is this refinery worth if this exchange with the pipeline company is not renewed? Its value would probably drop some—remember that oil through the pipeline is probably cheaper than oil through ships or trucks. So, if the refiner doesn't use the pipeline any longer, it will have to use these alternative supplies. This will reduce its value some—say from $1 million to $900,000. This $100,000 difference is the size of the transaction-specific investment made by the refining company.

However, the transaction-specific investment made by the pipeline firm is probably much larger. Suppose the pipeline is worth $750,000 as long as it is pumping oil to the refinery. But if it is not pumping oil, how much is it worth? Not very much. An oil pipeline that is not pumping oil has limited alternative uses. It has value either as scrap or (perhaps) as the world's largest enclosed water slide. If the value of the pipeline is only $10,000 if it is not pumping oil to the refinery, then the level of transaction specific investment made by the pipeline firm is substantially larger than that made by the firm that owns the refinery: $750,000 – $10,000, or $740,000 for the pipeline company versus $100,000 for the refining company.

So who is at greater risk of opportunism when the contract between the refinery and the pipeline company is renegotiated—the refinery or the pipeline company? Obviously, the pipeline company has more to lose. If it cannot come to an agreement with the oil refining company, it will lose $740,000. If the refinery cannot come to an agreement with the pipeline company, it will lose $100,000. Knowing this, the refining company can squeeze the pipeline company during the renegotiation by insisting on lower prices or more timely deliveries of higher-quality crude oil, and the pipeline company really can't do much about it.

Of course, managers in the pipeline firm are not stupid. They know that after the first five years of their exchange with the refining company they will be in a very difficult bargaining position. So, in anticipation, they will insist on much higher prices for building the oil pipeline in the first place than would otherwise be the case. This will drive up the cost of building the pipeline, perhaps to the point that it is no longer cheaper than getting crude oil from ships. If this is the case, then the pipeline will not be built, even though if it could be built and the threat of opportunism eliminated, both the refining company and the pipeline company would be better off.

One way to solve this problem is for the oil refining company to buy the oil pipeline company—that is, for the oil refinery to backward vertically integrate.[3] When this happens, the incentive for the oil refinery to exploit the vulnerability of the pipeline company will be reduced. After all, if the refinery business tries to rip-off the pipeline business, it only hurts itself, since it owns the pipeline business.

This, then, is the essence of opportunism-based explanations of when vertical integration creates value: Transaction-specific investments make parties to an exchange vulnerable to opportunism and vertical integration solves this vulnerability problem. Using language developed in Chapter 3, this approach suggests that vertical integration is valuable when it reduces threats from a firm's suppliers or buyers due to any transaction-specific investments a firm has made.

Vertical Integration and Firm Capabilities

A second approach to vertical integration decisions focuses on a firm's capabilities and its ability to generate sustained competitive advantages.[4] This approach has two broad implications. First, it suggests that firms should vertically integrate into those business activities where they possess valuable, rare, and costly-to-imitate resources and capabilities. This way, firms can appropriate at least some of the profits that using these capabilities to exploit environmental opportunities will create. Second, this approach also suggests that firms should not vertically integrate into business activities where they do not possess the resources necessary to gain competitive advantages. Such vertical integration decisions would not be a source of profits to a firm, since they do not possess any of the valuable, rare, or costly-to-imitate resources needed to gain competitive advantages in these business activities. Indeed, to the extent that some other firms have competitive advantages in these business activities, vertically integrating into them could put a firm at a competitive disadvantage.

This, then, is the essence of the capabilities approach to vertical integration: If a firm possesses valuable, rare, and costly-to-imitate resources in a business activity, it should vertically integrate into that activity; otherwise, no vertical integration. This perspective can sometimes lead to vertical integration decisions that conflict with decisions derived from opportunism-based explanations of vertical integration.

Consider, for example, firms acting as suppliers to Wal-Mart. As described in Chapter 4, Wal-Mart has a huge competitive advantage in the discount retail industry. In principle, firms that sell to Wal-Mart could vertically integrate forward into the discount retail market to sell their own products. That is, these firms could begin to compete against Wal-Mart. However, such efforts are not likely to be a source of competitive advantage for these firms. Wal-Mart's resources and capabilities are just too extensive and costly to imitate for most of these suppliers. So, instead of forward vertical integration, most of these firms sell their products through Wal-Mart.

Of course, the problem is that by relying so much on Wal-Mart, these firms are making significant transaction-specific investments. If they stop selling to Wal-Mart, they may go out of business. However, this decision will have a limited impact on Wal-Mart. Wal-Mart can go to any number of suppliers around the world who are willing to replace this failed firm. So, Wal-Mart's suppliers are at risk of opportunism in this exchange, and indeed, it is well known that Wal-Mart can squeeze its suppliers, in terms of the quality of the products it purchases, the price at which it purchases them, and the way in which these products are delivered.

So the tension between these two approaches to vertical integration becomes clear. Concerns about opportunism suggest that Wal-Mart's suppliers should vertically integrate forward. Concerns about having a competitive disadvantage if they do vertically integrate forward suggest that Wal-Mart's suppliers should not vertically integrate. So, should they or shouldn't they vertically integrate?

Not many of Wal-Mart's suppliers have been able to resolve this difficult problem. Most do not vertically integrate into the discount retail industry. However, they try to reduce the level of transaction-specific investment they make with Wal-Mart by supplying other discount retailers, both in the United States and abroad. They also try to use their special capabilities to differentiate their products so much that Wal-Mart's customers insist on Wal-Mart selling these products. And these firms constantly search for cheaper ways to make and distribute higher-quality products.

Vertical Integration and Flexibility

A third perspective on vertical integration focuses on the impact of this decision on a firm's flexibility. **Flexibility** refers to how costly it is for a firm to alter its strategic and organizational decisions. Flexibility is high when the cost of changing strategic choices is low; flexibility is low when the cost of changing strategic choices is high.

So, which is less flexible: vertical integration or no vertical integration? Research suggests that, in general, vertically integrating is less flexible than not vertically integrating.[5] This is because once a firm has vertically integrated, it has committed its organizational structure, its management controls, and its compensation policies to a particular vertically integrated way of doing business. Undoing this decision often means changing these aspects of an organization.

Suppose, for example, that a vertically integrated firm decides to get out of a particular business. To do this, this firm will have to sell or close its factories, (actions that can adversely affect both the employees it has to lay off and those that remain), alter its supply relationships, hurt customers that have come to rely on this firm as a partner, and change the internal reporting structure of the firm. On the other hand, if a non–vertically integrated firm decides to get out of a business, it simply stops. It cancels whatever contracts it might have had in place and ceases operations in that business. The cost of exiting a non–vertically integrated business is generally much lower than the cost of exiting a vertically integrated business.

Of course, flexibility is not always valuable. In fact, flexibility is only valuable when the decision-making setting a firm is facing is uncertain. A decision-making setting is **uncertain** when the future value of an exchange cannot be known when investments in that exchange are being made. In such settings, less vertical integration is better than more vertical integration. This is because vertically integrating into an exchange is less flexible than not vertically integrating into an exchange. If an exchange turns out not to be valuable, it is usually more costly for firms that have vertically integrated into an exchange to exit that exchange compared to firms that have not vertically integrated.

Consider, for example, a pharmaceutical firm making investments in biotechnology. The outcome of biotechnology research is very uncertain. If a pharmaceutical company vertically integrates into a particular type of biotechnology research by hiring particular types of scientists, building an expensive laboratory, and developing the other skills necessary to do this particular type of biotechnology research, it has made a very large investment. Now suppose that this research turns out not to be profitable. This firm has made huge investments that now have little value. As important, it has failed to make investments in other areas of biotechnology that could turn out to be valuable.

A flexibility-based approach to vertical integration suggests that, rather than vertically integrating into a business activity whose value is highly uncertain, firms should not vertically integrate and, instead, form a strategic alliance to manage this exchange. A strategic alliance is more flexible than vertical integration but still gives a firm enough information about an exchange to estimate its value over time.

An alliance has a second advantage in this setting. The downside risks associated with investing in a strategic alliance are known and fixed. They equal the cost of creating and maintaining the alliance. If an uncertain investment turns out not to be valuable, parties to this alliance know the maximum amount they can lose—an amount equal to the cost of creating and maintaining the alliance. On the other hand, if this exchange turns out to be very valuable, then maintaining an alliance can give a firm access to this huge upside potential. These aspects of strategic alliances will be discussed in more detail in Chapter 9.

Each of these explanations of vertical integration has received significant empirical attention in the academic literature. Some of these studies are described in the Research Made Relevant feature.

Research Made Relevant

*O*f the three explanations of verti- cal integration discussed here, opportunism-based explanations are the oldest, and thus have received the greatest empirical support. One review of this empirical work, by Professor Joe Mahoney of the University of Illinois, observes that the core asser- tion of this approach—that high levels of transaction-specific investment lead to higher levels of vertical integra- tion—receives consistent empirical support.

More recent work has begun to examine the trade-offs among these three explanations of vertical integra- tion by examining their effects on verti- cal integration simultaneously. For example, Professor Tim Folta of Purdue University examined the opportunism and flexibility approaches to vertical integration simultaneously. His results show that the basic assertion of the opportunism approach still holds. However, when he adds uncertainty to his empirical analysis, he finds that firms engage in less vertical integra-

Empirical Tests of Theories of Vertical Integration

tion than those in which they would otherwise engage. In other words, firms apparently worry not only about transaction-specific investments when they make vertical integration choices; they also worry about how costly it is to reverse those investments in the face of high uncertainty.

An even more recent study by Michael Leiblein of The Ohio State University and Doug Miller of Tulane University, examines all three of these explanations of vertical integration simultaneously. These authors study vertical integration decisions in the semiconductor manufacturing indus- try and find that all three explanations hold. That is, firms in this industry worry about transaction-specific investment, the capabilities they pos- sess, the capabilities they would like to possess, and the uncertainty of the markets within which they operate when they make vertical integration choices.

Sources: J. Mahoney (1992). "The choice of orga- nizational form: Vertical financial ownership versus other methods of vertical integration." *Strategic Management Journal*, 13, pp. 559–584; T. Folta (1998). "Governance and uncertainty: The trade-off between administrative control and commitment." *Strategic Management Journal*, 19, pp. 1007–1028; M. Leiblein and D. Miller (2003). "An empirical examination of transaction- and firm-level influences on the vertical boundaries of the firm." *Strategic Management Journal*, 24(9), pp. 839–859.

Applying the Theories to the Management of Call Centers

So, what do these three theories say about how call centers should be managed? Each of these theories will be discussed in turn.

Transaction-Specific Investments and Managing Call Centers

When applying opportunism-based explanations of vertical integration, start by looking for actual or potential transaction-specific investments that would need to be made in order to complete an exchange. High levels of such investments sug- gest the need for vertical integration; low levels of such investments suggest that vertically integrating this exchange is not necessary.

In the context of call centers, when this approach to providing customer ser- vice was first developed in the 1980s, it required substantial levels of transaction- specific investment. First, a great deal of special purpose equipment had to be pur- chased. And while this equipment could be used for any call center, it had little value except within a call center. Thus, this equipment was an example of a some- what specific investment.

More importantly, in order to provide service in call centers, call center employees would have to be fully aware of all the problems that are likely to emerge with the use of a firm's products. This requires a firm to study its products very closely and then to train call center employees to be able to respond to any problems customers might have. This training was sometimes very complex and very time-consuming and represented substantial transaction-specific investments on the part of call center employees. Only employees that worked full-time for a large corporation—where job security was usually high for productive workers—would be willing to make these kinds of specific investments. Thus, vertical integration into call center management made a great deal of sense.

However, as information technology improved, firms found it was possible to train call center employees much faster. Now, all call center employees had to do was follow scripts that were pre-written and pre-loaded on their computers. By asking a few pre-scripted questions, call center employees could diagnose most problems. And solutions to those problems were also included on an employee's computer. Only really unusual problems could not be handled by employees working off these computer scripts. Because the level of specific investment required to use these scripts was much lower, employees were willing to work for companies without the job security usually associated with large firms. Indeed, call centers became good part-time and temporary employment opportunities. Since the level of specific investment required to work in these call centers was much lower, not vertically integrating into call center management made a great deal of sense.

Capabilities and Managing Call Centers

In opportunism-based explanations of vertical integration, you start by looking for transaction-specific investments and then make vertical integration decisions based on these investments. In capability-based approaches, you start by looking for valuable, rare, and costly-to-imitate resources and capabilities, and then make vertical integration decisions appropriately.

In the early days of call center management, how well a firm operated its call centers could actually be a source of competitive advantage. During this time period, the technology was new, and the training required to answer a customer's questions was extensive. Firms that developed special capabilities in managing these processes could gain competitive advantages and thus would vertically integrate into call center management.

However, over time, as more and more call center management suppliers were created, and as the technology and training required to staff a call center became more widely available, the ability of a call center to be a source of competitive advantage for a firm dropped. That is, the ability to manage a call center was still valuable, but it was no longer rare or costly to imitate. In this setting, it is not surprising to see firms getting out of the call center management business, outsourcing this business to low-cost specialist firms, and focusing on those business functions where they might be able to gain a sustained competitive advantage.

Flexibility and Managing Call Centers

Opportunism logic suggests starting with a search for transaction-specific investments; capabilities logic suggests starting with a search for valuable, rare, and costly-to-imitate resources and capabilities. Flexibility logic suggests starting by looking for sources of uncertainty in an exchange.

One of the biggest uncertainties in providing customer service through call centers is the question: Can the people staffing the phones actually help a firm's customers? This is a particularly troubling concern for firms that are selling complex products that can have numerous different kinds of problems. A variety of technological solutions have been developed to try to address this uncertainty. But, if a firm vertically integrates into the call center management business, it is committing to a particular technological solution. This solution may not work, or may not work as well as some other solutions.

In the face of this uncertainty, maintaining relationships with several different call center management companies—each of whom have adopted different technological solutions to the problem of how to use call center employees to assist customers who are using very complex products—gives a firm technological flexibility that it would not otherwise have. Once a superior solution is identified, then a firm no longer needs this flexibility and may choose to vertically integrate into call center management or not—depending on opportunism and capabilities considerations.

Integrating Different Theories of Vertical Integration

At first glance, having three different explanations about how vertical integration can create value seems troubling. After all, won't these explanations sometimes contradict each other?

The answer to this question is: Yes. We have already seen such a contradiction in the case of opportunism and capabilities explanations of whether or not Wal-Mart suppliers should forward vertically integrate into the discount retail industry.

However, more often than not, these three explanations are complementary in nature. That is, applying these three approaches generally leads to the same conclusions about how a firm should vertically integrate, not different conclusions. Moreover, sometimes it is simply easier to apply one of these approaches to evaluate a firm's vertical integration choices than the other two. Having a "tool kit" that includes three explanations of vertical integration enables the analyst to choose the approach that is most likely to be a source of insight in a particular situation.

Even when these explanations make contradictory assertions about vertical integration, having multiple approaches can be helpful. In this context, having multiple explanations can highlight the trade-offs that a firm is making when choosing its vertical integration strategy. Thus, for example, if opportunism-based explanations suggest that vertical integration is necessary because of high transaction-specific investments, capabilities-based explanations caution about the cost of developing the resources and capabilities necessary to vertically integrate and flexibility concerns caution about the risks that committing to vertical integration imply, and the costs and benefits of whatever vertical integration decision is ultimately made can be understood very clearly.

Overall, having three explanations of vertical integration has several advantages for those looking to analyze the vertical integration choices of real firms. Of course, applying these explanations can create important ethical dilemmas for a firm, especially when it becomes clear that a firm needs to become less vertically integrated than it has historically been. Some of these dilemmas are discussed in the Ethics and Strategy feature.

VRIO ## Vertical Integration and Sustained Competitive Advantage

Of course, in order for vertical integration to be a source of sustained competitive advantage, not only must it be valuable (because it responds to threats of opportunism; enables a firm to exploit its own or other firms' valuable, rare,

Ethics and Strategy

*I*magine a firm that has successfully operated in a vertically integrated manner for decades. Employees come to work, they know their jobs, they know how to work together effectively, they know where to park. The job is not just the economic center of their lives; it has become the social center as well. Most of their friends work in the same company, in the same function, as they do. The future appears to be much as the past—stable employment and effective work, all aiming toward a comfortable and well-planned retirement. And then the firm adopts a new outsourcing strategy. It changes its vertical integration strategy by becoming less vertically integrated and purchasing services from outside suppliers that it used to obtain internally.

The economics of outsourcing can be compelling. Outsourcing can help firms reduce costs and focus their efforts on those business functions that are central to their competitive advantage. When done well, outsourcing creates value—value that firms can share with their owners, their stockholders.

Indeed, outsourcing is becoming a trend in business. In 2000, companies that specialize in providing outsourced services had worldwide sales of over $1

The Ethics of Outsourcing

trillion. As important, the size of this outsourced services market doubled from 1997 to 2000. By 2015, some observers predict that an additional 3.3 million jobs in the United States will be outsourced, many to operations overseas.

But what of the employees whose jobs are taken away? What of their lifetime of commitment, their steady and reliable work? What of their stable and secure retirement? Outsourcing often devastates lives, even as it creates economic value. Of course, some firms go out of their way to soften the impact of

outsourcing on their employees. Those that are near retirement age are often given an opportunity to retire early. Others receive severance payments in recognition of their years of service. Other firms hire "out placement" companies—firms that specialize in placing suddenly unemployed people in new jobs and new careers.

But all these efforts to soften the blow do not make the blow go away. Many employees assume that they have an implicit contract with the firms they work for. That contract is: "As long as I do my job well, I will have a job." That contract is being replaced with: "As long as a firm wants to employ me, I will have a job." In this world, it is not surprising that many employees now look first to maintain their employability in their current job—by receiving additional training and experiences that might be valuable at numerous other employers—and are concerned less with what they can do to improve the performance of the firm they work for.

Sources: S. Steele-Carlin (2003). "Outsourcing poised for growth in 2002." *FreelanceJobs News*.com, October 20; (2003). "Who wins in off shoring?" *McKinseyQuarterly*.com, October 20.

and costly-to-imitate resources; or because it gives a firm flexibility); it must also be rare and costly to imitate, and a firm must be organized to implement it correctly.

The Rarity of Vertical Integration

A firm's vertical integration strategy is rare when few competing firms are able to create value by vertically integrating in the same way. A firm's vertical integration strategy can be rare because it is one of a small number of competing firms that are able to vertically integrate efficiently or because it is one of a small number of firms that are able to adopt a non–vertically integrated approach to managing an exchange.

Rare Vertical Integration

A firm may be able to create value through vertical integration, when most of its competitors are not able to create value through vertical integration, for at least three reasons. Not surprisingly, these reasons parallel the three explanations of vertical integration presented in this chapter.

Rare Transaction-Specific Investment and Vertical Integration. First, a firm may have developed a new technology, or a new approach to doing business, that requires its business partners to make substantial transaction-specific investments. Firms that engage in these activities will find it in their self-interest to vertically integrate, while firms that have not engaged in these activities will not find it in their self-interest to vertically integrate. If these activities are rare and costly to imitate, they can be a source of competitive advantage for a vertically integrating firm.

For example, the opening case in this chapter suggests that many firms in the computer industry are outsourcing their call centers to India. However, one firm—Dell Computers—recently brought one of its call centers back from India and re–vertically integrated into this business. The call center Dell brought back within its boundaries provides technical support to its corporate customers.[6] The problems faced by corporate customers are typically much more complicated than the problems faced by individual consumers. Thus, it is much more difficult to provide call center employees the training they need to address corporate problems. Moreover, because corporate technologies change more rapidly than many consumer technologies, keeping call center employees up-to-date on how to service corporate customers is also more complicated than having call center employees provide services to its noncorporate customers. Because Dell needs the people staffing its corporate call centers to make substantial specific investments in its technology and in understanding its customers, it has found it necessary to bring these individuals within the boundaries of the firm and to re–vertically integrate the operation of this particular type of service center.

If Dell, through this vertical integration decision, is able to satisfy its customers more effectively than its competitors, and if the cost of managing this call center is not too high, then this vertical integration decision is both valuable and rare and thus a source of at least a temporary competitive advantage for Dell.

Rare Capabilities and Vertical Integration. A firm like Dell might also conclude that it has unusual skills, either in operating a call center, or in providing the training that is needed to staff certain kinds of call centers. If those capabilities are valuable and rare, then vertically integrating into businesses that exploit these capabilities can enable a firm to gain at least a temporary competitive advantage. Indeed, the belief that a firm possesses valuable and rare capabilities is often a justification for rare vertical integration decisions in an industry. Consider, for example, MTV's decision to enter the Indian market, described in the Global Perspectives feature.

Rare Uncertainty and Vertical Integration. Finally, a firm may be able to gain an advantage from vertically integrating when it resolves some uncertainty it faces sooner than its competition. Suppose, for example, that several firms in an industry all begin investing in a very uncertain technology. Flexibility logic suggests that, to the extent possible, these firms will prefer to not vertically integrate into the manufacturing of this technology until its designs and features stabilize and market demand for this technology is well established.

However, imagine that one of these firms is able to resolve these uncertainties before any other firm. This firm no longer needs to retain the flexibility that is so valuable under conditions of uncertainty. Instead, this firm might be able to,

Global Perspectives

MTV has a dominant brand in music television in the United States and much of western Europe. Given that this brand is valuable, rare, and costly to imitate in these markets, it is not surprising that MTV has decided to continue its international expansion by moving into Malaysia, Japan, India, and other countries in Asia. However, Viacom—MTV's corporate parent—is finding it necessary to modify much of its content as it tries to introduce MTV in these Asian markets.

For example, when MTV first entered India in 1991, it presented content originally produced for its U.S. station and for the rest of Asia. This included rock-and-roll videos, rap videos, and English-speaking vee-jays. Later, it presented reruns of *The Osbournes*. The only problem with this strategy was that Indian teenagers don't like rock-and-roll videos, rap videos, and English-speaking vee-jays, and were totally mystified by *The Osbournes*. Another successful U.S. MTV product—*MTV Grind*—about spring break, was too risqué for an Indian audience and was cancelled soon after it was first shown.

To respond to this local market, MTV has had to develop more locally oriented fare, including *Roadies*, a show based loosely on MTV's popular *Road*

Producing a Hindi Version of *The Osbournes*

Rules program. However, unlike *Road Rules*—where contestants ride across America in a comfortable RV—in *Roadies*, four young men and three young women ride across India on two-wheeled motor scooters. Moreover, all of MTV India's vee-jays now speak Hinglish—a combination of Hindi and English—and present popular Indian music videos.

An even more radical departure for MTV India is its new youth-oriented soap opera *Kitna Mast Hai Zindagi*, which means *It's a Beautiful Life*. What is most unusual about this

production is that, unlike most of the other programming on MTV India, this show is not produced by MTV itself. In an effort to gain a true "Indian" feel to this new soap, MTV India actually outsourced its production to an Indian production company. This company, Balaji Telefilms, already produces a successful prime time soap opera on another Indian cable channel.

These efforts are beginning to pay some dividends in the Indian market. In 2003, MTV India had revenues of about $25 million and generated "several million" in profits—a very small amont of money for $27 billion Viacom, but a respectful level of performance in a difficult market. However, MTV India has many challenges left if it is to reach a size and profitability level that will make it an important business for Viacom. For example, currently MTV India is broadcast in Hinglish and reaches the Hindi-speaking population. However, large regions of India speak Tamil, Telegu, and Punjabi, not Hindi. What if someone who speaks Telegu says, "I want my MTV"? How will MTV India respond?

Sources: M. Gunther (2004). "MTV's passage to India." *Fortune*, August 9, pp. 117 +. © 2004 Time Inc. All rights reserved.

say, design special purpose machines that can very efficiently manufacture this technology. Such machines are not flexible, but they can be very efficient.

Of course, for outside vendors to use these new machines, they would have to make substantial transaction-specific investments. Outside vendors may be reluctant to make these investments. In this setting, this firm may find it necessary to vertically integrate to be able to use its machines to produce this technology. Thus, this firm, by resolving uncertainty faster than its competitors, is able to gain some of the advantages of vertical integration sooner than its competitors. While the competition is still focusing on flexibility in the face of uncertainty, this firm gets to focus on production efficiency in meeting customers' product demands. This can obviously be a source of competitive advantage.

Rare Vertical Dis-Integration

Each of the examples of vertical integration and competitive advantage described so far focus on a firm's ability to vertically integrate to create competitive advantage. However, firms can also gain competitive advantages through their decisions to vertically dis-integrate, that is, through the decision to outsource an activity that used to be within the boundaries of the firm. Whenever a firm is among the first in its industry to conclude that the level of specific investment required to manage an economic exchange is no longer high, or that a particular exchange is no longer rare or costly to imitate, or that the level of uncertainty about the value of an exchange has increased, it may be among the first in its industry to vertically dis-integrate this exchange. Such activities, to the extent they are valuable, will be rare, and thus a source of at least a temporary competitive advantage.

The Imitability of Vertical Integration

The extent to which these rare vertical integration decisions can be sources of sustained competitive advantage depends, as always, on the imitability of the rare resources that gives a firm at least a temporary competitive advantage. Both direct duplication and substitution can be used to imitate another firm's valuable and rare vertical integration choices.

Direct Duplication of Vertical Integration

Direct duplication occurs when competitors develop or obtain the resources and capabilities that enable another firm to implement a valuable and rare vertical integration strategy. To the extent that these resources and capabilities are path dependent, socially complex, or causally ambiguous, they may be immune from direct duplication and thus can be a source of sustained competitive advantage.

With respect to outsourcing call centers to India, it seems that the very popularity of this strategy suggests that it is highly imitable. Indeed, this strategy is becoming so common that firms that move in the other direction by vertically integrating a call center and managing it in the United States (like Dell) make news.

But the fact that many firms are outsourcing their call centers to India does not mean that they are all equally successful in doing so. These differences in performance may reflect some subtle and complex capabilities that some of these outsourcing firms possess that others do not. These are the kinds of resources and capabilities that may be sources of sustained competitive advantage.

Some of the resources that might enable a firm to implement a valuable and rare vertical integration strategy may not be susceptible to direct duplication. These might include a firm's ability to analyze the attributes of its economic exchanges and its ability to conceive of and implement vertical integration strategies. Both of these capabilities may be socially complex and path dependent—built up over years of experience.

Substitutes for Vertical Integration

The major substitute for vertical integration—strategic alliances—is the major topic of Chapter 9. So an analysis of how strategic alliances can substitute for vertical integration will be delayed until then.

Organizing to Implement Vertical Integration

Organizing to implement vertical integration involves the same organizing tools as implementing any business or corporate strategy: organizational structure, management controls, and compensation policies.

Organizational Structure and Implementing Vertical Integration

The organizational structure that is used to implement a cost leadership and product differentiation strategy—the functional or U-form structure—is also used to implement a vertical integration strategy. Indeed, each of the exchanges included within the boundaries of a firm as a result of vertical integration decisions are incorporated into one of the functions in a functional organizational structure. Decisions about which manufacturing activities to vertically integrate into determine the range and responsibilities of the manufacturing function within a functionally organized firm; decisions about which marketing activities to vertically integrate into determine the range and responsibilities of the marketing function within a functionally organized firm; and so forth. Thus, in an important sense, vertical integration decisions made by a firm determine the structure of a functionally organized firm.

The CEO in this vertically integrated, functionally organized firm has the same two responsibilities that were first identified in Chapter 4: strategy formulation and strategy implementation. However, these two responsibilities take on added dimensions when implementing vertical integration decisions. In particular, while the CEO must take the lead in making decisions about whether or not each individual function should be vertically integrated into a firm, this person must also work to resolve conflicts that naturally arise between vertically integrated functions. The approach of one reluctant CEO to this management challenge is described in the Strategy in the Emerging Enterprise feature.

Resolving Functional Conflicts in a Vertically Integrated Firm

From a CEO's perspective, coordinating functional specialists to implement a vertical integration strategy almost always involves conflict resolution. Conflicts among functional managers in a U-form organization are both expected and normal. Indeed, if there is no conflict among certain functional managers in a U-form organization, then some of these managers probably are not doing their jobs. The task facing the CEO is not to pretend this conflict does not exist, or to ignore it, but to manage it in a way that facilitates strategy implementation.

Consider, for example, the relationship between manufacturing and sales managers. Typically, manufacturing managers prefer to manufacture a single product with long production runs. Sales managers, however, generally prefer to sell numerous customized products. Manufacturing managers generally do not like large inventories of finished products; sales managers generally prefer large inventories of finished products that facilitate rapid deliveries to customers. If these various interests of manufacturing and sales managers do not, at least sometimes, come into conflict in a vertically integrated U-form organization, then the manufacturing manager is not focusing enough on cost reduction and quality improvement in manufacturing or the sales manager is not focusing enough on meeting customer needs in a timely way, or both.

Strategy in the Emerging Enterprise

With revenues close to $1 billion a year, this woman heads one of the most successful multimedia companies in the United States. One of the businesses she owns—Harpo, Inc.—produces one of the most successful daytime television shows ever (with revenues of over $300 million a year); a magazine with the most successful launch ever and currently 2.5 million paid subscribers (more than *Vogue* and *Fortune*); and a movie production unit. One investment banker estimates that if Harpo, Inc. was a publicly traded firm, it would be valued at $575 million. Other properties she owns—including investments, real estate, a stake in the cable television channel Oxygen, and stock options in Viacom—generate another $468 million in revenues per year.

And Oprah Winfrey does not consider herself to be a CEO.

Certainly, her decision-making style is not typical of most CEOs. She has been quoted as describing her business decision-making as "leaps of faith" and "If I called a strategic planning meeting, there would be dead silence, and then people would fall out of their chairs laughing."

Oprah, Inc.

One the other hand, she has made other decisions that put her firmly in control of her empire. For example, in 1987, she hired a tough Chicago entertainment attorney—Jeff Jacobs—as president of Harpo, Inc. Where Oprah's business decisions are made from her gut and from her heart, Jacobs makes sure that the numbers add up to more revenues and profits for Harpo. She has also been unwilling to license her name to other firms, unlike Martha Stewart who licensed her name to Kmart. Oprah has made strategic alliances with King World (to distribute her TV show), with ABC (to broadcast her movies), with Hearst (to distribute her magazine), and with Oxygen (to distribute some other television programs). But she has never given up control of her business. And she has not taken her firm public. She was once quoted as saying "If I lost control of my business, I'd lose myself—or at least the ability to be myself."

To help control this growing business, Oprah and Jacobs hired a chief operating officer (COO), Tim Bennett, who then created several functional departments, including accounting, legal, and human resources, to help manage the firm. With 221 employees, an office, and a real organization, Harpo is a real company, and Oprah is a real CEO—albeit a CEO with a slightly different approach to making business decisions.

Sources: P. Sellers (2002). "The Business of being Oprah." *Fortune*, April 1, pp. 50 +; Oprah.com; Hoovers.com, "Harpo Inc.," October 20, 2003.

Numerous other conflicts arise among functional managers in a vertically integrated U-form organization. Accountants often focus on maximizing managerial accountability and close analysis of costs; R&D managers may fear that such accounting practices will interfere with innovation and creativity. Finance managers often focus on the relationship between a firm and its external capital markets; human resource managers are more concerned with the relationship between a firm and external labor markets.

In this context, the CEO's job is to help resolve conflicts in ways that facilitate the implementation of the firm's strategy. Functional managers do not have to "like" each other. However, if a firm's vertical integration strategy is correct, the reason that a function has been included within the boundaries of a firm is that this decision creates value for the firm. Allowing functional conflicts to get in the way of taking advantage of each of the functions within a firm's boundaries can destroy this potential value.

Management Controls and Implementing Vertical Integration

While having the correct organizational structure is important for firms implementing their vertical integration strategies, that structure must be supported by a variety of management control processes. Among the most important of these processes are the budgeting process and the management committee oversight process, which can also help CEOs resolve the functional conflicts that are common within vertically integrated firms.

The Budgeting Process

Budgeting is one of the most important control mechanisms available to CEOs in vertically integrated U-form organizations. Indeed, in most U-form companies, enormous management effort goes into the creation of budgets and the evaluation of performance relative to budgets. Budgets are developed for costs, revenues, and a variety of other activities performed by a firm's functional managers. Often, managerial compensation and promotion opportunities depend on the ability of a manager to meet budget expectations.

Although budgets are an important control tool, they can also have unintended negative consequences. For example, the use of budgets can lead functional managers to overemphasize short-term behavior that is easy to measure and underemphasize longer-term behavior that is more difficult to measure. Thus, for example, the strategically correct thing for a functional manager to do might be to increase expenditures for maintenance and management training, thereby ensuring that the function will have both the technology and the skilled people needed to do the job in the future. An overemphasis on meeting current budget requirements, however, might lead this manager to delay maintenance and training expenditures. By meeting short-term budgetary demands, this manager may be sacrificing the long-term viability of this function and thereby compromising the long-term viability of the firm.

CEOs can do a variety of things to counter the "short-termism" effects of the budgeting process. For example, research suggests that evaluating a functional manager's performance relative to budgets can be an effective control device when (1) the process used in developing budgets is open and participative, (2) the process reflects the economic reality facing functional managers and the firm, and (3) quantitative evaluations of a functional manger's performance are augmented by qualitative evaluations of that performance. Adopting an open and participative process for setting budgets helps ensure that budget targets are realistic and that functional managers understand and accept them. Including qualitative criteria for evaluation reduces the chances that functional managers will engage in behaviors that are very harmful in the long run but enable them to make budget in the short run.[7]

The Management Committee Oversight Process

In addition to budgets, vertically integrated U-form organizations can use various internal management committees as management control devices. Two particularly common internal management committees are the **executive committee** and the **operations committee** (although these committees have many different names in different organizations).

The executive committee in a U-form organization typically consists of the CEO and two or three key functional senior managers. It normally meets weekly and reviews the performance of the firm on a short-term basis. Functions represented on this committee generally include accounting, legal, and other functions (such as manufacturing or sales) that are most central to the firm's short-term business success. The fundamental purpose of the executive committee is to track the short-term performance of the firm, to note and correct any budget variances for functional managers, and to respond to any crises that might emerge. Obviously, the executive committee can help avoid many functional conflicts in a vertically integrated firm before they arise.

In addition to the executive committee, another group of managers meets regularly to help control the operations of the firm. Often called the operations committee, this committee typically meets monthly and usually consists of the CEO and each of the heads of the functional areas included in the firm. The executive committee is a subset of the operations committee.

The primary objective of the operations committee is to track firm performance over time intervals slightly longer than the weekly interval of primary interest to the executive committee and to monitor longer-term strategic investments and activities. Such investments might include plant expansions, the introduction of new products, and the implementation of cost-reduction or quality improvement programs. The operations committee provides a forum in which senior functional managers can come together to share concerns and opportunities and to coordinate efforts to implement strategies. Obviously, the operations committee can help resolve functional conflicts in a vertically integrated firm after they arise.

In addition to these two standing committees, various other committees and task forces can be organized within the U-form organization to manage specific projects and tasks. These additional groups are typically chaired by a member of the executive or operations committee and report to one or both of these standing committees as warranted.

Compensation in Implementing Vertical Integration Strategies

Organizational structure and management control systems can have an important impact on the ability of a firm to implement its vertical integration strategy. However, a firm's compensation policies can be important as well.

We have already seen how compensation can play a role in implementing cost leadership and product differentiation, and how compensation can be tied to budgets to help implement vertical integration. However, the three explanations of vertical integration presented in this chapter have important compensation implications as well. We will first discuss the compensation challenges these three explanations suggest and then discuss ways these challenges can be addressed.

Compensation Challenges

Opportunism-based Vertical Integration and Compensation Policy. For example, when opportunism-based approaches to vertical integration are applied to the exchange between a firm and its employees, this suggests that employees who make firm-specific investments in their jobs will often be able to create more value for a firm than employees who do not make firm-specific investments. Firm-specific investments are a type of transaction-specific investment. Where transaction-specific investments are investments that have more value in a particular exchange than in alternative exchanges, **firm-specific investments** are investments made by employees that have more value in a particular firm than in alternative firms.[8]

Examples of firm-specific investments include an employee's understanding of a particular firm's culture, his/her personal relationships with others in the firm, and an employee's knowledge about a firm's unique business processes. All this knowledge can be used by an employee to create a great deal of value in a firm. However, this knowledge has almost no value in other firms. The effort to create this knowledge is thus a firm-specific investment.

Despite the value that an employee's firm-specific investments can create, opportunism-based explanations of vertical integration suggest that employees will often be reluctant to make these investments because, once they do, they become vulnerable in their exchange with this firm. For example, an employee who has made very significant firm-specific investments may not be able to quit and go to work for another company, even if her or she is passed over for promotion, does not receive a raise, or is even actively discriminated against. This is because by quitting this firm, this employee loses all the investment he or she made in this particular firm. Since this employee has few employment options other than his or her current firm, this firm can treat this employee badly and the employee can do little about it. This is why employees are often reluctant to make firm-specific investments.

But the firm needs its employees to make such investments if it is to realize its full economic potential. Thus, one of the tasks of compensation policy is to create incentives for employees whose firm-specific investments could create great value to actually make those investments.

Capabilities and Compensation. Capability explanations of vertical integration also acknowledge the importance of firm-specific investments in creating value for a firm. Indeed, many of the valuable, rare, and costly-to-imitate resources and capabilities that can exist in a firm are a manifestation of firm-specific investments made by a firm's employees. However, where opportunism explanations of vertical integration tend to focus on firm-specific investments made by individual employees, capabilities explanations tend to focus on firm-specific investments made by groups of employees.[9]

In Chapter 3, it was suggested that one of the reasons that a firm's valuable and rare resources may be costly to imitate is that these resources are socially complex in nature. Socially complex resources reflect the teamwork, cooperation, and culture that have evolved within a firm—capabilities that can increase the value of a firm significantly, but capabilities that other firms will often find costly to imitate, at least in the short to medium term. Moreover, these are capabilities that exist because several employees—not just a single employee—have made specific investments in a firm.

From the point of view of designing a compensation policy, capabilities analysis suggests that not only should a firm's compensation policy encourage employees whose firm-specific investments could create value to actually make those investments; this theory also recognizes that these investments will often be collective in nature—that, for example, until all the members of a critical management team make firm-specific commitments to that team, that team's ability to create and sustain competitive advantages will be significantly limited.

Flexibility and Compensation. Flexibility explanations of vertical integration also have some important implications for compensation. In particular, since the creation of flexibility in a firm depends on employees being willing to engage in activities that have fixed and known downside risks and significant upside potential, it follows that compensation that has fixed and known downside risks and significant upside potential would encourage employees to choose and implement flexible vertical integration strategies.

Table 6.1   **Types of Compensation and Approaches to Making Vertical Integration Decisions**

Opportunism Explanations	Salary Cash Bonuses for individual performance Stock Grants for individual performance
Capabilities Explanations	Cash Bonuses for corporate or group performance Stock Grants for corporate or group performance
Flexibility Explanations	Stock Options for individual, corporate, or group performance

Compensation Alternatives

Table 6.1 lists several compensation alternatives and how they are related to each of the three explanations of vertical integration discussed in this chapter. Not surprisingly, opportunism-based explanations suggest that compensation that focuses on individual employees and how they can make firm-specific investments will be important for firms implementing their vertical integration strategies. Such individual compensation includes an employee's salary, cash bonuses based on individual performance, and **stock grants**—or payments to employees in a firm's stock—based on individual performance.

Capabilities explanations of vertical integration suggest that compensation that focuses on groups of employees making firm-specific investments in valuable, rare, and costly-to-imitate resources and capabilities will be particularly important for firms implementing their vertical integration strategies. Such collective compensation includes cash bonuses based on a firm's overall performance and stock grants based on a firm's overall performance.

Finally, flexibility logic suggests that compensation that has fixed and known downside risk and significant upside potential is important for firms implementing their vertical integration strategies. **Stock options**, where employees are given the right but not the obligation to purchase stock at predetermined prices, are a form of compensation that has these characteristics. Stock options can be granted based on an individual employee's performance or the performance of the firm as a whole.

The task facing CEOs looking to implement a vertical integration strategy through compensation policy is to determine what kinds of employee behavior they need to have for this strategy to create sustained competitive advantages and then to use the appropriate compensation policy. Not surprisingly, most CEOs find that all three explanations of vertical integration are important in their decision making and thus, not surprisingly, many firms adopt compensation policies that feature a mix of the compensation policies listed in Table 6.1. Thus, most firms use both individual and corporate-wide compensation schemes along with salaries, cash bonuses, stock grants, and stock options for employees who have the greatest impact on a firm's overall performance.

Vertical Integration in an International Context

Examples of vertical integration strategies that lead firms to begin operations beyond their home country borders—in particular, outsourcing to India—have already been featured in this chapter. Currently, the trend in vertical integration decisions in an international context seems to be for firms to reduce their level of

Table 6.2 **Vertical Integration Options When Pursuing International Market Opportunities**

Not Vertically Integrated	*Somewhat Vertically Integrated*	*Vertically Integrated*
Importing/Exporting	Licensing Strategic Alliances Joint Ventures	Foreign Direct Investment

vertical integration by outsourcing functions that used to be within their boundaries to independent foreign operations. However, in some settings, firms exploit international market opportunities not by outsourcing to independent foreign firms, but by entering those international markets in a vertically integrated way.

The vertical integration options available to firms pursuing an international strategy are listed in Table 6.2. These options range from non–vertically integrated (exporting/importing), to somewhat vertically integrated (licensing, strategic alliances, joint ventures), to fully vertically integrated (foreign direct investment). Each of these options is discussed briefly below.

Firms can maintain traditional arm's-length market relationships between themselves and their nondomestic customers and still implement international strategies. They do this by simply importing supplies from nondomestic sources or by exporting their products or services to nondomestic markets. In this way, firms limit any foreign direct investment into nondomestic markets. Of course, firms that adopt this non-vertically integrated approach generally have to work with some partner or partners to receive, market, and distribute their products in a nondomestic market. However, it is possible for exporting firms to use relatively simple contracts to manage their relationships with these foreign partners and thereby maintain arm's-length relationships with them.

The advantages of adopting a non–vertically integrated approach in engaging in an international strategy includes its relatively low cost and the limited risk exposure that firms that pursue international opportunities in this manner face. Firms that are just beginning to consider international strategies can use non–vertically integrated approaches to test international waters—to find out if there is demand for their current products or services, to develop some experience operating in nondomestic markets, or to begin to develop relationships that could be valuable in subsequent international strategy efforts. If firms discover that there is not much demand for their products or services in a nondomestic market, or if they discover that they do not have the resources and capabilities to effectively compete in those markets, they can simply cease their international operations. The direct cost of ceasing these operations can be quite low, especially if a firm's volume of international activity is small and the firm has not invested in plant and equipment internationally. Certainly, if a firm has limited its foreign direct investment, it does not risk losing this investment if it ceases international operations.

If a firm decides to move beyond non–vertically integrated approaches in pursuing international strategies, a wide range of somewhat vertically integrated approaches is available. These approaches range from simple **licensing arrangements**, where a domestic firm grants a firm in a nondomestic market the right to use its products and brand names to sell products in that nondomestic market; to full-blown joint ventures, where a domestic firm and a nondomestic firm create an independent organizational entity to manage international efforts. Again these options will be discussed in depth in Chapter 9.

Finally, firms may decide to integrate in their international operations by acquiring a firm in a nondomestic market or by forming a new wholly owned subsidiary to manage their operations in a nondomestic market. Obviously, both of these international investments involve substantial direct foreign investment by a firm over long periods of time. These investments are subject to both political and economic risks and should be undertaken only if the value they create is significant.

Although vertical integration in international operations can be expensive and risky, it can have some important advantages for internationalizing firms. First, this approach to internationalization can enable a firm to realize any sources of value that might exist in an international opportunity. Moreover, integration enables managers to use a wider range of organizational controls to limit the threats from any transaction-specific investments that have been made. Finally, unlike strategic alliances, where any profits from international operations must be shared with international partners, integrating into international operations enables firms to capture all the economic profits from their international operations.

SUMMARY

Vertical integration is defined as the number of stages in an industry's value chain that a firm has brought within its boundaries. Forward vertical integration is vertical integration that brings a firm closer to its ultimate customer; backward vertical integration is vertical integration that brings a firm closer to the sources of its raw materials. In making their vertical integration decisions for a particular business activity, firms can choose to be not vertically integrated, somewhat vertically integrated, or vertically integrated.

Vertical integration can create value in three different ways: First, by reducing opportunistic threats from a firm's buyers and suppliers due to any transaction-specific investments it may have made. A transaction-specific investment is an investment that has more value in a particular exchange than in any alternative exchanges. Second, vertical integration can create value by enabling a firm to exploit its valuable, rare, and costly-to-imitate resources and capabilities. Firms should vertically integrate into activities where they enjoy such advantages and should not vertically integrate into other activities. Third, vertical integration typically only creates value under conditions of low uncertainty. Under high uncertainty, vertical integration can commit a firm to a costly-to-reverse course of action and the flexibility of a non–vertically integrated approach may be preferred.

Often, these three different approaches to vertical integration will generate similar conclusions. However, even when they suggest different vertical integration strategies, they can still be helpful to management.

The ability of valuable vertical integration strategies to generate a sustained competitive advantage depends on how rare and costly to imitate these strategies are. Vertical integration strategies can be rare in two ways: (1) when a firm is vertically integrated while most competing firms are not vertically integrated and (2) when a firm is not vertically integrated while most competing firms are. These rare vertical integration strategies are possible when firms vary in the extent to which the strategies they pursue require transaction-specific investments; firms vary in the resources and capabilities they control; or firms vary in the level of uncertainty they face.

The ability to directly duplicate a firm's vertical integration strategies depends on how costly it is to directly duplicate the resources and capabilities that enable a firm to pursue these strategies. The closest substitute for vertical integration—strategic alliances—is discussed in more detail in Chapter 9.

Organizing to implement vertical integration depends on a firm's organizational structure, its management controls, and its compensation policies. The organizational structure most commonly used to implement vertical integration is the functional or U-form organization which involves cost leadership and product differentiation strategies. In a vertically integrated U-form organization, the CEO has to focus not only on deciding which functions to vertically integrate into, but also how to resolve conflicts that inevitably arise in a functionally organized vertically integrated firm. Two management controls that can be used to help implement vertical integration strategies and resolve these functional conflicts are the budgeting process and management oversight committees.

Each of the three explanations of vertical integration suggests different kinds of compensation policies that a firm looking to implement vertical integration should pursue. Opportunism-based explanations suggest individual-based compensation—including salaries and cash bonus and stock grants based on individual performance—while capabilities explanations suggests group-based compensation—including cash bonuses and stock grants based on corporate or group performance—and flexibility explanations suggest flexible compensation—including stock options based on individual, group, or corporate performance. Because all three approaches to vertical integration are often operating in a firm, it is not surprising that many firms employ all these devices in compensating employees whose actions are likely to have a significant impact on firm performance.

Firms in an international context also can choose to not be vertically integrated, somewhat vertically integrated, or vertically integrated. Firms choose to be not vertically integrated when they engage in arm's-length importing or exporting. They choose to be somewhat vertically integrated when they engage in licensing, strategic alliances, or joint ventures; and they choose vertical integration when they engage in foreign direct investment.

CHALLENGE QUESTIONS

1. Some firms have engaged in backward vertical integration strategies in order to appropriate the economic profits that would have been earned by suppliers selling to them. How is this motivation for backward vertical integration related to the opportunism logic for vertical integration described in this chapter? (*Hint*: Compare the competitive conditions under which firms may earn economic profits to the competitive conditions under which firms will be motivated to avoid opportunism through vertical integration.)

2. You are about to purchase a used car. What kinds of threats do you face

in this purchase? What can you do to protect yourself from these threats? How is buying a car like and unlike vertical integration decisions?

3. What are the competitive implications for firms if they assume that all potential exchange partners cannot be trusted?

4. Common conflicts between sales and manufacturing are mentioned in the text. What conflicts might exist between R&D and manufacturing? Between finance and manufacturing? Between marketing and sales? Between accounting and everyone else? What could a CEO do to help resolve these conflicts?

5. Under what conditions would you accept a lower-paying job instead of a higher-paying job? What implications does your answer have for your potential employer's compensation policy?

6. According to opportunism-based explanations of vertical integration, when should a firm pursue foreign direct investment? According to capabilities-based explanations, when should it pursue these investments? According to flexibility explanations, when should it pursue these investments?

PROBLEM SET

1. Which of the following two firms is more vertically integrated? How can you tell?

(a) Firm A has included manufacturing, sales, finance, and human resources within its boundaries and has outsourced legal and customer service.

(b) Firm B has included manufacturing, sales, legal, and customer service within its boundaries and has outsourced finance and human resources.

2. What is the level of transaction-specific investment for each firm in the following transactions? Who in these transactions is at greater risk of being taken unfair advantage of?

(a) Firm I has built a plant right next door to Firm II. Firm I's plant is worth $5 million if it supplies Firm II. It is worth $200,000 if it does not supply Firm II. Firm II has three alternative suppliers. If it receives supplies from Firm I, it is worth $10 million. If it does not receive supplies from Firm I, it is worth $9.8 million.

(b) Firm A has just purchased a new computer system that is only available from Firm B. Firm A has redesigned its entire production process around this new computer system. The old production process is worth $1 million, the new process is worth $12 million. Firm B has several hundred customers for its new computer system.

(c) Firm Alpha, a fast-food restaurant company, has a contract with Firm Beta, a movie studio. After negotiating with several other potential partners, Firm Alpha agreed to a contract that requires Firm Alpha to pay Firm Beta $5 million per year for the right to use characters from Firm Beta's movies in its packaged meals for children. Demand for children's movies has recently dropped.

(d) Firm I owns and runs a printing press. Firm J uses the services of a printing press. Historically, Firm I has sold its services to many customers. However, it was recently approached by Firm J to become its exclusive supplier of printing press services. Currently, Firm I is worth $1 million. If it became the sole supplier to Firm J, it would be worth $8 million. To complete this deal, Firm I would have to stop supplying its current customers and modify its machines to meet Firm J's needs. No other firm needs the same services as Firm J. Firm J contacted several other suppliers who said they would be willing to become a sole supplier for Firm J before deciding to propose this arrangement with Firm I.

3. What recommendation would you make in each of these situations, vertical integration or non–vertical integration, and why?

(a) Firm A needs a new and unique technology for its product line. There are no substitute technologies. Should Firm A make this technology or buy it?

(b) Firm I has been selling its products through a distributor for some time. It has become the market share leader. Unfortunately, this distributor has not been able to keep up with the evolving technology and customers are complaining. There are no alternative distributors available. Should Firm I keep its current distributor or should it begin distribution on its own?

(c) Firm Alpha has manufactured its own products for years. Recently, however, one of these products has become more and more like a commodity. Several firms are now able to manufacture this product at the same price and quality as Firm Alpha. However, they do not have Firm Alpha's brand name in the marketplace. Should Firm Alpha continue to manufacture this product or should it outsource it to one of these other firms?

(d) Firm I is convinced that a certain class of technologies holds real economic potential. However, it does not know, for sure, which particular version of this technology is going to dominate the market. There are eight competing versions of this technology currently, but ultimately, only one will dominate the market. Should Firm I invest in all eight of these technologies itself? Should it invest in just one of these technologies? Should it partner with other firms that are investing in these different technologies?

END NOTES

1. Coase, R. (1937). "The nature of the firm." *Economica*, 4, pp. 386–405.
2. This explanation of vertical integration is known as transactions cost economics in the academic literature. See Williamson, O. (1975). *Markets and hierarchies: Analysis and antitrust implications.* New York: Free Press; Williamson, O. (1985). *The economic institutions of capitalism.* New York: Free Press; and Klein, B., R. Crawford, and A. Alchian (1978). "Vertical integration, appropriable rents, and the competitive contracting process." *Journal of Law and Economics*, 21, pp. 297–326.
3. Another option—forming an alliance between these two firms—is discussed in more detail in Chapter 9.
4. This explanation of vertical integration is known as the capabilities-based theory of the firm in the academic literature. It draws heavily from the resource-based view described in Chapter 3. See Barney, J. B. (1991). "Firm resources and sustained competitive advantage." *Journal of Management*, 17, pp. 99–120; Barney, J. B. (1999). "How a firm's capabilities affect boundary decisions." *Sloan Management Review*, 40(3);

Conner, K. R., and C. K. Prahalad (1996). "A resource-based theory of the firm: Knowledge versus opportunism." *Organization Science*, 7, pp. 477–501.
5. This explanation of vertical integration is known as real-options theory in the academic literature. See Kogut, B. (1991). "Joint ventures and the option to expand and acquire." *Management Science*, 37, pp. 19–33.
6. Kripalani, M., and P. Engardio (2003). "The rise of India." *BusinessWeek*, December 8, pp. 66 +.
7. See Gupta, A. K. (1987). "SBU strategies, corporate-SBU relations and SBU effectiveness in strategy implementation." *Academy of Management Journal*, 30(3), pp. 477–500.
8. Becker, G. S. (1993). *Human capital: A theoretical and empirical analysis, with special reference to education.* Chicago: University of Chicago Press.
9. Barney, J. B. (1991). "Firm resources and sustained competitive advantage." *Journal of Management*, 17, pp. 99–120.

7

Corporate Diversification

X-Box Is Coming

Even its logo is foreboding: Two slashes of green, crossing, on a black background, as if an alien is trying to push through the sides of a box that has held it prisoner, revealing a terrifying world within. Microsoft's initial entry into the competitive world of video game consoles, X-Box was designed to thrill gamers and terrify competitors. It also represented a significant diversification move on the part of Microsoft.

Until X-Box, Microsoft was a software company. Its first products were applications software for Apple II computers. It then acquired the rights to a PC operating system called QDOS (for "Quick and Dirty Operating System"), renamed it MSDOS (for "Microsoft Disc Operating System"), and MSDOS became the standard of PC operating systems in the industry. MSDOS was later replaced by Windows, an operating system that emulated much of the user interface pioneered by Apple. However, because of the domination of MSDOS, Windows became the de facto standard operating system in PCs—and still is, despite the recent growth of an open-source operating system called Linux.

Microsoft followed up its PC operating system by diversifying into application software designed to operate effectively with Windows. Virtually every application

After reading this chapter, you should be able to:

1. Define corporate diversification and describe five types of corporate diversification.

2. Specify the two conditions that a corporate diversification strategy must meet in order to create economic value.

3. Define the concept of "economies of scope" and identify eight potential economies of scope a diversified firm might try to exploit.

4. Identify which of these economies of scope a firm's outside equity investors are able to realize on their own at low cost.

5. Specify the circumstances under which a firm's diversification strategy will be rare.

6. Indicate which of the economies of scope identified in this chapter are more likely to be subject to low-cost imitation and which are less likely to be subject to low-cost imitation.

7. Identify two potential substitutes for corporate diversification.

8. Identify economies of scope that can be realized through international operations.

---

developed by Microsoft—from Word, to Excel, to Power Point—has become the de facto standard application in the industry. More recently, Microsoft has diversified its software even more by developing both operating systems and applications for servers (larger computers used to connect multiple users most frequently purchased by companies), a variety of Internet applications (e.g., MSN), enterprise software for small and medium-sized firms (i.e., software that lets these firms do their bookkeeping efficiently), and Windows-type software for phones and PDAs (personal digital assistants or handheld computers).

In the process of developing this diversified portfolio of software, Microsoft has become a huge success. Its sales grew an average of 36 percent a year through the 1990s. Its current market value is $279 billion, and it generates $1 billion a month in profits. Given its success in developing and selling software, an obvious question becomes: Why did this software company decide to bring out hardware—the X-Box console—to compete in the video game market?

At least three reasons for this have been suggested. First, by the time Microsoft decided to enter the video game market, there were already several well-established video game development companies—not the least of which was Entertainment Arts (see Chapter 3). These firms had already demonstrated the ability to develop popular games. Given that Microsoft did not have these game development skills, it concluded that it could outsource game development to firms that did, and focus instead on the console.

Second, the video game software market, while it is software, is very different from any of the other software markets in which Microsoft operates. Microsoft's markets focus on using computers to accomplish very utilitarian tasks. Also, once users learn a Microsoft product, it is very unlikely that they will change. Video game software is more of a "hit" market—where firms have to introduce new games, these new games have to break new technical and playing ground, and old titles are constantly being replaced by new or updated titles. While computer operators might use the same copy of Windows or Word for several years and then update these copies when new versions come out, video game players are looking for new titles and new versions every year or more frequently.

The console market, on the other hand, is more like Microsoft's traditional software market. There has historically been a five-year product life cycle in consoles—once a console is developed, it remains largely unchanged for five years. This enables game developers to discover and then fully exploit the technical capabilities of a console in their games. Only after these technical capabilities are fully exploited do console manufacturers consider bringing out new ones.

Finally, Microsoft has been very interested in linking its current software products with the Internet. In a famous e-mail to Microsoft employees, founder Bill Gates argued that unless Microsoft learned how to integrate its software with the Internet it would struggle in the long run. X-Box is one area where this linkage is very natural. In fact, X-Box has become a leader in Internet-based video

gaming through its "X-Box Live" option. As a further entree into the Internet, X-Box is of strategic importance at Microsoft.

So far, the X-Box has not had a huge impact on Microsoft's performance. Current revenues for the games and home entertainment divisions at Microsoft hovers around $3.5 billion. However, these activities are yet to generate significant profits. Despite this lackluster performance, Microsoft remains committed to X-Box. Indeed, it currently has plans to introduce a new X-Box model after only four years, shortening by one year the traditional product life cycle in the video game console industry.

Sources: J. Greene (2004). "Microsoft's midlife crisis." *BusinessWeek*, April 19; R. Guth and S. Thurm (2004). "Microsoft to dole out its cash horde." *Wall Street Journal*, July 21, pp. A1 +; B. R. Schendler (1995). "What Bill Gates really wants." *Fortune*, January 16, pp. 34–63.

Microsoft is like most large firms in the United States and the world: It has diversified operations. Indeed, virtually all of the 500 largest firms in the United States and the 500 largest firms in the world are diversified, either by product or geographically. Large single-business firms are very unusual. However, like most of these large diversified firms, Microsoft has diversified along some dimensions, but not along others.

What Is Corporate Diversification?

A firm implements a **corporate diversification strategy** when it operates in multiple industries or markets simultaneously. When a firm operates in multiple industries simultaneously, it is said to be implementing a **product diversification strategy**. When a firm operates in multiple geographic markets simultaneously, it is said to be implementing a **geographic market diversification**

strategy. When a firm implements both of these types of diversification simultaneously, it is said to be implementing a **product-market diversification strategy**. Just how geographically diversified firms really are is examined in the Global Perspectives feature.

We have already seen glimpses of these diversification strategies in the discussion of vertical integration strategies in Chapter 6. Sometimes, when a firm vertically integrates backward or forward, it begins operations in a new product or geographic market. This happened to computer software firms when they began manning their own call centers. These firms moved from the "computer software development" business to the "call center management" business when they vertically integrated forward. In this sense, when firms vertically integrate, they may also be implementing a diversification strategy. However, the critical difference between the diversification strategies studied here and vertical integration (discussed in Chapter 6) is that in this chapter, product market diversification is the primary objective of these strategies, whereas in Chapter 6, such diversification was often a secondary consequence of pursuing a vertical integration strategy.

Types of Corporate Diversification

Firms vary in the extent to which they have diversified the mix of businesses they pursue. Perhaps the simplest way of characterizing differences in the level of corporate diversification focuses on the relatedness of the businesses pursued by a firm. As shown in Figure 7.1, firms can pursue a strategy of **limited corporate diversification**, of **related corporate diversification**, or of **unrelated corporate diversification**.

Figure 7.1 Levels and Types of Diversification

Global Perspectives

How Global Are Globally Diversified Firms?

The same headline seems to appear in every newspaper, in every business book, and in every business class: Business is Becoming More Global. The implication is clear: Firms ignore the global nature of their business at their own peril.

In one sense, it is clear that business is becoming more and more global. Large firms, whether headquartered in the United States or abroad, are seeing an ever-larger percentage of their revenues coming from nondomestic sources. Indeed, some firms—like McDonald's and Coca-Cola—are seen not just as global firms, but as exporters of U.S. culture around the world. On the other hand, a careful analysis of where large diversified firms actually sell their products and services tells a somewhat different story. One recent study found that "global diversification" is not really that "global."

In particular, these authors divided the world's economy into three great markets: North America, Europe, and Asia. They then examined the number of firms that have significant sales in just one of these three geographic markets, in two of these markets, and in all three of these markets. The "globalization of business" hypothesis suggests that large numbers of firms will have significant operations in all three of these markets. This is not the case.

Based on a list of 365 of the largest corporations in the world, this study found that only 9 (2.4 percent) had 20 percent or more of their sales in all three of these global regions, only 25 (5.0 percent) had 20 percent or more of their sales in two of these global regions, while 320 (84.2 percent) had 20 percent or more of their sales in just one of these global regions. This suggests that while it may not be uncommon for firms to sell outside their home country to neighboring countries, it is somewhat more uncommon for firms to have significant sales outside their geographic region.

The list of truly global firms, that is, firms that had significant sales in all three regional economies, includes many of the usual suspects, such as IBM, Sony, Philips Electronics, Nokia, Intel, Canon, and Coca-Cola. However,

Limited Corporate Diversification

A firm has implemented a strategy of **limited corporate diversification** when all or most of its business activities fall within a single industry and geographic market (see Panel A of Figure 7.1). Two kinds of firms are included in this corporate diversification category: **single-business firms** (firms with greater than 95 percent of their total sales in a single product market) and **dominant-business firms** (firms with between 70 percent and 95 percent of their total sales in a single product market).

Differences between single-business and dominant-business firms are represented in Panel A of Figure 7.1. The firm pursing a single-business corporate diversification strategy engages in only one business, Business A. An example of a single-business firm is the WD-40 Company of San Diego, California. This company manufactures and distributes only one product—the spray cleanser and lubricant WD-40. The dominant-business firm pursues two businesses, Business E and a smaller Business F that is tightly linked to Business E. An example of a dominant business firm is Donato's Pizza. Donato's Pizza does the vast majority of its business in a single product—pizza—in a single market—the United States.

several supposedly "global" firms did not show up on this list. For example, Toyota, Unilever, Motorola, Sun Microsystems, 3M, McDonald's, Michelin, and Kodak all have significant sales in two regions of the world, but not all three. For example, only 7.7 percent of Toyota's total sales comes from Europe; only 14 percent of Motorola's total sales comes from Europe; only 14.8 percent of McDonald's total sales comes from Asia; and only 17.2 percent of Kodak's sales comes from Asia.

The list of large firms that have significant sales in only one geographic region is also interesting. This list includes Wal-Mart (94.1 percent of sales in North America), General Motors (81.1 percent in North America), General Electric (59.1 percent in North America), Mitsubishi (86.8 percent in Asia), Volkswagen (68.2 percent in Europe), Ford (66.7 percent in North America) and Phillip Morris (57.9 percent in North America). Some of these firms—

including GM and GE—are thought of as truly international giants. But what this research shows is that even these giant international firms are still tied to their historical geographic homes.

These findings have significant implications for the management of international firms. First, they suggest that the products and services of most international firms are not equally accessible across the globe. This is true despite efforts by multinational firms to modify their products to be responsive to local demand. Second, these results suggest that many sources of competitive advantages for firms are valuable only within specific geographic regions and not broadly around the globe. Finally, because firms may have very different market positions in different geographic regions of the world, it may be necessary for these firms to adopt very different strategies in these regions. For exam-

ple, Toyota—a firm that has significant sales in Asia and North America—may be able to leverage its reputation for quality by introducing a new brand of luxury automobile—the Lexus. However, because Toyota has such a small market presence in Europe, it has less of a reputation for quality to build on in Europe and thus has been unable to successfully launch the Lexis brand there. Toyota may have to adopt a different approach to the European luxury market or wait to enter that market until its sales in Europe increase dramatically.

Sources: A. Rugman and A. Verbeke (2004). "A perspective on regional and global strategies of multinational enterprises." *Journal of International Business Studies*, 35, pp. 3–18; A. Rugman and A. Verbeke (2002). "A note on the transnational solution and the transaction cost theory of multinational strategic management." *Journal of International Business Studies*, 23, pp. 761–771.

However, Donato's also owns a subsidiary that makes a machine that automatically slices and puts pepperoni on pizzas. Not only does Donato's use this machine in its own pizzerias, it also sells this machine to food manufacturers that make frozen pepperoni pizza.

In an important sense, firms pursuing a strategy of limited corporate diversification are not leveraging their resources and capabilities beyond a single product or market. Thus, the analysis of limited corporate diversification is logically equivalent to the analysis of business-level strategies (discussed in Part 2 of this book). Because these kinds of strategies have already been discussed, the remainder of this chapter focuses on corporate strategies that involve higher levels of diversification.

Related Corporate Diversification

As a firm begins to engage in businesses in more than one product or market, it moves away from being a single-business or dominant-business firm and begins to adopt higher levels of corporate diversification. When less than 70 percent of a firm's revenue comes from a single product market and these multiple lines of business are linked, the firm has implemented a strategy of **related corporate diversification**.

The multiple businesses that a diversified firm pursues can be related in two ways (see Panel B in Figure 7.1). If all the businesses in which a firm operates share a significant number of inputs, production technologies, distribution channels, similar customers, and so forth, this corporate diversification strategy is called **related-constrained**. This strategy is termed "constrained" because corporate managers pursue business opportunities in new markets or industries only if those markets or industries share numerous resource and capability requirements with the businesses the firm is currently pursuing. Commonalities across businesses in a strategy of related-constrained diversification are represented by the linkages among Businesses K, L, M, and N in the related-constrained section of Figure 7.1.

PepsiCo is an example of a related-constrained diversified firm. While PepsiCo is operating in multiple businesses around the world, all of its businesses focus on providing snack-type products, either food or beverages. PepsiCo is not in the business of making or selling more traditional types of food—like pasta, or cheese, or breakfast cereal. Moreover, PepsiCo attempts to use a single, firm-wide capability to gain competitive advantages in each of its businesses—its ability to develop and exploit well-known brand names. Whether it's Pepsi, or Doritos, or Mountain Dew, or Big Red, PepsiCo is all about building brand names. In fact, PepsiCo has 16 brands that generate $1 billion or more in revenues each year. That is more so-called "power brands" than Nestlé, Procter & Gamble, or Coca-Cola![1]

If the different businesses that a single firm pursues are linked on only a couple of dimensions, or if different sets of businesses are linked along very different dimensions, that corporate diversification strategy is called **related-linked**. For example, Business Q and Business R may share similar production technology, Business R and Business S may share similar customers, Business S and Business T may share similar suppliers, and Business Q and Business T may have no common attributes. This strategy is represented in the related-linked section of Figure 7.1 by businesses with relatively few links between them and with different kinds of links between them (i.e., straight lines and curved lines).

An example of a related-linked diversified firm is Disney. Disney has evolved from a single-business firm (when it did nothing but produce animated motion pictures), to a dominant business firm (when it produced family-oriented motion pictures and operated a theme park), to a related-constrained diversified firm (when it produced family-oriented motion pictures, operated multiple theme parks, and sold products through its Disney Stores). Recently, it has become so diversified that it has taken on the attributes of related-linked diversification. While much of the Disney empire still builds on characters developed in its animated motion pictures, it also owns and operates businesses—including a movie studio that produces movies more appropriate for mature audiences, several hotels and resorts that have little or nothing to do with Disney characters, and a television network (ABC) that broadcasts non-Disney-produced content—that are less directly linked to these characters. This is not to suggest that Disney is pursuing an unrelated diversification strategy. After all, most of its businesses are in the entertainment industry, broadly defined. Rather, this is only to suggest that it is no longer possible to find a single thread—like a Mickey Mouse or a Lion King—that connects all of Disney's business enterprises. In this sense, Disney has become a related-linked diversified firm.[2]

Unrelated Corporate Diversification

Firms that pursue a strategy of related corporate diversification have some type of linkages among most, if not all, the different businesses they pursue. However, it is possible for firms to pursue numerous different businesses and for there to be *no* linkages among them (see Panel C of Figure 7.1). When less than 70 percent of a firm's revenues is generated in a single product market, and when a firm's businesses share few, if any, common attributes, then that firm is pursuing a strategy of **unrelated corporate diversification**.

General Electric is an example of a firm pursuing an unrelated diversification strategy. GE's mix of businesses includes commercial finance and leasing (revenues of $23 billion), insurance (revenues of $22.6 billion), turbines and other technologies to generate electricity (revenues of $18 billion), commercial finance including a large credit card business (revenues of $15 billion), jet engines (revenues of $15 billion), consumer and industrial products including light bulbs (revenues of $13 billion), medical imaging devices (revenues of $11.5 billion), entertainment businesses including NBC (revenues of $8.3 billion), advanced materials including artificial diamonds (revenues of $7.8 billion), equipment services including the leasing and management of railroad boxcars (revenues of $4.4 billion), and water treatment and security services (revenues of $3.5 billion). It is difficult to see how any of these businesses are closely related to each other. Indeed, GE tends to manage each of its businesses as if they were stand-alone entities—a management approach consistent with a firm implementing an unrelated diversified corporate strategy.[3]

The Value of Corporate Diversification

VRIO

In order for corporate diversification to be economically valuable, two conditions must hold. First, there must be some valuable economy of scope among the multiple businesses in which a firm is operating. Second, it must be less costly for managers in a firm to realize these economies of scope than for outside equity holders on their own. If outside investors could realize the value of a particular economy of scope on their own, and at low cost, then they would have few incentives to "hire" managers to realize this economy of scope for them. Each of these requirements for corporate diversification to add value for a firm will be considered below.

What Are Valuable Economies of Scope?

Economies of scope exist in a firm when the value of the products or services it sells increases as a function of the number of businesses that firm operates in. The term "scope" in this definition refers to the range of businesses in which a diversified firm operates. For this reason, only diversified firms can, by definition, exploit economies of scope. Economies of scope are valuable to the extent that they increase a firm's revenues or decrease its costs, compared to what would be the case if these economies of scope were not exploited.

A wide variety of potentially valuable sources of economies of scope have been identified in the literature. Some of the most important of these are listed in Table 7.1 and discussed below. How valuable economies of scope actually are, on average, has been the subject of a great deal of research summarized in the Research Made Relevant feature.

Research Made Relevant

In 1994, Lang and Stulz published a sensational article that suggested that, on average, when a firm began implementing a corporate diversification strategy, it destroyed about 25 percent of its market value. Lang and Stulz came to this conclusion by comparing the market performance of firms pursuing a corporate diversification strategy with portfolios of firms pursuing a limited diversification strategy. Taken together, the market performance of a portfolio of firms that were pursuing a limited diversification strategy was about 25 percent higher than the market performance of a single diversified firm operating in all of the businesses included in this portfolio. These results suggested that not only were economies of scope not valuable, but, on average, efforts to realize these economies actually destroyed economic value. Similar results were published by Comment and Jarrell using different measures of firm performance.

Not surprisingly, these results generated quite a stir. If Lang and Stulz were correct, then diversified firms—no matter what kind of diversification strategy they engaged in—destroyed an enormous amount of economic value. This could lead to a fundamental restructuring of the U.S. economy.

However, more recent research has significantly tempered Lang and Stutz's conclusions. Two new findings suggest that, even if there is a 25 percent discount, diversification can still add value. First, Villalonga and others found that firms pursuing diversification

How Valuable Are Economies of Scope, on Average?

strategies were generally performing more poorly before they began diversifying than firms that never pursued diversification strategies. Thus, while it might appear that diversification leads to a significant loss of economic value, in reality that loss of value occurred before these firms began implementing a diversification strategy. Indeed, some more recent research suggests that these relatively poor-performing firms may actually increase their market value over what would have been the case if they did not diversify.

Second, Miller found that firms that find it in their self-interest to diversify do so in a very predictable pattern. These firms tend to diversify into the most profitable new business first, the second most profitable business second, and so forth. Not surprisingly, the fiftieth

diversification move made by these firms might not generate huge additional profits. However, these profits—it turns out—are still, on average, positive. Since multiple rounds of diversification increase profits at a decreasing rate, the overall average profitability of diversified firms will generally be less than the overall average profitability of firms that do not pursue a diversification strategy—thus, a substantial difference between the market value of nondiversified and diversified firms might exist. However, this discount, per se, does not mean that the diversified firm is destroying economic value. Rather, it may mean only that a diversifying firm is creating value in smaller increments as it continues to diversify.

Currently, most scholars believe that exploiting economies of scope through corporate diversification, on average, increases a firm's market value. This does not mean, of course, that all diversification strategies will create economic value. Managers must carefully plan which economies of scope they will realize through their diversification moves and how to efficiently realize those economies through their organization.

Sources: H. P. Lang and R. Stulz (1994). "Tobin's *q*, corporate diversification, and firm performance." *Journal of Political Economy*, 102, pp. 1248–1280; R. Comment and G. Jarrell (1995). "Corporate focus and stock returns." *Journal of Financial Economics*, 37, pp. 67–87; D. Miller (2004). "Firms' technological resources and the performance effects of diversification: A longitudinal study." Forthcoming, *Strategic Management Journal;* B. Villalonga (2004). "Does diversification cause the 'diversification discount'?" *Financial Management*, 33(2), pp. 5–28.

Diversification to Exploit Operational Economies of Scope

Sometimes, economies of scope may reflect operational links among the businesses a firm engages in. **Operational economies of scope** typically take one of two forms: shared activities and shared core competencies.

Table 7.1   **Different Types of Economies of Scope**

1. Operational economies of scope
   - Shared activities
   - Core competencies

2. Financial economies of scope
   - Internal capital allocation
   - Risk reduction
   - Tax advantages

3. Anticompetitive economies of scope
   - Multipoint competition
   - Exploiting market power

4. Employee and stakeholder incentives for diversification
   - Maximizing management compensation

Shared Activities. In Chapter 3, it was suggested that value-chain analysis can be used to describe the specific business activities of a firm. This same value-chain analysis can also be used to describe the business activities that may be shared across several different businesses within a diversified firm. These **shared activities** are potential sources of operational economies of scope for diversified firms.

Consider, for example, the hypothetical firm presented in Figure 7.2. This diversified firm engages in three businesses: A, B, and C. However, these three

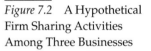

Figure 7.2   A Hypothetical Firm Sharing Activities Among Three Businesses

businesses share a variety of activities throughout their value chains. For example, all three draw on the same technology development operation. Product design and manufacturing are shared in businesses A and B and separate for business C. All three businesses share a common marketing and service operation. Business A has its own distribution system.

These kinds of shared activities are quite common among both related-constrained and related-linked diversified firms. At Texas Instruments, for example, a variety of electronics businesses share some research and development activities and often share common manufacturing locations. Procter & Gamble's numerous different consumer products businesses often share common manufacturing locations and rely on a common distribution network (through retail grocery stores).[4] Some of the most common shared activities in diversified firms, and their location in the value chain, are summarized in Table 7.2.

Many of the shared activities listed in Table 7.2 can have the effect of reducing a diversified firm's costs. For example, if a diversified firm has a purchasing function that is common to several of its different businesses it can often obtain volume discounts on its purchases that would otherwise not be possible. Also, by

Table 7.2   **Possible Shared Activities and Their Place in the Value Chain**

Value chain activity	Shared activities
Input activities	Common purchasing Common inventory control system Common warehousing facilities Common inventory delivery system Common quality assurance Common input requirements system Common suppliers
Production activities	Common product components Common product components manufacturing Common assembly facilities Common quality control system Common maintenance operation Common inventory control system
Warehousing and distribution	Common product delivery system Common warehouse facilities
Sales and marketing	Common advertising efforts Common promotional activities Cross-selling of products Common pricing systems Common marketing departments Common distribution channels Common sales forces Common sales offices Common order processing services
Dealer support and service	Common service network Common guarantees and warranties Common accounts receivable management systems Common dealer training Common dealer support services

Sources: Porter, M. E. (1985). *Competitive advantage*. New York: Free Press, Rumelt, R. P. (1974). *Strategy, structure, and economic performance*. Cambridge, MA: Harvard University Press, Ansoff, H. I. (1965). *Corporate strategy*. New York: McGraw-Hill.

manufacturing products that are used as inputs into several of a diversified firm's businesses, the total costs of producing these products in a firm can be reduced. A single sales force representing the products or services of several different businesses within a diversified firm can reduce the cost of selling these products or services. Firms such as IBM, Hewlett-Packard, and General Motors have all used shared activities to reduce their costs in these ways.

Failure to exploit shared activities across businesses can lead to out-of-control costs. For example, Kentucky Fried Chicken, when it was a division of PepsiCo, encouraged each of its regional business operations in North America to develop their own quality improvement plans. The result was enormous redundancy and at least three conflicting quality efforts—all leading to higher-than-necessary costs. In a similar way, Levi Strauss's unwillingness to centralize and coordinate order processing led to a situation where six separate order-processing computer systems operated simultaneously. This costly redundancy was ultimately replaced by a single, integrated ordering system shared across the entire corporation.[5]

Shared activities can also increase the revenues in diversified firms' businesses. This can happen in at least two ways. First, it may be that shared product development and sales activities may enable two or more businesses in a diversified firm to offer a bundled set of products to customers. Sometimes, the value of these "product bundles" is greater than the value of each product separately. This additional customer value can generate revenues greater than what would have been the case if the businesses were not together and sharing activities in a diversified firm.

In the telecommunications industry, for example, separate firms sell telephones, access to telephone lines, equipment to route calls in an office, mobile telephones, and paging services. A customer that requires all these services could contact five different companies. Each of these five different firms would likely possess its own unique technological standards and software, making the development of an integrated telecommunications system for the customer difficult at best. Alternatively, a single diversified firm sharing sales activities across these businesses could significantly reduce the search costs of potential customers. This one-stop shopping is likely to be valuable to customers, who might be willing to pay a slightly higher price for this convenience than they would pay if they purchased these services from five separate firms. Moreover, if this diversified firm also shares some technology development activities across its businesses, it might be able to offer an integrated telecommunications network to potential customers. The extra value of this integrated network for customers is very likely to be reflected in prices that are higher than would have been possible if each of these businesses were independent or if activities among these businesses were not shared. Most of the regional telephone operating companies in the United States—including Bell South and Southwestern Bell—are attempting to gain these economies of scope.[6]

Such product bundles are important in other firms as well. Many grocery stores now sell prepared foods alongside traditional grocery products in the belief that busy customers want access to all kinds of food products—in the same location.[7]

Second, shared activities can enhance business revenues by exploiting the strong, positive reputations of some of a firm's businesses in other of its businesses. For example, if one business has a strong positive reputation for high-quality manufacturing, other businesses sharing this manufacturing activity will gain some of the advantages of this reputation. And, if one business has a strong positive reputation for selling high-performance products, other businesses sharing sales and marketing activities with this business will gain some of the advantages of this reputation. In both cases, businesses that draw on the strong reputation of another business through shared activities with that business will have larger revenues than they would were they operating on their own.

The Limits of Activity Sharing. Despite the potential of activity sharing to be the basis of a valuable corporate diversification strategy, this approach has three important limits.[8] First, substantial organizational issues are often associated with a diversified firm's learning how to manage cross-business relationships. Managing these relationships effectively can be very difficult, and failure can lead to excess bureaucracy, inefficiency, and organizational gridlock. These issues are discussed in detail in Chapter 8.

Second, sharing activities may limit the ability of a particular business to meet its specific customers' needs. For example, if two businesses share manufacturing activities, they may reduce their manufacturing costs. However, to gain these cost advantages, these businesses may need to build products using somewhat standardized components that do not fully meet their individual customers' needs. Businesses that share distribution activities may have lower overall distribution costs but be unable to distribute their products to all their customers. Businesses that share sales activities may have lower overall sales costs but be unable to provide the specialized selling required in each business.

One diversified firm that has struggled with the ability to meet the specialized needs of customers in its different divisions is General Motors. To exploit economies of scope in the design of new automobiles, GM shared the design process across its several automobile divisions. The result, through much of the 1990s, was "cookie-cutter"–looking cars—the traditional distinctiveness of several GM divisions, including Oldsmobile and Cadillac, was all but lost.[9]

Third, if one business in a diversified firm has a poor reputation, sharing activities with that business can reduce the quality of the reputation of other businesses in the firm.

Taken together, these limits on activity sharing can more than offset any possible gains. Indeed, over the last decade, more and more diversified firms have been abandoning efforts at activity sharing in favor of managing each business's activities independently. For example, ABB, Inc. (a Swiss engineering firm) and CIBA-Geigy (a Swiss chemicals firm) have adopted explicit corporate policies that restrict almost all activity sharing across businesses.[10] Other diversified firms, including Nestlé and General Electric, restrict activity sharing to just one or two activities (such as research and development or management training). However, to the extent that a diversified firm can exploit shared activities while avoiding these problems, shared activities can add value to a firm.

Core Competencies. Recently, a second operational linkage among the businesses of a diversified firm has been described. Unlike shared activities, this linkage is based on different businesses in a diversified firm sharing less tangible resources such as managerial and technical know-how, experience, and wisdom. This source of operational economy of scope has been called a firm's core competence.[11] **Core competence** has been defined by Prahalad and Hamel as "the collective learning in the organization, especially how to coordinate diverse production skills and integrate multiple streams of technologies." Core competencies are complex sets of resources and capabilities that link different businesses in a diversified firm through managerial and technical know-how, experience, and wisdom.[12]

Two firms that have well-developed core competencies are 3M and Johnson & Johnson. 3M has a core competence in substrates, adhesives, and coatings.

Collectively, employees at 3M know more about developing and applying adhesives and coatings on different kinds of substrates than do employees in any other organization. Over the years, 3M has applied these resources and capabilities in a wide variety of products, including Post-it notes, magnetic tape, photographic film, pressure-sensitive tape, and coated abrasives. At first glance, these widely diversified products seem to have little or nothing in common. Yet they all draw on a single core set of resources and capabilities in substrates, adhesives, and coatings.

Johnson & Johnson has a core competence in developing or acquiring pharmaceutical and medical products and then marketing them to the public. Many of Johnson & Johnson's products are dominant in their market segments—Johnson & Johnson's in baby powder, Ethicon in surgical sutures, and Tylenol in pain relievers. And while these products range broadly from those sold directly to consumers (e.g., the BandAid brand of adhesive bandages) to highly sophisticated medical technologies sold only to doctors and hospitals (e.g., Ethicon sutures), all of Johnson & Johnson's products build on the same ability to identify, develop, acquire, and market products in the pharmaceutical and medical products industry.

To understand how core competencies can reduce a firm's costs or increase its revenues, consider how these core competencies emerge over time. Most firms begin operations in a single business. Imagine that a firm has carefully evaluated all of its current business opportunities and has fully funded all of those with a positive net present value. Any of the above-normal returns that this firm has left over after fully funding all its current positive net present value opportunities can be thought of as **free cash flow**.[13] Firms can spend this free cash in a variety of ways: They can spend it on benefits for managers; they can give it to shareholders through dividends or by buying back a firm's stock; they can use it to invest in new businesses.

Suppose a firm chooses to use this cash to invest in a new business. In other words, suppose this firm chooses to implement a diversification strategy. If this firm is seeking to maximize the return from implementing this diversification strategy, which of all the possible businesses that it could invest in should it invest in? Obviously, a profit-maximizing firm will choose to begin operations in a business where it has a competitive advantage. What kind of business is likely to generate this competitive advantage for this firm? The obvious answer is a business where the same underlying resources and capabilities that gave this firm an advantage in its original business are still valuable, rare, and costly to imitate. Consequently, this first diversification move sees the firm investing in a business that is closely related to its original business, in that both businesses draw on a common set of underlying resources and capabilities where the firm already has a competitive advantage.

Put another way, a firm that diversifies by exploiting its resource and capability advantages in its original business will have lower costs than firms that begin a new business without these resource and capability advantages, or higher revenues than firms lacking these advantages, or both. As long as this firm organizes itself to take advantage of these resource and capability advantages in its new business, it should earn high profits in its new business, along with the profits it will still be earning in its original business.[14] This can be true for even relatively small firms, as described in the Strategy in the Emerging Enterprise feature.

Of course, over time this diversified firm is likely to develop new resources and capabilities through its operations in the new business. These new resources and capabilities enhance the entire set of skills that a firm might be able to bring to still another business. Using the profits it has obtained in its previous businesses, this

Strategy in the Emerging Enterprise

W. L. Gore & Associates is best known for manufacturing a water- and wind-proof but breathable fabric that is used to insulate winter coats, hiking boots, and a myriad of other outdoor apparel products. This fabric—known as Gore-Tex—has a brand name in its market niche every bit as strong as any of the brand names controlled by PepsiCo. or Procter & Gamble. The "Gore-Tex" label attached to any outdoor garment promises water-proof comfort in even the harshest conditions.

But W. L. Gore & Associates did not start out in the outdoor fabric business. Indeed, for the first 10 years of its existence, W. L. Gore sold insulation for wires and similar industrial products using a molecular technology originally developed by DuPont—a technology most of us know as Teflon. Only 10 years after its initial founding did the founder's son, Bob Gore, discover that it was possible to stretch the Teflon molecule to form a strong and porous material that is chemically inert, has a low friction coefficient, functions within a wide temperature range, does not age, and is extremely strong. This is the material called Gore-Tex.

Gore-Tex and Guitar Strings

By extending its basic technology, W. L. Gore and Associates has been able to diversify well beyond its original wire insulation business. With 2003 sales of $1.35 billion, the company currently has operations in medical products (including synthetic blood vessels and patches for soft tissue regeneration), electronics products (including wiring board materials and computer chip components), industrial products (including filter bags for environmental protection and sealants for chemical manufacturing), and fabrics (including Gore-Tex fabric, Wind-Stopper fabric, and CleanStream filters).

And Gore continues to discover new ways to exploit its competence in the Teflon molecule. In 1997, a team of Gore engineers developed a cable made out of the Teflon molecule for use to control puppets at Disney's theme parks. Unfortunately, these cables did not perform up to expectations and were not sold to Disney. However, some guitar players discovered these cables and began using them as strings for their guitars. They found out that these "Gore-Tex" strings sounded great and lasted five times as long as alternative guitar strings. So Gore entered yet another market—the $100 million fretted-stringed-instrument business—with its Elixir brand of guitar strings. Currently, W. L. Gore is the second-largest manufacturer in this market.

The flexibility of the Teflon molecule—and W. L. Gore's ability to explore and exploit that flexibility—has created a diversified company whose original objective was simply to sell insulation for wires.

Sources: www.gore.com; D. Sacks (2003). "The Gore-Tex of guitar strings." *Fast Times,* December, p. 46.

---

firm is likely to enter another new business. Again, choosing from among all the new businesses it could enter, it is likely to begin operations in a business where it can exploit its now-expanded resource and capability advantages to obtain a competitive advantage, and so forth.

After a firm has engaged in this diversification strategy several times, the resources and capabilities that enable it to operate successfully in several businesses are its core competencies. A firm develops these core competencies by transferring the technical and management knowledge, experience, and wisdom it developed in earlier businesses to its new businesses. A firm that has just begun this diversification process has implemented a dominant-business strategy. If all of a firm's businesses share the same core competencies, then that firm has implemented a strategy of related-constrained diversification. If different businesses exploit different sets of resources and capabilities, that firm has implemented a strategy of related-linked diversification. In any case, these core competencies enable firms to have lower costs or higher revenues as they include more businesses in their diversified portfolio, compared to firms without these competencies.

Of course, not all firms develop core competencies in this logical and rational manner. That is, sometimes a firm's core competencies are examples of the emergent strategies described in Chapter 1. Indeed, as described in Chapter 1, Johnson & Johnson is an example of a firm that has a core competence that emerged over time. However, no matter how a firm develops core competencies, to the extent that they enable a diversified firm to have lower costs or larger revenues in its business operations, these competencies can be thought of as sources of economies of scope.

Some diversified firms realize the value of these kinds of core competencies through shared activities. For example, as suggested earlier, 3M has a core competence in substrates, adhesives, and coatings. To exploit this, 3M has adopted a multitiered product innovation process. In addition to product innovations within each business unit separately, 3M also supports a corporate research and development lab that seeks to exploit and expand its core competence in substrates, adhesives, and coatings. Since the corporate R&D laboratory is shared by all of 3M's different businesses, it can be thought of as a shared activity.

However, other firms realize the value of their core competencies without shared activities. While Johnson & Johnson has a core competence in developing, acquiring, and marketing pharmaceutical and medical products, it does not realize this core competence through shared activities. Indeed, each of J&J's businesses is run very independently. For example, while one of its most successful products is Tylenol, the fact that the company that manufactures and distributes Tylenol—McNeil—is actually a division of Johnson & Johnson is not printed on any Tylenol packaging. If you did not know that Tylenol was a J&J product, you could not tell from the bottles of Tylenol you buy.

While J&J does not use shared activities to realize the value of its core competencies, it does engage in other activities to realize this value. For example, it is not uncommon for members of the senior management team of each of the businesses in J&J's portfolio to have obtained managerial experience in some other J&J business. That is, J&J identifies high-potential managers in one of its businesses and uses this knowledge by giving these managers additional responsibilities in another J&J business. This ability to leverage its management talent across multiple businesses is an example of a firm's core competence, although the realization of the value of that competence does not depend on the existence of a shared activity.

Sometimes, because a firm's core competence is not reflected in specific shared activities, it is easy to conclude that it is not exploiting any economies of scope in its diversification strategy. Diversified firms that are exploiting core competencies as an economy of scope, but are not doing so with any shared activities, are sometimes called **seemingly unrelated diversified firms**. They may appear to be unrelated diversified firms, but are, in fact, related diversified firms without any shared activities.

One example of a seemingly unrelated diversified firm is the British company Virgin Group. Operating in a wide variety of businesses—everything from record producing, music retailing, air and rail travel, soft drinks, spirits, mobile phones, cosmetics, retail bridal shops, financial services, and providing gas and electricity, to hot air ballooning—the Virgin Group is clearly diversified. There are also few, if any, shared activities in this firm. However, there are at least two core competencies that cut across all the business activities in the group—the brand name "Virgin" and the eccentric marketing and management approach of Virgin's founder, Richard Branson. Branson is the CEO who walked down a "catwalk" in a wedding gown to help publicize the opening of Virgin Brides—the Virgin Group's line of retail bridal shops. Branson is also the CEO who had all of Virgin Air's airplanes repainted with the British "Union Jack" and the slogan "Britain's Real Airline" when British Airways eliminated the British Flag from its airplanes. Whether or not these two core competencies create sufficient value to justify the Virgin Group's continued existence, and whether or not they will continue beyond Branson's affiliation with the group, are still open questions.

Limits of Core Competencies. Just as there are limits to the value of shared activities as sources of economies of scope, so there are limits to core competencies as sources of these economies. The first of these limitations stems from important organizational issues to be discussed in Chapter 8. The way that a diversified firm is organized can either facilitate the exploitation of core competencies or prevent this exploitation from occurring.

A second limitation of core competencies is a result of the intangible nature of these economies of scope. Whereas shared activities are reflected in tangible operations in a diversified firm, core competencies may be reflected only in shared knowledge, experience, and wisdom across businesses. The intangible character of these relationships is emphasized when they are described as a **dominant logic** in a firm, or a common way of thinking about strategy across different businesses.[15]

The intangibility of core competencies can lead diversified firms to make two kinds of errors in managing relatedness. First, intangible core competencies can be illusory inventions by creative managers who link even the most completely unrelated businesses and thereby justify their diversification strategy. A firm that manufactures airplanes and running shoes can rationalize this diversification by claiming to have a core competence in managing transportation businesses. A firm operating in the professional football business and the movie business can rationalize this diversification by claiming to have a core competence in managing entertainment businesses. Such **invented competencies** are not real sources of economies of scope.

Second, a diversified firm's businesses may be linked by a core competence, but this competence may affect these businesses' costs or revenues in a trivial way. Thus, for example, all of a firm's businesses may be affected by government actions, but the impact of these actions on costs and revenues in different businesses may be quite small. A firm may have a core competence in managing relationships with the government, but this core competence will not reduce costs or enhance revenues for these particular businesses very much. Also, each of a diversified firm's businesses may use some advertising. However, if advertising does not have a major impact on revenues for these businesses, core competencies in advertising are not likely to significantly reduce a firm's costs or increase its revenues. In this case, a core competence may be a source of economies of scope, but the value of those economies may be very small.

Diversification to Exploit Financial Economies of Scope

A second class of motivations for diversification shifts attention away from operational linkages among a firm's businesses and toward financial advantages associated with diversification. Three financial implications of diversification have been studied: diversification and capital allocation, diversification and risk reduction, and tax advantages of diversification.

Diversification and Capital Allocation. Capital can be allocated to businesses in one of two ways. First, businesses operating as independent entities can compete for capital in the external capital market. They do this by providing a sufficiently high return to induce investors to purchase shares of their equity, by having a sufficiently high cash flow to repay principal and interest on debt, and in other ways. Alternatively, a business can be part of a diversified firm. That diversified firm competes in the external capital market and allocates capital among its various businesses. In a sense, diversification creates an **internal capital market** in which businesses in a diversified firm compete for corporate capital.[16]

For an internal capital market to create value for a diversified firm, it must offer some efficiency advantages over an external capital market. It has been suggested that a potential efficiency gain from internal capital markets depends on the greater amount and quality of information that a diversified firm possesses about the businesses it owns, compared with the information that external suppliers of capital possess. Owning a business gives a diversified firm access to detailed and accurate information about the actual performance of the business, its true future prospects, and thus the actual amount and cost of the capital that should be allocated to it. External sources of capital, in contrast, have relatively limited access to information and thus have a limited ability to judge the actual performance and future prospects of a business.

Some have questioned whether a diversified firm, as a source of capital, actually has more and better information about a business it owns, compared to external sources of capital. After all, independent businesses seeking capital have a strong incentive to provide sufficient information to external suppliers of capital to obtain required funds. However, a firm that owns a business may have at least two informational advantages over external sources of capital.

First, although an independent business has an incentive to provide information to external sources of capital, it also has an incentive to downplay or even not report any negative information about its performance and prospects. Such negative information would raise an independent firm's cost of capital. External sources of capital have limited ability to force a business to reveal all information about its performance and prospects and thus may provide capital at a lower cost than they would if they had full information. Ownership gives a firm the right to compel more complete disclosure, although even here full disclosure is not guaranteed. With this more complete information, a diversified firm can allocate just the right amount of capital, at the appropriate cost, to each business.

Second, an independent business may have an incentive not to reveal all the positive information about its performance and prospects. In Chapter 3, the ability of a firm to earn economic profits was shown to depend on the imitability of a firm's resources and capabilities. An independent business that informs external sources of capital about all of its sources of competitive advantage is also informing its potential competitors about these sources of advantage. This information sharing increases the probability that these sources of advantage will be imitated. Because of the competitive implications of sharing this information, firms may choose not to share it, and external sources of capital may underestimate the true performance and prospects of a business.

A diversified firm, however, may gain access to this additional information about its businesses without revealing it to potential competitors. This information enables the diversified firm to make more informed decisions about how much capital to allocate to a business and about the cost of that capital, compared to the external capital market.[17]

Over time, there should be fewer errors in funding businesses through internal capital markets, compared to funding businesses through external capital markets. Fewer funding errors, over time, suggest a slight capital allocation advantage for a diversified firm, compared to an external capital market. This advantage should be reflected in somewhat higher rates of return on invested capital for the diversified firm, compared to the rates of return on invested capital for external sources of capital.

However, the businesses within a diversified firm do not always gain cost-of-capital advantages by being part of a diversified firm's portfolio. Several authors have argued that because a diversified firm has lower overall risk (see the following discussion), it will have a lower cost of capital, which it can pass along to the businesses within its portfolio. Although the lower risks associated with a diversified firm may lower the firm's cost of capital, the appropriate cost of capital to businesses within the firm depends on the performance and prospects of each of those businesses. The firm's advantages in evaluating its businesses' performances and prospects result in more appropriate capital allocation, not just in lower cost of capital for those businesses. Indeed, a business's cost of capital may be lower than what it could have obtained in the external capital market (because the firm is able to more fully evaluate the positive aspects of that business), or it may be higher than what it could have obtained in the external capital market (because the firm is able to more fully evaluate the negative aspects of that business).

Of course, if these businesses also have lower cost or higher revenue expectations because they are part of a diversified firm, then those cost/revenue advantages will be reflected in the appropriate cost of capital for these businesses. In this sense, any operational economies of scope for businesses in a diversified firm may be recognized by a diversified firm exploiting financial economies of scope.

Limits on Internal Capital Markets. Although internal capital allocation has several potential advantages for a diversified firm, several limits of this process also exist. First, the level and type of diversification that a firm pursues can affect the efficiency of this allocation process. A firm that implements a strategy of unrelated diversification, where managers have to evaluate the performance and prospects of numerous very different businesses, puts a greater strain on the capital allocation skills of its managers than does a firm that implements related diversification. Indeed, in the extreme, the capital allocation efficiency of a firm pursuing broad-based unrelated diversification will probably not be superior to the capital allocation efficiency of the external capital market.

Second, the increased efficiency of internal capital allocation depends on managers in a diversified firm having better information for capital allocation than the information available to external sources. However, this higher-quality information is not guaranteed. The incentives that can lead managers to exaggerate their performance and prospects to external capital sources can also lead to this behavior within a diversified firm. Indeed, several examples of business managers falsifying performance records to gain access to more internal capital have been reported.[18] Research suggests that capital allocation requests by managers are routinely discounted in diversified firms in order to correct for these managers' inflated estimates of the performance and prospects of their businesses.[19]

Finally, not only do business managers have an incentive to inflate the performance and prospects of their business in a diversified firm, but managers in charge of capital allocation in these firms may have an incentive to continue investing in a business despite its poor performance and prospects. The reputation and status of these managers often depend on the success of these business investments, because often they initially approved them. These managers often continue throwing good money at these businesses in hope that they will someday improve, thereby justifying their original decision. Organizational psychologists call this process **escalation of commitment** and have presented numerous examples of managers' becoming irrationally committed to a particular investment.[20]

Indeed, research on the value of internal capital markets in diversified firms suggests that, on average, the limitations of these markets often outweigh their advantages. For example, even controlling for firm size, excessive investment in poorly performing businesses in a diversified firm reduces the market value of the average diversified firm.[21] However, the fact that many firms do not gain the advantages associated with internal capital markets does not necessarily imply that no firms gain these advantages. If only a few firms are able to obtain the advantages of internal capital markets while successfully avoiding their limitations, this financial economy of scope may be a source of at least a temporary competitive advantage.

Diversification and Risk Reduction. Another possible financial economy of scope for a diversified firm has already been briefly mentioned—that is, the riskiness of the cash flows of diversified firms is lower than the riskiness of the cash flows of undiversified firms. Consider, for example, the riskiness of two businesses operating separately, compared to the risk of a diversified firm operating in those same two businesses simultaneously. If both these businesses are very risky on their own, and the cash flows from these businesses are not highly correlated over time, then combining these two businesses into a single firm will generate a lower level of overall risk for the diversified firm than for each of these businesses on their own.

This lower level of risk is due to the low correlation between the cash flows associated with these two businesses. If Business I is having a bad year, Business II might be having a good year, and a firm that operates in both of these businesses simultaneously can have moderate levels of performance. In another year, Business II might be off while Business I is having a good year. Again, the firm operating in both these businesses can have moderate levels of performance. Firms that diversify to reduce risk will have relatively stable returns over time, especially as they diversify into many different businesses with cash flows that are not highly correlated over time.

Tax Advantages of Diversification. Another financial economy of scope from diversification stems from possible tax advantages of this corporate strategy. These possible tax advantages reflect one or a combination of two effects. First, a diversified firm can use losses in some of its businesses to offset profits in others, thereby reducing its overall tax liability. Of course, substantial losses in some of its businesses may overwhelm profits in other businesses, forcing businesses that would have remained solvent if they were independent to cease operation. However, as long as business losses are not too large, a diversified firm's tax liability can be reduced. Empirical research suggests that diversified firms do, sometimes, offset profits in some businesses with losses in others, although the tax savings of these activities are usually small.[22]

Second, because diversification can reduce the riskiness of a firm's cash flows, it can also reduce the probability that a firm will declare bankruptcy. This can increase a firm's debt capacity. This effect on debt capacity is greatest when the cash flows of a diversified firm's businesses are perfectly and negatively correlated. However, even when these cash flows are perfectly and positively correlated, there can still be a (modest) increase in debt capacity.

Debt capacity is particularly important in tax environments where interest payments on debt are tax deductible. In this context, diversified firms can increase their leverage up to their debt capacity and reduce their tax liability accordingly. Of course, if interest payments are not tax deductible, or if the marginal corporate tax rate is relatively small, then the tax advantages of diversification can be quite small. Recent empirical work suggests that diversified firms do have greater debt capacity than undiversified firms. However, low marginal corporate tax rates, at least in the United States, make the accompanying tax savings on average relatively small.[23]

Diversification to Exploit Anticompetitive Economies of Scope
A third group of motivations for diversification is based on the relationship between diversification strategies and various anticompetitive activities by firms. Two specific examples of these activities are (1) multipoint competition to facilitate mutual forbearance and tacit collusion and (2) exploiting market power.

Multipoint Competition. Multipoint competition exists when two or more diversified firms simultaneously compete in multiple markets. For example, Hewlett-Packard and IBM compete in both the personal computer market and the market for computer printers. Michelin and Goodyear compete in both the U.S. automobile tire market and the European automobile tire market. Disney and AOL/Time Warner compete in both the movie production and book publishing businesses.

Multipoint competition can serve to facilitate a particular type of tacit collusion called **mutual forbearance**. Firms engage in **tacit collusion** when they cooperate to reduce rivalry below the level expected under perfect competition. Consider the situation facing two diversified firms, A and B. These two firms operate in the same businesses, I, II, III, and IV (see Figure 7.3). In this context, any decisions that Firm A might make to compete aggressively in Businesses I and III must take into account the possibility that Firm B will respond by com-

Figure 7.3 Multipoint Competition Between Hypothetical Firms A and B

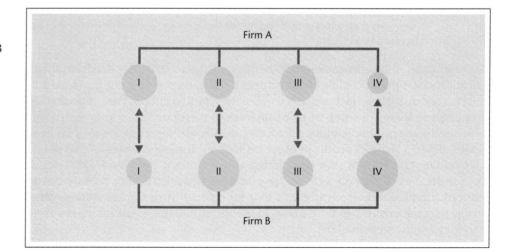

peting aggressively in Businesses II and IV and vice versa. The potential loss that each of these firms may experience in some of its businesses must be compared to the potential gain that each might obtain if it exploits competitive advantages in other of its businesses. If the present value of gains does not outweigh the present value of losses from retaliation, then both firms will avoid competitive activity. Refraining from competition is mutual forbearance.[24]

Mutual forbearance as a result of multipoint competition has occurred in several industries. For example, this form of tacit collusion has been described as existing between Michelin and Goodyear, Maxwell House and Folger's, Caterpillar and John Deere, and BIC and Gillette.[25] Another clear example of such cooperation can be found in the airline industry. For example, America West began service into the Houston Intercontinental Airport with very low introductory fares. Continental Airlines, the dominant firm at Houston Intercontinental, rapidly responded to America West's low Houston fares by reducing the price of its flights from Phoenix, Arizona, to several cities in the United States. Phoenix is the home airport of America West. Within just a few weeks, America West withdrew its low introductory fares in the Houston market, and Continental withdrew its reduced prices in the Phoenix market. The threat of retaliation across markets apparently led America West and Continental to tacitly collude on prices.[26]

However, sometimes multipoint competition does not lead to mutual forbearance. Consider, for example, the conflict between The Walt Disney Company and Time Warner in the early 1990s. As mentioned earlier, Disney operates in the theme park, movie and television production, and television broadcasting industries. Time Warner operates in the theme park and movie and television production industries and also operates a very large magazine business (*Time*, *People*, *Sports Illustrated*, and so forth). From 1988 through 1993, Disney spent over $40 million in advertising its theme parks in Time Warner magazines. Despite this substantial revenue, Time Warner began an aggressive advertising campaign aimed at wooing customers away from Disney theme parks to its own. Disney retaliated by canceling all of its advertising in Time Warner magazines. Time Warner responded to Disney's actions by canceling a corporate meeting to be held in Florida at Disney World. Disney responded to Time Warner's meeting cancellation by refusing to broadcast Time Warner theme park advertisements on its Los Angeles television station.[27]

Some recent research investigates the conditions under which mutual forbearance strategies are pursued, as well as conditions under which multipoint competition does not lead to mutual forbearance.[28] In general, the value of the threat of retaliation must be substantial for multipoint competition to lead to mutual forbearance. However, not only must the payoffs to mutual forbearance be substantial, but the firms pursuing this strategy must have strong strategic linkages among their diversified businesses. This suggests that firms pursuing mutual forbearance strategies based on multipoint competition are usually pursuing a form of related diversification.

Diversification and Market Power. Internal allocations of capital among a diversified firm's businesses may enable it to exploit in some of its businesses the market power advantages it enjoys in other of its businesses. For example, suppose that a firm is earning monopoly profits in a particular business. This firm can use some of these monopoly profits to subsidize the operations of another of its businesses. This cross-subsidization can take several forms, including **predatory pricing**— that is, setting prices so that they are less than the subsidized business's costs. The effect of this cross-subsidy may be to drive competitors out of the subsidized business and then to obtain monopoly profits in that subsidized business. In a sense, diversification enables a firm to apply its monopoly power in several different businesses. Economists call this a **deep pockets model** of diversification.[29]

Diversified firms with operations in regulated monopolies have been criticized for this kind of cross-subsidization. For example, most of the regional telephone companies in the United States are engaging in diversification strategies. The consent decree that forced the breakup of AT&T expressly forbade cross-subsidies between these regional companies' telephone monopolies and other business activities, under the assumption that such subsidies would give these firms an unfair competitive advantage in their diversified business activities.[30]

Although these market power economies of scope, in principle, may exist, relatively little empirical work documents their existence. Indeed, research on regulated utilities diversifying into nonregulated businesses in the 1980s suggests not that these firms use monopoly profits in their regulated businesses to unfairly subsidize nonregulated businesses, but that the poor management skills developed in the regulated businesses tend to make diversification less profitable rather than more profitable.[31] Nevertheless, the potential that large diversified large firms have to exercise market power and to behave in socially irresponsible ways has led some observers to call for actions to curtail both the economic and political power of these firms. These issues are discussed in the Ethics and Strategy feature.

Firm Size and Employee Incentives to Diversify

Employees may have incentives to diversify that are independent of any benefits from other sources of economies of scope. This is especially the case for employees in senior management positions and employees with long tenure in a particular firm. These employee incentives reflect the interest of employees to diversify because of the relationship between firm size and management compensation.

Research over the years demonstrates conclusively that the primary determinant of the compensation of top managers in a firm is not the economic performance of the firm but the size of the firm, usually measured in sales.[32] Thus, managers seeking to maximize their income should attempt to grow their firm. One of the easiest ways to grow a firm is through diversification, especially unrelated diversification through mergers and acquisitions. By making large acquisitions, a diversified firm can grow substantially in a short period of time, leading senior managers to earn higher incomes. All of this is independent of any economic profit that diversification may or may not generate. Senior managers need only worry about economic profit if the level of that profit is so low that unfriendly takeovers are a threat or so low that the board of directors may be forced to replace management.

Recently, the traditional relationship between firm size and management compensation has begun to break down. More and more, the compensation of senior managers is being tied to economic performance of firms. In particular, the use of stock and other forms of deferred compensation makes it in management's best interest to be concerned with a firm's economic performance. These changes in compensation do not necessarily imply that firms will abandon all forms of diversification. They do suggest that firms will abandon those forms of diversification that do not generate real economies of scope.

Can Equity Holders Realize These Economies of Scope on Their Own?

Earlier in this chapter, it was suggested that for a firm's diversification strategies to create value, two conditions must hold. First, these strategies must exploit valuable

Ethics and Strategy

*I*n 1999, a loose coalition of union members, environmentalists, youth, indigenous peoples, human rights activists, and small farmers took to the streets of Seattle, Washington, to protest a meeting of the World Trade Organization (WTO) and to fight against the growing global power of corporations. Government officials and corporate officers alike were confused by these protests. After all, hadn't world trade increased 11.5 times from 1950 to 1995 ($0.4 trillion to $5 trillion in constant 1997 dollars), and hadn't the total economic output of the entire world gone from $6.4 trillion in 1950 to $35.5 trillion in 1995 (again, in constant 1997 dollars)? Why protest a global economic system—a system that was enhancing the level of free trade and facilitating global economic efficiency—that was so clearly improving the economic well-being of the world's population?

The protestors' message to government and big business was that these aggregate growth numbers masked more truth than they told. Yes, there has been economic growth. But that growth has benefited only a small percentage of the world's population. Most of the population still struggles to survive. The combined net worth of 358 U.S. billionaires in the early 1990s ($760 billion) was equal to the combined net worth of the 2.5 billion poorest people on the earth! Eighty-three percent of the world's total income goes to the richest fifth of the population while the poorest fifth of the world's population receives only 1.4 percent of the world's total income. Currently, 45 to 70 million people worldwide have

Globalization and the Threat of the Multinational Firm

had to leave their home countries to find work in foreign lands and approximately 1.2 billion people around the world live on less than $1 a day. Even in relatively affluent societies like the United States, people are finding it increasingly difficult to meet their financial obligations. Falling real wages, economic insecurity, and corporate downsizing have led many people to work longer hours or hold two or three jobs. While the number of billionaires in the world continues to grow, the number of people facing mind-numbing and strength-robbing poverty grows even faster.

The causes of this apparent contradiction—global economic growth linked with growing global economic decay—are numerous and complex. However, one explanation focuses on the growing economic power of the diversified multi-national corporation. The size of these institutions can be immense—many international

diversified firms are larger than the entire economies of many nations. And these huge institutions, with a single-minded focus on maximizing their performance, can make profit-making decisions that adversely affect their suppliers, their customers, their employees, and the environment, all with relative impunity. Armed with the unspoken mantra that "Greed is Good," these corporations can justify almost any action, as long as it increases the wealth of its shareholders.

Of course, even if one accepts this hypothesis—and it is far from being universally accepted—solutions to the growing power of internationally diversified firms are not obvious. The problem is that one way that firms become large and powerful is by being able to meet customer demands effectively. Thus, firm size, per se, is not necessarily an indication that a firm is behaving in ways inconsistent with the public good. Government efforts to restrict the size of firms simply because they are large could easily have the effect of making citizens worse off. On the other hand, once firms are large and powerful, they may very well be tempted to exercise that power in ways that benefit themselves at great cost to society.

Whatever the causes and solutions to these problems, the protests in Seattle in 1999 have at least one clear message—global growth for growth's sake is no longer universally accepted as the correct objective of international economic policy.

Sources: D. C. Korten (2001). *When corporations rule the world*, 2nd ed. Bloomfield, CT: Kumarian Press; H. Demsetz (1973). "Industry structure, market rivalry, and public policy." *Journal of Law and Economics*, 16, pp. 1–9.

Table 7.3   **The Competitive Implications of Different Economies of Scope**

Type of Economy of Scope	Are They Valuable?	Can They be Realized by Equity Holders on Their Own?	Positive Returns to Equity Holders?
1. *Operational economies of scope*			
Shared activities	Possible	No	Possible
Core competencies	Possible	No	Possible
2. *Financial economies of scope*			
Internal capital allocation	Possible	No	Possible
Risk reduction	Possible	Yes	No
Tax advantages	Possible—small	No	Possible—small
3. *Anticompetitive economies of scope*			
Multipoint competition	Possible	No	Possible
Exploiting market power	Possible	No	Possible
4. *Employee incentives for diversification*			
Maximizing management compensation	No	No	No

economies of scope. Potentially valuable economies of scope were presented in Table 7.1 and discussed in the previous section. Second, it must be less costly for managers in a firm to realize these economies of scope than for outside equity holders on their own. If outside equity holders could realize a particular economy of scope on their own, without a firm's managers, at low cost, why would they want to hire managers to do this for them by investing in a firm and providing capital to managers to exploit an economy of scope?

Table 7.3 summarizes the discussion on the potential value of the different economies of scope listed in Table 7.1. It also suggests which of these economies of scope will be difficult for outside equity investors to exploit on their own and thus which bases of diversification are most likely to create positive returns for a firm's equity holders.

Most of the economies of scope listed in Table 7.3 cannot be realized by equity holders on their own. This is because most of them require activities that equity holders cannot engage in or information that equity holders do not possess. For example, shared activities, core competencies, multipoint competition, and exploiting market power all require the detailed coordination of business activities across multiple businesses in a firm. While equity holders may own a portfolio of equities, they are not in a position to coordinate business activities across this portfolio. In a similar way, internal capital allocation requires information about a business's prospects that is simply not available to a firm's outside equity holders.

Indeed, the only two economies of scope listed in Table 7.3 that do not have the potential for generating positive returns for a firm's equity holders are diversification in order to maximize the size of a firm—since firm size, per se, is not valuable—and diversification to reduce risk—since equity holders can do this on their own at very low cost by simply investing in a diversified portfolio of stocks. Indeed, while risk reduction is often a published rationale for many diversification moves, this rationale, by itself, is not directly consistent with the interests of a firm's equity holders. However, some scholars have suggested that this strategy may directly benefit other of a firm's stakeholders and thus indirectly benefit its equity holders. This possibility is discussed in detail in the Strategy in Depth feature.

Overall, this analysis of possible bases of diversification suggests that related diversification is more likely to be consistent with the interests of a firm's equity holders than unrelated diversification. This is because the one economy of scope listed in Table 7.3 that is the easiest for outside equity holders to duplicate—risk reduction—is the only economy of scope that an unrelated diversified firm can try to realize. All the other economies of scope listed in Table 7.3 require coordination and information sharing across businesses in a diversified firm that are very difficult to realize in unrelated diversified firms. Indeed, the preponderance of empirical research suggests that related diversified firms outperform unrelated diversified firms.[33]

Corporate Diversification and Sustained Competitive Advantage

VRIO

Table 7.3 describes those economies of scope that are likely to create real economic value for diversifying firms. It also suggests that related diversification can be valuable while unrelated diversification is usually not valuable. However, as we have seen with all the other strategies discussed in this book, the fact that a strategy is valuable does not necessarily imply that it will be a source of sustained competitive advantage. In order for diversification to be a source of sustained competitive advantage, it must be not only valuable but also rare and costly to imitate, and a firm must be organized to implement this strategy. The rarity and imitability of diversification are discussed in this section; organizational questions are deferred until the next.

The Rarity of Diversification

At first glance, it seems clear that diversification per se is usually not a rare firm strategy. Most large firms have adopted some form of diversification, if only the limited diversification of a dominant-business firm. Even many small and medium-sized firms have adopted different levels of diversification strategy.

However, the rarity of diversification depends not on diversification per se but on how rare the particular economies of scope associated with that diversification are. If only a few competing firms have exploited a particular economy of scope, that economy of scope can be rare. If numerous firms have done so, it will be common and not a source of competitive advantage.

The Imitability of Diversification

Both forms of imitation—direct duplication and substitution—are relevant in evaluating the ability of diversification strategies to generate sustained competitive advantages even if the economies of scope that they create are rare.

Direct Duplication of Diversification

The extent to which a valuable and rare corporate diversification strategy is immune from direct duplication depends on how costly it is for competing firms to realize this same economy of scope. As suggested in Table 7.4, some economies of scope are, in general, more costly to duplicate than others.

Strategy in Depth

Risk-Reducing Diversification and a Firm's Other Stakeholders

Although diversifying in order to reduce risk generally does not directly benefit outside equity investors in a firm, it can *indirectly* benefit outside equity investors through its impact on the willingness of other stakeholders in a firm to make firm-specific investments. A firm's **stakeholders** include all those groups and individuals who have an interest in how a firm performs. In this sense, a firm's equity investors are one of a firm's stakeholders. Other firm stakeholders include employees, suppliers, and customers.

Firm stakeholders make **firm-specific investments** when the value of the investments they make in a particular firm is much greater than the value of those same investments would be in other firms. Consider, for example, a firm's employees. An employee with a long tenure in a particular firm has generally made substantial **firm-specific human capital investments**. These investments include understanding a particular firm's culture, policies, and procedures; knowing the "right" people to contact to complete a task; and so forth. Such investments have significant value in the firm where they are made. Indeed, such firm-specific knowledge is generally necessary if an employee is to be able to help a firm conceive and implement valuable strategies.

However, the specific investments that an employee makes in a particular firm have almost no value in other firms. If a firm were to cease operations, employees would instantly lose almost all the value of any of the firm-specific investments they had made in that firm.

Suppliers and customers can also make these firm-specific investments. Suppliers make these investments when they customize their products or services to the specific requirements of a particular customer. They also make firm-specific investments when they forgo opportunities to sell to other firms in order to sell to a particular firm. Customers make firm-specific investments when they customize their operations to fully utilize the products or services of a particular firm. Also, by developing close relationships with a particular firm, customers may forgo the opportunity to develop relationships with other firms. These too are firm-specific investments made by customers. If a firm were to cease operations, suppliers and customers would instantly lose almost the entire value of the specific investments they have made in this firm.

Although the firm-specific investments made by employees, suppliers, and customers are risky—in the sense that almost their entire value is lost if the firm in which they are made ceases operations—they are extremely important if a firm is going to be able to generate economic profits. As was suggested in Chapter 3, valuable, rare, and costly-to-imitate resources and capabilities are more likely to be a source of sustained competitive advantage than resources and capabilities without these attributes. Firm-specific investments are more likely to have these attributes than non-firm-specific investments. Non-firm-specific investments are investments that can generate value in numerous different firms.

Thus, valuable, rare, and costly-to-imitate firm-specific investments

Table 7.4 **Costly Duplication of Economies of Scope**

Less costly-to-duplicate economies of scope	Costly-to-duplicate economies of scope
Shared activities	Core competencies
Risk reduction	Internal capital allocation
Tax advantages	Multipoint competition
Employee compensation	Exploiting market power

made by a firm's employees, suppliers, and customers can be the source of economic profits. And because a firm's outside equity holders are residual claimants on the cash flows generated by a firm, these economic profits benefit equity holders. Thus, a firm's outside equity holders generally will want a firm's employees, suppliers, and customers to make specific investments in a firm because those investments are likely to be sources of economic wealth for outside equity holders.

However, given the riskiness of firm-specific investments, employees, suppliers, and customers will generally only be willing to make these investments if some of the riskiness associated with making them can be reduced. Outside equity holders have little difficulty managing the risks associated with investing in a particular firm, because they can always create a portfolio of stocks that fully diversifies this risk at very low cost. This is why diversification that reduces the riskiness of a firm's cash flows does not generally directly benefit a firm's outside equity holders. However, a firm's employees, suppliers, and customers usually do not have these low-cost diversification opportunities. Employees, for example, are rarely able to make firm-specific human capital investments in a large enough number of different firms to

fully diversify the risks associated with making them. And although suppliers and customers can diversify their firm-specific investments to a greater degree than employees—through selling to multiple customers and through buying from multiple suppliers—the cost of this diversification for suppliers and customers is usually greater than the costs that are born by outside equity holders in diversifying their risk.

Because it is often very costly for a firm's employees, suppliers, and customers to diversify the risks associated with making firm-specific investments on their own, these stakeholders will often prefer that a firm's managers help manage this risk for them. Managers in a firm can do this by diversifying the portfolio of businesses in which a firm operates. If a firm is unwilling to diversify its portfolio of businesses, then that firm's employees, suppliers, and customers will generally be unwilling to make specific investments in that firm. Moreover, because these firm-specific investments can generate economic profits, and because economic profits can directly benefit a firm's outside equity holders, equity holders have an indirect incentive to encourage a firm to pursue a diversification strategy, even though that strategy does not directly benefit them.

Put differently, a firm's diversification strategy can be thought of as compensation for the firm-specific investments that a firm's employees, suppliers, and customers make in a firm. Outside equity holders have an incentive to encourage this compensation in return for access to some of the economic profits that these firm-specific investments can generate. In general, the greater the impact of the firm-specific investment made by a firm's employees, suppliers, and customers on the ability of a firm to generate economic profits, the more likely that pursuing a corporate diversification strategy is indirectly consistent with the interests of a firm's outside equity holders. In addition, the more limited the ability of a firm's employees, suppliers, and customers to diversify the risks associated with making firm-specific investments at low cost, the more that corporate diversification is consistent with the interests of outside equity investors.

Sources: J. B. Barney (1991). "Firm resources and sustained competitive advantage." *Journal of Management*, 17, pp. 99–120; R. M. Stulz (1996). "Rethinking risk management." *Journal of Applied Corporate Finance*, Fall, pp. 8–24; K. Miller (1998). "Economic exposure and integrated risk management." *Strategic Management Journal*, 33, pp. 756–779; R. Amit and B. Wernerfelt (1990). "Why do firms reduce business risk?" *Academy of Management Journal*, 33. pp. 520–533.

Shared activities, risk reduction, tax advantages, and employee compensation as bases for corporate diversification are usually relatively easy to duplicate. Because shared activities are based on tangible assets that a firm exploits across multiple businesses, such as common R&D labs, common sales forces, and common manufacturing, they are usually relatively easy to duplicate. The only duplication issues for shared activities concern developing the cooperative cross-business relationships that often facilitate the use of shared activities—issues discussed in the next chapter. Moreover, because risk reduction, tax advantages, and employee compensation motives for diversifying can be accomplished through both related and unrelated diversification, these motives for diversifying tend to be relatively easy to duplicate.

On the other hand, other economies of scope are much more difficult to duplicate. These difficult-to-duplicate economies of scope include core competencies, internal capital allocation efficiencies, multipoint competition, and exploitation of market power. Because core competencies are more intangible, their direct duplication is often challenging. The realization of capital allocation economies of scope requires very substantial information-processing capabilities. These capabilities are often very difficult to develop. Multipoint competition requires very close coordination between the different businesses in which a firm operates. This kind of coordination is socially complex and thus may often be immune from direct duplication. Finally, exploitation of market power may be costly to duplicate because it requires that a firm must possess significant market power in one of its lines of business. A firm that does not have this market power advantage would have to obtain it. The cost of doing so, in most situations, would be prohibitive.

Substitutes for Diversification

Two obvious substitutes for diversification exist. First, instead of obtaining cost or revenue advantages from exploiting economies of scope *across* businesses in a diversified firm, a firm may decide to simply grow and develop each of its businesses separately. In this sense, a firm that successfully implements a cost leadership strategy or a product differentiation strategy in a single business can obtain the same cost or revenue advantages it could have obtained by exploiting economies of scope, but without having to develop cross-business relations. Growing independent businesses within a diversified firm can be a substitute for exploiting economies of scope in a diversification strategy.

One firm that has chosen this strategy is Nestlé. Nestlé exploits few, if any, economies of scope among its different businesses. Rather, it has focused its efforts on growing each of its international operations to the point that they obtain cost or revenue advantages that could have otherwise been obtained in some form of related diversification. Thus, for example, Nestlé's operation in the United States is sufficiently large to exploit economies of scale in production, sales, and marketing, without reliance on economies of scope between U.S. operations and operations in other countries.[34]

A second substitute for exploiting economies of scope in diversification can be found in strategic alliances. By using a strategic alliance, firms may be able to gain the economies of scope they could have obtained if they had carefully exploited economies of scope across businesses they own. Thus, for example, instead of a firm exploiting research and development economies of scope between two businesses it owns, it could form a strategic alliance with a different firm and form a joint research and development lab. Instead of a firm exploiting sales economies of scope by linking its businesses through a common sales force, it might develop a sales agreement with another firm and obtain cost or revenue advantages in this way.

Corporate Diversification in an International Context

Each of the ways that a strategy of corporate diversification can add value, as summarized in Table 7.1, can also be an explanation of why firms pursuing an international strategy can also create value. This is because a firm pursuing an international strategy is pursuing, at least, a strategy of geographic diversification and perhaps a strategy of product-market diversification. In this sense, an international strategy can be thought of as a special case of a corporate diversification strategy. Indeed, some of the economies of scope listed in Table 7.1 are likely to be more valuable in an international context than in a domestic-only context. One of these economies of scope is described in the Global Perspectives feature.

However, pursuing international diversification opportunities can create unique challenges for a firm. Two of these challenges have to do with unique financial risks and the political risks associated with pursuing an international diversification strategy.

Financial Risks and International Diversification

As firms begin to pursue international strategies, they may expose themselves to financial risks that are less obvious within a single domestic market. In particular, currency fluctuations can significantly affect the value of a firm's international investments. Such fluctuations can turn what had been a losing investment into a profitable investment (this is the good news). They can also turn what had been a profitable investment into a losing investment (this is the bad news). In addition to currency fluctuations, different rates of inflation across countries can require very different managerial approaches, business strategies, and accounting practices. Certainly, when a firm first begins international operations, these financial risks can seem daunting.

Fortunately, it is now possible for firms to hedge many of these risks, through the use of a variety of financial instruments and strategies. The development of money markets, together with growing experience in operating in high-inflation economies, has substantially reduced the threat of these financial risks for firms pursuing international strategies. Of course, the benefits of these financial tools and experience in high-inflation environments do not accrue to firms automatically. Firms seeking to implement international strategies must develop the resources and capabilities they will need to manage these financial risks. Moreover, these hedging strategies can do nothing to reduce the business risks that firms assume when they enter into nondomestic markets. For example, it may be that consumers in a nondomestic market simply do not want to purchase a firm's products or services, in which case this economy of scope cannot be realized. Moreover, these financial strategies cannot manage political risks that can exist for firms pursuing an international strategy.

Political Risks and International Diversification

The political environment is an important consideration in all strategic decisions. Changes in the political rules of the game can have the effect of increasing some environmental threats, reducing others, and thereby changing the value of a firm's resources and capabilities. However, the political environment can be even more problematic as firms pursue international strategies.

Types of Political Risks

Politics can affect the value of a firm's international strategies at the macro and micro levels. At the macro level, broad changes in the political situation in a country can change the value of an investment. For example, after the Second World War, nationalist governments came to power in many countries in the Middle East. These governments expropriated, for little or no compensation, many of the

Global Perspectives

**Using International Strategies
to Avoid Taxes**

For firms not pursuing an international strategy, diversification can help reduce taxes because of its impact on a firm's debt capacity. The logic that links diversification, debt capacity, and taxes has already been discussed in this chapter: Because diversified firms generally have a low probability of bankruptcy, banks and other sources of debt are more willing to lend to these firms than they would otherwise; since interest payments on debt are tax deductible, a more highly leveraged firm, other factors being equal, will have lower taxes than a less leveraged firm. Thus, corporate diversification can affect a firm's tax liability. However, empirical work on the effect of diversification on tax liability suggests that, on average, this effect is not very large.

However, tax savings can be much more important for firms operating in an international context. Such firms can reduce their tax liability by using internal transfer prices to shift firm profits from high-tax locations to low-tax locations and can locate their operations in what are known as "tax havens."

As will be described in Chapter 8 in detail, a **transfer price** is the price that one part of a diversified firm charges another part of the firm for products or services. These transfer prices can have a substantial impact on the reported profits of a particular unit within a diversified firm. This impact of transfer pricing on a unit's reported profits is what creates the tax-reduction

opportunity in an international setting. Suppose one of these units (for example, the unit selling a product or service) is in a high-tax country, while the second unit (for example, the unit buying a product or service) is in a low-tax country. By setting the transfer price in this example very high, the corporation is essentially transferring profits that would otherwise be attributed to the first unit to the second unit. It is also shifting those profits from a high-tax country to a low-tax country, thereby reducing its tax liability.

Of course, national tax authorities (like the IRS) do not approve of such actions and try to prevent firms from using internal transfer prices to avoid paying taxes. They do this by making sure that a firm's internal

transfer prices are reasonable and justifiable. However, as we will see in Chapter 8, it is very difficult to calculate the "optimal transfer price" in most settings. Only when it is apparent that the sole purpose of setting a transfer price was to avoid taxes can firms be prevented from engaging in this strategy.

A second way that firms can use their international operations to avoid taxes is by establishing operations in what is known as a **tax haven**. A tax haven is a country that charges little or no corporate tax. In this tax avoidance strategy, a firm uses transfer prices, licensing fees, dividends, and other activities to book revenues and profits generated in high-tax countries to the operations in the tax haven. Countries that have emerged as tax havens over the last decade or so include Bermuda, the Cayman Islands, Granada, the Netherland Antilles, Liechtenstein, and Luxembourg. Currently, there are more foreign-owned firms registered in the Cayman Islands than there are people who live in the Cayman Islands. Banks on the Caymans have attracted over $300 billion in deposits from foreign investors, or roughly $9.4 million for each person who lives on the Caymans. Obviously, these tax havens are attracting a large number of firms and private investors.

Sources: "Cleaning up by cleaning up."
Euromoney, April, pp. 73–77; H. French (1991). "Offshore banking gets new scrutiny with BCCI scandal." *New York Times,* September 29, p. 7.

assets of oil and gas companies located in their countries. Expropriation of foreign company assets also occurred when the Shah of Iran was overthrown, when a communist government was elected in Chile, and when new governments came to power in Angola, Ethiopia, Peru, and Zambia.[35]

Government upheaval and the attendant risks to international firms are facts of life in some countries. Consider, for example, oil-rich Nigeria. Since its independence in 1960, Nigeria has experienced several successful coups d'état, one civil war, two civil governments, and six military regimes.[36] The prudent course of action for firms engaging in business activities in Nigeria is to expect the current government to change and to plan accordingly.

Of course, government changes are not always bad for international firms. The fall of the Soviet Union and the introduction of capitalism into eastern Europe have created enormous opportunities for firms pursuing international strategies. For example, Volkswagen has invested $6 billion in a Czech automobile firm; Opel (General Motors' European division) has invested $680 million in a car-manufacturing facility in the former East Germany; and General Electric has invested $150 million in a light-bulb manufacturing operation in Hungary since the fall of the Soviet Union.[37]

At the micro level, politics in a country can affect the fortunes of particular firms in particular industries. For example, the success of Japanese automobile companies in the U.S. market has subjected these firms to a variety of political challenges, including local-content legislation and voluntary import quotas. These political risks exist even though there have been no major macro changes in the political system in the United States.[38]

Quantifying Political Risks

Political scientists have attempted to quantify the political risk that firms seeking to implement international strategies are likely to face in different countries. Although different studies vary in detail, the country attributes listed in Table 7.5 summarize most of the important determinants of political risk for firms pursuing international strategies.[39] Firms can apply the criteria listed in the table by evaluating the political and economic conditions in a country and by adding up the scores associated with these conditions. The most recent rankings of the political risks associated with conducting business in different countries are interesting. Not surprisingly, countries in western Europe and North America are the least risky. The least risky country within which to do business in the entire world is Luxembourg, followed by Switzerland, Norway, Denmark, the United States, and Sweden. On the other hand, countries currently experiencing civil unrest and revolution are among the most risky. The most risky country in the world, overall, is North Korea. Other very risky countries include Afghanistan, Iraq, Cuba, the Marshall Islands, and Zaire. Countries in Asia range from very low risk (Singapore and Japan, numbers 17 and 18 overall) to very high risk (North Korea). Countries in Africa and South America, on the other hand, tend to be relatively risky.

Managing Political Risk

Unlike financial risks, there are relatively few tools for managing the political risks associated with pursuing an international strategy. Obviously, one option would be to pursue international opportunities only in countries where political risk is very small. However, it is often the case that significant business opportunities exist in politically risky countries precisely because they are politically risky. Alternatively, firms can limit their investment in politically risky environments. However, these limited investments may not enable a firm to take full advantage of whatever economies of scope might exist by engaging in business in that country.

One approach to managing political risk is to see each of the determinants of political risk as negotiation points as a firm enters into a new country market. In many circumstances, those in a nondomestic market have just as much interest in a firm doing business in a new market as does the firm contemplating entry. International firms can sometimes use this bargaining power to negotiate

Table 7.5   **Quantifying Political Risks from International Operations**

	Low	High
The political economic environment		
1. Stability of the political system	3	14
2. Imminent internal conflicts	0	14
3. External threats to stability	0	12
4. Degree of control of the economic system	5	9
5. Reliability of country as a trade partner	4	12
6. Constitutional guarantees	2	12
7. Effectiveness of public administration	3	12
8. Labor relations and social peace	3	15
Domestic economic conditions		
1. Size of the population	4	8
2. Per capita income	2	10
3. Economic growth over the last 5 years	2	7
4. Potential growth over the next 3 years	3	10
5. Inflation over the last 2 years	2	10
6. Availability of domestic capital markets to outsiders	3	7
7. Availability of high-quality local labor force	2	8
8. Possibility of employing foreign nationals	2	8
9. Availability of energy resources	2	14
10. Environmental pollution legal requirements	4	8
11. Transportation and communication infrastructure	2	14
External economic relations		
1. Import restrictions	2	10
2. Export restrictions	2	10
3. Restrictions on foreign investments	3	9
4. Freedom to set up or engage in partnerships	3	9
5. Legal protection for brands and products	3	9
6. Restrictions on monetary transfers	2	8
7. Revaluation of currency in the last 5 years	2	7
8. Balance-of-payments situation	2	9
9. Drain on hard currency through energy imports	3	14
10. Financial standing	3	8
11. Restrictions of the exchange of local and foreign currencies	2	8

Source: Adapted from E. Dichtl and H. G Koeglmayr (1986). "Country Risk Ratings." *Management Review*, 26(4), pp. 2–10. Reprinted with permission.

entry conditions that reduce, or even neutralize, some of the sources of political risk in a country. Of course, no matter how skilled a firm is in negotiating these entry conditions, a change of government or changes in laws can quickly nullify any agreements.

A final approach to managing political risk is to turn the threat into an opportunity. One firm that has been successful in this way is Schlumberger, an international oil services company. Schlumberger has headquarters in New

York, Paris, and the Caribbean; it is a truly international company. Schlumberger management has adopted a policy of strict neutrality in interactions with governments in the developing world. Because of this policy, the company has been able to avoid political entanglements and continues to do business where many firms find the political risks too great. Put differently, Schlumberger has developed valuable, rare, and costly-to-imitate resources and capabilities in managing political risks and is using these resources to generate high levels of economic performance.[40]

SUMMARY

Firms implement corporate diversification strategies that range from limited diversification (single-business, dominant-business) to related diversification (related-constrained, related-linked) to unrelated diversification. In order to be valuable, corporate diversification strategies must reduce costs or increase revenues by exploiting economies of scope that outside equity holders cannot realize on their own at low cost.

Several motivations for implementing diversification strategies exist, including exploiting operational economies of scope (shared activities, core competencies), exploiting financial economies of scope (internal capital allocation, risk reduction, obtaining tax advantages), exploiting anticompetitive economies of scope (multipoint competition, market power advantages), and employee incentives to diversify (maximizing management compensation). All of these reasons for diversifying, except diversifying to maximize management compensation, have the potential for creating economic value for a firm. Moreover, a firm's outside equity holders will find it costly to realize all of these bases for diversification, except risk reduction. Thus, neither diversifying to maximize management compensation nor diversifying to reduce risk is directly consistent with the wealth maximizing interests of a firm's equity holders. This analysis also suggests that, on average, related diversified firms will outperform unrelated diversified firms.

The ability of a diversification strategy to create sustained competitive advantages depends not only on the value of that strategy but also on its rarity and imitability. The rarity of a diversification strategy depends on the number of competing firms that are exploiting the same economies of scope through diversification. Imitation can occur either through direct duplication or through substitutes. Costly-to-duplicate economies of scope include core competencies, internal capital allocation, multipoint competition, and exploitation of market power. Other economies of scope are usually less costly to duplicate. Important substitutes for diversification are when relevant economies are obtained through the independent actions of businesses within a firm and when relevant economies are obtained through strategic alliances.

Firms that pursue international business opportunities are implementing a geographic diversification strategy and may be implementing a product-market diversification strategy. All the economies of scope that can exist for firms pursuing a diversification strategy within a country can also exist for firms pursuing a diversification strategy internationally. However, two unique challenges are associated with international diversification: financial risks and political risks.

This discussion set aside important organizational issues in implementing diversification strategies. These issues are examined in detail in the next chapter.

CHALLENGE QUESTIONS

1. One simple way to think about relatedness is to look at the products or services a firm manufactures. The more similar these products or services are, the more related is the firm's diversification strategy. However, will firms that exploit core competencies in their diversification strategies always produce products or services that are similar to each other? Why or why not?

2. A firm implementing a diversification strategy has just acquired what it claims is a strategically related target firm but announces that it is not going to change this recently acquired firm in any way. Will this type of diversifying acquisition enable the firm to realize any valuable economies of scope that could not be duplicated by outside investors on their own? Why or why not?

3. One of the reasons why internal capital markets may be more efficient than external capital markets is that firms may not want to reveal full information about their sources of competitive advantage to external capital markets, in order to reduce the threat of competitive imitation. This suggests that external capital markets may systematically undervalue firms with competitive advantages that are subject to imitation. Do you agree with this analysis? If yes, how could you trade on this information in your own investment activities? If no, why not?

4. A particular firm is owned by members of a single family. Most of the wealth of this family is derived from the operations of this firm, and the family does not want to "go public" with the firm by selling its equity position to outside investors. Will this firm pursue a highly related diversification strategy or a somewhat less related diversification strategy? Why?

5. Under what conditions will a related diversification strategy not be a source of competitive advantage for a firm?

6. Suppose a firm has invested heavily in an oil-rich country with an unstable government. If this government was to fall, this firm is likely to lose its investment in this country, and the price of crude oil is likely to go up substantially. Also, suppose this firm has purchased equity positions in a large number of other oil firms that do not have investments in this particular country. In what ways can these equity investments be thought of as a hedge against a firm losing its investment in the unstable country? What, if anything, does your analysis say about the ability of firms to manage political risks indirectly?

PROBLEM SET

1. Visit the corporate Web sites for the following firms. How would you characterize the corporate strategies of these companies? Are they following a strategy of limited diversification, related diversification, or unrelated diversification?

(a) ExxonMobil
(b) Google
(c) General Motors
(d) Jet Blue
(e) Citigroup
(f) Entertainment Arts
(g) IBM
(h) Dell
(i) Berkshire Hathaway

2. Consider the following list of strategies. In your view, which of these strategies are examples of potential economies of scope underlying a corporate diversification strategy?

For those strategies that are an economy of scope, which economy of scope are they? For those strategies that are not an economy of scope, why aren't they?

(a) The Coca-Cola Corporation replaces its old diet cola drink (Tab) with a new diet cola drink called Diet Coke.

(b) Apple Computer introduces an I-Pod MP3 player with a larger memory.

(c) PepsiCo distributes Lay's Potato Chips to the same stores where it sells Pepsi.

(d) Kmart extends is licensing arrangement with Martha Stewart for four years.

(e) Wal-Mart uses the same distribution system to supply its Wal-Mart stores, its Wal-Mart SuperCenters (Wal-Mart stores with grocery stores in them), and its Sam's Clubs.

(f) Head Ski Company introduces a line of tennis rackets.

(g) General Electric borrows money from BankAmerica at 3 percent interest and then makes capital available to its jet engine subsidiary at 8 percent interest.

(h) McDonald's acquires Boston Market and Chipotle (two restaurants where many customers sit in the restaurant to eat their meals).

(i) A venture capital firm invests in a firm in the biotechnology industry and a firm in the entertainment industry.

(j) Another venture capital firm invests in two firms in the biotechnology industry.

3. Consider the following facts. The standard deviation of the cash flows associated with Business I is .8. The larger this standard deviation, the riskier a business's future cash flows are likely to be. The standard deviation of the cash flows associated with Business II is 1.3. That is, Business II is riskier than Business I. Finally, the correlation between the cash flows of these two businesses over time is –.8. This means that when Business I is up, Business II tends to be down, and vice versa. Suppose one firm owns both of these businesses.

(a) Assuming that Business I constitutes 40 percent of this firm's revenues and Business II constitutes 60 percent of its revenues, calculate the riskiness of this firm's total revenues using the following equation:

$$sd_{I,II} = \sqrt{w^2 sd_I^2 + \left(1 - w\right)^2 sd_{II}^2 + 2w\left(1 + w\right)\left(r_{I,II} sd_I sd_{II}\right)}$$

Where $w = .40$; $sd_I = .8$, $sd_{II} = 1.3$, and $r_{I,II} = -.8$.

(b) Given this result, does it make sense for this firm to own both Business I and Business II? Why or why not?

END NOTES

1. See Sellers, Patricia (2004). "The brand king's challenge." *Fortune*, April 5, pp. 192 +.
2. The Walt Disney Company (A). Harvard Business School Case No. 1-388-147.
3. Useem, Jerry (2004). "Another boss, another revolution." *Fortune*, April 5, pp. 112 +.
4. See Burrows, P. (1995). "Now, TI means 'taking initiative'." *BusinessWeek*, May 15, pp. 120–121; and Rogers, A. (1992). "It's the execution that counts." *Fortune*, November 30, pp. 80–83; Wallas, J., and J. Erickson (1993). *Hard drive: Bill Gates and the making of the Microsoft empire*. New York: Harper Business; and Porter, M. E. (1981). "Disposable diaper industry in 1974." Harvard Business School Case No. 9-380-175. Whether or not Microsoft continues to share activities across operating systems and applications software was one of the key issues at stake in the Microsoft antitrust suit. A more general discussion of the value of shared activities can be found in St. John, C. H., and J. S. Harrison (1999). "Manufacturing-based relatedness, synergy, and coordination." *Strategic Management Journal*, 20, pp. 129–145.
5. See Fuchsberg, G. (1992). "Decentralized management can have its drawbacks." *Wall Street Journal*, December 9, p. B1.
6. See Crockett, R. (2000). "A Baby Bell's growth formula." *BusinessWeek*, March 6, pp. 50–52; and Crockett, R. (1999). "The last monopolist." *BusinessWeek*, April 12, p. 76.
7. de Lisser, E. (1993). "Catering to cooking-phobic customers, supermarkets stress carryout. " *Wall Street Journal*, April 5, p. B1.

8. See, for example, Davis, P., R. Robinson, J. Pearce, and S. Park (1992). "Business unit relatedness and performance: A look at the pulp and paper industry." *Strategic Management Journal*, 13, pp. 349–361.
9. Loomis, C. J. (1993). "Dinosaurs?" *Fortune*, May 3, pp. 36–42.
10. Rapoport, C. (1992). "A tough Swede invades the U.S." *Fortune*, June 29, pp. 776–779.
11. Prahalad, C. K., and G. Hamel (1990). "The core competence of the organization." *Harvard Business Review*, 90, p. 82.
12. See also Grant, R. M. (1988). "On 'dominant logic' relatedness and the link between diversity and performance." *Strategic Management Journal*, 9, pp. 639–642; Chatterjee, S., and B. Wernerfelt (1991). "The link between resources and type at diversification: Theory and evidence." *Strategic Management Journal*, 12, pp. 33–48; Markides, C., and P. J. Williamson (1994). "Related diversification, core competencies, and corporate performance." *Strategic Management Journal*, 15, pp. 149–165; Montgomery, C. A., and B. Wernerfelt (1991). "Sources of superior performance: Market share versus industry effects in the U.S. brewing industry." *Management Science*, 37, pp. 954–959; Liedtka, J. M. (1996). "Collaborating across lines of business for competitive advantage." *Academy of Management Executive*, 10(2), pp. 20–37; and Farjoun, M. (1998). "The independent and joint effects of the skill and physical bases of relatedness in diversification." *Strategic Management Journal*, 19, pp. 611–630.
13. Jensen, M. C. (1986). "Agency costs of free cash flow, corporate finance, and takeovers." *American Economic Review*, 76, pp. 323–329.
14. See Nayyar, P. (1990). "Information asymmetries: A source of competitive advantage for diversified service firms." *Strategic Management Journal*, 11, pp. 513–519; and Robins, J., and M. Wiersema (1995). "A resource-based approach to the multibusiness firm: Empirical analysis of portfolio interrelationships and corporate financial performance." *Strategic Management Journal*, 16, pp. 277–299, for a discussion of the evolution of core competencies.
15. Prahalad, C. K., and R. A. Bettis (1986). "The dominant logic: A new linkage between diversity and performance." *Strategic Management Journal*, 7(6), pp. 485–501.
16. See Williamson, O. E. (1975). *Markets and hierarchies: Analysis and antitrust implications*. New York: Free Press.
17. See Liebeskind, J. P. (1996). "Knowledge, strategy, and the theory of the firm." *Strategic Management Journal*, 17 (Winter Special Edition), pp. 93–107.
18. Perry, L. T., and J. B. Barney (1981). "Performance lies are hazardous to organizational health." *Organizational Dynamics*, 9(3), pp. 68–80.
19. Bethel, J. E. (1990). *The capital allocation process and managerial mobility: A theoretical and empirical investigation*. Unpublished doctoral dissertation, University of California at Los Angles.
20. Staw, B. M. (1981). "The escalation of commitment to a course of action." *Academy of Management Review*, 6, pp. 577–587.
21. See Comment, R., and G. Jarrell (1995). "Corporate focus and stock returns." *Journal of Financial Economics*, 37, pp. 67–87; Berger, P. G., and E. Otek (1995). "Diversification's effect on firm value." *Journal of Financial Economics*, 37, pp. 39–65; Maksimovic, V., and G. Phillips (1999). "Do conglomerate firms allocate resources inefficiently?" Working paper, University of Maryland; Matsusaka, J. G., and V. Nanda (1998). Internal capital markets and corporate refocusing." Working paper, University of Southern California; Palia, D. (1998). "Division-level overinvestment and agency conflicts in diversified firms." Working paper, Columbia University; Rajan, R., H. Servaes, and L. Zingales (1997). "The cost of diversity: The diversification discount and inefficient investment." Working paper, University of Chicago; Scharfstein, D. S. (1997). "The dark side of internal capital markets II: Evidence from diversified conglomerates." NBER [National Bureau of Economic Research]. Working paper; Shin, H. H., and R. M. Stulz (1998). "Are internal capital markets efficient?" *The Quarterly Journal of Economics*, May, pp. 551–552. But Houston and James (1998) show that internal capital markets can create competitive advantages for firms: Houston, J., and C. James (1998). "Some evidence that banks use internal capital markets to lower capital costs." *Journal of Applied Corporate Finance*, 11(2), pp. 70–78.
22. Scott, J. H. (1977). "On the theory of conglomerate mergers." *Journal of Finance*, 32, pp. 1235–1250.
23. See Brennan, M. (1979). "The pricing of contingent claims in discrete time models." *Journal of Finance*, 34, pp. 53–68; Cox, J., S. Ross, and M.

Rubinstein (1979). "Option pricing: A simplified approach." *Journal of Financial Economics*, 7, pp. 229–263; and Stapleton, R. C. (1982). "Mergers, debt capacity, and the valuation of corporate loans." In M. Keenan and L. J. White (eds.), *Mergers and acquisitions*. Lexington, MA: D. C. Heath, Chapter 2; and Galai, D., and R. W. Masulis (1976). "The option pricing model and the risk factor of stock." *Journal of Financial Economics*, 3, pp. 53–82.
24. See Karnani, A., and B. Wernerfelt (1985). "Multiple point competition." *Strategic Management Journal*, 6, pp. 87–96; Bernheim, R. D., and M. D. Whinston (1990). "Multimarket contact and collusive behavior." *Rand Journal of Economics*, 12, pp. 605–617; Tirole, J. (1988). *The theory of industrial organization*. Cambridge, MA: MIT Press; Gimeno, J., and C. Y. Woo (1999). "Multimarket contact, economies of scope, and firm performance." *Academy of Management Journal*, 43(3), pp. 239–259; Korn, H. J., and J. A. C. Baum (1999). "Chance, imitative, and strategic antecedents to multimarket contact." *Academy of Management Journal*, 42(2), pp. 171–193; Baum, J. A. C., and H. J. Korn (1999). "Dynamics of dyadic competitive interaction." *Strategic Management Journal*, 20, pp. 251–278; Gimeno, J. (1999). "Reciprocal threats in multimarket rivalry: Staking our 'spheres of influence' in the U.S. airline industry." *Strategic Management Journal*, 20, pp. 101–128; Gimeno, J., and C. Y. Woo (1996). "Hypercompetition in a multimarket environment: The role of strategic similarity and multimarket contact in competitive de-escalation." *Organization Science*, 7(3), pp. 322–341; Ma, H. (1998). "Mutual forbearance in international business." *Journal of International Management*, 4(2), pp. 129–147; McGrath, R. G., and M.-J. Chen (1998). "Multimarket maneuvering in uncertain spheres of influence: Resource diversion strategies." *Academy of Management Review*, 23(4), pp. 724–740; Chen, M.-J. (1996). "Competitor analysis and interfirm rivalry: Toward a theoretical integration." *Academy of Management Review*, 21(1), pp. 100–134; Chen, M.-J., and K. Stucker (1997). "Multinational management and multimarket rivalry: Toward a theoretical development of global competition." *Academy of Management Proceedings 1997*, pp. 2–6; and Young, G., K. G. Smith, and C. M. Grimm (1997). "Multimarket contact, resource heterogeneity, and rivalrous firm behavior." *Academy of Management Proceedings 1997*, pp. 55–59. This idea was originally proposed by Edwards, C. D. (1955). "Conglomerate bigness as a source of power." In *Business concentration and price policy*. NBER Conference Report. Princeton, NJ: Princeton University Press.
25. See Karnani, A., and B. Wernerfelt (1985). "Multiple point competition." *Strategic Management Journal*, 6, pp. 87–96.
26. This is documented by Gimeno, J. (1994). "Multipoint competition, market rivalry and firm performance: A test of the mutual forbearance hypothesis in the United States airline industry, 1984–1988." Unpublished doctoral dissertation, Purdue University.
27. See Landro, L., P. M. Reilly, and R. Turner (1993). "Cartoon clash: Disney relationship with Time Warner is a strained one." *Wall Street Journal*, April 14, p. A1; and Reilly, P. M., and R. Turner (1993). "Disney pulls ads in tiff with *Time*." *Wall Street Journal*, April 2, p. B1. The growth and consolidation of the entertainment industry since the early 1990s has made Disney and Time Warner (especially after its merger with AOL) large entertainment conglomerates. It will be interesting to see if these two larger firms will be able to find ways to tacitly collude or will continue the competition begun in the early 1990s.
28. The best work in this area has been done by Gimeno, J. (1994). "Multipoint competition, market rivalry and firm performance: A test of the mutual forbearance hypothesis in the United States airline industry, 1984–1988." Unpublished doctoral dissertation, Purdue University. See also Smith, F., and R. Wilson (1995). "The predictive validity of the Karnani and Wernerfelt model of multipoint competition." *Strategic Management Journal*, 16, pp. 143–160.
29. See Tirole, J. (1988). *The theory of industrial organization*. Cambridge, MA: MIT Press.
30. Carnevale, M. L. (1993). "Ring in the new: Telephone service seems on the brink of huge innovations." *Wall Street Journal*, February. 10, p. A1.
31. See Russo, M. V. (1992). "Power plays: Regulation, diversification, and backward integration in the electric utility industry." *Strategic Management Journal*, 13, pp. 13–27. Recent work by Jandik and Makhija indicates that when a regulated utility diversifies out of a

regulated industry, it often earns a more positive return than when an unregulated firm does this [Jandik, T., and A. K. Makhija (1999). "An Empirical Examination of the Atypical Diversification Practices of Electric Utilities: Internal Capital Markets and Regulation." Fisher College of Business, Ohio State University, working paper (September).] This work shows that regulators have the effect of making a regulated firm's internal capital market more efficient. Differences between Russo's (1992) findings and Jandik and Makhija's (1999) findings may have to do with when this work was done. Russo's (1992) research may have focused on a time period before regulatory agencies had learned how to improve a firm's internal capital market. However, even though Jandik and Makhija (1999) report positive returns from regulated firms diversifying, these positive returns do not reflect the market power advantages of these firms.

32. Finkelstein, S., and D. C. Hambrick (1989). "Chief executive compensation: A study of the intersection of markets and political processes." *Strategic Management Journal*, 10, pp. 121–134.

33. See William, J., B. L. Paez, and L. Sanders (1988). "Conglomerates revisited." *Strategic Management Journal*, 9, pp. 403–414; Geringer, J. M., S. Tallman, and D. M. Olsen (2000). "Product and international diversification among Japanese multinational firms." *Strategic Management Journal*, 21, pp. 51–80; Nail, L. A., W. L. Megginson, and C. Maquieira (1998). "How stock-swap mergers affect shareholder (and bondholder) wealth: More evidence of the value of corporate 'focus'." *Journal of Applied Corporate Finance*, 11(2), pp. 95–106; G. R. Carroll; L. S. Bigelow; M.-D. L. Seidel; L. B. Tsai (1966)." "The fates of *De Novo* and *De Alio* producers in the American automobile industry 1885—1981." *Strategic Management Journal*, 17 (Special Summer Issue), pp. 117–138; Nguyen, T. H., A. Seror, and T. M. Devinney (1990). "Diversification strategy and performance in Canadian manufacturing firms." *Strategic Management Journal*, 11, pp. 411–418; and Amit, R., and J. Livnat (1988). "Diversification strategies, business cycles and economic performance." *Strategic Management Journal*, 9, pp. 99–110, for a discussion of corporate diversification in the economy over time.

34. The Nestlé story is summarized in Templeman, J. (1993). "Nestlé: A giant in a hurry." *BusinessWeek*, March 22, pp. 50–54.

35. See Rugman, A., and R. Hodgetts (1995). *Business: A strategic management approach*. New York: McGraw-Hill.

36. Glynn, M. A. (1993). "Strategic planning in Nigeria versus U.S.: A case of anticipating the (next) coup." *Academy of Management Executive* 7(3), pp. 82–83.

37. See Roth, T. (1990). "Bid size showed VW's eagerness to buy Skoda." *Wall Street Journal*, December 11, p. A15; and Tully, S. (1990). "GE in Hungary: Let there be light." *Fortune*, October 22, pp. 137–142.

38. See Ring, P. S., S. A. Lenway, and M. Govekar (1990). "Management of the political imperative in international business." *Strategic Management Journal*, 11, pp. 141–151.

39. Dichtl, E., and H. G. Koeglmayr (1986). "Country risk ratings." *Management Review*, 26(4), pp. 2–10; O'Leary, M. (2002) "Analysts take an optimistic view." *Euromoney*, September, pp. 208–216; Hoti, S. (2004). "Snapshot images of country risk ratings: An international comparison." Unpublished, Department of Economics, University of Western Australia.

40. See Auletta, K. (1983). "A certain poetry—Parts I and II." *The New Yorker*, June 6, pp. 46–109; June 13, pp. 50–91.

8

Organizing to Implement Corporate Diversification

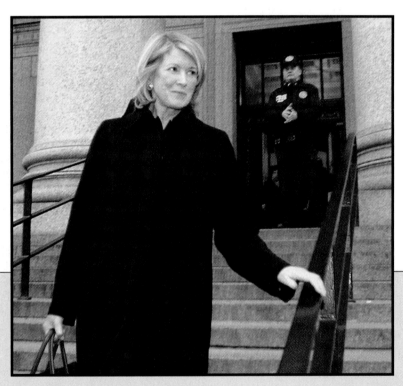

During 2002 and 2003, it seemed like you couldn't open the newspaper without reading about yet another example of corporate corruption. The list of former senior managers recently convicted, currently on trial, or awaiting trial is depressingly long: Samuel D. Walsa (ImClone Systems, Inc.); Frank Quattrone (an investment banker at Credit Suisse First Boston); Dennis Kozlowski and Mark H. Swartz (Tyco International); Bernard J. Ebbers and Scott D. Sullivan

Corporate Crooks

(WorldCom, Inc.); Richard Scrushy (HealthSouth Corp.); Andrew Fastow and David W. Delainey (Enron); and Martha Stewart (Martha Stewart Living Inc.). And this corruption isn't limited to just the United States Calisto Tanzi, founder and former CEO of the Italian dairy and food products firm Parmalat, has

been jailed, along with his son and several members of Parmalat's top management team, for corruption and accounting fraud.

What is wrong? Is the current generation of senior managers simply less honest or less ethical than previous generations? Or has the level of dishonesty remained the same, but the effectiveness of government enforcement improved? And why did it take so many years for the transgressions of Enron and WorldCom and other firms to be revealed?

Learning Objectives

After reading this chapter, you should be able to:

1. Describe the multidivisional, or M-form, structure and how it is used to implement a corporate diversification strategy.

2. Describe the roles of the board of directors, institutional investors, the senior executive, corporate staff, division general managers, and shared activity managers in making the M-form structure work.

3. Describe how three management control processes—measuring divisional performance, allocating corporate capital, and transferring intermediate products—are used to help implement a corporate diversification strategy.

4. Describe the role of management compensation in helping to implement a corporate diversification strategy.

Where were the checks and balances supposedly built into the capitalist system? Where were the boards of directors, the banks, institutional investors, external auditors, the press?

One explanation of the current level of business corruption begins by observing that the economic climate of the 1990s led to growth expectations that were greater than what could be sustained by the underlying business models of many large firms. Faced with the choice between dampening those expectations (and having the price of their firm's stock drop significantly) or

"cooking the books" to keep the price up, many managers took the latter course. This was a particularly tempting option since many of these managers owned a great deal of their company's stock. As these first efforts at "earnings management" were augmented by even more creative forms of accounting, companies and managers created an accounting "house of cards" so fragile that even the smallest of events could send it tumbling down.

And then it came crashing down, and the list of managerial felons grew ever longer.

Obviously, the components of corporate governance that were supposed to rein in these kinds of abuses—the boards of directors, banks, institutional investors, external auditors, the press— failed too many times, and new legislation that strengthened the control of corporations was passed, at least in the United States.

But this episode in the history of the corporation strikes another cautionary note. Despite the lengthy list of corporate

245

misdeeds uncovered during the first years of the twenty-first century, the vast majority of corporations in the United States and around the world followed the rules, did not engage in unethical practices, and continued to manage their businesses in fiscally sound ways. Put differently, our recent experiences remind us both of the importance of diligence in monitoring the business practices of large firms and of the fact that most of that monitoring effort reveals remarkably few unethical practices.

Sources: "On Trial." *BusinessWeek,* January 12, 2004, pp. 80–81; Alessandra Galloni, David Reilly, and Carrick Mollenkamp (2004). "Italy's Parmalat probe looks to Bank of America in London." *Wall Street Journal,* March 8, p. B6; Gail Edmondson, David Fairlamb, and Nanete Byrnes (2004). "The milk just keeps on spilling." *BusinessWeek,* January 26, pp. 54 +.

This chapter is about how the large diversified firm—the kind of firm at the center of so much of the business corruption recently reported in the popular press—is managed and governed efficiently. The chapter explains how many of the checks and balances described in the opening case act to assure that the corporation is managed in a way that is consistent with the interests of its owners—equity holders—as well as the interests of its other stakeholders. The three components of organizing to implement any strategy, first identified in Chapter 3—organizational structure, management controls, and compensation policy—are also important in implementing corporate diversification strategies.

VRIO

Organizational Structure and Implementing Corporate Diversification

The most common organizational structure for implementing a corporate diversification strategy is the **M-form**, or **multidivisional**, structure. A typical M-form structure, as it would appear in a firm's annual report, is presented in Figure 8.1.

Figure 8.1 An Example of M-Form Organizational Structure as Depicted in a Firm's Annual Report

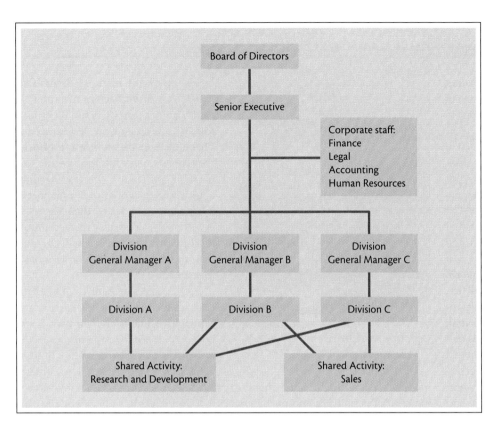

Board of Directors

Senior Executive

Corporate staff:
Finance
Legal
Accounting
Human Resources

Division
General Manager A

Division
General Manager B

Division
General Manager C

Division A

Division B

Division C

Shared Activity:
Research and Development

Shared Activity:
Sales

Figure 8.2 An M-Form Structure Redrawn to Emphasize Roles and Responsibilities

This same structure is redrawn in Figure 8.2 to emphasize the roles and responsibilities of each of the major components of the M-form organization.[1]

In the multidivisional structure, each business that the firm engages in is managed through a division. Different firms have different names for these **divisions**—strategic business units (SBUs), business groups, companies. Whatever their names, the divisions in an M-form organization are true **profit-and-loss centers**: Profits and losses are calculated at the level of the division in these firms.

Different firms use different criteria for defining the boundaries of profit-and-loss centers. For example, General Electric defines its divisions in terms of the types of products each one manufactures and sells (for example, consumer electronics, nuclear, medical imaging, and so forth). Nestlé defines its divisions with reference to the geographic scope of each of its businesses (North America, South America, and so forth). General Motors defines its divisions in terms of the brand names of its products (Cadillac, Chevrolet, Saturn, and so forth). However they are defined, divisions in an M-form organization should be large enough to represent identifiable business entities but small enough so that each one can be managed effectively by a division general manager. Indeed, each division in an M-form organization typically adopts a U-form structure (see the discussion of the U-form structure in Chapters 4, 5, and 6), and the division general manager takes on the role of a U-form senior executive for his or her division.

The M-form structure is designed to create checks and balances for managers that increase the probability that a diversified firm will be managed in ways consistent with the interests of its equity holders. The roles of each of the major elements of the M-form structure in accomplishing this objective are summarized in Table 8.1 and discussed below. Some of the conflicts of interest that might emerge between a firm's equity holders and its managers are described in the Strategy in Depth feature.

Strategy in Depth

*I*n Chapter 7, it was suggested that sometimes it is in the best interest of equity holders to delegate to managers the day-to-day management of their equity investments in a firm. This will be the case when equity investors cannot realize a valuable economy of scope on their own while managers *can* realize that economy of scope.

Several authors suggest that whenever one party to an exchange delegates decision-making authority to a second party, an **agency relationship** has been created between these parties. The party delegating this decision-making authority is called the **principal**; the party to whom this authority is delegated is called the **agent**. In the context of corporate diversification, an agency relationship exists between a firm's outside equity holders (as principals) and its managers (as agents) to the extent that equity holders delegate the day-to-day management of their investment to those managers.

The agency relationship between equity holders and managers can be very effective as long as managers make investment decisions that are consistent with equity holders' interests. Thus, if equity holders are interested in maximizing the rate of return on their investment in a firm and if managers make their investment decisions with this objective in mind, then equity holders will have few concerns about delegating the day-to-day management of their investments to managers. Unfortunately, in numerous situations the interests of a firm's outside equity holders and its managers do not coincide. When parties in an agency relationship differ in their decision-making objectives, **agency problems** arise. Two common agency problems

Agency Conflicts Between Managers and Equity Holders

have been identified: investment in managerial perquisites and managerial risk aversion.

Managers can decide to take some of a firm's capital and invest it in **managerial perquisites** that do not add economic value to the firm but do directly benefit those managers. Examples of such investments include lavish offices, fleets of corporate jets, and corporate vacation homes. Dennis Kozlowski, former CEO of Tyco International, is accused of "stealing" $600 million in these kinds of managerial perquisites from his firm. The list of goods and services that Kozlowski lavished on himself and those close to him is truly astounding—a multimillion-dollar birthday party for his wife, a $6,000 wastebasket, a $15,000 umbrella stand, a $144,000 loan to a board member, toga-clad waiters at an event, and so on.

As outrageous as some of these managerial perquisites can be, the second source of agency problems—managerial risk aversion—is probably

more important in most diversified firms. As discussed in Chapter 7, equity holders can diversify their portfolio of investments at very low cost. Through their diversification efforts, they can eliminate all firm-specific risk in their portfolios. In this setting, equity holders would prefer managers make more risky rather than less risky investments, since the expected return on risky investments is usually greater than the expected return on less risky investments.

Managers, in contrast, have limited ability to diversify their human capital investments in their firm. Some portion of these investments is specific to a particular firm and has limited value in alternative uses. The value of a manager's human capital investment in a firm depends critically on the continued existence of the firm. Thus managers are *not* indifferent to the riskiness of investment opportunities in a firm. Very risky investments may jeopardize a firm's survival and thus eliminate the value of a manager's human capital investments. These incentives can lead managers to be more risk averse in their decision making than equity holders would like them to be.

One of the purposes of the M-form structure, and indeed of all aspects of organizing to implement corporate diversification, is to reduce these agency problems.

Sources: M. C. Jensen and W. H. Meckling (1976). "Theory of the firm: Managerial behavior, agency costs, and ownership structure." *Journal of Financial Economics.* 3, pp. 305–360; J. Useem (2003). "The biggest show." *Fortune,* December 8, pp157+; R. Lambert (1986). "Executive effort and selection of risky projects." *Rand Journal of Economics,* 13(2), pp. 369–378.

Table 8.1   **The Roles and Responsibilities of Major Components of the M-Form Structure**

Component	Activity
Board of directors	Monitor decision-making in a firm to ensure that it is consistent with the interests of outside equity holders
Institutional investors	Monitor decision-making to ensure that it is consistent with the interests of major institutional equity investors
Senior executives	Formulate corporate strategies consistent with equity holders' interests and assure strategy implementation Strategy formulation: ■ Decide the businesses in which the firm will operate ■ Decide how the firm should compete in those businesses ■ Specify the economies of scope around which the diversified firm will operate Strategy implementation: ■ Encourage cooperation across divisions to exploit economies of scope ■ Evaluate performance of divisions ■ Allocate capital across divisions
Corporate staff	Provides information to the senior executive about internal and external environments for strategy formulation and implementation
Division general managers	Formulate divisional strategies consistent with corporate strategies and assure strategy implementation Strategy formulation: ■ Decide how the division will compete in its business, given the corporate strategy Strategy implementation: ■ Coordinate the decisions and actions of functional managers reporting to the division general manager to implement divisional strategy ■ Compete for corporate capital allocations ■ Cooperate with other divisions to exploit corporate economies of scope
Shared activity managers	Support the operations of multiple divisions

The Board of Directors

One of the major components of an M-form organization is a firm's **board of directors**. In principle, all of a firm's senior managers report to the board. The board's primary responsibility is to monitor decision making in the firm, to ensure that it is consistent with the interests of outside equity holders.

Research Made Relevant

**The Effectiveness
of Boards of Directors**

There has been a great deal of research on when boards of directors are more or less effective in ensuring that firms are managed in ways consistent with the interests of equity holders. Three issues have received particular attention: The roles of insiders (i.e., managers) and outsiders on the board; whether or not the board chair and the senior executive should be the same or different people; and whether the board should be active or passive.

With respect to insiders and outsiders on the board, in one way this seems like a simple problem. Because the primary role of the board of directors is to monitor managerial decisions to ensure that they are consistent with the interests of equity holders, it follows that the board should consist primarily of outsiders because they face no conflict of interest in evaluating managerial performance. Obviously, managers, as inside members of the board, face significant conflicts of interest in evaluating their own performance.

Research on outsider members of boards of directors tends to support this point of view. Outside directors, as compared to insiders, tend to focus more on monitoring a firm's economic performance than on other measures of firm performance. Obviously, a firm's economic performance is most relevant to its equity investors. Outside board members are also more likely than inside members to dismiss CEOs following poor performance. Also, outside board members have a stronger incentive than inside members to maintain their reputations as effective monitors. This incentive by itself can lead to more effective monitoring by outside board

members. Moreover, the monitoring effectiveness of outside board members seems to be enhanced when they personally own a substantial amount of a firm's equity.

However, the fact that outside members face fewer conflicts of interest in evaluating managerial performance compared to management insiders on the board does not mean that there is no appropriate role for inside board members. Managers bring something to the board that cannot be easily duplicated by outsiders—detailed information about the decision-making activities inside the firm. This is precisely the information that outsiders need to effectively monitor the activities of a firm, and it is information available to them only if they work closely with insiders (managers). One way to gain access to this information is to include managers as members of the board of directors. Thus, while most work suggests that a board of directors should be composed primarily of outsiders, there is an important role for insiders/managers to play as members of a firm's board.

There is currently some debate about whether the roles of board chair and CEO should be combined or sepa-

A board of directors typically consists of 10 to 15 individuals drawn from a firm's top management group and from individuals outside the firm. A firm's **senior executive** (often identified by the title president or chief executive officer or CEO), its chief financial officer (CFO), and a few other senior managers are usually on the board—although managers on the board are typically outnumbered by outsiders. The firm's senior executive is often but not always the **chairman of the board** (a term used here to denote both female and male senior executives). The task of managerial board members—including the board chair—is to provide other board members information and insights about critical decisions being made in the firm and the effect those decisions are likely to have on a firm's equity holders. The task of outsiders on the board is to evaluate the past, current, and future performance of the firm, and of its senior managers, to ensure that the actions taken in the firm are consistent with equity holders' interests.[2]

rated and, if separated, what kinds of people should occupy these positions. Some have argued that the roles of CEO and chairman of the board should definitely be separated and that the role of the chairman should be filled by an outside (nonmanagerial) member of the board of directors. These arguments are based on the assumption that only an outside member of the board can ensure the independent monitoring of managerial decision making. Others have argued that effective monitoring often requires more information than what would be available to outsiders and thus that the roles of board chair and CEO should be combined and filled by a firm's senior manager.

Empirical research on this question suggests that whether these roles of CEO and chairman should be combined or not depends on the complexity of the information analysis and monitoring task facing the CEO and chairman. Brian Boyd has found that combining the roles of CEO and chairman is positively correlated with firm performance when firms operate in slow-growth and simple competitive environments—environments that do not overtax the cognitive capability of a single individual. This finding suggests that combining these roles does not necessarily increase conflicts between a firm and its equity holders. This research also found that separating the roles of CEO and board chair is positively correlated with firm performance when firms operate in high-growth and very complex environments. In such environments, a single individual cannot fulfill all the responsibilities of both CEO and chairman and thus the two roles need to be held by separate individuals.

Finally, with respect to active versus passive boards, historically the boards of major firms have been relatively passive and would take dramatic action, such as firing the senior executive, only if a firm's performance was significantly below expectations for long periods of time. However, more recently, boards have become more active proponents of equity holders' interests. This recent surge in board activity reflects a new economic reality: If a board does not become more active in monitoring firm performance, then other monitoring mechanisms will. Consequently, the board of directors has become progressively more influential in representing the interests of a firm's equity holders.

However, board activity can go too far. To the extent that the board begins to operate a business on a day-to-day basis, it goes beyond its capabilities. Boards rarely have sufficient detailed information to manage a firm directly. When it is necessary to change a firm's senior executive, boards will usually not take on the responsibilities of that executive, but rather will rapidly identify a single individual—either an insider or outsider—to take over this position.

Sources: E. Zajac and J. Westphal (1994). "The costs and benefits of managerial incentives and monitoring in large U.S. corporations: When is more not better?" *Strategic Management Journal*, 15, pp. 121–142; P. Rechner and D. Dalton (1991). "CEO duality and organizational performance: A longitudinal analysis." *Strategic Management Journal*, 12, pp. 155–160; S. Finkelstein and R. D'Aveni (1994). "CEO duality as a double-edged sword: How boards of directors balance entrenchment avoidance and unity of command." *Academy of Management Journal*, 37, pp. 1079–1108; B. K. Boyd (1995). "CEO duality and firm performance: A contingency model." *Strategic Management Journal*, 16, pp. 301–312; F. Kesner and R. B. Johnson (1990). "An investigation of the relationship between board composition and stockholder suits." *Strategic Management Journal*, 11, pp. 327–336.

Boards of directors are typically organized into several subcommittees. An **audit committee** is responsible for ensuring the accuracy of accounting and financial statements. A **finance committee** maintains the relationship between the firm and external capital markets. A **nominating committee** nominates new board members. A **personnel and compensation committee** evaluates and compensates the performance of a firm's senior executive and other senior managers. Often, membership on these standing committees is reserved for external board members. Other standing committees reflect specific issues for a particular firm and are typically open to external and internal board members.[3]

Over the years, a great deal of research has been conducted about the effectiveness of boards of directors in ensuring that a firm's managers make decisions in ways consistent with the interests of its equity holders. Some of this work is summarized in the Research Made Relevant feature.

Global Perspectives

How common is it for large diversified firms around the world to be owned or dominated by single families? Most people are surprised to find out just how common family-dominated firms are in the United States. Indeed, one-third of the firms in the Standard & Poor's 500 have their founding families still involved in day-to-day management. Such firms include Marriott, Walgreens, Wrigley, Alberto-Culver, Campbell Soup, Dell Computer, and Wal-Mart.

However, as important as these family-dominated firms are in the U.S. economy, they are not the dominant force that such firms are in many countries around the world. In fact, one recent study found that they can be a very important force in the economy of many countries. For example, in New Zealand, 9 of the 20 largest firms in the economy are family dominated; in Argentina, 13 of the 20 largest firms in the economy are family dominated; in Mexico, all 20 of the 20 largest firms in the economy are

The Family Firm in the United States and the World

family dominated. By comparison, only 4 of the 20 largest firms in the United States are family dominated, and only 1 of the 20 largest firms in the United Kingdom is family dominated.

These results suggest that the model of corporate governance that is

normally taught in the United States—with large numbers of shareholders owning stock in professionally managed firms—is actually the exception around the world. In many countries—including Argentina, Belgium, Canada, Denmark, Greece, Hong Kong, Israel, Mexico, New Zealand, Portugal, Singapore, South Korea, Sweden, and Switzerland—over one-third of the 20 largest firms are dominated by family owners.

Family ownership of large diversified corporations has advantages and disadvantages. On the positive side, many of the agency problems (see the Strategy in Depth feature) that exist in professionally managed firms are less important in family-dominated firms. After all, managers in family-dominated firms are not "playing" with other people's money, they are "playing" with their own family's money. Family-dominated firms can also make strategic decisions faster than large bureaucratic firms, they tend to create a sense of loyalty among

Institutional Owners

Historically, the typical large diversified firm has had its equity owned in small blocks by millions of individual investors. The exception to this general rule was family-owned or -dominated firms, a phenomenon that is discussed in more detail in the Global Perspectives feature. When a firm's ownership is spread among millions of small investors, it is difficult for any one of these investors to have a large enough ownership position to influence management decisions directly. The only course of action open to such investors if they disagree with management decisions is to sell their stock.

However, the growth of institutional owners has changed the ownership structure of many large diversified firms over the last several years. **Institutional owners** are usually pension funds, mutual funds, insurance companies, or other groups of individual investors that have joined together to manage their investments. In 1970, institutions owned 32 percent of the equity traded in the United States. By 1990, institutions owned 48 percent of this equity. In 2002, they owned 62 percent of the equity traded in the United States.[4]

their employees, and they tend to invest for long-term growth rather than being forced to respond to short-term fluctuations in the stock market. Indeed, in the United States over the last 10 years, family-dominated firms have outperformed non-family-dominated firms—in terms of income growth—21 percent to 11.5 percent.

On the other hand, family-dominated firms have some significant limitations as well. First, since senior leadership positions in these firms, and especially those outside the United States, tend to be reserved for family members, such firms often do not have access to the broader professional management skills available to non-family-dominated firms. Also, since family interests tend to weigh heavily in strategic decision making in these firms, outside investors will often be reluctant to invest in such firms. This suggests that family-dominated firms may often face important capital constraints. Finally, because much

of a particular family's wealth tends to be tied up in the family firm, it is difficult for family members to purchase equities and other investments to diversify their personal investment portfolios. Thus, in order to obtain the benefits of portfolio diversification for their family owners, family-dominated firms often engage in a strategy of unrelated diversification. As was suggested in Chapter 7, this is a very expensive way for a firm's owners to diversify their risk.

Overall, while family-dominated businesses can have advantages and disadvantages, research indicates that the predominance of family-dominated businesses in a country's economy is negatively correlated with the overall level of growth in that economy. Countries whose economies are dominated by family-owned businesses tend to grow less quickly than countries whose economies are not dominated by family-owned businesses. This negative correlation probably reflects the

primary reason that family firms are still important in many economies around the world. When individuals in a country are not confident that the legal and political system will protect their personal property rights, they develop alternative ways to protect those rights. Large and powerful family firms are another way of protecting personal property rights. This suggests that the sanctity of personal property rights in a country explains both the level of economic growth in that country and the extent to which family firms dominate a country's economy.

Sources: R. Morck and B. Yeung (2004). "Family control and the rent-seeking society." *Entrepreneurship: Theory and Practice*, Summer, pp. 391–409; R. LaPorta, F. Lopez-de-Salinas, A. Shleifer, and R. Vishny (1999). "Corporate ownership around the world." *Journal of Finance*, 54, pp. 471–520; J. Weber, L. Lavelle, T. Lowry, W. Zellner, and A. Barrett (2003). "Family, Inc." *BusinessWeek*, November 10, pp. 100 +.

Institutional investors can use their investment clout to insist that a firm's management behaves in ways consistent with the interests of equity holders. Observers who assume that institutional investors are interested more in maximizing the short-term value of their portfolios than in the long-term performance of firms in those portfolios fear that such power will force firms to make only short-term investments. Recent research in the United States and Japan, however, suggests that institutional investors are not unduly myopic. Rather, as suggested earlier, these investors use approximately the same logic equity investors use when evaluating the performance of a firm. For example, one group of researchers examined the impact of institutional ownership on research and development investments in R&D–intensive industries. R&D investments tend to be longer term in orientation. If institutional investors are myopic, they should influence firms to invest in relatively less R&D, in favor of investments that generate shorter-term profits. This research showed that high levels of institutional ownership did not adversely affect the level of R&D in a firm. These findings are consistent with the notion that institutional investors are not inappropriately concerned with the short term in their monitoring activities.[5]

More generally, other researchers have shown that high levels of institutional ownership leads firms to sell strategically unrelated businesses. This effect of institutional investors is enhanced if, in addition, outside directors on a firm's board have substantial equity investments in the firm. Given the discussion of the value of unrelated diversification in Chapter 7, it seems clear that these divestment actions are typically consistent with maximizing the present value of a firm.[6]

The Senior Executive

As suggested in Table 8.1, the senior executive (the president or CEO) in an M-form organization has two responsibilities: strategy formulation and strategy implementation. Strategy formulation entails deciding which set of businesses a diversified firm will operate in and strategy implementation focuses on encouraging behavior in a firm that is consistent with this strategy. Each of these responsibilities of the senior executive are discussed in turn.

Strategy Formulation

At the broadest level, deciding which businesses a diversified firm should operate in is equivalent to discovering and developing valuable economies of scope among a firm's current and potential businesses. If these economies of scope are also rare and costly to imitate, they can be a source of sustained competitive advantage for a diversified firm.

The senior executive is uniquely positioned to discover, develop, and nurture valuable economies of scope in a diversified firm. Every other manager in this kind of firm either has a divisional point of view (for example, division general managers and shared activity managers) or is a functional specialist (for example, corporate staff and functional managers within divisions). Only the senior executive has a truly corporate perspective. However, the senior executive in an M-form organization should involve numerous other divisional and functional managers in strategy formulation to ensure complete and accurate information as input to the process and a broad understanding of and commitment to that strategy once it has been formulated.

Strategy Implementation

As is the case for senior executives in a U-form structure, strategy implementation in an M-form almost always involves resolving conflicts among groups of managers. However, instead of simply resolving conflicts between functional managers (as is the case in a U-form), senior executives in M-form organizations must resolve conflicts within and between each of the major managerial components of the M-form structure: corporate staff, division general managers, and shared activity managers. Various corporate staff managers may disagree about the economic relevance of their staff functions, corporate staff may come into conflict with division general managers over various corporate programs and activities, division general managers may disagree with how capital is allocated across divisions, division general managers may come into conflict with shared activity managers about how shared activities should be managed, shared activity managers may disagree with corporate staff about their mutual roles and responsibilities, and so forth.

Obviously, the numerous and often conflicting relationships among groups of managers in an M-form organization can place significant strategy implementation burdens on the senior executive.[7] While resolving these numerous conflicts, however, the senior executive needs to keep in mind the reasons why the firm began pursuing a diversification strategy in the first place: to exploit real economies of scope that outside investors cannot realize on their own. Any strategy implementation decisions that jeopardize the realization of these real economies of scope are inconsistent with the underlying strategic objectives of a diversified firm. These issues are analyzed in detail later in this chapter, in the discussion of management control systems in the M-form organization.

The Office of the President: Chairman, CEO, and COO

It is often the case that the roles and responsibilities of the senior executive in an M-form organization are greater than what can be reasonably managed by a single individual. This is especially likely if a firm is broadly diversified across numerous complex products and markets. In this situation, it is not uncommon for the tasks of the senior executive to be divided among two or three people: the **chairman of the board**, the **chief executive officer**, and the **chief operating officer (COO)**. The primary responsibilities of each of these roles in an M-form organization are listed in Table 8.2. Together, these roles are known as the **office of the president**. In general, as the tasks facing the office of the president become more demanding and complex, the more likely it is that the roles and responsibilities of this office will be divided among two or three people.

Corporate Staff

The primary responsibility of **corporate staff** is to provide information about the firm's external and internal environments to the firm's senior executive. This information is vital for both the strategy formulation and the strategy implementation responsibilities of the senior executive. Corporate staff functions that provide information about a firm's external environment include finance, investor relations, legal affairs, regulatory affairs, and corporate advertising. Corporate staff functions that provide information about a firm's internal environment include accounting and corporate human resources. These corporate staff functions report directly to a firm's senior executive and are a conduit of information to that executive.

Corporate and Divisional Staff

Many organizations re-create some corporate staff functions within each division of the organization. This is particularly true for internally oriented corporate staff functions such as accounting and human resources. At the division level, divisional staff managers usually have a direct, "solid-line" reporting relationship to their respective corporate staff functional managers and a less formal, "dotted-line" reporting relationship to their division general manager. The reporting relationship between the divisional staff manager and the corporate staff manager is the link that enables the corporate staff manager to collect the information that the senior executive requires for strategy formulation and implementation. The senior executive can also use this corporate staff–division staff relationship to communicate corporate policies and procedures to the divisions, although these policies can also be communicated directly by the senior executive to division general managers.

Table 8.2 **Responsibilities of Three Different Roles in the Office of the President**

Chairman of the board	Supervision of the board of directors in its monitoring role
Chief executive officer	Strategy formulation
Chief operating officer	Strategy implementation

Although divisional staff managers usually have a less formal relationship with their division general managers, in practice division general managers can have an important influence on the activities of divisional staff. After all, divisional staff managers may formally report to corporate staff managers, but they spend most of their time interacting with their division general managers and with the other functional managers who report to their division general managers. These divided loyalties can sometimes affect the timelines and accuracy of the information transmitted from divisional staff managers to corporate staff managers and thus affect the timeliness and accuracy of the information the senior executive uses for strategy formulation and implementation.

Nowhere are these divided loyalties potentially more problematic than in accounting staff functions. Obviously, it is vitally important for the senior executive in an M-form organization to receive timely and accurate information about divisional performance. If the timeliness and accuracy of that information are inappropriately affected by division general managers, the effectiveness of senior management can be adversely affected. Moreover, in some situations, division general managers can have very strong incentives to affect the timeliness and accuracy of divisional performance information, especially if a division general manager's compensation depends on this information or if the capital allocated to a division depends on this information.

Efficient monitoring by the senior executive requires that corporate staff, and especially the accounting corporate staff function, remain organizationally independent of division general managers—thus the importance of the solid-line relationship between divisional staff managers and corporate staff managers. Nevertheless, the ability of corporate staff to obtain accurate performance information from divisions also depends on close cooperative working relationships between corporate staff, divisional staff, and division general managers—thus the importance of the dotted-line relationship between divisional staff managers and division general managers. How one maintains the balance between, on the one hand, the distance and objectivity needed to evaluate a division's performance and, on the other hand, the cooperation and teamwork needed to gain access to the information required to evaluate a division's performance distinguishes excellent from mediocre corporate staff managers.

Overinvolvement in Managing Division Operations

Over and above the failure to maintain a balance between objectivity and cooperation in evaluating divisional performance, the one sure way that corporate staff can fail in a multidivisional firm is to become too involved in the day-to-day operations of divisions. In an M-form structure, the management of such day-to-day operations is delegated to division general managers and to functional managers who report to division general managers. Corporate staff managers collect and transmit information; they do not manage divisional operations.

One way to ensure that corporate staff does not become too involved in managing the day-to-day operations of divisions is to keep corporate staff small. This is certainly true for some of the best-managed diversified firms in the world. For example, just 1.5 percent of Johnson & Johnson's 82,700 employees work at the firm's headquarters, and only some of those individuals are members of the corporate staff. Hanson Industries has in its U.S. headquarters 120 people who help manage a diversified firm with $8 billion in revenues. Clayton, Dubilier, and Rice, a management buyout firm, has only 11 headquarters staff members overseeing eight businesses with collective sales of over $6 billion.[8]

Division General Manager

Division general managers in an M-form organization have primary responsibility for managing a firm's businesses from day to day. Division general managers have full profit-and-loss responsibility and typically have multiple functional managers reporting to them. As general managers, they have both strategy formulation and strategy implementation responsibilities. On the strategy formulation side, division general managers choose strategies for their divisions, within the broader strategic context established by the senior executive of the firm. Many of the analytical tools described in Parts 1 and 2 of this book can be used by division general managers to make these strategy formulation decisions.

The strategy implementation responsibilities of division general managers in an M-form organization parallel the strategy implementation responsibilities of senior executives in U-form organizations. In particular, division general managers must be able to coordinate the activities of often-conflicting functional managers in order to implement a division's strategies.

In addition to their responsibilities as a U-form senior executive, division general managers in an M-form organization have two additional responsibilities: to compete for corporate capital and to cooperate with other divisions to exploit corporate economies of scope. Division general managers compete for corporate capital by promising high rates of return on capital invested by the corporation in their business. In most firms, divisions that have demonstrated the ability to generate high rates of return on earlier capital investments gain access to more capital or to lower-cost capital, compared to divisions that have not demonstrated a history of such performance.

Division general managers cooperate to exploit economies of scope by working with shared activity managers, corporate staff managers, and the senior executive in the firm to isolate, understand, and use the economies of scope around which the diversified firm was originally organized. Division general managers can even become involved in discovering new economies of scope that were not anticipated when the firm's diversification strategy was originally implemented but nevertheless may be both valuable and costly for outside investors to create on their own.

Of course, a careful reader will recognize a fundamental conflict between the last two responsibilities of division general managers in an M-form organization. These managers are required to compete for corporate capital and to cooperate to exploit economies of scope at the same time. Competition is important, because it leads division general managers to focus on generating high levels of economic performance from their divisions. If each division is generating high levels of economic performance, then the diversified firm as a whole is likely to do well also. However, cooperation is important to exploit economies of scope that are the economic justification for implementing a diversification strategy in the first place. If divisions do not cooperate in exploiting these economies, there are few, if any, justifications for implementing a corporate diversification strategy, and the diversified firm should be split into multiple independent entities. The need to simultaneously compete and cooperate puts significant managerial burdens on division general managers. It is likely that this ability is both rare and costly to imitate across most diversified firms.[9]

Shared Activity Managers

One of the potential economies of scope identified in Chapter 7 was shared activities. Divisions in an M-form organization exploit this economy of scope when one or more of the stages in their value chains are managed in common. Typical examples of activities shared across two or more divisions in a multidivisional firm include common sales forces, common distribution systems, common manufacturing facilities, and common research and development efforts (also see Table 7.2). The primary responsibility of the individuals who manage shared activities is to support the operations of the divisions that share the activity.

The way in which M-form structure is often depicted in company annual reports (as in Figure 8.1) tends to obscure the operational role of shared activities. In this version of the M-form organizational chart, no distinction is made between corporate staff functions and shared activity functions. Moreover, it appears that managers of shared activities report directly to a firm's senior executive, just like corporate staff. These ambiguities are resolved by redrawing the M-form organizational chart to emphasize the roles and responsibilities of different units within the M-form (as in Figure 8.2). In this more accurate representation of how an M-form actually functions, corporate staff groups are separated from shared activity managers, and each is shown reporting to its primary internal "customer." That "internal customer" is the senior executive for corporate staff groups and two or more division general managers for shared activity managers.

Shared Activities as Cost Centers

Shared activities are often managed as cost centers in an M-form structure. That is, rather than having profit-and-loss responsibility, **cost centers** are assigned a budget and manage their operations to that budget. When this is the case, shared activity managers do not attempt to create profits when they provide services to the divisions they support. Rather, these services are priced to internal customers in such a way that the shared activity just covers its cost of operating.

Because cost center shared activities do not have to generate profits from their operations, the cost of the services they provide to divisions can be less than the cost of similar services provided either by a division itself or by outside suppliers. If a shared activity is managed as a cost center, and the cost of services from this shared activity is *greater than* the cost of similar services provided by alternative sources, then either this shared activity is not being well managed, or it was not a real economy of scope in the first place. However, when the cost of services from a shared activity is *less than* the cost of comparable services provided by a division itself or by an outside supplier, then division general managers have a strong incentive to use the services of shared activities, thereby exploiting an economy of scope that may have been one of the original reasons why a firm implemented a corporate diversification strategy.

Shared Activities as Profit Centers

Some diversified firms are beginning to manage shared activities as profit centers, rather than as cost centers. Moreover, rather than requiring divisions to use the services of shared activities, divisions retain the right to purchase services from internal shared activities or from outside suppliers or to provide services for themselves. In this setting, managers of shared activities are required to compete for their internal customers on the basis of the price and quality of the services they provide.[10]

One firm that has taken this profit center approach to managing shared activities is ABB, Inc., a Swiss engineering firm. ABB eliminated almost all its corporate staff and reorganized its remaining staff functions into shared activities. Shared activities in ABB compete to provide services to ABB divisions. Not only do some traditional shared activities—such as research and development and sales—compete for internal customers, but many traditional corporate staff functions—such as human resources, marketing, and finance—do as well. ABB's approach to managing shared activities has resulted in a relatively small corporate staff and in increasingly specialized and customized shared activities.[11]

Of course, the greatest risk associated with treating shared activities as profit centers and letting them compete for divisional customers is that divisions may choose to obtain no services or support from shared activities. Although this course of action may be in the self-interest of each division, it may not be in the best interest of the corporation as a whole if, in fact, shared activities are an important economy of scope around which the diversified firm is organized.

In the end, whether a shared activity is managed as a cost center or as a profit center, the task facing the managers of shared activities is the same: to provide such highly customized and high-quality services to divisional customers at a reasonable cost that those internal customers will not want to seek alternative suppliers outside the firm or provide those services themselves. In an M-form organization, the best way to ensure that shared activity economies of scope are realized is for shared activity managers to satisfy their internal customers.

Management Controls and Implementing Corporate Diversification

The M-form structure presented in Figures 8.2 and 8.3 is complex and multifaceted. However, no organizational structure by itself is able to fully implement a corporate diversification strategy. The M-form structure must be supplemented with a variety of management controls. Three of the most important management controls in an M-form structure—systems for evaluating divisional performance, for allocating capital across divisions, and for transferring intermediate products between divisions—are discussed in this section.[12]

Evaluating Divisional Performance

Because divisions in an M-form structure are profit-and-loss centers, evaluating divisional performance should, in principle, be straightforward: Divisions that are very profitable should be evaluated more positively than divisions that are less profitable. In practice, this seemingly simple task is surprisingly complex. Two problems typically arise: (1) How should division profitability be measured? and (2) How should economy-of-scope linkages between divisions be factored into divisional performance measures?

Measuring Divisional Performance

Accounting Measures of Divisional Performance. Both accounting and economic measures of performance can be used in measuring the performance of divisions within a diversified firm. Common accounting measures of divisional performance include the return on the assets controlled by a division, the return on a division's sales, and a division's sales growth. These accounting measures of divisional performance are then compared with some standard to see if a division's performance exceeds or falls short of that standard. Diversified firms use three different standards of comparison when evaluating the performance of a division: (1) a hurdle rate that is common across all the different business units in a firm, (2) a division's budgeted level of performance (which may vary by division), and (3) the average level of profitability of firms in a division's industry.

Each of these standards of comparison has its strengths and weaknesses. For example, if a corporation has a single hurdle rate of profitability that all divisions must meet or exceed, there is little ambiguity about the performance objectives of divisions. On the other hand, such a single standard ignores important differences in performance that might exist across divisions.

Comparing a division's actual performance to its budgeted performance allows the performance expectations of different divisions to vary, but the budgeting process is time-consuming and fraught with political intrigue. One study showed that corporate managers routinely discount the sales projections and capital requests of division managers on the assumption that division managers are trying to "game" the budgeting system.[13] Moreover, division budgets are usually based on a single set of assumptions about how the economy is going to evolve, how competition in a division's industry is going to evolve, and what actions that division is going to take in its industry. When these assumptions no longer hold, budgets are redone—a costly and time-consuming process that has little to do with generating value in a firm.

Finally, while comparing a division's performance with the average level of profitability of firms in a division's industry also allows performance expectations to vary across divisions within a diversified firm, this approach lets other firms determine what is and is not excellent performance for a division within a diversified firm. This approach can also be manipulated: By choosing just the "right" firms with which to compare a division's performance, almost any division can be made to look like it's performing better than its industry average.[14]

No matter what standard of comparison is used to evaluate a division's accounting performance, most accounting measures of divisional performance have a common limitation. All these measures have a short-term bias. This short-term bias reflects the fact that all these measures treat investments in resources and capabilities that have the potential for generating value in the long run as costs during a particular year. In order to reduce costs in a given year, division managers may sometimes forgo investing in these resources and capabilities, even if they could be a source of sustained competitive advantage for a division in the long run.

Economic Measures of Divisional Performance. Given the limitations of accounting measures of divisional performance, several firms have begun adopting economic methods of evaluating this performance. Economic methods build on accounting methods, but adjust those methods to incorporate short-term investments that may generate long-term benefits. Economic methods also compare a division's performance with a firm's cost of capital (see Chapter 1). This avoids some of the gaming that can characterize the use of other standards of comparison in applying accounting measures of divisional performance.

Perhaps the most popular of these economically oriented measures of division performance is known as **economic value added** or **EVA**.[15] EVA is calculated by subtracting the cost of capital employed in a division from that division's earnings in the following manner:

$$EVA = \text{adjusted accounting earnings}$$
$$- (\text{weighted average cost of capital} \times \text{total capital employed by a division})$$

Several of the terms in the EVA formula require some discussion. For example, the calculation of economic value added begins with a division's "adjusted" accounting earnings. These are a division's traditional accounting earnings, adjusted so that they approximate what would be a division's economic earnings. Several adjustments to a division's accounting statements have been described in the literature. For example, traditional accounting practices require R&D spending to be deducted each year from a division's earnings. This can lead division general managers to underinvest in longer-term R&D efforts. In the EVA measure of divisional performance, R&D spending is added back into a division's performance, and R&D is then treated as an asset and depreciated over some period of time.

One consulting firm (Stern Stewart) that specializes in implementing EVA-based divisional evaluation systems in multidivisional firms makes up to 40 "adjustments" to a division's standard accounting earnings so that they more closely approximate economic earnings. Many of these adjustments are proprietary to this consulting firm. However, the most important adjustments—like how R&D should be treated—are broadly known.

The terms in parentheses in the EVA equation reflect the cost of investing in a division. Rather than using some alternative standard of comparison, EVA applies financial theory and multiplies the amount of money invested in a division by a firm's weighted average cost of capital. A firm's weighted average cost of capital is the amount of money a firm could earn if it invested in any of its other divisions. In this sense, a firm's weighted average cost of capital can be thought of as the opportunity cost of investing in a particular division, as opposed to investing in any other division in the firm.

By adjusting a division's earnings, and accounting for the cost of investing in a division, economic value added is a much more accurate estimate of a division's economic performance than are traditional accounting measures of performance. The number of diversified firms evaluating their divisions with EVA-based measures of divisional performance is impressive and growing. These firms include AT&T, Coca-Cola, Quaker Oats, CSX, Briggs and Stratton, and Allied Signal. At Allied Signal, divisions that do not earn their cost of capital are awarded the infamous "leaky bucket" award. If this performance is not improved, division general managers are replaced. The use of EVA has been touted as the key to creating economic wealth in a diversified corporation. Even the U.S. Postal Service is exploring the application of EVA to its operations.[16]

Economies of Scope and the Ambiguity of Divisional Performance

Whether a firm uses accounting measures to evaluate the performance of a division or uses economic measures of performance like EVA, divisional performance in a well-managed diversified firm can never be evaluated unambiguously. Consider a simple example.

Suppose that in a particular multidivisional firm there are only two divisions (Division A and Division B) and one shared activity (research and development). Also, suppose that the two divisions are managed as profit-and-loss centers and that the R&D shared activity is managed as a cost center. To support this R&D effort, each division pays $10 million per year and has been doing so for 10 years. Finally, suppose that after 10 years of effort (and investment) the R&D group develops a valuable new technology that perfectly addresses Division A's business needs.

Obviously, no matter how divisional performance is measured, it is likely to be the case that Division A's performance will rise relative to Division B's performance. In this situation, what percentage of Division A's improved performance should be allocated to Division A, what percentage should be allocated to the R&D group, and what percentage should be allocated to Division B?

The managers in each part of this diversified firm can make compelling arguments in their favor. Division general manager A can reasonably argue that without Division A's efforts to exploit the new technology, the full value of the technology would never have been realized. The R&D manager can reasonably argue that without the R&D effort, there would not have been a technology to exploit in the first place. Finally, division general manager B can reasonably argue that without the dedicated long-term investment of Division B in R&D, there would have been no new technology and no performance increase for Division A.

That all three of these arguments can be made suggests that, to the extent that a firm exploits real economies of scope in implementing a diversification strategy, it will not be possible to unambiguously evaluate the performance of individual divisions in that firm. The fact that there are economies of scope in a diversified firm means that all of the businesses a firm operates in are more valuable bundled together than they would be if kept separate from one another. Efforts to evaluate the performance of these businesses as if they were separate from one another are futile.

One solution to this problem is to force businesses in a diversified firm to operate independently of each other. If each business operates independently, then it will be possible to unambiguously evaluate its performance. Of course, to the extent that this independence is enforced, the diversified firm is unlikely to be able to realize the very economies of scope that were the justification for the diversification strategy in the first place.

Divisional performance ambiguity is bad enough when shared activities are the primary economy of scope that a diversified firm is trying to exploit. This ambiguity increases dramatically when the economy of scope is based on intangible core competencies. In this situation, it is shared learning and experience that justify a firm's diversification efforts. The intangible nature of these economies of scope multiplies the difficulty of the divisional evaluation task.

Even firms that apply rigorous EVA measures of divisional performance are unable to fully resolve these performance ambiguity difficulties. For example, the Coca-Cola division of the Coca-Cola Company has made enormous investments in the Coke brand name over the years, and the Diet Coke division has exploited some of that brand name capital in its own marketing efforts. Of course, it is not clear that all of Diet Coke's success can be attributed to the Coke brand name. After all, Diet Coke has developed its own creative advertising, has developed its own loyal group of customers, and so forth. How much of Diet Coke's success—as measured through that division's economic value added—should be allocated to the Coke brand name (an investment made long before Diet Coke was even conceived), and how much should be allocated to the Diet Coke division's efforts? EVA measures of divisional performance do not resolve ambiguities created when economies of scope exist across divisions.[17]

In the end, the quantitative evaluation of divisional performance—with either accounting or economic measures—must be supplemented by the experience and judgment of senior executives in a diversified firm. Only by evaluating a division's performance numbers in the context of a broader, more subjective evaluation of the division's performance can a true picture of divisional performance be developed.

Allocating Corporate Capital

Another potentially valuable economy of scope outlined in Chapter 7 (besides shared activities and core competencies) is internal capital allocation. In that discussion, it was suggested that for internal capital allocation to be a justification for diversification, the information made available to senior executives allocating capital in a diversified firm must be superior, in both amount and quality, to the information available to external sources of capital in the external capital market. Both the quality and the quantity of the information available in an internal capital market depend on the organization of the diversified firm.

One of the primary limitations of internal capital markets is that division general managers have a strong incentive to overstate their division's prospects and understate its problems, in order to gain access to more capital at lower costs.

Having an independent corporate accounting function in a diversified firm can help address this problem. However, given the ambiguities inherent in evaluating divisional performance in a well-managed diversified firm, independent corporate accountants do not resolve all these informational problems.

In the face of these challenges, some firms use a process called **zero-based budgeting** to help allocate capital. In zero-based budgeting, corporate executives create a list of all capital allocation requests from divisions in a firm, rank them from "most important" to "least important," and then fund all the projects a firm can afford, given the amount of capital it has available. In principle, with zero-based budgeting, no project will receive funding for the future simply because it received funding in the past. Rather, each project has to stand on its own merits each year by being included among the important projects the firm can afford to fund.

While zero-based budgeting has some attractive features, it has some important limitations as well. For example, evaluating and ranking all projects in a diversified firm from "most important" to "least important" is a very difficult task. It requires corporate executives to have a very complete understanding of the strategic role of each of the projects being proposed by a division, as well as an understanding of how these projects will affect the short-term performance of divisions.

In the end, no matter what process firms use to allocate capital, allocating capital inside a firm in a way that is more efficient than what could be done by external capital markets requires the use of information that is not available to those external markets. Typically, that information will be intangible, tacit, and complex. Corporate managers looking to realize this economy of scope must find a way to use this kind of information effectively.[18] The difficulty of managing this process effectively may be one of the reasons why internal capital allocation often fails to qualify as a valuable economy of scope in diversified firms.[19]

Transferring Intermediate Products

The existence of economies of scope across multiple divisions in a diversified firm often means that products or services produced in one division are used as inputs for products or services produced by a second division. Such products or services are called **intermediate products or services**. Intermediate products or services can be transferred between any of the units in an M-form organization. This transfer is, perhaps, most important and problematic when it occurs between profit center divisions.

The transfer of intermediate products or services among divisions is usually managed through a **transfer-pricing system**: One division "sells" its product or service to a second division for a transfer price. Unlike a market price, which is typically determined by market forces of supply and demand, transfer prices are set by a firm's corporate management to accomplish corporate objectives.

Setting Optimal Transfer Prices

From an economic point of view, the rule for establishing the optimal transfer price in a diversified firm is quite simple: The transfer price should be the value of the opportunities forgone when one division's product or service is transferred to another division. Consider the following example. Division A's marginal cost of production is $5 per unit, but Division A can sell all of its output to outside customers for $6 per unit. If Division A can sell all of its output to outside customers for $6 per unit, the value of the opportunity forgone of transferring a unit of production from Division A to Division B is $6—the amount of money that Division A forgoes by transferring its production to Division B instead of selling it to the market.

However, if Division A is selling all the units it can to external customers for $6 per unit but still has some excess manufacturing capacity, the value of the opportunity forgone in transferring the product from Division A to Division B is only $5 per unit—Division A's marginal cost of production. Because the external market cannot absorb any more of Division A's product at $6 per unit, the value of the opportunity forgone when Division A transfers units of production to Division B is not $6 per unit (Division A can't get that price) but only $5 per unit.[20]

When transfer prices are set equal to opportunity costs, selling divisions will produce output up to the point that the marginal cost of the last unit produced equals the transfer price. Moreover, buying divisions will buy units from other divisions in the firm as long as the net revenues from doing so just cover the transfer price. These transfer prices will lead profit-maximizing divisions to optimize the diversified firm's profits.

Difficulties in Setting Optimal Transfer Prices

Setting transfer prices equal to opportunity costs sounds simple enough, but it is very difficult to do in real diversified firms. Establishing optimal transfer prices requires information about the value of the opportunities forgone by the "selling" division. This, in turn, requires information about this division's marginal costs, its manufacturing capacity, external demand for its products, and so forth. Much of this information is difficult to obtain. Moreover, it is rarely stable. As market conditions change, demand for a division's products can change, marginal costs can change, and the value of opportunities forgone can change. Also, to the extent that a selling division customizes the products or services it transfers to other divisions in a diversified firm, the value of the opportunities forgone by this selling division become even more difficult to calculate.

Even if this information could be obtained and updated rapidly, division general managers in selling divisions have strong incentives to manipulate the information in ways that increase the perceived value of the opportunities forgone by their division. These division general managers can thus increase the transfer price for the products or services they sell to internal customers and thereby appropriate for their division profits that should have been allocated to buying divisions.

Setting Transfer Prices in Practice

Because it is rarely possible for firms to establish an optimal transfer-pricing scheme, most diversified firms must adopt some form of transfer pricing that attempts to approximate optimal prices. Several of these transfer-pricing schemes are described in Table 8.3. However, no matter what particular schemes a firm uses, the transfer prices it generates will, at times, create inefficiencies and conflicts in a diversified firm. Some of these inefficiencies and conflicts are described in Table 8.4.[21]

The inefficiencies and conflicts created by transfer-pricing schemes that only approximate optimal transfer prices mean that few diversified firms are ever fully satisfied with how they set transfer prices. Indeed, one study found that as the level of resource sharing in a diversified firm increases (thereby increasing the importance of transfer-pricing mechanisms), the level of job satisfaction for division general managers decreases.[22]

It is not unusual for a diversified firm to change its transfer-pricing mechanisms every few years in an attempt to find the "right" transfer-pricing mechanism. Economic theory tells us what the "right" transfer-pricing mechanism is: Transfer prices should equal opportunity cost. However, this "correct" transfer-price mechanism cannot be implemented in most firms. Firms that continually change their transfer-pricing mechanisms generally find that all

Table 8.3   **Alternative Transfer Pricing Schemes**

Exchange autonomy	■ Buying and selling division general managers are free to negotiate transfer price without corporate involvement. ■ Transfer price is set equal to the selling division's price to external customers.
Mandated full cost	■ Transfer price is set equal to the selling division's actual cost of production. ■ Transfer price is set equal to the selling division's standard cost (that is, the cost of production if the selling division were operating at maximum efficiency).
Mandated market based	■ Transfer price is set equal to the market price in the selling division's market.
Dual pricing	■ Transfer price for the buying division is set equal to the selling division's actual or standard costs. ■ Transfer price for the selling division is set equal to the price to external customers or to the market price in the selling division's market.

Source: R. Eccles (1985). *The transfer pricing problem: A theory for practice.* Lexington, MA: Lexington Books. Used with permission of Rowman and Littlefield Publishing Group.

these systems have some weaknesses. In choosing which system to use, a firm should be less concerned about finding the right transfer-pricing mechanism and more concerned about choosing a transfer-pricing policy that creates the fewest management problems—or at least the kinds of problems that the firm can manage effectively. Indeed, some scholars have suggested that the search for optimal transfer pricing should be abandoned in favor of treating transfer pricing as a conflict resolution process. Viewed in this way, transfer pricing highlights differences between divisions and thus makes it possible to begin to resolve those differences in a mutually beneficial way.[23]

Table 8.4   **Weaknesses of Alternative Transfer-Pricing Schemes**

1. Buying and selling divisions negotiate transfer price.
   - ■ What about the negotiating and haggling costs?
   - ■ The corporation risks not exploiting economies of scope if the right transfer price cannot be negotiated.

2. Transfer price is set equal to the selling division's price to external customers.
   - ■ Which customers? Different selling division customers may get different prices.
   - ■ Shouldn't the volume created by the buying division for a selling division be reflected in a lower transfer price?
   - ■ The selling division doesn't have marketing expenses when selling to another division. Shouldn't that be reflected in a lower transfer price?

3. Transfer price is set equal to the selling division's actual costs.
   - ■ What are those actual costs, and who gets to determine them?
   - ■ *All* the selling division's costs, or only the costs relevant to the products being purchased by the buying division?

4. Transfer price is set equal to the selling division's standard costs.
   - ■ Standard costs are the costs the selling division would incur if it were running at maximum efficiency. This hypothetical capacity subsidizes the buying division.

5. Transfer price is set equal to the market price.
   - ■ If the product in question is highly differentiated, there is no simple "market price."
   - ■ Shouldn't the volume created by the buying division for a selling division be reflected in a lower transfer price?
   - ■ The selling division doesn't have marketing expenses when selling to a buying division. Shouldn't that be reflected in a lower transfer price?

6. Transfer price is set equal to actual costs for the selling division and to market price for the buying division.
   - ■ This combination of schemes simply combines other problems of setting transfer prices.

Overall, the three management control processes described here—measuring divisional performance, allocating corporate capital, and transferring intermediate products—suggest that the implementation of a corporate diversification requires a great deal of management skill and experience. They also suggest that sometimes diversified firms may find themselves operating businesses that no longer fit with the firm's overall corporate strategy. What happens when a division no longer fits with a firm's corporate strategy is described in the Strategy in the Emerging Enterprise feature.

Compensation Policies and Implementing Corporate Diversification

A firm's compensation policies constitute a final set of tools for implementing corporation diversification. Traditionally, the compensation of corporate managers in a diversified firm has been only loosely connected to the firm's economic performance. One important study examined the relationship between executive compensation and firm performance and found that differences in CEO cash compensation (salary plus cash bonus) are not very responsive to differences in firm performance.[24] In particular, this study showed that a CEO of a firm whose equity holders lost, collectively, $400 million in a year earned average cash compensation worth $800,000, while a CEO of a firm whose equity holders gained, collectively, $400 million in a year earned average cash compensation worth $1,040,000. Thus, an $800 million difference in the performance of a firm only had, on average, a $204,000 impact on the size of a CEO's salary and cash bonus. Put differently, for every million dollars of improved firm performance, CEOs, on average, get paid an additional $255. After taxes, increasing a firm's performance by a million dollars is roughly equal in value to a good dinner at a nice restaurant.

However, this same study was able to show that if a substantial percentage of a CEO's compensation came in the form of stock and stock options in the firm, changes in compensation would be closely linked with changes in the firm performance. In particular, the $800 million difference in firm performance just described would be associated with a $1.2 million difference in the value of CEO compensation, if CEO compensation included stock and stock options in addition to cash compensation. In this setting, an additional million dollars of firm performance increases a CEO's salary by $667.

These and similar findings reported elsewhere have led more and more diversified firms to include stock and stock options as part of the compensation package for the CEO. As important, many firms now extend this noncash compensation to other senior managers in a diversified firm, including division general managers. For example, the top 1,300 managers at General Dynamics receive stock and stock options as part of their compensation package. Moreover, the cash bonuses of these managers also depend on General Dynamics' stock market performance. At Johnson & Johnson, all division general managers receive a five-component compensation package. The level of only one of those components, salary, does not vary with the economic profitability of the business over which a division general manager presides. The level of the other four components—a cash bonus, stock grants, stock options, and a deferred income package—varies with the economic performance of a particular division. Moreover, the value of some of these variable components of compensation also depends on Johnson & Johnson's long-term economic performance.[25]

To the extent that compensation in diversified firms gives managers incentives to make decisions consistent with stockholders' interests, they can be an important part of the process of implementing corporate diversification. However, the sheer size of the compensation paid to some CEOs raises ethical issues for some. These ethical issues are discussed in the Ethics and Strategy feature on page 269.

Strategy in the Emerging Enterprise

A corporate spin-off exists when a large, typically diversified firm divests itself of a business in which it has historically been operating and the divested business operates as an independent entity. Thus, corporate spin-offs are different from asset divestitures, where a firm sells some of its assets, including perhaps a particular business, to another firm. Spin-offs are a way that new firms can enter into the economy.

Spin-offs can occur in numerous ways. For example, a business might be sold to its managers and employees who then manage and work in this independently operating firm. Alternatively, a business unit within a diversified firm may be sold to the public through an **initial public offering**, or **IPO**. Sometimes, the corporation spinning a business unit off will retain some ownership stake in the spin-off; other times, this corporation will sever all financial links with the spun-off firm.

In general, there are three broad reasons why large diversified firms might spin off businesses they own. First, the efficient management of these businesses may require very specific skills that are not available in a diversified firm. For example, suppose a diversified manufacturing firm finds itself operating in an R&D-intensive industry. The management skills required to manage manufacturing efficiently can be very different from the management skills required to manage R&D. If a diversified firm's skills do not match the skills required in a particular business, that business might be spun off.

Second, anticipated economies of scope between a business and the rest of a diversified firm may turn out to not be valuable. For example, PepsiCo acquired Kentucky Fried Chicken, Pizza Hut, and

Transforming Big Business into Entrepreneurship

Taco Bell, anticipating important marketing synergies between these fast-food restaurants and PepsiCo's soft drink business. Despite numerous efforts to realize these synergies, they were not forthcoming. Indeed, several of these fast-food restaurants began losing market share because they were forced to sell Pepsi rather than Coca-Cola products. After a few years, PepsiCo spun off its restaurants into a separate business.

Finally, it may be necessary to spin a business off in order to fund other of a firm's businesses. Large diversified firms may face capital constraints due to, among other things, their high level of debt. In this setting, firms may need to spin off a business in order to raise capital to invest in other parts of the firm. Moreover, spinning off a part of the business that is particularly costly in terms of the capital it consumes may not only be a source of funds for other parts of this firm's business; it can also reduce the demand for that capital within a firm.

Research in corporate finance suggests that corporations are most likely to spin off businesses that are unrelated to a firm's corporate diversification strategy; those that are poorly performing compared to other businesses a firm operates in; and relatively small businesses. Also, the amount of merger and acquisition activity in a particular industry will determine which businesses are spun off. The greater the level of this activity in an industry, the more likely that a business owned by a corporation in such an industry will be spun off. This is because the level of merger and acquisition activity in an industry is an indicator of the number of people and firms that might be interested in purchasing a spun-off business. On the other hand, when there is not much merger and acquisition activity in an industry, businesses in that industry are less likely to be spun off, even if they are unrelated to a firm's corporate diversification strategy, are poorly performing, or small. In such settings, large firms are not likely to obtain the full value associated with spinning off a business and thus are reluctant to do so.

Whatever the conditions that lead a large diversified firm to spin off one of its businesses, this process is important for creating new firms in the economy.

Sources: F. Schlingemann, R. Stulz, and R. Walkling (2002). "Divestitures and the liquidity of the market for corporate assets." *Journal of Financial Economics*, 64, pp. 117–144; G. Hite, J. Owens, and R. Rogers (1987). "The market for inter-firm asset sales: Partial sell-offs and total liquidations." *Journal of Financial Economics*, 18, pp. 229–252; P. Berger and E. Ofek (1999). "Causes and consequences of corporate focusing programs." *Review of Financial Studies*, 12, pp. 311–345.

Organizing to Implement Corporate Diversification in an International Context

Since international strategies are really just a special case of corporate diversification strategies, it follows that many of the issues firms face in implementing corporate diversification strategies would also exist for firms implementing international strategies. It also follows that many of the organizational tools used to implement corporate diversification strategies can be used to implement international strategies.

Despite these similarities, there are some differences between how corporate diversification within a country and corporate diversification across multiple countries is implemented. Differences in organizational structure, management controls, and compensation policies will all be briefly discussed.

Firms pursuing an international strategy have four basic organizational structural alternatives, listed in Table 8.5 and discussed later. Although each of these structures has some special features, they are all special cases of the M-form structure.

Some firms organize their international operations as a **decentralized federation**. In this organizational structure, each country in which a firm operates is organized as a full profit-and-loss division headed by a division general manager who is typically the president of the company in that particular country. In a decentralized federation, there are very few shared activities or other economies of scope among different divisions or country companies; corporate headquarters plays a limited strategic role. Corporate staff functions are generally limited to the collection of accounting and other performance information from divisions or country companies and to reporting this aggregate information to appropriate government officials and to financial markets. Most employees within the divisions or country companies in a decentralized federation may not even be aware that they are part of a larger, internationally diversified firm. Both strategic and operational decision making are delegated to division general managers or country company presidents in a decentralized federation organizational structure. There are relatively few examples of pure decentralized federations in today's world economy, but firms like Nestlé, CIBA-Geigy, and Electrolux have many of the attributes of this type of structure.

A second structural option for international firms is the **coordinated federation**. In a coordinated federation, each country operation is organized as a full profit-and-loss center, and division general managers can be presidents of country companies. However, unlike the case in a decentralized federation, strategic and operational decisions are not fully delegated to division general managers. Operational decisions are delegated to division general managers or country presidents, but broader strategic decisions are made at corporate headquarters.

Table 8.5 **Structural Options for Firms Pursuing International Strategies**

Decentralized federation	Strategic and operational decisions are delegated to divisions or country companies.
Coordinated federation	Operational decisions are delegated to divisions or country companies; strategic decisions are retained at corporate headquarters.
Centralized hub	Strategic and operational decisions are retained at corporate headquarters.
Transnational structure	Strategic and operational decisions are delegated to those operational entities that maximize responsiveness to local conditions and international integration.

Sources: C. A. Bartlett, and S. Ghoshal (1989). *Managing across borders: The transnational solution.* Boston: Harvard Business School Press.

Ethics and Strategy

Steve Jobs, CEO of Apple Computer, was hailed as a modern-day hero when he refused to accept any salary upon returning, in 1997, to the firm he founded. At the time, Apple was going through some rough times. People were being laid off, investments in new technologies curtailed. And Steve Jobs, being sensitive to the economic condition of the firm—and being already independently wealthy—decided to take the radical step of receiving no salary.

However, six years later, in 2003, Steve Jobs—although he still received no regular salary—received $74.8 million in total compensation. Assuming that Mr. Jobs worked 50 hours a week and took two weeks' vacation, this means that he earned just under $30,000 an hour in 2003. Even if this total is considered as compensation for his six years of service at Apple, Steve Jobs still earned—based on his 2003 compensation—the equivalent of $5,000 per hour since he returned to Apple in 1997.

But Jobs did not receive the highest hourly pay of a CEO in 2003. He was only number two. Number one was Reuben Mark, CEO of Colgate-Palmolive. Again, assuming he worked 50 hours a week for 50 weeks, Mr. Mark earned $56,440 per hour. Of this income, $5.1 million came in the form of salary and bonus and $136 million came in the form of long-term compensation—stock, stock options, and so forth.

Of course, what is remarkable about the hourly incomes of Steve Jobs and Reuben Mark is that they are not all that remarkable. The CEO of United

When Is Enough Too Much?

Technologies earned $28,200 per hour, the CEO of Cendant earned $21,700 per hour, the CEO of Citigroup earned $21,640 per hour, and so forth. Indeed, the average hourly wage of the top 20 highest paid CEOs in the United States in 2003 was $18,619. To put that in a different context, the median family income in the United States in 2002 was $42,409. This means that the average top paid CEO in the United States in 2003 needed to work just over two hours and fifteen minutes to earn as much as the median family in the United States.

These levels of compensation would seem more reasonable if they were closely tied to the performance of a firm. Of course, some are. For example, during his time as CEO of Colgate-Palmolive, Mr. Mark helped increase this firm's stock price by 286 percent, compared to the 114 percent gain of the

Standard & Poor's 500 Stock Index over the same time period. But the overall correlation between CEO compensation and firm performance is not very high. For example, Margaret Whitman (CEO of eBay) was paid "only" $3.4 million even though shareholders of eBay earned a 292 percent return in 2003, while Larry Elison (CEO of Oracle) was paid $746.7 million even though shareholders of Oracle lost 54 percent of the value of their investment in the firm. Warren Buffett (CEO of Berkshire Hathaway) was paid only $1 million while his investors received a 19 percent return on their investment; Jozef Straus (CEO of JDS Uniphase) was paid $151.9 million while his investors received a negative 91 percent return on their investment.

Apologists for these high levels of CEO compensation suggest that they simply reflect the result of market forces in the labor market for CEOs. An alternative explanation is that high CEO compensation, especially when it is unrelated to a firm's performance, may reflect more of a CEO's power and influence over his/her board of directors than any competitive market process. If the latter explanation is true, such levels of CEO compensation may not be consistent with the interests of a firm's equity holders.

Moreover, all of this begs the simple moral question: Is anyone really worth $56,000 an hour?

Sources: L. Lavelle (2004). "Executive pay." *BusinessWeek*, April 19, pp. 106 +; S. Finkelstein and D. C. Hambrick (1996). "Chief executive compensation: A study of the intersection of markets and political processes." *Strategic Management Journal*, 10, pp. 121–134.

Moreover, coordinated federations attempt to exploit various shared activities and other economies of scope among their divisions or country companies. It is not uncommon for coordinated federations to have corporately sponsored central research and development laboratories, corporately sponsored manufacturing and technology development initiatives, and corporately sponsored management training and development operations. There are numerous examples of coordinated federations in today's world economy, including General Electric, General Motors, IBM, and Coca-Cola.

A third structural option for international firms is the **centralized hub**. In centralized hubs, operations in different companies may be organized into profit-and-loss centers, and division general managers may be country company presidents. However, most of the strategic and operational decision making in these firms takes place at the corporate center. The role of divisions or country companies in centralized hubs is simply to implement the strategies, tactics, and policies that have been chosen at headquarters. Of course, divisions or country companies are also a source of information for headquarters staff when these decisions are being made. However, in centralized hubs, strategic and operational decision rights are retained at the corporate center. Many Japanese and Korean firms are managed as centralized hubs, including Toyota, Mitsubishi, and NEC (in Japan) and Goldstar, Daewoo, and Hyundai (in Korea).

A fourth structural option for international firms is the **transnational structure**. This structure is most appropriate for implementing the transnational strategy described in previous chapters. In many ways, the transnational structure is similar to the coordinated federation. In both, strategic decision-making responsibility is largely retained at the corporate center, and operational decision making is largely delegated to division general managers or country presidents. However, important differences also exist.

In a coordinated federation structure, shared activities and other cross-divisional or cross-country economies of scope are managed by the corporate center. Thus, for many of these firms, if research and development is seen as a potentially valuable economy of scope, a central research and development laboratory is created and managed by the corporate center. In the transnational structure, these centers of corporate economies of scope may be managed by the corporate center. However, they are more likely to be managed by specific divisions or country companies within the corporation. Thus, for example, if one division or country company develops valuable, rare, and costly-to-imitate research and development capabilities in its ongoing business activities in a particular country, that division or country company could become the center of research and development activity for the entire corporation. If one division or country company develops valuable, rare, and costly-to-imitate manufacturing technology development skills in its ongoing business activities in a particular country, that division or country company could become the center for manufacturing technology development for the entire corporation.

The role of corporate headquarters in a transnational structure is to constantly scan business operations across different countries for resources and capabilities that might be a source of competitive advantage for other divisions or country companies in the firm. Once these special skills are located, corporate staff must then determine the best way to exploit these economies of scope—whether they should be developed within a single division or country company (to gain economies of scale) and then transferred to other divisions or country companies, or developed through an alliance between two or more divisions or country companies (to gain economies of scale) and then transferred to other divisions or country companies, or redeveloped for the entire firm at corporate headquarters. These options are not available to decentralized federations (which always allow individual divisions or country companies to develop their own competencies), coordinated federations, or centralized hubs (which always develop corporate-wide economies of scope at the corporate level). Firms that have been successful in adopting this transnational structure include Ford (Ford Europe has become a leader for automobile design in all of the Ford Motor Company) and Ericson (Ericson's Australian subsidiary developed this Swedish company's first electronic telecommunication switch, and corporate headquarters was able to help transfer this technology to other Ericson subsidiaries).

It should be clear that the choice among these four approaches to managing international strategies depends on the trade-offs that firms are willing to make between local responsiveness and international integration (see Figure 8.3). Firms that seek to maximize their local responsiveness will tend to choose a decentralized federation structure. Firms that seek to maximize international integration in their operations will typically opt for centralized hub structures. Firms that seek to balance the need for local responsiveness and international integration will typically choose centralized federations. Firms that attempt to optimize both local responsiveness and international integration will choose a transnational organizational structure.

Of course, none of the organizational structures described in Table 8.5 can stand alone without the support of a variety of management control systems and management compensation policies. All the management control processes discussed previously, including evaluating the performance of divisions, allocating capital, and managing the exchange of intermediate products among divisions, are also important for firms organizing to implement an international strategy. Moreover, the same management compensation challenges and opportunities discussed previously apply in the organization of international strategies as well.

However, as is often the case when organizing processes originally developed to manage diversification within a domestic market are extended to the management of international diversification, many of the management challenges highlighted earlier in this chapter are exacerbated in an international context. This puts an even greater burden on senior managers in an internationally diversified firm to choose control systems and compensation policies that create incentives for division general managers or country presidents to appropriately cooperate to realize the economies of scope that originally motivated the implementation of an international strategy.

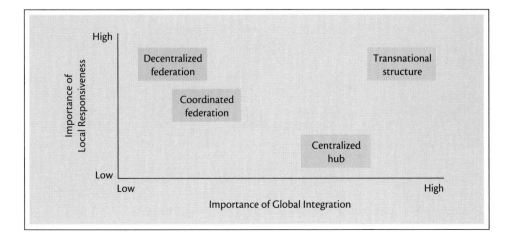

Figure 8.3 Local Responsiveness, International Integration, and Organizational Structure

Sources: From R. Grant (1991). *Contemporary strategy analysis.* Cambridge, MA: Basil Blackwell. Reprinted with permission.

SUMMARY

To be valuable, diversification strategies must exploit valuable economies of scope that cannot be duplicated by outside investors at low cost. However, to realize the value of these economies of scope, firms must organize themselves appropriately. A firm's organizational structure, its management control processes, and its compensation policies are all relevant in implementing a corporate diversification strategy.

The best organizational structure for implementing a diversification leveraging strategy is the multidivisional, or M-form, structure. The M-form structure has several critical components including the board of directors, institutional investors, the senior executive, corporate staff, division general managers, and shared activity managers.

This organizational structure is supported by a variety of management control processes. Three critical management control processes for firms implementing diversification strategies are (1) evaluating the performance of divisions, (2) allocating capital across divisions, and (3) transferring intermediate products between divisions. The existence of economies of scope in firms implementing corporate diversification strategies significantly complicates the management of these processes.

Finally, a firm's compensation policies are also important for firms implementing a diversification strategy. Historically, management compensation has been only loosely connected to a firm's economic performance, but the last few years have seen the increased popularity of using stock and stock options to help compensate managers. Such compensation schemes help reduce conflicts between managers and outside investors, but the absolute level of CEO compensation is still very high, at least in the United States.

These same implementation issues exist for firms looking to diversify their operations internationally. In this international context, firms can choose between a decentralized federation, a coordinated federation, a centralized hub, and a transnational organizational structure. The effectiveness of these different approaches depends on the relative importance of local responsiveness and global integration.

CHALLENGE QUESTIONS

1. Agency theory has been criticized for assuming that managers, left on their own, will behave in ways that reduce the wealth of outside equity holders when, in fact, most managers are highly responsible stewards of the assets they control. This alternative view of managers has been called *stewardship theory*. Do you agree with this criticism of agency theory? Why or why not?

2. Suppose that the concept of the stewardship theory is correct and that most managers, most of the time, behave responsibly and make decisions that maximize the present value of the assets they control. What implications, if any, would this supposition have on organizing to implement diversification strategies?

3. The M-form structure enables firms to pursue complex corporate diversification strategies by delegating different management responsibilities to different individuals and groups within a firm. Will there come a time when a firm becomes too large and too complex to be managed even through an M-form structure? In other words, is there a natural limit to the efficient size of a diversified firm?

4. Most observers agree that centrally planned economies fail because it is impossible for bureaucrats in large government hierarchies to coordinate different sectors of an economy as efficiently as market mechanisms do. Many diversified firms, however, are as large as some economies and use private sector hierarchies to coordinate diverse business activities in a firm. Are these large, private sector hierarchies somehow different from the government hierarchies of centrally planned economies? If yes, in what way? If no, why do these large, private sector hierarchies continue to exist?

5. Suppose that the optimal transfer price between one business and all other business activities in a firm is the market price. What does this condition say about whether this firm should own this business?

6. Suppose a firm pursuing an international diversification strategy requires neither local responsiveness nor global integration to realize valuable economies of scope that cannot be duplicated by outside equity holders at low cost. What type of organizational structure should this firm pursue?

PROBLEM SET

1. Which elements of the M-form structure (the board of directors, the office of the CEO, corporate staff, division general managers, shared activity managers) should be involved in the following business activities? If more than one of these groups should be involved, indicate their relative level of involvement (e.g., 20 percent office of the CEO, 10 percent shared activity manager, 70 percent division general manager). Justify your answers.

(a) Determining the compensation of the CEO.
(b) Determining the compensation of the Corporate Vice President of Human Resources.
(c) Determining the compensation of a Vice President of Human Resources in a particular business division.
(d) Deciding to sell a business division.
(e) Deciding to buy a relatively small firm whose activities are closely related to the activities of one of the firm's current divisions.
(f) Deciding to buy a larger firm that is not closely related to the activities of any of a firm's current divisions.
(g) Evaluating the performance of the Vice President of Sales, a manager whose sales staff sells the products of three divisions in the firm.
(h) Evaluating the performance of the Vice President of Sales, a manager whose sales staff sells the products of only one division in the firm.
(i) How much money to invest in a corporate R&D function.

(j) How much money to invest in an R&D function that supports the operations of two divisions within the firm.

(k) Whether or not to fire an R&D scientist.

(l) Whether or not to fire the Vice President of Accounting in a particular division.

(m) Whether or not to fire the corporation's Vice President of Accounting.

(n) The decision to take a firm public by selling stock in the firm to the general public for the first time.

2. Consider the following facts. Division A in a firm has generated $847,000 of profits on $24 million worth of sales, using $32 million worth of dedicated assets. The cost of capital for this firm is 9 percent, and the firm has invested $7.3 million in this division.

(a) Calculate the ROS and ROA of Division A. If the hurdle rate for ROS and ROA in this firm are, respectively, .06 and .04, has this division performed well?

(b) Calculate the EVA of Division A (assuming that the reported profits have already been adjusted). Based on this EVA has this division performed well?

(c) Suppose you were CEO of this firm, how would you choose between ROS/ROA and EVA for evaluating this division?

3. Suppose that Division A sells an intermediate product to Division B. Choose one of the ways of determining transfer prices described in this chapter (not setting transfer prices equal to the selling firm's opportunity costs) and show how Division Manager A can use this mechanism to justify a higher transfer price, while Division Manager B can use this mechanism to justify a lower transfer price. Repeat this exercise with another approach to setting transfer prices described in the chapter.

END NOTES

1. The structure and function of the multidimensional firm was first described by Chandler, A. (1962). *Strategy and structure: Chapters in the history of the industrial enterprise.* Cambridge, MA: MIT Press; The economic logic underlying the multidimensional firm was first described by Williamson, O. E. (1975). *Markets and hierarchies: Analysis and antitrust implications.* New York: Free Press; Empirical examinations of the impact of the M-form or firm performance include Armour, H. O., and D. J. Teece (1980). "Vertical integration and technological innovation." *Review of Economics and Statistics,* 60, pp. 470–474; There continues to be some debate about the efficiency of the M-form structure. See Freeland, R. F. (1966). "The myth of the M-form? Governance, consent, and organizational change." *American Journal of Sociology,* 102(2), pp. 483–626; and Shanley, M. (1996). "Straw men and M-form myths: Comment on Freeland." *American Journal of Sociology,* 102(2), pp. 527–536.

2. See Finkelstein, S., and R. D'Aveni (1994). "CEO duality as a double-edged sword: How boards of directors balance entrenchment avoidance and unity of command." *Academy of Management Journal,* 37, pp. 1079–1108.

3. Kesner, I. F. (1988). "Director's characteristics and committee membership: An investigation of type, occupation, tenure and gender." *Academy of Management Journal,* 31, pp. 66–84; Zahra, S. A., and J. A. Pearce II (1989). "Boards of directors and corporate financial performance: A review and integrative model." *Journal of Management,* 15, pp. 291–334.

4. *Investor Relations Business* (2000). "Reversal of fortune: Institutional ownership is declining," May 1, pp. 8–9; Federal Reserve Board (2004). "Flow of funds report."

5. See Hansen, G. S., and C. W. L. Hill (1991). "Are institutional investors myopic? A time-series study of four technology-driven industries." *Strategic Management Journal,* 12, pp. 1–16.

6. See Bergh, D. (1995). "Size and relatedness of units sold: An agency theory and resource-based perspective." *Strategic Management Journal,* 16, pp. 221–239; and Bethel, J., and J. Liebeskind (1993). "The effects of ownership structure on corporate restructuring." *Strategic Management Journal,* 14, pp. 15–31.

7. Burdens that are well described by Westley, F., and H. Mintzberg (1989). "Visionary leadership and strategic management." *Strategic Management Journal,* 10, pp. 17–32.

8. See Dumaine, B. (1992). "Is big still good?" *Fortune,* April 20, pp. 50–60.

9. See Golden, B. (1992). "SBU strategy and performance: The moderating effects of the corporate–SBU relationship." *Strategic Management Journal,* 13, pp. 145–158; Berger, P., and E. Otek (1995). "Diversification effect on firm value." *Journal of Financial Economics,* 37, pp. 36–65; Lang, H. P., and R. Stulz (1994). "Tobin's q, corporate diversification, and firm performance." *Journal of Political Economy,* 102, pp. 1248–1280; Rumelt, R. (1991). "How much does industry matter?" *Strategic Management Journal,* 12, pp. 167–185.

10. See Halal, W. (1994). "From hierarchy to enterprise: Internal markets are the new foundation of management." *The Academy of Management Executive,* 8(4), pp. 69–83.

11. Bartlett, C., and S. Ghoshal (1993). "Beyond the M-form: Toward a managerial theory of the firm." *Strategic Management Journal,* 14, pp. 23–46.

12. See Simons, R. (1994). "How new top managers use control systems as levers of strategic renewal." *Strategic Management Journal,* 15, pp. 169–189.

13. Bethel, J. E. (1990). "The capital allocation process and managerial mobility: A theoretical and empirical investigation." Unpublished doctoral dissertation, UCLA.

14. Some of these are described in Duffy, M. (1989). "ZBB, MBO, PPB, and their effectiveness within the planning/marketing process." *Strategic Management Journal*, 12, pp. 155–160.

15. See Stern, J., B. Stewart, and D. Chew (1995). "The EVA financial management system." *Journal of Applied Corporate Finance*, 8, pp. 32–46; and Tully, S. (1993). "The real key to creating wealth." *Fortune*, September 20, pp. 38–50.

16. Applications of EVA are described in Tully, S. (1993). "The real key to creating wealth." *Fortune*, September 20, pp. 38–50; Tully, S. (1995). "So, Mr. Bossidy, we know you can cut. Now show us how to grow." *Fortune*, August 21, pp. 70–80; Tully, S. (1995). "Can EVA deliver profits to the post office?" *Fortune*, July 10, p. 22.

17. A special issue of the *Journal of Applied Corporate Finance* in 1994 addressed many of these issues.

18. See Priem, R. (1990). "Top management team group factors, consensus, and firm performance." *Strategic Management Journal*, 11, pp. 469–478; and Wooldridge, B., and S. Floyd (1990). "The strategy process, middle management involvement, and organizational performance." *Strategic Management Journal*, 11, pp. 231–241.

19. A point made by Westley, F. (1900). "Middle managers and strategy: Microdynamics of inclusion." *Strategic Management Journal*, 11, pp. 337–351; Lamont, O. (1997). "Cash flow and investment: Evidence from internal capital markets." *The Journal of Finance*. 52(1), pp. 83–109; Shin, H. H., and R. M. Stulz (1998). "Are internal capital markets efficient?" *Quarterly Journal of Economics*, May,

pp. 531–552; and Stein, J. C. (1997). "Internal capital markets and the competition for corporate resources." *The Journal of Finance*, 52(1), pp. 111–133.

20. See Brickley, J., C. Smith, and J. Zimmerman (1996). *Organizational architecture and managerial economics approach*. Homewood, IL: Irwin; and Eccles, R. (1985). *The transfer pricing problem: A theory for practice*. Lexington, MA: Lexington Books.

21. See Cyert, R., and J. G. March (1963). *A behavioral theory of the firm*. Upper Saddle River, NJ: Prentice Hall; Swieringa, R. J., and J. H. Waterhouse (1982). "Organizational views of transfer pricing." *Accounting, Organizations & Society*, 7(2), pp. 149–165; and Eccles, R. (1985). *The transfer pricing problem: A theory for practice*. Lexington, MA: Lexington Books.

22. Gupta, A. K., and V. Govindarajan (1986). "Resource sharing among SBUs: Strategic antecedents and administrative implications." *Academy of Management Journal*, 29, pp. 695–714.

23. A point made by Swieringa, R. J., and J. H. Waterhouse (1982). "Organizational views of transfer pricing." *Accounting, Organizations and Society*, 7(2), pp. 149–165.

24. Jensen, M. C., and K. J. Murphy (1990). "Performance pay and top management incentives." *Journal of Political Economy*, 98, pp. 225–264.

25. See Dial, J., and K. J. Murphy (1995). "Incentive, downsizing, and value creation at General Dynamics." *Journal of Financial Economics*, 37, pp. 261–314, on General Dynamics' compensation scheme, and Aguilar, F. J., and A. Bhambri (1983). "Johnson & Johnson (A)." Harvard Business School Case No. 384-053, on Johnson & Johnson's compensation scheme.

9

Strategic Alliances

Sex and the City, *The Sopranos,* and *Band of Brothers*—all these programs have at least three things in common. First, they have all been among the most critically acclaimed programs on television. *Sex and the City* routinely earned the Emmy for Best Comedy Series, *The Sopranos* was nominated for the Best Dramatic Series Emmy every year it was on television, and *Band of Brothers*—a ten-part mini-series that documents the history of the 101st Airborne during World War II—won numerous Emmys the

Original Programming at HBO

year it was broadcast. Second, they have been among the most-watched shows on cable television. Indeed, in its fourth year, *The Sopranos* became the most-watched series ever on premium cable television and led

HBO to its highest ratings ever. Finally, all three of these shows were co-produced by HBO—a division of AOL Time Warner—through HBO's Original Programming Division.

This has not always been the case. Originally, HBO presented only material produced by others—in particular, movies. Indeed, for many years, competition between HBO and other premium cable channels focused exclusively on which of these channels would gain the broadcast rights to which movies. The resulting competition

Learning Objectives

After reading this chapter, you should be able to:

1. Define a strategic alliance and give three specific examples of strategic alliances.

2. Describe nine different ways that alliances can create value for firms and how these nine sources of value can be grouped into three large categories.

3. Describe how adverse selection, moral hazard, and hold-up can threaten the ability of alliances to generate value.

4. Describe the conditions under which a strategic alliance can be rare and costly to directly duplicate.

5. Describe the conditions under which "going it alone" and acquisitions are not likely to be substitutes for alliances.

6. Describe how contracts, equity investments, firm reputations, joint ventures, and trust can all reduce the threat of cheating in strategic alliances.

7. Describe the role of strategic alliances in an international context.

led to substantial increases in rights fees—the fee a cable channel pays a movie's producers for the right to broadcast that movie. This competition hurt the profitability of many premium cable channels, including HBO.

However, beginning in the mid-1990s, HBO began producing, or co-producing, its own programming. This began slowly, with a few low-budget movies and sports programs (e.g., *NFL This Week* and various boxing matches). However, by the late 1990s, original programming had become an important part of HBO's weekly schedule. Most of this original programming was produced through partnerships between HBO Original Productions and independent production companies, including Steven Spielberg's production company Dreamworks and Tom Hanks's production company Playtone. And in the summer of 2003, HBO announced that it would enter into similar partnerships to begin producing movies for theatrical release.

The entry of HBO into partnerships to produce original programming has increased its prof-

itability. It has also shifted the basis of competition in the premium cable market from "Who can broadcast the biggest movies?"—a competition that was making movie producers wealthy but reducing the profits of premium cable channel companies—to "Who can develop the most cutting-edge, provocative, and popular entertainment on television?"

This shift in strategy at HBO has also had an impact on the content of broadcast network shows. ABC, NBC, CBS, Fox, and the WB have all had to increase the quality and "cutting-edge" feel of their series and other programs if these programs are to attract viewers away from the shows broadcast on HBO. Shows like *Frasier, Will and Grace, NYPD Blue, Law and Order, The West Wing, 24,* and *Boomtown* have all incorporated comedic and dramatic elements first pioneered on television in shows co-produced by HBO.

While HBO is now committed to using partnerships to co-produce much of its entertainment programming, other premium channels have not yet made such a commitment. For example, Cinemax (a division of HBO), Starz (a 12-channel premium service), and the Sundance Channel all have very little self-produced content. Indeed, the only other premium cable chan-nels that are following HBO's lead are Showtime—the second-largest premium cable channel—and the Independent Film Channel—which has begun investing in the production of independent films for theatrical release.

Sources: www.AOLTW.com; www.HBO.com.

H BO's decision to begin producing its own shows is an example of a backward vertical integration decision—the kind of decision discussed in Chapter 6. However, rather than fully incorporating the production process within its boundaries, HBO uses partnerships with independent producers to create virtually all of its original content. These partnerships are an example of strategic alliances.

The use of strategic alliances to manage economic exchanges has grown substantially over the last several years. In the early 1990s, strategic alliances were relatively uncommon, except in a few industries—including the entertainment industry. However, by the late 1990s, they had become much more common in a wide variety of industries. High-technology firms like IBM and Cisco were creating alliances with hundreds of partners. Over 450 alliances between large pharmaceutical firms and biotechnology firms were created in 1997 and 1998 alone. Even firms in more traditional industries—including firms in the U.S. automobile indus-try—began using alliances to manage their international expansion. Currently, alliances account for over 35 percent of the revenue of the largest 1,000 firms in the United States.[1]

What Is a Strategic Alliance?

A **strategic alliance** exists whenever two or more independent organizations cooperate in the development, manufacture, or sale of products or services. As shown in Figure 9.1, strategic alliances can be grouped into three broad categories: nonequity alliances, equity alliances, and joint ventures.

In a **nonequity alliance**, cooperating firms agree to work together to develop, manufacture, or sell products or services, but they do not take equity positions in each other or form an independent organizational unit to manage their cooperative efforts. Rather, these cooperative relations are managed through the use of various forms of contracts. **Licensing agreements** (where one firm allows others to use its brand name to sell products), **supply agreements** (where one firm agrees to supply others), and **distribution agreements** (where one firm agrees to distribute the products of others) are examples of nonequity strategic alliances. Most of the alliances between HBO and independent producers take the form of nonequity supply agreements.

In an **equity alliance**, cooperating firms supplement contracts with equity holdings in alliance partners. For example, when General Motors began importing small cars manufactured by Isuzu, not only did these partners have supply con-

Figure 9.1 Types of
Strategic Alliances

tracts in place, but GM purchased 34.2 percent of Isuzu's stock. Ford had a similar relationship with Mazda, and DaimlerChrysler had a similar relationship with Mitsubishi.[2] Equity alliances are also very common in the biotechnology industry. Large pharmaceutical firms like Pfizer and Merck own equity positions in several start-up biotechnology companies.

In a **joint venture**, cooperating firms create a legally independent firm in which they invest and from which they share any profits that are created. Some of these joint ventures can be very large. For example, Dow and Corning's joint venture Dow-Corning is a *Fortune* 500 company on its own. SBC and BellSouth are co-owners of the joint venture Cingular, one of the largest wireless phone companies in the United States—especially after its recent acquisition of AT&T Wireless Service. And CFM—a joint venture between General Electric and SNECMA (a French Aerospace firm)—is one of the world's leading manufacturers of jet engines for commercial aircraft. If you have ever flown on a Boeing 737, then you have placed your life in the hands of this joint venture because it manufactures the engines for virtually all of these aircraft.

How Do Strategic Alliances Create Value?

Like all the strategies discussed in this book, strategic alliances create value by exploiting opportunities and neutralizing threats facing a firm. Some of the most important opportunities that can be exploited by strategic alliances are listed in Table 9.1. Threats to strategic alliances are discussed later in this chapter.

Strategic Alliance Opportunties

Opportunities associated with strategic alliances fall into three large categories. First, these alliances can be used by a firm to improve the performance of their current operations. Second, alliances can be used to create a competitive environment favorable to superior firm performance. Finally, they can be used to facilitate a firm's entry into or exit from new markets or industries.

Table 9.1   **Ways Strategic Alliances Can Create Economic Value**

Helping firms improve the performance of their current operations
1. Exploiting economies of scale
2. Learning from competitors
3. Managing risk and sharing costs

Creating a competitive environment favorable to superior performance
4. Facilitating the development of technology standards
5. Facilitating tacit collusion

Facilitating entry and exit
6. Low-cost entry into new industries and new industry segments
7. Low-cost exit from industries and industry segments
8. Managing uncertainty
9. Low-cost entry into new markets

Improving Current Operations

One way that firms can use strategic alliances to improve their current operations is to use alliances to realize economies of scale. The concept of economies of scale was first introduced in Chapter 2. **Economies of scale** exist when the per unit cost of production falls as the volume of production increases. Thus, for example, while the per unit cost of producing one Bic pen would be very high, the per unit costs of producing 50 million Bic pens can be very low.

To realize economies of scale, firms have to have a large volume of production, or at least a volume of production large enough so that the cost advantages associated with scale can be realized. Sometimes—as was described in Chapters 2 and 4—a firm can realize these economies of scale by itself; other times, it can't. When a firm cannot realize the cost savings from economies of scale all by itself, it may join in a strategic alliance with other firms. Jointly, these firms may have sufficient volume to be able to gain the cost advantages of economies of scale.

But, why wouldn't a firm be able to realize these economies all by itself? There are several reasons why a firm may have to turn to alliance partners to help realize economies of scale. For example, if the volume of production required to realize these economies is very large, a single firm might have to dominate an entire industry in order to obtain these advantages. It is often very difficult for a single firm to obtain such a dominant position in an industry. And even if it does so, it may be subject to anti-monopoly regulation by the government. Also, while a particular part or technology may be very important to several firms, no one of these firms may generate sufficient demand for this part or technology to realize economies of scale in its development and production. In this setting as well, independent firms may join together to form an alliance to realize economies of scale in the development and production of the part or technology.

Firms can also use alliances to improve their current operations by learning from their competitors. As suggested in Chapter 3, different firms in an industry may have different resources and capabilities. These resources can give some firms competitive advantages over others. Firms that are at a competitive disadvantage may want to form alliances with the firms that have an advantage in order to learn about their resources and capabilities.

General Motors formed this kind of alliance with Toyota. In the early 1990s, GM and Toyota jointly invested in a previously closed General Motors plant in Fremont, California. This joint venture—called NUMI—was to build compact cars to be distributed through GM's distribution network. But why did GM decide to build these cars in an alliance with Toyota? Obviously, it could have built them in any of its own plants. However, GM was very interested in learning about how Toyota was able to manufacture high-quality small cars at a profit. Indeed, in the NUMI plant, Toyota agreed to take total responsibility for the manufacturing process, using former General Motors employees to install and operate the "lean manufacturing" system that had enabled Toyota to become the quality leader in the small-car segment of the automobile industry. However, Toyota also agreed to let GM managers work in the plant and directly observe how Toyota managed this production process. Since its inception, GM has rotated thousands of its managers from other GM plants through the NUMI plant so that they can be exposed to Toyota's lean manufacturing methods.

It's clear why GM would want this alliance with Toyota. But, why would Toyota want this alliance with GM? Certainly, Toyota was not looking to learn about lean manufacturing, per se. However, since Toyota was contemplating entering the United States by building its own manufacturing facilities, it did need to learn how to implement lean manufacturing in the United States with U.S. employees. Thus, Toyota also had something to learn from this alliance.

When both parties to an alliance are seeking to learn something from that alliance, an interesting dynamic called a "learning race" can evolve. This dynamic is described in more detail in the Strategy in Depth feature.

Finally, firms can use alliances to improve their current operations through sharing costs and risks. Indeed, most of HBO's alliances with independent producers are created to share costs and risks. Producing new television shows can be costly. Development and production costs can run into the hundreds of millions of dollars, especially for long and complicated mini-series like HBO's *Band of Brothers*. And, despite audience testing and careful market analyses, the production of these new shows is also very risky. Even bankable stars like Dustin Hoffman and Warren Beatty—remember *Ishtar*?—and Ben Affleck and Jennifer Lopez—remember *Gigli*?—cannot guarantee success.

In this context, it is not surprising that HBO decides to not "go it alone" in its production efforts. If HBO was to be the sole producer of its original programming, not only would it have to absorb all the production costs, but it would also bear all the risk if a production turned out not to be successful. Of course, by getting other firms involved in its production efforts, HBO also has to share whatever profits a particular production generates. Apparently, HBO has concluded that sharing this upside potential is more than compensated for by sharing the costs and risks of these productions.

Creating a Favorable Competitive Environment

Firms can also use strategic alliances to create a competitive environment that is more conducive to superior performance. This can be done in at least two ways. First, firms can use alliances to help set technology standards in an industry. With these standards in place, technology-based products can be developed and consumers can be confident that the products they buy will be useful for some time to come.

Such technologic standards are particularly important in what are called **network industries**. Such industries are characterized by **increasing returns to scale**. Consider, for example, fax machines. How valuable is one fax machine, all by itself? Obviously, not very valuable. Two fax machines that can talk to each other are a little more valuable, three that can talk to each other are still more valuable, and so forth. The value of each individual fax machine depends on the total number of fax machines that can talk to each other that are in operation. This is

Strategy in Depth

A **learning race** exists in a strategic alliance when both parties to that alliance seek to learn from each other, but when the rate at which these two firms learn varies. In this setting, the first firm to learn what it wants to learn from an alliance has the option to begin to underinvest in, and perhaps even withdraw from, an alliance. In this way, the firm that learns the fastest is able to prevent the slow-learning firm from learning all it wanted from an alliance. If, outside of this alliance, these firms are competitors, winning a learning race can create a sustained competitive advantage for the fast-learning firm over the slow-learning firm.

There are a variety of reasons why firms in an alliance may vary in the rate they learn from each other. First, they may be looking to learn different things, and some things are easier to learn than others. For example,

Winning Learning Races

in the GM–Toyota example, GM wanted to learn about how to use "lean manufacturing" to build high-quality small cars profitably. Toyota wanted to learn how to apply the "lean manufacturing" skills it already possessed in the United States. Which of these is easier to learn—about "lean manufacturing" or about how to apply "lean manufacturing" in the United States?

An argument can be made that GM's learning task was much more complicated than Toyota's. At the very least, in order for GM to apply knowledge about "lean manufacturing" gleaned from Toyota, it would have to transfer that knowledge to several of its currently operating plants. Using this knowledge would require these plants to change their current operations—a difficult and time-consuming process. Toyota, on the other hand, only had to transfer its knowledge of how to operate a "lean manufacturing" operation in the United States to its other U.S. plants—plants that at the time this alliance was first created had yet to be built. Because GM's learning task was

what is meant by increasing returns to scale—the value (or returns) on each product increases as the number of these products (or scale) increases.

Now, if there are 100 million fax machines in operation, but none of these machines can talk to each other, none of these machines has any value whatsoever—except as a large paper weight. For their full value to be realized, they must be able to talk to each other. And to talk to each other, they must all adopt the same—or at least compatible—communication standards. This is why setting technology standards is so important in network industries.

There are two ways that these standards can be set. First, different firms can introduce different standards, and consumers can decide which they prefer. This is how the standard for home videotapes was set. Sony sold one type of videotape machine—the Betamax—and Matsushita sold a second type of videotape machine—VHS. These two technologies were incompatible. Some consumers preferred Beta and purchased Sony's technology. Others preferred VHS and bought Matsushita's technology. However, since Matsushita licensed its VHS technology to numerous other firms, while Sony refused to do so, more and more consumers started buying VHS machines, until VHS became the de facto standard. This was the case even though most observers agreed that Beta was superior to VHS on several dimensions.

Of course, the biggest problem with letting customers and competition set technology standards is that customers may end up purchasing technologies that more complicated than Toyota's, it is very likely that Toyota's rate of learning was greater than GM's.

Second, firms may differ in terms of their ability to learn. This ability has been called a firm's **absorptive capacity**. Firms with high levels of absorptive capacity will learn at higher rates than firms with low levels of absorptive capacity, even if these two firms are trying to learn exactly the same things in an alliance. Absorptive capacity has been shown to be an important organizational capability in a wide variety of settings.

Third, firms can engage in activities to try to slow the rate of learning of their alliance partners. For example, while firms might make their technology available to an alliance partner—thereby fulfilling the alliance agreement—they may not provide all the know-how necessary to exploit this technology. This can slow a partner's

learning. Also, a firm might withhold critical employees from an alliance, thereby slowing the learning of an alliance partner. All these actions, to the extent that they slow the rate of a partner's learning without also slowing the rate at which the firm engaging in these activities learns, can help this firm win a learning race.

While learning race dynamics have been described in a wide variety of settings, they are particularly common in relations between entrepreneurial and large firms. In these alliances, entrepreneurial firms are often looking to learn about all the managerial functions required to bring a product to market, including manufacturing, sales, distribution, and so forth. This is a difficult learning task. Large firms in these alliances, on the other hand, often are only looking to learn about the entrepreneurial firm's technology. This is a

less difficult learning task. Because the learning task facing entrepreneurial firms is more challenging than that facing their large-firm partners, larger firms in these alliances typically win the learning race. Once these large firms learn what they want from their alliance partners, they often underinvest or even withdraw from these alliances. This is why, in one study, almost 80 percent of the managers in entrepreneurial firms felt unfairly exploited by their large-firm alliance partners.

Sources: S. A. Alvarez and J. B. Barney (2001). "How entrepreneurial firms can benefit from alliances with large partners." *Academy of Management Executive*, 15, pp. 139–148; G. Hamel (1991). "Competition for competence and inter-partner learning within international alliances." *Strategic Management Journal*, 12, pp. 83–103; W. Cohen and D. Levinthal (1990). "Absorptive capacity: A new perspective on learning and innovation." *Administrative Science Quarterly*, 35, pp. 128–152.

---

are incompatible with the standard that is ultimately set in the industry. What about all those consumers who purchased Beta products? For this reason, customers may be unwilling to invest in a new technology until the standards of that technology are established.

This is where strategic alliances come in. Sometimes, firms form strategic alliances, the sole purpose of which is to evaluate and then choose a technology standard in an industry. With such a standard in place, technologies can be turned into products that customers are likely to be more willing to purchase, since they know that they will compatible with industry standards for at least some period of time. Thus, in this setting—network industries with increasing returns to scale where standards are important—strategic alliances can be used to create a more favorable competitive environment.

Such alliances have been important in setting standards in a wide variety of industries, including the mobile telephone industry. The history of standard-setting in this industry, and how it has affected competition in the mobile phone industry around the world, is described in the Global Perspectives feature.

Another incentive for cooperating in strategic alliances is that such activities may facilitate the development of tacit collusion. As explained in Chapter 3, **collusion** exists when two or more firms in an industry coordinate their strategic choices to reduce competition in an industry. This reduction in competition usually

Global Perspectives

The mobile telephone industry is a classic example of a network industry—that is, an industry with increasing returns to scale where standards are important. The more people that own mobile phones that can talk to each other, the more valuable those mobile phones are. Because of the role that standards play in realizing these increasing returns to scale, standard-setting has been an important determinant of competition in the mobile phone industry around the world.

However, this standard-setting process has been anything but smooth; nor has there been agreement around the world about what the technological standard in the industry should be. While alliances can facilitate the creation of standards, sometimes sets of competing alliances can make it more difficult, not less difficult, to create a standard for an entire industry. This has been the case in the worldwide mobile telecommunications industry.

The first round of technical standards in mobile telephones was developed in the early 1980s. In the United States, the federal government adopted Ameritech's AMPS standard and required all mobile phone operators to use this analogue system. In Europe, two analogue standards emerged: NMT-450, developed by an alliance between Ericsson and Nokia, dominant in the Scandinavian countries and much of continental Europe; and TACS, developed by an alliance between Vodaphone and Cellnet for operations in the United Kingdom and Italy. Many

Can You Hear Me Now?

mobile phones operating in the United Kingdom still use the TACS standard. And in Japan, two additional analogue standards were created—NTT, created by Nippon Telephone and Telegraph, and JTACS, created in by an alliance that involved Toyota Motor Corporation. None of these standards were compatible with each other. A person with a phone that operated on, say, the NMT-450 standard could not talk to a person with a phone operating on, say, the AMPS standard.

The emergence of digital technology in the late 1980s led to a new round of standard-setting. In the United States, several potential standards were allowed to compete. The two dominant competing digital standards in the United States were known as TDMA and CDMA. In Europe, an alliance among all the major mobile phone companies, with government support, devel-

oped a single pan-European standard known as GSM—Global System for Mobile Communication. In Japan, two competing digital standards emerged: PDC, supported by an alliance that included Nissan Motors, and PHS, a system that relies on a dense network of antennas each with a very restricted range to provide mobile telephone services. Countries around the world have generally adopted one or more of these standard technologies. As was the case with analog standards, none of these digital standards are compatible.

This cacophony of standards has led to a search for a third-generation standard that would be applicable around the world. This standard—known as 3G—would have to be backward compatible (i.e., previous standards would have to be able to operate in conjunction with the new standard) and facilitate the full range of digital communications technology around the world. Two standards are currently competing for the right to become the worldwide 3G standard: UMTS, a standard supported by an alliance of European and Japanese mobile telecommunications companies, and CDMA-2000, a standard supported by most American mobile telecommunications companies. How this standards competition will unfold is still not entirely known.

Sources: www.cellular-news.com/history_of_telecoms/; C. Arnst, S. Jackson, and M. Shari (1995). "The last frontier: Telecommunications in developing countries." *BusinessWeek*, September 18, pp. 98 +; T. Rapport (1996). *Wireless communications: principles and practices.* Upper Saddle River, NJ: Prentice Hall.

makes it easier for colluding firms to earn high levels of performance. A common example of collusion is when firms cooperate to reduce the quantity of products being produced in an industry in order to drive prices for these products up. **Explicit collusion** exists when firms directly communicate with each other to coordinate their levels of production, their prices, and so forth. Explicit collusion is illegal in most countries.

Since managers that engage in explicit collusion can end up in jail, most collusion that exists in the economy must be tacit in character. **Tacit collusion** exists when firms coordinate their production and pricing decisions, not by directly communicating with each other, but by exchanging signals with other firms about their intent to cooperate. Examples of such signals might include public announcements about price increases, public announcements about reductions in a firm's productive output, public announcements about decisions not to pursue a new technology, and so forth.

Sometimes, signals of intent to collude are very ambiguous. For example, when firms in an industry do not reduce their prices in response to a decrease in demand, they may be sending a signal that they want to collude, or they may be attempting to exploit their product differentiation to maintain high margins. When firms do not reduce their prices in response to reduced supply costs, they may be sending a signal that they want to collude, or they may be individually maximizing their economic performance. In both these cases, a firm's intent to collude or not, as implied by its activities, is ambiguous at best.

In this context, strategic alliances can facilitate tacit collusion. Separate firms, even if they are in the same industry, can form strategic alliances. Although communication between these firms cannot legally include sharing information about prices and costs for products or services that are produced outside the alliance, such interaction does help create the social setting within which tacit collusion may develop.[3] As suggested in the Research Made Relevant feature, most early research on strategic alliances focused on their implications for tacit collusion. More recently, research suggests that alliances do not usually facilitate tacit collusion, although this is still a possibility.

Facilitating Entry and Exit

A final way that strategic alliances can be used to create value is by facilitating either a firm's entry into a new market or industry or its exit from a market or industry. Strategic alliances are particularly valuable in this context when the value of market entry or exit is uncertain. Entry into an industry can require skills, abilities, and products that a potential entrant does not possess. Strategic alliances can help a firm enter a new industry by avoiding the high costs of creating these skills, abilities, and products.

For example, recently DuPont wanted to enter into the electronics industry. However, building the skills and abilities needed to develop competitive products in this industry can be very difficult and costly. Rather than absorb these costs, DuPont developed a strategic alliance (DuPont/Philips Optical) with an established electronics firm, Philips, to distribute some of Philips's products in the United States. In this way DuPont was able to enter into a new industry (electronics) without having to absorb all the costs of creating electronics resources and abilities from the ground up.

Of course, for this joint venture to succeed, Philips must have had an incentive to cooperate with DuPont. Where DuPont was looking to reduce its cost of

Research Made Relevant

Several authors have concluded that joint ventures, as a form of alliance, do increase the probability of tacit collusion in an industry. As reviewed in books by Scherer and Barney, one study found that joint ventures created two industrial groups, besides U.S. Steel, in the U.S. iron and steel industry in the early 1900s. In this sense, joint ventures in the steel industry were a substitute for U.S. Steel's vertical integration and had the effect of creating an oligopoly in what (without joint ventures) would have been a more competitive market. Other studies found that over 50 percent of joint venture parents belong to the same industry. After examining 885 joint venture bids for oil and gas leases, yet another study found only 16 instances where joint venture partners competed with one another on another tract in the same sale. These results suggest that joint ventures might encourage subsequent tacit collusion among firms in the same industry.

In a particularly influential study, Pfeffer and Nowak found that joint ventures were most likely in industries of moderate concentration. These authors argued that in highly concentrated industries—where there

Do Strategic Alliances Facilitate Tacit Collusion?

were only a small number of competing firms—joint ventures were not necessary to create conditions conducive to collusion. In highly fragmented industries, the high levels of industry concentration conducive to tacit collusion could not be created by joint ventures. Only when joint venture activity could effectively create concentrated industries—that is, only when industries were moderately concentrated—were joint ventures likely.

Scherer and Barney also review more recent work that disputes these findings. Joint ventures between firms in the same industry may be valuable for a variety of reasons that have little or nothing to do with collusion. Moreover, by using a lower level of aggregation, several authors have disputed the finding that joint ventures are most likely in moderately concentrated industries. The original study defined industries using very broad industry categories—"the electronics industry," "the automobile industry," and so forth. By defining industries less broadly—"consumer electronics" and "automobile part manufacturers"—subsequent work found that 73 percent of the joint ventures had parent firms coming from different industries. Although joint ventures between firms in the same industry (defined at this lower level of aggregation) may have collusive implications, subsequent work has shown that these kinds of joint ventures are relatively rare.

Sources: F. M. Scherer (1980). *Industrial market structure and economic performance.* Boston: Houghton Mifflin; J. B. Barney (2002). *Gaining and sustaining competitive advantage,* 2nd ed. Upper Saddle River, NJ: Prentice Hall; J. Pfeffer and P. Nowak (1976). "Patterns of joint venture activity: Implications for anti-trust research." *Antitrust Bulletin,* 21, pp. 315–339.

entry into a new industry, Philips was looking to reduce its cost of continued entry into a new market: the United States. Philips used its alliance with DuPont to sell in the United States the compact discs it already was selling in Europe.[4] The role of alliances in facilitating entry into new geographic markets will be discussed in more detail later in this chapter.

Alliances to facilitate entry into new industries can be valuable even when the skills needed in these industries are not as complex and difficult to learn as skills in the electronics industry. For example, rather than develop their own frozen novelty foods, Welch Foods, Inc., and Leaf, Inc. (maker of Heath candy bars), asked Eskimo Pie to formulate products for this industry. Eskimo Pie developed Welch's frozen grape juice bar and the Heath toffee ice cream bar. These firms then split the profits derived from these products.[5] As long as the cost of using an alliance to enter a new industry is less than the cost of learning new skills and capabilities, an alliance can be a valuable strategic opportunity.

Some firms use strategic alliances as a mechanism to withdraw from industries or industry segments in a low-cost way. Firms are motivated to withdraw from an industry or industry segment when their level of performance in that business is less than what was expected and when there are few prospects of its improving. Often, when a firm desires to exit an industry or industry segment, it will need to dispose of the assets it has developed to compete in that industry or industry segment. These assets often include tangible resources and capabilities such as factories, distribution centers, and product technologies, and intangible resources and capabilities such as brand name, relationships with suppliers and customers, a loyal and committed workforce, and so forth.

Firms will often have difficulty in obtaining the full economic value of these tangible and intangible assets as they exit an industry or industry segment. This reflects an important information asymmetry that exists between the firms that currently own these assets and firms that may want to purchase these assets. By forming an alliance with a firm that may want to purchase its assets, a firm is giving its partner an opportunity to directly observe how valuable those assets are. If those assets are actually valuable, then this "sneak preview" can lead the assets to be more appropriately priced and thereby facilitate the exit of the firm that is looking to sell its assets. These issues will be discussed in more detail in Chapter 10's discussion of mergers and acquisitions.

One firm that has used strategic alliances to facilitate its exit from an industry or industry segment is Corning. In the late 1980s, Corning entered into the medical diagnostics industry. After several years, however, Corning concluded that its resources and capabilities could be more productively used in other businesses. For this reason, it began to extract itself from the medical diagnostics business. However, to make sure it received the full value of the assets it had created in the medical diagnostics business, upon exiting, it formed a strategic alliance with the Swiss specialty chemical company Ciba-Geigy. Ciba-Geigy paid $75 million to purchase half of Corning's medical diagnostics business. A couple of years later, Corning finished exiting from the medical diagnostics business by selling its remaining assets in this industry to Ciba-Geigy. However, where Ciba-Geigy had paid $75 million for the first half of Corning's assets, it paid $150 million for the second half. Corning's alliance with Ciba-Geigy had made it possible for Ciba-Geigy to fully value Corning's medical diagnostics capabilities. Any information asymmetry that might have existed was reduced, and Corning was able to get more of the full value of its assets upon exiting this industry.[6]

Finally, firms may use strategic alliances to manage **uncertainty**. Under conditions of high uncertainty, firms may not be able to tell, at a particular point in time, which of several different strategies they should pursue. Firms in this setting have an incentive to retain the flexibility to move quickly into a particular market or industry once the full value of that strategy is revealed. In this sense, strategic alliances enable a firm to maintain a point of entry into a market or industry, without incurring the costs associated with full-scale entry.

Based on this logic, strategic alliances have been analyzed as **real options**.[7] In this sense, a joint venture is an option that a firm buys, under conditions of uncertainty, to retain the ability to move quickly into a market or industry if valuable opportunities present themselves. One way in which firms can move quickly into a market is simply to buy out their partner(s) in the joint venture. Moreover, by investing in a joint venture, a firm may gain access to the information it needs to evaluate full-scale entry into a market. In this approach to analyzing strategic alliances, firms that invest in alliances as options will acquire their alliance partners only after the market signals an unexpected increase in value of the venture—that is, only after uncertainty is reduced and the true, positive value of entering into a market is known. Empirical findings are consistent with these expectations.[8]

Given these observations, it is not surprising to see firms in new and uncertain environments develop numerous strategic alliances. This is one of the reasons that strategic alliances are so common in the biotechnology industry. While there is relatively little uncertainty that at least some drugs created through biotechnology will ultimately prove to be very valuable, which specific drugs will turn out to be the most valuable is very uncertain. Rather than investing in a small number of biotechnology drugs on their own, pharmaceutical companies have invested in numerous strategic alliances with small biotechnology firms. Each of these smaller firms represents a particular "bet" about the value of biotechnology in a particular class of drugs. If one of these "bets" turns out to be valuable, then the large pharmaceutical firm that has invested in that firm has the right, but not the obligation, to purchase the rest of this company. In this sense, from the point of view of the pharmaceutical firms, alliances between large pharmaceutical firms and small biotechnology firms can be thought of as real options.

Alliance Threats: Incentives to Cheat on Strategic Alliances

Just as there are incentives to cooperate in strategic alliances, there are also incentives to cheat on these cooperative agreements. Indeed, research shows that as many as one-third of all strategic alliances do not meet the expectations of at least one alliance partner.[9] While some of these alliance "failures" may be due to firms forming alliances that do not have the potential for creating value, some are also due to parties to an alliance cheating—that is, not cooperating in a way that maximizes the value of the alliance. Cheating can occur in at least the three different ways presented in Table 9.2: adverse selection, moral hazard, and holdup.[10]

Adverse Selection

Potential cooperative partners can misrepresent the skills, abilities, and other resources that they will bring to an alliance. This form of cheating, called **adverse selection**, exists when an alliance partner promises to bring to an alliance certain resources that it either does not control or cannot acquire. For example, a local firm engages in adverse selection when it promises to make available to alliance

Table 9.2   **Ways to Cheat in Strategic Alliances**

- *Adverse selection*: Potential partners misrepresent the value of the skills and abilities they bring to the alliance.
- *Moral hazard*: Partners provide to the alliance skills and abilities of lower quality than they promised.
- *Holdup:* Partners exploit the transaction-specific investments made by others in the alliance.

partners a local distribution network that does not currently exist. Firms that engage in adverse selection are not competent alliance partners.

Adverse selection in a strategic alliance is likely only when it is difficult or costly to observe the resources or capabilities that a partner brings to an alliance. If potential partners can easily see that a firm is misrepresenting the resources and capabilities it possesses, they will not create a strategic alliance with that firm. Armed with such understanding, they will seek a different alliance partner, develop the needed skills and resources internally, or perhaps forgo this particular business opportunity.

However, evaluating the veracity of the claims of potential alliance partners is often not easy. The ability to evaluate these claims depends on information that a firm may not possess. To fully evaluate claims about a potential partner's political contacts, for example, a firm needs its own political contacts; to fully evaluate claims about potential partners' market knowledge, a firm needs significant market knowledge. A firm that can completely, and at low cost, evaluate the resources and capabilities of potential alliance partners probably does not really need these partners in a strategic alliance. The fact that a firm is seeking an alliance partner is in some sense an indication that the firm has limited abilities to evaluate potential partners.

In general, the less tangible the resources and capabilities that are to be brought to a strategic alliance, the more costly it will be to estimate their value before an alliance is created, and the more likely it is that adverse selection will occur. Firms considering alliances with partners that bring intangible resources such as "knowledge of local conditions" or "contacts with key political figures" will need to guard against this form of cheating.

Moral Hazard

Partners in an alliance may possess high-quality resources and capabilities of significant value in an alliance but fail to make those resources and capabilities available to alliance partners. This form of cheating is called **moral hazard**. For example, a partner in an engineering strategic alliance may agree to send only its most talented and best trained engineers to work in the alliance but then actually send less talented, poorly trained engineers. These less qualified engineers may not be able to contribute substantially to making the alliance successful, but they may be able to learn a great deal from the highly qualified engineers provided by other alliance partners. In this way, the less qualified engineers effectively transfer wealth from other alliance partners to their own firm.[11]

Often both parties in a failed alliance accuse each other of moral hazard. This was the case in the recently abandoned alliance between Disney and Pixar, described in the Strategy in the Emerging Enterprise feature.

The existence of moral hazard in a strategic alliance does not necessarily mean that any of the parties to that alliance are malicious or dishonest. Rather, what often happens is that market conditions change after an alliance is formed, requiring one or more partners to an alliance to change their strategies.

For example, in the early days of the personal computer industry, Compaq Computer Corporation relied on a network of independent distributors to sell its computers. However, as competition in the personal computer industry increased, Internet, mail order, and so-called computer superstores became much more valuable distribution networks, and alliances between Compaq and its traditional distributors became strained. Over time, Compaq's traditional distributors were

Strategy in the Emerging Enterprise

*I*n 1994, Pixar was a struggling start-up company in northern California that was trying to compete in an industry that really didn't yet exist—the computer graphics animated motion picture industry. Headed by the former founder of Apple Computer, Steven Jobs, Pixar was desperately looking for a partner that could help finance and distribute its new brand of animated movies. Who better, Pixar thought, than the world's leader in animated feature length films—Disney? And thus, a strategic alliance between Pixar and Disney was formed.

In the alliance, Disney agreed to help finance and distribute Pixar's films. In return, they would share in any profits these films generated. Also, Disney would retain the right to produce any sequels to Pixar's films—after first offering Pixar the right to make these sequels. This agreement gave Disney a great deal of control of any characters that Pixar created in movies distributed through Pixar's alliance with Disney. Of course, at the time the alliance was originally formed, there were no such characters. Indeed, Pixar had yet to produce any movies. So, because Pixar was a weak alliance partner, Disney was able to gain control of any characters Pixar developed in the future. Disney, after all, had the track record of success.

A funny thing happened over the next ten years. Pixar produced blockbuster animated features like *Toy Story* ($362 million in revenues in 1995); *A Bug's Life* ($363 million in revenues in 1998); *Toy Story 2* ($485 million in revenues in 1999); *Monsters, Inc.* ($524 million in revenues in 2001); and *Finding Nemo*

Disney and Pixar Have a Falling Out

($844 million in revenues in 2003). During this same time period, Disney's traditional animated fare performed much more poorly—*Treasure Planet* generated only $112 million in revenues in 2002, *The Emperor's New Groove* only $169 million in revenues in 2000, and *Brother Bear* only $126 million in revenues in 2003. Disney's "big hit" during this time period was *Lilo & Stitch*, with 2002 revenues of $269 million—smaller than any of the movies produced by Pixar.

Oops! The firm with the "proven track record" of producing hit animated features—Disney—stumbled badly, and the upstart company with no track record—Pixar—had all the success. Since Disney did not have many of its own characters upon which to base sequels, it began to eye Pixar's characters. And Disney's approach to making sequels made Pixar's man-

agers blanche—poor production values, poorly developed story lines, limited distribution, lower-quality talent. Do you remember seeing the "direct to video hit," *The Lion King: Another Viewpoint*?

Fast forward to 2004. It's time to renew this alliance. But now Pixar has the upper hand, because it has the track record. Disney comes knocking and asks Pixar to redo the alliance. What does Pixar say, "Okay, but . . . we want control of our characters, we want Disney to act just as a distributor"—in other words, "We want Disney out of our business!" Disney balks at these demands, and Pixar—well, Pixar just cancelled the alliance.

But Disney is not done. It still controls the rights to characters created by Pixar while the old alliance with Disney was in place. So, in 2004, Disney announced that it would be producing *Toy Story 3* without Pixar's involvement. Whether this new production will be up to the standards established by Pixar, or be more similar to Disney's track record from 2000 on is yet to be seen. But for now, Disney seems to need Pixar more than Pixar needs Disney.

One final irony in this alliance. Some observers have suggested that Disney's inability to maintain its alliance with Pixar was one of the reasons that Comcast was able to launch an unfriendly takeover bid for Disney in February of 2004.

Sources: S. Levy and D. Jefferson (2004). "Hey Mickey, buzz off!" *BusinessWeek*, February 9, pp. 4; T. Lowry et al. (2004). "Megamedia mergers: How dangerous?" *BusinessWeek*, February 23, pp. 34 +.

unable to obtain all the inventory they wanted in a timely manner. Indeed, to satisfy the needs of large accounts, some traditional distributors actually purchased Compaq computers from local computer superstores and then shipped them to their customers. Compaq's shift from independent dealers to alternative distributors looked like moral hazard—at least from the point of view of the independent dealers. However, from Compaq's perspective, this change simply reflected economic realities in the personal computer industry.[12]

Holdup

Even if alliance partners don't engage in either adverse selection or moral hazard, another form of cheating may evolve. Once a strategic alliance has been created, partner firms may make investments that have value only in the context of that alliance and in no other economic exchanges. These are the transaction-specific investments mentioned in Chapter 6. For example, managers from one alliance partner may have to develop close, trusting relationships with managers from other alliance partners. These close relationships are very valuable in the context of the alliance but have limited economic value in other economic exchanges. Also, one partner may have to customize its manufacturing equipment, distribution network, and key organizational policies to cooperate with other partners. These modifications have significant value in the context of the alliance but do not help the firm, and may even hurt it, in economic exchanges outside the alliance. As was the case in Chapter 6, whenever an investment's value in its first-best use (in this case, within the alliance) is much greater than its value in its second-best use (in this case, outside the alliance), that investment is said to be **transaction specific**.[13]

When one firm makes more transaction-specific investments in a strategic alliance than partner firms make, that firm may be subject to the form of cheating called **holdup**. Holdup occurs when a firm that has not made significant transaction-specific investments demands returns from an alliance that are higher than what the partners agreed to when they created the alliance.

For example, suppose two alliance partners agree to a fifty–fifty split of the costs and profits associated with an alliance. To make the alliance work, Firm A has to customize its production process. Firm B, however, does not have to modify itself to cooperate with Firm A. The value to Firm A of this customized production process, if it is used in the strategic alliance, is $5,000. However, outside the alliance, this customized process is only worth $200 (as scrap).

Obviously, Firm A has made a transaction-specific investment in this alliance and Firm B has not. Consequently, Firm A may be subject to holdup by Firm B. In particular, Firm B may threaten to leave the alliance unless Firm A agrees to give Firm B part of the $5,000 value that Firm A obtains by using the modified production process in the alliance. Rather than lose all the value that could be generated by its investment, Firm A may be willing to give up some of its $5,000 to avoid gaining only $200. Indeed, if Firm B extracts up to the value of Firm A's production process in its next-best use (here, only $200), Firm A will still be better off continuing in this relationship rather than dissolving it. Thus, even though Firm A and Firm B agree on a fifty–fifty split from this strategic alliance, the agreement may be modified if one party to the alliance makes significant transaction-specific investments. Research on international joint ventures suggests that the existence of transaction-specific investments in these relationships often leads to holdup problems.[14]

Although holdup is a form of cheating in strategic alliances, the threat of holdup can also be a motivation for creating an alliance. Bauxite-smelting companies often join in joint ventures with mining companies in order to exploit economies of scale in mining. However, these firms have another option: They could choose to operate large and efficient mines by themselves and then sell the excess bauxite (over and above their needs for their own smelters) on the open market. Unfortunately, bauxite is not a homogeneous commodity. Moreover, different kinds of bauxite require different smelting technologies. In order for one firm to sell its excess bauxite on the market, other smelting firms would have to make enormous investments, the sole purpose of which would be to refine that particular firm's bauxite. These investments would be transaction specific and subject these other smelters to holdup problems.

In this context, a strategic alliance can be thought of as a way of reducing the threat of holdup by creating an explicit management framework for resolving holdup problems. In other words, although holdup problems might still exist in these strategic alliances, the alliance framework may still be a better way in which to manage these problems than attempting to manage them in arm's-length market relationships. Some of the ethical dimensions of adverse selection, moral hazard, and holdup are discussed in the Ethics and Strategy feature.

Strategic Alliances and Sustained Competitive Advantage

V R I O

The ability of strategic alliances to be sources of sustained competitive advantage, like all the other strategies discussed in this book, to be sources of sustained competitive advantage can be analyzed by using the VRIO framework developed in Chapter 3. An alliance is economically valuable when it exploits any of the opportunities listed in Table 9.1 but avoids the threats in Table 9.2. In addition, for a strategic alliance to be a source of sustained competitive advantage, it must be rare and costly to imitate.

The Rarity of Strategic Alliances

The rarity of strategic alliances does not only depend on the number of competing firms that have already implemented an alliance. It also depends on whether or not the benefits that firms obtain from their alliances are common across firms competing in an industry.

Consider, for example, the automobile industry in the United States. Over the last several years, strategic alliances have become very common in this industry, especially with Japanese auto firms. GM developed an alliance with Toyota that has already been described; Ford developed an alliance with Mazda before it purchased this Japanese firm outright; and DaimlerChrysler developed an alliance with Mitsubishi. Given the frequency with which alliances have developed in this industry, it is tempting to conclude that strategic alliances are rare and thus not a source of competitive advantage.

Closer examination, however, suggests that these alliances may have been created for different reasons. For example, until recently, GM and Toyota have cooperated only in building a single line of cars, the Chevrolet Nova. GM has been less interested in learning design skills from Toyota and has been more interested in learning about manufacturing high-quality small cars profitably. Ford and Mazda,

Ethics and Strategy

So, firms in strategic alliances can cheat on their alliance partners by engaging in adverse selection, moral hazard, or holdup. These three activities all have at least one thing in common—they all involve one alliance partner lying to another. And these lies can often pay off big, in the form of the lying firm appropriating more than its "fair share" of the value created in an alliance. Are alliances one place in the economy where the adage "cheaters never prosper" does not hold?

There is little doubt that, in the short run, firms that cheat on their alliance partners can gain some advantages. But research suggests that cheating does not pay in the long run, because firms that cheat on their alliance partners will find it difficult to form alliances with new partners and thus have many valuable exchange opportunities foreclosed to them.

One study that examined the long-term return to "cheaters" in strategic alliances examined alliances using a simple game called the "Prisoner's Dilemma." In a "Prisoner's Dilemma" game, firms have two options: to continue cooperating in a strategic alliance, or to "cheat" on that alliance through adverse selection, moral hazard, or

When It Comes to Alliances, Do "Cheaters Never Prosper?"

holdup. The payoffs to firms in this game depend on the decisions made by both firms. As shown in Table 9.3, if both firms decide to cooperate, they each get a good size payoff from the alliance ($3,000 in Table 9.3); if they both decide to cheat on the alliance, they each get a very small payoff ($1,000 in Table 9.3); and if one decides to cheat while the other decides to cooperate, then the cheating firm gets a very big payoff ($5,000 in Table 9.3) while the cooperating firm gets a very small payoff ($0 in Table 9.3).

If Firms One and Two in this game are going to engage in only one strategic alliance, then they have a very strong incentive to "cheat." The worst that could happen if they cheat is that they earn a $1,000 payoff; but there is a possibility of a $5,000 payoff. However, research has shown that if a firm is contemplating engaging in multiple strategic alliances over time, then the optimal strategy is to cooperate in all its alliances. This is true even if all these alliances are not with the same partner firm.

The specific "winning" strategy in repeated "Prisoner Dilemma" games is called a "tit-for-tat" strategy. "Tit-for-tat" means that Firm One will cooperate in an alliance as long as Firm Two cooperates. However, as soon as Firm Two cheats on an alliance, Firm One cheats as well. "Tit-for-tat" works well in this setting because adopting a cooperative posture in an alliance ensures that, most of the time, the alliance will generate a high payoff (of $3,000 in Table 9.3). However, by immediately responding to cheaters by cheating, the firm implementing a "tit-for-tat" strategy also minimizes the times when it will earn the lowest payoff in the table ($0). So, "tit-for-tat" maximizes the upside potential of an alliance while minimizing its downside.

All this analysis suggests that while cheating on an alliance can give a firm competitive advantages in the short to medium term; in the long run, "cheaters never prosper."

Sources: R. M. Axelrod (1984). *The evolution of cooperation.* New York: Basic Books; D. Ernst and J. Bleek (1993). *Collaborating to compete.* New York: Wiley.

Table 9.3 **Returns from Cooperating and Cheating in a "Prisoner's Dilemma"**

Firm One		Strategic Alliance	
		Cooperates	Cheats
	Cooperates	I: $3,000 II: $3,000	I: $5,000 II. $0
Firm Two	Cheats	I: $0 II: $5,000	I: $1,000 II: $1,000

in contrast, have worked closely together in designing new cars and have joint manufacturing operations. Indeed, Ford and Mazda have worked so closely together that Ford finally purchased Mazda. Mitsubishi has acted primarily as a supplier to DaimlerChrysler, and (until recently) there has been relatively little joint development or manufacturing. Thus, although all three U.S. firms have strategic alliances, the alliances serve different purposes and therefore each may be rare.[15]

One of the reasons why the benefits that accrue from a particular strategic alliance may be rare is that relatively few firms may have the complementary resources and abilities needed to form an alliance. This is particularly likely when an alliance is formed to enter into a new market and especially a new foreign market. In many less developed economies, only one local firm or very few local firms may exist with the local knowledge, contacts, and distribution network needed to facilitate entry into that market. Moreover, sometimes the government acts to limit the number of these local firms. Although several firms may seek entry into this market, only a very small number will be able to form a strategic alliance with the local entity and therefore the benefits that accrue to the allied firms will likely be rare.

The Imitability of Strategic Alliances

As discussed in Chapter 3, the resources and capabilities that enable firms to conceive and implement valuable strategies may be imitated in two ways: direct duplication and substitution. Both duplication and substitution are important considerations in analyzing the imitability of strategic alliances.

Direct Duplication of Strategic Alliances

Recent research suggests that successful strategic alliances are often based on socially complex relations among alliance partners.[16] In this sense, successful strategic alliances often go well beyond simple legal contracts and are characterized by socially complex phenomena such as a trusting relationship between alliance partners, friendship, and even (perhaps) a willingness to suspend narrow self-interest for the longer-term good of the relationship.

Some research has shown that the development of trusting relationships between alliance partners is both difficult and essential to the success of strategic alliances. In one study, the most common reason that alliances fail to meet the expectations of partner firms was the partners' inability to trust one another. Interpersonal communication, tolerance for cultural differences, patience, and willingness to sacrifice short-term profits for longer-term success were all important determinants of the level of trust among alliance partners.[17]

Of course, not all firms in an industry are likely to have the organizational and relationship-building skills required for successful alliance building. If these skills and abilities are rare among a set of competing firms and costly to develop, then firms that are able to exploit these abilities by creating alliances may gain competitive advantages. Examples of firms that have developed these specialized skills include Corning and Cisco, firms with several hundred strategic alliances each.[18]

Substitutes for Strategic Alliances

Even if the purpose and objectives of a strategic alliance are valuable and rare, and even if the relationships on which an alliance is created are socially complex and costly to imitate, that alliance will still not generate a sustained competitive advantage if low-cost substitutes are available. At least two possible substitutes for strategic alliances exist: "going it alone" and acquisitions.[19]

"Going It Alone". Firms "go it alone" when they attempt to develop all the resources and capabilities they need to exploit market opportunities and neutralize market threats by themselves. Sometimes "going it alone" can create the same—or even more—value than using alliances to exploit opportunities and neutralize threats. In these settings, "going it alone" is a substitute for a strategic alliance. However, in other settings, using an alliance can create substantially more value than "going it alone." In these settings, "going it alone" is not a substitute for a strategic alliance.

So, when will firms prefer an alliance over "going it alone?" Not surprisingly, the three explanations of vertical integration, discussed in Chapter 6, are relevant here as well. These three explanations focused on the threat of opportunism, the impact of firm resources and capabilities, and the role of uncertainty. If you need to review these three explanations, they are described in detail in Chapter 6. They are relevant here because "going it alone"—as a potential substitute for a strategic alliance—is an example of vertical integration. The implications of these three explanations for when strategic alliances will be preferred over "going it alone" are summarized in Table 9.4. If any of the conditions listed in Table 9.4 exist, then "going it alone" will not be a substitute for strategic alliances.

Recall from Chapter 6 that opportunism-based explanations of vertical integration suggest that firms will want to vertically integrate an economic exchange when they have made high levels of transaction specific investment in that exchange. That is, using language developed in this chapter, firms will want to vertically integrate an economic exchange when using an alliance to manage that exchange could subject them to holdup. Extending this logic to strategic alliances suggests that strategic alliances will be preferred over "going it alone" and other alternatives when the level of transaction-specific investment required to complete an exchange is moderate. If the level of this specific investment is low, then market forms of exchange will be preferred; if the level of this specific investment is high, then "going it alone" in a vertically integrated way will be preferred; if the level of this specific investment is moderate, then some sort of strategic alliance will be preferred. Thus, when the level of specific exchange in a transaction is moderate, then "going it alone" is not a substitute for a strategic alliance.

Capabilities explanations suggest that an alliance will be preferred over "going it alone" when an exchange partner possesses valuable, rare, and costly-to-imitate resources and capabilities. A firm without these capabilities may find them to be too costly to develop on their own. If a firm must have access to capabilities it cannot develop on its own, it must use an alliance to gain access to those capabilities. In this setting, "going it alone" is not a substitute for a strategic alliance.[20]

Finally, it has already been suggested that, under conditions of high uncertainty, firms may be unwilling to commit to a particular course of action by engaging

Table 9.4   **When Alliances Will Be Preferred Over "Going It Alone"**

Alliances will be preferred over "going it alone" when:

1. The level of transaction-specific investment required to complete an exchange is moderate.
2. An exchange partner possesses valuable, rare, and costly-to-imitate resources and capabilities.
3. There is great uncertainty about the future value of an exchange.

in an exchange within a firm. In such settings, firms may choose the strategic flexibility associated with alliances. As suggested earlier in this chapter, alliances can be thought of as real options that give a firm the right, but not the obligation, to invest further in an exchange—perhaps by bringing it within the boundaries of a firm—if that exchange turns out to be valuable sometime in the future. Thus, under conditions of high uncertainty, "going it alone" is not a substitute for strategic alliances.

Acquisitions. The acquisition of other firms can also be a substitute for alliances. In this case, rather than developing a strategic alliance or attempting to develop and exploit the relevant resources by "going it alone," a firm seeking to exploit the opportunities listed in Table 9.1 may simply acquire another firm that already possesses the relevant resources and capabilities. However, such acquisitions have four characteristics that often limit the extent to which they can act as substitutes for strategic alliances. These are summarized in Table 9.5.[21]

First, there may be legal constraints on acquisitions. These are especially likely if firms are seeking advantages by combining with other firms in their own industry. Thus, for example, using acquisitions as a substitute for strategic alliances in the aluminum industry would lead to a very concentrated industry and subject some of these firms to serious antitrust liabilities. These firms have acquisitions foreclosed to them and must look elsewhere to gain advantages from cooperating with their competition.

Second, as has already been suggested, strategic alliances enable a firm to retain its flexibility either to enter or not to enter into a new business. Acquisitions limit that flexibility, because they represent a strong commitment to engage in a certain business activity. Consequently, under conditions of high uncertainty, firms may choose strategic alliances over acquisitions as a way to exploit opportunities while maintaining the flexibility that alliances create.

Third, firms may choose strategic alliances over acquisitions because of the unwanted organizational baggage that often comes with an acquisition. Sometimes, the value created by combining firms depends on combining particular functions, divisions, or other assets in the firms. A strategic alliance can focus on exploiting the value of combining just those parts of firms that create the most value. Acquisitions, in contrast, generally include the entire organization, both the parts of a firm where value is likely to be created and parts of a firm where value is not likely to be created.

From the point of view of the acquiring firm, parts of a firm that do not create value are essentially unwanted baggage. These parts of the firm may be sold off subsequent to an acquisition. However, this sell-off may be costly and time-consuming. If enough baggage exists, firms may determine that an acquisition is not a viable option, even though important economic value could be created between a firm and a potential acquisition target. To gain this value, an alternative approach—a strategic alliance—may be preferred. These issues will be explored in more detail in Chapter 10.

Table 9.5 **Reasons Why Strategic Alliances May Be More Attractive than Acquisitions to Realize Exchange Opportunities**

Alliances will be preferred to acquisitions when:

1. There are legal constraints on acquisitions.
2. Acquisitions limit a firm's flexibility under conditions of high uncertainty.
3. There is substantial unwanted organizational "baggage" in an acquired firm.
4. The value of a firm's resources and capabilities depends on its independence.

Finally, sometimes a firm's resources and capabilities are valuable because that firm is independent. In this setting, the act of acquiring a firm can actually reduce the value of a firm. When this is the case, any value between two firms is best realized through an alliance, not an acquisition. For example, the international growth of numerous marketing-oriented companies in the 1980s led to strong pressures for advertising agencies to develop global marketing capabilities. During the 1990s, many domestic-only advertising firms acquired nondomestic agencies to form a few large international advertising agencies. However, one firm that was reluctant to be acquired in order to be part of an international advertising network was the French advertising company Publicis. Over and above the personal interests of its owners to retain control of the company, Publicis wanted to remain an independent French agency in order to retain its stable of French and French-speaking clients—including Renault and Nestlé. These firms had indicated that they preferred working with a French advertising agency and that they would look for alternative suppliers if Publicis were acquired by a foreign firm. Because much of the value that Publicis created in a potential acquisition depended on obtaining access to its stable of clients, the act of acquiring Publicis would have had the effect of destroying the very thing that made the acquisition attractive. For this reason, rather than allowing itself to be acquired by foreign advertising agencies, Publicis developed a complex equity strategic alliance and joint venture with a U.S. advertising firm, Foote, Coyne, and Belding. Although, ultimately, this alliance was not successful in providing an international network for either of these two partner firms, an acquisition of Publicis by Foote, Coyne, and Belding would almost certainly have destroyed some of the economic value that Publicis enjoyed as a stand-alone company.

Organizing to Implement Strategic Alliances

V R I O

One of the most important determinants of the success of strategic alliances is their organization. The primary purpose of organizing a strategic alliance is to enable partners in the alliance to gain all the benefits associated with cooperation while minimizing the probability that cooperating firms will cheat on their cooperative agreements. The organizing skills required in managing alliances are, in many ways, unique. It often takes some time for firms to learn these skills and thus to realize the full potential of their alliances. This is why some firms are able to gain competitive advantages from managing alliances more effectively than their competitors. Indeed, sometimes firms may have to choose alternatives to alliances—including "going it alone" and acquisitions—even when those alternatives are not preferred simply because they do not have the skills required to organize and manage alliances.

A variety of tools and mechanisms can be used to help realize the value and minimize the threat of cheating in alliances. These include: contracts, equity investments, firm reputations, joint ventures, and trust.

Explicit Contracts and Legal Sanctions

One way to avoid cheating in strategic alliances is for parties to an alliance to anticipate the ways in which cheating may occur (including adverse selection, moral hazard, and holdup) and to write explicit contracts that define legal liability if cheating does occur. Writing these contracts, together with the close monitoring of contractual compliance and the threat of legal sanctions, can reduce the probability of cheating. Earlier in this chapter, such strategic alliances were called non-equity alliances.

However, contracts sometimes fail to anticipate all forms of cheating that might occur in a relationship—and firms may cheat on cooperative agreements in subtle ways that are difficult to evaluate in terms of contractual requirements. Thus, for example, a contract may require parties in a strategic alliance to make available to the alliance certain proprietary technologies or processes. However, it may be very difficult to communicate the subtleties of these technologies or processes to alliance partners. Does this failure in communication represent a clear violation of contractual requirements, or does it represent a good-faith effort by alliance partners? Moreover, how can one partner tell whether it is obtaining all the necessary information about a technology or process when it is unaware of all the information that exists in another firm? Hence, although contracts are an important component of most strategic alliances, they do not resolve all the problems associated with cheating.

Although most contracts associated with strategic alliances are highly customized, these different contracts do have some common features. These common features are described in detail in Table 9.6. In general, firms contemplating a strategic alliance that will be at least partially governed by a contract will have to include clauses that address the issues presented in Table 9.6.

Table 9.6   **Common Clauses in Contracts Used to Govern Strategic Alliances**

Establishment Issues

Shareholdings

If an equity alliance or joint venture is to be formed, what percentage of equity is to be purchased by each firm involved in the alliance.

Voting rights

The number of votes assigned to each partner in an alliance. May or may not be equal to shareholding percentages.

Dividend percentage

How the profits from an alliance will be allocated among cooperating firms. May or may not be equal to shareholding percentages.

Minority protection

Description of the kinds of decisions that can be vetoed by firms with a minority interest in an alliance.

Board of directors

Initial board of directors, plus mechanisms for dismissing and appointing board members.

Articles of association

Procedures for passing resolutions, share issuance, share disposal, etc.

Place of incorporation

If a joint venture, geographic location of incorporation.

Advisors

Lawyers, accountants, and other consultants to the alliance.

Identification of parties

Legal entities directly involved in an alliance.

Operating Issues

Performance clauses

Duties and obligations of alliance partners, including warranties and minimum performance levels expected.

Noncompete clauses

Partners are restricted from entering the primary business of the alliance.

Nonsolicitation clauses

Partners are restricted from recruiting employees from each other.

Confidentiality clauses

Proprietary information from partners or from the alliance cannot be shared outside the alliance.

Licensing intellectual property rights

Who owns the intellectual property created by an alliance and how this property is licensed to other firms.

Liability

Liability of the alliance and liability of cooperating partners.

Changes to the contract

Process by which the contract can be amended.

Dispute resolution

Process by which disputes among partners will be resolved.

Termination Issues

Preemption rights

If one partner wishes to sell its shares, it must first offer them to the other partner.

Variations on preemption rights

Partners are forbidden to ever discuss the sale of their shares to an outsider without first informing their partner of their intention to do so.

Call options

When one partner can force the other partner to sell its shares to it. Includes discussion on how these shares will be valued and the circumstances under which a call option can be exercised.

Put options

A partner has the right to force another partner to buy its alliance shares.

Drag-along rights

One partner can arrange a sale to an outside firm and force the other partner to sell shares as well.

Tag-along rights

A partner can prevent the sale of the second partner's shares to an outside firm unless that outside firm also buys the first partner's shares.

Initial public offering (IPO)

Circumstances under which an IPO will be pursued.

Termination

Conditions under which contract can be terminated and consequences of termination for partners.

Sources: Adapted from E. Campbell and J. Reuer (2000). "Note on the legal negotiation of strategic alliance agreements." Unpublished working paper, Fontainbleau, France: INSEAD.

Equity Investments

The effectiveness of contracts can be enhanced by having partners in an alliance make equity investments in each other. When Firm A buys a substantial equity position in its alliance partner, Firm B, the market value of Firm A now depends, to some extent, on the economic performance of that partner. The incentive of Firm A to cheat Firm B falls, for to do so would be to reduce the economic performance of Firm B and thus the value of Firm A's investment in its partner. These kinds of strategic alliances are called equity alliances.

Many firms use cross-equity investments to help manage their strategic alliances. These arrangements are particularly common in Japan, where a firm's largest equity holders often include several of its key suppliers, including its main banks. These equity investments, because they reduce the threat of cheating in alliances with suppliers, can reduce these firms' supply costs. In turn, not only do firms have equity positions in their suppliers, but suppliers often have substantial equity positions in the firms to which they sell.[22]

Firm Reputations

A third constraint on incentives to cheat in strategic alliances exists in the effect that a reputation for cheating has on a firm's future opportunities. Although it is often difficult to anticipate all the different ways in which an alliance partner may cheat, it is often easier to describe after the fact how an alliance partner has cheated. Information about an alliance partner that has cheated is likely to become widely known. A firm with a reputation as a cheater is not likely to be able to develop strategic alliances with other partners in the future, despite any special resources or capabilities that it might be able to bring to an alliance. In this way, cheating in a current alliance may foreclose opportunities for developing other valuable alliances. For this reason, firms may decide not to cheat in their current alliances.[23]

There is substantial evidence that the effect of reputation on future business opportunities is important. Firms go to great lengths to make sure that they do not develop this negative reputation. Nevertheless, this reputational control of cheating in strategic alliances does have several limitations.[24]

First, subtle cheating in a strategic alliance may not become public, and if it does become public, the responsibility for the failure of the strategic alliance may be very ambiguous. In one equity joint venture attempting to perfect the design of a new turbine for power generation, financial troubles made one partner considerably more anxious than the other partner to complete product development. The financially healthy and thus patient partner believed that if the alliance required an additional infusion of capital, the financially troubled partner would have to abandon the alliance and would have to sell its part of the alliance at a relatively low price. The patient partner thus encouraged alliance engineers to work slowly and carefully in the guise of developing the technology to reach its full potential. The financially troubled and thus impatient partner encouraged alliance engineers to work quickly, perhaps sacrificing some quality to develop the technology sooner. Eventually, the impatient partner ran out of money, sold its share of the alliance to the patient partner at a reduced price and accused the patient partner of not acting in good faith to facilitate the rapid development of the new technology. The patient partner accused the other firm of pushing the technology too quickly, thereby sacrificing quality and, perhaps, worker safety. In some sense, both firms were cheating on their agreement to develop the new technology cooperatively. However, this cheating was subtle and difficult to spot and had relatively little impact on the reputation of either firm or on the ability of either firm to establish alliances in the future. It is likely that most observers would simply conclude that the patient partner obtained a windfall because of the impatient partner's bad luck.[25]

Second, although one partner to an alliance may be unambiguously cheating on the relationship, one or both of the firms may not be sufficiently connected into a network with other firms to make this information public. When information about cheating remains private, public reputations are not tarnished and future opportunities are not forgone. This is especially likely to happen if one or both alliance partners operate in less developed economies where information about partner behavior may not be rapidly diffused to other firms or to other countries.

Finally, the effect of a tarnished reputation, as long as cheating in an alliance is unambiguous and publicly known, may foreclose future opportunities for a firm, but it does little to address the current losses experienced by the firm that was cheated. Moreover, any of the forms of cheating discussed earlier—adverse selection, moral hazard, or holdup—can result in substantial losses for a firm currently in an alliance. Indeed, the wealth created by cheating in a current alliance may be large enough to make a firm willing to forgo future alliances. In this case, a tarnished reputation may be of minor consequence to a cheating firm.[26]

Joint Ventures

A fourth way to reduce the threat of cheating is for partners in a strategic alliance to invest in a joint venture. Creating a separate legal entity, in which alliance partners invest and from whose profits they earn returns on their investments, reduces some of the risks of cheating in strategic alliances. When a joint venture is created, the ability of partners to earn returns on their investments depends on the economic success of the joint venture. Partners in joint ventures have limited interests in behaving in ways that hurt the performance of the joint venture, because such behaviors end up hurting themselves. Moreover, unlike reputational consequences of cheating, cheating in a joint venture does not just foreclose future alliance opportunities; it can hurt the cheating firm in the current period as well.

Given the advantages of joint ventures in controlling cheating, it is not surprising that when the probability of cheating in a cooperative relationship is greatest, a joint venture is usually the preferred form of cooperation. There are some clear economies of scale in bauxite mining, for example. However, transaction-specific investments would lead to significant holdup problems in selling excess bauxite in the open market, and legal constraints prevent the acquisition of other smelter companies to create an intraorganizational demand for excess bauxite. Holdup problems would continue to exist in any mining strategic alliances that might be created. Nonequity alliances, equity alliances, and reputational effects are not likely to restrain cheating in this situation, because the returns on holdup, once transaction-specific investments are in place, can be very large. Thus, most of the strategic alliances created to mine bauxite take the form of joint ventures. Only this form of strategic alliance is likely to create incentives strong enough to significantly reduce the probability of cheating.[27]

Despite these strengths, joint ventures are not able to costlessly reduce all cheating in an alliance. Sometimes the value of cheating in a joint venture is sufficiently large that a firm cheats even though doing so hurts the joint venture and forecloses future opportunities. For example, through a joint venture, a particular firm may gain access to a technology that would be valuable if used in another of its lines of business. This firm may be tempted to transfer this technology to this other line of business even if it has agreed not to do so and even if doing so would limit the performance of its joint venture. Because the profits earned in this other line of business may have a greater value than the returns that could have been earned in the joint venture and the returns that could have been earned in the future with other strategic alliances, cheating may occur in a joint venture.

Trust

It is sometimes the case that alliance partners rely only on legalistic and narrowly economic approaches to manage their alliance. However, recent work seems to suggest that although successful alliance partners do not ignore legal and economic disincentives to cheating, they strongly support these narrower linkages with a rich set of interpersonal relations and trust. Trust, in combination with contracts, can help reduce the threat of cheating. More important, trust may enable partners to explore exchange opportunities that they could not explore if only legal and economic organizing mechanisms were in place.[28]

At first glance, this argument may seem far-fetched. However, some research offers support for this approach to managing strategic alliances, suggesting that successful alliance partners typically do not specify all the terms and conditions in their relationship in a legal contract and do not specify all possible forms of cheating and their consequences. Moreover, when joint ventures are formed, partners do not always insist on simple fifty–fifty splits of equity ownership and profit sharing. Rather, successful alliances involve trust, a willingness to be flexible, a willingness to learn, and a willingness to let the alliance develop in ways that the partners could not have anticipated.[29]

Commitment, coordination, and trust are all important determinants of alliance success. Put another way, a strategic alliance is a relationship that evolves over time. Allowing the lawyers and economists to too-rigorously define, a priori, the boundaries of that relationship may limit it and stunt its development.[30]

This "trust" approach also has implications for the extent to which strategic alliances may be sources of sustained competitive advantage for firms. The ability to move into strategic alliances in this trusting way may be very valuable over the long run. There is strong reason to believe that this ability is not uniformly distributed across all firms that might have an interest in forming strategic alliances and that this ability may be history-dependent and socially complex and thus costly to imitate. Firms with these skills may be able to gain sustained competitive advantages from their alliance relationships. The observation that just a few firms, including Corning and Cisco, are well known for their strategic alliance successes is consistent with the observation that these alliance management skills may be valuable, rare, and costly to imitate.

Strategic Alliances in an International Context

As suggested in Table 9.1, strategic alliances are especially important for firms looking to enter into new foreign markets. In this context, one partner typically brings products or services (as resources) to the alliance, and the other partner brings local knowledge, local distribution networks, and local political influence (as resources) to the relationship. The development of local distribution networks can be a costly and difficult process. Such actions generally require a great deal of knowledge about local conditions. Local alliance partners may already possess this knowledge. They may even already have a local distribution network in place. By cooperating with local partners, firms can substantially reduce the cost of entry into these markets.

Of course, some governments require new entrants to have local alliance partners. Governments see such relationships not only as a way to facilitate entry of foreign firms into their market place, but also as a way that domestic firms can learn from foreign firms. This has been the case with General Electric's entry into the Chinese electricity production market. The Chinese government has required GE, if it wants to sell its generators in China, to form joint ventures with local Chinese companies. This has enabled GE to sell over $900 million worth of generators in the Chinese market.

However, recently, China began to require GE to provide its Chinese joint venture partners information about its generator technology and information about how to manufacture that technology. GE has spent over $500 million developing its new line of generators and obviously does not want to share this knowledge with firms that might some day become its competitors. But the Chinese government is now saying: "If you want to sell in China, you need to share your technology." Several other firms, besides GE, have had to share technology with their Chinese alliance partners to continue doing business in China as well, including Motorola, Microsoft, Seimens, and Nokia.[31] These actions by the Chinese government have the effect of increasing the cost of entry into the Chinese market.

All the potential threats that exist in alliances—from adverse selection to moral hazard, from holdup to learning races—can exist in an international context. Indeed, while it is often the case that there will be important information asymmetries between firms in an alliance, these asymmetries are likely to be much greater when alliance partners come from different countries, operate in different cultures, and speak different languages.

Ironically, it is precisely these kinds of threats that often motivate firms to engage in alliances in exploiting international opportunities. These same kinds of threats exist if a firm vertically integrates into its international operations—either on its own or by acquiring another firm. However, once a firm has vertically integrated, it can be relatively costly for it to extract itself from this investment if it turns out that it has been unfairly taken advantage of in deciding to begin operations in a country. On the other hand, it is much less costly for a firm to withdraw from an international alliance. For these reasons, it is not unusual to observe firms, as they begin to explore international opportunities, to do so first by engaging in market-based forms of exchange (through simple importing or exporting), followed by nonequity alliances (including licensing agreements). Only after a firm has developed trust and confidence in its international partners will it be willing to engage in equity alliances and, perhaps, joint ventures. In the end, if it makes economic sense to do so, a firm may even decide to vertically integrate into its international operations. However, this is often the last step in exploiting international opportunities, not the first step.

Thus, while all the threats associated with alliances exist in an international context, so do all the tools that can be used to reduce these threats. Over time, firms can even develop very strong and trusting relationships with their international alliance partners—relationships that create all the economic value of vertical integration but do so at much lower cost.

SUMMARY

Strategic alliances exist whenever two or more organizations cooperate in the development, manufac- ture, or sale of products or services. Strategic alliances can be grouped into three large categories: nonequity alliances, equity alliances, and joint ventures.

There are three broad reasons why firms join in strategic alliances: to improve the performance of their current operations, to improve the competitive environment within which they are operating, and to facilitate entry or exit into markets and industries. Just as there are incentives to cooperate in strategic alliances, there are also incentives to cheat. Cheating generally takes one or a combination of three forms: adverse selection, moral hazard, or holdup.

Strategic alliances can be a source of sustained competitive advantage. The rarity of alliances depends not only on the number of competing firms that have developed an alliance but also on the benefits that firms gain through their alliances.

Imitation through direct duplication of an alliance may be costly because of the socially complex relations that underlie an alliance. However, imitation through substitution is more likely. Two substitutes for alliances may be "going it alone," where firms develop and exploit the relevant sets of resources and capabilities on their own, and acquisitions. Opportunism, capabilities, and uncertainty all have an impact on when "going it alone" will and will not be a substitute for a strategic alliance. Acquisitions may be a substitute for strategic alliances when there are no legal constraints in acquisitions, strategic flexibility is not an important consideration, when the acquired firm has relatively little unwanted "organizational baggage," and when the value of a firm's resources and capabilities does not depend on its remaining independent. However, when these conditions do not exist, acquisitions are not a substitute for alliances.

The key issue facing firms in organizing their alliances is to facilitate cooperation while avoiding the threat of cheating. Contracts, equity investments, firm reputations, joint ventures, and trust can all reduce the threat of cheating in different contexts. These tools can also be used to reduce the threats to alliances in an international context.

CHALLENGE QUESTIONS

1. One reason why firms might want to pursue a strategic alliance strategy is to exploit economies of scale. Exploiting economies of scale should reduce a firm's costs. Does this mean that a firm pursuing an alliance strategy to exploit economies of scale is actually pursuing a cost leadership strategy? Why or why not?

2. Consider the joint venture between General Motors and Toyota. GM has been interested in learning how to profitably manufacture high-quality small cars from its alliance with Toyota. Toyota has been interested in gaining access to GM's U.S. distribution network and in reducing the political liability associated with local content laws.

Which of these firms do you think is more likely to accomplish its objectives, and why? What implications, if any, does your answer have for a possible "learning race" in this alliance?

3. Some have argued that strategic alliances are one way in which firms can help facilitate the development of a tacit collusion strategy. In your view, what are the critical differences between tacit collusion strategies and strategic alliance strategies? How can one tell whether two firms are engaging in an alliance to facilitate collusion or are engaging in an alliance for other purposes?

4. Some have argued that alliances can be used to help firms evaluate the economic potential of entering into a new industry or market. Under what conditions will a firm seeking to evaluate these opportunities need to invest in an alliance to accomplish this evaluation? Why couldn't such a firm simply hire some smart managers, consultants, and industry experts to evaluate the economic potential of entering into a new industry? What, if anything, about an alliance makes this a better way to evaluate entry opportunities than alternatives?

5. If adverse selection, moral hazard, and holdup are such significant problems for firms pursuing alliance strategies, why do firms even bother with alliances? Why don't they instead adopt a "go it alone" strategy to replace strategic alliances?

PROBLEM SET

1. Which of the following firms faces the greater threat of "cheating" in the alliances described, and why?

(a) Firm I and Firm II form a strategic alliance. As part of the alliance, Firm I agrees to build a new plant right next to Firm II's primary facility. In return, Firm II promises to buy most of the output of this new plant. Who is at risk, Firm I or Firm II?

(b) Firm A and Firm B form a strategic alliance. As part of the alliance, Firm A promises to begin selling products it already sells around the world in the home country of Firm B. In return, Firm B promises to provide Firm A with crucial contacts in its home country's government. These contacts are essential if Firm A is going to be able to sell in Firm B's home country. Who is at risk, Firm A or Firm B?

(c) Firm 1 and Firm 2 form a strategic alliance. As part of the alliance, Firm 1 promises to provide Firm 2 access to some new and untested technology that Firm 2 will use in its products. In return, Firm 2 will share some of the profits from its sales with Firm 1. Who is at risk, Firm 1 or Firm 2?

2. For each of the strategic alliances described in the above question, what actions could be taken to reduce the likelihood that partner firms will "cheat" in these alliances?

3. Examine the Web sites of the following strategic alliances and determine which of the sources of value presented in Table 9.1 are present:

(a) Dow-Corning (an alliance between Dow Chemical and Corning)
(b) CFM (an alliance between General Electric and SNECMA)
(c) Cingular (an alliance between SBC and BellSouth)
(d) NCAA (an alliance among colleges and universities in the United States)
(e) Visa (an alliance among banks in the United States)
(f) The alliance among United, Delta, Singapore Airlines, AeroMexico, Alitalia, and Korean Air.

END NOTES

1. See J. L. Badaracco and N. Hasagava (1988). "General Motors' Asian alliances." Harvard Business School, Case no. 9-388-094; D. Ernst and J. Bleeke (1993). *Collaborating to compete: Using strategic alliances and acquisitions in the global marketplace*. New York: Wiley; L. Doz & G. Hamel (1998). *Alliance advantage: The art of creating value through partnering*, Boston: Harvard Business School Press, xiii; R. D. Ireland, M. A. Hitt, & D. Vaidyanath (2202). Alliance management as a source of competitive advantage, *Journal of Management*, 28: 413–446; J. G. Coombs & D. J. Ketchen, 1999, Exploring interfirm cooperation and performance: Toward a reconciliation of predictions from the resource-based view and organizational economies, *Strategic Management Journal*, 20: 867–888.

2. Badaracco, J. L., and N. Hasegawa (1988). "General Motors' Asian alliances." Harvard Business School Case No. 9-388-094.

3. See Burgers, W. P., C. W. L. Hill, and W. C. Kim (1993). "A theory of global strategic alliances: The case of the global auto industry." *Strategic Management Journal*, 14, pp. 419–432.

4. See Freeman, A., and R. Hudson (1980). "Dupont and Philips plan joint venture to make, market laser disc products." *Wall Street Journal*, December 22, p. 10.

5. Teitelbaum, R. S. (1992). "Eskimo pie." *Fortune*, June 15, p. 123.

6. Nanda, A., and C. A. Bartlett (1990). "Corning Incorporated: A network of alliances." Harvard Business School Case No. 9-391-102.

7. See Knight, F. H. (1965). *Risk, uncertainty, and profit*. New York: John Wiley & Sons, Inc., on uncertainty; Kogut, B. (1991). "Joint ventures and the option to expand and acquire." *Management Science*, 37, pp. 19–33; Burgers, W. P., C. W. L. Hill, and W. C. Kim (1993). "A theory of global strategic alliances: The case of the global auto industry." *Strategic Management Journal*, 14, pp. 419–432; Noldeke, G., and K. M. Schmidt (1998). "Sequential investments and options to own." *Rand Journal of Economics*, 29(4), pp. 633–653; and Folta, T. B. (1998). "Governance and uncertainty: The tradeoff between administrative control and commitment." *Strategic Management Journal*, 19, pp. 1007–1028.

8. See Kogut, B. (1991). "Joint ventures and the option to expand and acquire. " *Management Science*, 37, pp. 19–33; and Balakrishnan, S., and M. Koza (1993). "Information asymmetry, adverse selection and joint-ventures." *Journal of Economic Behavior & Organization*, 20, pp. 99–117.

9. See, for example, Ernst, D., and J. Bleeke (1993). *Collaborating to compete: Using strategic alliances and acquisition in the global marketplace*. New York: John Wiley & Sons, Inc.

10. These terms are defined in Barney, J. B., and W. G. Ouchi (1986). *Organizational economics*. San Francisco: Jossey-Bass; and Holmstrom, B. (1979). "Moral hazard and observability." *Bell Journal of Economics*, 10(1), pp. 74–91. Problems of cheating in economic exchanges, in general, and in alliances in particular, are discussed by Gulati, R., and H. Singh (1998). "The architecture of cooperation: Managing coordination costs and appropriation concerns in strategic alliances." *Administrative Science Quarterly*, 43, pp. 781–814; Williamson, O. E. (1991). "Comparative economic organization: The analysis of discrete structural alternatives." *Administrative Science Quarterly*, 36, pp. 269–296; Osborn, R. N., and C. C. Baughn (1990). "Forms of interorganizational governance for multinational alliances." *Academy of Management Journal*, 33(3), pp. 503–519; Hagedorn, J., and R. Narula (1996). "Choosing organizational modes of strategic technology partnering: International and sectoral differences." *Journal of International Business Studies*, second quarter, pp. 265–284; Hagedorn, J. (1996). "Trends and patterns in strategic technology partnering since the early seventies." *Review of Industrial Organization*, 11, pp. 601–616; Kent, D. H. (1991). "Joint ventures vs. non-joint ventures: An empirical investigation." *Strategic Management Journal*, 12, pp. 387–393; and Shane, S. A. (1998). "Making new franchise systems work." *Strategic Management Journal*, 19, pp. 697–707.

11. Such alliance difficulties are described in Ouchi, W. G. (1984). *The M-form society: How American teamwork can capture the competitive edge*. Reading, MA: Addison-Wesley; and Bresser, R. K. (1988). "Cooperative strategy." *Strategic Management Journal*, 9, pp. 475–492.

12. Pope, K. (1993). "Dealers accuse Compaq of jilting them." *Wall Street Journal*, February 26, pp. 8, B1 +.

13. Williamson, O. E. (1975). *Markets and hierarchies: Analysis and antitrust implications*. New York: Free Press; Klein, B., R. Crawford, and A. Alchian (1978). "Vertical integration, appropriable rents, and the competitive contracting process." *Journal of Law and Economics*, 21, pp. 297–326.

14. See, for example, Yan, A., and B. Gray (1994). "Bargaining power, management control, and performance in United States-China joint ventures: A comparative case study." *Academy of Management Journal*, 37, pp. 1478–1517.

15. See Badaracco, J. L., and N. Hasegawa (1988). "General Motors' Asian alliances." Harvard Business School Case No. 9-388-094, on GM and Toyota; Patterson, G. A. (1991). "Mazda hopes to crack Japan's top tier." *Wall Street Journal*, September 20, pp. B1 +; and Williams, M., and M. Kanabayashi (1993). "Mazda and Ford drop proposal to build cars together in Europe." *Wall Street Journal*, March 4, p. A14, on Ford and Mazda; and Ennis, P. (1991). "Mitsubishi group wary of deeper ties to Chrysler." *Tokyo Business Today*, 59, July, p. 10, on DaimlerChrysler and Mitsubishi.

16. See, for example, Ernst, D., and J. Bleeke (1993). *Collaborating to compete: Using strategic alliances and acquisition in the global marketplace*. New York: John Wiley & Sons, Inc.; and Barney, J. B., and M. H. Hansen (1994). "Trustworthiness as a source of competitive advantage." *Strategic Management Journal*, 15, winter (special issue), pp. 175–190.

17. Ernst, D., and J. Bleeke (1993). *Collaborating to compete: Using strategic alliances and acquisition in the global marketplace*. New York: John Wiley & Sons, Inc.

18. Bartlett, C., and S. Ghoshal (1993). "Beyond the M-form: Toward a managerial theory of the firm." *Strategic Management Journal*, 14, pp. 23–46.

19. See Nagarajan, A., and W. Mitchell (1998). "Evolutionary diffusion: Internal and external methods used to acquire encompassing, complementary, and incremental technological changes in the lithotripsy industry." *Strategic Management Journal*, 19, pp. 1063–1077; Hagedoorn, J., and B. Sadowski (1999). "The transition from strategic technology alliances to mergers and acquisitions: An exploratory study." *Journal of Management Studies*, 36(1), pp. 87—107; and Newburry, W., and Y. Zeira (1997). "Generic differences between equity international joint ventures (EIJVs), international acquisitions (IAs) and International Greenfield investments (IGIs): Implications for parent companies." *Journal of World Business*, 32(2), pp. 87–102, on alliance substitutes.

20. Barney, J. B. (1999). "How a firm's capabilities affect boundary decisions." *Sloan Management Review*, 40(3), pp. 137–145.

21. See Hennart, J. F. (1988). "A transaction cost theory of equity joint ventures." *Strategic Management Journal*, 9, pp. 361–374; Kogut, B. (1988). "Joint ventures: Theoretical and empirical perspectives." *Strategic Management Journal*, 9, pp. 319–332; and Barney, J. B. (1999). "How a firm's capabilities affect boundary decisions." *Sloan Management Review*, 40(3), pp. 137–145, for a discussion of these limitations.

22. See Ouchi, W. G. (1984). *The M-form society: How American teamwork can capture the competitive edge*. Reading, MA: Addison-Wesley; and Barney, J. B. (1990). "Profit sharing bonuses and the cost of debt: Business finance and compensation policy in Japanese electronics firms." *Asia Pacific Journal of Management*, 7, pp. 49–64.

23. This is an argument developed by Barney, J. B., and M. H. Hansen (1994). "Trustworthiness as a source of competitive advantage." *Strategic Management Journal*, 15, winter (special issue), pp. 175–190; Weigelt, K., and C. Camerer (1988). "Reputation and corporate strategy: A review of recent theory and applications." *Strategic Management Journal*, 9, pp. 443–454; and Granovetter, M. (1985). "Economic action and social structure: The problem of embeddedness." *American Journal of Sociology*, 3, pp. 481–510.

24. See, for example, Eichenseher, J., and D. Shields (1985). "Reputation and corporate strategy: A review of recent theory and applications." *Strategic Management Journal*, 9, pp. 443–454; Beatty, R., and R. Ritter (1986). "Investment banking, reputation, and the underpricing of initial public offerings." *Journal of Financial Economics*, 15, pp. 213–232; Kalleberg, A. L., and T. Reve (1992). "Contracts and commitment: Economic and Sociological Perspectives on Employment Relations." *Human Relations*, 45(9), pp. 1103–1132; Larson, A. (1992). "Network dyads in entrepreneurial settings: A study of the governance of exchange relationships." *Administrative Science Quarterly*, March, pp. 76–104; Stuart, T. E., H. Hoang, and R. C. Hybels (1999).

"Interorganizational endorsements and the performance of entrepreneurial ventures." *Administrative Science Quarterly*, 44, pp. 315–349; Stuart, T. E. (1998). "Network positions and propensities to collaborate: An investigation of strategic alliance formation in a high-technology industry." *Administrative Science Quarterly*, 43(3), pp. 668–698; and Gulati, R. (1998). "Alliances and networks." *Strategic Management Journal*, 19, pp. 293–317.

25. Personal communication, April 8, 1986.
26. This same theoretic approach to firm reputation is discussed in Tirole, J. (1988). *The theory of industrial organization.* Cambridge, MA: MIT Press.
27. Scherer, F. M. (1980). *Industrial Market structure and economic performance.* Boston: Houghton Mifflin.
28. See again, Ernst, D., and J. Bleeke (1993). *Collaborating to compete: Using strategic alliances and acquisition in the global marketplace.* New York: John Wiley & Sons, Inc.; and Barney, J. B., and M. H. Hansen (1994). "Trustworthiness as a source of competitive advantage." *Strategic Management Journal*, 15, winter (special issue), pp. 175–190. In fact, there is a great deal of literature on the role of trust in strategic alliances. Some of the most interesting of this work can be found in Holm, D. B., K. Eriksson, and J. Johanson (1999). "Creating value through mutual commitment to business network relationships." *Strategic Management Journal*, 20, pp. 467–486; Lorenzoni, G., and A. Lipparini (1999). "The leveraging of interfirm relationships as a distinctive organizational capability: A longitudinal study." *Strategic Management Journal*, 20(4), pp. 317–338; Blois, K. J. (1999). "Trust in business to business relationships: An evaluation of its status." *Journal of Management Studies*, 36(2), pp. 197–215; Chiles, T. H., and J. F. McMackin (1996). "Integrating variable risk preferences, trust, and transaction cost economics." *Academy of Management Review*, 21(1), pp. 73–99; Larzelere, R. E., and T. L. Huston (1980). "The dyadic trust scale: Toward understanding interpersonal trust in close relationships." *Journal of Marriage and the Family*, August, pp. 595–604; Butler, J. K., Jr. (1983). "Reciprocity of trust between professionals and their secretaries." *Psychological Reports*, 53, pp. 411–416; Zaheer, A., and N. Venkatraman (1995). "Relational governance as an interorganizational strategy: An empirical test of the role of trust in economic exchange." *Strategic Management Journal*, 16, pp. 373–392; Butler, J. K., Jr., and R. S. Cantrell (1984). "A behavioral decision theory approach to modeling dyadic trust in superiors and subordinates." *Psychological Reports*, 55, pp. 19–28; Carney, M. (1998). "The competitiveness of networked production: The role of trust and asset specificity." *Journal of Management Studies*, 35(4), pp. 457–479.
29. Ernst, D., and J. Bleeke (1993). *Collaborating to compete: Using strategic alliances and acquisition in the global marketplace.* New York: John Wiley & Sons, Inc.
30. See Mohr, J., and R. Spekman (1994). "Characteristics of partnership success: Partnership attributes, communication behavior, and conflict resolution techniques." *Strategic Management Journal*, 15, pp. 135–152; and Zaheer, A., and N. Venkatraman (1995). "Relational governance as an interorganizational strategy: An empirical test of the role of trust in economic exchange." *Strategic Management Journal*, 16, pp. 373–392.
31. Kranhold, Kathryn (2004). "China's price for market entry: Give us your technology, too." *Wall Street Journal*, February 26, pp. A1 +.

10

Mergers and Acquisitions

It's as baffling as any mystery novel. One acquisition works while an apparently very similar acquisition does not work. How can this be?

Here are the facts: Two struggling Japanese automakers—Mitsubishi and Nissan—were acquired. DaimlerChrysler, a German and American company, acquired 37 percent of Mitsubishi's stock (a controlling interest) for $2.4 billion in 2001; Renault, a French company, acquired 38 percent of Nissan for $6 billion in 1998.

Before they were acquired, both Mitsubishi and Nissan had significant difficulties. Mitsubishi

The Case of the Twin Mergers

had a staggering debt load; it had few products under development, and miniscule sales in the most important car market in the world—the United States. Mitsubishi is, however, a member of one of the oldest and most powerful *keiretsu* in Japan. Its close links with other Japanese firms

suggested that Mitsubishi would probably have access to the low-cost capital it needed to invest in its turnaround.

If anything, Nissan was in worse shape. Indeed, $19 billion in debt, a faded brand name, and no products under development led DaimlerChrysler to turn its back on a potential acquisition of Nissan in favor of acquiring Mitsubishi. Renault was the only suitor left.

Learning Objectives

After reading this chapter, you should be able to:

1. Describe different types of mergers and acquisitions.

2. Estimate the return to the stockholders of bidding and target firms when there is no strategic relatedness between firms.

3. Describe different sources of relatedness between bidding and target firms.

4. Estimate the return to stockholders of bidding and target firms when there is strategic relatedness between firms.

5. Describe five reasons why bidding firms might still engage in acquisitions, even if on average they do not create value for a bidding firm's stockholders.

6. Describe three ways that bidding firms might be able to generate high returns for their equity holders through implementing mergers or acquisitions.

7. Describe the major challenges that firms integrating acquisitions are likely to face.

8. Discuss unique challenges to merger and acquisition strategies in an international context.

As soon as these acquisitions were complete, DaimlerChrysler reorganized and restructured Mitsubishi while Renault reorganized and restructured Nissan. By 2003, DaimlerChrysler had cut Mitsubishi's supplier costs by 15 percent, cut the workforce by 16 percent, doubled research and development spending compared to 2000, and hired several new world-class designers. More over, the Chrysler division of DaimlerChrysler had begun cooperating with Mitsubishi to develop new platforms for small and medium-sized cars. Soon, automobile platforms developed with Mitsubishi would be the basis for new models of the Dodge Neon, the Dodge Stratus, the Chrysler Sebring, a new Jeep SUV, and a new Chrysler PT Cruiser. Together, these cars represented about 20 percent of Chrysler's annual sales. At the end of this restructuring, Mitsubishi seemed poised to join with DaimlerChrysler to create a worldwide power in the automobile industry.

Over this same time period, Renault made its own changes in

Nissan. It closed five Nissan plants, reduced Nissan's workforce by 23,000, and began manufacturing more models in Nissan's efficient U.S. factories. These changes and investments led Nissan to lose $6.2 billion in 2000. Moreover, unlike Mitsubishi, Nissan was part of a relatively weak *keiretsu* in Japan. This meant that Nissan had to rely much more on Renault, and on its own capabilities, for the capital it needed to invest to become a world-class auto manufacturer. While a Renault–Nissan combination was not likely to be able to wield the worldwide clout of

DaimlerChrysler and Mitsubishi, it nevertheless appeared that Nissan was poised to restore some of the luster it had lost over the previous decade.

Jump to 2004. Nissan reported record profits. Its product line-up included such well-received models as the new Nissan 350Z sports car and the full-size Titan pickup. Nissan's market share in the U.S. market continued to improve, and it enjoyed some of the highest profit margins on its products in the industry. Mitsubishi, on the other hand, reported a $660 million loss. Its sales in the United States fell 26 percent and it had only 1.5 percent of the U.S. car market. Executives at DaimlerChrysler were beginning to despair. One Daimler executive was quoted as saying: "It's an absolute disaster. We can't sell it. It's worth nothing!" DaimlerChrysler almost seemed ready to write off its $2.4 billion investment in Mitsubishi, while Renault's investment in Nissan was beginning to show real dividends.

Why the difference between these two acquisitions? Some observers argued that DaimlerChrysler's efforts to restructure Mitsubishi never went far enough. Some actions not taken by Mitsubishi that might have helped turn things around included closing one plant in Japan, one plant in Australia, phasing out money-losing models in Japan, and shifting production to low-cost factories in China. However, while these actions might have improved Mitsubishi's financial position, other observers suggest a more subtle difference between the acquisition of Mitsubishi and the acquisition of Nissan.

Because Nissan was a member of a weak *keiretsu*, senior managers at Nissan knew that if they did not successfully turn this company around, it would go out of business. Literally, the entire livelihood for these Nissan managers was at risk, dependent on reawakening this once very successful company. On the other hand, since Mitsubishi was part of a much stronger *keiretsu*, its survival as an organization was never really in jeopardy. Historically, members of the Mitsubishi *keiretsu* have provided each other the cash and other resources they need to survive in even the most difficult times. Because their survival was never at risk, some senior managers at Mitsubishi were able to resist the cultural changes that are always part of a corporate restructuring. Despite the efforts of senior managers brought to Mitsubishi by DaimlerChrysler, these pockets of cultural resistance remained. Most observers agree that until Mitsubishi transforms its culture—a culture that is so reluctant to share bad news with senior managers that information about quality defects that should have led to product recalls was squelched for over 10 years—it will not be as successful an acquisition as Nissan.

Sources : G. Edmundson (2004). "Japan: A tale of two mergers." *BusinessWeek*, May 10, p. 42; D. Welch and G. Edmundson (2004). "A shaky automotive *menage a trois.*" *BusinessWeek*, May 10, pp. 40–41.

Mergers and acquisitions are one very common way that a firm can accomplish its vertical integration and diversification objectives. This can be seen in the opening case. Both DaimlerChrysler and Renault were looking to diversify their operations internationally to give themselves a more global reach than they traditionally had. DaimlerChrysler's acquisition of Mitsubishi and Renault's acquisition of Nissan accomplished this objective quite well. In addition, the Chrysler division of DaimlerChrysler was looking to outsource some aspects of the car development process—including the design of new automotive platforms. It needed a partner to work with and the recently acquired Mitsubishi became that partner. So, this acquisition also helped a division of DaimlerChrysler to accomplish its vertical integration objectives.

However, the story of the acquisitions of Mitsubishi and Nissan is a cautionary tale as well. While a firm may be able to accomplish its vertical integration and diversification objectives through mergers or acquisitions, it is sometimes difficult to generate real economic profit from doing so. Indeed, one of the strongest empirical findings in the fields of strategic management and finance is that, on average, the equity holders of target firms in mergers and acquisitions make money while the equity holders of bidding firms in these same mergers and acquisitions usually only "break even."

What Are Mergers and Acquisitions?

The terms "mergers" and "acquisitions" are often used interchangeably, even though they are not synonyms. A firm engages in an **acquisition** when it purchases a second firm. The form of this purchase can vary. For example, an acquiring firm can use cash it has generated from its ongoing businesses to purchase a target firm; it can go into debt to purchase a target firm; it can use its own equity to purchase a target firm; or it can use a mix of these mechanisms to purchase a target firm. Also, an acquiring firm can purchase all of a target firm's assets, it can purchase a majority of those assets (greater than 51 percent), or it can purchase a **controlling share** of those assets (i.e., enough assets so that the acquiring firm is able to make all the management and strategic decisions in the target firm).

Acquisitions also vary on several other dimensions. For example, **friendly acquisitions** occur when the management of the target firm wants the firm to be acquired. **Unfriendly acquisitions** occur when the management of the target firm does not want the firm to be acquired. Some unfriendly acquisitions are also known as **hostile takeovers**. Some acquisitions are accomplished through direct negotiations between an acquiring firm's managers and the managers of a target firm. This is especially common when a target firm is **privately held** (i.e., when it has not sold shares on the public stock market) or **closely held** (i.e., when it has not sold very many shares on the public stock market). Other acquisitions are accomplished by the acquiring firm publicly announcing that it is willing to purchase the outstanding shares of a potential target for a particular price. This price is normally greater than the current market price of the target firm's shares. The difference between the current market price of a target firm's shares and the price a potential acquirer offers to pay for those shares is known as an **acquisition premium**. This approach to purchasing a firm is called a **tender offer**. Tender offers can be made either with or without the support of the management of the target firm. Obviously, tender offers with the support of the target firm's management are typically friendly in character; those made without the support of the target firm's management are typically unfriendly.

It is usually the case that larger firms—in terms of sales or assets—acquire smaller firms. This was the case both for DaimlerChrysler's acquisition of Mitsubishi and Renault's acquisition of Nissan. On the other hand, when the assets of two similar-sized firms are combined, this transaction is called a **merger**. Mergers can be accomplished in many of the same ways as acquisitions, that is, using cash or stock to purchase a percentage of another firm's assets. Typically, however, mergers will not be unfriendly. In a merger, one firm purchases some percentage of a second firm's assets while the second firm simultaneously purchases some percentage of the first firm's assets. For example, DaimlerChrysler—the firm that purchased Mitsubishi (in the opening case)—was created as a merger between Daimler-Benz (the maker of Mercedes-Benz) and Chrysler. Daimler-Benz invested some of its capital in Chrysler, and Chrysler invested some of its capital in Daimler-Benz.

While mergers typically begin as a transaction between equals, that is, between firms of equal size and profitability, they often evolve after a merger such that one firm is more dominant in the management of the merged firm than the other. For example, most observers believe that Daimler (the German part of DaimlerChrysler) has become more dominant in the management of the combined firm than Chrysler (the American part). Indeed, while Daimler management may be willing to "write off" their interests in Mitsubishi as a bad investment, Chrysler management is very reluctant to do so, since they have worked with Mitsubishi to help develop platforms for many of Chrysler's best-selling cars. How long a Daimler-dominated DaimlerChrysler will put up with a "bad" investment that only helps the Chrysler part of the firm is an open question.[1] Put differently, while mergers usually start out as something different from acquisitions, they usually end up looking more like acquisitions than mergers.

VRIO The Value of Mergers and Acquisitions

That merger and acquisition strategies are an important strategic option open to firms pursuing diversification and vertical integration strategies can hardly be disputed. The number of firms that have used merger and acquisition strategies to become diversified over the last few years is staggering. Worldwide, the total value of announced merger and acquisition activities was over $1.5 trillion in 2000, 2001, and 2002. And while the total level of these activities moderated somewhat in 2003, mergers and acquisitions have certainly not disappeared. For example, in 2003, over 200 publicly traded firms in the United States engaged in merger and acquisition activities. These firms ranged in size from Cardinal Health and Johnson & Johnson—two of the largest health care firms in the world—to Inflazyme Pharmaceuticals—a relatively small biotechnology start-up that acquired Glycodesign, Inc. Nor were these acquisitions limited to just a few industries. At least 26 occurred in health-related industries, 43 in the financial services industries, 20 in the mining and raw materials extraction industries, and 28 in high-technology industries.

The list of firms that engaged in mergers and acquisitions in 2003 was long and varied. For example, on October 29, 2003, Applied Micro Circuits purchased JNI Corporation for $7.00 cash per share, in a deal valued at $209.2 million. JNI made enterprise storage connectivity products that Applied Micro Circuits used in its products. On October 28, 2003, palmOne Inc. (maker of the famous Palm Pilot lines of PDAs) purchased Handspring, Inc. (maker of another PDA brand, Treo). On March 26, 2003, K2 (the ski and in-line skate manufacturer) extended its operations into the sporting goods industry by purchasing Rawlings Sporting Goods (manufacturer of, among other things, most of the baseball gloves used in major league baseball). Each Rawlings shareholder received 1.08 shares of K2 stock. On September 3, 2003, Univision Communications (the leading broadcaster of Spanish-language programming on television) purchased Hispanic Broadcasting Corporation (a firm that owns over 40 Spanish-language radio stations). On September 26, 2003, Linamar Corp. (a firm that sells machined parts to the worldwide automobile industry) purchased Mclaren Performance Technologies (the firm that was originally created to develop and build race engines for Mclaren Formula One race cars) for $.8875 per share. And on March 3, 2003, Penn National Gaming (an owner and operator of riverboat casinos and other gambling venues) expanded its geographic reach by acquiring Hollywood Casinos for $12.75 a share.

That mergers and acquisitions are common is clear. What is less clear is that they actually generate value for firms implementing these strategies. Two cases will be examined here: mergers and acquisitions between strategically unrelated firms and mergers and acquisitions between strategically related firms.

Mergers and Acquisitions: The Unrelated Case

Imagine the following scenario: One firm (the target) is the object of an acquisition effort, and 10 firms (the bidders) are interested in making this acquisition. Suppose the **current market value** of the target firm is $10,000—that is, the price of each of this firm's shares times the number of shares outstanding equals $10,000. Also, suppose the current market value of each of the bidding firms is $15,000.[2] Finally, suppose there is no strategic relatedness between these bidding firms and the target. This means that the value of any one of these bidding firms when combined with the target firm exactly equals the sum of the value of these firms as separate entities. In this example, since the current market value of the target is $10,000, and the current market value of the bidding firms is $15,000, the value of this target when combined with any of these bidders would be $25,000 ($10,000 + $15,000). Given this information, at what price will this target be acquired, and what are the economic performance implications for bidding and target firms at this price?

In this, and all acquisition situations, bidding firms will be willing to pay a price for a target up to the value that the target firm adds to the bidder once it is acquired. This price is simply the difference between the value of the two firms combined (in this case $25,000) and the value of the bidding firm by itself (in this case $15,000). Notice that this price does not depend on the value of the target firm acting as an independent business but, rather, depends on the value that the target firm creates when it is combined with the bidding firm. Any price for a target less than this value (i.e., less than $10,000) will be a source of economic profit for a bidding firm; any price equal to this value (i.e., equal to $10,000) will be a source of zero economic profits; and any price greater than this value (i.e., greater than $10,000) will be a source of economic losses for the bidding firm that acquires the target.

It is not hard to see that the price of this acquisition will quickly rise to $10,000 and that at this price the bidding firm that acquires the target will earn zero economic profits. The price of this acquisition will quickly rise to $10,000 because any bid less than $10,000 will generate economic profits for a successful bidder. These potential profits, in turn, will generate entry into the bidding war for a target. Because entry into the acquisition contest is very likely, the price of the acquisition will quickly rise to its value, and economic profits will not be created.

Moreover, at this $10,000 price, the target firm's equity holders will also gain zero economic profits. Indeed, for them, all that has occurred is that the market value of the target firm has been capitalized in the form of a cash payment from the bidder to the target. The target was worth $10,000, and that is exactly what these equity holders will receive.

Mergers and Acquisitions: The Related Case

The conclusion that the acquisition of strategically unrelated targets will generate only zero economic profits for both the bidding and the target firms is not surprising. It is very consistent with the discussion of the economic consequences of unrelated diversification in Chapter 7. There it was argued that there is no economic justification for a corporate diversification strategy that does not build on some type of economy of scope across the businesses within which a firm operates, and thus that unrelated diversification is not an economically viable corporate strategy. So, if there is any hope that mergers and acquisitions will be a source of superior performance for bidding firms, it must be because of some sort of strategic relatedness or economy of scope between bidding and target firms.

Types of Strategic Relatedness

Of course, bidding and target firms can be strategically related in a wide variety of ways. Three particularly important lists of these potential linkages are discussed here.[3]

The FTC Categories. Because mergers and acquisitions can have the effect of increasing (or decreasing) the level of concentration in an industry, the Federal Trade Commission (FTC) is charged with the responsibility of evaluating the competitive implications of proposed mergers or acquisitions. In principle, the FTC will disallow any acquisition involving firms with headquarters in the United States that could have the potential for generating monopoly (or oligopoly) profits in an industry. To help in this regulatory effort, the FTC has developed a typology of mergers and acquisitions (see Table 10.1). Each category in this typology can be thought of as a different way in which a bidding firm and a target firm can be related in a merger or acquisition.

According to the FTC, a firm engages in a **vertical merger** when it vertically integrates, either forward or backward, through its acquisition efforts. Vertical mergers could include a firm purchasing critical suppliers of raw materials (backward vertical integration) or acquiring customers and distribution networks (forward vertical integration). Applied Micro Circuits' acquisition of JDI is an example of a backward vertical integration. Disney's acquisition of Capital Cities/ABC can be understood as an attempt by Disney to forward vertically integrate into the entertainment distribution industry, while its acquisition of ESPN can be seen as backward vertical integration into the entertainment production business.[4]

A firm engages in a **horizontal merger** when it acquires a former competitor; palmOne's acquisition of Handspring is an example of a horizontal merger.

Table 10.1 **FTC Categories of Mergers and Acquisitions**

■ Vertical merger	A firm acquires former suppliers or customers.
■ Horizontal merger	A firm acquires a former competitor.
■ Product extension merger	A firm gains access to complementary products through an acquisition.
■ Market extension merger	A firm gains access to complementary markets through an acquisition.
■ Conglomerate merger	There is no strategic relatedness between a bidding and a target firm.

Obviously, the FTC is particularly concerned with the competitive implications of horizontal mergers because these strategies can have the most direct and obvious anticompetitive implications in an industry. For example, the FTC raised antitrust concerns in the proposed merger between Oracle and PeopleSoft, because these firms, collectively, dominated the enterprise software market. Similar concerns were raised in the proposed merger between British Petroleum and Arco and the proposed merger between Mobil and Exxon.

The third type of merger identified by the FTC is a **product extension merger**. In a product extension merger, firms acquire complementary products through their merger and acquisition activities. Examples include K2's acquisition of Rawlings Sporting Goods, Univision's acquisition of Hispanic Broadcasting, and Linamar's acquisition of Mclaren Performance Technology.

The fourth type of merger identified by the FTC is a **market extension merger**. Here, the primary objective is to gain access to new geographic markets. Examples include Penn National Gaming's acquisition of Hollywood Casinos.

The final type of merger or acquisition identified by the FTC is a **conglomerate merger**. For the FTC, conglomerate mergers are a residual category. If there are no vertical, horizontal, product extension, or market extension links between firms, the FTC defines the merger or acquisition activity between firms as a conglomerate merger. Given our earlier conclusion that mergers or acquisitions between strategically *unrelated* firms will not generate economic profits for either bidders or targets, it should not be surprising that there are currently relatively few examples of conglomerate mergers or acquisitions; however, at various times in history, they have been relatively common. In the 1960s, for example, many acquisitions took the form of conglomerate mergers. Research has shown that the fraction of single-business firms in the *Fortune* 500 dropped from 22.8 percent in 1959 to 14.8 percent in 1969, while the fraction of firms in the *Fortune* 500 pursuing unrelated diversification strategies rose from 7.3 percent to 18.7 percent during the same time period. These findings are consistent with an increase in the number of conglomerate mergers and acquisitions during the 1960s.[5]

Despite the popularity of conglomerate mergers in the 1960s, many mergers or acquisitions among strategically unrelated firms are divested shortly after they are completed. One study estimated that over one-third of the conglomerate mergers of the 1960s were divested by the early 1980s. Another study showed that over 50 percent of these acquisitions were subsequently divested. These results are all consistent with our earlier conclusion that mergers or acquisitions involving strategically unrelated firms are not a source of economic profits.[6]

Other Types of Strategic Relatedness. Although the FTC categories of mergers and acquisitions provide some information about possible motives underlying these corporate strategies, they do not capture the full complexity of the links that might exist between bidding and target firms. Several authors have attempted to develop more complete lists of possible sources of relatedness between bidding and target firms. One of these lists, developed by Professor Michael Lubatkin, is summarized in Table 10.2. This list includes **technical economies** (in marketing, production, and similar forms of relatedness), **pecuniary economies** (market power), and **diversification economies** (in portfolio management and risk reduction) as possible bases of strategic relatedness between bidding and target firms.

A second important list of possible sources of strategic relatedness between bidding and target firms was developed by Michael Jensen and Richard Ruback after a comprehensive review of empirical research on the economic returns to mergers and acquisitions. This list is summarized in Table 10.3 and includes the following factors as

Table 10.2   Lubatkin's List of Potential Sources of Strategic Relatedness Between Bidding and Target Firms

Technical economies	Scale economies that occur when the physical processes inside a firm are altered so that the same amounts of input produce a higher quantity of outputs. Sources of technical economies include marketing, production, experience, scheduling, banking, and compensation.
Pecuniary economies	Economies achieved by the ability of firms to dictate prices by exerting market power.
Diversification economies	Economies achieved by improving a firm's performance relative to its risk attributes or lowering its risk attributes relative to its performance. Sources of diversification economies include portfolio management and risk reduction.

Sources: M. Lubatkin (1983). "Mergers and the performance of the acquiring firm." *Academy of Management Review*, 8, pp. 218–225. © 1983 by Academy of Management. Reproduced with permission.

possible sources of economic gains in mergers and acquisitions: potential reductions in production or distribution costs (from economies of scale, vertical integration, reduction in agency costs, and so forth); the realization of financial opportunities (such as gaining access to underutilized tax shields, avoiding bankruptcy costs); the creation of market power; and the ability to eliminate inefficient management in the target firm.

To be economically valuable, links between bidding and target firms must meet the same criteria as diversification strategies (see Chapter 7). First, these links must build on real economies of scope between bidding and target firms. These economies of scope can reflect either cost savings or revenue enhancements that are created by combining firms. Second, not only must this economy of scope exist but it must be less costly for the merged firm to realize than for outside equity holders to realize on their own. As is the case with corporate diversification strategies, by investing in a diversified portfolio of stocks, outside equity investors can gain many

Table 10.3   Jensen and Ruback's List of Reasons Why Bidding Firms Might Want to Engage in Merger and Acquisition Strategies

To reduce production or distribution costs:
1. Through economies of scale.
2. Through vertical integration.
3. Through the adoption of more efficient production or organizational technology.
4. Through the increased utilization of the bidder's management team.
5. Through a reduction of agency costs by bringing organization-specific assets under common ownership.

Financial motivations:
1. To gain access to underutilized tax shields.
2. To avoid bankruptcy costs.
3. To increase leverage opportunities.
4. To gain other tax advantages.

To gain market power in product markets.

To eliminate inefficient target management.

Sources: M. C. Jensen and R. S. Ruback (1983). "The market for corporate control: The scientific evidence." *Journal of Financial Economics*, 11, pp. 5–50. Vol. II. © 1983.

of the economies associated with a merger or acquisition on their own. Moreover, investors can realize some of these economies of scope at almost zero cost. In this situation, it makes little sense for investors to "hire" managers in firms to realize these economies of scope for them through a merger or acquisition. Rather, firms should pursue merger and acquisition strategies only to obtain valuable economies of scope that outside investors find too costly to create on their own.

Economic Profits in Related Acquisitions

If bidding and target firms are strategically related, then the economic value of these two firms combined is greater than their economic value as separate entities. To see how this changes returns to merger and acquisition strategies, consider the following scenario: As before, there is one target firm and ten bidding firms. The market value of the target firm as a stand-alone entity is $10,000, and the market value of the bidding firms as stand-alone entities is $15,000. However, unlike the earlier scenario in this chapter, the bidding and target firms are strategically related. Any of the types of relatedness identified in Tables 10.1, 10.2, or 10.3 could be the source of these economies of scope. They imply that when any of the bidding firms and the target are combined, the market value of this combined entity will be $32,000—note that $32,000 is greater than the sum of $15,000 and $10,000. At what price will this target firm be acquired, and what are the economic profit implications for bidding and target firms at this price?

As before, bidding firms will be willing to pay a price for a target up to the value that a target firm adds once it is acquired. Thus, the maximum price bidding firms are willing to pay is still the difference between the value of the combined entity (here, $32,000) and the value of a bidding firm on its own (here, $15,000), or $17,000.

As was the case for the strategically unrelated acquisition, it is not hard to see that the price for actually acquiring the target firm in this scenario will rapidly rise to $17,000, because any bid less than $17,000 has the potential for generating profits for a bidding firm. Suppose that one bidding firm offers $13,000 for the target. For this $13,000, the bidding firm gains access to a target that will generate $17,000 of value once it is acquired. Thus, to this bidding firm, the target is worth $17,000, and a bid of $13,000 will generate $4,000 economic profit. Of course, these potential profits will motivate entry into the competitive bidding process. Entry will continue until the price of this target equals $17,000. Any price greater than $17,000 would mean that a bidding firm is actually losing money on its acquisition.[7]

At this $17,000 price, the successful bidding firm earns zero economic profits. After all, this firm has acquired an asset that will generate $17,000 of value and has paid $17,000 to do so. However, the owners of the target firm will earn an economic profit worth $7,000. As a stand-alone firm, the target is worth $10,000; when combined with a bidding firm, it is worth $17,000. The difference between the value of the target as a stand-alone entity and its value in combination with a bidding firm is the value of the economic profit that can be appropriated by the owners of the target firm.

Thus, the existence of strategic relatedness between bidding and target firms is not a sufficient condition for the equity holders of bidding firms to earn economic profits from their acquisition strategies. If the economic potential of acquiring a particular target firm is widely known and if several potential bidding firms can all obtain this value by acquiring a target, the equity holders of bidding firms will, at best, earn only zero economic profits from implementing an acquisition strategy. In this setting, a "strategically related" merger or acquisition will create economic value, but this value will be distributed in the form of economic profits to the equity holders of acquired target firms.

Since so much of the value created in a merger or acquisition is appropriated by the stockholders of the target firm, it is not surprising that many small and entrepreneurial firms look to be acquired as one way to compensate their owners for taking the risks associated with founding these firms. This phenomenon is discussed in more detail in the Strategy in the Emerging Enterprise feature.

Strategy in the Emerging Enterprise

Imagine you are an entrepreneur. You have mortgaged your home, taken out loans, run up your credit cards, and put all you own on the line in order to help grow a small company. And finally, after years of effort, things start going well. Your product or service starts to sell, customers start to appreciate your unique value proposition, and you actually begin to pay yourself a reasonable salary. What do you do next to help grow your company?

Some entrepreneurs in this situation decide that maintaining their control of the firm is very important. These entrepreneurs may compensate certain critical employees with equity in the firm, but typically limit the number of outsiders who make equity investments in their firm. To grow these closely held firms, these entrepreneurs must rely on capital generated from their ongoing operations (called **retained earnings**) and debt capital provided by banks, customers, and suppliers. Entrepreneurs who decide to maintain control of their companies are compensated for taking the risks associated with starting a firm through the salary they pay themselves.

Other entrepreneurs get more outside equity investors involved in providing the capital a firm needs to grow. These outside investors might include wealthy individuals—called **business angels**—looking to invest in entrepreneurial ventures or **venture capital firms**. Venture capital firms typically raise money from numerous smaller investors which they then

Cashing Out

invest in a portfolio of entrepreneurial firms. Over time, many of these firms decide to "go public" by engaging in what is called an **initial public offering**, or **IPO**. In an IPO, a firm, typically working with an investment banker, sells its equity to the public at large. Entrepreneurs who decide to sell equity in their firm are compensated for taking the risks associated with starting a firm through the sale of their equity on the public markets through an IPO. An entrepreneur who receives compensation for risk-taking in this manner is said to be **cashing out**.

Finally, still other entrepreneurs may decide to not use an IPO to cash out, but rather to have their firm acquired by another, typically larger, firm. In this scenario, entrepreneurs are compensated by the acquiring firm for

taking the risks associated with starting a firm. Indeed, because the demand for IPOs has been volatile since the technology bubble burst of 2000, more and more smaller and entrepreneurial firms are looking to be acquired as a way for their founders to cash out. Moreover, since the stockholders of target firms typically appropriate a large percentage of the total value created by an acquisition, and since the founders of these entrepreneurial firms are also often large stockholders, being acquired is often a source of great wealth for an entrepreneurial firm's founders.

The choice between keeping a firm private, going public, or being acquired is a difficult and multidimensional one. Issues including the personal preferences of a firm's founders, demand for IPOs, how much capital a firm will need in order to continue to grow its business, and what other resources—besides capital—it will need to create additional value all play a role. In general, firms that do not need a great deal of money or other resources to grow will choose to remain private. Those that need only money to grow will choose IPOs, while those that need managerial or technical resources controlled by another firm to grow will typically be acquired. Of course, all this changes if entrepreneurs decide to maintain control of their firms because they want to.

Sources: R. Hennessey (2004). "Underwriters cut prices on IPOs as market softens." *Wall Street Journal*, May 27, p. C4; F. Vogelstein (2003). "Can Google grow up?" *Fortune*, December 8, pp. 102 +.

What Does Research Say About Returns to Mergers and Acqusitions?

The empirical implications of this discussion of returns to bidding and target firms in strategically related and strategically unrelated mergers and acquisitions have been examined in a variety of academic literatures. One study reviewed over 40 empirical merger and acquisition studies in the finance literature. This study concluded that acquisitions, on average, increased the market value of target firms by about 25 percent and left the market value of bidding firms unchanged. The authors of this report concluded that "corporate takeovers generate positive gains, … target firm equity holders benefit, and … bidding firm equity holders do not lose."[8] The way these studies evaluate the return to acquisition strategies is discussed in the Strategy in Depth feature.

Strategy researchers have also attempted to examine in more detail the sources of value creation in mergers and acquisitions and the question of whether these sources of value creation affect whether bidders or targets appropriate this value. For example, two well-known studies examined the impact of the type and degree of strategic relatedness (defined using the FTC typology summarized in Table 10.1) between bidding and target firms on the economic consequences of mergers and acquisitions.[9] These studies found that the more strategically related bidding and target firms are, the more economic value mergers and acquisitions create. However, like the finance studies, this work found that this economic value was appropriated by the owners of the target firm, regardless of the type or degree of relatedness between bidding and target firms. Bidding firms—even when they attempt to acquire strategically related targets—earn, on average, zero economic profits from their merger and acquisition strategies.

Why Are There So Many Mergers and Acquisitions?

Given the overwhelming empirical evidence that most of the economic value created in mergers and acquisitions is appropriated by the owners of the target firm most of the time, an important question becomes: " Why do managers of bidding firms continue to engage in merger and acquisition strategies?" Some possible explanations are summarized in Table 10.4 and discussed in this section.

To Ensure Survival
Even if mergers and acquisitions, on average, generate only zero economic profits for bidding firms, it may be necessary for bidding firms to engage in these activities to ensure their survival. In particular, if all of a bidding firm's competitors have been able to improve their efficiency and effectiveness

Table 10.4   **Possible Motivations to Engage in Mergers and Acquisitions Even Though They Usually Do Not Generate Profits for Bidding Firms**

1. To ensure survival
2. Free cash flow
3. Agency problems
4. Managerial hubris
5. The potential for above-normal profits

Strategy in Depth

*B*y far, the most popular way to evaluate the performance effects of acquisitions for bidding firms is called **event study analysis**. Rooted in the field of financial economics, event study analysis compares the actual performance of a stock after an acquisition has been announced to the expected performance of that stock, if no acquisition had been announced. Any performance greater (or less) than what was expected in a short period of time around when an acquisition is announced is attributed to that acquisition. This **cumulative abnormal return** or **CAR** can be positive or negative, depending on whether the stock in question performs better or worse than what was expected without an acquisition.

The CAR created by an acquisition is calculated in several stages. First, the expected performance of a stock, without an acquisition, is estimated with the following regression equation:

$$E(R_{j,t}) = a_j + b_j R_{m,t} + e_{j,t}$$

Where $E(R_{j,t})$ is the expected return of stock j during time t, a_j is a constant (approximately equal to the rate of return on risk-free equities), b_j is an empirical estimate of the financial parameter β (equal to the covariance between the returns of a particular firm's stock and the average return of all stocks in the market, over time), $R_{m,t}$ is the actual average rate of return of all stocks in the market over time, and $e_{j,t}$ is an error term. The form of this equation is derived from the capital asset pricing model in finance. In this model, $E(R_{j,t})$ is simply the expected performance of a stock, given

Evaluating the Performance Effects of Acquisitions

the historical relationship between that stock and the overall performance of the stock market.

To calculate the unexpected performance of a stock, this expected level of performance is simply subtracted from the actual level of performance for a stock. This is done in the following equation:

$$XR_{j,t} = R_{j,t} - (a_j + b_j R_{m,t})$$

where $R_{j,t}$ is the actual performance of stock j during time t, and $XR_{j,t}$ is the unexpected performance of stock j during time t.

In calculating the CAR for a particular acquisition, it is necessary to sum the unexpected returns ($XR_{j,t}$) for a stock across the t periods when the stock market is responding to news about this acquisition. Most analyses of acquisitions examine the market's reaction one day before an acquisition is formally announced to three days after it is announced. The sum of these

unexpected returns over this time period is the CAR attributable to this acquisition.

This methodology has been applied to literally thousands of acquisition episodes. For example, when Manulife Financial purchased John Hancock Financial, Manulife's CAR was −10%, while John Hancock's CAR was +6%. When Anthem acquired Wellpoint, Anthem's CAR was −10% and Wellpoint's was +7%. When Bank of America acquired FleetBoston Financial, Bank of America's CAR was −9% and FleetBoston's was +24%. And when UnitedHealth acquired Mid Atlantic Medical, UnitedHealth's CAR was −4% and Mid Atlantic Medical's was +11%.

While the event study method has been used widely, it does have some important limitations. First, it is based entirely on the capital asset pricing model and there is some reason to believe that this model is not a particularly good predictor of a firm's expected stock price. Second, it assumes that a firm's equity holders can anticipate all the benefits associated with making an acquisition at the time that acquisition is made. Some scholars have argued that value creation continues long after an acquisition is announced as parties in this exchange discover value-creating opportunities that could not have been anticipated.

Sources: A. Arikan (2004). "Long-term returns to acquisitions: The case of purchasing tangible and intangible assets." Unpublished, Fisher College of Business, Ohio State University; S. J. Brown and J. B. Warner (1985). "Using daily stock returns: The case of event studies." *Journal of Financial Economics*, 14, pp. 3–31; D. Henry, M. Der Hovanseian, and D. Foust (2003). "M&A deals: Show me." *BusinessWeek*, November 10, pp. 38 +.

through a particular type of acquisition, then failing to make such an acquisition may put a firm at a competitive disadvantage. Here, the purpose of a merger or acquisition is not to gain competitive advantages but rather to gain competitive parity.

Many recent mergers among banks in the United States seem to have competitive parity and normal economic profits as an objective. Most bank managers recognize that changing bank regulations, increased competition from nonbanking financial institutions, and soft demand are likely to lead to a consolidation of the U.S. banking industry. To survive in this consolidated industry, many U.S. banks will have to merge. As the number of banks engaging in mergers and acquisitions goes up, the ability to earn superior profits from those strategies goes down. These lower returns from acquisitions have already reduced the economic value of some of the most aggressive acquiring banks. Despite these lower returns, acquisitions are likely to continue for the foreseeable future, as banks seek survival opportunities in a consolidated industry.[10]

Free Cash Flow

Another reason why firms may continue to invest in merger and acquisition strategies is that these strategies, on average, can be expected to generate at least competitive parity for bidding firms. This zero economic profit may be a more attractive investment for some firms than alternative strategic investments. This is particularly the case for firms that generate free cash flow.[11]

Free cash flow is simply the amount of cash a firm has to invest after all positive net present-value investments in its ongoing businesses have been funded. Free cash flow is created when a firm's ongoing business operations are very profitable but offer few opportunities for additional investment. One firm that seems to have generated a great deal of free cash flow over the last several years is Philip Morris. Philip Morris's retail tobacco operations are extremely profitable. However, regulatory constraints, health concerns, and slowing growth in demand limit investment opportunities in the tobacco industry. Thus, the amount of cash generated by Philip Morris's ongoing tobacco business has probably been larger than the sum of its positive net present-value investments in that business. This difference is free cash flow for Philip Morris.[12]

A firm that generates a great deal of free cash flow must decide what to do with this money. One obvious alternative would be to give it to stockholders in the form of dividends or stock buybacks. However, in some situations (for example, when stockholders face high marginal tax rates), stockholders may prefer a firm to retain this cash flow and invest it for them. When this is the case, how should a firm invest its free cash flow?

Because (by definition) no positive net present-value investment opportunities in a firm's ongoing business operations are available, firms have only two investment options: to invest their free cash flow in strategies that generated competitive parity or in strategies that generate competitive disadvantages. In this context, merger and acquisition strategies are a viable option, for bidding firms, on average, can expect to generate at least competitive parity. Put differently, while mergers and acquisitions may not be a source of superior profits, there are worse things you could do with your free cash flow.

Agency Problems

Another reason why firms might continue to engage in mergers and acquisitions, despite earning only competitive parity from doing so, is that mergers and acquisitions benefit managers directly, independent of any value they may or may not create for a bidding firm's stockholders. As suggested in Chapter 8, these conflicts of interest are a manifestation of agency problems between a firm's managers and its stockholders.

Merger and acquisition strategies can benefit managers—even if they do not directly benefit a bidding firm's equity holders—in at least two ways. First, managers can use mergers and acquisitions to help diversify their human capital investments in their firm. As discussed in Chapter 7, managers have difficulty diversifying their firm-specific human capital investments when a firm operates in a narrow range of businesses. By acquiring firms with cash flows that are not perfectly correlated with the cash flows of a firm's current businesses, managers can reduce the probability of bankruptcy for their firm and thus partially diversify their human capital investments in their firm.

Second, managers can use mergers and acquisitions to quickly increase firm size, measured in either sales or assets. If management compensation is closely linked to firm size, managers who increase firm size are able to increase their compensation. Of all the ways to increase the size of a firm quickly, growth through mergers and acquisitions is perhaps the easiest. Even if there are no economies of scope between a bidding and a target firm, an acquisition ensures that the bidding firm will grow by the size of the target (measured in either sales or assets). If there are economies of scope between a bidding and a target firm, the size of the bidding firm can grow at an even faster rate, as can the value of management's compensation, even though, on average, acquisitions do not generate wealth for the owners of the bidding firm.

Managerial Hubris

Another reason why managers may choose to continue to invest in mergers and acquisitions, despite the fact that, on average, they gain no profits from doing so, is the existence of what has been called **managerial hubris**.[13] This is the unrealistic belief held by managers in bidding firms that they can manage the assets of a target firm more efficiently than the target firm's current management. This notion can lead bidding firms to engage in acquisition strategies even though there may not be positive economic profits from doing so.

The existence of managerial hubris suggests that the economic value of bidding firms will fall once they announce a merger or acquisition strategy. Although managers in bidding firms might truly believe that they can manage a target firm's assets more efficiently than the target firm's managers, investors in the capital markets are much less likely to be caught up in this hubris. In this context, a commitment to a merger or acquisition strategy is a strong signal that a bidding firm's management has deluded itself about its abilities to manage a target firm's assets. Such delusions will certainly adversely affect the economic value of the bidding firm.

Of course, empirical work on mergers and acquisitions discussed earlier in this chapter has concluded that although bidding firms do not obtain profits from their merger and acquisition strategies, they also do not, on average, reduce their economic value from implementing these strategies. This is inconsistent with the "hubris hypothesis." However, the fact that, on average, bidding firms do not lose economic value does not mean that *some* bidding firms do not lose economic value. Thus, although it is unlikely that all merger and acquisition strategies are motivated by managerial hubris, it is likely that at least some of them are.[14]

The Potential for Economic Profits

A final reason why managers might continue to pursue merger and acquisition strategies is the potential that these strategies offer for generating profits for at least some bidding firms. The empirical research on returns to bidding firms in mergers and acquisitions is very strong. On average, bidding firms do not gain profits from their merger and acquisition strategies. However, the fact that bidding firms, *on average*, do not earn profits on these strategies does not mean that *all* bidding firms will *always* fail to earn profits. In some situations bidding firms may be able to gain competitive advantages from merger and acquisition activities. These situations are discussed in the following section.

Mergers and Acquisitions and Sustained Competitive Advantage

V R I O

We have already seen that the economies of scope that motivate mergers and acquisitions between strategically related bidding and target firms can be valuable. However, the ability of these economies to generate profits and competitive advantages for bidding firms depends not only on their economic value but also on the competitiveness of the market for corporate control through which these valuable economies are realized. The **market for corporate control** is the market that is created when multiple firms actively seek to acquire one or several firms. Only when the market for corporate control is imperfectly competitive might it be possible for bidding firms to earn profits from implementing a merger or acquisition strategy. To see how the competitiveness of the market for corporate control can affect returns to merger and acquisition strategies, we will consider three scenarios involving bidding and target firms and examine their implications for the managers of these firms.[15]

Valuable, Rare, and Private Economies of Scope

An imperfectly competitive market for corporate control can exist when a target is worth more to one bidder than it is to any other bidders and when no other firms—including bidders and targets—are aware of this additional value. In this setting, the price of a target will rise to reflect public expectations about the value of the target. Once the target is acquired, however, the performance of the special bidder that acquires the target will be greater than generally expected, and this level of performance will generate profits for the equity holders of the bidding firm.

Consider a simple case. Suppose the market value of bidder Firm A combined with target firms is $12,000, whereas the market value of all other bidders combined with targets is $10,000. No other firms (bidders or targets) are aware of Firm A's unique relationship with these targets, but they are aware of the value of all other bidders combined with targets (that is, $10,000). Suppose also that the market value of all bidding firms, as stand-alone entities, is $7,000. In this setting, Firm A will be willing to pay up to $5,000 to acquire a target ($12,000 − $7,000), and all other bidders will only be willing to pay up to $3,000 to acquire a target ($10,000 − $7,000).

Because publicly available information suggests that acquiring a target is worth $3,000 more than the target's stand-alone price, the price of targets will rapidly rise to this level, ensuring that if bidding firms, apart from Firm A, acquire a target, they will obtain no profits. If there is only one target in this market for corporate control, then Firm A will be able to bid slightly more than $3,000 (perhaps $3,001) for this target. No other firms will bid higher than Firm A because, from their point of view, the acquisition is simply not worth more than $3,000. At this $3,001 price, Firm A will earn a profit of $1,999—Firm A had to spend only $3,001 for a firm that brings $5,000 in value above its stand-alone market price. Alternatively, if there are multiple targets, then several bidding firms, including Firm A, will pay $3,000 for their targets. At this price, these bidding firms will all earn zero economic profits, except for Firm A, which will earn an economic profit equal to $2,000. That is, only Firm A will gain a competitive advantage from acquiring a target in this market.

In order for Firm A to obtain this profit, the value of Firm A's economy of scope with target firms must be greater than the value of any other bidding firms with that target. This special value will generally reflect unusual resources and capabilities possessed by Firm A—resources and capabilities that are more valuable in combination with target firms than are the resources and capabilities that other bidding firms possess. Put differently, to be a source of economic profits and competitive advantage, Firm A's link with targets must be based on firm resources and capabilities that are rare among those firms competing in this market for corporate control.

However, not only does Firm A have to possess valuable and rare links with bidding firms to gain economic profits and competitive advantages from its acquisition strategies, but information about these special economies of scope must not be known by other firms. If other bidding firms know about the additional value associated with acquiring a target, they are likely to try to duplicate this value for themselves. Typically, they would accomplish this by imitating the type of relatedness that exists between Firm A and its targets, by developing the resources and capabilities that enabled Firm A to have its valuable economies of scope with targets. Once other bidders developed the resources and capabilities necessary to obtain this more valuable economy of scope, they would be able to enter into bidding, thereby increasing the likelihood that the equity holders of successful bidding firms would earn no economic profits.

Target firms must also be unaware of Firm A's special resources and capabilities if Firm A is to obtain competitive advantages from an acquisition. If target firms were aware of this extra value available to Firm A, along with the sources of this value, they could inform other bidding firms. These bidding firms could then adjust their bids to reflect this higher value, and competitive bidding would reduce profits to bidders. Target firms are likely to inform bidding firms in this way because increasing the number of bidders with more valuable economies of scope increases the likelihood that target firms will extract all the economic value created in a merger or acquisition.[16]

Valuable, Rare, and Costly-to-Imitate Economies of Scope

The existence of firms that have valuable, rare, and private economies of scope with targets is not the only way that the market for corporate control can be imperfectly competitive. If other bidders cannot imitate one bidder's valuable and rare economies with targets, then competition in this market for corporate control will be imperfect, and the equity holders of this special bidding firm will earn economic profits. In this case, the existence of valuable and rare economies does not need to be private, because other bidding firms cannot imitate these economies, and therefore bids that substantially reduce the profits for the equity holders of the special bidding firm are not forthcoming.

Typically, bidding firms will be unable to imitate one bidder's valuable and rare economies of scope with targets when the strategic relatedness between the special bidder and the targets stems from some rare and costly-to-imitate resources or capabilities controlled by the special bidding firm. Any of the costly-to-imitate resources and capabilities discussed in Chapter 3 could create costly-to-imitate economies of scope between a firm and a target. If, in addition, these economies are valuable and rare, they can be a source of profits to the equity holders of the special bidding firm. This can happen even if all firms in this market for corporate control are aware of the more valuable economies of scope available to this firm and its sources. Although information about this special economy of scope is publicly available, equity holders of special bidding firms will earn a profit when acquisition occurs. The equity holders of target firms will not obtain all of this profit, because competitive bidding dynamics cannot unfold when the sources of a more valuable economy of scope are costly to imitate.

Of course, it may be possible for a valuable, rare, and costly-to-imitate economy of scope between a bidding and a target firm to also be private. Indeed, it is often the case that those attributes of a firm that are costly to imitate are also difficult to describe and thus can be held as proprietary information. In that case, the analysis of profits associated with valuable, rare, and private economies of scope presented earlier applies.

Unexpected Valuable Economies of Scope Between Bidding and Target Firms

Thus far, this discussion has adopted, for convenience, the strong assumption that the present value of the strategic relatedness between bidders and targets is known with certainty by individual bidders. This is, in principle, possible but certainly not likely. Most modern acquisitions and mergers are massively complex, involving numerous unknown and complicated relationships between firms. In these settings, unexpected events after an acquisition has been completed may make an acquisition or merger more valuable than bidders and targets anticipated it would be. The price that bidding firms will pay to acquire a target will equal the expected value of the target only when the target is combined with the bidder. The difference between the unexpected value of an acquisition actually obtained by a bidder and the price the bidder paid for the acquisition is a profit for the equity holders of the bidding firm.

Of course, by definition, bidding firms cannot expect to obtain unexpected value from an acquisition. Unexpected value, in this context, is a surprise, a manifestation of a bidding firm's good luck, not its skill in acquiring targets. For example, when the British advertising firm WPP acquired J. Walter Thompson for $550 million, it discovered some property owned by J. Walter Thomson in Tokyo. No one knew of this property when the firm was acquired. It turned out to be worth over $100 million after taxes, a financial windfall that helped offset the high cost of this acquisition. When asked, Martin Sorrel, president of WPP and the architect of this acquisition, admitted that this $100 million windfall was simply good luck.[17]

Implications for Bidding Firm Managers

The existence of valuable, rare, and private economies of scope between bidding and target firms, and of valuable, rare, and costly-to-imitate economies of scope between bidding and target firms suggests that although, on average, most bidding firms do not generate competitive advantages from their acquisition strategies, in some special circumstances it may be possible for them to do so. Thus, the task facing managers in firms contemplating merger and acquisition strategies is to choose strategies that have the greatest likelihood of being able to generate profits for their equity holders. Several important managerial prescriptions can be derived from this discussion. These "rules" for bidding firm managers are summarized in Table 10.5.

Search for Rare Economies of Scope

One of the main reasons why bidding firms do not obtain competitive advantages from acquiring strategically related target firms is that several other bidding firms value the target firm in the same way. When multiple bidders all value a target in the same way, competitive bidding is likely. Competitive bidding, in turn, drives out the potential for superior performance. To avoid this problem, bidding firms should seek to acquire targets with which they enjoy valuable and rare linkages.

Operationally, the search for rare economies of scope suggests that managers in bidding firms need to consider not only the value of a target firm when combined with their own company, but also the value of a target firm when combined with other potential bidders. This is important because it is the difference between the value of a particular bidding firm's relationship with a target and the value of other bidding firms' relationships with that target that defines the size of the potential economic profits from an acquisition.

In practice, the search for valuable and rare economies of scope is likely to become a search for valuable and rare resources already controlled by a firm that are synergistically related to a target. For example, if a bidding firm has a unique reputation in its product market, and if the target firm's products could benefit by association with that reputation, then the target firm may be more valuable to this particular bidder than to other bidders (firms that do not possess this special reputation). Also, if a particular bidder possesses the largest market share in its industry, the best distribution system, or restricted access to certain key raw materials, and if the target firm would benefit from being associated with these valuable and rare resources, then the acquisition of this target may be a source of economic profits.

The search for valuable and rare economies of scope as a basis of mergers and acquisitions tends to rule out certain interfirm linkages as sources of economic profits. For example, most acquisitions can lead to a reduction in overhead costs, because much of the corporate overhead associated with the target firm can be eliminated subsequent to acquisition. However, the ability to eliminate these overhead costs is not unique to any one bidder, and thus the value created by these reduced costs will usually be captured by the equity holders of the target firm.

Table 10.5　**Rules for Bidding Firm Managers**

1. Search for valuable and rare economies of scope.
2. Keep information away from other bidders.
3. Keep information away from targets.
4. Avoid winning bidding wars.
5. Close the deal quickly.
6. Operate in "thinly traded" acquisition markets.

Keep Information Away from Other Bidders

One of the keys to earning superior performance in an acquisition strategy is to avoid multiple bidders for a single target. One way to accomplish this is to keep information about the bidding process, and about the sources of economies of scope between a bidder and target that underlie this bidding process, as private as possible. In order for other firms to become involved in bidding for a target, they must be aware of the value of the economies of scope between themselves and that target. If only one bidding firm knows this information, and if this bidding firm can close the deal before the full value of the target is known, then it may gain a competitive advantage from completing this acquisition.

Of course, in many circumstances, keeping all this information private is difficult. Often, it is illegal. For example, when seeking to acquire a publicly traded firm, potential bidders must meet disclosure requirements that effectively reduce the amount of private information a bidder can retain. In these circumstances, unless a bidding firm has some valuable, rare, and costly-to-imitate economy of scope with a target firm, the possibility of economic profits coming from an acquisition is very low. It is not surprising that the research conducted on mergers and acquisitions of firms traded on public stock exchanges governed by the U.S. Securities and Exchange Commission (SEC) disclosure rules suggests that, most of the time, bidding firms do not earn economic profits from implementing their acquisition strategies.

However, not all potential targets are publicly traded. Privately held firms may be acquired in an information environment that can create opportunities for above-normal performance for bidding firms. Moreover, even when acquiring a publicly traded firm, a bidder does not have to release all the information it has about the potential value of that target in combination with itself. Indeed, if some of this value reflects a bidding firm's taken-for-granted "invisible" assets, it may not be possible to communicate this information. In this case, as well, there may be opportunities for competitive advantages for bidding firms.

Keep Information Away from Targets

Not only should bidding firms keep information about the value of their economy of scope with a target away from other bidders; they should also keep this information away from target firms. Suppose that the value of a target firm to a bidding firm is $8,000 but the bidding firm, in an attempt to earn economic profits, has bid only $5,000 for the target. If the target knows that it is actually worth $8,000, it is very likely to hold out for a higher bid. In fact, the target may contact other potential bidding firms and tell them of the opportunity created by the $5,000 bid. As the number of bidders goes up, the possibility of superior economic performance for bidders goes down. Therefore, to keep the possibility of these profits alive, bidding firms must not fully reveal the value of their economies of scope with a target firm. Again, in some circumstances, it is very difficult, or even illegal, to attempt to limit the flow of information to target firms. In these settings, superior economic performance for bidding firms is very unlikely.

Limiting the amount of information that flows to the target firm may have some other consequences as well. For example, it has been shown that a complete sharing of information, insights, and perspectives before an acquisition is completed increases the probability that economies of scope will actually be realized once it is completed.[18] By limiting the flow of information between itself and a target, a bidding firm may actually be increasing the cost of integrating the target into its ongoing business, thereby jeopardizing at least some of the superior economic performance that limiting information flow is designed to create. Bidding firms will need to carefully balance the economic benefits of limiting the information they share with the target firm against the costs that limiting information flow may create.

Avoid Winning Bidding Wars

It should be reasonably clear that if a number of firms bid for the same target, the probability that the firm that successfully acquires the target will gain competitive advantages is very low. Indeed, to ensure that competitive bidding occurs, target firms can actively encourage other bidding firms to enter into the bidding process. The implications of these arguments are clear: Bidding firms should generally avoid winning a bidding war. To "win" a bidding war, a bidding firm will often have to pay a price at least equal to the full value of the target. Many times, given the emotions of an intense bidding contest, the winning bid may actually be larger than the true value of the target. Completing this type of acquisition will certainly reduce the economic performance of the bidding firm.

The only time it might make sense to "win" a bidding war is when the winning firm possesses a rare and private or a rare and costly-to-imitate economy of scope with a target that is more valuable than the strategic relatedness that exists between any other bidders and that target. In this setting, the winning firm may be able to earn a profit if it is able to fully realize the value of its relationship with the target.

Close the Deal Quickly

Another rule of thumb for obtaining superior performance from implementing merger and acquisition strategies is to close the deal quickly. All the economic processes that make it difficult for bidding firms to earn economic profits from acquiring a strategically related target take time to unfold. It takes time for other bidders to become aware of the economic value associated with acquiring a target; it takes time for the target to recruit other bidders; information leakage becomes more of a problem over time; and so forth. A bidding firm that begins and ends the bidding process quickly may forestall some of these processes and thereby retain some superior performance for itself.

The admonition to close the deal quickly should not be taken to mean that bidding firms need to make their acquisition decisions quickly. Indeed, the search for valuable and rare economies of scope should be undertaken with great care. There should be little rush in isolating and evaluating acquisition candidates. However, once a target firm has been located and valued, bidding firms have a strong incentive to reduce the period of time between the first bid and the completion of the deal. The longer this period of negotiation the less likely it is that the bidding firm will earn economic profits from the acquisition.

Complete Acquisitions in "Thinly Traded" Markets

Finally, an acquisition strategy can be a source of economic profits to bidding firms if these firms implement this corporate strategy in what could be described as "thinly traded markets." In general, a **thinly traded market** is a market where there are only a small number of buyers and sellers, where information about opportunities in this market is not widely known, and where interests besides purely maximizing the value of a firm can be important. In the context of mergers and acquisitions, thinly traded markets are markets where only a few (often only one) firms are implementing acquisition strategies. These unique firms may be the only firms that understand the full value of the acquisition opportunities in this market. Even target firm managers may not fully understand the value of the economic opportunities in these markets, and if they do, they may have other interests besides maximizing the value of their firm if it becomes the object of a takeover.

In general, thinly traded merger and acquisition markets are highly fragmented. Competition in these markets occurs at the local level, as one local small firm competes with other local small firms for a common group of geographically defined customers. Most of these small firms are privately held. Many are sole proprietorships. Examples of these thinly traded markets have included, at various points in history, the printing industry, the fast-food industry, the used car industry, the dry cleaning industry, and the barber shop/hair salon industry.

As was suggested in Chapter 2, the major opportunity in all highly fragmented industries is consolidation. In the context of mergers and acquisitions, consolidation can occur by one firm (or a small number of firms) buying numerous independent firms to realize economies of scope in these industries. Often, these economies of scope reflect economies of scale in these industries—economies of scale that were not realized in a highly fragmented setting. As long as the number of firms implementing this consolidation strategy is small, then the market for corporate control in these markets will probably be less than perfectly competitive and opportunities for profits from implementing an acquisition strategy may be possible.

More generally, if a merger or acquisition contest is played out through full-page ads in the *Wall Street Journal*, the ability of bidding firms to gain competitive advantages from their acquisitions is limited. Such highly public acquisitions are likely to lead to very competitive markets for corporate control. Competitive markets for corporate control, in turn, assure that the equity holders of the target firm will appropriate any value that could be created by an acquisition. However, if these contests occur in obscure, out-of-the-way industries, it is more likely that bidding firms will be able to earn profits from their acquisitions.

Service Corporation International: An Example

Empirical research on mergers and acquisitions suggests that it is not easy for bidding firms to earn economic profits from these strategies. However, it may be possible for some bidding firms, some of the time, to do so. One firm that has been successful in gaining competitive advantages from its merger and acquisition strategies is Service Corporation International (SCI). SCI is in the funeral home and cemetery business. It grew from a collection of five funeral homes in 1967 to being the largest owner of cemeteries and funeral homes in the United States today. It has done this through an aggressive and what was until recently a highly profitable acquisitions program in this historically fragmented industry.

The valuable and rare economy of scope that SCI brought to the funeral home industry is the application of traditional business practices in a highly fragmented and not often professionally managed industry. SCI-owned funeral homes operate with gross margins approaching 30 percent, nearly three times the gross margins of independently owned funeral homes. Among other things, higher margins reflected savings from centralized purchasing services, centralized embalming and professional services, and the sharing of underutilized resources (including hearses) among funeral homes within geographic regions. SCI's scale advantages made a particular funeral home more valuable to SCI than to one of SCI's smaller competitors, and more valuable than if a particular funeral home was left as a stand-alone business.

Moreover, the funeral homes that SCI targeted for acquisition were, typically, family owned and lacked heirs to continue the business. Many of the owner or operators of these funeral homes were not fully aware of the value of their operations to SCI (they are morticians more than business managers), nor were they just interested in maximizing the sale price of their funeral homes. Rather, they were often looking to maintain continuity of service in a community, secure employment for

Global Perspectives

Ford's Acquisition of Jaguar

In the late 1980s, managers at Ford Motor Company faced a problem. While Ford had been able to get its quality on par with the best manufacturers—through its "Quality Is Job One" program—worldwide competition in small and medium-sized cars had reduced the profit margin on Ford's small-car lines to almost nothing. The only cars that continued to deliver high profit margins to Ford were its luxury cars—the Lincoln and related cars. Unfortunately, Lincoln was an aging brand. It was being rapidly displaced in the highly profitable luxury car market by Mercedes-Benz and BMW—German automobiles that had more traction among younger car buyers than Lincoln. Moreover, Nissan (through its Infiniti division), Honda (through its Acura division), and Toyota (through its Lexus division) were beginning to invest in the luxury car market.

At the same time, managers at Jaguar also faced a problem. They were about to go out of business. Despite having a well-known brand and beautifully designed cars, Jaguar's quality problems had just about driven this firm out of business; its poor quality was legendary. The joke was that you had to buy two brand-new Jaguars—one to drive and one for parts. To give its customers some sense of security, Jaguar introduced a free towing service for new-car buyers. The service would tow your broken-down Jaguar to a Jaguar dealer free. The usage rate of this free towing service among Jaguar owners was 118 percent—essentially every Jaguar owner had to have his or her new car towed in for repairs and some more than once. In the J. D. Power ratings of initial quality, Jaguar in the early 1990s was ranked ahead of only one other firm—Yugo. Yugo manufactured very low-quality, cheap cars for sale in Europe and import into the United States. Unfortunately, while Jaguar was manufacturing very low-quality cars for sale around the world, they were not cheap! What a deal—a luxury car price with Yugo quality!

The match between Ford and Jaguar seemed perfect. Ford needed a new luxury brand to compete with Mercedes, BMW, Lexus, and so forth; Jaguar had such a brand. Jaguar desperately needed to learn how to manufacture quality automobiles; Ford now knew how to do that. Assuming Ford could use its manufacturing skills with Jaguar without destroying the value of Jaguar's brand name, it seemed likely that a Ford acquisition of Jaguar would create real economic value.

But who would appropriate that value—Ford's stockholders or Jaguar's stockholders? To answer this question, it is necessary to understand if any other firms would profit from acquiring Jaguar in about the same way as Ford. What about General Motors? GM faced the same profit squeeze in small cars as Ford. It also had its own

their loyal employees, and ensure a comfortable (if not lavish) retirement for themselves. Being acquired by SCI was likely to be the only alternative to closing the funeral home once an owner or operator retired. Extracting less than the full value of the home when selling to SCI often seemed preferable to other alternatives.

Because SCI's acquisition of funeral homes exploited real and valuable economies of scope, this strategy had the potential for generating superior economic performance. Because SCI was, for many years, the only firm implementing this strategy in the funeral home industry, because the funeral homes that SCI acquired were generally not publicly traded, and because the owner or operators of these funeral homes often had interests besides simply maximizing the price of their operation when they sold it, it seems likely that SCI's acquisition strategy generated superior economic performance for many years. However, in the last several years, information about SCI's acquisition strategy has become widely aging luxury line of cars—the Cadillac. And GM had also recently begun improving its manufacturing quality dramatically. Would GM be interested in purchasing Jaguar?

It turns out that while GM never made a formal offer for Jaguar, it did hold discussions about a possible acquisition. The bid that Ford made to take over Jaguar had to anticipate the possibility that GM was also interested. Initially, Ford paid $2.5 billion for Jaguar; since the acquisition, Ford has invested another $3.5 billion. Together, the almost $6 billion invested in Jaguar is almost $2.5 billion more than Jaguar's market price when it was a stand-alone company. This means that in order for this acquisition to pay off for Ford's stockholders, Ford must create more than $2.5 billion of extra value from its acquisition of Jaguar.

What has Ford done with Jaguar? First, and foremost, it helped Jaguar improve its quality problems. Indeed, Jaguar went from having the second-worst initial quality of any car manufacturer ranked by J. D. Powers in 1992 to having the best initial quality in 1999. Since 1999, Jaguar's rankings have dropped some, but it is still among the world's elite in initial qual-

ity rankings. However, it is reasonable to expect that much of the value created through this quality effort was anticipated in the price for Jaguar. That is, the value created here is part of the $2.5 billion premium paid for Jaguar. For it to be a source of profits for Ford's stockholders, Ford must create value in excess of this $2.5 billion.

Ford also helped Jaguar develop new models, including the mid-size "S-Type" and the smaller "X-Type" Jaguars. While these vehicles have dramatically increased Jaguar's volume of production, some observers worry that these automobile lines blur the distinction between the Ford and Jaguar brands. This is especially a problem for the "X-Type" or "baby Jag"—a car that looks disturbingly like a Hyundai Sonata. While it seems reasonable to assume that the premium paid for Jaguar anticipated Ford's ability to help Jaguar introduce some new models, the specific details of these models and their ultimate success would have been difficult to anticipate at the time Jaguar was acquired. If these models turn out to be successful, they may be a source of superior profits for Ford's shareholders.

More recently, Ford has used additional acquisitions to round out its

line of luxury cars—including its recent acquisition of Volvo and Range Rover. Ford is currently experimenting with the creation of single dealerships that sell Jaguars, Volvos, and Range Rovers. In this way, Ford's customers can gain access to a full line of luxury cars in a single location. It is also likely that these additional acquisitions were not anticipated at the time Ford acquired Jaguar. If this "one-stop-shop" approach to luxury car shopping ends up creating value, this value is also likely to be a source of superior performance to Ford's shareholders.

Of course, all this discussion begs a more fundamental question: Did Ford have to acquire Jaguar to obtain all the value described here? Couldn't Ford have created its own new luxury brand, the same way that Nissan, Honda, and Toyota did? And, which would have been cheaper—Ford paying a $2.5 billion premium for Jaguar or developing its own new luxury brand?

Sources: T. Luehrman (1991). "Jaguar plc, 1989." Harvard Business School Case No. 9-291-034; J. D. Powers (1999). "Jaguar is top make in initial quality." *Special Power Report*; J. Flint (2004). "Tarnished jewels." www.forbes.com, 01/27/04; D. Kiley (2001). "$29,950 soon can buy you a 'baby Jag." *USA Today*, February 14, p. 1.

known. This has led other funeral homes to begin bidding to acquire formerly independent funeral homes. Moreover, independent funeral home owners have become more aware of their full value to SCI. Although SCI's economy of scope with independent funeral homes is still valuable, it is no longer rare and thus no longer a source of economic profits to SCI. Put differently, the imperfectly competitive market for corporate control that SCI was able to exploit for almost 10 years has become more perfectly competitive. Future acquisitions by SCI are not likely to be a source of sustained competitive advantage and economic profit. For these reasons, SCI is currently reevaluating its corporate strategy, attempting to discover a new way that it might be able to generate superior profits.[19]

This same form of analysis can be applied to virtually any merger and acquisition strategy. Consider, for example, the acquisition discussed in the Global Perspectives feature.

Implications for Target Firm Managers

Although bidding firm managers can do several things to attempt to maximize the probability of earning economic profits from their merger and acquisition strategies, target firm managers can attempt to counter these efforts, to ensure that the owners of target firms appropriate whatever value is created by a merger or acquisition. These "rules" for target firm managers are summarized in Table 10.6

Seek Information from Bidders

One way a bidder can attempt to obtain superior performance from implementing an acquisition strategy is to keep information about the source and value of the strategic relatedness that exists between the bidder and target private. If that relationship is actually worth $12,000 but targets believe it is only worth $8,000, then a target might be willing to settle for a bid of $8,000 and thereby forgo the extra $4,000 it could have extracted from the bidder. Once the target knows that its true value to the bidder is $12,000, it is in a much better position to obtain this full value when the acquisition is completed. Therefore, not only should a bidding firm inform itself about the value of a target, target firms must inform themselves about their value to potential bidders. In this way, they can help obtain the full value of their assets.

Invite Other Bidders to Join the Bidding Competition

Once a target firm is fully aware of the nature and value of the economies of scope that exist between it and current bidding firms, it can exploit this information by seeking other firms that may have the same relationship with it and then informing these firms of a potential acquisition opportunity. By inviting other firms into the bidding process, the target firm increases the competitiveness of the market for corporate control, thereby increasing the probability that the value created by an acquisition will be fully captured by the target firm.

Delay But Do Not Stop the Acquisition

As suggested earlier, bidding firms have a strong incentive to expedite the acquisition process, to prevent other bidders from becoming involved in an acquisition. Of course, the target firm wants other bidding firms to enter the process. To increase the probability of receiving more than one bid, target firms have a strong incentive to delay an acquisition.

The objective, however, should be to delay an acquisition to create a more competitive market for corporate control, not to stop an acquisition. If a valuable economy of scope exists between a bidding and a target firm, the merger of these two firms will create economic value. If the market for corporate control within which this merger occurs is competitive, then the equity holders of the target firm will appropriate the full value of this economy of scope. Preventing an acquisition in this setting can be very costly to the equity holders of the target firm.

Table 10.6   **Rules for Target Firm Managers**

1. Seek information from bidders.
2. Invite other bidders to join the bidding competition.
3. Delay but do not stop the acquisition.

Target firm managers can engage in a wide variety of activities to delay the completion of an acquisition. Some common responses of target firm management to takeover efforts, along with their economic implications for the equity holders of target firms, are discussed in the Research Made Relevant feature.

Research Made Relevant

*M*anagers in potential target firms can respond to takeover attempts in a variety of ways. As suggested in Table 10.7, some of these responses increase the wealth of target firm shareholders, some have no impact on target firm shareholders, and others decrease the wealth of target firm shareholders.

Management responses that have the effect of reducing the value of target firms include greenmail, standstill agreements, and "poison pills." Each of these is an anti-takeover action target firm managers can take that reduces the wealth of target firm equity holders. **Greenmail** is a maneuver in which a target firm's management purchases any of the target firm's stock owned by a bidder and does so for a price that is greater than the current market value of that stock. Greenmail effectively ends a bidding

The Wealth Effects of Management Responses to Takeover Attempts

firm's effort to acquire a particular target and does so in a way that can

greatly reduce the wealth of a target firm's equity holders. Not only do these equity holders not appropriate any economic value that could have been created if an acquisition had been completed, but they have to bear the cost of the premium price that management pays to buy its stock back from the bidding firm.

Not surprisingly, target firms that resort to greenmail substantially reduce the economic wealth of their equity holders. One study found that the value of target firms that pay greenmail drops, on average, 1.76 percent. Another study reported a 2.85 percent drop in the value of such firms. These reductions in value are greater if greenmail leads to the cancellation of a takeover effort. Indeed, this second study found that such episodes led to a 5.50 percent reduction in the value of target firms. These reductions in value as a response to greenmail activities stand in marked contrast to the generally positive market response to efforts by a firm to repurchase its own shares in nongreenmail situations.

Standstill agreements are often negotiated in conjunction with greenmail. A standstill agreement is a contract between a target and a bidding firm wherein the bidding firm agrees not to attempt to take over the target for some period of time. When a target firm negotiates a standstill agreement, it prevents the current acquisition effort from being completed, and it reduces the number of bidders that might become involved in future acquisition efforts. Thus, the equity holders of this target firm forgo

Table 10.7   **The Wealth Effects of Target Firm Management Responses to Acquisition Efforts**

1. Responses that reduce the wealth of target firm equity holders:
   - Greenmail
   - Standstill agreements
   - Poison pills

2. Responses that do not affect the wealth of target firm equity holders:
   - Shark repellents
   - Pac Man defense
   - Crown jewel sale
   - Law suits

3. Responses that increase the wealth of target firm equity holders:
   - Search for white knights
   - Creation of bidding auctions
   - Golden parachutes

(continued)

any value that could have been created if the current acquisition had occurred, and they also lose some of the value that they could have appropriated in future acquisition episodes by the target's inviting multiple bidders into a market for corporate control.

Standstill agreements, either alone or in conjunction with greenmail, reduce the economic value of a target firm. One study found that standstill agreements that were unaccompanied by stock repurchase agreements reduced the value of a target firm by 4.05 percent. Such agreements, in combination with stock repurchases, reduced the value of a target firm by 4.52 percent.

So-called **poison pills** include any of a variety of actions that target firm managers can take to make the acquisition of the target prohibitively expensive. In one common poison-pill maneuver, a target firm issues rights to its current stockholders indicating that if the firm is acquired in an unfriendly takeover, it will distribute a special cash dividend to stockholders. This cash dividend effectively increases the cost of acquiring the target and can discourage otherwise interested bidding firms from attempting to acquire this target. Another poison-pill tactic substitutes the distribution of additional shares of a target firm's stock, at very low prices, for the special cash dividend. Issuing this low-price stock to current stockholders effectively undermines the value of a bidding firm's equity investment in a target and thus increases the cost of the acquisition. Other poison pills involve granting current stockholders other rights—rights that effectively increase the cost of an unfriendly takeover.

Although poison pills are creative devices that target firms can use to prevent an acquisition, they generally have not been very effective. If a bidding firm and a target firm are strategically related, the value that can be created in an acquisition can be substantial, and most of this value will be appropriated by the stockholders of the target firm. Thus, target firm stockholders have a strong incentive to see that the target firm is acquired, and they are amenable to direct offers made by a bidding firm to them as individual investors; these are called **tender offers**. However, to the extent that poison pills actually do prevent mergers and acquisitions, they are usually bad for the equity holders of target firms.

Target firm management can also engage in a wide variety of actions that have little or no impact on the wealth of a target firm's equity holders. One class of these responses is known as shark repellents. **Shark repellents** include a variety of relatively minor corporate governance changes that, in principle, are supposed to make it somewhat more difficult to acquire a target firm. Common examples of shark repellents include **supermajority voting rules** (which specify that more than 50 percent of the target firm's board of directors must approve a takeover) and state incorporation laws (in some states, incorporation laws make it difficult to acquire a firm incorporated in that state). However, if the value created by an acquisition is sufficiently large, these shark repellents will neither slow an acquisition attempt significantly nor prevent it from being completed.

Another response that does not affect the wealth of target firm equity holders is known as the **Pac Man defense**. Targets using this tactic fend off an acquisition by taking over the firm or firms bidding for them. Just as in the old video game, the hunted becomes the hunter; the target turns the tables on current and potential bidders. It should not be too surprising that the Pac Man defense does not, on average, either hurt or help the stockholders of target firms. In this defense, targets become bidders, and we know from empirical literature that, on average, bidding firms earn only zero economic profits from their acquisition efforts. Thus, one would expect that, on average, the Pac Man defense would generate only zero economic profits for the stockholders of target firms implementing it.

Another ineffective and inconsequential response is called a **crown jewel sale**. The idea behind a crown jewel sale is that, sometimes, a bidding firm is interested in just a few of the businesses currently being operated by the target firm. These businesses are the target firm's "crown jewels." To prevent an acquisition, the target firm can sell off these crown jewels, either directly to the bidding firm or by setting up a separate company to own and operate these businesses. In this way, the bidding firm is likely to be less interested in acquiring the target.

A final, relatively ineffective defense that most target firm managers pursue is filing lawsuits against bidding firms. Indeed, at least in the United States, the filing of a lawsuit has been almost automatic as soon as an acquisition effort is announced. These suits, however, usually do not delay or stop an acquisition or merger.

Finally, as suggested in Table 10.7, some of the actions that the management of target firms can take to delay (but not stop) an acquisition actually benefit target firm equity holders. The first of these is the search for a **white knight**—another bidding firm that agrees to acquire a particular target in the place of the original bidding firm. Target firm management may prefer to be acquired by some bidding firms more than by others. For example, it may be that some bidding firms possess much more valuable economies of scope with a target firm than other bidding firms. It may also be that some bidding firms will take a longer-term view in managing a target firm's assets than other bidding firms. In both cases, target firm managers are likely to prefer some bidding firms over others.

Whatever motivation a target firm's management has, inviting a white knight to bid on a target firm has the effect of increasing by at least one the number of firms bidding for a target. If there is currently only one bidder, inviting a white knight into the bidding competition doubles the number of firms actually bidding for a target. As the number of bidders increases, the competitiveness of the market for corporate control and the likelihood that the equity holders of the target firm will appropriate all the value created by an acquisition also increase. On average, the entrance of a white knight into a competitive bidding contest for a target firm increases the wealth of target firm equity holders by 17 percent.

If adding one firm into the competitive bidding process increases the wealth of target firm equity holders

some, then adding more firms to the process is likely to increase this wealth even more. Target firms can accomplish this outcome by creating an **auction** among bidding firms. On average, the creation of an auction among multiple bidders increases the wealth of target firm equity holders by 20 percent.

A third action that the managers of a target firm can take to increase the wealth of their equity holders from an acquisition effort is the institution of **golden parachutes**. A golden parachute is a compensation arrangement between a firm and its senior management team that promises these individuals a substantial cash payment if their firm is acquired and they lose their jobs in the process. These cash payments can appear to be very large but are actually quite small in comparison to the total value that can be created if a merger or acquisition is completed. In this sense, golden parachutes are a small price to pay to give a potential target firm's top managers incentives not to stand in the way of completing a takeover of their firm. Put differently, golden parachutes reduce agency problems for the equity holders of a potential target firm by aligning the interests of top managers with the interests of that firm's stockholders. On average, when a firm announces golden parachute compensation packages for its top management team, the value of this potential target firm's equity increases by 7 percent.

Overall, there is substantial evidence that delaying an acquisition long enough to ensure that a competitive market for corporate control

emerges can significantly benefit the equity holders of target firms. One study found that when target firms did not delay the completion of an acquisition, their equity holders experienced, on average, a 36 percent increase in the value of their stock once the acquisition was complete. If, on the other hand, target firms *did* delay the completion of the acquisition, this average increase in value jumped to 65 percent.

Of course, target firm managers can delay too long. Delaying too long can create opportunity costs for their firm's equity holders, for these individuals do not actually realize the gain from an acquisition until it is completed. Also, long delays can jeopardize the completion of an acquisition, in which case the equity holders of the target firm do not realize any gains from the acquisition.

Sources: R. Walkling and M. Long (1984). "Agency theory, managerial welfare, and takeover bid resistance." *Rand Journal of Economics*, 15(1), pp. 54–68; R. D. Kosnik (1987). "Greenmail: A study of board performance in corporate governance." *Administrative Science Quarterly*, 32, pp. 163–185; J. Walsh (1989). "Doing a deal: Merger and acquisition negotiations and their impact upon target company top management turnover." *Strategic Management Journal*, 10, pp. 307–322; L. Y. Dann and H. DeAngelo (1983). Standstill agreements, privately negotiated stock repurchases, and the market for corporate control." *Journal of Financial Economics*, 11, pp. 275–300; M. Bradey and L. Wakeman (1983). "The wealth effects of targeted share repurchases." *Journal of Financial Economics*, 11, pp. 301–328; H. Singh and F. Haricento (1989). "Top management tenure, corporate ownership and the magnitude of golden parachutes." *Strategic Management Journal*, 10, pp. 143–156; T. A. Turk (1987). "The determinants of management responses to interfirm tender offers and their effect on shareholder wealth." Unpublished doctoral dissertation, Graduate School of Management, University of California at Irvine.

| VRIO |

Organizing to Implement a Merger or Acquisition

To realize the full value of any strategic relatedness that exists between a bidding and a target firm, the merged organizations must be appropriately organized. The realization of each of the types of strategic relatedness discussed earlier in this chapter requires at least some coordination and integration between the bidding and target firms after an acquisition has occurred. For example, to realize economies of scale from an acquisition, bidding and target firms must coordinate in the combined firm the functions that are sensitive to economies of scale. To realize the value of any technology that a bidding firm acquires from a target firm, the combined firm must use this technology in developing, manufacturing, or selling its products. To exploit underutilized leverage capacity in the target firm, the balance sheets of the bidding and target firms must be merged, and the resulting firm must then seek additional debt funding. To realize the opportunity of replacing the target firm's inefficient management with more efficient management from the bidding firm, these management changes must actually take place.

Post-acquisition coordination and integration is essential if bidding and target firms are to realize the full potential of the strategic relatedness that drove the acquisition in the first place. If a bidding firm decides not to coordinate or integrate any of its business activities with the activities of a target firm, then why was this target firm acquired? Just as corporate diversification requires the active management of linkages among different parts of a firm, mergers and acquisitions (as one way in which corporate diversification strategies can be created) require the active management of linkages between a bidding and a target firm.

Given that most merger and acquisition strategies are used to create corporate diversification strategies, the organizational approaches previously described for implementing diversification are relevant for implementing merger and acquisition strategies as well. Thus, mergers and acquisitions designed to create diversification strategies should be managed through the M-form structure. The management control systems and compensation policies associated with implementing diversification strategies should also be applied in organizing to implement merger and acquisition strategies. On the other hand, mergers and acquisitions designed to create vertical integration strategies should be managed through the U-form structure, with management controls and compensation policies consistent with this strategy.

Although, in general, organizing to implement merger and acquisition strategies can be seen as a special case of organizing to implement corporate diversification strategies or vertical integration strategies, implementing merger and acquisition strategies can create special problems. Most of these problems reflect the fact that operational, functional, strategic, and cultural differences between bidding and target firms involved in a merger or acquisition are likely to be much greater than these same differences between the different parts of a diversified or vertically integrated business that was not created through acquisition. The reason for this difference is that the firms involved in a merger or acquisition have had a separate existence, separate histories, separate management philosophies, and separate strategies.

Differences between bidding and target firms can manifest themselves in a wide variety of ways. For example, they may own and operate different computer systems, different telephone systems, and other conflicting technologies. These firms might have very different human resource policies and practices. One firm might have a very generous retirement and health care program; the other, a less generous program. One firm's compensation system might focus on high salaries; the other firm's compensation system might focus on large cash bonuses and stock options. Also, these firms might have very different relationships with customers. At one firm, customers might be thought of as business partners; in another, the relationship with customers might be more arm's-length in character. Integrating bidding and target firms may require the resolution of numerous differences.

Perhaps the most significant challenge in integrating bidding and target firms has to do with cultural differences.[20] In Chapter 3, it was suggested that it can often be difficult to change a firm's organizational culture. The fact that a firm has been acquired does not mean that the culture in that firm will rapidly change to become more like the culture of the bidding firm; cultural conflicts can last for very long periods of time. Indeed, the difference between the relative success of Renault's acquisition of Nissan and DaimlerChrysler's acquisition of Mitsubishi—discussed in the opening case of this chapter—has largely been attributed to the inability of Mitsubishi to modify its traditional management culture.

Cultural differences were apparently an important part of the post-merger integration challenges in the merger between Bank One and First Chicago Bank. Bank One had many operations and offices in small and medium-sized cities in the Midwest. First Chicago, on the other hand, was a more urban bank. Different kinds of employees may have been attracted to these different firms, leading to significant cultural clashes as these two firms sought to rationalize their combined operations.[21] Most reports suggest that First Chicago employees have come to dominate this "merger." Whether similar challenges will arise between the recently merged Bank One and J. P. Morgan is yet to seen.

Operational, functional, strategic, and cultural differences between bidding and target firms can all be compounded by the merger and acquisition process—especially if that process was unfriendly. Unfriendly takeovers can generate, in target firm management, anger and animosity toward the management of the bidding firm. Research has shown that top management turnover is much higher in firms that have been taken over compared to firms not subject to takeovers, reflecting one approach to resolving these management conflicts.[22]

The difficulties often associated with organizing to implement a merger and acquisition strategy can be thought of as an additional cost of the acquisition process. Bidding firms, in addition to estimating the value of the strategic relatedness between themselves and a target firm, also need to estimate the cost of organizing to implement an acquisition. The value that a target firm brings to a bidding firm through an acquisition should be discounted by the cost of organizing to implement this strategy. In some circumstances, it may be the case that the cost of organizing to realize the value of strategic relatedness between a bidding firm and a target may be greater than the value of that strategic relatedness, in which case the acquisition should not occur. For this reason, many observers argue that potential economies of scope between bidding and target firms are often not fully realized. For example, despite the numerous multimedia mergers in the 1990s (Time Warner, Turner Broadcasting, and AOL; The Walt Disney Company, Capital Cities/ABC, and ESPN; GE and NBC; Westinghouse and CBS), only Viacom and News Corporation seem to have been able to realize any important economies of scope.[23]

Although organizing to implement mergers and acquisitions can be a source of significant cost, it can also be a source of value and opportunity. Some scholars have suggested that value creation can continue to occur in a merger or acquisition long after the formal acquisition is complete.[24] As bidding and target firms continue to coordinate and integrate their operations, unanticipated opportunities for value creation can be discovered. These sources of value could not have been anticipated at the time a firm was originally acquired (and thus are, at least partially, a manifestation of a bidding firm's good luck), but bidding firms can influence the probability of discovering these unanticipated sources of value by learning to cooperate effectively with target firms while organizing to implement a merger or acquisition strategy.

Mergers and Acquisitions in an International Context

All the issues associated with mergers and acquisitions described thus far also apply to those that occur in an international setting. For example, firms exploring international merger and acquisition opportunities will need to follow the guidelines in Table 10.5 if they hope to gain competitive advantages from these strategies, while international targets need to follow the guidelines in Table 10.6 if they are to extract as much of the value created by an acquisition as possible. However, there is one aspect of international mergers and acquisitions that requires additional discussion: Challenges created for post-merger integration caused by cultural differences between countries.

We have already seen that post-merger integration usually involves resolving conflicts between the cultures of merged or acquired firms. However, when these organizational cultures reflect deep-seated country cultures, post-merger integration can be even more difficult. Thus, the integration of merged firms in an international context is often confounded by the need to discover how different country cultures can work together.

The most influential study of cultures around the world, by Geert Hofstede, suggests that cultures can be described as varying along the five dimensions presented in Figure 10.1.[25] Differences along each of these dimensions create potential challenges when integrating acquisitions conducted across country and cultural borders. These differences are rarely easy to resolve.

For example, a firm that operates in an individualistic culture may have a compensation scheme that celebrates individual achievement. If this firm acquires a company that operates in a collectivist culture, imposing an individualistic compensation policy can lead to misunderstanding and disagreement. Senior managers in a firm that operates in a culture that respects power may assume that their orders to employees in a firm that operates in a culture that only tolerates power will be carried out, while these employees will not do anything until they hear the boss's justification of those orders. A firm used to innovation and risk-seeking may be very frustrated if it acquires a company that operates in a culture that avoids uncertainty rather than celebrates it. Employees that work in a firm that operates in a culture that values material possessions and hard work to obtain those possessions may be shocked to see employees in an acquired firm that operates in a culture that values the quality of life over material possessions go home at 5:00 P.M.—even if the work for the day is not done. Finally, employees that work in a firm that operates in a culture that values looking to the future may find it very difficult to work with employees in a firm that operates in a culture that values looking to the past.

Of course, acquiring firms can engage in specific activities to modify some aspects of the culture of the firms they acquire. However, to the extent that the

Figure 10.1   Dimensions of Culture and Their Implications for Integration in International Acquisitions

Individualism ◄———————— **Social Orientation** ————————► Collectivism
Individual interests   *Relative importance of individual*   *Group interests*
dominate   *and group interests*   *dominate*

Examples of Cultural Clashes in Post-Merger Integration:

Individualistic firm has individually oriented compensation policies while the collectivist firm has group-based compensation policies; individualistic firm has employees that make quick decisions on their own while the collectivist firm has employees who consult with others before making decisions.

Power Respect ◄———————— **Power Orientation** ————————► Power Tolerance
Authority determined by a   *Basis on which power and*   *Authority determined by*
person's position in a firm   *authority are granted to others*   *its perceived correctness*

Examples of Cultural Clashes in Post-Merger Integration:

Employees in power respect firm do what they are told while employees in power tolerance firm wait to hear justifications before they do what they are told; employees in power respect firm are deferential to senior managers while employees in power tolerance firms may or may not be deferential depending on how effective senior managers have been in the past.

Uncertainty Acceptance ◄———————— **Uncertainty Orientation** ————————► Uncertainty Avoidance
Change and new opportunities   *Emotional response to*   *Change and new opportunities*
valued   *change and new opportunities*   *not valued*

Examples of Cultural Clashes in Post-Merger Integration:

Employees in uncertainty acceptance firms are encouraged to think "outside the box" while employees in uncertainty avoidance firms are encouraged to reinforce the boundaries of the "box"; employees in uncertainty acceptance firms understand that failure sometimes accompanies risk-taking while employees in the uncertainty avoidance firm punish risk-takers for being foolish.

Aggressive Goal Behavior ◄———————— **Goal Orientation** ————————► Passive Goal Behavior
Value material possessions   *Source of motivation to*   *Value quality of life and welfare*
                                  accomplish goals   *of others*

Examples of Cultural Clashes in Post-Merger Integration:

Employees in aggressive goal behavior firms willing to work long hours to accomplish objectives while employees in passive goal behavior firms will leave when work begins to interfere with the quality of life; employees in aggressive goal behavior firms look for tangible results from their work while employees in passive goal behavior firms are more interested in how others in a firm are faring.

Long-Term Outlook ◄———————— **Time Orientation** ————————► Short-Term Outlook
Value patience, determination, *Short- or long-term outlook*   *Tend to focus on the present or*
and hard work   *the past*

Examples of Cultural Clashes in Post-Merger Integration:

Employees in long-term outlook firms have long-term goals and objectives while employees in short-term outlook firms tend to be satisfied with the status quo; employees in long term outlook firms focus on the benefits of hard work while employees in short-term outlook firms focus on the benefits of traditional ways of doing things.

Source: G. Hofstede, 1980. *Culture's consequences: International differences in work-related values.*

organizational cultures of these acquired firms reflect differences in national cultures, there are few things that can be done to modify them. In such settings, acquiring firms must look to sources of value creation in an acquisition that do not depend on the integration of the organizational cultures of the bidding and target firms.

SUMMARY

Firms can use mergers and acquisition and vertical integration between strategically unrelated firms sitions to create corporate diversification and vertical integration strategies. Mergers or acquisitions between strategically unrelated firms can be expected to generate only competitive parity for both bidders and targets. Thus, firms contemplating merger and acquisition strategies must search for strategically related targets.

Several sources of strategic relatedness have been discussed in literature. On average, the acquisition of strategically related targets does create economic value, but most of that value is captured by the equity holders of target firms. The equity holders of bidding firms generally gain competitive parity even when bidding firms acquire strategically related targets. Empirical research on mergers and acquisitions is consistent with these expectations. On average, acquisitions do create value, but that value is captured by target firms, and acquisitions do not hurt bidding firms.

Given that most mergers and acquisitions generate only zero economic profits for bidding firms, an important question becomes: " Why are there so many mergers and acquisitions?" Explanations include (1) the desire to ensure firm survival, (2) the existence of free cash flow, (3) agency problems between bidding firm managers and equity holders, (4) managerial hubris, and (5) the possibility that some bidding firms might earn economic profits from implementing merger and acquisition strategies.

To gain competitive advantages and economic profits from mergers or acquisitions, these strategies must be either valuable, rare, and private or valuable, rare, and costly to imitate. In addition, a bidding firm may exploit unanticipated sources of strategic relatedness with a target. These unanticipated sources of relatedness can also be a source of economic profits for a bidding firm. These observations have several implications for the managers of bidding and target firms.

Organizing to implement a merger or acquisition strategy can be seen as a special case of organizing to implement a corporate diversification or vertical integration strategy. However, historical differences between bidding and target firms may make the integration of different parts of a firm created through acquisitions more difficult than if a firm is not created through acquisitions. Cultural differences between bidding and target firms are particularly problematic. Bidding firms need to estimate the cost of organizing to implement a merger or acquisition strategy and discount the value of a target by that cost. However, organizing to implement a merger or acquisition can also be a way that bidding and target firms can discover unanticipated economies of scope.

Post-merger integration challenges are likely to be particularly important for mergers and acquisitions in an international context. Important differences between the country cultures of different firms can raise the cost of post-merger integration. In these settings, it may be necessary for acquiring firms to find economies of scope to exploit that do not require the integration of cultures.

CHALLENGE QUESTIONS

1. Consider the following scenario: A firm acquires a strategically related target after successfully fending off four other bidding firms. Under what conditions, if any, can the firm that acquired this target expect to earn an economic profit from doing so?

2. Consider this scenario: A firm acquires a strategically related target; there were no other bidding firms. Is this acquisition situation necessarily different from the situation described in question 1? Under what conditions, if any, can the firm that acquired this target expect to earn an economic profit from doing so?

3. Some researchers have argued that the existence of free cash flow can lead managers in a firm to make inappro-priate acquisition decisions. To avoid these problems, these authors have argued that firms should increase their debt-to-equity ratio and "soak up" free cash flow through interest and principal payments. Is free cash flow a significant problem for many firms? What are the strengths and weaknesses of increased leverage as a response to free cash flow problems in a firm?

4. The hubris hypothesis suggests that managers continue to engage in acquisitions, even though on average they do not generate economic profits, because of the unrealistic belief on the part of these managers that they can manage a target firm's assets more efficiently than that firm's current management. This type of systematic nonrationality usually does not last too long in competitive market conditions: Firms led by managers with these unrealistic beliefs change, are acquired, or go bankrupt in the long run. Are there any attributes of the market for corporate control that suggest that managerial hubris could exist in this market, despite its performance-reducing implications for bidding firms? If yes, what are these attributes? If no, can the hubris hypothesis be a legitimate explanation for continuing acquisition activity?

5. It has been shown that so-called poison pills rarely prevent a takeover from occurring. In fact, sometimes when a firm announces that it is instituting a poison pill, its stock price goes up. Why could that happen?

PROBLEM SET

1. For each of the following scenarios, estimate how much value an acquisition will create, how much of that value will be appropriated by each of the bidding firms, and how much of that value will be appropriated by each of the target firms. In each of these scenarios, assume that firms do not face significant capital constraints.

(a) A bidding firm, A, is worth $27,000 as a stand-alone entity. A target firm, B, is worth $12,000 as a stand-alone entity, but $18,000 if it is acquired and integrated with Firm A. Several other firms are interested in acquiring Firm B, and Firm B is also worth $18,000 if it is acquired by these other firms. If A acquired B, would this acquisition create value? If yes, how much? How much of this value would the equity holders of A receive? How much would the equity holders of B receive?

(b) The same scenario as in a, except that the value of B, if it is acquired by the other firms interested in it, is only $12,000.

(c) The same scenario as in a, except that the value of B, if it is acquired by the other firms interested in it, is $16,000.

(d) The same scenario as in b, except that Firm B contacts several other firms and explains to them how they can create the same value with Firm B that Firm A does.

(e) The same scenario as in b, except that Firm B sues Firm A. After suing Firm A, Firm B installs a "supermajority" rule in how its board of directors operates. After putting this new rule in place, Firm B offers to buy back any stock purchased by Firm A for 20 percent above the current market price.

END NOTES

1. See Welch, David, and Gail Edmondson (2004). "A Shaky automotive
   Menage à Trois." *BusinessWeek*, May 10, pp. 40–41.
2. Here, and throughout this chapter, it is assumed that capital markets
   are semi-strong efficient, that is, all publicly available information
   about the value of a firm's assets is reflected in the market price of
   those assets. One implication of semi-strong efficiency is that firms
   will be able to gain access to the capital they need to pursue any strategy that generates positive present value. See Fama, E. F. (1970).
   "Efficient capital markets: A review of theory and empirical work."
   Journal of Finance, 25, pp. 383–417.
3. See Trautwein, I. (1990). "Merger motives and merger prescriptions."
   Strategic Management Journal, 11, pp. 283–295; and Walter, G., and J. B.
   Barney (1990). "Management objectives in mergers and acquisition."
   Strategic Management Journal, 11, pp. 79–86. The three lists of potential
   links between bidding and target firms were developed by the Federal
   Trade Commission; Lubatkin, M. (1983). "Mergers and the performance of the acquiring firm." *Academy of Management Review*, 8,
   pp. 218–225; and Jensen, M. C., and R. S. Ruback (1983). "The market
   for corporate control: The scientific evidence." *Journal of Financial
   Economics*, 11, pp. 5–50.
4. See Huey, J. (1995). "Eisner explains everything." *Fortune*, April 17,
   pp. 44–68; and Lefton, T. (1996). "Fitting ABC and ESPN into Disney:
   Hands in glove." *Brandweek*, 37(18), April 29, pp. 30–40.
5. See Rumelt, R. (1974). *Strategy, structure, and economic performance*.
   Cambridge, MA: Harvard University Press.
6. The first study was by Ravenscraft, D. J., and F. M. Scherer (1987). *Mergers,
   sell-offs, and economic efficiency*. Washington, DC: Brookings Institution. The
   second study was by Porter, M. E. (1987). "From competitive advantage to
   corporate strategy." *Harvard Business Review*, 3, pp. 43–59.
7. This is because, if the combined firm is worth $32,000, the bidder
   firm is worth $15,000 on its own. If a bidder pays, say, $20,000
   for this target, it will be paying $20,000 for a firm that can only
   add $17,000 in value. So, a $20,000 bid would lead to a $3,000
   economic loss.
8. This is Jensen, M. C., and R. S. Ruback (1983). "The market for corporate
   control: The scientific evidence." *Journal of Financial Economics*, 11, pp. 5–50.
9. See Lubatkin, M. (1987). "Merger strategies and stockholder value."
   Strategic Management Journal, 8, pp. 39—53; and Singh, H., and C. A.
   Montgomery (1987). "Corporate acquisition strategies and economic
   performance." *Strategic Management Journal*, 8, pp. 377–386.
10. See Grant, L. (1995). "Here comes Hugh." *Fortune*, August 21,
    pp. 43–52; Serwer, A. E. (1995). "Why bank mergers are good for your
    savings account." *Fortune*, October 2, p. 32; and Deogun, N. (2000).
    "Europe catches merger fever as global volume sets record."
    Wall Street Journal, January 3, p. R8.
11. The concept of free cash flow has been emphasized in Jensen, M. C.
    (1986). "Agency costs of free cash flow, corporate finance, and
    takeovers." *American Economic Review*, 76, pp. 323–329; and Jensen, M.
    (1988). "Takeovers: Their causes and consequences." *Journal of
    Economic Perspectives*, 2, pp. 21–48.
12. See Miles, R. H., and K. S. Cameron (1982). *Coffin nails and corporate
    strategies*. Upper Saddle River, NJ: Prentice Hall.
13. Roll, R. (1986). "The hubris hypothesis of corporate takeovers." *Journal
    of Business*, 59, pp. 205–216.
14. See Dodd, P. (1980). "Merger proposals, managerial discretion and
    stockholder wealth." *Journal of Financial Economics*, 8, pp. 105–138;
    Eger, C. E. (1983). "An empirical test of the redistribution effect in pure
    exchange mergers." *Journal of Financial and Quantitative Analysis*, 18,
    pp. 547–572; Firth, M. (1980). "Takeovers, shareholder returns, and the
    theory of the firm." *Quarterly Journal of Economics*, 94, pp. 235–260;
    Varaiya, N. (1985). "A test of Roll's hubris hypothesis of corporate
    takeovers." Working paper, Southern Methodist University, School of
    Business; Ruback, R. S., and W. H. Mikkelson (1984). "Corporate
    investments in common stock." Working paper, Massachusetts
    Institute of Technology, Sloan School of Business; Ruback, R. S. (1982).
    "The Conoco takeover and stockholder returns." *Sloan Management
    Review*, 14, pp. 13–33.
15. This section of the chapter draws on Barney, J. B. (1988). "Returns to
    bidding firms in mergers and acquisitions: Reconsidering the related-
    ness hypothesis." *Strategic Management Journal*, 9, pp. 71–78.
16. See Turk, T. A. (1987). "The determinants of management responses to
    interfirm tender offers and their effect on shareholder wealth."
    Unpublished doctoral dissertation, Graduate School of Management,
    University of California at Irvine. In fact, this is an example of an
    anti-takeover action that can increase the value of a target firm.
    These anti-takeover actions are discussed later in this chapter.
17. See Bower, J. (1996). "WPP-integrating icons." Harvard Business
    School Case No. 9-396-249.
18. See Jemison, D. B., and S. B. Sitkin (1986). "Corporate acquisitions: A
    process perspective." *Academy of Management Review*, 11, pp. 145–163.
19. Blackwell, R. D. (1998). "Service Corporation International." Presented
    to The Cullman Symposium, October, Columbus, OH.
20. Cartwright, S., and C. Cooper (1993). "The role of culture compatibil-
    ity in successful organizational marriage." *The Academy of Management
    Executive*, 7(2), pp. 57–70; Chatterjee, S., M. Lubatkin, D. Schweiger,
    and Y. Weber (1992). "Cultural differences and shareholder value in
    related mergers: Linking equity and human capital." *Strategic
    Management Journal*, 13, pp. 319–334.
21. See Deogun, N. (2000). "Europe catches merger fever as global volume
    sets record." *Wall Street Journal*, January 3, p. R8.
22. See Walsh, J., and J. Ellwood (1991). "Mergers, acquisitions, and the
    pruning of managerial deadwood." *Strategic Management Journal*, 12,
    pp. 201–217; and Walsh, J. (1988). "Top management turnover following
    mergers and acquisitions." *Strategic Management Journal*, 9, pp. 173–183.
23. Landro, L. (1995). "Giants talk synergy but few make it work." *Wall
    Street Journal*, September 25, pp. B1 +.
24. See Haspeslagh, P., and D. Jemison (1991). *Managing acquisitions:
    Creating value through corporate renewal*. New York: Free Press.
25. See Hofstede, G. (1980). *Culture's consequences: International differences
    in work-related values*. Beverly Hills, CA: Sage Publications.

Analyzing Cases and Preparing for Class Discussions

This book, properly understood, is really about how to analyze cases. Just reading the book, however, is no more likely to fully develop one's skills as a strategist than reading a book about golf will make one a golfer. Practice in applying the concepts and tools is essential. Cases provide the opportunity for this necessary practice.

Why the Case Method?

The core of many strategic management courses is the case method of instruction. Under the case method, you will study and discuss the real-world challenges and dilemmas that face managers in firms. Cases are typically accounts of situations that a firm or manager has faced at a given point in time. By necessity, cases do not possess the same degree of complexity that a manager faces in the real world, but they do provide a concrete set of facts that suggest challenges and opportunities that real managers have faced. Very few cases have clear answers. The case method encourages you to engage problems directly and propose solutions or strategies in the face of incomplete information. To succeed at the case method, you must develop the capability to analyze and synthesize data that are sometimes ambiguous and conflicting. You must be able to prioritize issues and opportunities and make decisions in the face of ambiguous and incomplete information. Finally, you must be able to persuade others to adopt your point of view.

In an applied field like strategic management the real test of learning is how well you can apply knowledge to real-world situations. Strategic management cases offer you the opportunity to develop judgment and wisdom in applying your conceptual knowledge. By taking the relatively unstructured information in a case and by applying the concepts they have learned, students develop judgment in applying concepts. Alfred North Whitehead discussed the importance of application to knowledge:

> This discussion rejects the doctrine that students should first learn passively, and then, having learned, should apply knowledge. . . . For the very meaning of the things known is wrapped up in their relationship beyond themselves. This unapplied knowledge is knowledge shorn of its meaning.

Alfred North Whitehead (1947). *Essays in Science and Philosophy*. New York: Philosophical Library, Inc. pp. 218–219.

Thus, knowledge is gained as you apply concepts. In the case method, you do not passively absorb wisdom imparted from your instructor, but actively develop it as you wrestle with the real-world situations described in cases.

How to Analyze Cases

Before discussing how to analyze a case, it may be useful to comment on how *not* to prepare a case. We see two common failings in case preparation that often go hand-in-hand. First, students often do not apply conceptual frameworks in a rigorous and systematic manner. Second, many students do not devote sufficient time to reading, analyzing, and discussing a case before class. Many students succumb to the temptation to quickly read a case and quickly latch on to the most visible issues that present themselves. Thus, they come to class prepared to make only a few superficial observations about a case. Often, they entirely miss the deeper issues around why a firm is in the situation that it is in and how it can better its performance. Applying the frameworks systematically may take more time and effort in the beginning, but it will generally lead to deeper insights about the cases and a more profound understanding of the concepts in the chapters. As you gain experience in this systematic approach to analyzing cases, many of you will find that your preparation time will decrease. This appendix offers a framework that will assist you as you analyze cases. The framework is important, but no framework can substitute for hard work. There are no great shortcuts to analyzing cases, and there is no single right method for preparing a case. The following approach, however, may help you develop your ability to analyze cases.

1. **Skim through the case very quickly.** Pay particular attention to the exhibits. The objective in this step is to gain familiarity with the broad facts of the case. What are the apparent challenges or opportunities the company faces? What information is provided? You may find it especially useful to focus on the first and last few paragraphs of the case in this step.

2. **Read the case more carefully and make notes, underline, etc.** What appear to be important facts? The conceptual frameworks in the chapters will be essential in helping you identify what are key facts. Throughout the course, you will want to address central questions such as the following:

   - What is the firm's performance?
   - What is the firm's mission? Strategy? Goals?
   - What are the resources involved in the firm's value chain and how do they compare to competitors on cost and differentiation?
   - Does the firm have a competitive advantage?
   - Are the firm's advantages and disadvantages temporary or sustainable?
   - What is the value of the firm's resources?
   - Are the firm's resources rare?
   - Are the firm's resources costly to imitate?
   - Is the firm organized sufficiently to exploit its resources?

Depending on the case, you may also want to consider other frameworks and questions where appropriate. Each chapter provides concepts and frameworks that you may want to consider. For example:

   - What are the five forces? How do they influence industry opportunities and threats? (Chapter 2)
   - What are the sources of cost differences in an industry? (Chapter 4)
   - What are the bases and potential bases for product differentiation in an industry? (Chapter 5)

Each chapter suggests more specific questions and concepts than those above. You will want to consider these concepts in detail. In some cases, the instructor may offer direction about which concepts to apply to a given case. In other instances, you may be left to use your judgment in choosing which concepts to focus on in analyzing a case.

3. **Define the basic issues.** This is perhaps the most important step and also the stage of analysis that requires the most wisdom and judgment. Cases are rarely like tidy problem sets where the issues or problems are explicitly stated and the tools needed to address those issues are prescribed. Generally, you need to determine what the key issues are. In doing this, it may help for you to begin by asking: What are the fundamental issues in the case? Which concepts matter most in providing insight into those issues? One trap to avoid in defining basic issues is doing what some decision-making scholars label "plunging-in," which is drawing conclusions without first thinking about the crux of the issues involved in a decision.[i] Many students have a tendency to seize the first issues that are prominently mentioned in a case. As an antidote to this trap, you may want to consider a case from the perspective of different conceptual frames.

4. **Develop and elaborate your analysis of the key issues.** As with all of the steps, there is no substitute for painstaking work in this stage. You need to take the key issues you have defined in Step 3, examine the facts that you have noted in Step 2, and assess what are the key facts. What does quantitative analysis reveal? Here it is not just ratio analysis that we are concerned with. Just as body temperature, blood pressure, and pulse rate may reveal something about a person's health but little about the causes of a sickness, ratio analysis typically tells us more about the health of a company than the causes of its performance. You should assemble facts and analysis to support your point of view. Opinions unsupported by factual evidence and analysis are generally not persuasive. This stage of the analysis involves organizing the facts in the case. You will want to develop specific hypotheses about what factors relate to success in a particular setting. Often, you will find it helpful to draw diagrams to clarify your thinking.

5. **Draw conclusions and formulate a set of recommendations.** You may be uncomfortable in drawing conclusions and making recommendations because you do not have complete information. This is an eternal dilemma for managers. Managers who wait for complete information to do something, however, usually act too late. Nevertheless, you should strive to do the most complete analysis that you can under reasonable time constraints. Recommendations should also flow naturally from your analysis. Too often, students formulate their recommendations in an ad hoc way. In formulating recommendations, you should be clear about priorities and the sequence of actions that you recommend.

6. **Prepare for class discussion.** Students who diligently work through the five steps above and rigorously examine a case should be well prepared for class discussion. You may find it helpful to make some notes and bring them to

---

[i]J. E. Russo and P. J. H. Schoemaker (1989). *Decision Traps: The Ten Barriers to Brilliant Decision-Making and How to Overcome Them.* New York: Fireside.

class. Over the years, we have observed that many of the students who are low contributors to class discussions bring few or no notes to class. Once in class, a case discussion usually begins with a provocative question from the instructor. Many instructors will "cold call"—a question directed to a specific student who has not been forewarned. Students who have thoroughly analyzed and discussed the case before coming to class will be much better prepared for these surprise calls. They will also be better prepared to contribute to the analysis, argument, and persuasion that will take place in the class discussion. Discussions can move rapidly. You will hear new insights from fellow students. Preparation helps you to absorb, learn, and contribute to the insights that emerge from class discussion.

Summary

Students who embark in the case method soon learn that analyzing cases is a complex process. Having a clear conceptual approach like the VRIO framework does not eliminate the complexity. This systematic approach, however, does allow the analyst to manage the complexity of real-world business situations. In the end, though, neither cases nor real-world businesses conclude their analyses with tidy solutions that resolve all the uncertainties and ambiguities a business faces. However, the case method coupled with a good theory like the VRIO approach and hard work do make it more likely that you will generate valuable insights into the strategic challenges of firms and develop the strategic skills needed to lead a firm.

Illustration/
Photo Credits

Illustration for part openers by P.J. Loughran
Illustration for boxed features by Gary Hovland

Part 1

Chapter 1
2   AFP Photo/John G. Mabanglo

Chapter 2
32   Chris Windsor/Getty Images, Inc.–Photodisc

Chapter 3
74   Electronic Arts

Part 2

Chapter 4
114   Alan Schein Photography/Corbis/Bettmann

Chapter 5
144   Getty Images, Inc.–Photodisc

Part 3

Chapter 6
178   Gautam Singh/AP Wide World Photos

Chapter 7
206   Laura Rauch/AP Wide World Photos

Chapter 8
244   AP Wide World Photos

Chapter 9
276   Annie Leibovitz/Contact Press Images Inc.

Chapter 10
308   left: Ron Kimball Photography, right: AP Wide World Photos

G l o s s a r y

above average accounting performance when a firm's accounting performance is greater than the industry average

above normal economic performance when a firm earns above its cost of capital

absorptive capacity the ability of firms to learn

accounting performance a measure of a firm's competitive advantage calculated by using information from its published profit-and-loss and balance sheet statements

accounting ratios numbers taken from a firm's financial statements that are manipulated in ways that describe various aspects of the firm's performance

acquisition when a firm purchases another firm

acquisition premium the difference between the current market price of a target firm's shares and the price a potential acquirer offers to pay for those shares

activity ratios accounting ratios that focus on the level of activity in a firm's business

ad valorem tariffs where a tariff is calculated as a percentage of the market value of an import, regardless of its weight or volume

adverse selection when an alliance partner promises to bring to an alliance certain resources that it either does not control or cannot acquire

agency problems when parties in an agency relationship differ in their decision-making objectives

agency relationship when one party to an exchange delegates decision-making authority to a second party

agent the party to whom the decision-making authority is delegated

architectural competence the ability of a firm to use organizational structure and other organizing mechanisms to facilitate coordination among scientific disciplines to conduct research

auction a mechanism for establishing the price of an asset, in mergers and acquisitions, when multiple firms bid for a single target firm

audit committee sub-group of the board of directors responsible for ensuring the accuracy of accounting and financial statements

average accounting performance when a firm's accounting performance is equal to the industry average

backward vertical integration when a firm incorporates more stages of the value chain within its boundaries and those stages bring it closer to gaining access to raw materials

barriers to entry attributes of an industry's structure that increase the cost of entry

below average accounting performance when a firm's accounting performance is less than the industry average

below normal economic performance when a firm earns less than its cost of capital

board of directors a group of 10 to 15 individuals drawn from a firm's top management and from people outside the firm, whose primary responsibilities are to monitor decisions made in the firm and ensure that they are consistent with the interests of outside equity holders

business angels wealthy individuals who act as outside investors in a typically entrepreneurial firm

business cycle the alternating pattern of prosperity followed by recession followed by prosperity

business strategy a firm's theory of how to gain competitive advantage in a single business or industry

buyers those who purchase a firm's products or services

capabilities a subset of a firm's resources, defined as tangible and intangible assets that enable a firm to take full advantage of other resources it controls

cashing out the compensation paid to an entrepreneur for risk-taking associated with starting a firm

causally ambiguous Where imitating firms do not understand the relationship between the resources and capabilities controlled by a firm and that firm's competitive advantage

centralized hub where each country in which a firm operates is organized as a full profit-and-loss division headed by a division general manager and where strategic and operational decisions are retained at headquarters

chairman of the board the person that presides over the board of directors; may or may not be the same person as a firm's senior executive

chairman of the board (duties of) supervision of the board of directors in its ratifying and monitoring roles

chief executive officer (CEO) the person to whom all functional managers report in a U-form organization; the person to whom all all divisional personal and corporate staff report to in an M-form organization

chief executive officer (CEO) (duties of) strategy formulation and implementation

chief operating officer (COO) (duties of) strategy implementation

closely held firm a firm that has not sold very many of its shares on the public stock market

co-brand Tying the brand of a product to the brand of another firm's or division's product

collusion when two or more firms in an industry coordinate their strategic choices to reduce competition in that industry

compensation policies the ways that firms pay employees

competitive advantage when a firm creates more economic value than rival firms

competitive disadvantage when a firm generates less economic value than rival firms

competitive dynamics how one firm responds to the strategic actions of competing firms

competitive parity when a firm creates the same economic value as rival firms

competitor any firm, group, or individual trying to reduce a firm's competitive advantage

complementary resources and capabilities resources and capabilities that have limited ability to generate competitive advantage in isolation, but in combination with other resources can enable a firm to realize its full potential for competitive advantage

complementor a firm is a complementor when its customers value its products more when they have this other firm's products than when they have a particular firm's products alone

compound tariffs where both market values and the weight or volume are used in calculating a tariff

conduct refers to the strategies that firms in an industry implement

conglomerate merger a merger or acquisition where there are no vertical, horizontal, product extension, or market extension links between the firms

consolidation strategy strategy that reduces the number of firms in an industry by exploiting economies of scale

controlling share when an acquiring firm purchases enough of a target firm's assets to be able to make all the management and strategic decisions in the target firm

coordinated federation where each country in which a firm operates is organized as a full profit-and-loss division headed by a division general manager and where operational decisions are delegated to these divisions or countries, but strategic decisions are retained at headquarters

core competence the collective learning in an organization, especially how to coordinate diverse production skills and integrate multiple streams of technologies

corporate spin-off exists when a large, typically diversified firm divests itself of a business in which it has historically been operating and the divested business operates as an independent entity

corporate staff provides information about a firm's external and internal environments to the firm's senior executive

corporate strategy a firm's theory of how to gain competitive advantage by operating in several businesses simultaneously

cost centers divisions are assigned a budget and manage their operations to that budget

cost leadership business strategy focuses on gaining advantages by reducing costs below those of competitors

cost of capital the rate of return that a firm promises to pay its suppliers of capital to induce them to invest in a firm

cost of debt equals the interest that a firm must pay its debt holders to induce them to lend money to the firm

cost of equity equals the rate of return a firm must promise to its equity holders to induce them to invest in the firm

crown jewel sale where a bidding firm is interested in just a few of the businesses being operated by the target firm, known as its crown jewels, and the target firm sells these businesses

culture the values, beliefs, and norms that guide behavior in a society and in a firm

cumulative abnormal return (CAR) performance that is greater (or less) than what was expected in a short period of time around when an acquisition is announced

current market value the price of each of a firm's shares times the number of shares outstanding

customer-switching costs exist when customers make investments in order to use a firm's particular products or services and when these investments are not useful in using other firms' products

debt capital from banks and bondholders

decentralized federation where each country in which a firm operates is organized as a full profit-and-loss division headed by a division general manager and where strategic and operational decisions are delegated to these country managers

declining industry an industry that has experienced an absolute decline in unit sales over a sustained period of time

deep pockets model a firm that takes advantage of its monopoly power in one business to subsidize several different businesses

demographics the distribution of individuals in a society in terms of age, sex, marital status, income, ethnicity, and other personal attributes that may determine their buying patterns

depression a severe recession that lasts for several years

direct duplication the attempt to imitate other firms by developing resources that have the same strategic effects as the resources controlled by those other firms

diseconomies of scale when a firm's costs begin to rise as a function of that firm's volume of production

distinctive competence a valuable and rare resource or capability

distribution agreements when one firm agrees to distribute the products of others

diversification economies sources of relatedness in a diversified firm

divestment selling a business with which a firm had been operating

division each business that a firm engages in, also called strategic business units (SBUs) or business group

dominant-business firms firms with between 70 percent and 95 percent of their total sales in a single product market

dominant logic a common way of thinking about strategy across different businesses in a diversified firm

economic climate the overall health of the economic systems within which a firm operates

economic measures of competitive advantage measures that compare a firm's level of return to its cost of capital instead of to the average level of return in the industry

economic value the difference between the perceived benefits gained by a customer that purchases a firm's products or services and the full economic cost of these products or services

economic value added (EVA) calculated by subtracting the cost of the capital employed in a division from that division's earnings

economies of scale when the per unit cost of production falls as the volume of production increases

economies of scope exist in a firm when the value of the products or services it sells increases as a function of the number of different businesses in which that firm operates

emerging industries newly created or newly re-created industries formed by technological innovations, change in demand, or the emergence of new customer needs

emergent strategies theories of how to gain competitive advantage in an industry that emerge over time or have been radically reshaped once they are initially implemented

environmental threat any individual, group, or organization outside a firm that seeks to reduce the level of that firm's performance

equity capital from individuals and institutions that purchase a firm's stocks

equity alliance where cooperating firms supplement contracts with equity holdings in alliance partners

escalation of commitment an increased commitment by managers to an incorrect course of action even as its limitations become manifest

event study analysis a way to evaluate the performance effects of acquisitions for bidding firms

executive committee typically consists of the CEO and two or three functional senior managers

explicit collusion exists when firms directly communicate with each other to coordinate their levels of production, their prices, and so forth (illegal in most countries)

external analysis identification and examination of the critical threats and opportunities in a firm's competitive environment

finance committee sub-group of the board of directors that maintains the relationship between the firm and external capital markets

financial resources include all the money, from whatever source, that firms use to conceive and implement strategies

firm-specific human capital investments investments made by employees in a particular firm over time, including understanding the culture, policies, and procedures, and knowing the people to contact to complete a task, that have limited value in other firms

firm-specific investments when the value of stakeholders' investments in a particular form is much greater than the value those same investments would be in other firms

first-mover advantages advantages that come to firms that make important strategic and technological decisions early in the development of an industry

five forces framework identifies the five most common threats faced by firms in their local competitive environments and the conditions under which these threats are more or less likely to be present

flexibility how costly it is for a firm to alter its strategic and organizational decisions

formal management controls include a firm's budgeting and reporting activities that keep people higher up in a firm's organizational chart informed about the actions taken by people lower down in the organizational chart

formal reporting structure a description of who in the organization reports to whom

forward vertical integration when a firm incorporates more stages of the value chain within its boundaries and those stages bring it closer to interacting directly with final customers

fragmented industries industries in which a large number of small or medium-sized firms operate and no small set of firms has dominant market share or creates dominant technologies

free cash flow the amount of cash a firm has to invest after all positive net present-value investments in its ongoing businesses have been funded

friendly acquisitions when the management of a target firm wants the firm to be acquired

functional manager a manager who leads a particular function within a firm, such as manufacturing, marketing, finance, accounting, or sales

functional organizational structure the structure a firm uses to implement business-level strategies it might pursue where each function in the firm reports to the CEO

general environment broad trends in the context within which a firm operates that can have an impact on a firm's strategic choices

generic business strategies another name for business-level strategies, which are cost leadership and product differentiation

geographic market diversification strategy when a firm operates in multiple geographic markets simultaneously

global opportunities opportunities for a firm to optimize production, distribution, and other business functions throughout the world in all the markets in which it operates

golden parachutes incentive compensation paid to senior managers if the firm they manage is acquired

greenmail a maneuver in which a target firm's management purchases any of the target firm's stock owned by a bidder for a price that is greater than its current market value

harvest when firms engage in a long, systematic, phased withdrawal from a declining industry, extracting as much value as possible

hedonic price that part of the price of a product or service that is attributable to a particular characteristic of that product or service

holdup when one firm makes more transaction-specific investments in an exchange than partner firms make and the firm that has not made these investments tries to exploit the firm that has

horizontal merger when a firm acquires a former competitor

hostile takeovers when the management of a target firm does not want the firm to be acquired

human capital resources the training, experience, judgment, intelligence, relationships, and insight of individual managers and workers in a firm

imperfectly imitable resources and capabilities that are more costly for other firms to imitate, compared to firms that already possess them

increasing returns to scale in network industries, the value of a product or service increases as the number of people using these products or services increases

inelastic in supply where the quantity of supply is fixed and does not respond to price increases, such as the total supply of land, which is relatively fixed and cannot be significantly increased in response to higher demand and prices

industry structure attributes of an industry that determines its competitiveness; measured by such factors as the number of competitors in an industry, the heterogeneity of products in an industry, and the cost of entry and exit in an industry

informal management controls include a firm's culture and the willingness of employees to monitor each others' behavior

initial public offering (IPO) when the stock of a privately held firm, or a division of a corporation, is first sold to the general public

institutional owners pension funds, corporations and others that invest other peoples' money in firm equities

intermediate products or services products or services produced in one division that are used as inputs for products or services produced by a second division

internal analysis identification of a firm's organizational strengths and weaknesses and of the resources and capabilities that are likely to be sources of competitive advantage

invented competencies illusory inventions by creative managers to justify poor diversification moves by linking intangible core competencies to completely unrelated businesses

joint venture where cooperating firms create a legally independent firm in which they invest and from which they share any profits that are created

learning curve a concept which formalizes the relationship between cumulative volumes of production and falling per unit costs

leverage ratios accounting ratios that focus on the level of a firm's financial flexibility

licensing agreements where one firm allows others to use its brand name to sell products in return for some fee or percentage of profits

limited corporate diversification when all or most of a firm's business activities fall within a single industry and geographic market

liquidity ratios accounting ratios that focus on the ability of a firm to meet its short-term financial obligations

management control systems include a range of formal and informal mechanisms to ensure that managers are behaving in ways consistent with a firm's strategies

managerial hubris the unrealistic belief held by managers in bidding firms that they can manage the assets of a target firm more efficiently than the target firm's current management

managerial know-how the often-taken-for-granted knowledge and information that are needed to compete in an industry on a day-to-day basis

managerial perquisites activities that do not add economic value to the firm, but directly benefit the managers who make them

market extension merger where firms make acquisitions in new geographical markets

market for corporate control the market that is created when multiple firms actively seek to acquire one or several firms

market leader the firm with the largest market share in an industry

matrix structures where one employee reports to two or more people

mature industries an industry in which, over time, ways of doing business have become widely understood, technologies have diffused through competitors, and the rate of innovation in new products and technologies drops

merger when the assets of two similar-sized firms are combined

M-form an organizational structure for implementing a corporate diversification strategy, where each business a firm engages in is managed through a separate profit-and-loss division

mission a firm's long-term purpose

mission statement written statement defining both what a firm aspires to be in the long run and what it wants to avoid in the meantime

monopolistically competitive industries where there are large numbers of competing firms and low-cost entry and exit, but products in these industries are not homogeneous with respect to cost or product attributes; firms are said to enjoy a "monopoly" in that part of the market they dominate

monopolistic industries industries that consist of only a single firm

moral hazard where partners in an exchange possess high-quality resources and capabilities of significant value to the exchange but fail to make them available to the other partners

multinational opportunities opportunities for a firm to operate simultaneously in several national or regional markets, but where these operations are independent of each other

multipoint competition when two or more diversified firms simultaneously compete in the same multiple markets

mutual forbearance a form of tacit collusion where firms tacitly agree to not compete in one industry in order to avoid competition in a second industry

network industries industries where single technical standards and increasing returns to scale tend to dominate; competition in these industries tends to focus on which of several competing standards will be chosen

new entrants firms that have either recently begun operations in an industry or that threaten to begin operations in an industry soon

niche strategy when a firm reduces its scope of operations and focuses on narrow segments of a declining industry

nominating committee sub-group of the board of directors that nominates new board members

nonequity alliance where cooperating firms agree to work together to develop, manufacture, or sell products or services, but they do not take equity positions in each other or form an independent organizational unit to manage their cooperative efforts

nontariff trade barriers the establishment of product performance standards that cannot be met by imports, the restriction of access to domestic distribution channels, imposition of local purchasing requirements for government purchases, or implementation of a variety of environmental and labor regulations that foreign firms must meet in order to do business in a country

normal economic performance when a firm earns its cost of capital

objectives specific, measurable targets a firm can use to evaluate the extent to which it is realizing its mission

office of the president together, the roles of chairman of the board, CEO, and COO

oligopolies industries characterized by a small number of competing firms, by homogeneous products, and by costly entry and exit

operational economies of scope shared activities and shared core competencies in a diversified firm

operations committee typically meets monthly and usually consists of the CEO and each of the heads of the functional areas included in the firm

opportunism when a firm is unfairly exploited in an exchange

organizational chart a table that summarizes the formal reporting structure within a firm

organizational resources a firm's formal reporting structure; its formal and informal planning, controlling, and coordinating systems; its culture and reputation; and informal relations among groups within a firm and between a firm and those in its environment

pac man defense fending off an acquisition by a firm acquiring the firm or firms bidding for it

path dependence when events early in the evolution of a process have significant effects on subsequent events

pecuniary economies sources of relatedness in market power between bidding and target firms

perfectly competitive industry when there are large numbers of competing firms, the products being sold are homogeneous with respect to cost and product attributes, and entry and exit are very low cost

personnel and compensation committee sub-group of the board of directors that evaluates and compensates the performance of a firm's senior executive and other senior managers

physical resources all the physical technology used in a firm

poison pills a variety of actions that target firm managers can take to make the acquisition of the target prohibitively expensive

policy choices choices firms make about the kinds of products or services they will sell—choices that have an impact on relative cost and product differentiation position

policy of experimentation exists when firms are committed to engage in several related product differentiation efforts simultaneously

predatory pricing setting prices so that they are less than a business's costs

price takers where the price of the products or services a firm sells is determined by market conditions and not by the decisions of firms

principal the party who delegates the decision-making authority

privately held a firm that has stock that is not traded on public stock markets and is not a division of a larger company

processes the activities a firm engages in to design, produce, and sell its products or services

process innovation a firm's effort to refine and improve its current processes

process manufacturing when manufacturing is accomplished in a continuous system; examples include manufacturing in chemical, oil refining, and paper and pulp industries

product differentiation a business strategy whereby firms attempt to gain a competitive advantage by increasing the perceived value of their products or services relative to the perceived value of other firms' products or services

product diversification strategy when a firm operates in multiple industries simultaneously

product extension merger where firms acquire complementary products through their merger and acquisition activities

productive inputs any supplies used by a firm in conducting its business activities, such as labor, capital, land, and raw materials, among other things

product-market diversification strategy when a firm implements both product and geographic market diversification simultaneously

profitability ratios accounting ratios with some measure of profit in the numerator and some measure of firm size or assets in the denominator

profit-and-loss centers where profits and losses are calculated at the level of the division in a firm

proprietary technology secret or patented technology that gives incumbent firms important advantages over potential entrants

Question of Imitability "Do firms without a resource or capability face a cost disadvantage in obtaining or developing it compared to firms that already possess it?"

Question of Organization "Is a firm organized to exploit the full competitive potential of its resources and capabilities?"

Question of Rarity "How many competing firms already possess particular valuable resources and capabilities?"

Question of Value "Does a resource enable a firm to exploit an external opportunity or neutralize an external threat?"

quotas a numerical limit on the number of particular items that are allowed to be imported into a country

real options investments in real assets that create the opportunity for additional investments in the future

recession a period of relatively low prosperity, when demand for goods and services is low and unemployment is high

related-constrained diversification a strategy wherein all the businesses in which a firm operates share a significant number of inputs, product technologies, distribution channels, similar customers, and so forth

related corporate diversification when less than 70 percent of a firm's revenue comes from a single product market and its multiple lines of business are linked

related-linked a strategy wherein the different businesses that a single firm pursues are linked on only a couple of dimensions, or where different sets of businesses are linked along very different dimensions

reputation beliefs customers hold about a firm

Resource-based View (RBV) a model of firm performance that focuses on the resources and capabilities controlled by a firm as sources of competitive advantage

resource heterogeneity implies that for a given business activity, some firms may be more skilled in accomplishing this activity than other firms

resource immobility resources controlled by some firms may not diffuse to other firms

resources the tangible and intangible assets that a firm controls, which it can use to conceive of and implement its strategies

retained earnings capital generated from a firm's ongoing operations and retained by a firm

rivalry the intensity of competition among a firm's direct competitors

seemingly unrelated diversified diversified firms that are exploiting core competencies as an economy of scope, but are not doing so with any shared activities

senior executive the president or CEO of a firm

shakeout period exists when total supply in an industry is reduced by bankruptcies, acquisitions, and business closings

shared activities potential sources of operational economies of scope for diversified firms

shark repellents a variety of relatively minor corporate governance changes that, in principle, are supposed to make it somewhat more difficult to acquire a target firm

single-business firms firms with greater than 95 percent of their total sales in a single product market

"Skunk Works" temporary teams whose creative efforts are intensive and focused

socially complex resorces and capabilities that involve interpersonal, social, or cultural links among individuals

social welfare the overall good of society

specific tariffs where a tariff is calculated as a percentage of the weight or volume of the goods being imported, regardless of their market value

stakeholders all groups and individuals who have an interest in how a firm performs

standstill agreements a contract between a target and a bidding firm wherein the bidding firm agrees not to attempt to take over the target for some period of time

stock grants payments to employees in a firm's stock

stock options where employees are given the right but not the obligation to purchase stock at predetermined prices

strategic alliance exists whenever two or more independent organizations cooperate in the development, manufacture, or sale of products or services

strategic management process a sequential set of analyses that can increase the likelihood of a firm's choosing a strategy that generates competitive advantages

strategy a firm's theory about how to gain competitive advantage

strategy implementation occurs when a firm adopts organizational policies and practices that are consistent with its strategy

strengths valuable resources and capabilities

structure-conduct-performance model (S-C-P) theory which suggests that industry structure determines a firm's conduct which in turn determines its performance

substitutes products or services that meet approximately the same customer needs but do so in different ways

substitution developing or acquiring strategically equivalent, but different resources as a competing firm

supermajority voting rules an example of a shark repellent that specifies that more than 50 percent of the target firm's board of directors must approve a takeover

suppliers those who make a wide variety of raw materials, labor, and other critical assets available to firms

supply agreements where one firm agrees to supply others

sustainable distinctive competencies valuable, rare, and costly to imitate resources or capabilities

sustained competitive advantage a competitive advantage that lasts for a long period of time; an advantage that is not competed away through strategic imitation

tacit collusion exists when firms coordinate their production and pricing decisions, not by directly communicating with each other, but by exchanging signals with other firms about their intent to cooperate; special case of tacit cooperation

tacit cooperation actions a firm takes that have the effect of reducing the level of rivalry in an industry and that do not require firms in an industry to directly communicate or negotiate with each other

tactics the specific actions a firm takes to implement its strategies

tariffs taxes levied on goods or services imported into a country

tax haven a country that charges little or no corporate tax

technical economies sources of relatedness in marketing, production, and similar activities between bidding and target firms

technological hardware the machines and other hardware used by firms

technological leadership strategy when firms make early investments in particular technologies in an industry

technological software the quality of labor–management relations, an organization's culture, and the quality of managerial controls in a firm

temporary competitive advantage a competitive advantage that lasts for a short period of time

temporary cross-divisional and cross-functional teams groups of individuals from different businesses and different functional areas who are brought together to cooperate on a particular new product or service

tender offer when a bidding firm offers to purchase the shares of a target firm directly by offering a higher than market price for those shares to current shareholders

thinly traded market a market where there are only a small number of buyers and sellers, where information about opportunities in this market is not widely known, and where interests besides purely maximizing the value of a firm can be important

transaction specific investment when the value of an investment in its first-best use is much greater than its value in its second-best use; any investment in an exchange that has significantly more value in the current exchange than it does in alternative exchanges

transfer price the price that one part of a diversified firm charges another part of the firm for intermediate products or services

transnational opportunity where firms treat their global operations as an integrated network of distributed and interdependent resources and capabilities

transnational structure where each country in which a firm operates is organized as a full profit-and-loss division headed by a division general manager and where strategic and operational decisions are delegated to operational entities that maximize local responsiveness and international integration

U-form structure organization where different functional heads report directly to CEO; used to implement business level strategies

uncertainty when the future value of an exchange cannot be known when investments in that exchange are being made

unfriendly acquisition when the management of the target firm does not want the firm to be acquired

unrelated corporate diversification where less than 70 percent of a firm's revenues is generated in a single product market, and when a firm's businesses share few, if any, common attributes

value added as a percentage of sales measures that percentage of a firm's sales that is generated by activities done within the boundaries of a firm; a measure of vertical integration

value chain that set of activities that must be accomplished to bring a product or service from raw materials to the point that it can be sold to a final customer

venture capital firms outside investment funds looking to invest in entrepreneurial ventures

vertical integration the number of steps in the value chain that a firm accomplishes within its boundaries

vertical merger when a firm vertically integrates, either forward or backward, through its acquisition efforts

visionary firms firms whose mission is central to all they do

VRIO framework four questions that must be asked about a resource or capability to determine its competitive potential

weaknesses resources and capabilities that are not valuable

weighted average cost of capital (WACC) the percentage of a firm's total capital that is debt times the cost of debt plus the percentage of a firm's total capital that is equity times the cost of equity

white knight another bidding firm that agrees to acquire a particular target in place of the original bidding firm

zero-based budgeting where corporate executives create a list of all capital allocation requests from divisions in a firm, rank them from most important to least important, and then fund all the projects the firm can afford, given the amount of capital it has available

Company Index

Name Index

Subject Index